PHILIP'S

STREET MAPS

East Yorkshire
Northern Lincolnshire

www.philips-maps.co.uk
First published in 2002 by
Philip's, a division of
Octopus Publishing Group Ltd
www.octopusbooks.co.uk
2-4 Heron Quays, London E14 4JP
An Hachette UK Company
www.hachettelivre.co.uk

Third edition 2009
First impression 2009
EYLCA

978-0-540-09492-9 (spiral)

© Philip's 2009

Ordnance Survey®

This product includes mapping data licensed
from Ordnance Survey® with the permission
of the Controller of Her Majesty's Stationery
Office. © Crown copyright 2009. All rights
reserved. Licence number 100011710.

Ordnance Survey and the OS Symbol are
registered trademarks of Ordnance Survey, the
national mapping agency of Great Britain.

Speed camera data provided by
PocketGPSWorld.com Ltd

Post Office is a trade mark of Post Office Ltd in
the UK and other countries.

Printed by Toppan, China

Contents

Digital Data

The exceptionally high-quality mapping found in this atlas is available as digital data in TIFF format, which is easily convertible to other bitmapped (raster) image formats.

The index is also available in digital form as a standard database table. It contains all the details found in the printed index together with the National Grid reference for the map square in which each entry is named.

For further information and to discuss your requirements, please contact victoria.dawbarn@philips-maps.co.uk

Mobile safety cameras

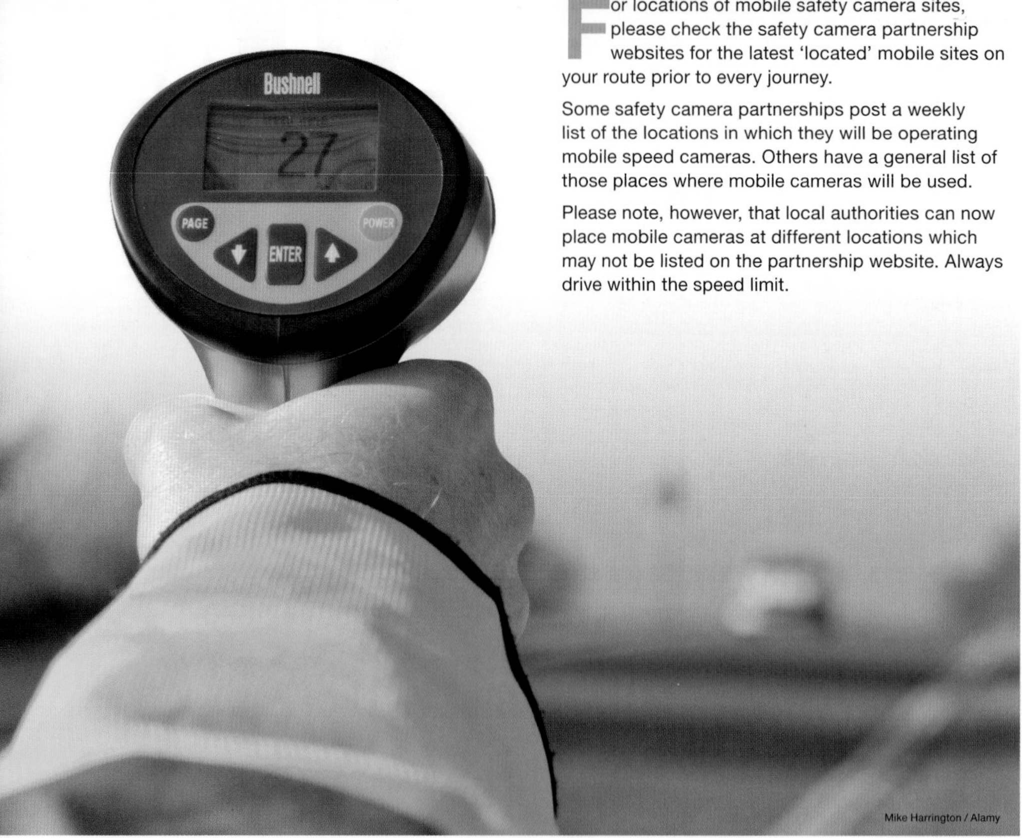

Mike Harrington / Alamy

For locations of mobile safety camera sites, please check the safety camera partnership websites for the latest 'located' mobile sites on your route prior to every journey.

Some safety camera partnerships post a weekly list of the locations in which they will be operating mobile speed cameras. Others have a general list of those places where mobile cameras will be used.

Please note, however, that local authorities can now place mobile cameras at different locations which may not be listed on the partnership website. Always drive within the speed limit.

Useful websites

East Riding safety camera partnership
www.eastriding.gov.uk/safetycamerapartnership

Lincolnshire safety camera partnership
www.lincssafetycamera.com

Nottinghamshire safety camera partnership
http://www.nottspeed.com

South Yorkshire safety camera partnership
www.safetycamera.org/home

West Yorkshire safety camera partnership
www.safetycameraswestyorkshire.co.uk

Further information
www.dvla.gov.uk
www.thinkroadsafety.gov.uk
www.dft.gov.uk
www.road-safe.org

Key to map symbols

Motorway with junction number (22)	
Primary route – dual/single carriageway	
A road – dual/single carriageway	
B road – dual/single carriageway	
Minor road – dual/single carriageway	
Other minor road – dual/single carriageway	
Road under construction	
Tunnel, covered road	
Speed cameras – single, multiple	
Rural track, private road or narrow road in urban area	
Gate or obstruction to traffic – restrictions may not apply at all times or to all vehicles	
Path, bridleway, byway open to all traffic, restricted byway	
Pedestrianised area	
BS22 Postcode boundaries	
County or unitary authority boundaries	
Railway with station	
Tunnel	
Railway under construction	
Metro station	
Private railway station	
Miniature railway	
Tramway, tramway under construction	
Tram stop, tram stop under construction	
Bus, coach station	

Ambulance station	
Coastguard station	
Fire station	
Police station	
Accident and Emergency entrance to hospital	
H Hospital	
+ Place of worship	
i Information centre – open all year	
P Shopping centre, parking	
P&R PO Park and Ride, Post Office	
Camping site, caravan site	
Golf course, picnic site	
Church ROMAN FORT Non-Roman antiquity, Roman antiquity	
Univ Important buildings, schools, colleges, universities and hospitals	
Woods, built-up area	
River Medway Water name	
River, weir	
Stream	
Canal, lock, tunnel	
Water	
Tidal water	

Adjoining page indicators and overlap bands – the colour of the arrow and band indicates the scale of the adjoining or overlapping page (see scales below)

The dark grey border on the inside edge of some pages indicates that the mapping does not continue onto the adjacent page

The small numbers around the edges of the maps identify the 1-kilometre National Grid lines

Enlarged maps only

Railway or bus station building	
Place of interest	
Parkland	

Abbreviations

Acad	Academy	Meml	Memorial
Allot Gdns	Allotments	Mon	Monument
Cemy	Cemetery	Mus	Museum
C Ctr	Civic centre	Obsy	Observatory
CH	Club house	Pal	Royal palace
Coll	College	PH	Public house
Crem	Crematorium	Recn Gd	Recreation ground
Ent	Enterprise		
Ex H	Exhibition hall	Resr	Reservoir
Ind Est	Industrial Estate	Ret Pk	Retail park
IRB Sta	Inshore rescue boat station	Sch	School
		Sh Ctr	Shopping centre
Inst	Institute	TH	Town hall / house
Ct	Law court	Trad Est	Trading estate
L Ctr	Leisure centre	Univ	University
LC	Level crossing	W Twr	Water tower
Liby	Library	Wks	Works
Mkt	Market	YH	Youth hostel

The map scale on the pages numbered in green is 1¾ inches to 1 mile
2.76 cm to 1 km • 1:36 206

The map scale on the pages numbered in blue is 3½ inches to 1 mile
5.52 cm to 1 km • 1:18 103

The map scale on the pages numbered in red is 7 inches to 1 mile
11.04 cm to 1 km • 1:9 051

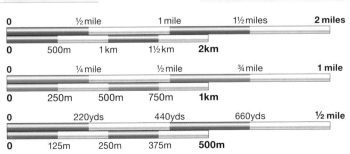

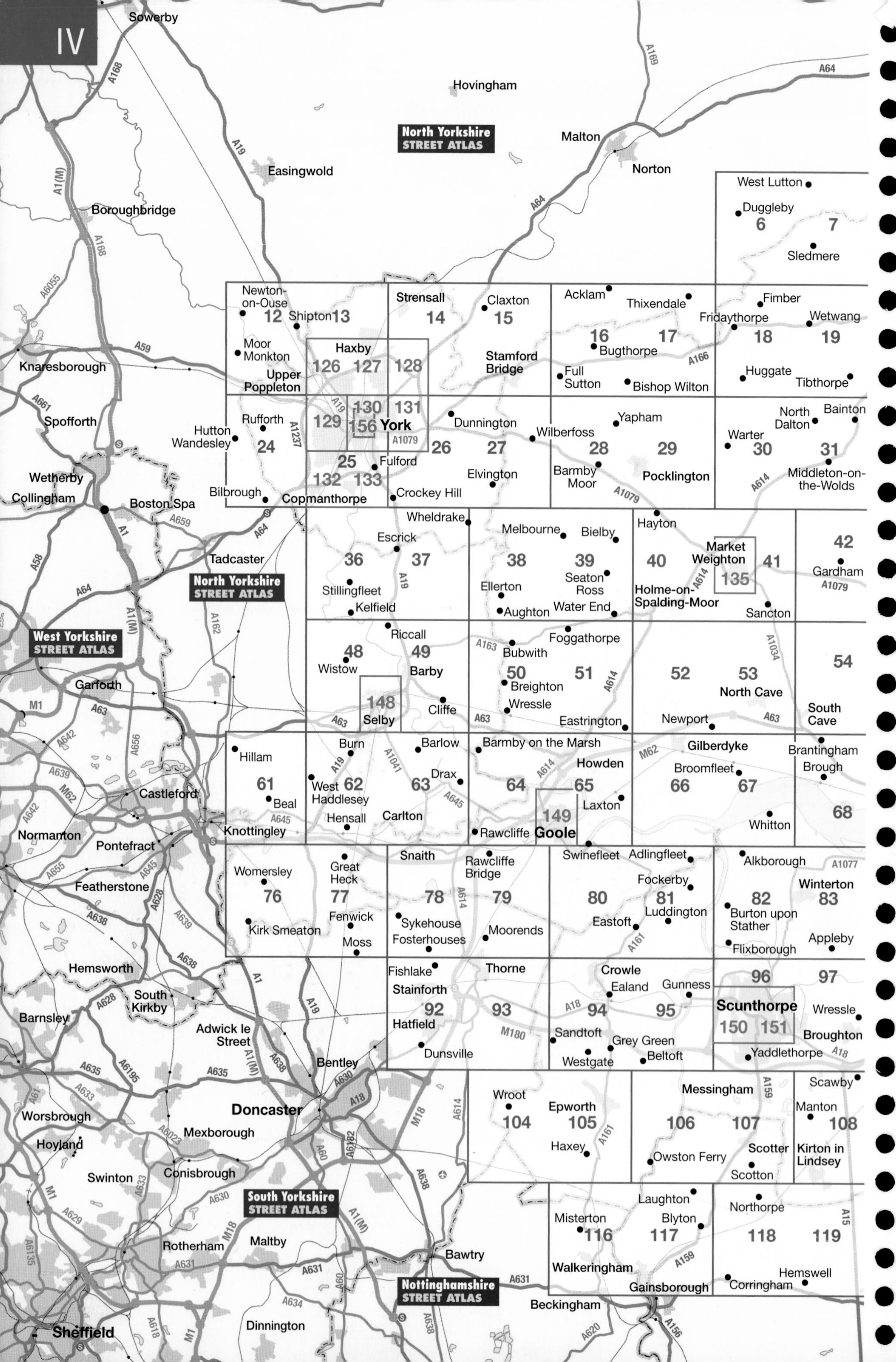

Sowerby
Hovingham
North Yorkshire STREET ATLAS
Malton
Norton
Easingwold
Boroughbridge
West Lutton
Duggleby
6
7
Sledmere
Newton-on-Ouse
12
Shipton
13
Strensall
14
Claxton
15
Acklam
Thixendale
Fimber
Fridaythorpe
Wetwang
16
17
18
19
Bugthorpe
Moor Monkton
Haxby
126
127
128
Stamford Bridge
Full Sutton
Bishop Wilton
Huggate
Tibthorpe
Knaresborough
Upper Poppleton
Spofforth
Rufforth
Hutton Wandesley
24
129
130
131
156
York
Dunnington
Wilberfoss
Yapham
28
29
North Dalton
Bainton
Warter
30
31
26
27
25
Fulford
132
133
Elvington
Barmby Moor
Pocklington
Middleton-on-the-Wolds
Wetherby
Collingham
Boston Spa
Bilbrough
Copmanthorpe
Crockey Hill
Wheldrake
Melbourne
Bielby
Hayton
Escrick
36
37
38
39
40
Market Weighton
41
135
42
Gardham
Tadcaster
North Yorkshire STREET ATLAS
Stillingfleet
Kelfield
Ellerton
Seaton Ross
Aughton
Water End
Holme-on-Spalding-Moor
Sancton
West Yorkshire STREET ATLAS
Riccall
Foggathorpe
48
49
Wistow
Barby
Bubwith
54
Garforth
148
Selby
Cliffe
50
51
Breighton
Wressle
Eastrington
52
53
North Cave
Newport
South Cave
Hillam
Burn
Barlow
Barmby on the Marsh
Howden
Gilberdyke
Brantingham
Broomfleet
Brough
61
62
63
64
65
66
67
68
Beal
West Haddlesey
Drax
Laxton
149
Castleford
Hensall
Carlton
Rawcliffe
Goole
Whitton
Normanton
Knottingley
Pontefract
Snaith
Rawcliffe Bridge
Swinefleet
Adlingfleet
Alkborough
Great Heck
Womersley
Fockerby
Winterton
76
77
78
79
80
81
82
83
Featherstone
Luddington
Burton upon Stather
Eastoft
Fenwick
Sykehouse
Kirk Smeaton
Moss
Fosterhouses
Moorends
Appleby
Flixborough
Hemsworth
Fishlake
Thorne
Crowle
96
97
Stainforth
Ealand
Gunness
South Kirkby
Barnsley
92
93
94
95
Scunthorpe
Wressle
Hatfield
150
151
Adwick le Street
Sandtoft
Broughton
Grey Green
Yaddlethorpe
Dunsville
Westgate
Beltoft
Bentley
Scawby
Wroot
Messingham
Manton
Doncaster
Epworth
Worsbrough
104
105
106
107
108
Mexborough
Hoyland
Haxey
Scotter
Kirton in Lindsey
Owston Ferry
Scotton
Swinton
Conisbrough
South Yorkshire STREET ATLAS
Laughton
Northorpe
Misterton
Blyton
116
117
118
119
Rotherham
Maltby
Walkeringham
Bawtry
Hemswell
Gainsborough
Corringham
Nottinghamshire STREET ATLAS
Beckingham
Sheffield
Dinnington

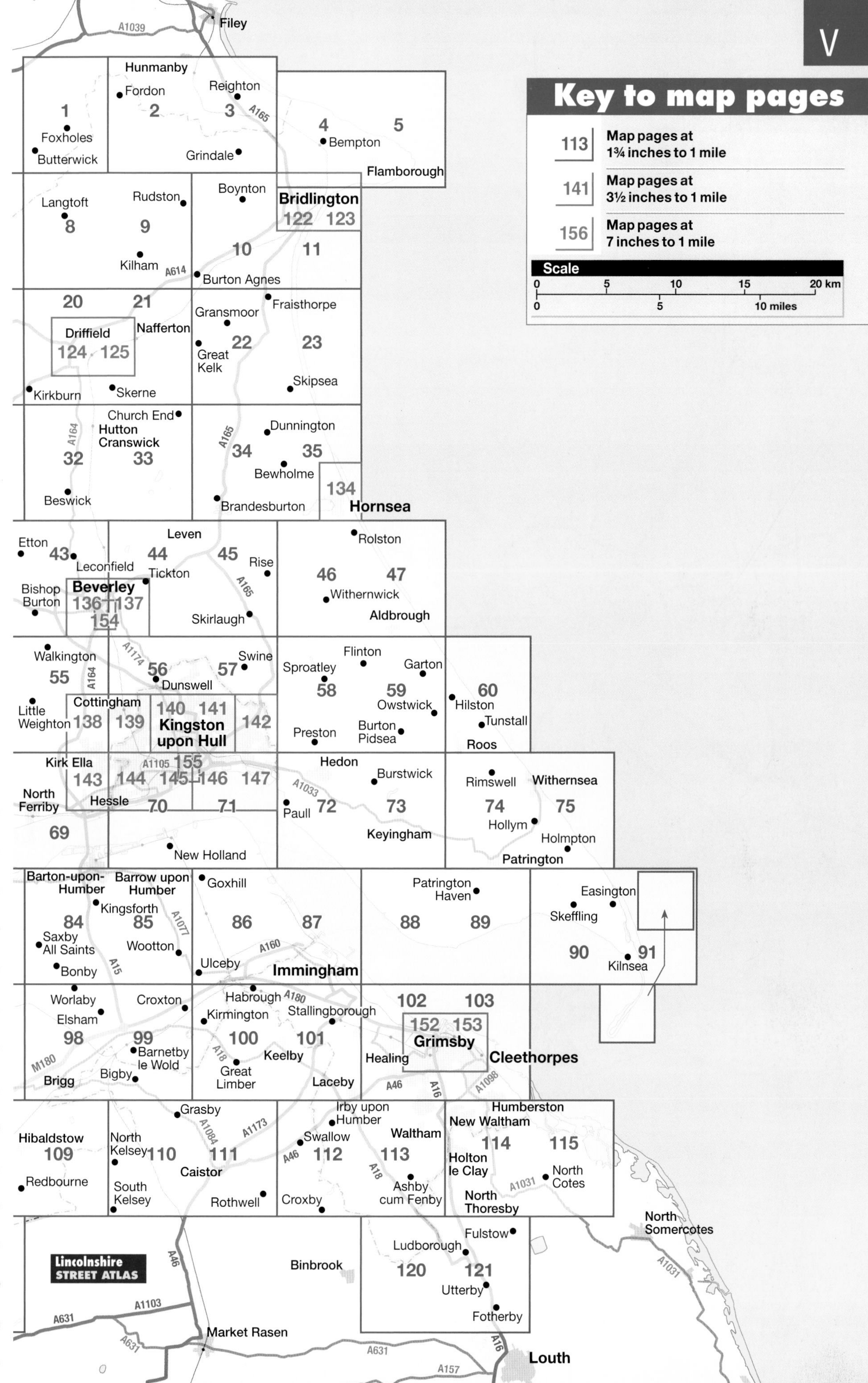

V

Key to map pages

113	Map pages at 1¾ inches to 1 mile
141	Map pages at 3½ inches to 1 mile
156	Map pages at 7 inches to 1 mile

Scale

0 — 5 — 10 — 15 — 20 km
0 — 5 — 10 miles

Filey

Hunmanby
Fordon
Reighton
1 Foxholes
Butterwick
2
Grindale
3
4 Bempton
5
Flamborough

Langtoft
Rudston
Boynton
Bridlington
122 123
8
9
Kilham
10
11
Burton Agnes

20 **21**
Gransmoor
Fraisthorpe
Driffield
Nafferton
124 125
Great Kelk
22
23
Kirkburn
Skerne
Skipsea

Church End
Hutton
Cranswick
Dunnington
32
33
34
35
Bewholme
Beswick
Brandesburton
134
Hornsea

Etton
Leven
Rolston
43
44
45
Rise
Leconfield
Tickton
46
47
Bishop Burton
Beverley
136 137
154
Withernwick
Skirlaugh
Aldbrough

Walkington
Swine
Flinton
Garton
55
56
57
Sproatley
58
59
60
Dunswell
Owstwick
Hilston
Cottingham
140 141
142
Preston
Burton Pidsea
Tunstall
Little Weighton
138 139
Kingston upon Hull
Roos

Kirk Ella
Hedon
Rimswell
Withernsea
143
144 145 146 147
155
Burstwick
74
75
North Ferriby
Hessle
70
71
72
73
Hollym
Holmpton
69
Paull
Keyingham
Patrington
New Holland

Barton-upon-Humber
Barrow upon Humber
Goxhill
Patrington Haven
Easington
84
Kingsforth
85
86
87
88
89
Skeffling
Saxby All Saints
Wootton
90
91
Bonby
Ulceby
Immingham
Kilnsea

Worlaby
Croxton
Habrough
Stallingborough
102
103
Elsham
Kirmington
152 153
98
99
100
101
Grimsby
Brigg
Barnetby le Wold
Keelby
Healing
Cleethorpes
Bigby
Great Limber
Laceby

Grasby
Irby upon Humber
Humberston
New Waltham
Hibaldstow
North Kelsey
Swallow
Waltham
114
115
109
110
111
112
113
Holton le Clay
North Cotes
Redbourne
Caistor
Croxby
Ashby cum Fenby
North Thoresby
South Kelsey
Rothwell

Fulstow
North Somercotes
Lincolnshire STREET ATLAS
Ludborough
Binbrook
120
121
Utterby
Fotherby
Market Rasen
Louth

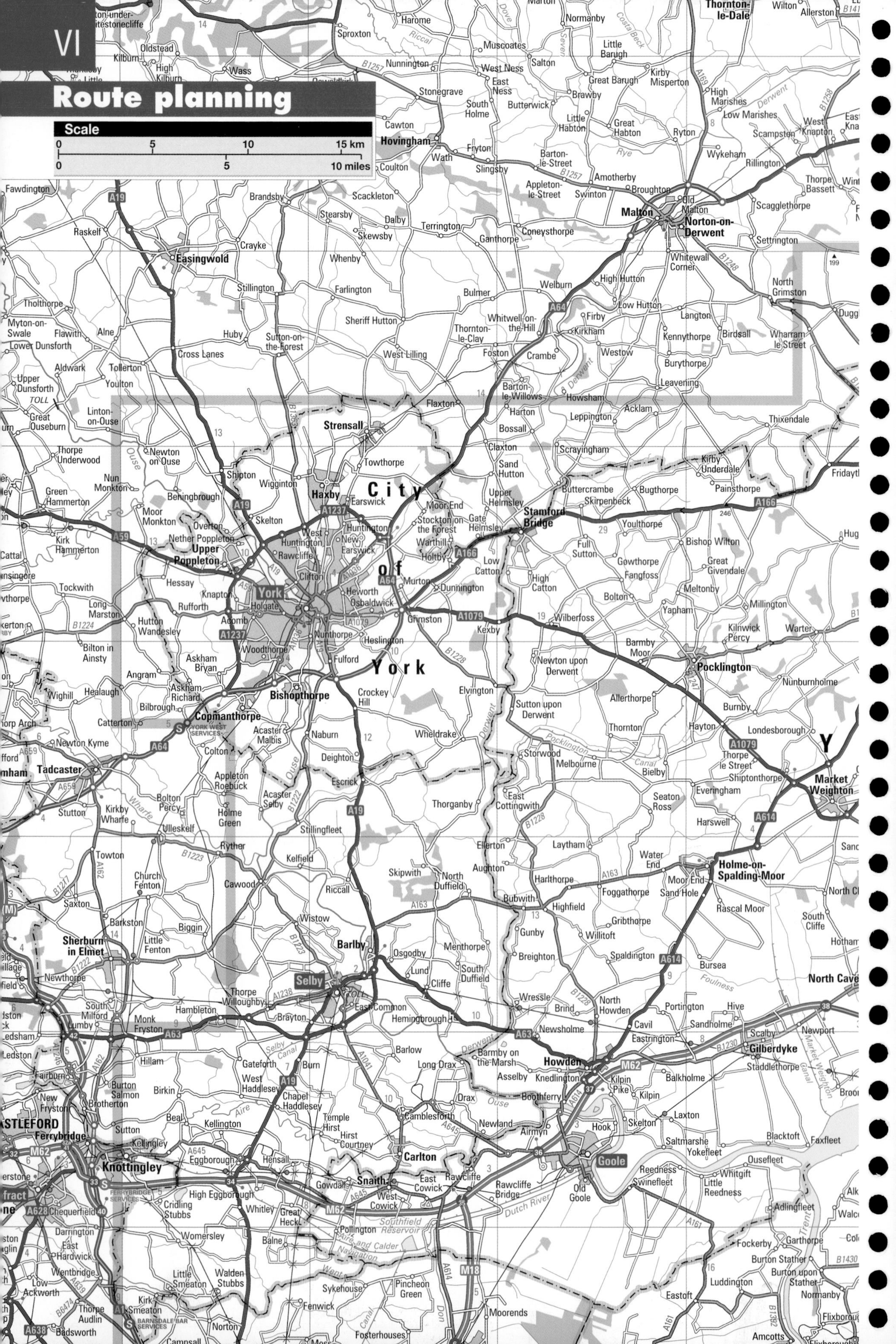
VI
Route planning
Scale
0
5
10
15 km
0
5
10 miles
City of York
York
Malton
Norton-on-Derwent
Easingwold
Hovingham
Strensall
Haxby
Upper Poppleton
Stamford Bridge
Pocklington
Market Weighton
Holme-on-Spalding-Moor
Bishopthorpe
Copmanthorpe
Tadcaster
Sherburn in Elmet
Selby
Barlby
Howden
Gilberdyke
Goole
Snaith
Carlton
Knottingley
Ferrybridge
North Cave
Thornton-le-Dale
Sheriff Hutton
Stillington
Flaxton
Wheldrake
Escrick
Riccall
Cawood
Elvington
Dunnington
Heslington
Fulford
Acomb
Holgate
Osbaldwick
Heworth
Huntington
Clifton
Rawcliffe
Skelton
Nether Poppleton
Rufforth
Wilberfoss
Kexby
Stillingfleet
Hemingbrough
Drax
Camblesforth
Rawcliffe
Airmyn
Old Goole
Swinefleet
Reedness
Eastrington
Newport
Kirk Smeaton
Womersley
Pollington
Moorends
Fosterhouses
Eastoft
Luddington
Garthorpe
A19
A64
A1079
A166
A59
A1237
A63
A614
A162
A645
A163
M62
M18
A1
B1228
B1222
B1223
Ouse
Derwent
Wharfe
Aire
Foulness
Trent
Dutch River
Pocklington Canal
Selby Canal
Aire and Calder Navigation
Southfield Reservoir
York West Services
Ferrybridge Services
Barnsdale Bar Services

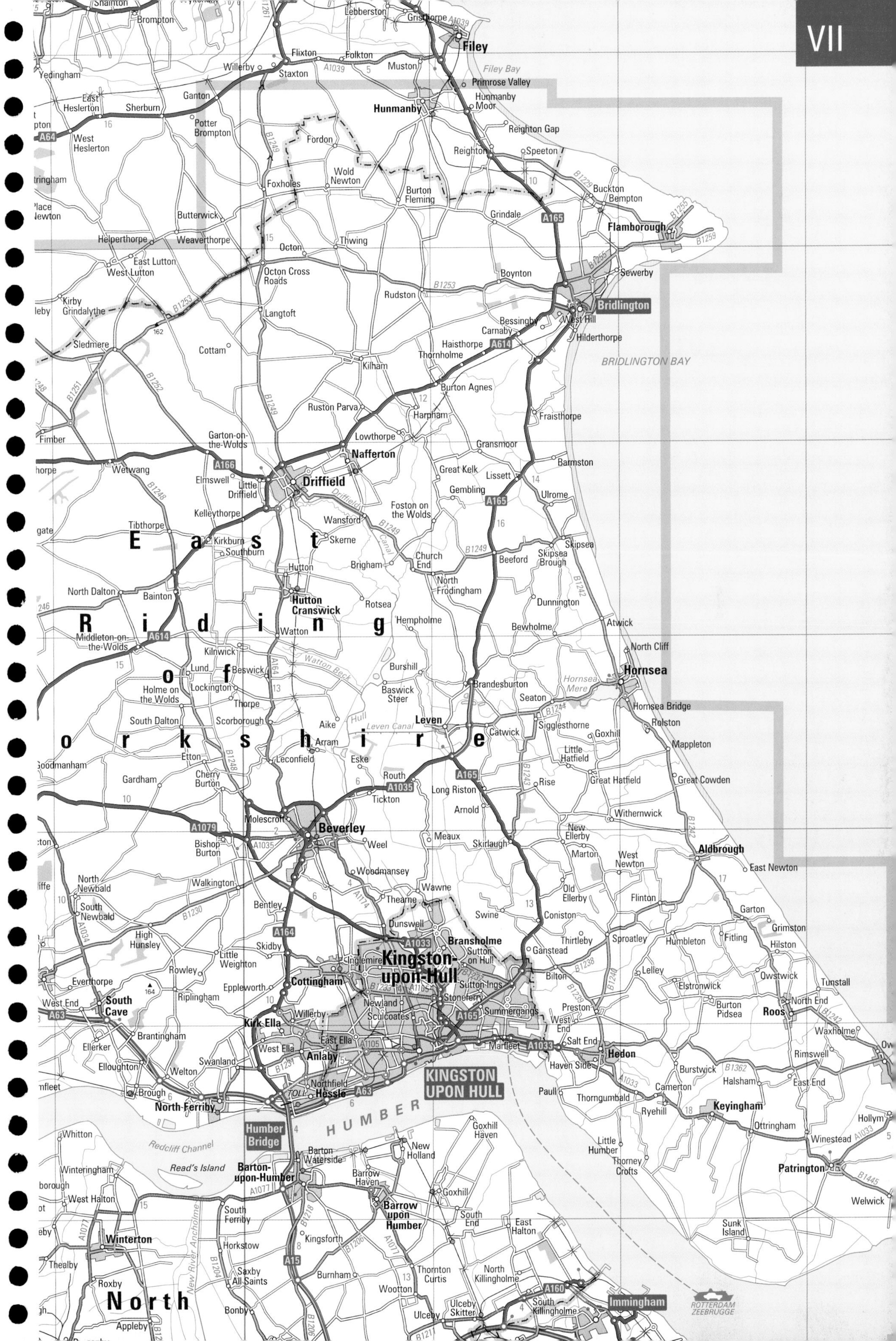
Shainton
Brompton
Lebberston
Gristhorpe
Filey
Flixton
Folkton
Willerby
Staxton
Muston
Yedingham
Filey Bay
Primrose Valley
East Heslerton
Sherburn
Ganton
Hunmanby
Hunmanby Moor
Potter Brompton
Reighton Gap
West Heslerton
Fordon
Reighton
Speeton
Foxholes
Wold Newton
Burton Fleming
Bempton
Buckton
Butterwick
Grindale
Flamborough
Helperthorpe
Weaverthorpe
Thwing
Octon
East Lutton
West Lutton
Octon Cross Roads
Boynton
Sewerby
Kirby Grindalythe
Rudston
Bridlington
Langtoft
Bessingby
West Hill
Carnaby
Hilderthorpe
Sledmere
Haisthorpe
Cottam
Thornholme
BRIDLINGTON BAY
Kilham
Burton Agnes
Ruston Parva
Harpham
Fraisthorpe
Fimber
Garton-on-the-Wolds
Lowthorpe
Gransmoor
Nafferton
Barmston
Wetwang
Elmswell
Great Kelk
Lissett
Little Driffield
Driffield
Gembling
Ulrome
Kelleythorpe
Foston on the Wolds
Wansford
Tibthorpe
Skerne
Skipsea
Kirkburn
Southburn
Church End
Beeford
Skipsea Brough
Brigham
Hutton
North Frodingham
North Dalton
Bainton
Hutton Cranswick
Dunnington
Rotsea
Hempholme
Atwick
Middleton-on-the-Wolds
Watton
Bewholme
North Cliff
Kilnwick
Watton Beck
Lund
Beswick
Burshill
Hornsea
Hornsea Mere
Holme on the Wolds
Lockington
Brandesburton
Baswick Steer
Seaton
Thorpe
Hornsea Bridge
South Dalton
Scorborough
Aike
Leven
Leven Canal
Catwick
Sigglesthorne
Rolston
Goxhill
Arram
Mappleton
Etton
Leconfield
Eske
Little Hatfield
Goodmanham
Gardham
Cherry Burton
Routh
Long Riston
Rise
Great Hatfield
Great Cowden
Tickton
Arnold
Molescroft
Withernwick
Beverley
New Ellerby
Bishop Burton
Weel
Meaux
Skirlaugh
Aldbrough
Marton
West Newton
East Newton
North Newbald
Walkington
Woodmansey
Wawne
Old Ellerby
South Newbald
Thearne
Bentley
Flinton
Swine
Coniston
Garton
Grimston
Dunswell
High Hunsley
Thirtleby
Sproatley
Humbleton
Fitling
Hilston
Bransholme
Skidby
Ganstead
Kingston-upon-Hull
Inglemire
Sutton on Hull
Little Weighton
Rowley
Bilton
Lelley
Owstwick
Everthorpe
Tunstall
Cottingham
Sutton Ings
Elstronwick
Riplingham
Eppleworth
West End
South Cave
Stoneferry
Newland
Preston
Burton Pidsea
North End
Roos
Willerby
Sculcoates
Summergangs
West End
Waxholme
Kirk Ella
Brantingham
East Ella
Salt End
Ellerker
West Ella
Marfleet
Hedon
Rimswell
Anlaby
Swanland
Haven Side
Elloughton
Burstwick
Halsham
East End
Welton
KINGSTON UPON HULL
Camerton
Brough
Northfield
Paull
Thorngumbald
Hessle
North Ferriby
Ryehill
Keyingham
HUMBER
Humber Bridge
Goxhill Haven
Hollym
Whitton
Ottringham
Winestead
Redcliff Channel
New Holland
Little Humber
Read's Island
Barton Waterside
Thorney Crofts
Winteringham
Barton-upon-Humber
Barrow Haven
Patrington
West Halton
Goxhill
Welwick
Barrow upon Humber
South Ferriby
South End
East Halton
Sunk Island
Winterton
Kingsforth
Horkstow
New River Ancholme
Thealby
Thornton Curtis
North Killingholme
Saxby All Saints
Burnham
Roxby
Wootton
Immingham
North
Bonby
Ulceby Skitter
South Killingholme
Appleby
Ulceby
ROTTERDAM ZEEBRUGGE

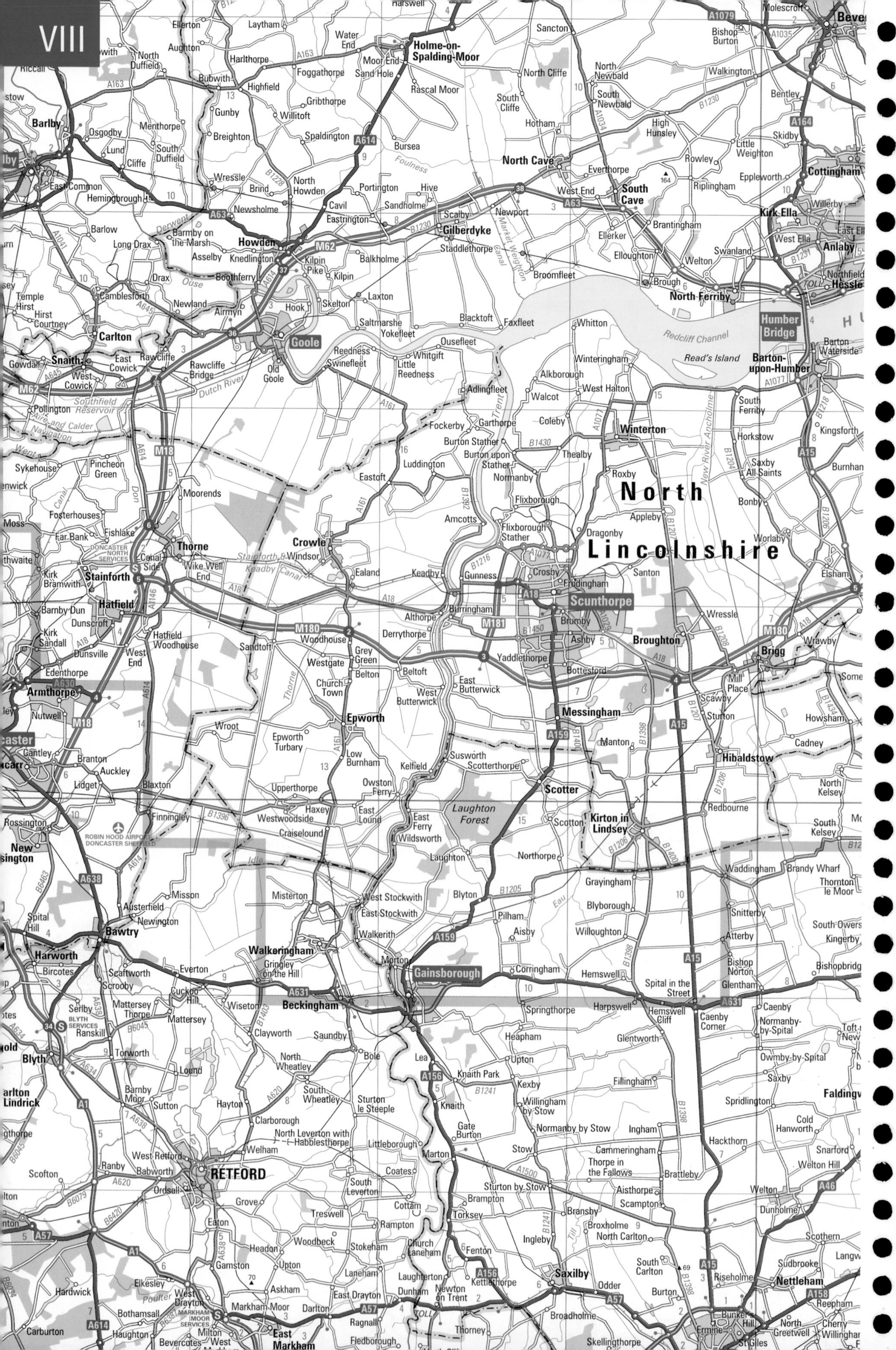
Ellerton
Laytham
Harswell
Holme-on-Spalding-Moor
Water End
Moor End
Sand Hole
Sancton
Molescroft
Beverley
Bishop Burton
North Duffield
Aughton
Harlthorpe
Foggathorpe
Rascal Moor
North Cliffe
North Newbald
South Newbald
Walkington
Bentley
Riccall
Bubwith
Highfield
Gribthorpe
Willitoft
South Cliffe
Hotham
High Hunsley
Skidby
Little Weighton
Barlby
Osgodby
Menthorpe
Gunby
Breighton
Spaldington
Bursea
Foulness
Lund
South Duffield
Cliffe
Wressle
North Howden
Portington
Hive
North Cave
Everthorpe
Rowley
Eppleworth
Cottingham
East Common
Hemingbrough
Brind
Newsholme
Cavil
Eastrington
Sandholme
Scalby
Gilberdyke
Newport
West End
South Cave
Riplingham
Kirk Ella
Willerby
Barlow
Long Drax
Barmby on the Marsh
Asselby
Howden
Knedlington
Balkholme
Staddlethorpe
Market Weighton Canal
Ellerker
Brantingham
Ellough
Welton
Swanland
West Ella
Anlaby
Kilpin Pike
Kilpin
Drax
Boothferry
Broomfleet
Brough
North Ferriby
Hessle
Northfield
Temple Hirst
Hirst Courtney
Camblesforth
Newland
Airmyn
Hook
Skelton
Laxton
Saltmarshe
Yokefleet
Blacktoft
Faxfleet
Whitton
Humber Bridge
Carlton
Goole
Redcliff Channel
Read's Island
Barton Waterside
Barton-upon-Humber
Gowdall
Snaith
East Cowick
Rawcliffe
Rawcliffe Bridge
West Cowick
Old Goole
Reedness
Swinefleet
Whitgift
Little Reedness
Ousefleet
Winteringham
Alkborough
West Halton
Walcot
Adlingfleet
Southfield Reservoir
Dutch River
Pollington
Aire and Calder Navigation
Went
Fockerby
Garthorpe
Coleby
Winterton
South Ferriby
Horkstow
Kingsforth
Burton Stather
Burton upon Stather
Thealby
Sykehouse
Pincheon Green
Luddington
Normanby
Roxby
Saxby All Saints
Burnham
Fenwick
Eastoft
North Lincolnshire
Bonby
Moorends
Flixborough
Fosterhouses
Fishlake
Amcotts
Appleby
Flixborough Stather
Dragonby
Worlaby
Far Bank
Doncaster North Services
Thorne
Crowle
Canal Side
Wike Well End
Stainforth & Keadby Canal
Windsor
Kirk Bramwith
Stainforth
Eaaland
Keadby
Gunness
Crosby
Frodingham
Santon
Elsham
Scunthorpe
Wressle
Barnby Dun
Hatfield
Burringham
Brumby
Dunscroft
Kirk Sandall
Hatfield Woodhouse
Sandtoft
Woodhouse
Althorpe
Derrythorpe
Ashby
Broughton
Wrawby
Dunsville
West End
Grey Green
Westgate
Belton
Yaddlethorpe
Brigg
Edenthorpe
Beltoft
Bottesford
Mill Place
Armthorpe
Church Town
East Butterwick
West Butterwick
Scawby
Nutwell
Epworth
Messingham
Sturton
Howsham
Wroot
Epworth Turbary
Manton
Cadney
Doncaster
Cantley
Branton
Auckley
Low Burnham
Kelfield
Susworth
Scotterthorpe
Hibaldstow
Lidget
Blaxton
Upperthorpe
Owston Ferry
Scotter
North Kelsey
Rossington
Finningley
Westwoodside
Haxey
East Lound
Laughton Forest
Scotton
Kirton in Lindsey
Redbourne
Robin Hood Airport Doncaster Sheffield
Craiselound
East Ferry
Wildsworth
South Kelsey
New Rossington
Laughton
Northorpe
Idle
Misson
Misterton
West Stockwith
Blyton
Grayingham
Waddingham
Brandy Wharf
Thornton le Moor
Austerfield
Newington
East Stockwith
Pilham
Eau
Blyborough
Snitterby
Spital Hill
Bawtry
Walkerith
Aisby
Willoughton
South Owersby
Kingerby
Atterby
Harworth
Walkeringham
Morton
Bishop Norton
Bishopbridge
Bircotes
Scaftworth
Everton
Gringley on the Hill
Gainsborough
Corringham
Hemswell
Spital in the Street
Glentham
Scrooby
Cuckoo Hill
Wiseton
Beckingham
Springthorpe
Harpswell
Hemswell Cliff
Caenby Corner
Caenby
Normanby-by-Spital
Serlby
Mattersey Thorpe
Mattersey
Blyth Services
Ranskill
Clayworth
Saundby
Heapham
Glentworth
Owmby-by-Spital
Torworth
North Wheatley
Bole
Lea
Upton
Blyth
Lound
Knaith Park
Kexby
Fillingham
Saxby
Carlton in Lindrick
Barnby Moor
Sutton
Hayton
South Wheatley
Sturton le Steeple
Knaith
Willingham by Stow
Spridlington
Faldingworth
Clarborough
Gate Burton
Normanby by Stow
Ingham
Cold Hanworth
North Leverton with Habblesthorpe
Littleborough
Cammeringham
Hackthorn
Welham
Stow
Snarford
West Retford
Marton
Thorpe in the Fallows
Welton Hill
Scofton
Ranby
Babworth
Retford
Coates
Brattleby
Ordsall
South Leverton
Sturton by Stow
Aisthorpe
Welton
Grove
Cottam
Brampton
Scampton
Dunholme
Treswell
Torksey
Bransby
Eaton
Rampton
Broxholme
North Carlton
Headon
Woodbeck
Church Laneham
Ingleby
Scothern
Stokeham
Fenton
Langworth
Gamston
Upton
Laneham
Saxilby
South Carlton
Sudbrooke
Riseholme
Nettleham
Hardwick
Elkesley
Askham
Laughterton
Kettlethorpe
Odder
Burton
Reepham
West Drayton
Markham Moor
Darlton
East Drayton
Dunham
Newton on Trent
Poulter
Bothamsall
Markham Moor Services
Ragnall
Broadholme
Bunker's Hill
North Greetwell
Cherry Willingham
Carburton
Haughton
Milton
East Markham
Fledborough
Thorney
Bevercotes
West
Skellingthorpe
Ermine
St Giles
Derwent
Ouse
Trent
Don
Canal
Thorne
Till
New River Ancholme
A1079
A1035
A163
A614
A63
A1034
B1230
A164
A1041
M62
A645
A161
B1228
A1077
B1430
B1392
B1204
B1206
A15
M18
A614
B1216
A18
M180
M181
B1450
A1029
B1207
B1208
A630
A1146
B1434
A159
B1400
B1398
B1396
B6463
A638
B1205
B1206
A631
B1403
B6045
A634
A620
A156
B1241
A1500
A57
A1
B6079
B6420
B6387
A614
A46
A158
B1231
B1218
Ouse
164
70
69

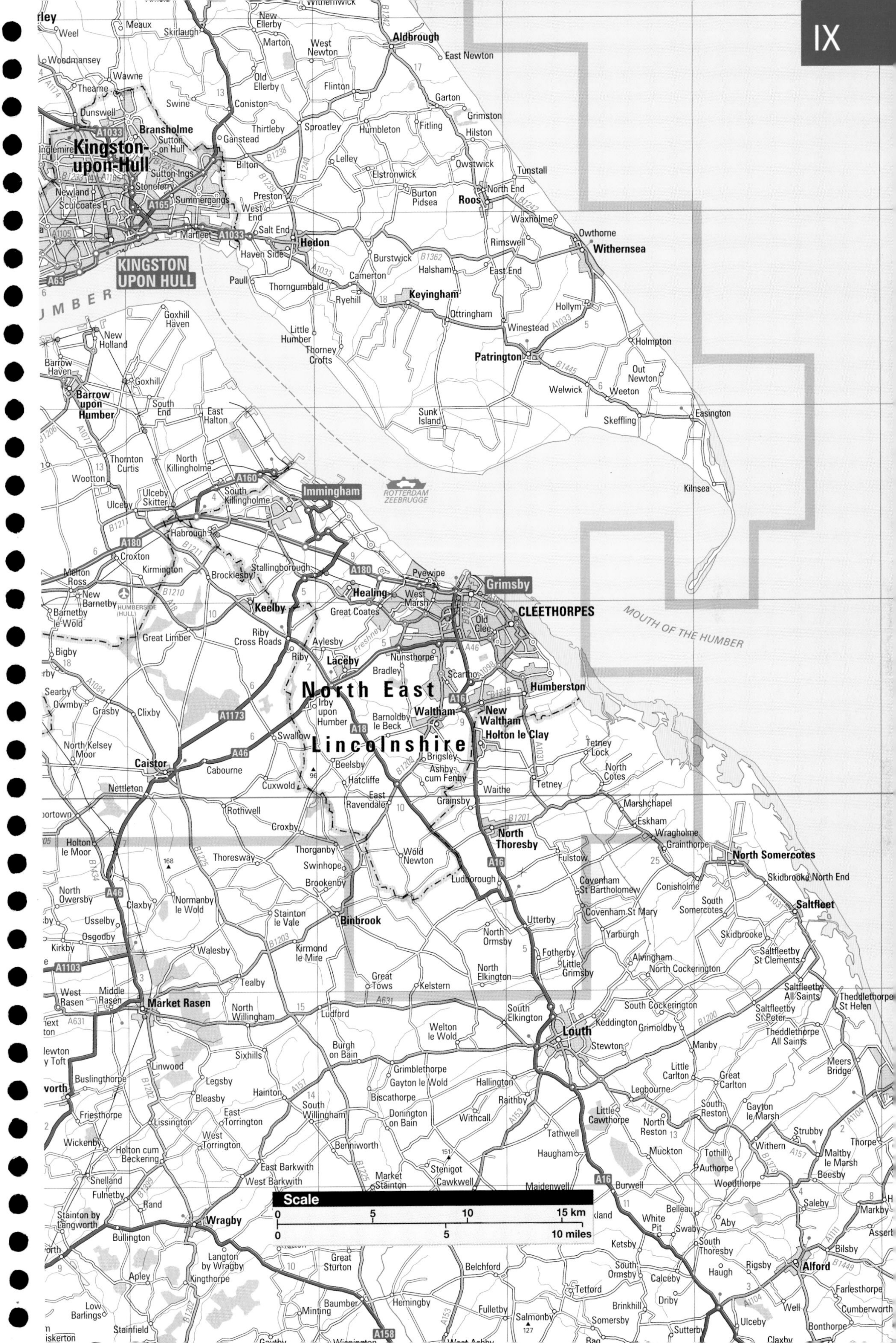
Aldbrough
East Newton
New Ellerby
Marton
West Newton
Meaux
Skirlaugh
Weel
Woodmansey
Wawne
Thearne
Old Ellerby
Flinton
Garton
Grimston
Hilston
Swine
Coniston
Dunswell
Thirtleby
Sproatley
Humbleton
Fitling
Bransholme
Kingston-upon-Hull
Sutton on Hull
Ganstead
Bilton
Lelley
Elstronwick
Owstwick
Tunstall
Sutton Ings
Stoneferry
Newland
Sculcoates
Summergangs
Preston
Burton Pidsea
Roos
North End
West End
Waxholme
Salt End
Hedon
Marfleet
Haven Side
Rimswell
Owthorne
Withernsea
Burstwick
Halsham
East End
KINGSTON UPON HULL
Paull
Thorngumbald
Camerton
Ryehill
Keyingham
Hollym
HUMBER
Ottringham
Winestead
Little Humber
Thorney Crofts
Holmpton
Patrington
Goxhill Haven
New Holland
Barrow Haven
Goxhill
Barrow upon Humber
South End
East Halton
Out Newton
Welwick
Weeton
Sunk Island
Skeffling
Easington
Thornton Curtis
North Killingholme
Wootton
Immingham
ROTTERDAM ZEEBRUGGE
Kilnsea
Ulceby Skitter
South Killingholme
Ulceby
Habrough
Croxton
Kirmington
Brocklesby
Stallingborough
Pyewipe
Melton Ross
New Barnetby
HUMBERSIDE (HULL)
Barnetby le Wold
Keelby
Healing
West Marsh
Grimsby
CLEETHORPES
Great Coates
Old Clee
MOUTH OF THE HUMBER
Great Limber
Riby Cross Roads
Aylesby
Bigby
Riby
Laceby
Nunsthorpe
Bradley
Scartho
Humberston
Searby
Owmby
North East Lincolnshire
Grasby
Clixby
Irby upon Humber
Barnoldby le Beck
Waltham
New Waltham
Holton le Clay
Swallow
North Kelsey Moor
Tetney Lock
Caistor
Cabourne
Beelsby
Brigsley
Ashby cum Fenby
North Cotes
Hatcliffe
Cuxwold
East Ravendale
Waithe
Tetney
Nettleton
Grainsby
Marshchapel
Rothwell
Eskham
Croxby
North Thoresby
Wragholme
Grainthorpe
Holton le Moor
Thorganby
Wold Newton
North Somercotes
Thoresway
Swinhope
Fulstow
Brookenby
Ludborough
Skidbrooke North End
North Owersby
Covenham St Bartholomew
Conisholme
Claxby
Normanby le Wold
South Somercotes
Saltfleet
Stainton le Vale
Binbrook
Covenham St Mary
Usselby
Osgodby
Utterby
Yarburgh
North Ormsby
Skidbrooke
Walesby
Kirmond le Mire
Fotherby
Little Grimsby
Alvingham
Saltfleetby St Clements
Kirkby
North Cockerington
North Elkington
Tealby
Great Tows
Kelstern
Saltfleetby All Saints
West Rasen
Middle Rasen
Market Rasen
Theddlethorpe St Helen
North Willingham
South Cockerington
Ludford
South Elkington
Keddington
Grimoldby
Saltfleetby St Peter
Welton le Wold
Louth
Theddlethorpe All Saints
Burgh on Bain
Stewton
Manby
Sixhills
Linwood
Grimblethorpe
Little Carlton
Meers Bridge
Gayton le Wold
Hallington
Great Carlton
Buslingthorpe
Legsby
Hainton
Biscathorpe
Raithby
Legbourne
Bleasby
South Willingham
Little Cawthorpe
South Reston
Gayton le Marsh
Friesthorpe
East Torrington
Donington on Bain
Withcall
North Reston
Lissington
West Torrington
Tathwell
Strubby
Wickenby
Muckton
Thorpe
Holton cum Beckering
Benniworth
Haugham
Tothill
Withern
Maltby le Marsh
Beesby
East Barkwith
Stenigot
Authorpe
Snelland
West Barkwith
Market Stainton
Cawkwell
Maidenwell
Burwell
Woodthorpe
Fulnetby
Rand
Scale
0 5 10 15 km
0 5 10 miles
Saleby
Markby
Stainton by Langworth
Wragby
Belleau
White Pit
Aby
Swaby
Bullington
South Thoresby
Asserby
Bilsby
Langton by Wragby
Great Sturton
Ketsby
Apley
Kingthorpe
Belchford
South Ormsby
Calceby
Haugh
Rigsby
Alford
Tetford
Driby
Brinkhill
Farlesthorpe
Low Barlings
Baumber
Hemingby
Minting
Fulletby
Salmonby
Somersby
Well
Ulceby
Cumberworth
Stainfield
Sutterby
Bonthorpe
Claxby

Administrative and Postcode boundaries

County and unitary authority boundaries

Postcode boundaries

Area covered by this atlas

Scale

0 5 10 15 20 25 30 35 40 km

0 5 10 15 20 25 miles

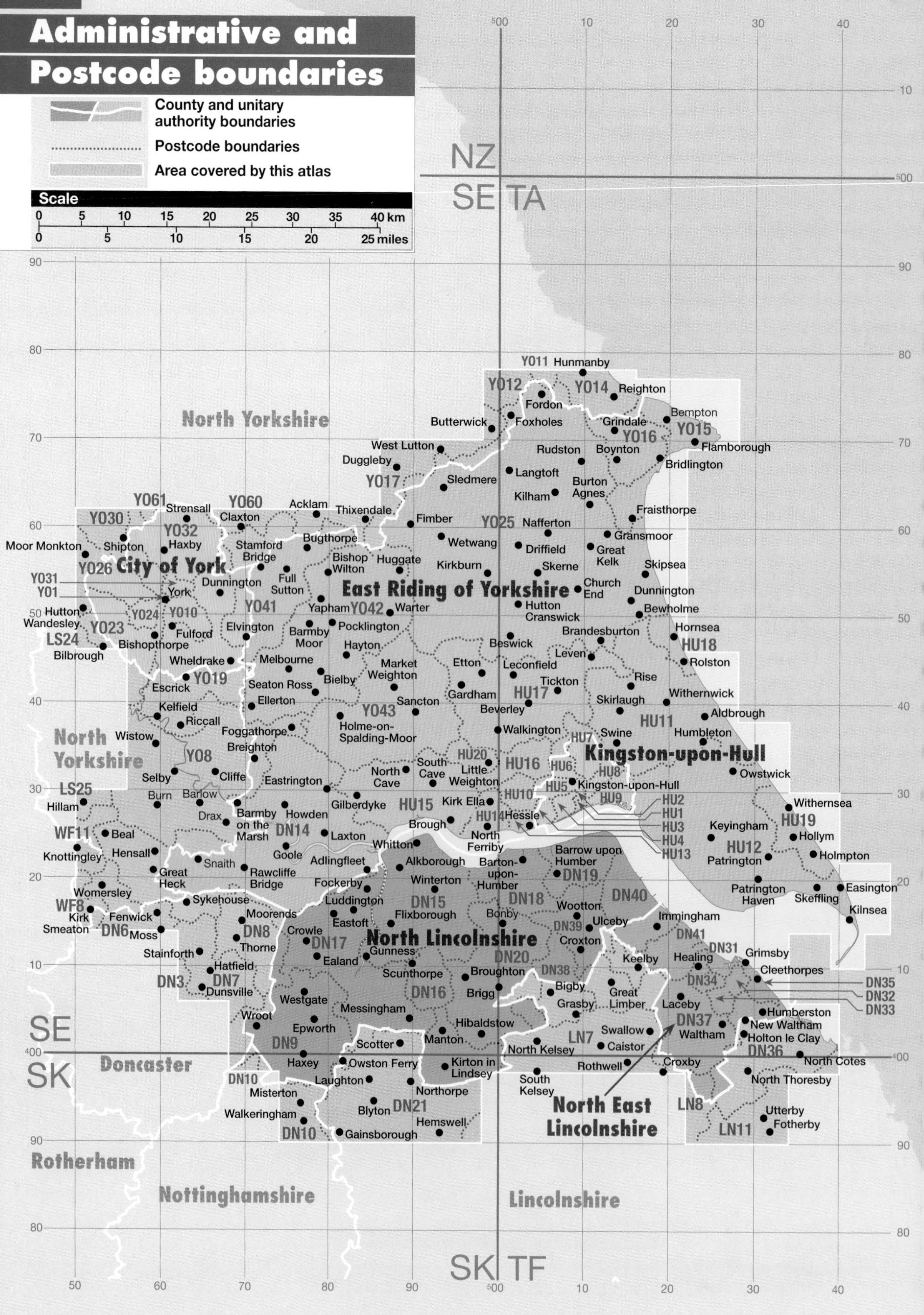

Scale: 1¾ inches to 1 mile

2

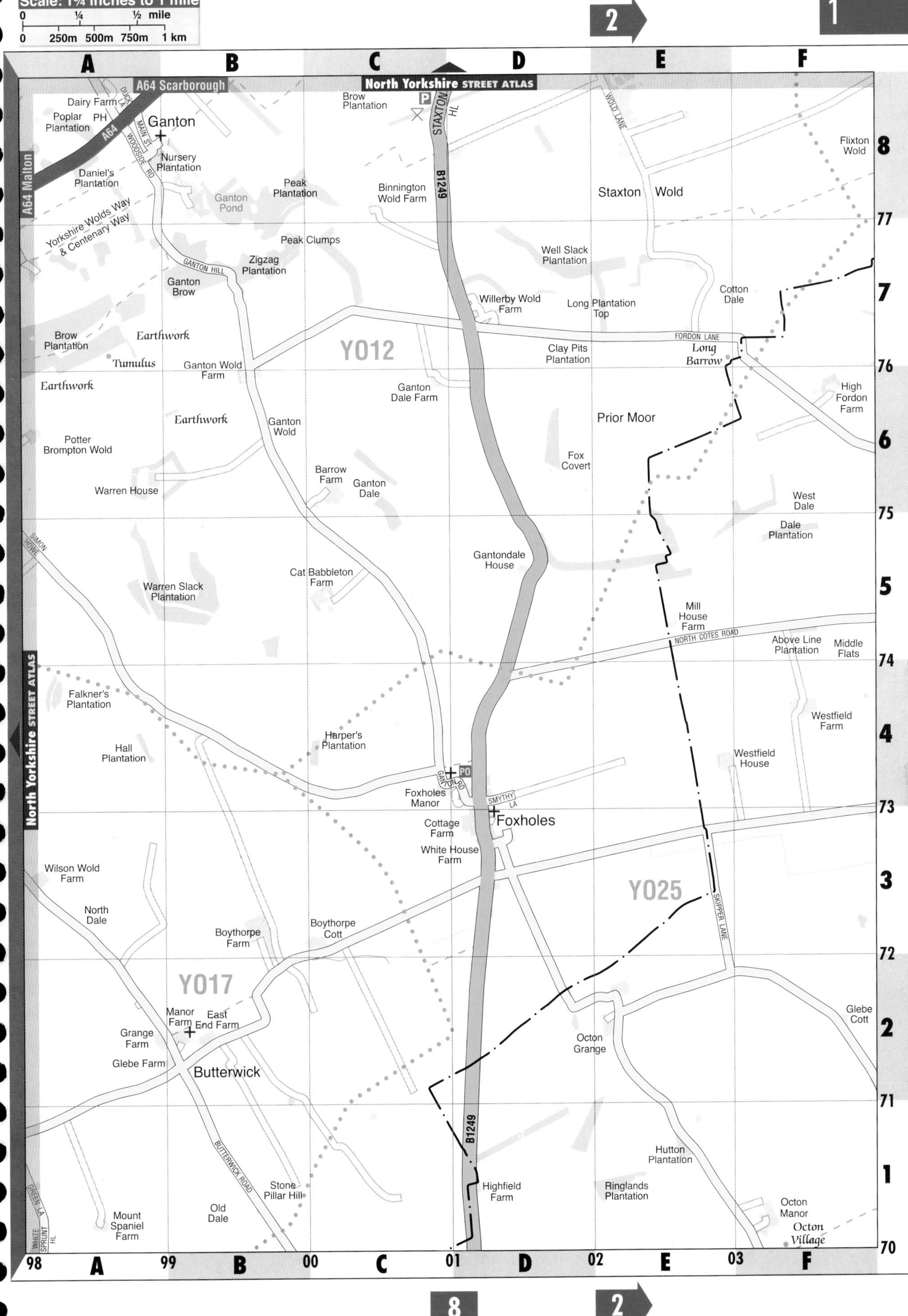

A64 Scarborough
North Yorkshire STREET ATLAS
A64 Malton
Dairy Farm
Poplar Plantation
PH
Ganton
Nursery Plantation
Daniel's Plantation
Ganton Pond
Peak Plantation
Brow Plantation
Binnington Wold Farm
STAXTON HL
B1249
Staxton Wold
Flixton Wold
Yorkshire Wolds Way & Centenary Way
Peak Clumps
Zigzag Plantation
GANTON HILL
Ganton Brow
Well Slack Plantation
Willerby Wold Farm
Long Plantation Top
Cotton Dale
Brow Plantation
Earthwork
Tumulus
YO12
Ganton Wold Farm
Clay Pits Plantation
FORDON LANE
Long Barrow
Earthwork
Ganton Dale Farm
Earthwork
Ganton Wold
Prior Moor
High Fordon Farm
Potter Brompton Wold
Fox Covert
Barrow Farm
Ganton Dale
Warren House
West Dale
Dale Plantation
SIMON HOWE
Gantondale House
Cat Babbleton Farm
Warren Slack Plantation
Mill House Farm
NORTH COTES ROAD
Above Line Plantation
Middle Flats
Falkner's Plantation
Westfield Farm
Harper's Plantation
Hall Plantation
Westfield House
GANTON RD
PO
Foxholes Manor
SMYTHY LA
Foxholes
Cottage Farm
White House Farm
Wilson Wold Farm
YO25
North Dale
Boythorpe Farm
Boythorpe Cott
SKIPPER LANE
YO17
Manor Farm
East End Farm
Glebe Cott
Grange Farm
Octon Grange
Glebe Farm
Butterwick
B1249
Hutton Plantation
BUTTERWICK ROAD
Stone Pillar Hill
Highfield Farm
Ringlands Plantation
GREEN LA
Mount Spaniel Farm
Old Dale
Octon Manor
Octon Village
WHITE SPRUNT HL
A B C D E F
98 99 00 01 02 03
70 71 72 73 74 75 76 77
1 2 3 4 5 6 7 8

8
2

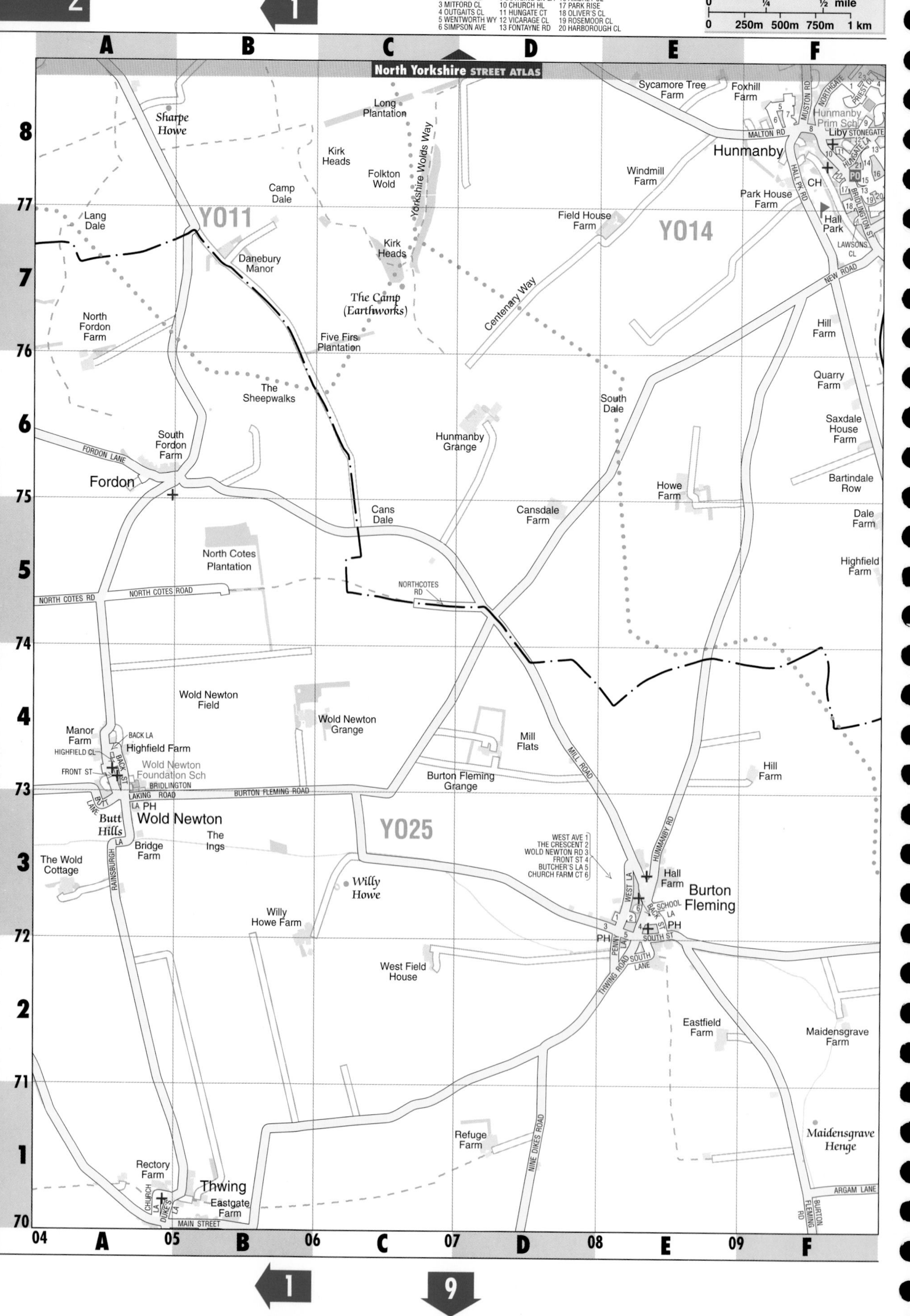

F8
1 OWSTON RD
2 MITFORD RD
3 MITFORD CL
4 OUTGAITS CL
5 WENTWORTH WY
6 SIMPSON AVE
7 HIGH CFT
8 CASTLE HL
9 BOWLING GN LA
10 CHURCH HL
11 HUNGATE CT
12 VICARAGE CL
13 FONTAYNE RD
14 BARDNEY RD
15 ROWEDALE CL
16 AMBREY CL
17 PARK RISE
18 OLIVER'S CL
19 ROSEMOOR CL
20 HARBOROUGH CL
21 EASTFIELD
22 GARTON LA

Scale: 1¾ inches to 1 mile

0   ¼   ½   mile
0   250m   500m   750m   1 km

North Yorkshire STREET ATLAS

A   **B**   **C**   **D**   **E**   **F**

8

Sharpe Howe

Long Plantation

Sycamore Tree Farm

Foxhill Farm

MUSTON RD

NORTHGATE

PRISTE LA

Hunmanby Prim Sch

Liby STONEGATE

MALTON RD

Hunmanby

HALL PK RD

CH

PO

BRIDLINGTON ST

77

Camp Dale

Kirk Heads

Folkton Wold

YO11

Lang Dale

Danebury Manor

Windmill Farm

Field House Farm

YO14

Park House Farm

Hall Park

LAWSONS CL

NEW ROAD

7

Kirk Heads

The Camp (Earthworks)

Yorkshire Wolds Way

Centenary Way

Hill Farm

North Fordon Farm

Five Firs Plantation

76

The Sheepwalks

Quarry Farm

Saxdale House Farm

South Dale

6

South Fordon Farm

Hunmanby Grange

Bartindale Row

FORDON LANE

Dale Farm

75

Fordon

Cans Dale

Cansdale Farm

Howe Farm

Highfield Farm

5

North Cotes Plantation

NORTHCOTES RD

NORTH COTES RD

NORTH COTES ROAD

74

4

Wold Newton Field

Wold Newton Grange

Mill Flats

MILL ROAD

Hill Farm

Manor Farm

BACK LA

Highfield Farm

HIGHFIELD CL

FRONT ST

Wold Newton Foundation Sch

BRIDLINGTON

Burton Fleming Grange

73

Wold Newton

LAKING ROAD

BURTON FLEMING ROAD

LA PH

YO25

WEST AVE 1
THE CRESCENT 2
WOLD NEWTON RD 3
FRONT ST 4
BUTCHER'S LA 5
CHURCH FARM CT 6

Butt Hills

RAINSBURGH LA

The Ings

Bridge Farm

BACK LA

HUNMANBY RD

WEST LA

Hall Farm

SCHOOL LA

Burton Fleming

3

The Wold Cottage

Willy Howe

PH

SOUTH ST

PH

72

Willy Howe Farm

West Field House

THWING ROAD

SOUTH LANE

PENNY LANE

2

Eastfield Farm

Maidensgrave Farm

71

1

Refuge Farm

NINE DIKES ROAD

Maidensgrave Henge

Rectory Farm

Thwing

Eastgate Farm

CHURCH LA

DIKES LA

MAIN STREET

ARGAM LANE

BURTON FLEMING RD

70

04   **A**   05   **B**   06   **C**   07   **D**   08   **E**   09   **F**

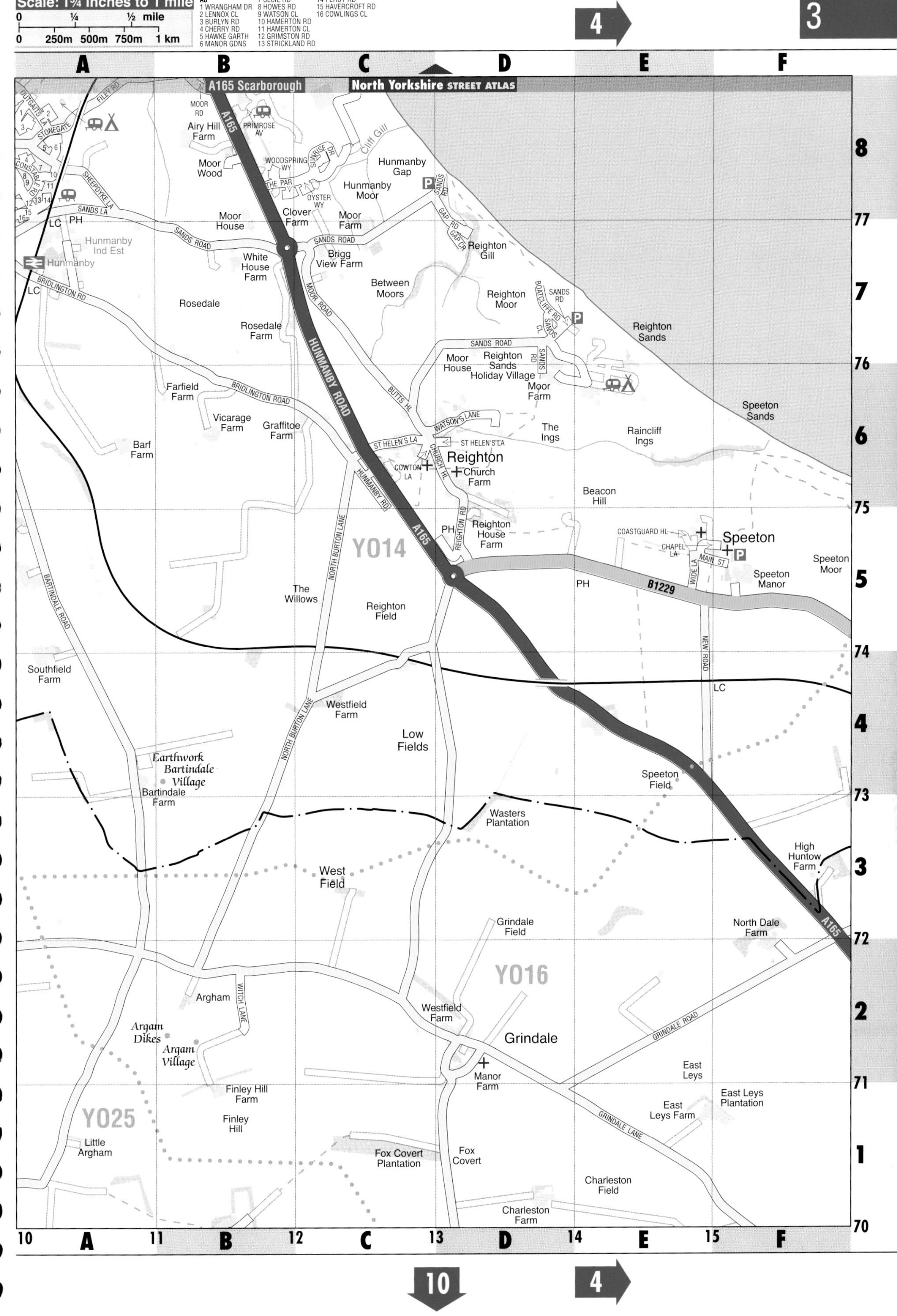
Scale: 1¾ inches to 1 mile
0 ¼ ½ mile
0 250m 500m 750m 1 km
A8
1 WRANGHAM DR
2 LENNOX CL
3 BURLYN RD
4 CHERRY RD
5 HAWKE GARTH
6 MANOR GDNS
7 CECIL RD
8 HOWES RD
9 WATSON CL
10 HAMERTON RD
11 HAMERTON CL
12 GRIMSTON RD
13 STRICKLAND RD
14 PERCY RD
15 HAVERCROFT RD
16 COWLINGS CL
4
A165 Scarborough
North Yorkshire STREET ATLAS
Airy Hill Farm
Moor Wood
Moor House
Clover Farm
Moor Farm
Hunmanby Gap
Hunmanby Moor
White House Farm
Brigg View Farm
Hunmanby Ind Est
Hunmanby
Rosedale
Rosedale Farm
Between Moors
Reighton Gill
Reighton Moor
Reighton Sands
Moor House
Reighton Sands Holiday Village
Moor Farm
Farfield Farm
Vicarage Farm
Graffitoe Farm
Barf Farm
The Ings
Raincliff Ings
Speeton Sands
Reighton
Church Farm
Beacon Hill
Reighton House Farm
Speeton
Speeton Moor
Speeton Manor
YO14
The Willows
Reighton Field
Southfield Farm
Westfield Farm
Low Fields
Earthwork Bartindale Village
Bartindale Farm
Speeton Field
Wasters Plantation
High Huntow Farm
West Field
Grindale Field
North Dale Farm
YO16
Argham
Westfield Farm
Grindale
Argam Dikes
Argam Village
Manor Farm
East Leys
East Leys Plantation
East Leys Farm
Finley Hill Farm
Finley Hill
YO25
Little Argham
Fox Covert Plantation
Fox Covert
Charleston Field
Charleston Farm
HUNMANBY ROAD
BRIDLINGTON ROAD
SANDS ROAD
SANDS LA
SHEEPDYKE LA
FILEY RD
STONEGATE
OUTGATES LA
MOOR RD
PRIMROSE AV
WOODSPRING WY
SUNRISE DR
THE PAR
OYSTER WY
SANDS RD
GAP RD
GAP CR
Cliff Gill
MOOR ROAD
BUTTS HL
WATSON'S LANE
ST HELEN'S LA
CHURCH HL
COWTON LA
REIGHTON RD
BOATCLIFFE RD
NORTH BURTON LANE
BARTINDALE ROAD
COASTGUARD HL
CHAPEL LA
MAIN ST
WIDE LA
NEW ROAD
B1229
A165
WITCH LANE
GRINDALE ROAD
GRINDALE LANE
A B C D E F
10 11 12 13 14 15
8 77 7 76 6 75 5 74 4 73 3 72 2 71 1 70
10
4

Scale: 1¾ inches to 1 mile

0 ¼ ½ mile
0 250m 500m 750m 1 km

A B C D E F

8
76
7
75
6
74
5
73
4
72
3
71
2
70
1
69

King & Queen Rocks
Speeton Cliffs
Dulcey Dock
Buckton Cliffs
Speeton Moor
Great Moor
Crab Rocks
B1229
Buckton Hall
Visitor Centre
Scale Nab
Speeton Gate
Mast
Standard Hill
Bempton Cliffs Nature Reserve
The Leys
Cat Nab
Greenlands Farm
Grange Farm
Bempton Grange
Norway Farm
The Moor
Wandale Farm
Dykes End
Gull Nook
Cliff Lane
White House Farm
Buckton
Bempton Prim Sch
Forge Cl
PH
Bydales Plantation
Metlands
YO15
Dykes Plantation
Main St
Green La
Bempton
Stonepit Lane
Wold Farm
Mast
Grindale Road
High St
School
PO
Eden Gd
Flamborough Road
B1229
Danes' Dyke
A165
Bolam Lane
Bempton
LC
LC
Butterwicks Farm
Bempton Lane
YO16
Mill Farm
Newsham Field
Sewerby Mill Farm
Norlands
Newsham Hill La
Lynhams
CROFTS HILL
The Crofts
East Huntow
Norlands La
Bempton Lane
Short Lane
High Barn
Quarry Farm
Lynhams Rd
Bream Wood
North Mount
Field House
Jewison Lane
Long Acres Farm
Daneswood Farm
West Huntow
Scarborough Road
Pinfold Lane
Derwent Gd
Cote Walls Plantation
LC
Sheeprake La
Flamborough Rd
Bridlington Rd
Gell-spring Plantation
Home Farm
The Grange
Hill Field
Stackyard Plantation
Marton Gate
PH
Moor Road
Marton
Leys Plantation
Long Wood
Dyke Wood
Nature Reserve
Danes Dyke Farm
Dykes End
Grindale Lane
A165
B1255 Marton Gate
Charity Farm
Church La
High Sewerby Rd
Moor Rd
CH
Sewerby Hall

122
123

C4
1 WALMSLEY CL
2 GRANGE CL
3 COLLINGWOOD RD
4 THE MEADOWS
5 RINGLEY MDWS

D4
1 THE PADDOCK
2 SPRING LA
3 ST MICHAEL'S WK
4 BYEDALES
5 GILLUS LA
6 CHURCH LA
7 ACREDYKES
8 VICARAGE LA
9 CLARK CR

For full street detail of the highlighted area see pages 122 and 123.

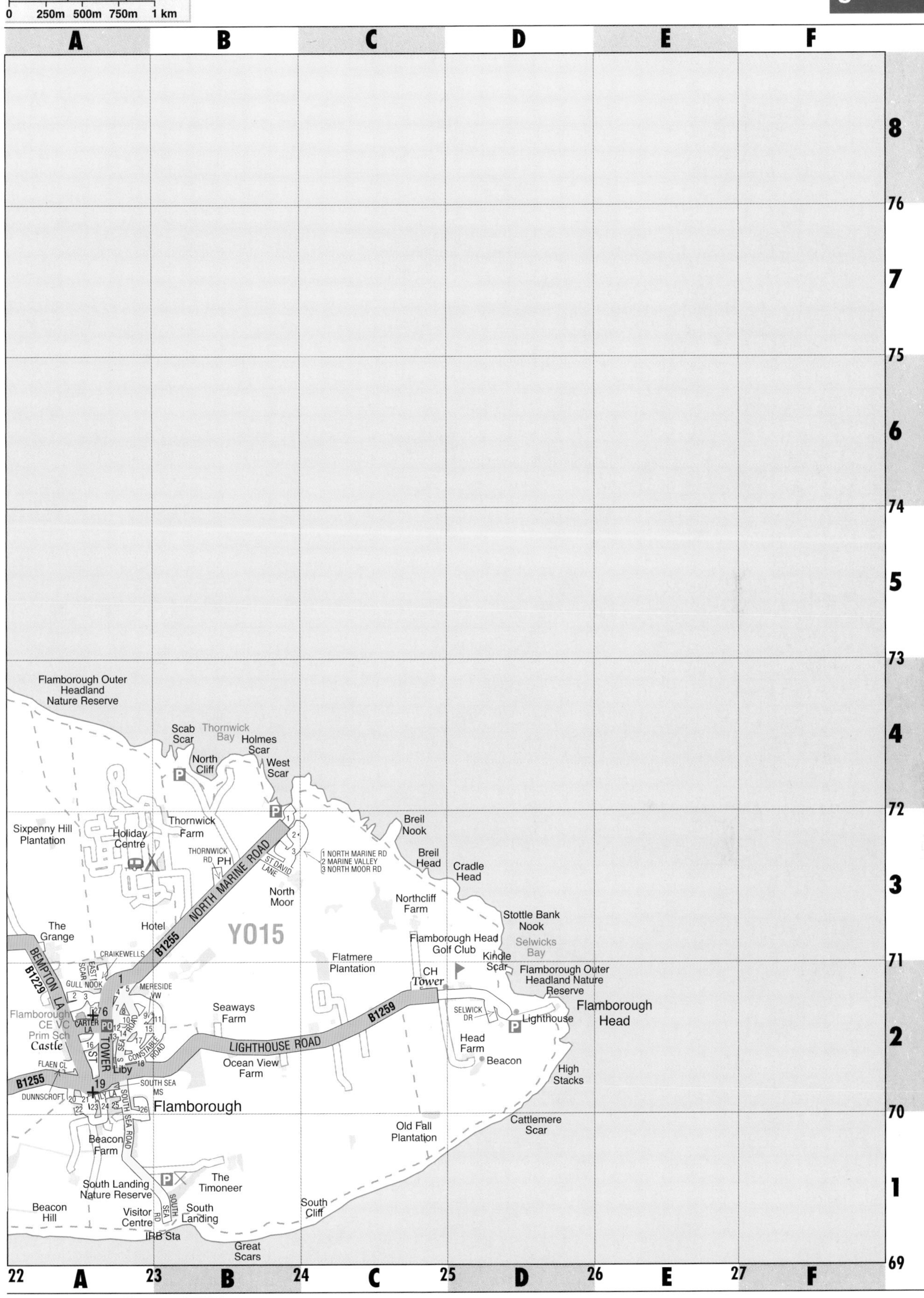

A2
1 WOODCOCK RD
2 BEECH GR
3 BEECH AVE
4 GARENDS RD
5 NORTH END
6 CHAPEL ST
7 HIGH ST
8 GREENSIDE
9 MERESIDE
10 SCHOOL LA
11 OGLE RD
12 POST OFFICE ST
13 DOG AND DUCK SQ
14 ALLISON LA
15 STYLEFIELD RD
16 CASTLE CR
17 STOTTLEBINK
18 CONSTABLE CL
19 CHURCH ST
20 WATER LA
21 WEST ST
22 HARTENDALE CL
23 BUTLERS LA
24 CHURCH LA
25 CHURCH CL
26 SOUTH SEA AVE
27 CHAPEL CL

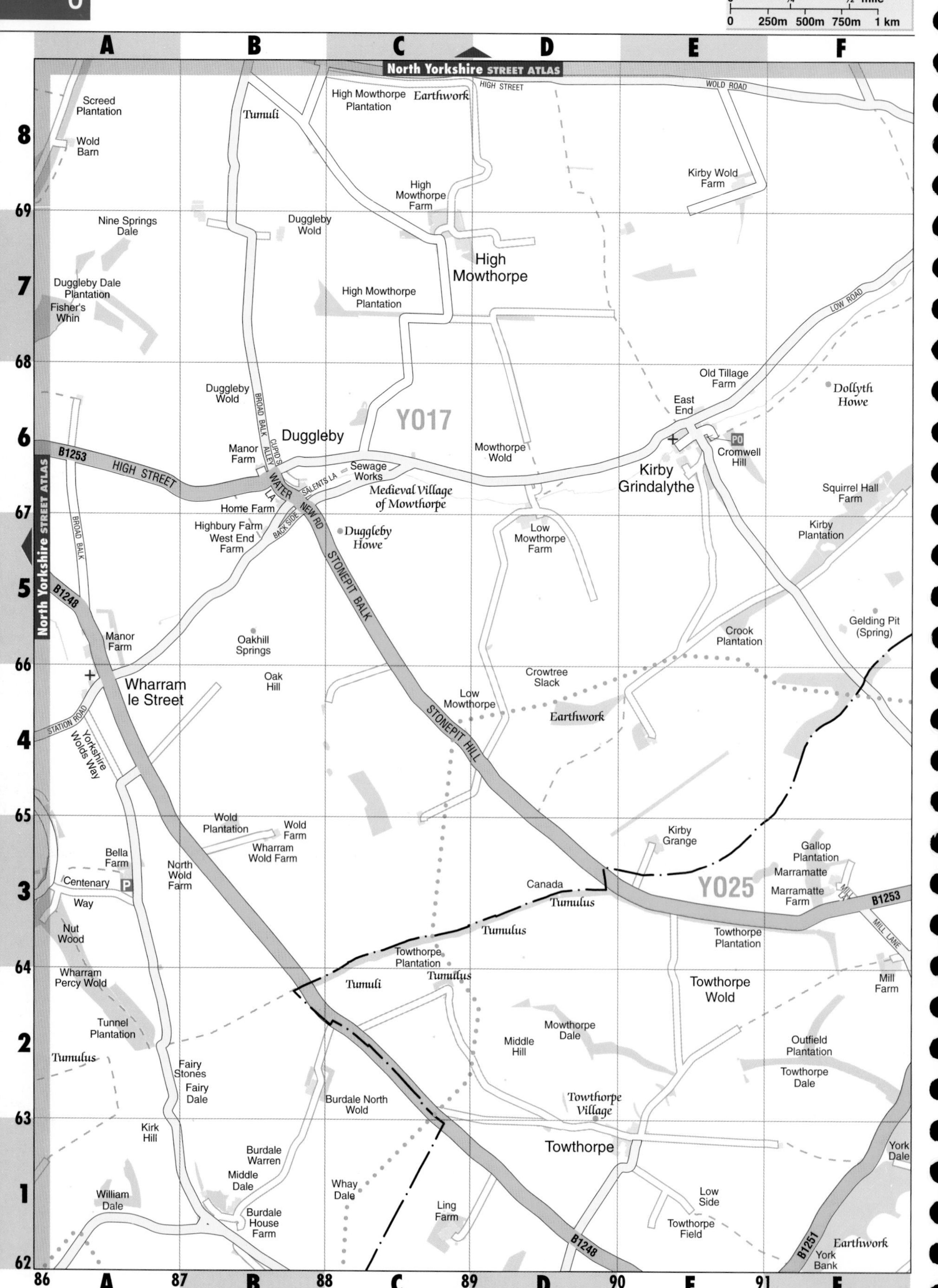

Scale: 1¾ inches to 1 mile

0   ¼   ½   mile
0   250m 500m 750m 1 km

North Yorkshire STREET ATLAS

North Yorkshire STREET ATLAS

Screed Plantation

Wold Barn

Nine Springs Dale

Duggleby Dale Plantation

Fisher's Whin

Tumuli

High Mowthorpe Plantation

Earthwork

HIGH STREET

WOLD ROAD

Duggleby Wold

High Mowthorpe Farm

High Mowthorpe

Kirby Wold Farm

High Mowthorpe Plantation

LOW ROAD

Duggleby Wold

B1253 HIGH STREET

Manor Farm

Duggleby

YO17

Old Tillage Farm

East End

Dollyth Howe

Cromwell Hill

BROAD BALK

CUPIDS ALLEY

WATER LA

SALENTS LA

Sewage Works

Mowthorpe Wold

Kirby Grindalythe

PO

Squirrel Hall Farm

Home Farm

Medieval Village of Mowthorpe

Kirby Plantation

BROAD BALK

NEW RD

BACK SIDE

Highbury Farm West End Farm

Duggleby Howe

Low Mowthorpe Farm

B1248

Manor Farm

Oakhill Springs

STONEPIT BALK

Crook Plantation

Gelding Pit (Spring)

Wharram le Street

Oak Hill

Crowtree Slack

Low Mowthorpe

STATION ROAD

Yorkshire Wolds Way

STONEPIT HILL

Earthwork

Wold Plantation

Wold Farm

Kirby Grange

Gallop Plantation

Marramatte

YO25

B1253

Bella Farm

Centenary Way

P

North Wold Farm

Wharram Wold Farm

Canada

Tumulus

Towthorpe Plantation

Marramatte Farm

MILL LANE

MILL LANE

Nut Wood

Tumulus

Towthorpe Plantation

Towthorpe Wold

Towthorpe Plantation

Mill Farm

Wharram Percy Wold

Tumuli

Tumulus

Towthorpe Wold

Outfield Plantation

Tunnel Plantation

Mowthorpe Dale

Towthorpe Dale

Tumulus

Fairy Stones

Middle Hill

Fairy Dale

Burdale North Wold

Towthorpe Village

York Dale

Kirk Hill

Burdale Warren

Towthorpe

Low Side

Middle Dale

Whay Dale

Ling Farm

Towthorpe Field

B1248

William Dale

Burdale House Farm

B1251

York Bank

Earthwork

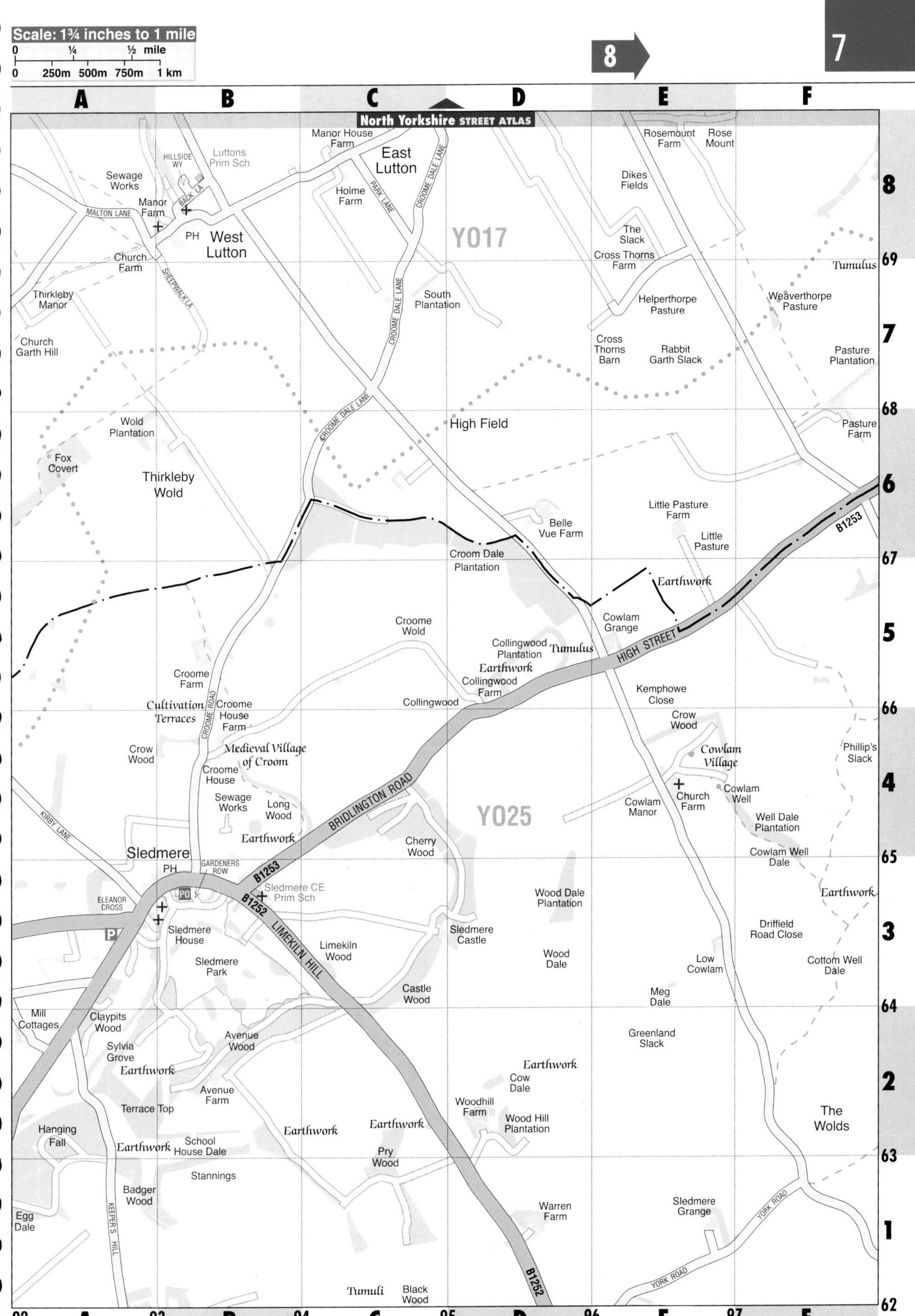

North Yorkshire STREET ATLAS

A   B   C   D   E   F

Manor House Farm

East Lutton

Rosemount Farm   Rose Mount

Sewage Works

HILLSIDE WY

Luttons Prim Sch

Dikes Fields

8

Holme Farm

BACK LA

Manor Farm

PH

West Lutton

PARK LANE

CROOME DALE LANE

YO17

The Slack

Cross Thorns Farm

69   Tumulus

MALTON LANE

Church Farm

SWEEPWALK LA

South Plantation

Helperthorpe Pasture

Weaverthorpe Pasture

Thirkleby Manor

Cross Thorns Barn

Rabbit Garth Slack

7

Pasture Plantation

Church Garth Hill

CROOME DALE LANE

68   Pasture Farm

Wold Plantation

High Field

Fox Covert

Thirkleby Wold

6

Little Pasture Farm

B1253

Belle Vue Farm

Little Pasture

67

Croom Dale Plantation

Earthwork

Cowlam Grange

HIGH STREET

5

Croome Wold

Collingwood Plantation   Tumulus

Croome Farm

Earthwork   Collingwood Farm

Kemphowe Close

Crow Wood

66

Cultivation Terraces

CROOME ROAD

Croome House Farm

Collingwood

Phillip's Slack

Crow Wood

Medieval Village of Croom

YO25

Cowlam Village

4

KIRBY LANE

Croome House

Cowlam Manor

Church Farm

Cowlam Well

Sewage Works

Long Wood

Cowlam Well Dale

BRIDLINGTON ROAD

Earthwork

Well Dale Plantation

Cherry Wood

Sledmere

PH

GARDENERS ROW

65

Wood Dale Plantation

Earthwork

B1253

Sledmere CE Prim Sch

B1252

ELEANOR CROSS

PO

P

Sledmere House

Wood Dale

Low Cowlam

Driffield Road Close

3

Cottom Well Dale

LIMEKILN HILL

Limekiln Wood

Sledmere Castle

Meg Dale

Sledmere Park

Castle Wood

Greenland Slack

64

Mill Cottages

Claypits Wood

Avenue Wood

Sylvia Grove

Earthwork

Earthwork   Cow Dale

2

Avenue Farm

Earthwork   Earthwork

Woodhill Farm

Wood Hill Plantation

The Wolds

Terrace Top

Hanging Fall

Earthwork   School House Dale

Earthwork

Pry Wood

63

KEEPER'S HILL

Stannings

Badger Wood

Sledmere Grange

YORK ROAD

Egg Dale

1

B1252

Tumuli   Black Wood

Warren Farm

YORK ROAD

92   A   93   B   94   C   95   D   96   E   97   F   62

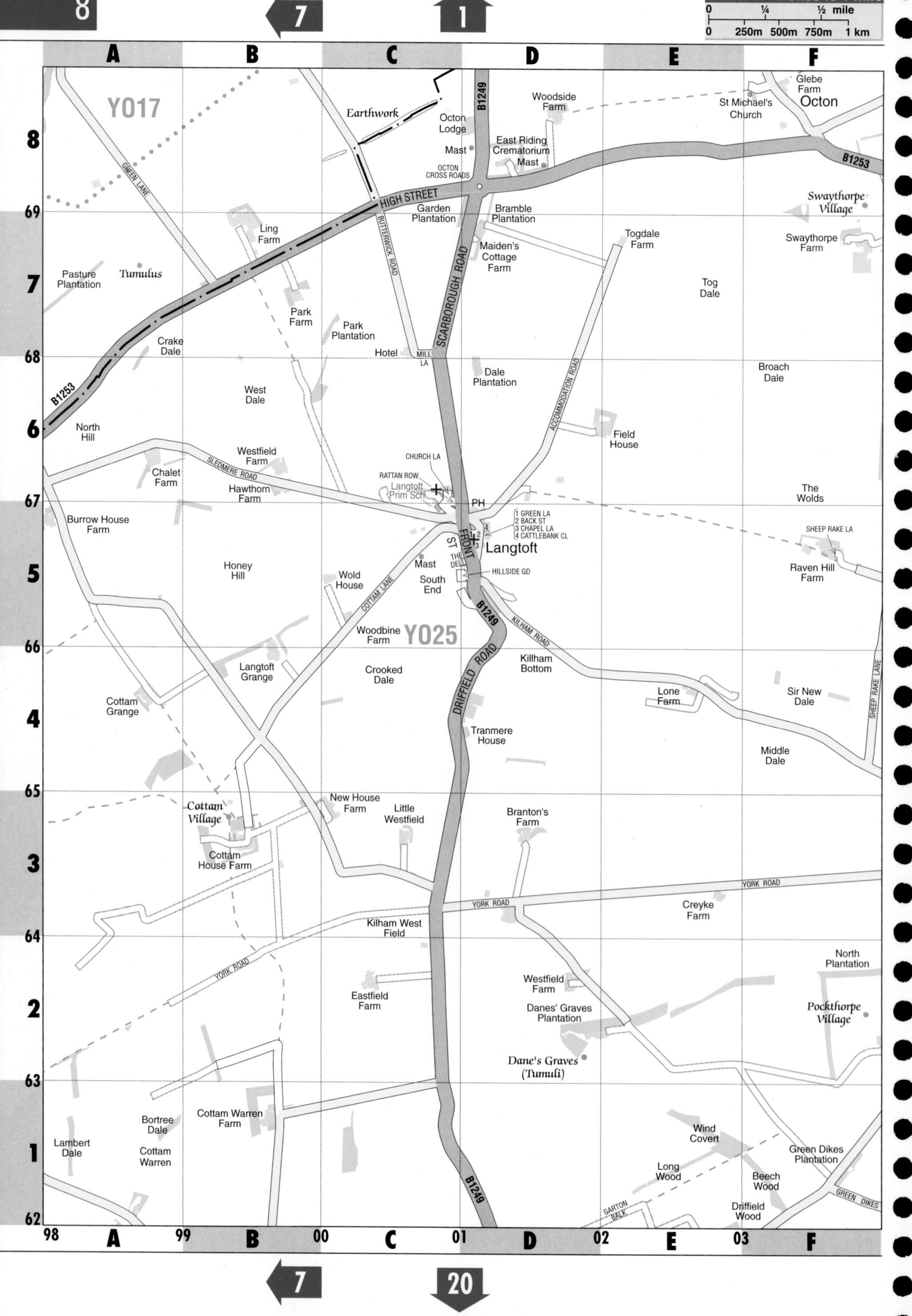
7
1
Scale: 1¾ inches to 1 mile
0 ¼ ½ mile
0 250m 500m 750m 1 km
A B C D E F
YO17
Earthwork
Octon Lodge
Mast
OCTON CROSS ROADS
B1249
Woodside Farm
East Riding Crematorium
Mast
Glebe Farm
St Michael's Church
Octon
B1253
Swaythorpe Village
Swaythorpe Farm
GREEN LANE
HIGH STREET
Garden Plantation
Bramble Plantation
Ling Farm
BUTTERWICK ROAD
Maiden's Cottage Farm
Togdale Farm
Pasture Plantation
Tumulus
Tog Dale
Park Farm
Park Plantation
SCARBOROUGH ROAD
Crake Dale
Hotel
MILL LA
B1253
Dale Plantation
Broach Dale
West Dale
ACCOMMODATION ROAD
North Hill
Field House
Westfield Farm
CHURCH LA
Chalet Farm
SLEDMERE ROAD
RATTAN ROW
Langtoft Prim Sch
Hawthorn Farm
PH
The Wolds
1 GREEN LA
2 BACK ST
3 CHAPEL LA
4 CATTLEBANK CL
Burrow House Farm
FRONT ST
Langtoft
SHEEP RAKE LA
THE DELL
Mast
Honey Hill
Wold House
South End
HILLSIDE GD
Raven Hill Farm
COTTAM LANE
B1249
KILHAM ROAD
Woodbine Farm
YO25
Killham Bottom
Langtoft Grange
Crooked Dale
DRIFFIELD ROAD
Cottam Grange
Lone Farm
Sir New Dale
SHEEP RAKE LANE
Tranmere House
Middle Dale
New House Farm
Cottam Village
Little Westfield
Branton's Farm
Cottam House Farm
YORK ROAD
YORK ROAD
Creyke Farm
Kilham West Field
YORK ROAD
North Plantation
Westfield Farm
Eastfield Farm
Danes' Graves Plantation
Pockthorpe Village
Dane's Graves (Tumuli)
Cottam Warren Farm
Bortree Dale
Wind Covert
Lambert Dale
Cottam Warren
Green Dikes Plantation
Long Wood
Beech Wood
B1249
GREEN DIKES
GARTON BALK
Driffield Wood
8
69
7
68
6
67
5
66
4
65
3
64
2
63
1
62
98
99
00
01
02
03
7
20

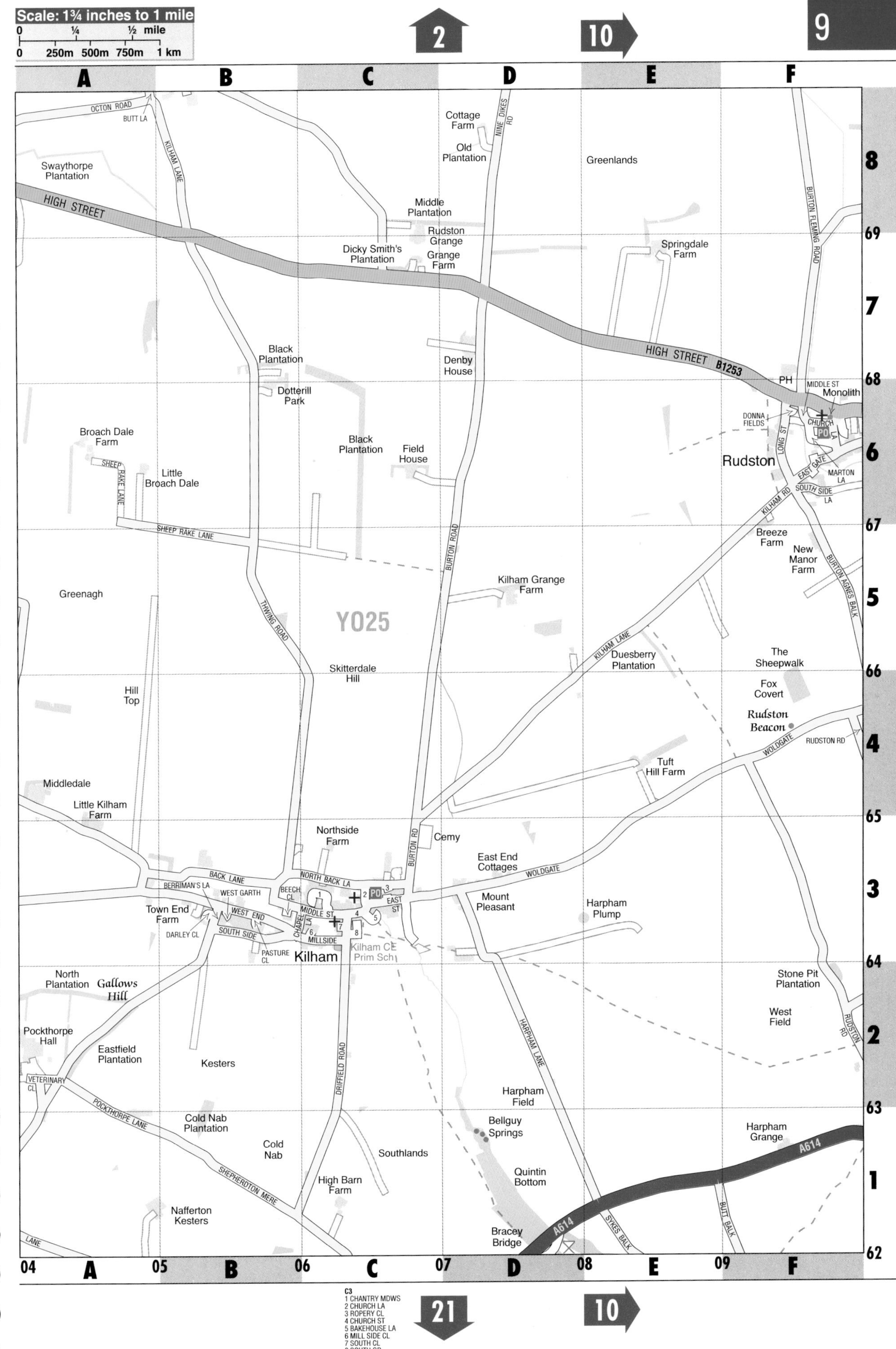

0   ¼   ½   mile
0   250m 500m 750m 1 km

2
10

A B C D E F

OCTON ROAD
BUTT LA
KILHAM LANE

Swaythorpe
Plantation

HIGH STREET

Cottage
Farm

NINE DIKES RD

Old
Plantation

Greenlands

8

Middle
Plantation

Rudston
Grange

69

BURTON FLEMING ROAD

Dicky Smith's
Plantation

Grange
Farm

Springdale
Farm

7

HIGH STREET B1253

Black
Plantation

Denby
House

PH MIDDLE ST
Monolith

68

Dotterill
Park

DONNA
FIELDS

CHURCH
PO

LONG ST

Broach Dale
Farm

Black
Plantation

Field
House

Rudston

EAST GATE

MARTON
LA

6

SHEEP RAKE LANE

Little
Broach Dale

SOUTH SIDE
LA

SHEEP RAKE LANE

Breeze
Farm

New
Manor
Farm

67

BURTON AGNES BALK

Greenagh

Kilham Grange
Farm

KILHAM LANE

Duesberry
Plantation

The
Sheepwalk

5

YO25

KILHAM LANE

THWING ROAD

Fox
Covert

66

Skitterdale
Hill

BURTON ROAD

Rudston
Beacon

WOLDGATE

RUDSTON RD

Hill
Top

4

Middledale

Tuft
Hill Farm

65

Little Kilham
Farm

Northside
Farm

BURTON RD

Cemy

East End
Cottages

WOLDGATE

3

BACK LANE
NORTH BACK LA

BERRIMAN'S LA
WEST GARTH
BEECH CL

PO

EAST ST

Mount
Pleasant

Harpham
Plump

Town End
Farm

WEST END

MIDDLE ST

SOUTH SIDE

DARLEY CL

MILLSIDE

Kilham

PASTURE CL

Kilham CE
Prim Sch

HARPHAM LANE

Stone Pit
Plantation

64

North
Plantation

Gallows
Hill

West
Field

2

RUDSTON RD

Pockthorpe
Hall

Eastfield
Plantation

Kesters

DRIFFIELD ROAD

VETERINARY
CL

Harpham
Field

63

POCKTHORPE LANE

Cold Nab
Plantation

Harpham
Grange

A614

SHEPHERDTON MERE

Cold
Nab

Southlands

Bellguy
Springs

Quintin
Bottom

1

Nafferton
Kesters

High Barn
Farm

A614

SYKES BALK

BUTT BALK

LANE

Bracey
Bridge

62

04 A 05 B 06 C 07 D 08 E 09 F

C3
1 CHANTRY MDWS
2 CHURCH LA
3 ROPERY CL
4 CHURCH ST
5 BAKEHOUSE LA
6 MILL SIDE CL
7 SOUTH CL
8 SOUTH GR

21
10

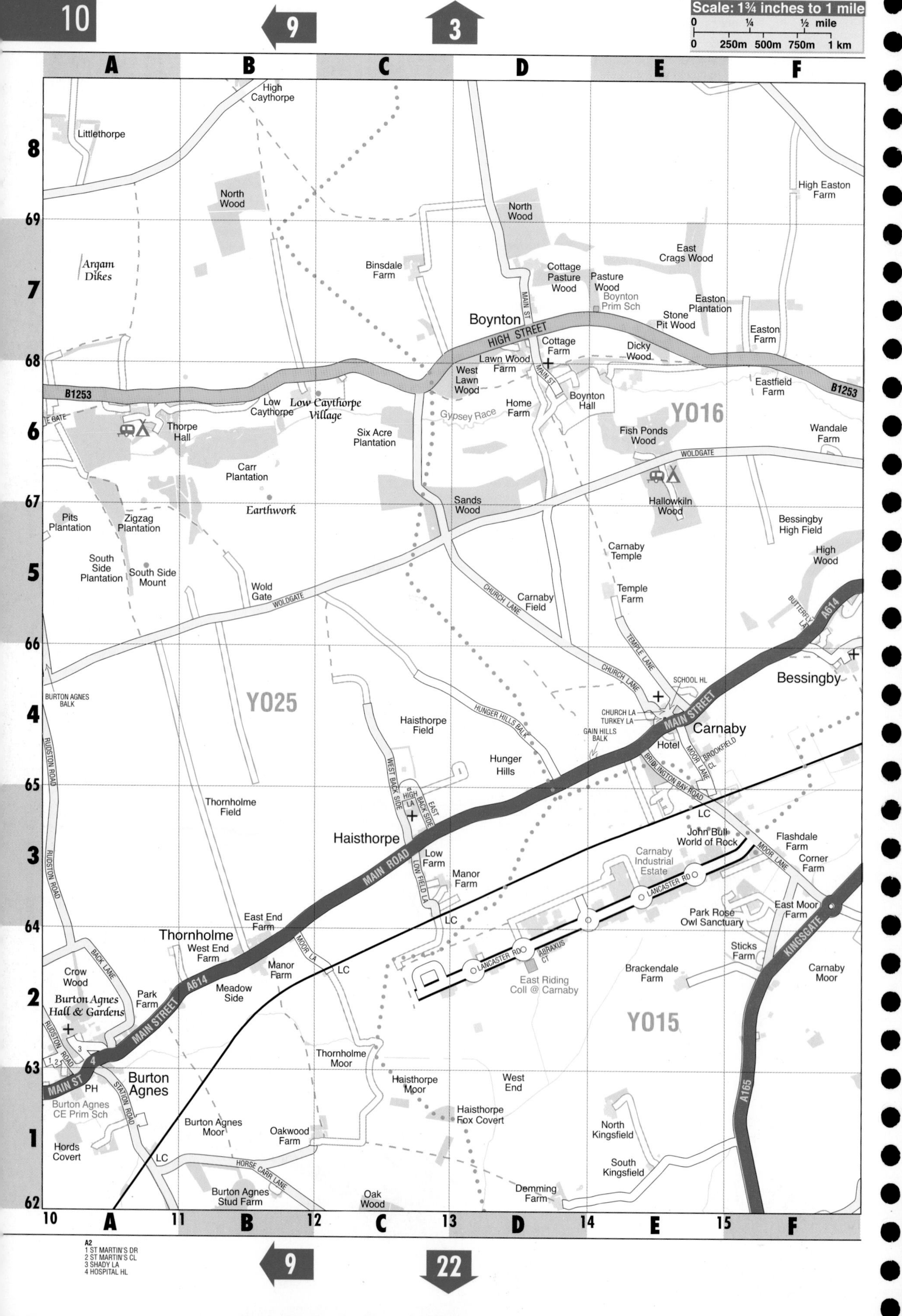
9
3
Scale: 1¾ inches to 1 mile
0 ¼ ½ mile
0 250m 500m 750m 1 km
A B C D E F
High Caythorpe
Littlethorpe
North Wood
North Wood
High Easton Farm
Argam Dikes
Binsdale Farm
Cottage Pasture Wood
Pasture Wood
Boynton Prim Sch
East Crags Wood
Easton Plantation
Stone Pit Wood
Boynton
HIGH STREET
MAIN ST
Easton Farm
Cottage Farm
Dicky Wood
Lawn Wood Farm
West Lawn Wood
B1253
Eastfield Farm
Low Caythorpe
Low Caythorpe Village
Home Farm
Boynton Hall
YO16
Gypsey Race
Thorpe Hall
Six Acre Plantation
Fish Ponds Wood
Wandale Farm
WOLDGATE
Carr Plantation
Hallowkiln Wood
Sands Wood
Earthwork
Pits Plantation
Zigzag Plantation
Bessingby High Field
Carnaby Temple
High Wood
South Side Plantation
South Side Mount
Wold Gate
CHURCH LANE
Carnaby Field
Temple Farm
BUTTERFLY LA
A614
TEMPLE LANE
Bessingby
SCHOOL HL
BURTON AGNES BALK
YO25
HUNGER HILLS BALK
Haisthorpe Field
CHURCH LA
TURKEY LA
GAIN HILLS BALK
MAIN STREET
Carnaby
Hotel
BROOKFIELD CL
MOOR LANE
BRIDLINGTON BAY ROAD
Hunger Hills
RUDSTON ROAD
WEST BACK SIDE
HIGH LA
EAST BACK SIDE
Thornholme Field
LC
John Bull World of Rock
Flashdale Farm
Haisthorpe
Carnaby Industrial Estate
Corner Farm
MAIN ROAD
Low Farm
LOW FIELD LA
Manor Farm
LANCASTER RD
East Moor Farm
Park Rose Owl Sanctuary
KINGSGATE
East End Farm
Thornholme
West End Farm
MOOR LA
Manor Farm
ABRAXUS CT
Sticks Farm
Brackendale Farm
Carnaby Moor
Crow Wood
BACK LANE
Meadow Side
East Riding Coll @ Carnaby
Burton Agnes Hall & Gardens
Park Farm
YO15
Thornholme Moor
MAIN ST
PH
Burton Agnes
STATION ROAD
Burton Agnes CE Prim Sch
Haisthorpe Moor
West End
Haisthorpe Fox Covert
A165
Burton Agnes Moor
Oakwood Farm
North Kingsfield
Hords Covert
South Kingsfield
HORSE CARR LANE
Burton Agnes Stud Farm
Oak Wood
Demming Farm
8 69 7 68 6 67 5 66 4 65 3 64 2 63 1 62
10 11 12 13 14 15
A2
1 ST MARTIN'S DR
2 ST MARTIN'S CL
3 SHADY LA
4 HOSPITAL HL
9
22

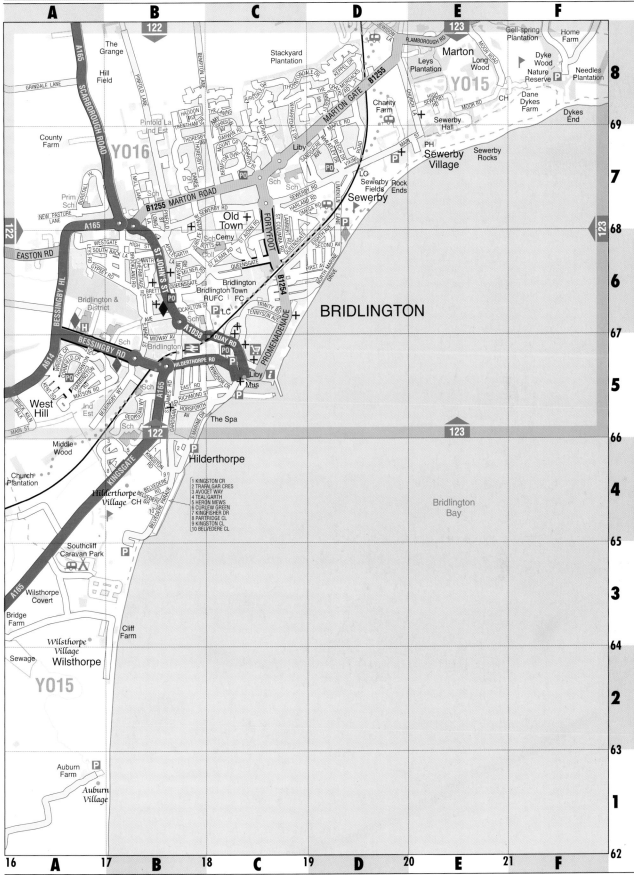

For full street detail of the highlighted area see pages 122 and 123.

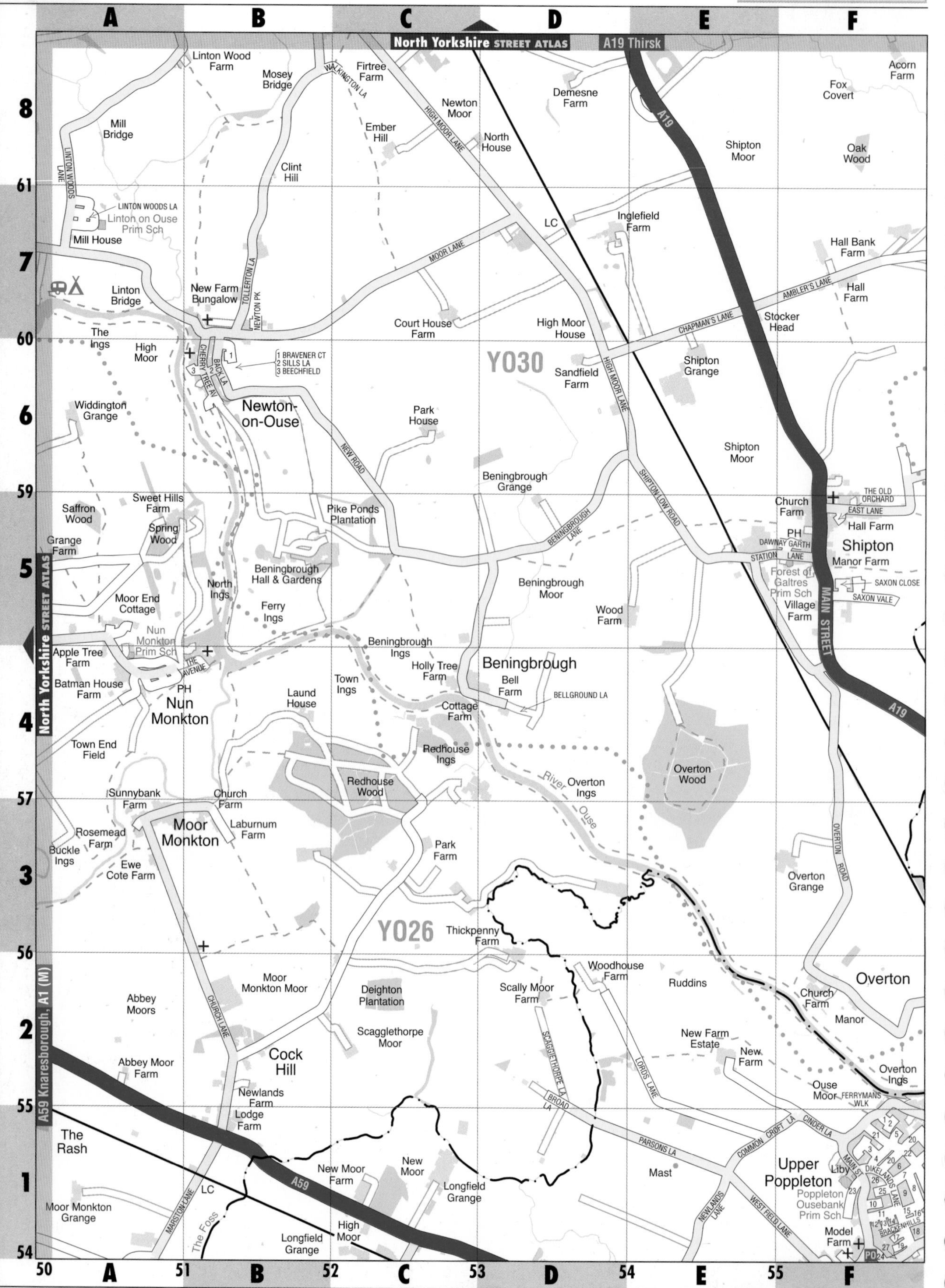

North Yorkshire STREET ATLAS

A B C D E F

A19 Thirsk

8

61

7

60

6

59

5

4

57

3

56

2

55

1

54

50 A 51 B 52 C 53 D 54 E 55 F

North Yorkshire STREET ATLAS

Linton Wood Farm
Mosey Bridge
WARKINGTON LA
Firtree Farm
Newton Moor
Demesne Farm
Fox Covert
Acorn Farm

Mill Bridge
Clint Hill
Ember Hill
HIGH MOOR LANE
North House
Shipton Moor
Oak Wood

LINTON WOODS LA
Linton Woods
Linton on Ouse Prim Sch
MOOR LANE
LC
Inglefield Farm
A19
Hall Bank Farm

Mill House
Linton Bridge
New Farm Bungalow
TOLLERTON LA
NEWTON PK
Court House Farm
High Moor House
CHAPMAN'S LANE
AMBLER'S LANE
Hall Farm
Stocker Head

The Ings
High Moor
CHERRY TREE LA
BACK LA
1 BRAVENER CT
2 SILLS LA
3 BEECHFIELD
YO30
Sandfield Farm
HIGH MOOR LANE
Shipton Grange

Widdington Grange
Newton-on-Ouse
NEW ROAD
Park House
Beningbrough Grange
Shipton Moor
THE OLD ORCHARD
EAST LANE

Saffron Wood
Sweet Hills Farm
Pike Ponds Plantation
BENINGBROUGH LANE
Church Farm
Hall Farm
Shipton

Grange Farm
Spring Wood
North Ings
Beningbrough Hall & Gardens
Ferry Ings
SHIPTON LOW ROAD
PH
DAWNAY GARTH LANE
STATION
MAIN STREET
Manor Farm

Moor End Cottage
Nun Monkton Prim Sch
Beningbrough Moor
Wood Farm
Forest of Galtres Prim Sch
Village Farm
SAXON CLOSE
SAXON VALE

Apple Tree Farm
THE AVENUE
Beningbrough Ings
Holly Tree Farm
Beningbrough
Bell Farm
BELLGROUND LA

Batman House Farm
PH
Nun Monkton
Town Ings
Laund House
Cottage Farm

Town End Field
Redhouse Ings
Overton Wood
OVERTON ROAD

Sunnybank Farm
Church Farm
Redhouse Wood
River Ouse
Overton Ings
Overton Grange

Rosemead Farm
Moor Monkton
Laburnum Farm
Park Farm

Buckle Ings
Ewe Cote Farm
YO26
Thickpenny Farm
Overton

Abbey Moors
Moor Monkton Moor
Deighton Plantation
Scally Moor Farm
Woodhouse Farm
Ruddins
Church Farm
Manor

Abbey Moor Farm
CHURCH LANE
Scagglethorpe Moor
SCAGGLETHORPE LA
LORDS LANE
New Farm Estate
New Farm
Overton Ings

Cock Hill
Newlands Farm
Lodge Farm
BROAD LA
Ouse Moor
FERRYMANS WLK

A59 Knaresborough, A1 (M)
The Rash
MARSTON LANE
LC
A59
New Moor Farm
New Moor
Longfield Grange
PARSONS LA
Mast
COMMON LA
CROFT LA
CINDER LA
Upper Poppleton
Liby

Moor Monkton Grange
The Foss
Longfield Grange
High Moor
NEWLANDS LANE
WEST FIELD LANE
MAIN ST
DIKELANDS LANE
Poppleton Ousebank Prim Sch
Model Farm

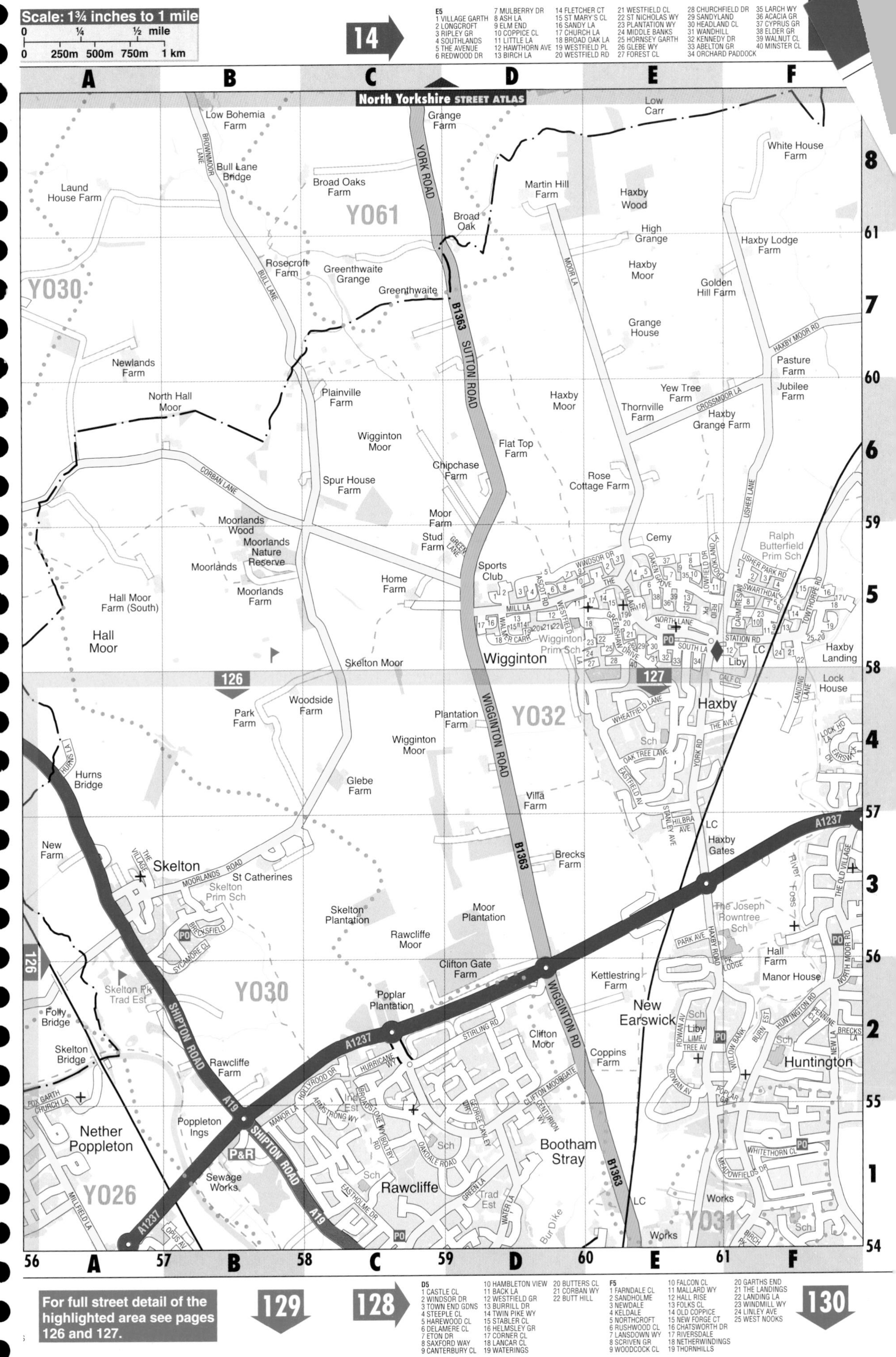

Scale: 1¾ inches to 1 mile
0 ¼ ½ mile
0 250m 500m 750m 1 km
14
E5
1 VILLAGE GARTH
2 LONGCROFT
3 RIPLEY GR
4 SOUTHLANDS
5 THE AVENUE
6 REDWOOD DR
7 MULBERRY DR
8 ASH LA
9 ELM END
10 COPPICE CL
11 LITTLE LA
12 HAWTHORN AVE
13 BIRCH LA
14 FLETCHER CT
15 ST MARY'S CL
16 SANDY LA
17 CHURCH LA
18 BROAD OAK LA
19 WESTFIELD PL
20 WESTFIELD RD
21 WESTFIELD CL
22 ST NICHOLAS WY
23 PLANTATION WY
24 MIDDLE BANKS
25 HORNSEY GARTH
26 GLEBE WY
27 FOREST CL
28 CHURCHFIELD DR
29 SANDYLAND
30 HEADLAND CL
31 WANDHILL
32 KENNEDY DR
33 ABELTON GR
34 ORCHARD PADDOCK
35 LARCH WY
36 ACACIA GR
37 CYPRUS GR
38 ELDER GR
39 WALNUT CL
40 MINSTER CL
A B C D E F
North Yorkshire STREET ATLAS
Low Bohemia Farm
Grange Farm
Low Carr
White House Farm
BROWNMOOR LANE
Bull Lane Bridge
Laund House Farm
Broad Oaks Farm
YORK ROAD
Martin Hill Farm
Haxby Wood
YO61
Broad Oak
High Grange
Haxby Lodge Farm
YO30
Rosecroft Farm
Greenthwaite Grange
Greenthwaite
BULL LANE
MOOR LA
Haxby Moor
Golden Hill Farm
B1363
SUTTON ROAD
Grange House
HAXBY MOOR RD
Newlands Farm
Pasture Farm
Yew Tree Farm
Jubilee Farm
North Hall Moor
Plainville Farm
Haxby Moor
Thornville Farm
CROSSMOOR LA
Haxby Grange Farm
Wigginton Moor
Flat Top Farm
CORBAN LANE
Chipchase Farm
Spur House Farm
Rose Cottage Farm
USHER LANE
Moor Farm
Moorlands Wood
Moorlands Nature Reserve
Stud Farm
GREEN LANE
Cemy
Ralph Butterfield Prim Sch
Moorlands
Sports Club
WINDSOR DR
USHER PARK RD
Home Farm
Moorlands Farm
Hall Moor Farm (South)
MILL LA
THE VILLAGE
OAKEN GROVE
SWARTHDALE
TOWTHORPE RD
WALKER CARR
WESTFIELD
GRENDALE DRIVE
NORTH LANE
STATION RD
Hall Moor
Wigginton Prim Sch
SOUTH LA
PO
LC
Liby
Haxby Landing
Skelton Moor
Wigginton
126
127
CALF CL
Lock House
Park Farm
Woodside Farm
Plantation Farm
YO32
WHEATFIELD LANE
Haxby
LANDING LANE
Wigginton Moor
Sch
THE AVE
LOCK HO LA
WIGGINTON ROAD
OAK TREE LANE
EARSWICK
HURNS LA
Hurns Bridge
Glebe Farm
EASTFIELD AV
YORK RD
Villa Farm
STANLEY AVE
HILBRA AVE
A1237
New Farm
Skelton
MOORLANDS ROAD
Brecks Farm
LC
Haxby Gates
THE VILLAGE
St Catherines
Skelton Prim Sch
River Foss
THE OLD VILLAGE
Skelton Plantation
Moor Plantation
The Joseph Rowntree Sch
BRECKSFIELD
Rawcliffe Moor
PARK AVE
HAXBY ROAD
SYCAMORE CL
Clifton Gate Farm
Hall Farm
NORTH MOOR RD
Kettlestring Farm
Manor House
Skelton Pk Trad Est
YO30
LODGE
Folly Bridge
SHIPTON ROAD
Poplar Plantation
WIGGINTON RD
New Earswick
HUNTINGTON RD
PENNINE
Clifton Moor
ROWAN AV
Liby
BURN EST
BRECKS LA
STIRLING RD
TREE AV
WILLOW BANK
NEW LA
Skelton Bridge
Rawcliffe Farm
HURRICANE WY
Coppins Farm
Huntington
FOX GARTH
CHURCH LA
HOLLYROOD DR
ARMSTRONG WY
Ind Est
GEORGE CAYLEY DR
CLIFTON MOORGATE
CENTURION WY
POPLAR GR
Nether Poppleton
Poppleton Ings
MANOR LA
BROADSTONE WY
BOLTBY RD
Sch
Bootham Stray
WHITETHORN CL
P&R
SHIPTON ROAD
A19
OAKDALE ROAD
MEADOWFIELDS DR
YO26
Sewage Works
Sch
Rawcliffe
GREEN LA
Trad Est
LC
Works
MILLFIELD LA
A1237
EASTHOLME DR
WATER LA
Bur Dike
YO31
Works
OPUS AV
PO
BIRCH PK
8
61
7
60
6
59
5
58
4
57
3
56
2
55
1
54
56 A 57 B 58 C 59 D 60 E 61 F
For full street detail of the highlighted area see pages 126 and 127.
129
128
D5
1 CASTLE CL
2 WINDSOR DR
3 TOWN END GDNS
4 STEEPLE CL
5 HAREWOOD CL
6 DELAMERE CL
7 ETON DR
8 SAXFORD WAY
9 CANTERBURY CL
10 HAMBLETON VIEW
11 BACK LA
12 WESTFIELD GR
13 BURRILL DR
14 TWIN PIKE WY
15 STABLER CL
16 HELMSLEY GR
17 CORNER CL
18 LANCAR CL
19 WATERINGS
20 BUTTERS CL
21 CORBAN WY
22 BUTT HILL
F5
1 FARNDALE CL
2 SANDHOLME
3 NEWDALE
4 KELDALE
5 NORTHCROFT
6 RUSHWOOD CL
7 LANSDOWN WY
8 SCRIVEN GR
9 WOODCOCK CL
10 FALCON CL
11 MALLARD WY
12 HALL RISE
13 FOLKS CL
14 OLD COPPICE
15 NEW FORGE CT
16 CHATSWORTH DR
17 RIVERSDALE
18 NETHERWINDINGS
19 THORNHILLS
20 GARTHS END
21 THE LANDINGS
22 LANDING LA
23 WINDMILL WY
24 LINLEY AVE
25 WEST NOOKS
130

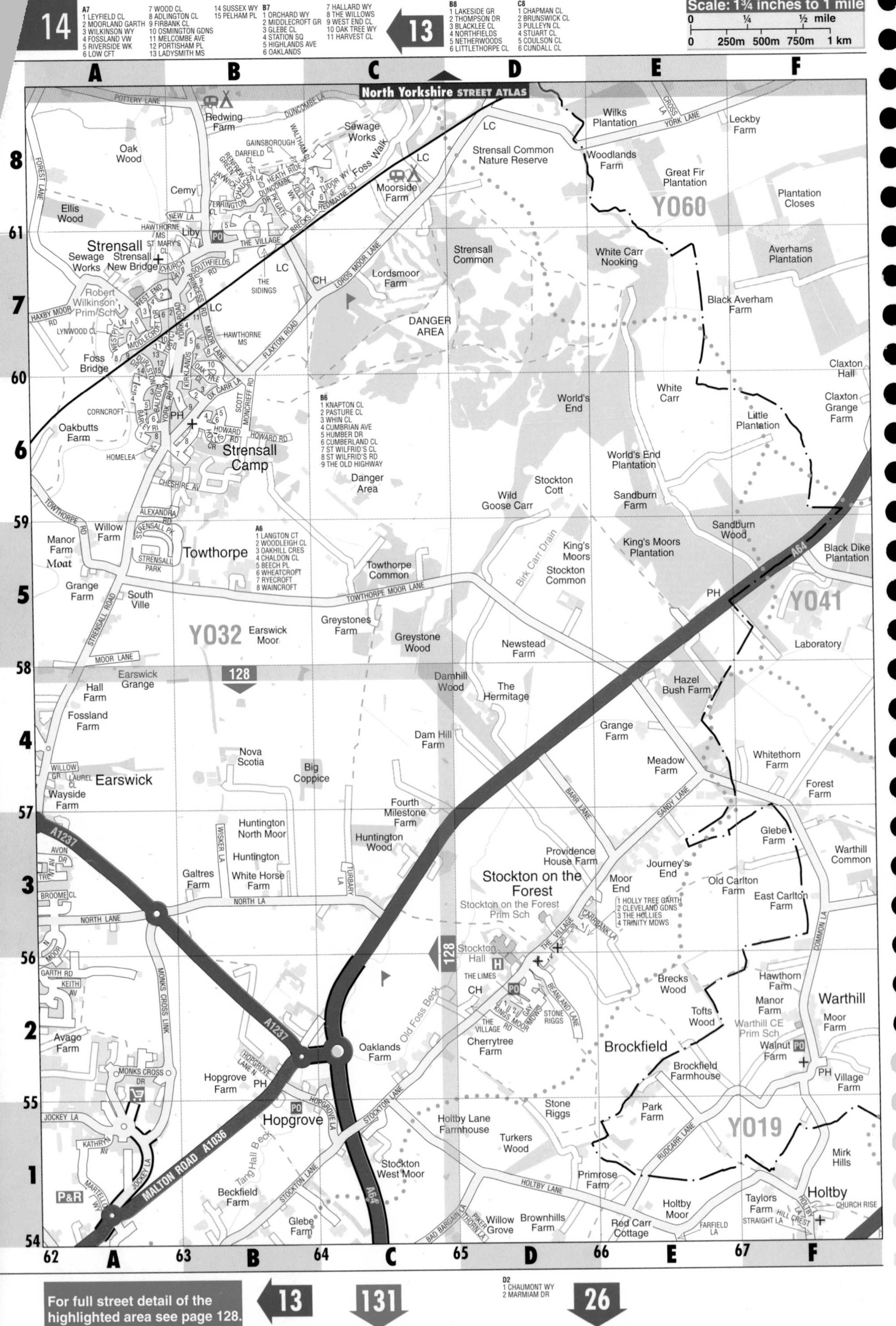
A7
1 LEYFIELD CL
2 MOORLAND GARTH
3 WILKINSON WY
4 FOSSLAND VW
5 RIVERSIDE WK
6 LOW CFT
7 WOOD CL
8 ADLINGTON CL
9 FIRBANK CL
10 OSMINGTON GDNS
11 MELCOMBE AVE
12 PORTISHAM PL
13 LADYSMITH MS
14 SUSSEX WY
15 PELHAM PL
B7
1 ORCHARD WY
2 MIDDLECROFT GR
3 GLEBE CL
4 STATION SQ
5 HIGHLANDS AVE
6 OAKLANDS
7 HALLARD WY
8 THE WILLOWS
9 WEST END CL
10 OAK TREE WY
11 HARVEST CL
13
B8
1 LAKESIDE GR
2 THOMPSON DR
3 BLACKLEE CL
4 NORTHFIELDS
5 NETHERWOODS
6 LITTLETHORPE CL
C8
1 CHAPMAN CL
2 BRUNSWICK CL
3 PULLEYN CL
4 STUART CL
5 COULSON CL
6 CUNDALL CL
Scale: 1¾ inches to 1 mile
0 ¼ ½ mile
0 250m 500m 750m 1 km
North Yorkshire STREET ATLAS
A B C D E F
8 61 7 60 6 59 5 58 4 57 3 56 2 55 1 54
62 63 64 65 66 67
Redwing Farm
Sewage Works
Oak Wood
Ellis Wood
Cemy
Strensall
Sewage Works
Strensall New Bridge
Robert Wilkinson Prim Sch
Foss Bridge
Oakbutts Farm
Foss Walk
Moorside Farm
Lordsmoor Farm
Strensall Common Nature Reserve
Strensall Common
DANGER AREA
Wilks Plantation
Woodlands Farm
Leckby Farm
Great Fir Plantation
Plantation Closes
YO60
White Carr Nooking
Averhams Plantation
Black Averham Farm
Claxton Hall
Claxton Grange Farm
White Carr
World's End
Little Plantation
World's End Plantation
Strensall Camp
B6
1 KNAPTON CL
2 PASTURE CL
3 WHIN CL
4 CUMBRIAN AVE
5 HUMBER DR
6 CUMBERLAND CL
7 ST WILFRID'S CL
8 ST WILFRID'S RD
9 THE OLD HIGHWAY
Danger Area
Wild Goose Carr
Stockton Cott
Sandburn Farm
Sandburn Wood
Black Dike Plantation
Manor Farm
Moat
Willow Farm
Towthorpe
A6
1 LANGTON CT
2 WOODLEIGH CL
3 OAKHILL CRES
4 CHALDON CL
5 BEECH PL
6 WHEATCROFT
7 RYECROFT
8 WAINCROFT
Towthorpe Common
King's Moors
Stockton Common
King's Moors Plantation
YO41
Grange Farm
South Ville
YO32
Earswick Moor
Greystones Farm
Greystone Wood
Newstead Farm
Laboratory
Earswick Grange
128
Damhill Wood
The Hermitage
Hazel Bush Farm
Hall Farm
Fossland Farm
Dam Hill Farm
Grange Farm
Nova Scotia
Big Coppice
Meadow Farm
Whitethorn Farm
Forest Farm
Earswick
Wayside Farm
Fourth Milestone Farm
Huntington North Moor
Huntington Wood
Glebe Farm
Warthill Common
Galtres Farm
Huntington
White Horse Farm
Providence House Farm
Stockton on the Forest
Stockton on the Forest Prim Sch
Moor End
Journey's End
Old Carlton Farm
East Carlton Farm
1 HOLLY TREE GARTH
2 CLEVELAND GDNS
3 THE HOLLIES
4 TRINITY MDWS
Stockton Hall
THE LIMES
CH
Brecks Wood
Hawthorn Farm
Manor Farm
Warthill
Tofts Wood
Warthill CE Prim Sch
Moor Farm
Avago Farm
Oaklands Farm
Cherrytree Farm
Brockfield
Walnut Farm
Brockfield Farmhouse
Village Farm
Hopgrove Farm
Hopgrove
Holtby Lane Farmhouse
Stone Riggs
Park Farm
YO19
Turkers Wood
Mirk Hills
Stockton West Moor
Primrose Farm
Beckfield Farm
Glebe Farm
Willow Grove
Brownhills Farm
Red Carr Cottage
Holtby Moor
Taylors Farm
Holtby
A1237
A1036
A64
MALTON ROAD
HOLTBY LANE
STOCKTON LANE
TOWTHORPE MOOR LANE
NORTH LA
NORTH LANE
MOOR LANE
SANDY LANE
BARR LANE
YORK LANE
P&R
A B C D E F
For full street detail of the highlighted area see page 128.
13
131
D2
1 CHAUMONT WY
2 MARMIAM DR
26

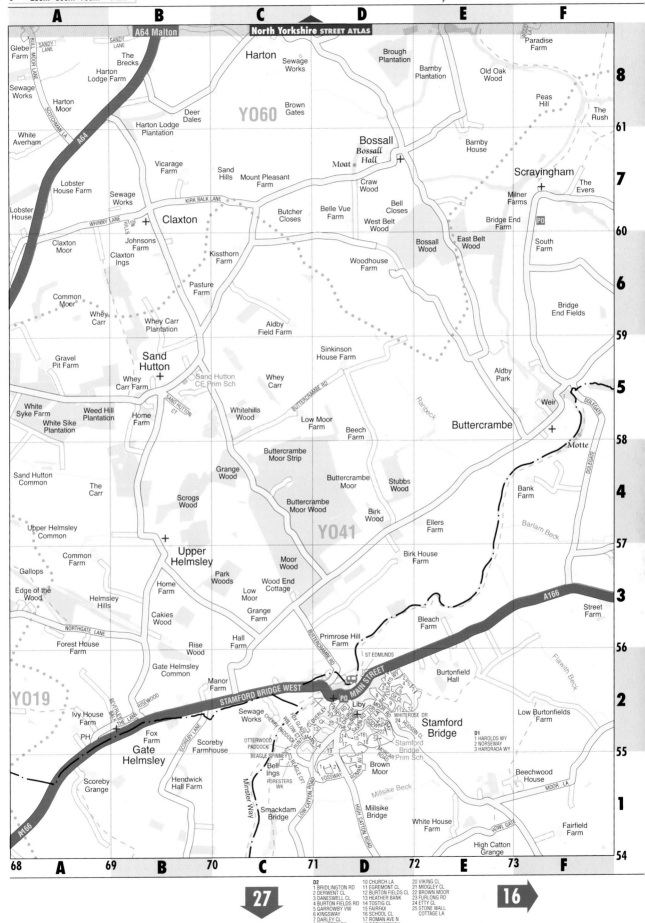

A   B   C   D   E   F

A64 Malton

Glebe Farm
SANDY LANE
The Brecks
SANDY LANE
Harton
Sewage Works
Brough Plantation
Barnby Plantation
Old Oak Wood
Paradise Farm

8

BULL MOOR LANE
Harton Lodge Farm
Deer Dales
Brown Gates
Peas Hill
The Rush

Sewage Works
Harton Moor
Harton Lodge Plantation
YO60
Barnby House

61

SCOTCHMAN LA
White Averham
A64
Bossall
Bossall Hall
Moat
Scrayingham

7

Lobster House Farm
Vicarage Farm
Sand Hills
Mount Pleasant Farm
Craw Wood
Milner Farms
The Evers

Sewage Works
KIRK BALK LANE
Belle Vue Farm
Bell Closes
Bridge End Farm
PO

60

Lobster House
WHINNY LANE
Claxton
Butcher Closes
West Belt Wood
Bossall Wood
East Belt Wood
South Farm

GN HILLS LN
Johnsons Farm
Bridge End Fields

6

Claxton Moor
Claxton Ings
Kissthorn Farm
Woodhouse Farm

Common Moor
Pasture Farm
Aldby Field Farm

59

Whey Carr
Whey Carr Plantation
Sinkinson House Farm
Aldby Park

Gravel Pit Farm
Sand Hutton
Rantbeck
Weir
DOLEGATE

5

White Syke Farm
Whey Carr Farm
Sand Hutton CE Prim Sch
Whitehills Wood
BUTTERCRAMBE RD
Low Moor Farm
Buttercrambe
Motte

White Sike Plantation
Weed Hill Plantation
Home Farm
SAND HUTTON CT
Whey Carr
Beech Farm

58

Sand Hutton Common
The Carr
Grange Wood
Buttercrambe Moor Strip
Buttercrambe Moor
Stubbs Wood
Bank Farm
DOLEGATE

4

Scrogs Wood
Buttercrambe Moor Wood
Birk Wood
Barlam Beck

Upper Helmsley Common
YO41
Ellers Farm

57

Gallops
Common Farm
Park Woods
Moor Wood
Birk House Farm

Edge of the Wood
Upper Helmsley
Low Moor
Wood End Cottage
A166
Street Farm

3

Home Farm
Helmsley Hills
Grange Farm
Bleach Farm

NORTHGATE LANE
Cakies Wood
Hall Farm
Primrose Hill Farm

Forest House Farm
Rise Wood
BUTTERCRAMBE RD
ST EDMUNDS
Burtonfield Hall

56

Gate Helmsley Common
Manor Farm
STAMFORD BRIDGE WEST
PO MAIN STREET
Liby

YO19
Sewage Works
Stamford Bridge
Low Burtonfields Farm

2

BEVERLEY WALK
RISEWOOD
WHITEROSE DR
Stamford Bridge Prim Sch
D1
1 HAROLDS WY
2 NORSEWAY
3 HARDRADA WY

Ivy House Farm
THE LANE
Fox Farm
OTTERWOOD PADDOCK
Brown Moor

PH
Scoreby Farmhouse
CHERRY PADDOCK
BEAGLE SPINNEY
FORESTERS WK
Beechwood House
MOOR LA

55

Gate Helmsley
SCOREBY LANE
Scoreby
Bell Ings
Millsike Beck

A166
Scoreby Grange
Hendwick Hall Farm
Minster Way
Smackdam Bridge
High Catton Road
Millsike Bridge
White House Farm
HOWL GATE
Fairfield Farm

1

High Catton Grange

54

68   A   69   B   70   C   71   D   72   E   73   F

D2
1 BRIDLINGTON RD
2 DERWENT CL
3 DANESWELL CL
4 BURTON FIELDS RD
5 GARROWBY VW
6 KINGSWAY
7 DARLEY CL
8 WHARTON RD
9 ST JOHN'S RD
10 CHURCH LA
11 EGREMONT CL
12 BURTON FIELDS CL
13 HEATHER BANK
14 TOSTIG CL
15 FAIRFAX
16 SCHOOL CL
17 ROMAN AVE N
18 GODWINSWAY
19 BUTTS CL
20 VIKING CL
21 MIDGLEY CL
22 BROWN MOOR
23 FURLONG RD
24 ETTY CL
25 STONE WALL COTTAGE LA

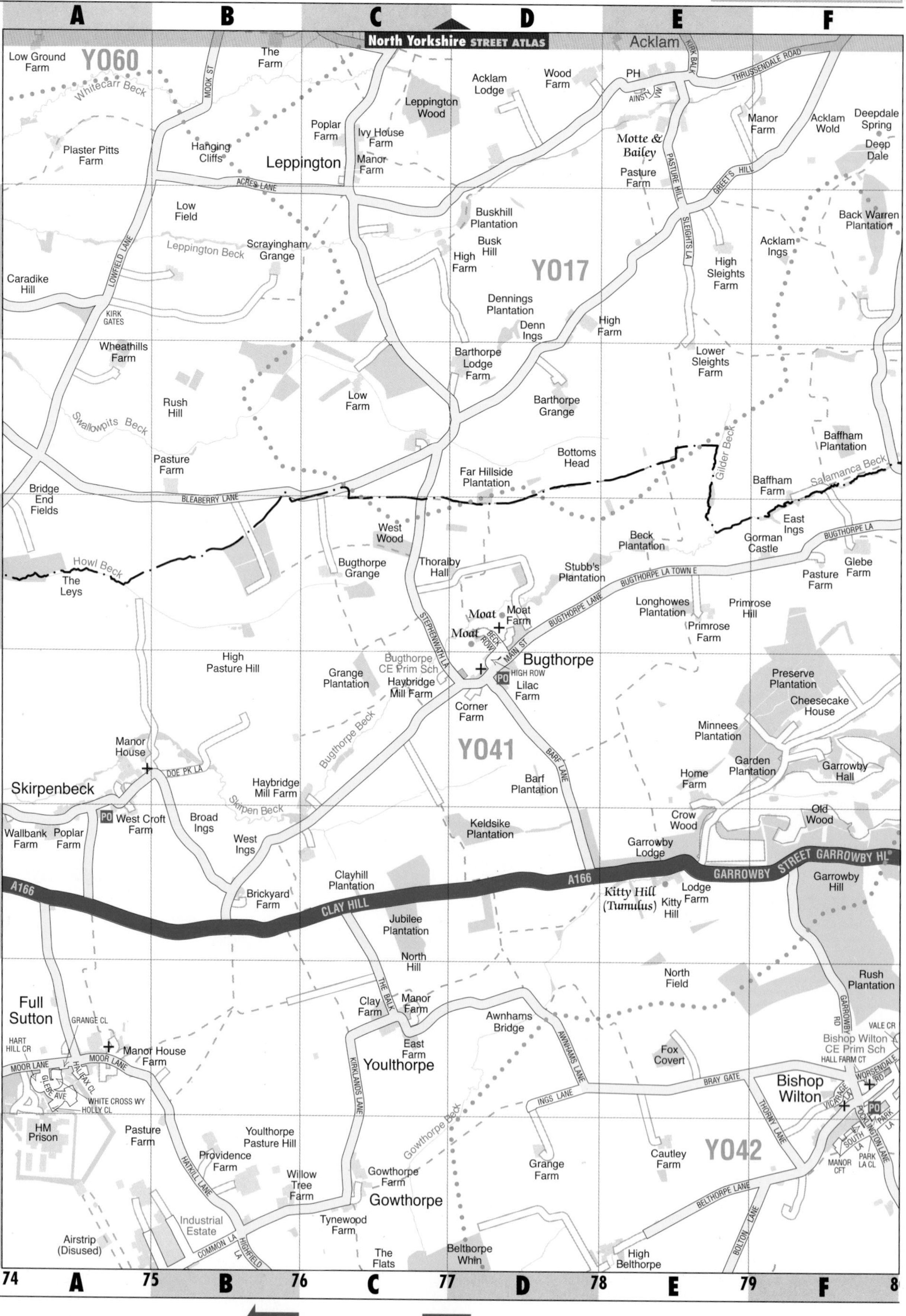

Scale: 1¾ inches to 1 mile
0   ¼   ½ mile
0   250m 500m 750m 1 km

North Yorkshire STREET ATLAS

A B C D E F

Acklam

8

YO60

Low Ground Farm
Whitecarr Beck
Plaster Pitts Farm
Hanging Cliffs
The Farm
Poplar Farm
Leppington Wood
Ivy House Farm
Acklam Lodge
Wood Farm
PH
Motte & Bailey
Manor Farm
Acklam Wold
Deepdale Spring
Deep Dale

61

Leppington
ACRES LANE
Manor Farm
Pasture Farm

7

Caradike Hill
Low Field
Scrayingham Grange
Leppington Beck
Buskhill Plantation
Busk Hill
High Farm
YO17
Dennings Plantation
High Farm
High Sleights Farm
Acklam Ings
Back Warren Plantation

60

KIRK GATES
Wheathills Farm
Denn Ings
Barthorpe Lodge Farm
Lower Sleights Farm

6

Rush Hill
Swallowpits Beck
Low Farm
Barthorpe Grange
Baffham Plantation
Pasture Farm
Bottoms Head
Baffham Farm
Salamanca Beck

59

Bridge End Fields
BLEABERRY LANE
Far Hillside Plantation
Glider Beck
Beck Plantation
Gorman Castle
East Ings
Bugthorpe La
Pasture Farm
Glebe Farm

5

Howl Beck
The Leys
West Wood
Bugthorpe Grange
Thoralby Hall
Stubb's Plantation
BUGTHORPE LA TOWN E
Primrose Hill

BUGTHORPE LANE
Longhowes Plantation
Primrose Farm

Moat
Moat Farm
Moat

58

High Pasture Hill
Grange Plantation
Bugthorpe CE Prim Sch
Haybridge Mill Farm
STEPHENWATH LA
BECK ROW
MAIN ST
Bugthorpe
HIGH ROW
PO
Lilac Farm

Preserve Plantation
Cheesecake House

4

Manor House
DOE PK LA
Bugthorpe Beck
Corner Farm
YO41
Minnees Plantation
Garden Plantation
Garrowby Hall

Skirpenbeck
Haybridge Mill Farm
Skipen Beck
Barf Plantation
BARF LANE
Home Farm

57

Wallbank Farm
Poplar Farm
PO
West Croft Farm
Broad Ings
West Ings
Keldsike Plantation
Crow Wood
Old Wood

Garrowby Lodge
GARROWBY STREET GARROWBY HL

3

A166
Brickyard Farm
CLAY HILL
Clayhill Plantation
A166
Kitty Hill (Tumulus)
Lodge Farm
Kitty Hill
Garrowby Hill

56

Jubilee Plantation
North Hill
THE BANK
Manor Farm
North Field
Rush Plantation

2

Full Sutton
GRANGE CL
HART HILL CR
MOOR LANE
HALFRAY CL
Manor House Farm
MANOR LANE
Clay Farm
East Farm
KIRKLANDS LANE
Youlthorpe
Awnhams Bridge
AWNHAMS LANE
Fox Covert
GARROWBY RD
VALE CR
Bishop Wilton CE Prim Sch
HALL FARM CT
Bishop Wilton
HORSEDALE RD

55

GLEBE AVE
WHITE CROSS WY
HOLLY CL
HM Prison
Pasture Farm
Youlthorpe Pasture Hill
Providence Farm
Gowthorpe Beck
INGS LANE
Grange Farm
BRAY GATE
Cautley Farm
YO42
THORNY LANE
VICARAGE
MANOR CFT
PO
SOUTH
PARK LA CL

1

Willow Tree Farm
Gowthorpe
Tynewood Farm
HATKIL LANE
HIGHFIELD
Industrial Estate
COMMON LA
The Flats
Belthorpe Whin
BELTHORPE LANE
High Belthorpe
BOLTON LANE

54

Airstrip (Disused)

74 A 75 B 76 C 77 D 78 E 79 F 8

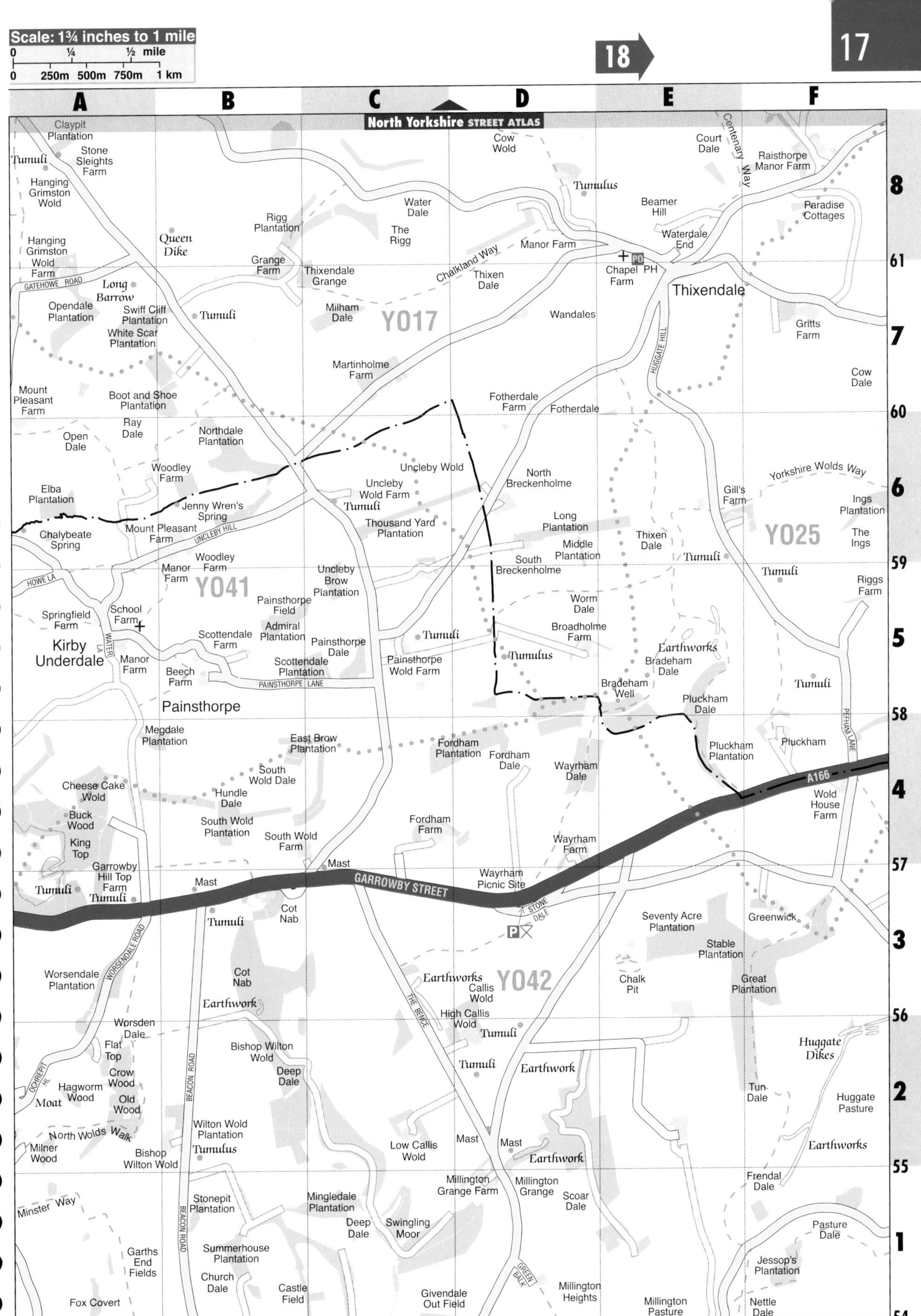

Scale: 1¾ inches to 1 mile

0 — ¼ — ½ mile
0 — 250m — 500m — 750m — 1 km

A B C D E F

Claypit Plantation
Tumuli
Stone Sleights Farm
Hanging Grimston Wold
Hanging Grimston Wold Farm
GATEHOWE ROAD
Long Barrow
Queen Dike
Rigg Plantation
Grange Farm
Thixendale Grange
Water Dale
The Rigg
Cow Wold
Tumulus
Court Dale
Centenary Way
Raisthorpe Manor Farm
Paradise Cottages
8
Chalkland Way
Manor Farm
Thixen Dale
Beamer Hill
Waterdale End
Chapel PH Farm
PO
Thixendale
61
Opendale Plantation
Swiff Cliff Plantation
White Scar Plantation
Milham Dale
YO17
Wandales
HUGGATE HILL
Gritts Farm
7
Tumuli
Martinholme Farm
Fotherdale Farm
Fotherdale
Cow Dale
Mount Pleasant Farm
Boot and Shoe Plantation
Ray Dale
Northdale Plantation
North Breckenholme
Gill's Farm
Yorkshire Wolds Way
60
Open Dale
Woodley Farm
Uncleby Wold
Uncleby Wold Farm
Tumuli
Thousand Yard Plantation
North Breckenholme
Long Plantation
Middle Plantation
Thixen Dale
Tumuli
YO25
Ings Plantation
The Ings
6
Elba Plantation
Jenny Wren's Spring
Chalybeate Spring
Mount Pleasant Farm
UNCLEBY HILL
WATER LA
Woodley Farm
Manor Farm
YO41
Uncleby Brow Plantation
South Breckenholme
Tumuli
Riggs Farm
59
HOWE LA
Springfield Farm
School Farm
Painsthorpe Field
Admiral Plantation
Painsthorpe Dale
Tumulus
Worm Dale
Broadholme Farm
Earthworks
Bradeham Dale
Tumuli
5
Kirby Underdale
Scottendale Farm
Manor Farm
Beech Farm
Scottendale Plantation
PAINSTHORPE LANE
Painsthorpe Wold Farm
Tumuli
Bradeham Well
Pluckham Dale
PEHAM LANE
Painsthorpe
Megdale Plantation
East Brow Plantation
Fordham Plantation
Fordham Dale
Wayrham Dale
Pluckham Plantation
Pluckham
58
A166
Cheese Cake Wold
Buck Wood
King Top
Garrowby Hill Top Farm
Tumuli
South Wold Dale
Hundle Dale
South Wold Plantation
South Wold Farm
Fordham Farm
Wayrham Farm
Wold House Farm
4
Mast
GARROWBY STREET
Wayrham Picnic Site
STONE DALE
57
Tumuli
Mast
Tumuli
Cot Nab
P ✕
Seventy Acre Plantation
Stable Plantation
Greenwick
3
Worsendale Plantation
WORSENDALE ROAD
Cot Nab
Earthwork
THE BENCE
Earthworks
Callis Wold
YO42
High Callis Wold
Chalk Pit
Great Plantation
Worsden Dale
Flat Top
Crow Wood
Old Wood
OGHREPT HIL
Hagworm Wood
Moat
Bishop Wilton Wold
Deep Dale
Tumuli
Earthwork
Huggate Dikes
56
Tun Dale
Huggate Pasture
2
Milner Wood
North Wolds Walk
Bishop Wilton Wold
BEACON ROAD
Wilton Wold Plantation
Tumulus
Low Callis Wold
Mast
Mast
Earthwork
Earthworks
Frendal Dale
55
Minster Way
Stonepit Plantation
Mingledale Plantation
Deep Dale
Swingling Moor
Millington Grange Farm
Millington Grange
Scoar Dale
Pasture Dale
1
Garths End Fields
Summerhouse Plantation
Church Dale
Castle Field
Givendale Out Field
GREAT BALK
Millington Heights
Millington Pasture
Jessop's Plantation
Nettle Dale
Fox Covert
54

A 81 B 82 C 83 D 84 E 85 F

17
6

Scale: 1¾ inches to 1 mile

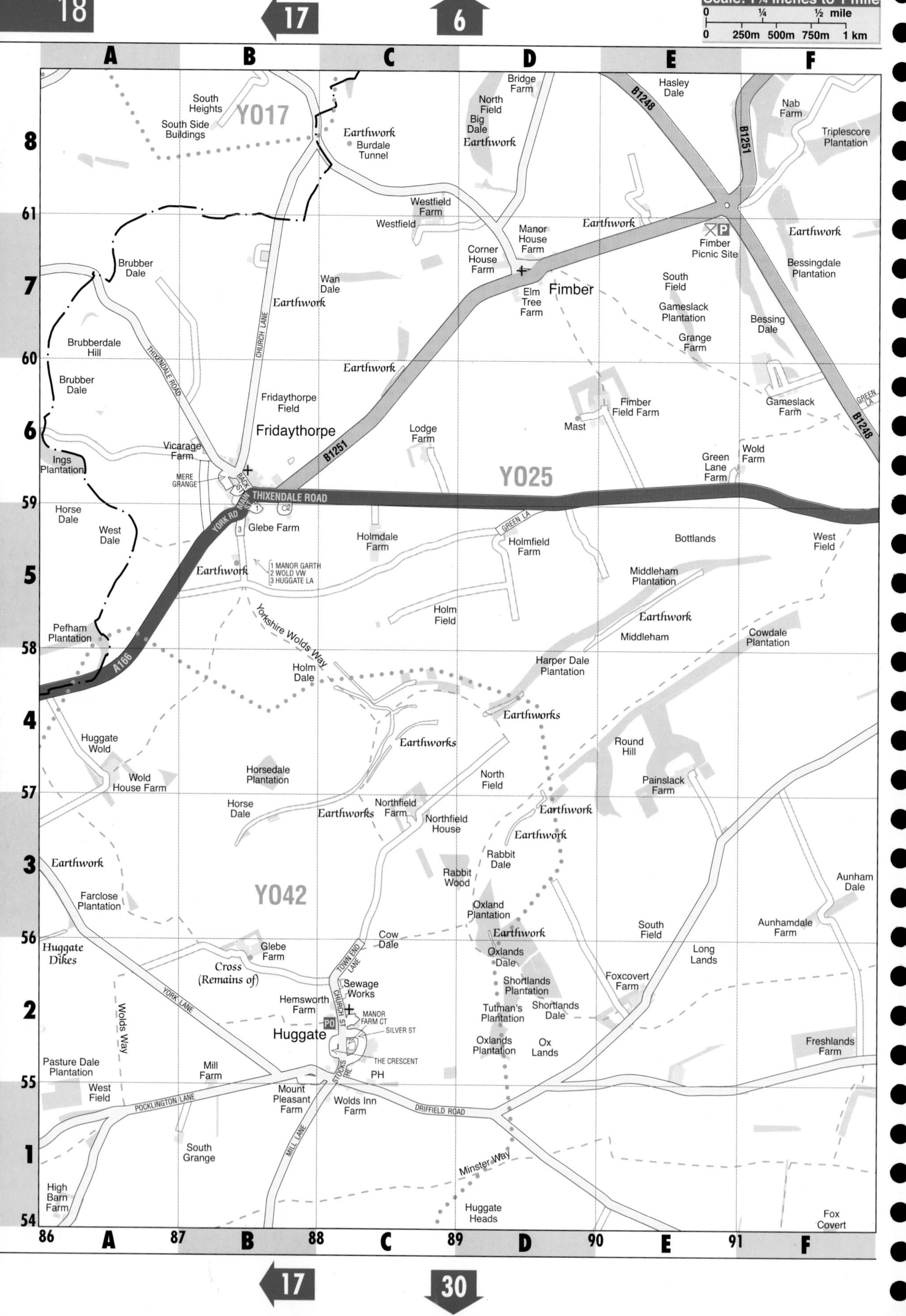
0
¼
½ mile
0
250m
500m
750m
1 km
A
B
C
D
E
F
South Heights
South Side Buildings
YO17
Earthwork
Burdale Tunnel
Bridge Farm
North Field
Big Dale
Earthwork
Hasley Dale
B1248
Nab Farm
B1251
Triplescore Plantation
Westfield Farm
Westfield
Manor House Farm
Earthwork
Fimber Picnic Site
Earthwork
Brubber Dale
Corner House Farm
Bessingdale Plantation
Wan Dale
Elm Tree Farm
Fimber
South Field
Earthwork
Gameslack Plantation
Bessing Dale
Brubberdale Hill
THIXENDALE ROAD
CHURCH LANE
Grange Farm
Earthwork
Brubber Dale
Fridaythorpe Field
Fimber Field Farm
Gameslack Farm
GREEN LA
Lodge Farm
Mast
Fridaythorpe
B1251
B1248
Vicarage Farm
Ings Plantation
MERE GRANGE
BACK ST
YO25
Green Lane Farm
Wold Farm
MAIN ST
THIXENDALE ROAD
Horse Dale
YORK RD
Glebe Farm
GREEN LA
West Dale
Holmdale Farm
Holmfield Farm
Bottlands
West Field
Earthwork
1 MANOR GARTH
2 WOLD VW
3 HUGGATE LA
Middleham Plantation
Holm Field
Earthwork
Yorkshire Wolds Way
Middleham
Pefham Plantation
Cowdale Plantation
A166
Holm Dale
Harper Dale Plantation
Earthworks
Huggate Wold
Earthworks
Round Hill
Horsedale Plantation
North Field
Wold House Farm
Painslack Farm
Horse Dale
Northfield Farm
Earthworks
Northfield House
Earthwork
Earthwork
Earthwork
Rabbit Dale
Rabbit Wood
Aunham Dale
YO42
Farclose Plantation
Oxland Plantation
Cow Dale
Earthwork
South Field
Aunhamdale Farm
Huggate Dikes
Glebe Farm
TOWN END LANE
Oxlands Dale
Long Lands
Cross (Remains of)
Sewage Works
Shortlands Plantation
Foxcovert Farm
Wolds Way
YORK LANE
Hemsworth Farm
CHURCH ST
MANOR FARM CT
Tutman's Plantation
Shortlands Dale
PO
SILVER ST
Huggate
Oxlands Plantation
Ox Lands
Freshlands Farm
Pasture Dale Plantation
THE CRESCENT
Mill Farm
STOCKS HL
PH
West Field
Mount Pleasant Farm
POCKLINGTON LANE
Wolds Inn Farm
DRIFFIELD ROAD
MILL LANE
South Grange
Minster Way
High Barn Farm
Huggate Heads
Fox Covert
8
61
7
60
6
59
5
58
4
57
3
56
2
55
1
54
86
87
88
89
90
91

17
30

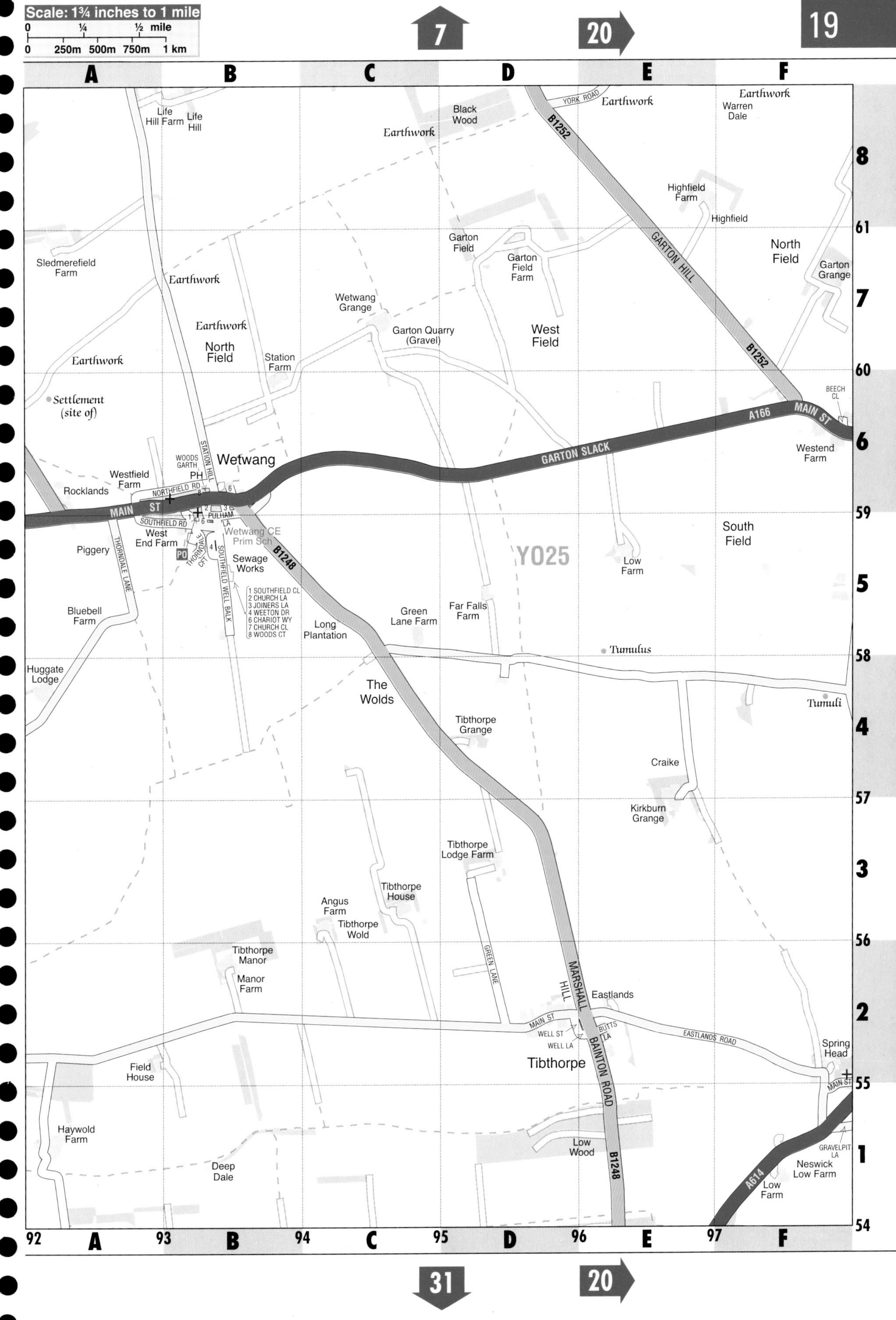
Scale: 1¾ inches to 1 mile
0 ¼ ½ mile
0 250m 500m 750m 1 km
7
20
A B C D E F
Life Hill Farm
Life Hill
Black Wood
Earthwork
YORK ROAD
Earthwork
B1252
Earthwork
Warren Dale
Highfield Farm
Highfield
Garton Field
Garton Field Farm
GARTON HILL
North Field
Garton Grange
Sledmerefield Farm
Earthwork
Earthwork
Wetwang Grange
Garton Quarry (Gravel)
West Field
North Field
Station Farm
Earthwork
B1252
Settlement (site of)
BEECH CL
A166
MAIN ST
WOODS GARTH
STATION HILL
Wetwang
PH
GARTON SLACK
Westend Farm
Westfield Farm
Rocklands
NORTHFIELD RD
MAIN ST
PULHAM LA
SOUTHFIELD RD
West End Farm
Wetwang CE Prim Sch
B1248
South Field
Piggery
THORNDALE LANE
PO
THORNDALE CFT
SOUTHFIELD WELL BALK
Sewage Works
YO25
Low Farm
1 SOUTHFIELD CL
2 CHURCH LA
3 JOINERS LA
4 WEETON DR
6 CHARIOT WY
7 CHURCH CL
8 WOODS CT
Bluebell Farm
Long Plantation
Green Lane Farm
Far Falls Farm
Tumulus
Huggate Lodge
The Wolds
Tumuli
Tibthorpe Grange
Craike
Kirkburn Grange
Tibthorpe Lodge Farm
Tibthorpe House
Angus Farm
Tibthorpe Wold
GREEN LANE
Tibthorpe Manor
Manor Farm
MARSHALL HILL
Eastlands
MAIN ST
WELL ST
WELL LA
BUTTS LA
EASTLANDS ROAD
BAINTON ROAD
Spring Head
Field House
Tibthorpe
MAIN ST
Haywold Farm
Low Wood
GRAVELPIT LA
Deep Dale
B1248
Neswick Low Farm
A614
Low Farm
8
61
7
60
6
59
5
58
4
57
3
56
2
55
1
54
92 93 94 95 96 97
31
20

19
8

Scale: 1¾ inches to 1 mile
0 ¼ ½ mile
0 250m 500m 750m 1 km

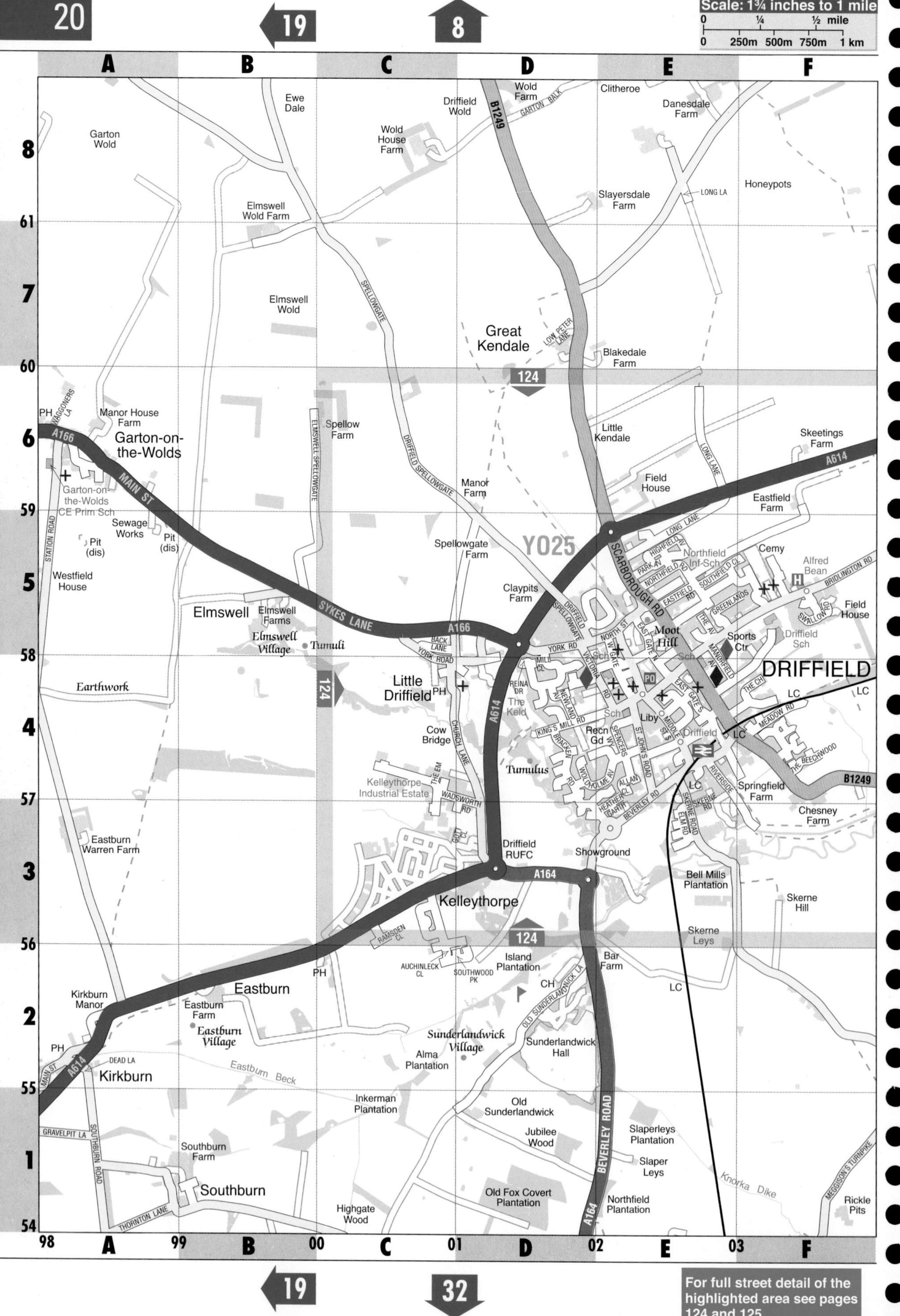

For full street detail of the highlighted area see pages 124 and 125.

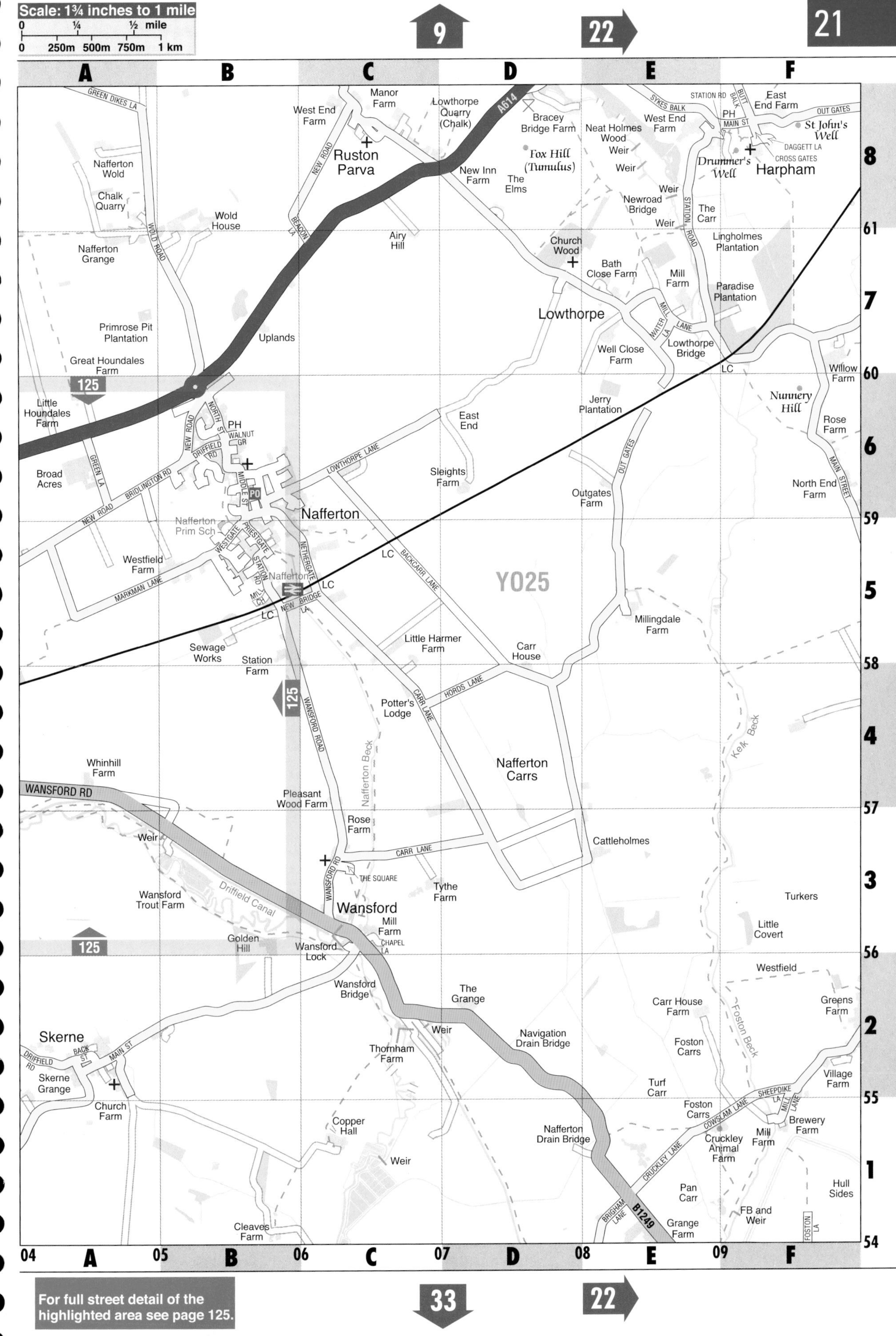

Scale: 1¾ inches to 1 mile

0   ¼   ½   mile
0   250m   500m   750m   1 km

9

22

GREEN DIKES LA

Nafferton Wold

Chalk Quarry

Nafferton Grange

Primrose Pit Plantation

Great Houndales Farm

Little Houndales Farm

Broad Acres

Wold House

WOLD ROAD

NEW ROAD

West End Farm

Manor Farm

Ruston Parva

Airy Hill

BEACON LA

Lowthorpe Quarry (Chalk)

A614

New Inn Farm

The Elms

Bracey Bridge Farm

Fox Hill (Tumulus)

Neat Holmes Wood

Weir

Church Wood

Bath Close Farm

Lowthorpe

Weir

Newroad Bridge

Weir

Mill Farm

Well Close Farm

Lowthorpe Bridge

STATION RD

SYKES BALK

BUTT BALK

MAIN ST

PH

West End Farm

St John's Well

Drummer's Well

Harpham

DAGGETT LA

CROSS GATES

East End Farm

OUT GATES

The Carr

Lingholmes Plantation

Paradise Plantation

WATER LANE

MILL LANE

STATION ROAD

Willow Farm

Nunnery Hill

Rose Farm

North End Farm

MAIN STREET

61

7

60

6

59

8

Uplands

125

NORTH ST

DRIFFIELD RD

NEW ROAD

GREEN LA

PH

WALNUT GR

Nafferton Prim Sch

Westfield Farm

WESTGATE

CHESTGATE

BRIDLINGTON RD

MIDDLE ST

PO

Nafferton

STATION RD

NETHERGATE

MARKMAN LANE

LOWTHORPE LANE

East End

Sleights Farm

Jerry Plantation

OUT GATES

Outgates Farm

Millingdale Farm

YO25

Carr House

BACKCARR LANE

LC

LC

LC

Nafferton

MILL LA

NEW BRIDGE

Sewage Works

Station Farm

125

WANSFORD ROAD

Little Harmer Farm

HORDS LANE

CARR LANE

Potter's Lodge

Nafferton Carrs

Nafferton Beck

Pleasant Wood Farm

Rose Farm

CARR LANE

Cattleholmes

Kelk Beck

5

58

4

57

3

56

Whinhill Farm

WANSFORD RD

Weir

Wansford Trout Farm

Driffield Canal

125

Golden Hill

Wansford Lock

WANSFORD RD

THE SQUARE

Wansford

Tythe Farm

Mill Farm

CHAPEL LA

Wansford Bridge

The Grange

Weir

Navigation Drain Bridge

Carr House Farm

Foston Carrs

Turf Carr

Foston Carrs

Westfield

Foston Beck

Turkers

Little Covert

Greens Farm

Village Farm

SHEEPDIKE LANE

MILL LANE

2

55

1

54

Skerne

DRIFFIELD RD

BACK ST

MAIN ST

Skerne Grange

Church Farm

Copper Hall

Weir

Thornham Farm

Nafferton Drain Bridge

Cleaves Farm

BRIGHAM LANE

B1249

Grange Farm

Pan Carr

FOSTON LA

Cruckley Animal Farm

COWSLAM LANE

CRUCKLEY LANE

Mill Farm

Brewery Farm

FB and Weir

Hull Sides

04   A   05   B   06   C   07   D   08   E   09   F

For full street detail of the highlighted area see page 125.

33

22

Scale: 1¾ inches to 1 mile
0   ¼   ½ mile
0   250m 500m 750m 1 km

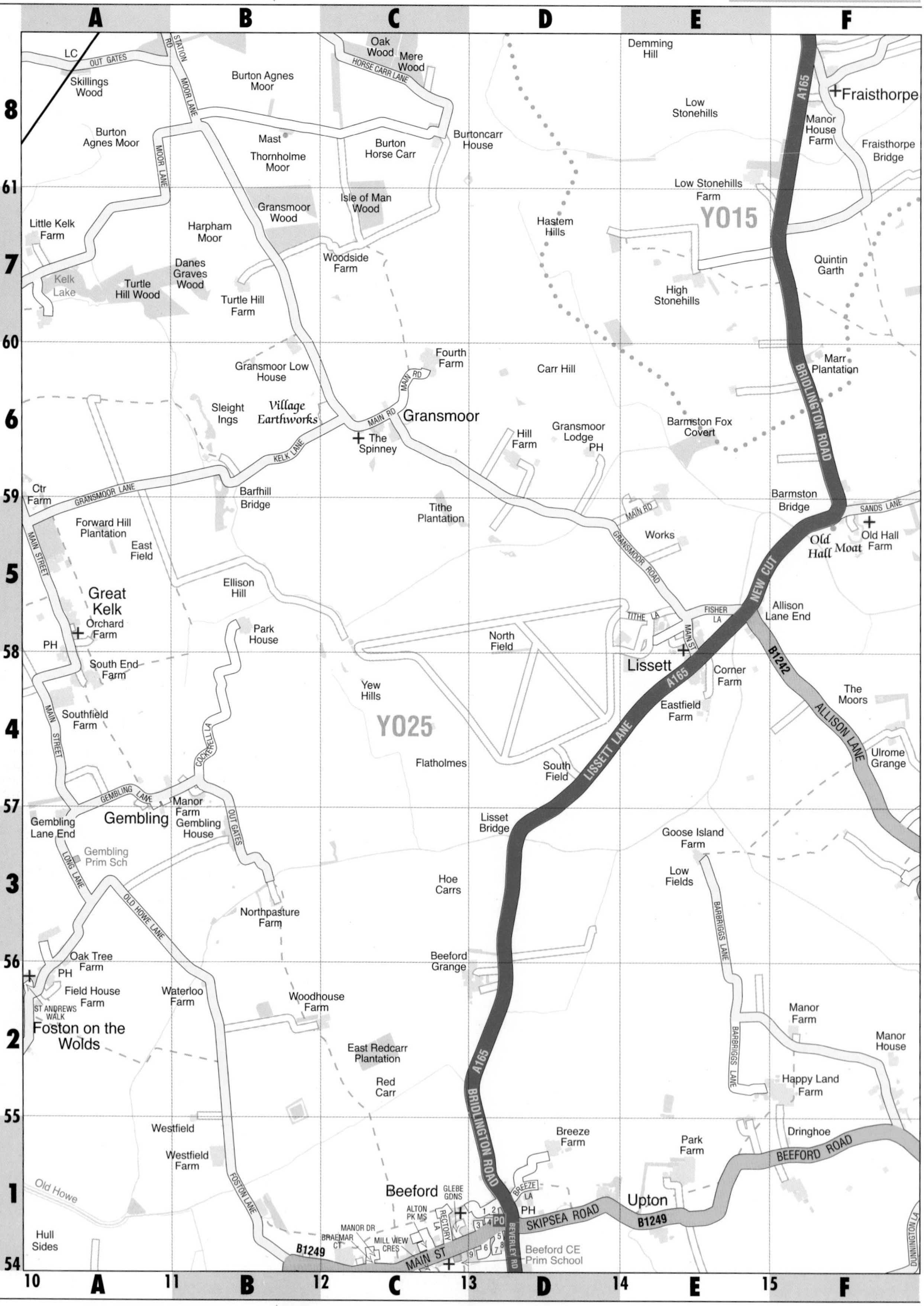

A B C D E F

8 LC OUT GATES
Skillings Wood
STATION RD
MOOR LANE
Burton Agnes Moor
Mast
Oak Wood
Mere Wood
HORSE CARR LANE
Demming Hill
Low Stonehills
Manor House Farm
Fraisthorpe
Fraisthorpe Bridge
A165
BRIDLINGTON ROAD

61 Burton Agnes Moor
Thornholme Moor
Burton Horse Carr
Burtoncarr House
Low Stonehills Farm
YO15

7 Little Kelk Farm
Harpham Moor
Gransmoor Wood
Isle of Man Wood
Woodside Farm
Hastem Hills
High Stonehills
Quintin Garth

60 Kelk Lake
Turtle Hill Wood
Danes Graves Wood
Turtle Hill Farm

6 Gransmoor Low House
Sleight Ings
Village Earthworks
MAIN RD
Fourth Farm
Gransmoor
Hill Farm
Carr Hill
Gransmoor Lodge PH
Barmston Fox Covert
Marr Plantation

59 Ctr Farm
GRANSMOOR LANE
Barfhill Bridge
KELK LANE
The Spinney
Tithe Plantation
GRANSMOOR ROAD
MAIN RD
Works
Barmston Bridge
SANDS LANE
Old Hall Moat
Old Hall Farm

5 Forward Hill Plantation
East Field
Ellison Hill
MAIN STREET
TITHE LA
FISHER LA
MAIN ST
NEW CUT
Allison Lane End
B1242
ALLISON LANE

Great Kelk
Orchard Farm
Park House
North Field
Lissett
A165
Corner Farm
The Moors

58 PH
South End Farm
Yew Hills
YO25
Eastfield Farm
Ulrome Grange

4 Southfield Farm
MAIN ST
COCKERELL LA
OUT GATES
Flatholmes
South Field
LISSETT LANE

57 Gembling Lane End
GEMBLING LANE
Manor Farm
Gembling House
Gembling
Lisset Bridge
Goose Island Farm
Low Fields

3 LONG LANE
OLD HOWE LANE
Gembling Prim Sch
Hoe Carrs
BARBRIGGS LANE

Northpasture Farm
Beeford Grange

56 Oak Tree Farm
PH
Field House Farm
Waterloo Farm
Woodhouse Farm
Manor Farm
Manor House

2 ST ANDREWS WALK
Foston on the Wolds
East Redcarr Plantation
Red Carr
A165
BRIDLINGTON ROAD
Breeze Farm
Happy Land Farm
Park Farm

55 Old Howe
Westfield
Westfield Farm
FOSTON LANE
Breeze Farm
BREEZE LA
Dringhoe
BEEFORD ROAD

1 Hull Sides
Beeford
GLEBE GDNS
ALTON PK MS
MANOR DR
MILL VIEW CRES
RECTORY LA
PO
PH
BEVERLEY RD
SKIPSEA ROAD
Upton
B1249
DUNNINGTON LA

54 B1249
BRAEMAR CT
MAIN ST
Beeford CE Prim School

10 A 11 B 12 C 13 D 14 E 15 F

D1
1 CHURCH LA
2 ST LEONARD'S CL
3 WHARRAM FIELD
4 NEWSAM CL
5 MEADOW CL
6 ASHLEIGH DR
7 BARONWOOD CR
8 WELBURN CT
9 RECTORY VW

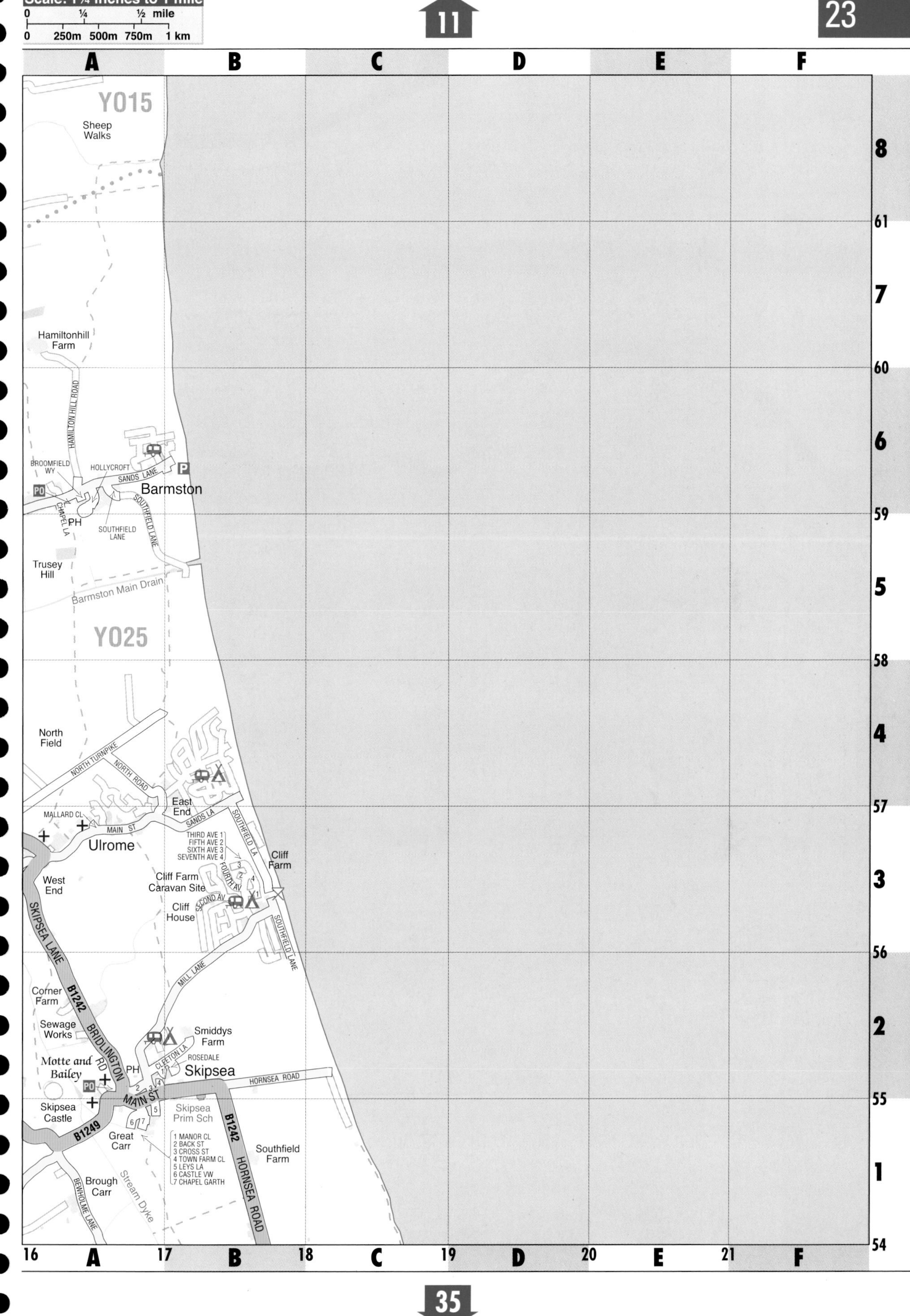

A B C D E F

8

61

7

60

6

59

5

58

4

57

3

56

2

55

1

54

YO15

Sheep Walks

Hamiltonhill Farm

BROOMFIELD WY
HOLLYCROFT
HAMILTONHILL ROAD
SANDS LANE
P
PO
CHAPEL LA
PH
SOUTHFIELD LANE
SOUTHFIELD LANE
Barmston

Trusey Hill

Barmston Main Drain

YO25

North Field

NORTH TURNPIKE
NORTH ROAD
MALLARD CL
MAIN ST
East End
SANDS LA
SOUTHFIELD LA
THIRD AVE 1
FIFTH AVE 2
SIXTH AVE 3
SEVENTH AVE 4
Cliff Farm
Ulrome
Cliff Farm Caravan Site
FOURTH AV
Cliff House
SECOND AV
West End
SOUTHFIELD LANE
MILL LANE

SKIPSEA LANE
B1242
BRIDLINGTON RD
Corner Farm
Sewage Works
Smiddys Farm
PH
CLETON LA
ROSEDALE
Motte and Bailey
PO
Skipsea
HORNSEA ROAD

Skipsea Castle
B1249
MAIN ST
5
6 7
Great Carr
Skipsea Prim Sch
1 MANOR CL
2 BACK ST
3 CROSS ST
4 TOWN FARM CL
5 LEYS LA
6 CASTLE VW
7 CHAPEL GARTH
B1242
Southfield Farm
HORNSEA ROAD

Brough Carr
Stream Dyke
BEWHOLME LANE

16 A 17 B 18 C 19 D 20 E 21 F

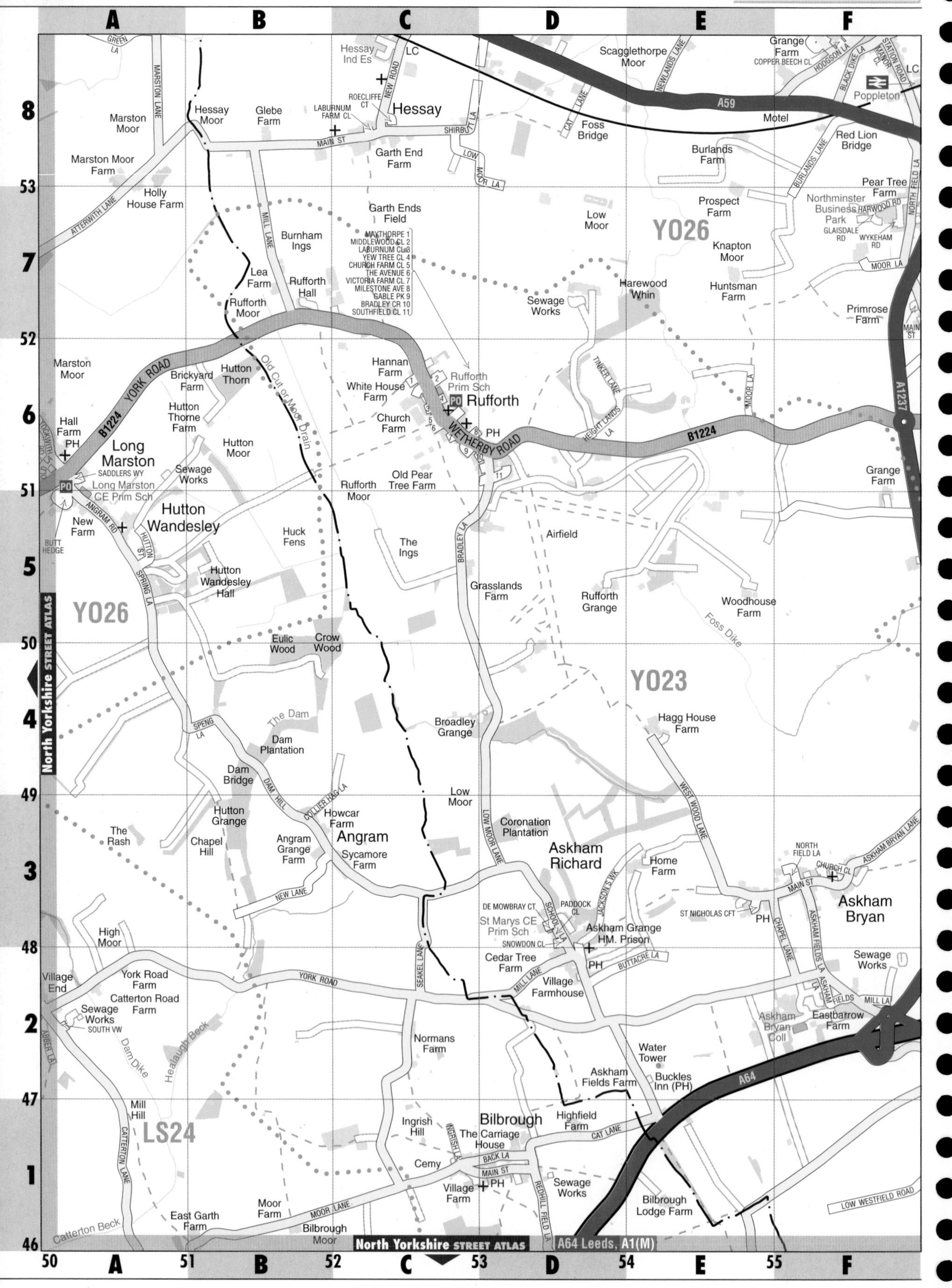

North Yorkshire STREET ATLAS

A   **B**   **C**   **D**   **E**   **F**

GREEN LA

Hessay Ind Es
LC

MARSTON LANE

8

Marston Moor

Hessay Moor

Glebe Farm

ROECLIFFE CT
LABURNUM FARM CL

NEW ROAD

Hessay

Scagglethorpe Moor

NEWLANDS LANE

A59

Grange Farm
COPPER BEECH CL

BLACK DIKE LA

HODGSON LA

STATION ROAD

MANOR RD

LC

Poppleton

Motel

Marston Moor Farm

ATTERWITH LANE

Holly House Farm

MAIN ST

SHIRBUTT LA

Garth End Farm

LOW MOOR LA

Foss Bridge

Burlands Farm

Red Lion Bridge

Pear Tree Farm

BURLANDS LANE

HARWOOD RD

Northminster Business Park

NORTH FIELD LA

53

Burnham Ings

MILL LANE

Garth Ends Field

Low Moor

YO26

Prospect Farm

GLAISDALE RD

WYKEHAM RD

7

Lea Farm

Rufforth Moor

Rufforth Hall

MAWTHORPE 1
MIDDLEWOOD CL 2
LABURNUM CL 3
YEW TREE CL 4
CHURCH FARM CL 5
THE AVENUE 6
VICTORIA FARM CL 7
MILESTONE AVE 8
GABLE PK 9
BRADLEY CR 10
SOUTHFIELD CL 11

Sewage Works

Harewood Whin

Knapton Moor

Huntsman Farm

MOOR LA

Primrose Farm

52

Marston Moor

YORK ROAD

Brickyard Farm

Hutton Thorn

Old Cut or Moor Drain

Hannan Farm

White House Farm

Rufforth Prim Sch

Rufforth

TIMBER LANE

A1237

MAIN ST

6

B1224

Hall Farm PH

Hutton Thorne Farm

Hutton Moor

Church Farm

WETHERBY ROAD

PH

HEIGHT LANDS LA

B1224

Grange Farm

51

ROCKWITH LA

Long Marston

PO

SADDLERS WY

Sewage Works

Rufforth Moor

Old Pear Tree Farm

Long Marston CE Prim Sch

ANGRAM RD

HUTTON ST

SPRING LA

Hutton Wandesley

Huck Fens

BRADLEY LA

Airfield

5

New Farm

BUTT HEDGE

Hutton Wandesley Hall

The Ings

Grasslands Farm

Rufforth Grange

Woodhouse Farm

Foss Dike

YO26

Eulic Wood

Crow Wood

YO23

50

The Dam

Hagg House Farm

North Yorkshire STREET ATLAS

4

SPENG LA

Dam Plantation

Broadley Grange

WEST WOOD LANE

DAM HILL

49

Dam Bridge

Hutton Grange

COLLIER HAGG LA

Howcar Farm

Low Moor

Coronation Plantation

NORTH FIELD LA

CHURCH CL

ASKHAM BRYAN LANE

3

The Rash

Chapel Hill

Angram Grange Farm

Angram

Sycamore Farm

LOW MOOR LANE

Askham Richard

JACKSON'S YK

Home Farm

MAIN ST

Askham Bryan

NEW LANE

PH

CHAPEL LANE

St Nicholas CFT

48

High Moor

York Road Farm

DE MOWBRAY CT

St Marys CE Prim Sch

SCHOOL LA

PADDOCK CL

Askham Grange HM Prison

Sewage Works

ASKHAM FIELDS LA

ASKHAM FIELDS LA

Catterton Road Farm

YORK ROAD

SNOWDON CL

Cedar Tree Farm

PH

BUTTACRE LA

Askham Bryan Coll

MILL LA

Village End

Sewage Works
SOUTH VW

Village Farmhouse

MILL LANE

Askham Bryan Farm

Eastbarrow Farm

2

ABBEY LA

Headaup Beck

Dam Dike

Normans Farm

SEAKEL LANE

Water Tower

A64

47

Mill Hill

Askham Fields Farm

Buckles Inn (PH)

LS24

CATTERTON LANE

Ingrish Hill

Bilbrough

Highfield Farm

CAT LANE

REDHILL FIELD LA

1

The Carriage House

BACK LA

Cemy

MAIN ST

Village Farm

PH

INGRISH LA

Sewage Works

Bilbrough Lodge Farm

LOW WESTFIELD ROAD

East Garth Farm

Moor Farm

MOOR LANE

Bilbrough Moor

North Yorkshire STREET ATLAS

A64 Leeds, A1(M)

46

Catterton Beck

Scale: 1¾ inches to 1 mile
0 ¼ ½ mile
0 250m 500m 750m 1 km

126 127 131

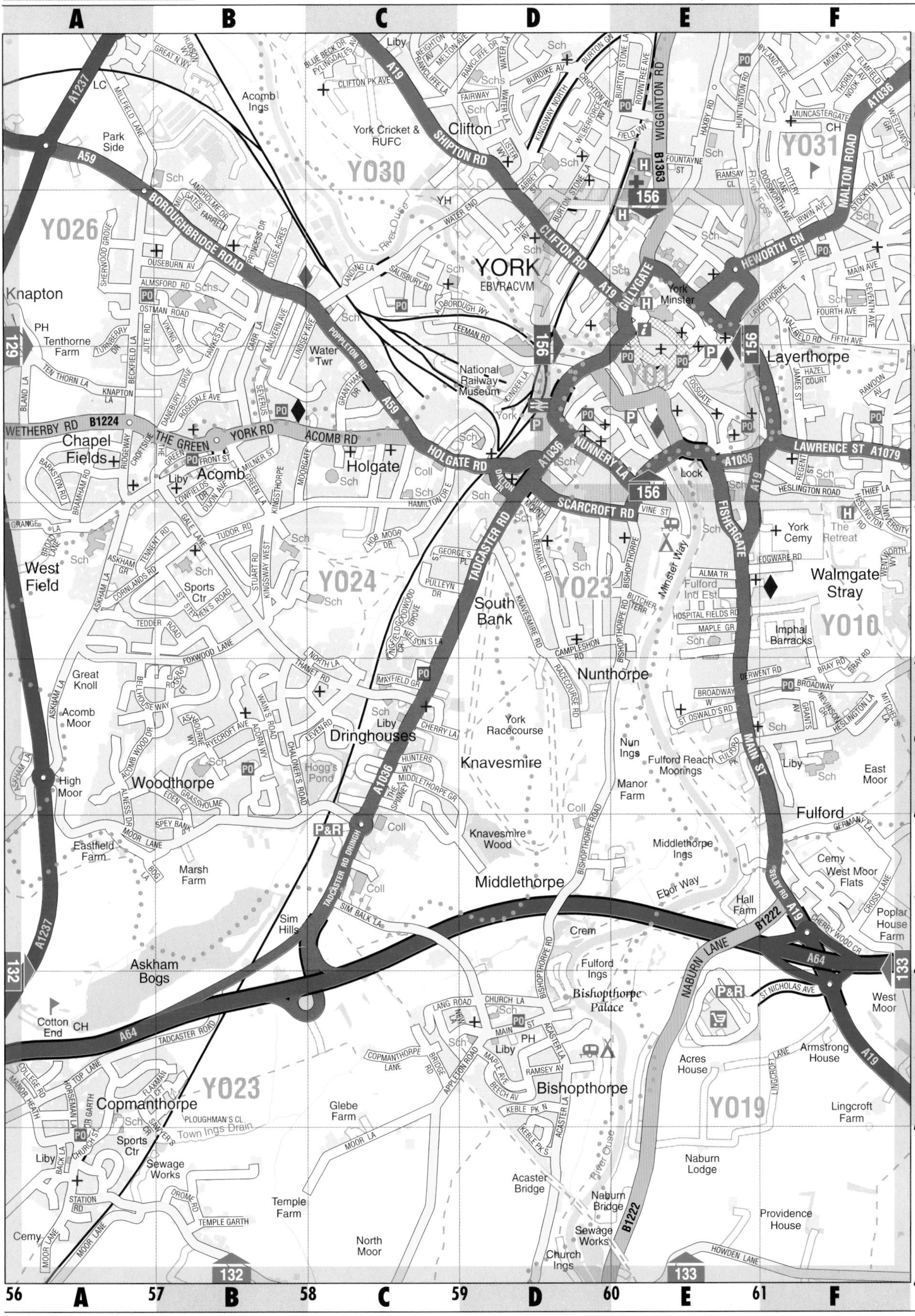

For full street detail of the highlighted area see pages 129, 130, 132 and 133.

36

26

For full street detail of the highlighted area see page 156.

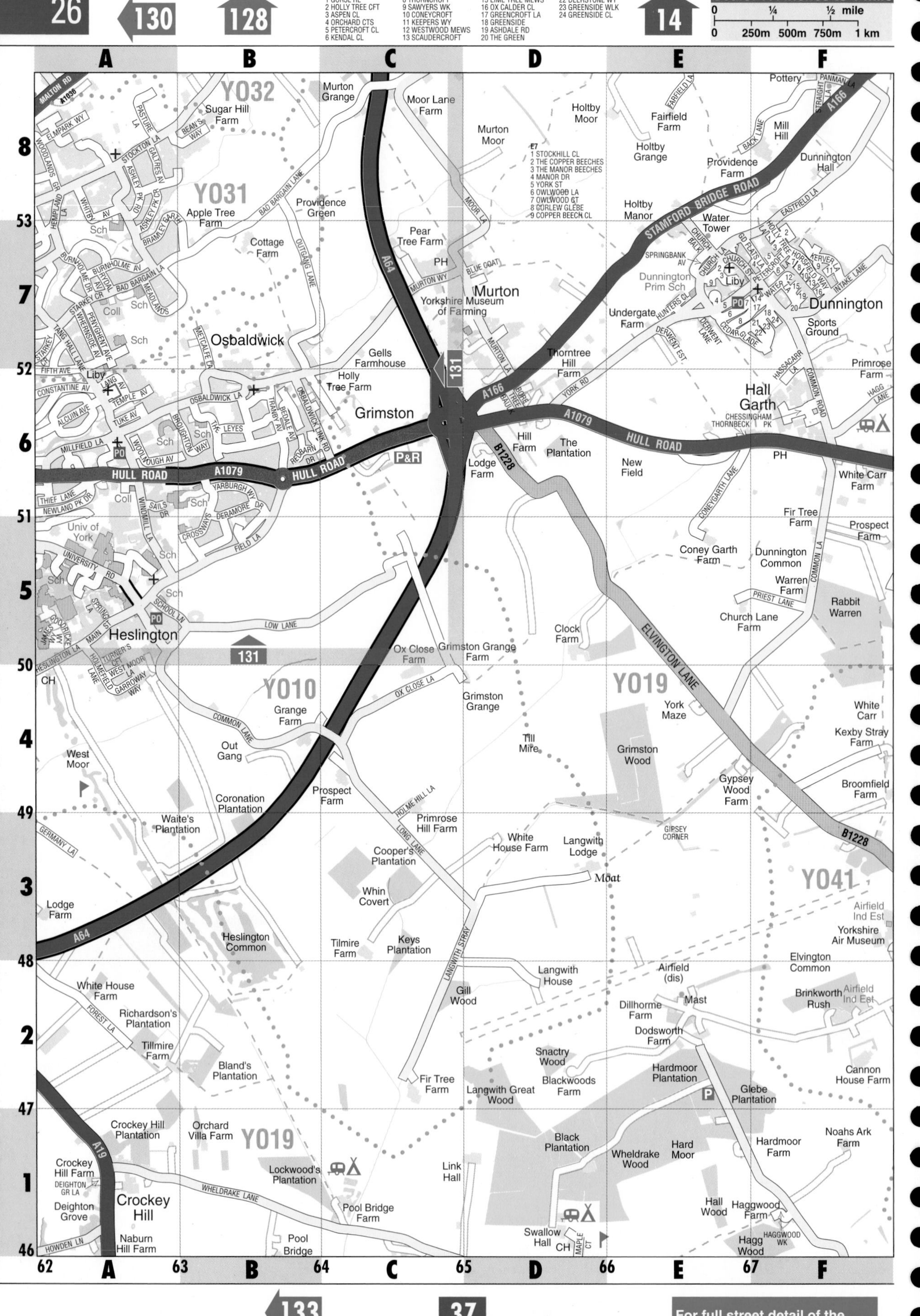

F7
1 GORSE HL
2 HOLLY TREE CFT
3 ASPEN CL
4 ORCHARD CTS
5 PETERCROFT CL
6 KENDAL CL

7 UNDERCROFT
8 THORNCROFT
9 SAWYERS WK
10 CONEYCROFT
11 KEEPERS WY
12 WESTWOOD MEWS
13 SCAUDERCROFT

14 GREENCROFT CT
15 LIME TREE MEWS
16 OX CALDER CL
17 GREENCROFT LA
18 GREENSIDE
19 ASHDALE RD
20 THE GREEN

21 HUNTERS WOOD WY
22 DEERSTONE WY
23 GREENSIDE WLK
24 GREENSIDE CL

F7
1 STOCKHILL CL
2 THE COPPER BEECHES
3 THE MANOR BEECHES
4 MANOR DR
5 YORK ST
6 OWLWOOD LA
7 OWLWOOD GT
8 CURLEW GLEBE
9 COPPER BEECH CL

For full street detail of the highlighted area see page 131.

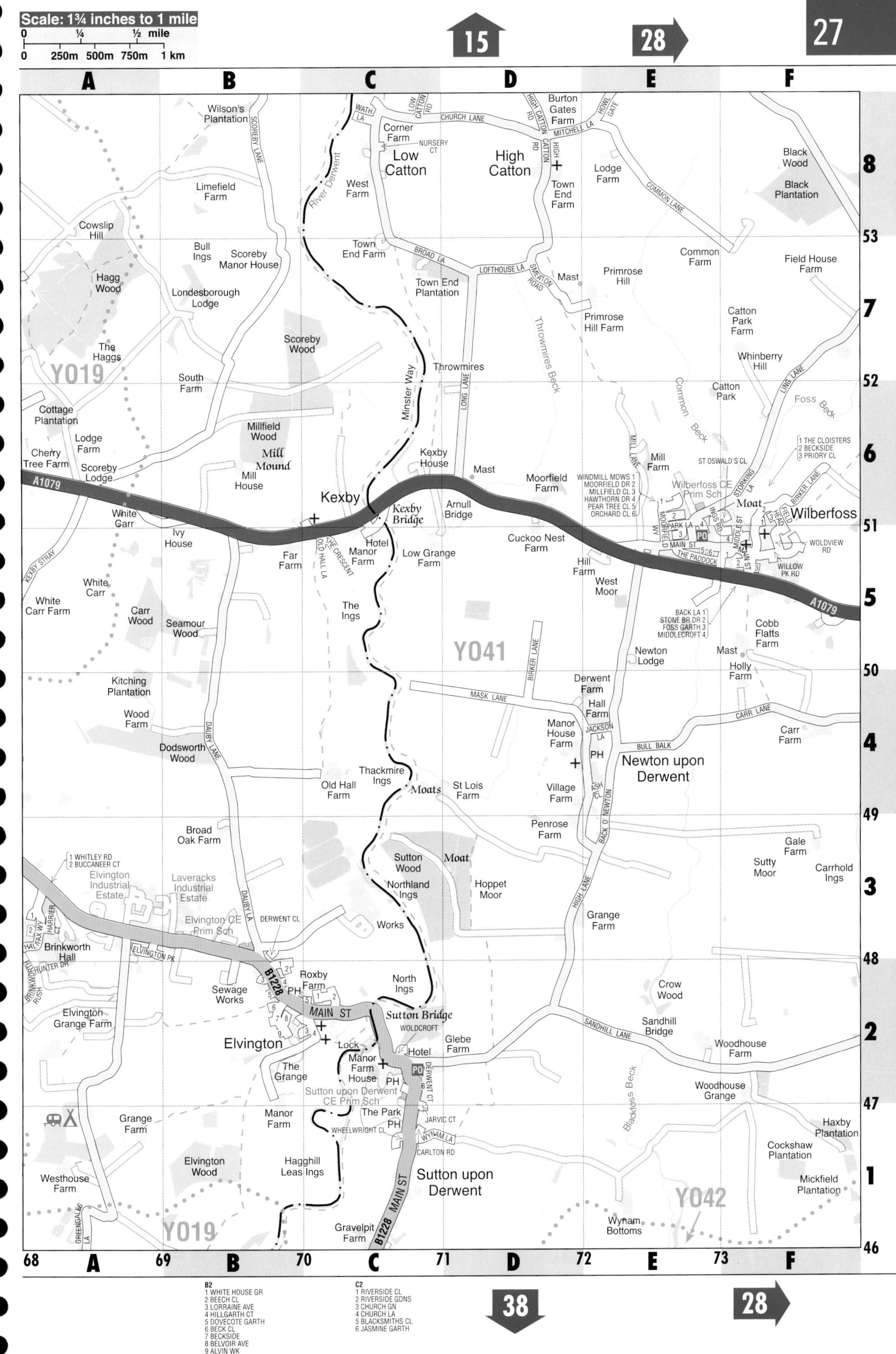

Scale: 1¾ inches to 1 mile

0   ¼   ½ mile
0   250m 500m 750m 1 km

A   B   C   D   E   F

8
53
7
52
6
51
5
50
4
49
3
48
2
47
1
46

Wilson's Plantation

Limefield Farm

Cowslip Hill

Hagg Wood

The Haggs

Y019

Cottage Plantation

Cherry Tree Farm

Lodge Farm

Scoreby Lodge

A1079

White Carr

Ivy House

White Carr Farm

White Carr

Carr Wood

Seamour Wood

Kitching Plantation

Wood Farm

Dodsworth Wood

Bull Ings

Scoreby Manor House

Londesborough Lodge

South Farm

Scoreby Wood

Millfield Wood

Mill Mound

Mill House

Far Farm

Old Hall La

Ivy Crescent

Dairy Lane

Old Hall Farm

Broad Oak Farm

Scoreby Lane

River Derwent

Wath La

Corner Farm

West Farm

Low Catton

Town End Farm

Town End Plantation

Minster Way

Throwmires

Long Lane

Broad La

Nursery Ct

Church Lane

High Catton

Town End Farm

Lofthouse La

Mast

Burton Gates Farm

High Catton Rd

High Catton Rd

Mitchell La

Howe Gate

Lodge Farm

Town End Farm

Common Lane

Black Wood

Black Plantation

Common Farm

Field House Farm

Primrose Hill

Primrose Hill Farm

Catton Park Farm

Whinberry Hill

Catton Park

Common Beck

Throwmires Beck

Skelton Road

Birker Lane

Kexby House

Mast

Kexby

Kexby Bridge

Arnull Bridge

Hotel Manor Farm

Low Grange Farm

The Ings

Y041

Mask Lane

Moorfield Farm

Cuckoo Nest Farm

Hill Farm

West Moor

Mill Lane

Moorfield Lane

Windmill Mdws 1
Moorfield Dr 2
Millfield Cl 3
Hawthorn Dr 4
Pear Tree Cl 5
Orchard Cl 6

St Oswald's Cl

Storking La

Main St

Ings Rd

The Paddock

Middle St

Wilberfoss CE Prim Sch

PO

Moat

Wilberfoss

1 The Cloisters
2 Beckside
3 Priory Cl

Birker Lane

Field La

Foss Beck

Woldview Rd

Willow Pk Rd

A1079

Lings Lane

Newton Lodge

Derwent Farm

Hall Farm

Manor House Farm

Jackson La

PH

Ash Cl

Back O Newton

Bull Balk

Carr Lane

Newton upon Derwent

Holly Farm

Mast

Cobb Flatts Farm

Back La 1
Stone Br Dr 2
Foss Garth 3
Middlecroft 4

Carr Farm

Thackmire Ings

Moats

St Lois Farm

Village Farm

Penrose Farm

Gale Farm

Sutty Moor

Carrhold Ings

Sutton Wood

Northland Ings

Moat

Hoppet Moor

Works

Grange Farm

High Lane

Crow Wood

Sandhill Lane

Sandhill Bridge

Broad Oak Farm

1 Whitley Rd
2 Buccaneer Ct

Elvington Industrial Estate

Laveracks Industrial Estate

Elvington CE Prim Sch

Derwent Cl

Dairy La

Halifax Way

Harrier Dr

Brinkworth Rush

Hurricane Rd

Brinkworth Hall

Elvington Grange Farm

Elvington Pk

B1228

PH

Sewage Works

Roxby Farm

Main St

Elvington

The Grange

Manor Farm

Hagghill Leas Ings

Westhouse Farm

Grange Farm

Elvington Wood

North Ings

Sutton Bridge

Woldcroft

Lock

Manor Farm House

Sutton upon Derwent CE Prim Sch

PH

The Park

PH

Wheelwright La

Glebe Farm

Hotel

PO

Derwent Ct

Jarvic Ct

William La

Carlton Rd

B1228

Main St

Sutton upon Derwent

Y042

Blacktoss Beck

Woodhouse Farm

Woodhouse Grange

Haxby Plantation

Cockshaw Plantation

Mickfield Plantation

Gravelpit Farm

Wynam Bottoms

Greendale La

Y019

68   69   70   71   72   73

A   B   C   D   E   F

B2
1 WHITE HOUSE GR
2 BEECH CL
3 LORRAINE AVE
4 HILLGARTH CT
5 DOVECOTE GARTH
6 BECK CL
7 BECKSIDE
8 BELVOIR AVE
9 ALVIN WK

C2
1 RIVERSIDE CL
2 RIVERSIDE GDNS
3 CHURCH GN
4 CHURCH LA
5 BLACKSMITHS CL
6 JASMINE GARTH

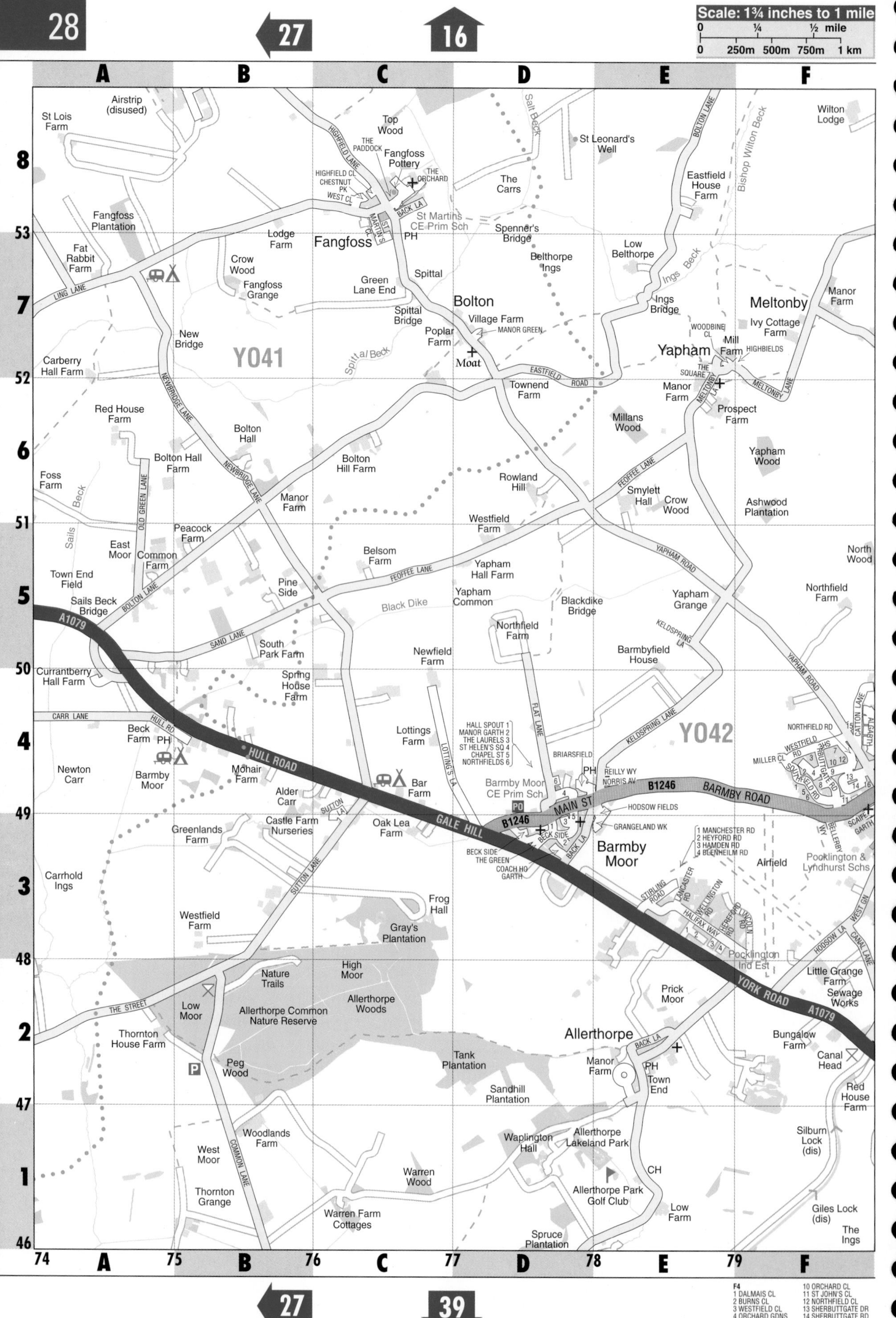

A   B   C   D   E   F

St Lois Farm
Airstrip (disused)
Top Wood
St Leonard's Well
Wilton Lodge

THE PADDOCK
Fangfoss Pottery
THE ORCHARD
The Carrs
Eastfield House Farm

Fangfoss Plantation
HIGHFIELD CL
CHESTNUT PK
WEST CL
BACK LA
St Martins CE Prim Sch
Spenner's Bridge
Low Belthorpe

Fat Rabbit Farm
Fangfoss
PH
Spittal
Belthorpe Ings
Manor Farm

Crow Wood
Green Lane End
Bolton
Ings Bridge
Meltonby
Ivy Cottage Farm

Carberry Hall Farm
Lodge Farm
Fangfoss Grange
Spittal Bridge
Village Farm
WOODBINE CL
Yapham
Mill Farm
HIGHFIELDS
Manor Farm

New Bridge
YO41
Poplar Farm
MANOR GREEN
THE SQUARE
Prospect Farm

Red House Farm
Spittal Beck
Moat
Townend Farm
EASTFIELD ROAD
Manor Farm
Yapham Wood

Foss Farm
Bolton Hall
Bolton Hill Farm
Millans Wood
Ashwood Plantation

East Moor
Common Farm
Peacock Farm
Rowland Hill
Smylett Hall
Crow Wood
North Wood

Town End Field
Sails Beck Bridge
Pine Side
Belsom Farm
Westfield Farm
Yapham Hall Farm
Yapham Common
YAPHAM ROAD
Yapham Grange
Northfield Farm

A1079
Currantberry Hall Farm
FEOFFE LANE
Black Dike
Yapham Hall Farm
Blackdike Bridge
KELDSPRING LA
Northfield RD
CATTON CL

CARR LANE
South Park Farm
Newfield Farm
Northfield Farm
Barmbyfield House
YO42
NORTHFIELD RD
WESTFIELD
MILLER CL

Beck Farm
PH
HULL RD
Spring House Farm
Lottings Farm
HALL SPOUT 1
MANOR GARTH 2
THE LAURELS 3
ST HELEN'S SQ 4
CHAPEL ST 5
NORTHFIELDS 6
BRIARSFIELD
REILLY WY
NORRIS AV
SHERBUTTGATE

Newton Carr
Barmby Moor
Mohair Farm
Alder Carr
Bar Farm
Barmby Moor CE Prim Sch
P
B1246
BARMBY ROAD

Carrhold Ings
Greenlands Farm
Castle Farm Nurseries
Oak Lea Farm
GALE HILL
B1246
BECK SIDE
MAIN ST
HODSOW FIELDS
GRANGELAND WK
1 MANCHESTER RD
2 HEYFORD RD
3 HAMDEN RD
4 BLENHEIM RD
Airfield
Pocklington & Lyndhurst Schs

Westfield Farm
SUTTON LANE
Frog Hall
Gray's Plantation
BECK SIDE
THE GREEN
COACH HO GARTH
Barmby Moor
STIRLING ROAD
LANCASTER RD
WELLINGTON RD
Pocklington Ind Est

THE STREET
Nature Trails
High Moor
Allerthorpe Woods
Allerthorpe
HALIFAX WAY
YORK ROAD
Little Grange Farm
Sewage Works

Thornton House Farm
Low Moor
Allerthorpe Common Nature Reserve
Tank Plantation
Manor Farm
PH Town End
Prick Moor
Bungalow Farm
Canal Head
A1079

P
Peg Wood
Sandhill Plantation
Waplington Hall
Allerthorpe Lakeland Park
CH
Silburn Lock (dis)
Red House Farm

Woodlands Farm
West Moor
COMMON LANE
Warren Wood
Allerthorpe Park Golf Club
Low Farm
Giles Lock (dis)
The Ings

Thornton Grange
Warren Farm Cottages
Spruce Plantation

74   A   75   B   76   C   77   D   78   E   79   F

53 / 7 / 52 / 6 / 51 / 5 / 50 / 4 / 49 / 3 / 48 / 2 / 47 / 1 / 46
8

F4
1 DALMAIS CL
2 BURNS CL
3 WESTFIELD CL
4 ORCHARD GDNS
5 WELLINGTON CL
6 MEADOWFIELD CL
7 NORTHFIELD RISE
8 HALIFAX CL
9 ORCHARD WY
10 ORCHARD CL
11 ST JOHN'S CL
12 NORTHFIELD CL
13 SHERBUTTGATE DR
14 SHERBUTTGATE RD
15 ANDREW'S CT
16 ARCHIBALD CL

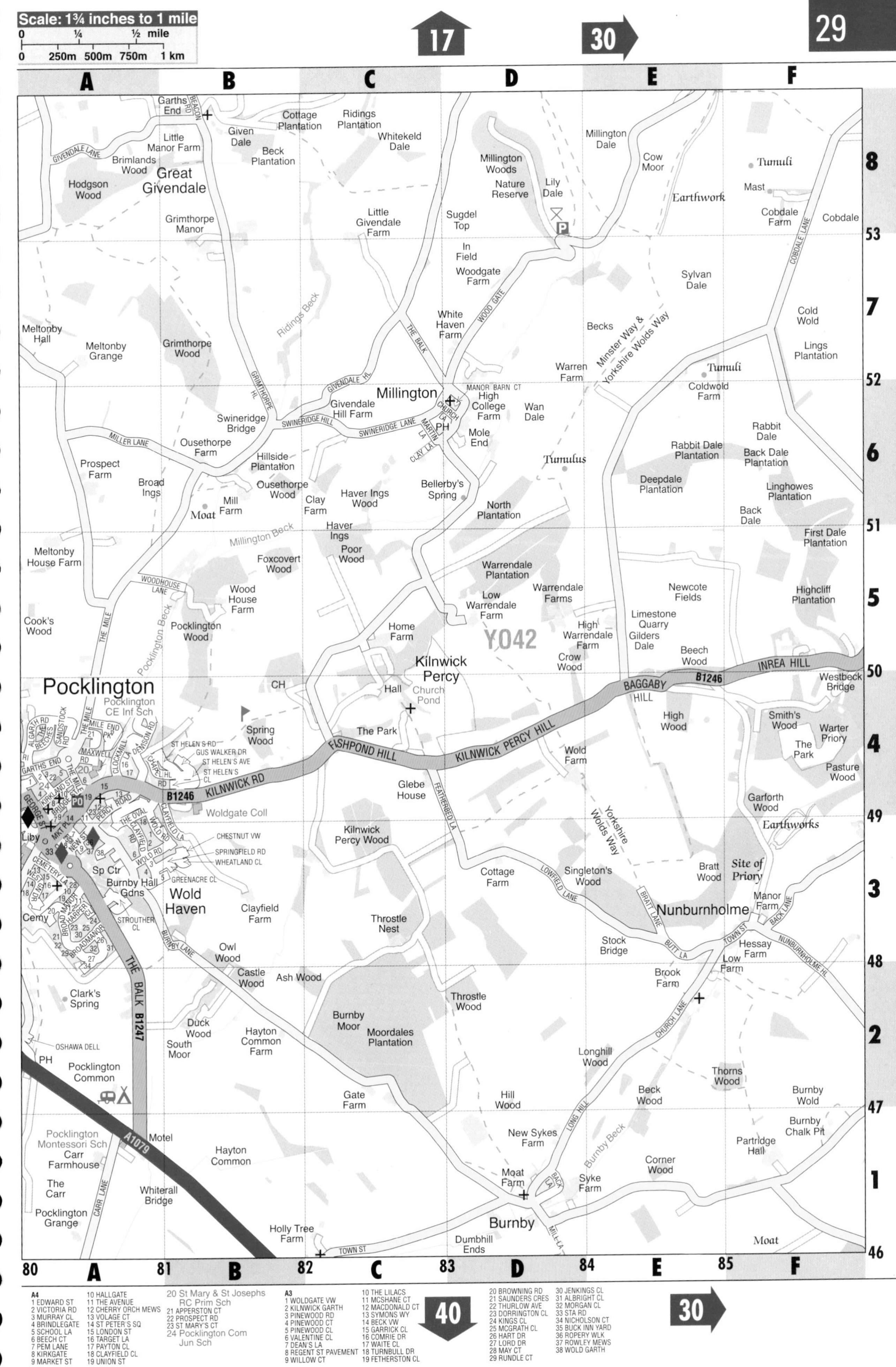

A   B   C   D   E   F

8

Garths End

Little Manor Farm

Cottage Plantation

Ridings Plantation

Whitekeld Dale

Millington Woods

Millington Dale

Cow Moor

Tumuli

Mast

Cobdale Farm

Cobdale

Hodgson Wood

Givendale Lane

Brimlands Wood

Great Givendale

Given Dale

Beck Plantation

Nature Reserve

Lily Dale

Earthwork

53

Grimthorpe Manor

Little Givendale Farm

Sugdel Top

In Field

Woodgate Farm

P

Sylvan Dale

7

Meltonby Hall

Meltonby Grange

Grimthorpe Wood

Ridings Beck

THE BALK

White Haven Farm

WOOD GATE

Becks

Minster Way & Yorkshire Wolds Way

Warren Farm

Coldwold Farm

Tumuli

Cold Wold

Lings Plantation

52

GRIMTHORPE

Swineridge Bridge

Givendale Hill Farm

Millington

MANOR BARN CT

CHURCH

High College Farm

PH

Wan Dale

Mole End

Tumulus

Rabbit Dale Plantation

Back Dale Plantation

Rabbit Dale

6

Prospect Farm

MILLER LANE

SWINERIDGE HILL

GIVENDALE RD

SWINERIDGE LANE

MARTIN LA

CLAY LA

Hillside Plantation

Deepdale Plantation

Linghowes Plantation

Broad Ings

Ousethorpe Farm

Ousethorpe Wood

Clay Farm

Haver Ings Wood

Bellerby's Spring

North Plantation

Back Dale

51

Mill Farm

Moat

Haver Ings Poor Wood

Warrendale Plantation

Limestone Quarry

Newcote Fields

Highcliff Plantation

First Dale Plantation

5

Meltonby House Farm

WOODHOUSE LANE

Foxcovert Wood

Pocklington Beck

Wood House Farm

Millington Beck

Low Warrendale Farm

Warrendale Farms

Gilders Dale

Beech Wood

Cook's Wood

THE MILE

Pocklington Wood

Home Farm

YO42

High Warrendale Farm

Crow Wood

BAGGABY HILL

B1246

INREA HILL

Westbeck Bridge

50

Pocklington

Pocklington CE Inf Sch

CH

Kilnwick Percy

Hall

Church Pond

Smith's Wood

Warter Priory

The Park

Pasture Wood

Spring Wood

FISHPOND HILL

The Park

KILNWICK PERCY HILL

High Wood

4

ALGARTH RD

SANDSTOCK

THE MILE PK

RECTRS

MAXWELL

ST HELEN'S RD

GUS WALKER DR

ST HELEN'S AVE

ST HELEN'S CL

B1246

KILNWICK RD

Woldgate Coll

Glebe House

FEATHERBED LA

Wold Farm

Garforth Wood

Earthworks

49

GEORGE ST

Liby

CLOCKMILL

PO

PERCY ROAD

CLAYFIELD LA

CHESTNUT VW

SPRINGFIELD RD

WHEATLAND CL

Kilnwick Percy Wood

LOWFIELD LANE

Yorkshire Wolds Way

Bratt Wood

Site of Priory

Manor Farm

BACK LANE

3

CEMETERY

Cemy

BURNBY LANE

Sp Ctr

Burnby Hall Gdns

GREENACRE CL

STROUTHER CL

Wold Haven

Clayfield Farm

Throstle Nest

Cottage Farm

BRATT LANE

BUTT LA

TOWN ST

Nunburnholme

NUNBURNHOLME RD

Stock Bridge

Hessay Farm

Low Farm

48

Clark's Spring

THE BALK

B1247

Owl Wood

Castle Wood

Ash Wood

Burnby Moor

Moordales Plantation

Throstle Wood

Singleton's Wood

Brook Farm

2

OSHAWA DELL

PH

Pocklington Common

Duck Wood

South Moor

Hayton Common Farm

Longhill Wood

CHURCH LANE

Thorns Wood

Burnby Wold

47

Pocklington Montessori Sch

A1079

Motel

Carr Farmhouse

Hayton Common

Gate Farm

Hill Wood

New Sykes Farm

Beck Wood

Corner Wood

Partridge Hall

Burnby Chalk Pit

Burnby Beck

LONG HILL

Ropery Wlk

The Carr

CARR LANE

Whiterall Bridge

Moat Farm

BACK LA

Syke Farm

1

Pocklington Grange

Holly Tree Farm

TOWN ST

Burnby

Dumbhill Ends

MILL LA

Moat

46

80   A   81   B   82   C   83   D   84   E   85   F

30

40

30

A4
1 EDWARD ST
2 VICTORIA RD
3 MURRAY CL
4 BRINDLEGATE
5 SCHOOL LA
6 BEECH CT
7 PEM LANE
8 KIRKGATE
9 MARKET ST
10 HALLGATE
11 THE AVENUE
12 CHERRY ORCH MEWS
13 VOLAGE CT
14 ST PETER'S SQ
15 LONDON ST
16 TARGET LA
17 PAYTON CL
18 CLAYFIELD CL
19 UNION ST

20 St Mary & St Josephs RC Prim Sch
21 APPERSTON CT
22 PROSPECT RD
23 ST MARY'S CT
24 Pocklington Com Jun Sch

A3
1 WOLDGATE VW
2 KILNWICK GARTH
3 PINEWOOD RD
4 PINEWOOD CT
5 PINEWOOD CL
6 VALENTINE CL
7 DEAN'S LA
8 REGENT ST PAVEMENT
9 WILLOW CT
10 THE LILACS
11 MCSHANE CT
12 MACDONALD CT
13 SYMONS WY
14 BECK VW
15 GARRICK CL
16 COMRIE CT
17 WAITE CL
18 TURNBULL DR
19 FETHERSTON CL

20 BROWNING RD
21 SAUNDERS CRES
22 THURLOW AVE
23 DORRINGTON CL
24 KINGS CL
25 MCGRATH CL
26 HART DR
27 LORD DR
28 MAY CL
29 RUNDLE CT
30 JENKINGS CL
31 ALBRIGHT CL
32 MORGAN CL
33 STA RD
34 NICHOLSON CT
35 BUCK INN YARD
36 ROPERY WLK
37 ROWLEY MEWS
38 WOLD GARTH

29
18

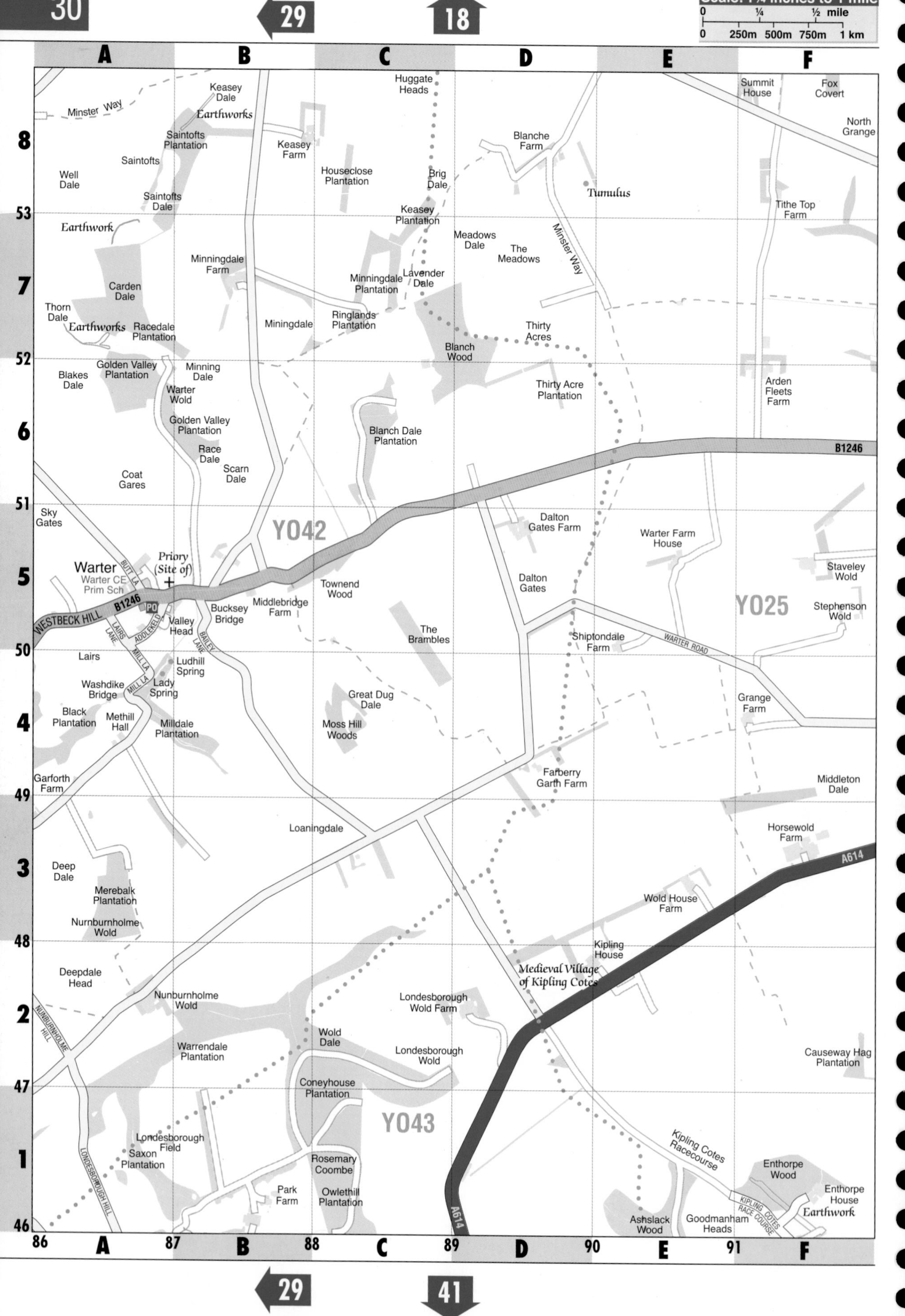
Scale: 1¾ inches to 1 mile
0 ¼ ½ mile
0 250m 500m 750m 1 km
A B C D E F
8 53 7 52 6 51 5 50 4 49 3 48 2 47 1 46
86 87 88 89 90 91
Keasey Dale
Minster Way
Earthworks
Saintofts Plantation
Saintofts
Well Dale
Saintofts Dale
Earthwork
Huggate Heads
Keasey Farm
Houseclose Plantation
Brig Dale
Keasey Plantation
Blanche Farm
Tumulus
Summit House
Fox Covert
North Grange
Tithe Top Farm
Meadows Dale
The Meadows
Minster Way
Minningdale Farm
Minningdale Plantation
Lavender Dale
Carden Dale
Thorn Dale
Earthworks
Racedale Plantation
Miningdale
Ringlands Plantation
Thirty Acres
Blanch Wood
Blakes Dale
Golden Valley Plantation
Minning Dale
Warter Wold
Thirty Acre Plantation
Arden Fleets Farm
Golden Valley Plantation
Blanch Dale Plantation
Race Dale
Scarn Dale
Coat Gares
B1246
Sky Gates
YO42
Dalton Gates Farm
Warter Farm House
Warter
Warter CE Prim Sch
Priory (Site of)
BUTT LA
Staveley Wold
Townend Wood
Middlebridge Farm
Dalton Gates
YO25
Stephenson Wold
WESTBECK HILL
B1246
PO
Bucksey Bridge
Valley Head
ADDLEKELD
LAIRS LANE
BAILEY LANE
The Brambles
Shiptondale Farm
WARTER ROAD
Lairs
MILL LA
Ludhill Spring
Washdike Bridge
Lady Spring
Great Dug Dale
Grange Farm
Black Plantation
Methill Hall
Milldale Plantation
Moss Hill Woods
Garforth Farm
Farberry Garth Farm
Middleton Dale
Loaningdale
Horsewold Farm
Deep Dale
A614
Merebalk Plantation
Wold House Farm
Nunburnholme Wold
Kipling House
Deepdale Head
Medieval Village of Kipling Cotes
Nunburnholme Wold
Londesborough Wold Farm
NUNBURNHOLME HILL
Warrendale Plantation
Wold Dale
Londesborough Wold
Causeway Hag Plantation
Coneyhouse Plantation
YO43
Londesborough Field
Saxon Plantation
LONDESBOROUGH HILL
Rosemary Coombe
Kipling Cotes Racecourse
Enthorpe Wood
Enthorpe House
Earthwork
Park Farm
Owlethill Plantation
A614
Ashslack Wood
Goodmanham Heads
KIPLING COTES RACE COURSE

29
41

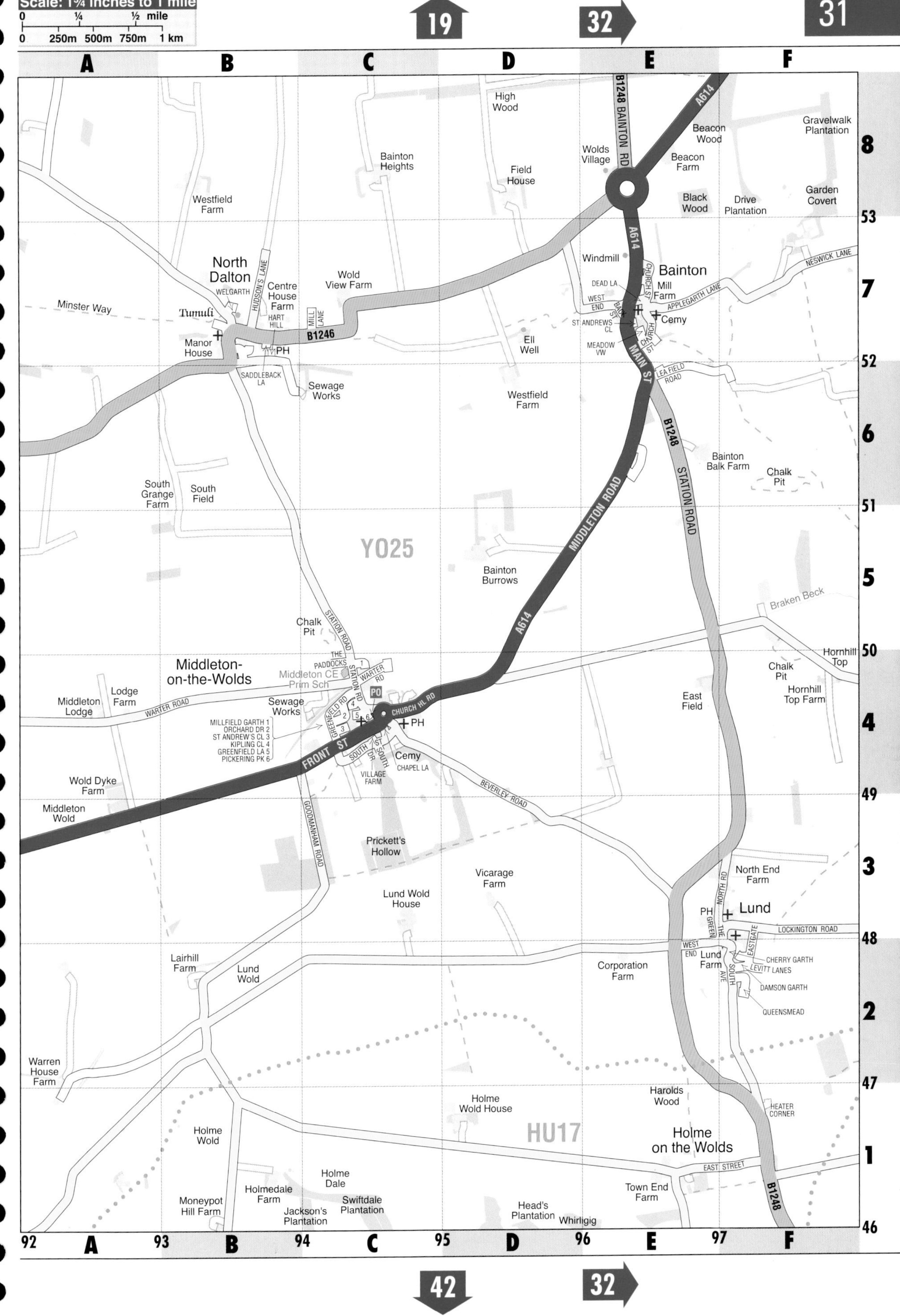
Scale: 1¾ inches to 1 mile
0 ¼ ½ mile
0 250m 500m 750m 1 km
19
32
A B C D E F
8
53
7
52
6
51
5
50
4
49
3
48
2
47
1
46
92 93 94 95 96 97
High Wood
Bainton Heights
Field House
Wolds Village
B1248 BAINTON RD
A614
Beacon Wood
Beacon Farm
Gravelwalk Plantation
Black Wood
Drive Plantation
Garden Covert
Westfield Farm
North Dalton
WELGARTH
HUDSON'S LANE
Centre House Farm
HART HILL
MILL LANE
B1246
Wold View Farm
Minster Way
Tumuli
Manor House
PH
SADDLEBACK LA
Sewage Works
Windmill
Bainton
Mill Farm
DEAD LA
WEST END
BACK ST
CHURCH ST
ST ANDREWS CL
MEADOW VW
Cemy
APPLEGARTH LANE
NESWICK LANE
Ell Well
MAIN ST
LEA FIELD ROAD
Westfield Farm
B1248
Bainton Balk Farm
Chalk Pit
South Grange Farm
South Field
STATION ROAD
MIDDLETON ROAD
YO25
Bainton Burrows
Braken Beck
Chalk Pit
Hornhill Top
Middleton-on-the-Wolds
THE PADDOCKS
Middleton CE Prim Sch
WARTER RD
PO
Chalk Pit
Hornhill Top Farm
East Field
Middleton Lodge
Lodge Farm
WARTER ROAD
Sewage Works
GREENFIELD RD
CHURCH HL RD
PH
MILLFIELD GARTH 1
ORCHARD DR 2
ST ANDREW'S CL 3
KIPLING CL 4
GREENFIELD LA 5
PICKERING PK 6
FRONT ST
SOUTH DR
SOUTH ST
Cemy
CHAPEL LA
VILLAGE FARM
BEVERLEY ROAD
Wold Dyke Farm
Middleton Wold
GOODMANHAM ROAD
Prickett's Hollow
Vicarage Farm
Lund Wold House
North End Farm
NORTH RD
Lund
PH
THE GREEN
LOCKINGTON ROAD
WEST END
Lund Farm
EASTGATE
CHERRY GARTH
LEVITT LANES
SOUTH AVE
DAMSON GARTH
QUEENSMEAD
Corporation Farm
Lairhill Farm
Lund Wold
Warren House Farm
Harolds Wood
HEATER CORNER
Holme Wold House
HU17
Holme Wold
Holme on the Wolds
EAST STREET
Holme Dale
Holmedale Farm
Swiftdale Plantation
Town End Farm
Moneypot Hill Farm
Jackson's Plantation
Head's Plantation
Whirligig
42
32

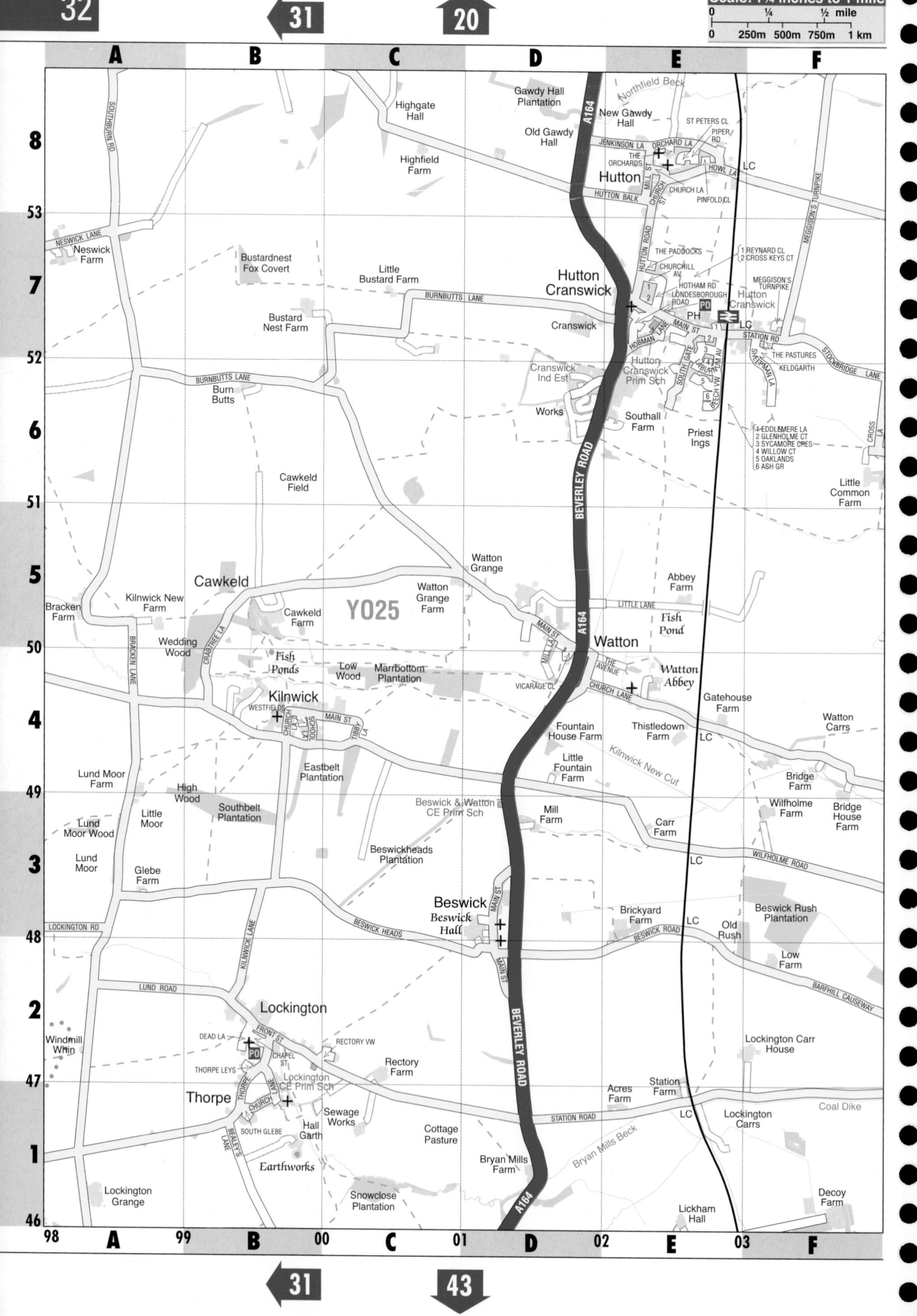

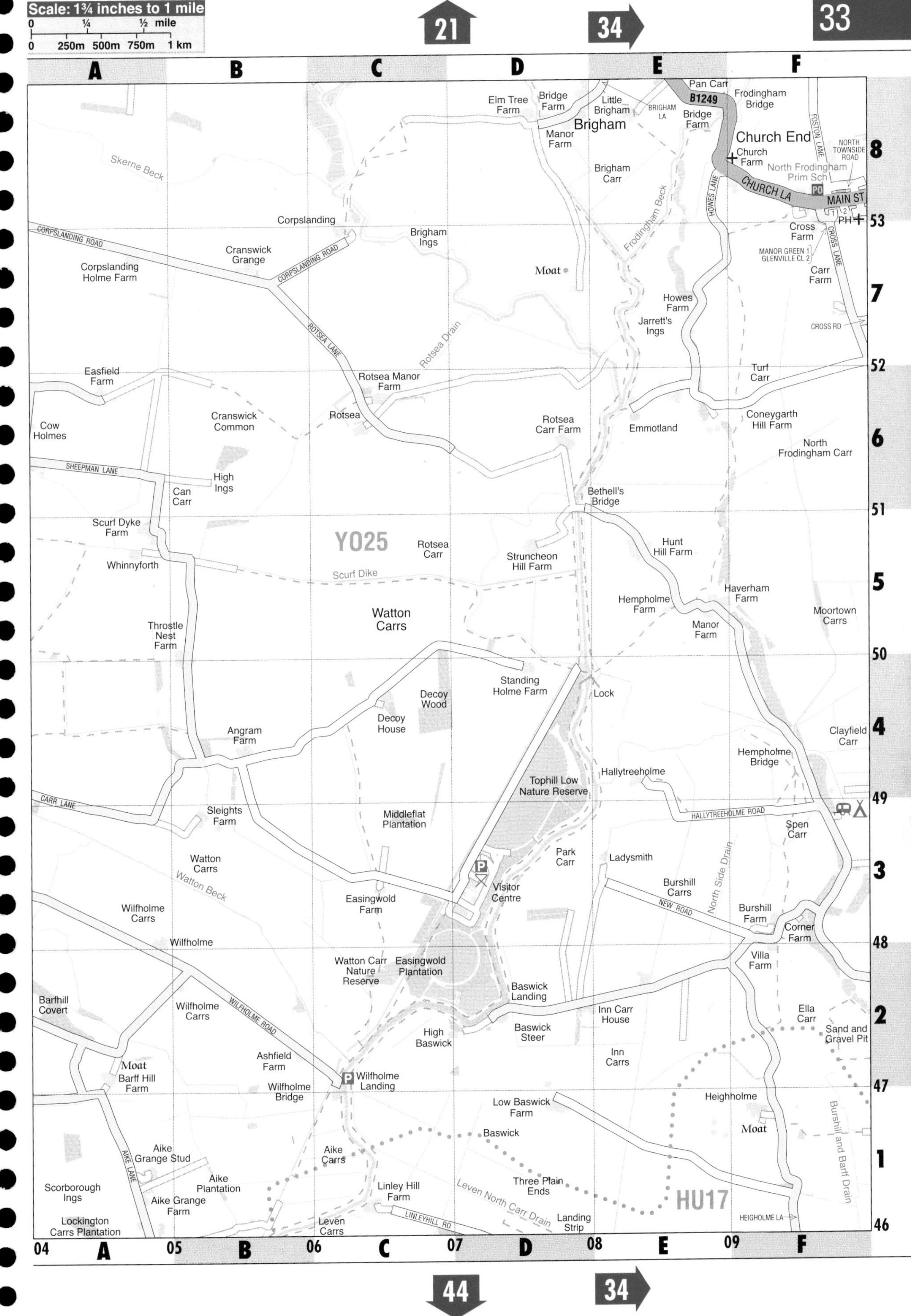

A   B   C   D   E   F

Skerne Beck

Elm Tree Farm
Bridge Farm
Little Brigham
Pan Carr
Frodingham Bridge
B1249
Manor Farm
Brigham
Brigham LA
Bridge Farm

Church End
Church Farm
North Frodingham Prim Sch
CHURCH LA
MAIN ST
PH

8

53

Corpslanding Road
Cranswick Grange
Corpslanding
Corpslanding Road
Brigham Ings
Brigham Carr

Cross Farm

MANOR GREEN 1
GLENVILLE CL 2
Carr Farm

Corpslanding Holme Farm

Moat

Howes Farm

7

CROSS RD

Easfield Farm

Rotsea Manor Farm

Rotsea

Jarrett's Ings

Turf Carr

52

Cow Holmes

SHEEPMAN LANE

Cranswick Common
Rotsea Carr Farm
Emmotland
Coneygarth Hill Farm
North Frodingham Carr

6

Can Carr

High Ings

51

Scurf Dyke Farm

YO25

Rotsea Carr

Bethell's Bridge

Hunt Hill Farm

Whinnyforth

Scurf Dike

Struncheon Hill Farm

Hempholme Farm

Haverham Farm

5

Watton Carrs

Manor Farm

Moortown Carrs

Throstle Nest Farm

50

Standing Holme Farm
Decoy Wood
Lock

Clayfield Carr

4

Angram Farm

Decoy House

Hempholme Bridge

Carr Lane

Sleights Farm

Middleflat Plantation

Tophill Low Nature Reserve

Hallytreeholme

Hallytreeholme Road

49

Spen Carr

Watton Carrs

Watton Beck

Park Carr

Ladysmith

Burshill Carrs

North Side Drain

3

Wilfholme Carrs

Visitor Centre

Burshill Farm

Wilfholme

Easingwold Farm

New Road

Corner Farm

48

Villa Farm

Barfhill Covert

Watton Carr Nature Reserve
Easingwold Plantation
Baswick Landing

Inn Carr House

Ella Carr

2

Wilfholme Carrs

Baswick Steer

Sand and Gravel Pit

Moat
Barff Hill Farm

Ashfield Farm

High Baswick

Inn Carrs

Heigholme

47

Wilfholme Bridge
Wilfholme Landing

Low Baswick Farm

Moat

Aike Lane

Aike Grange Stud

Aike Carrs

Baswick

Burshill and Barff Drain

1

Scorborough Ings

Aike Plantation

Linley Hill Farm

Three Plain Ends

HU17

Lockington Carrs Plantation

Aike Grange Farm

Leven Carrs

Linleyhill Rd

Leven North Carr Drain

Landing Strip

Heigholme La

46

04   A   05   B   06   C   07   D   08   E   09   F

44

34

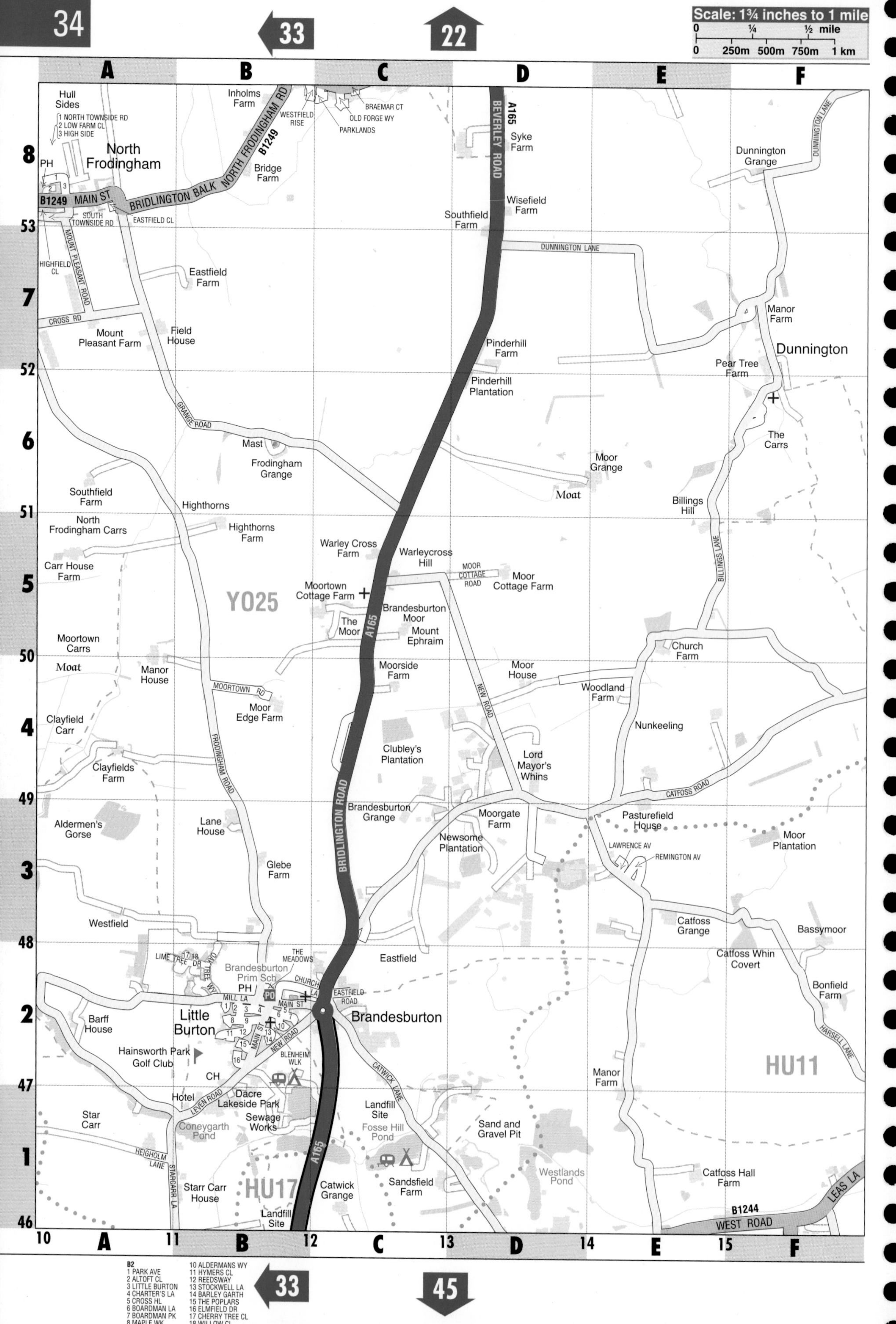
33
22
Scale: 1¾ inches to 1 mile
0 ¼ ½ mile
0 250m 500m 750m 1 km
A
B
C
D
E
F
Hull Sides
1 NORTH TOWNSIDE RD
2 LOW FARM CL
3 HIGH SIDE
Inholms Farm
WESTFIELD RISE
BRAEMAR CT
OLD FORGE WY
PARKLANDS
NORTH FRODINGHAM RD
B1249
A165
BEVERLEY ROAD
Syke Farm
Dunnington Grange
DUNNINGTON LANE
8
PH
North Frodingham
Bridge Farm
B1249 MAIN ST
BRIDLINGTON BALK
SOUTH TOWNSIDE RD
EASTFIELD CL
Wisefield Farm
Southfield Farm
53
DUNNINGTON LANE
HIGHFIELD CL
MOUNT PLEASANT ROAD
Eastfield Farm
7
CROSS RD
Mount Pleasant Farm
Field House
Manor Farm
Pinderhill Farm
Dunnington
Pear Tree Farm
52
Pinderhill Plantation
GRANGE ROAD
6
Mast
Frodingham Grange
The Carrs
Moor Grange
Southfield Farm
Moat
Billings Hill
51
Highthorns
North Frodingham Carrs
Highthorns Farm
Warley Cross Farm
Warleycross Hill
BILLINGS LANE
Carr House Farm
MOOR COTTAGE ROAD
Moor Cottage Farm
5
Moortown Cottage Farm
YO25
Brandesburton Moor
The Moor
A165
Mount Ephraim
Moortown Carrs
Church Farm
50
Moat
Manor House
Moorside Farm
Moor House
MOORTOWN RD
Woodland Farm
NEW ROAD
Moor Edge Farm
4
Clayfield Carr
Nunkeeling
Clubley's Plantation
Lord Mayor's Whins
Clayfields Farm
FRODINGHAM ROAD
49
CATFOSS ROAD
BRIDLINGTON ROAD
Brandesburton Grange
Moorgate Farm
Pasturefield House
Aldermen's Gorse
Lane House
Newsome Plantation
Moor Plantation
LAWRENCE AV
REMINGTON AV
3
Glebe Farm
Westfield
Catfoss Grange
Bassymoor
48
LIME TREE DR
17 18
WOOD
THE MEADOWS
Eastfield
Catfoss Whin Covert
Brandesburton Prim Sch
PH
CHURCH LA
PO
EASTFIELD ROAD
Bonfield Farm
MILL LA
MAIN ST
2
Barff House
Little Burton
Brandesburton
MAIN ST
NEW ROAD
HARSELL LANE
Hainsworth Park Golf Club
BLENHEIM WLK
CATWICK LANE
HU11
CH
47
Hotel
Dacre Lakeside Park
Manor Farm
Landfill Site
LEVEN ROAD
Star Carr
Sewage Works
Coneygarth Pond
Fosse Hill Pond
Sand and Gravel Pit
1
HEIGHOLM LANE
Westlands Pond
STARCARR LA
Catfoss Hall Farm
Starr Carr House
HU17
Catwick Grange
Sandsfield Farm
LEAS LA
B1244
WEST ROAD
46
Landfill Site
10
A
11
B
12
C
13
D
14
E
15
F
B2
1 PARK AVE
2 ALTOFT CL
3 LITTLE BURTON
4 CHARTER'S LA
5 CROSS HL
6 BOARDMAN LA
7 BOARDMAN PK
8 MAPLE WK
9 ST QUINTIN PK
10 ALDERMANS WY
11 HYMERS CL
12 REEDSWAY
13 STOCKWELL LA
14 BARLEY GARTH
15 THE POPLARS
16 ELMFIELD DR
17 CHERRY TREE CL
18 WILLOW CL
33
45

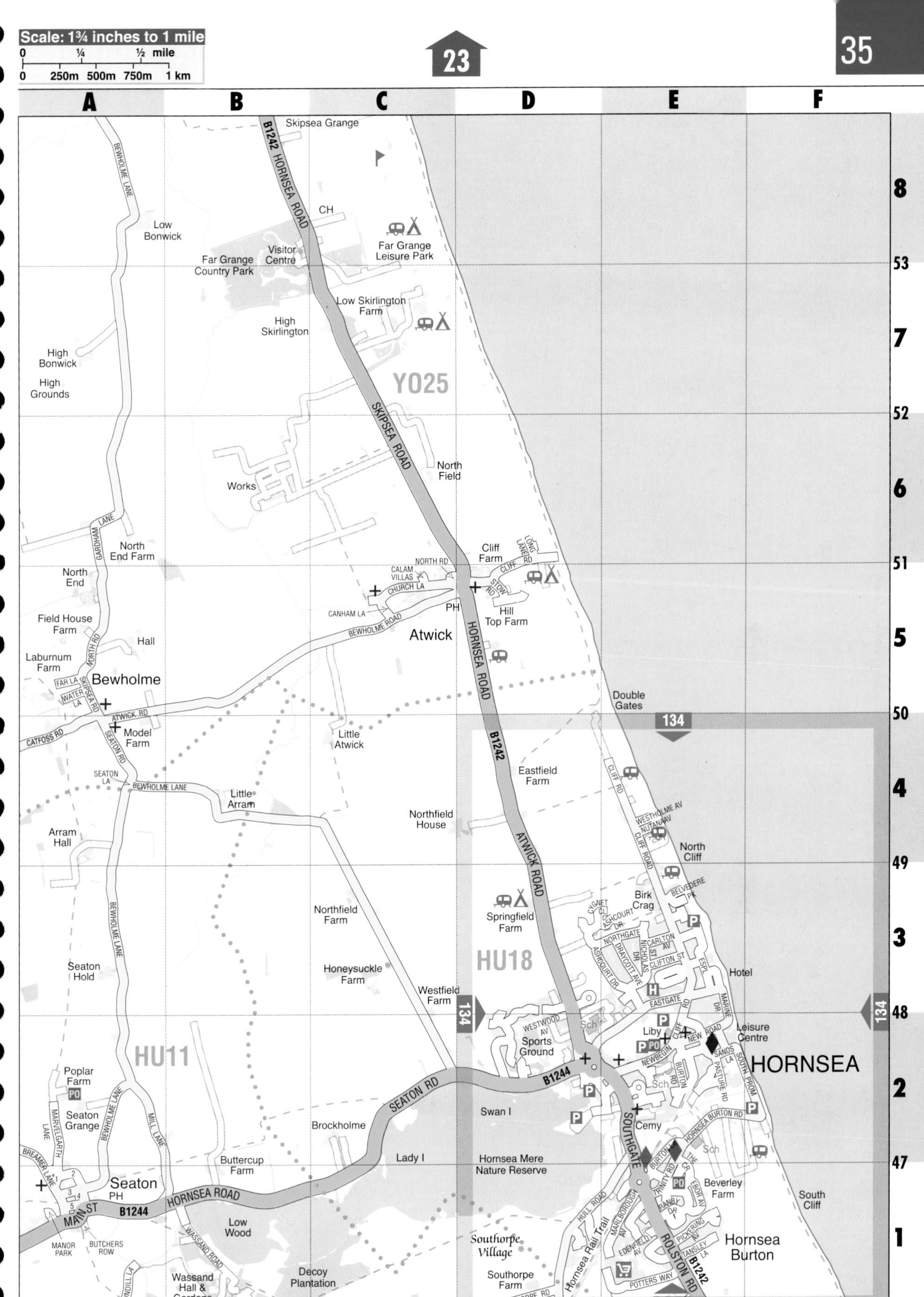

For full street detail of the highlighted area see page 134.

A1
1 COMMON LA
2 NICHOLSON LA
3 BACK LA
4 WITTYS PADDOCK
5 MIDDLE LA

132

C7
1 THE CRESENT
2 LILAC AVE
3 PLEASANT AVE
4 BEECH AVE
5 CHERRY TREE DR
6 CUNDALL DR
7 THE WILLOWS
8 OAK AVE
9 THE CLOSE
10 ELM AVE

D8
1 MAIN ST
2 FERRY FARM CL
3 MAYPOLE GR
4 ST MATTHEW'S CT

133

Scale: 1¾ inches to 1 mile

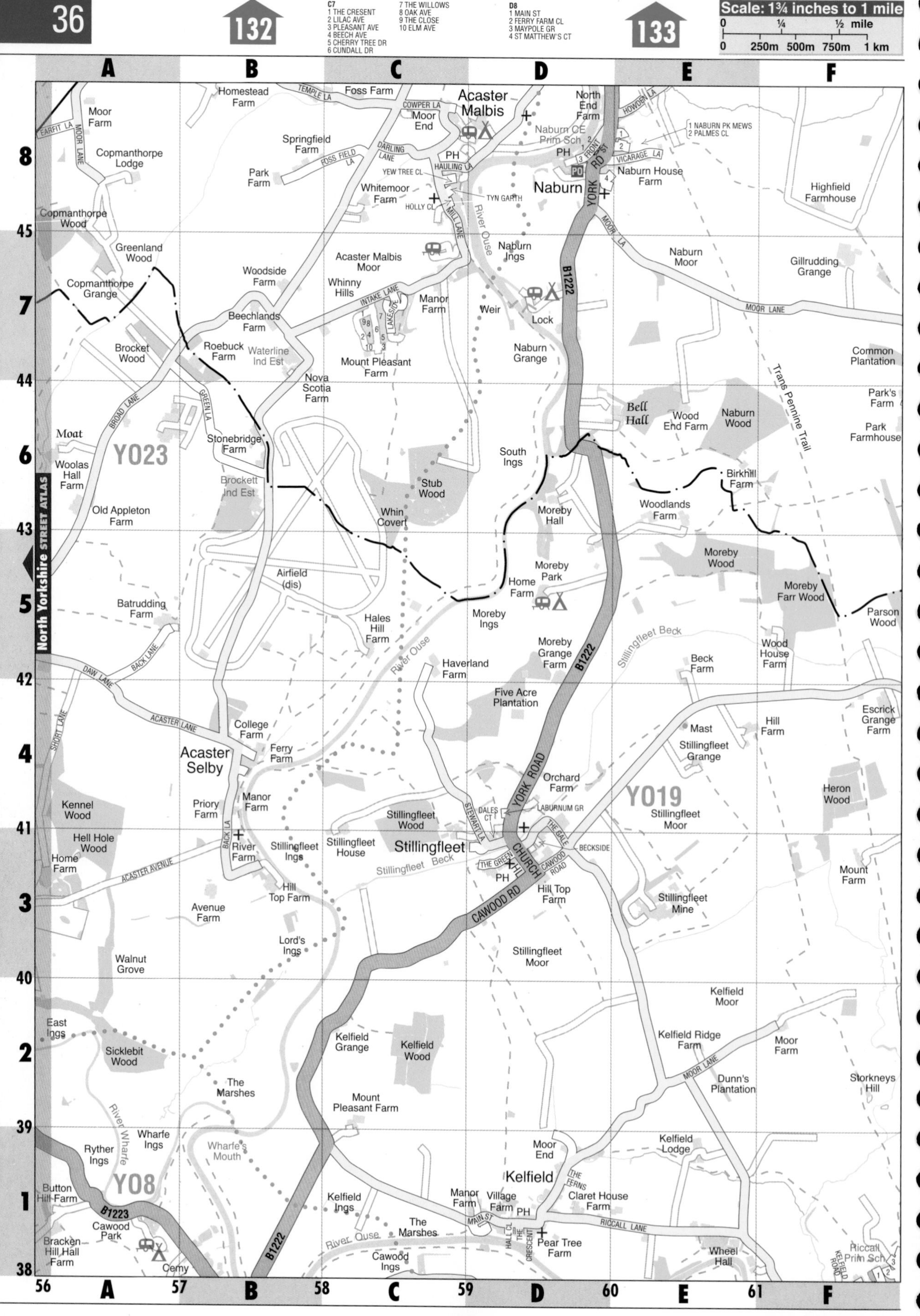

48

F1
1 COPPERGATE
2 ELMS CL
3 NORTHFIELD LA

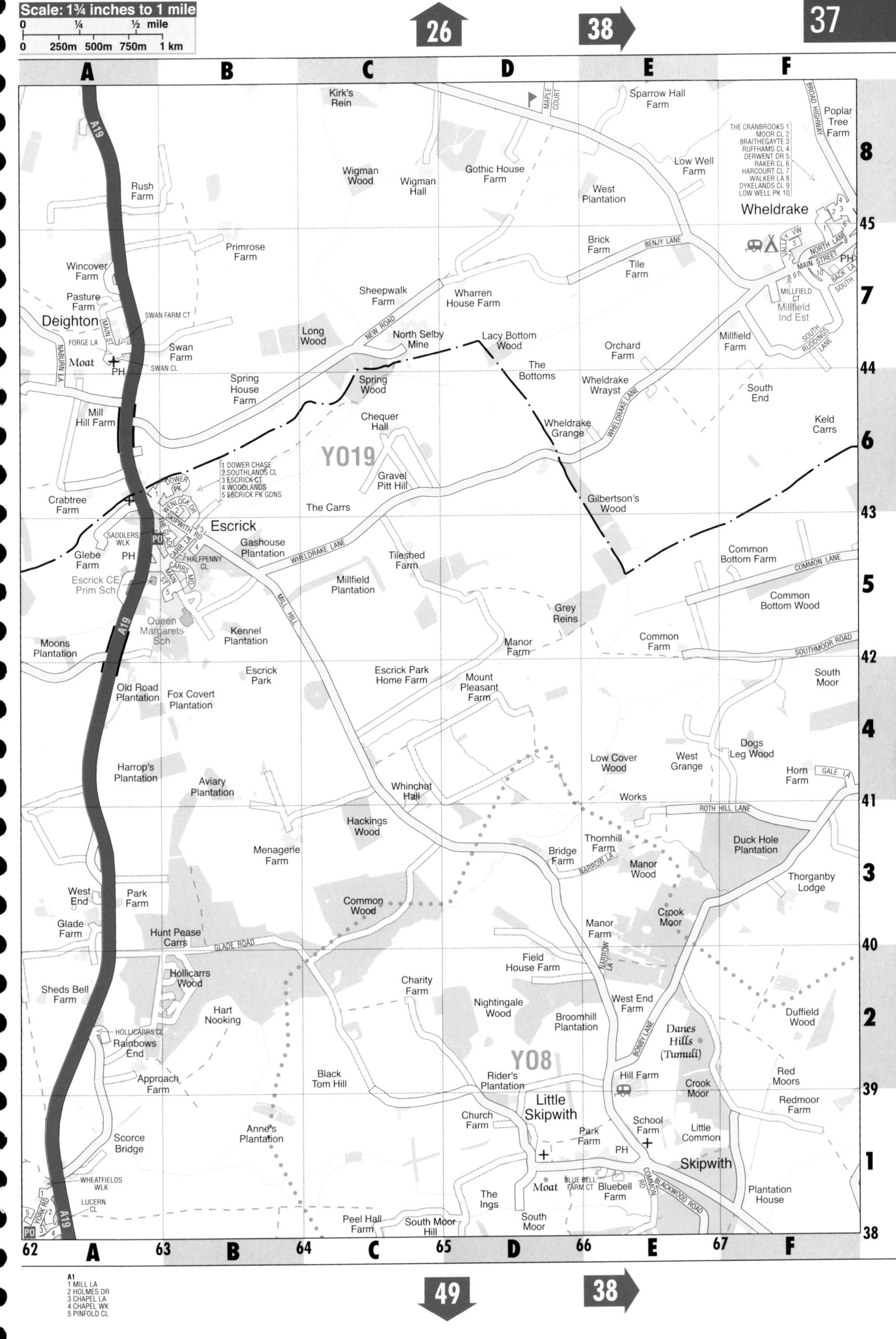

37
27

Scale: 1¾ inches to 1 mile

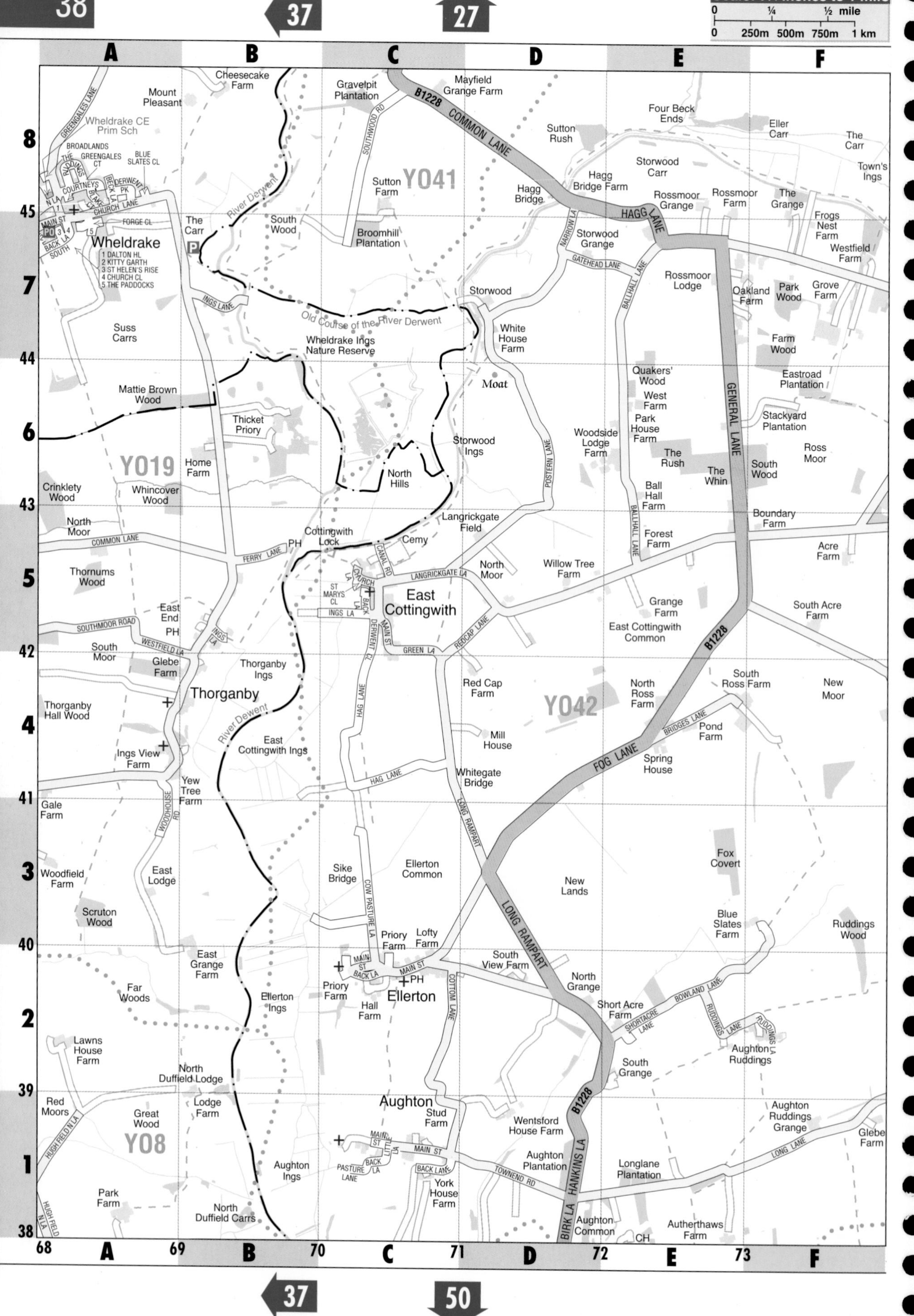

A B C D E F
8 45 7 44 6 43 5 42 4 41 3 40 2 39 1 38
68 69 70 71 72 73
Cheesecake Farm
Mount Pleasant
Wheldrake CE Prim Sch
Gravelpit Plantation
Mayfield Grange Farm
B1228 COMMON LANE
Four Beck Ends
Eller Carr
The Carr
Town's Ings
Sutton Rush
Storwood Carr
Hagg Bridge Farm
Hagg Bridge
Sutton Farm
YO41
Rossmoor Grange
Rossmoor Farm
The Grange
Frogs Nest Farm
Westfield Farm
HAGG LANE
South Wood
Broomhill Plantation
The Carr
River Derwent
Wheldrake
Storwood Grange
GATEHEAD LANE
NARROW LA
BALLHALL LANE
Rossmoor Lodge
Oakland Farm
Park Wood
Grove Farm
1 DALTON HL
2 KITTY GARTH
3 ST HELEN'S RISE
4 CHURCH CL
5 THE PADDOCKS
BROADLANDS
GREENGALES CT
BLUE SLATES CL
COURTNEYS
CHURCH LANE
FORGE CL
MAIN ST
BACK LA
Storwood
INGS LANE
Old Course of the River Derwent
Suss Carrs
Wheldrake Ings Nature Reserve
White House Farm
Farm Wood
Moat
Quakers' Wood
Eastroad Plantation
Mattie Brown Wood
West Farm
GENERAL LANE
Stackyard Plantation
Thicket Priory
Storwood Ings
Woodside Lodge Farm
Park House Farm
Ross Moor
YO19
Home Farm
North Hills
The Rush
The Whin
South Wood
Crinklety Wood
Whincover Wood
POSTERN LANE
Ball Hall Farm
North Moor
Langrickgate Field
Boundary Farm
COMMON LANE
Cottingwith Lock
PH
Cemy
Forest Farm
Acre Farm
FERRY LANE
CANAL RD
Thornums Wood
North Moor
Willow Tree Farm
LANGRICKGATE LA
ST MARYS CL
East Cottingwith
CHURCH LA
Grange Farm
South Acre Farm
East End
INGS LA
SOUTHMOOR ROAD
PH
WESTFIELD LA
REDCAP LANE
East Cottingwith Common
B1228
South Moor
GREEN LA
DERWENT CL
Glebe Farm
Thorganby Ings
Red Cap Farm
South Ross Farm
New Moor
North Ross Farm
YO42
Thorganby
Thorganby Hall Wood
BRIDGES LANE
Pond Farm
Mill House
Ings View Farm
East Cottingwith Ings
Spring House
FOG LANE
Whitegate Bridge
HAG LANE
Yew Tree Farm
Gale Farm
WOODHOUSE RD
LONG RAMPART
Fox Covert
Woodfield Farm
East Lodge
Sike Bridge
Ellerton Common
New Lands
Scruton Wood
COW PASTURE LA
Blue Slates Farm
Ruddings Wood
Priory Farm
Lofty Farm
East Grange Farm
South View Farm
North Grange
Far Woods
Priory Farm
Ellerton Ings
Ellerton
Short Acre Farm
BOWLAND LANE
Hall Farm
COTTOM LANE
SHORTACRE LANE
RUDDINGS LANE
Lawns House Farm
South Grange
Aughton Ruddings
North Duffield Lodge
Red Moors
Lodge Farm
Aughton
Stud Farm
Aughton Ruddings Grange
Great Wood
Wentsford House Farm
YO8
Glebe Farm
MAIN ST
LITTLE LA
Aughton Plantation
LONG LANE
HIGHFIELD LA
PASTURE LANE
BACK LA
Aughton Ings
BACK LANE
TOWNEND RD
Longlane Plantation
HANKINS LA
York House Farm
Park Farm
North Duffield Carrs
Aughton Common
Autherthaws Farm
BIRK LA
CH
HIGHFIELD LA

37
50

Scale: 1¾ inches to 1 mile

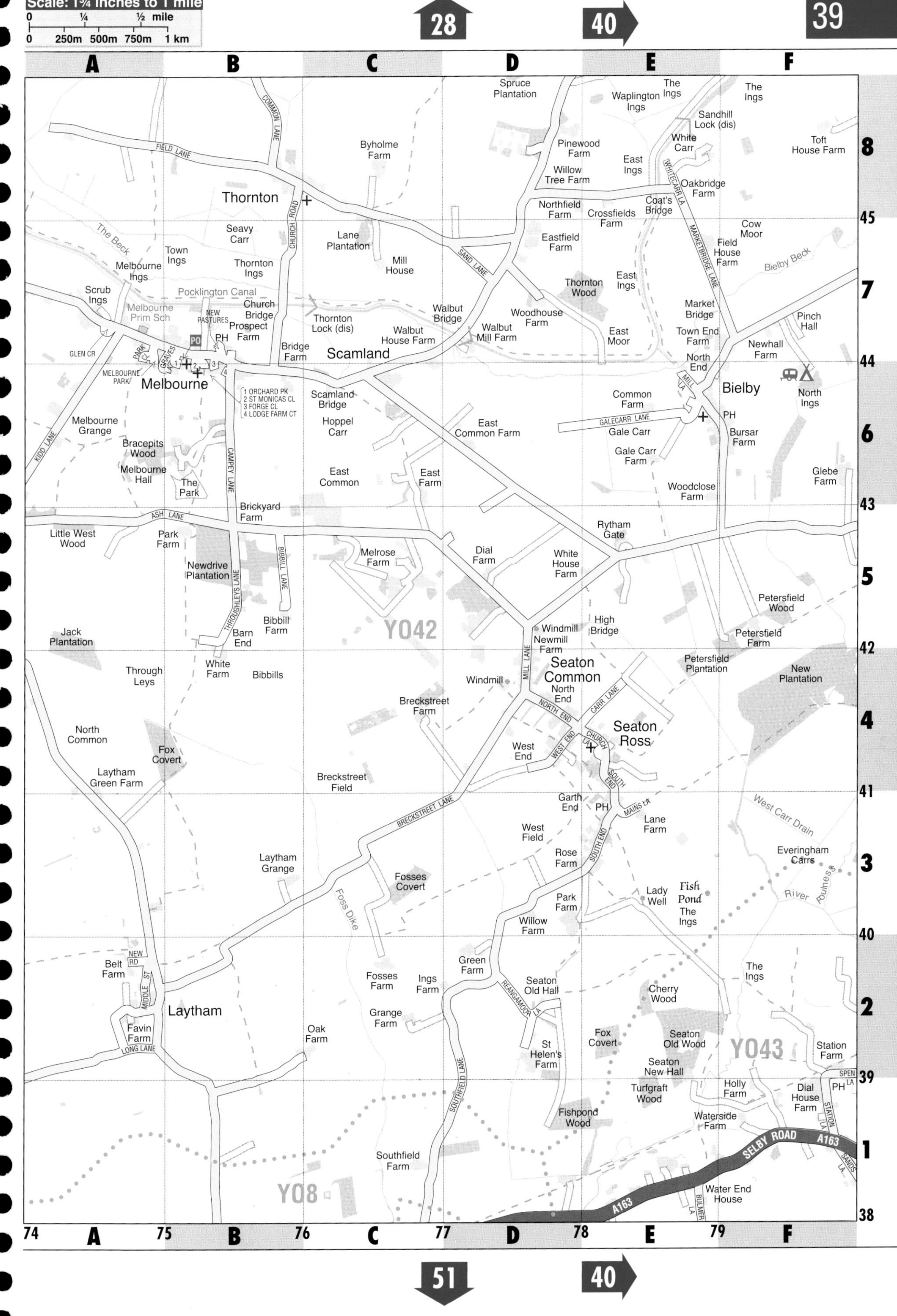
28
40
A
B
C
D
E
F
Thornton
Melbourne
Scamland
Bielby
Seaton Common
Seaton Ross
Laytham
Field Lane
Common Lane
Church Road
Sand Lane
Pocklington Canal
The Beck
Bielby Beck
Byholme Farm
Spruce Plantation
Waplington Ings
The Ings
Sandhill Lock (dis)
White Carr
Toft House Farm
Pinewood Farm
Willow Tree Farm
East Ings
Oakbridge Farm
Northfield Farm
Crossfields Farm
Coat's Bridge
Seavy Carr
Lane Plantation
Mill House
Eastfield Farm
Cow Moor
Field House Farm
Town Ings
Melbourne Ings
Thornton Ings
Thornton Wood
Scrub Ings
Melbourne Prim Sch
Church Bridge
Prospect Farm
Thornton Lock (dis)
Walbut Bridge
Woodhouse Farm
Walbut House Farm
Walbut Mill Farm
East Moor
Market Bridge
Town End Farm
Pinch Hall
Newhall Farm
North End
North Ings
Bridge Farm
Glen Cr
Melbourne Park
1 Orchard Pk
2 St Monicas Cl
3 Forge Cl
4 Lodge Farm Ct
Scamland Bridge
Hoppel Carr
East Common Farm
Common Farm
Galecarr Lane
Gale Carr
Gale Carr Farm
Bursar Farm
Melbourne Grange
Bracepits Wood
Melbourne Hall
The Park
Kidd Lane
Campey Lane
East Common
East Farm
Glebe Farm
Woodclose Farm
Brickyard Farm
Ash Lane
Little West Wood
Park Farm
Newdrive Plantation
Bibbill Lane
Melrose Farm
Dial Farm
White House Farm
Rytham Gate
Petersfield Wood
Throughleys Lane
Jack Plantation
Barn End
Bibbill Farm
YO42
Windmill
Newmill Farm
High Bridge
Petersfield Farm
Mill Lane
Petersfield Plantation
New Plantation
Through Leys
White Farm
Bibbills
Breckstreet Farm
North End
Carr Lane
North Common
Fox Covert
West End
Church La
Laytham Green Farm
Breckstreet Field
South End
Breckstreet Lane
Garth End
PH
Mains La
Lane Farm
West Carr Drain
West Field
Rose Farm
Everingham Carrs
Laytham Grange
Fosses Covert
Foss Dike
Lady Well
Fish Pond
The Ings
River Foulness
Park Farm
Willow Farm
Belt Farm
New Rd
Middle St
Green Farm
Fosses Farm
Ings Farm
Seaton Old Hall
Reangamoor La
Cherry Wood
Grange Farm
Oak Farm
Favin Farm
Long Lane
St Helen's Farm
Fox Covert
Seaton Old Wood
Seaton New Hall
YO43
Station Farm
Spen La
Southfield Lane
Turfgraft Wood
Holly Farm
Dial House Farm
Station La
Fishpond Wood
Waterside Farm
Selby Road A163
Sands La
Southfield Farm
YO8
Water End House
Bulmer La
A163
PO
8
45
7
44
6
43
5
42
4
41
3
40
2
39
1
38
74
75
76
77
78
79
51
40

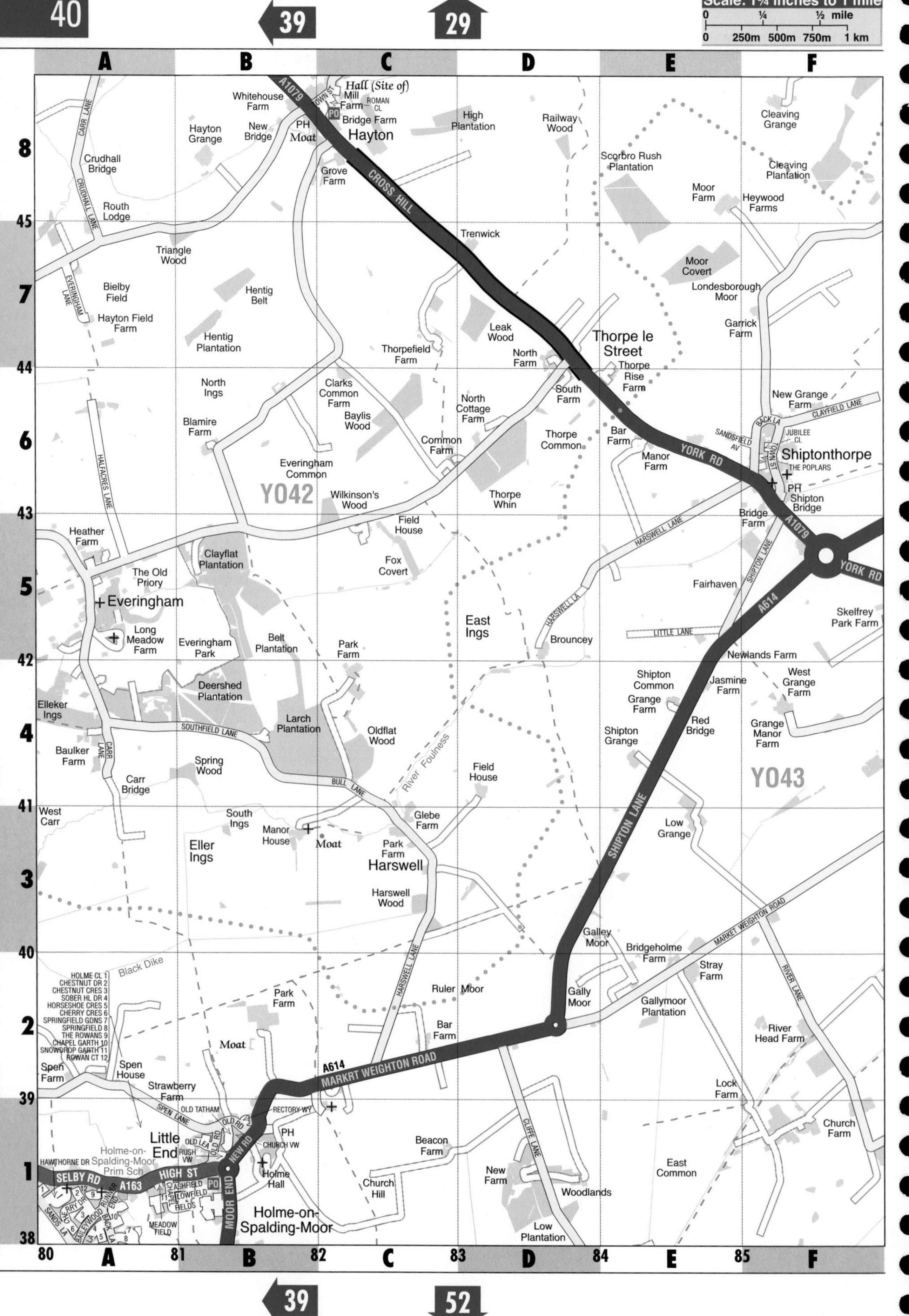

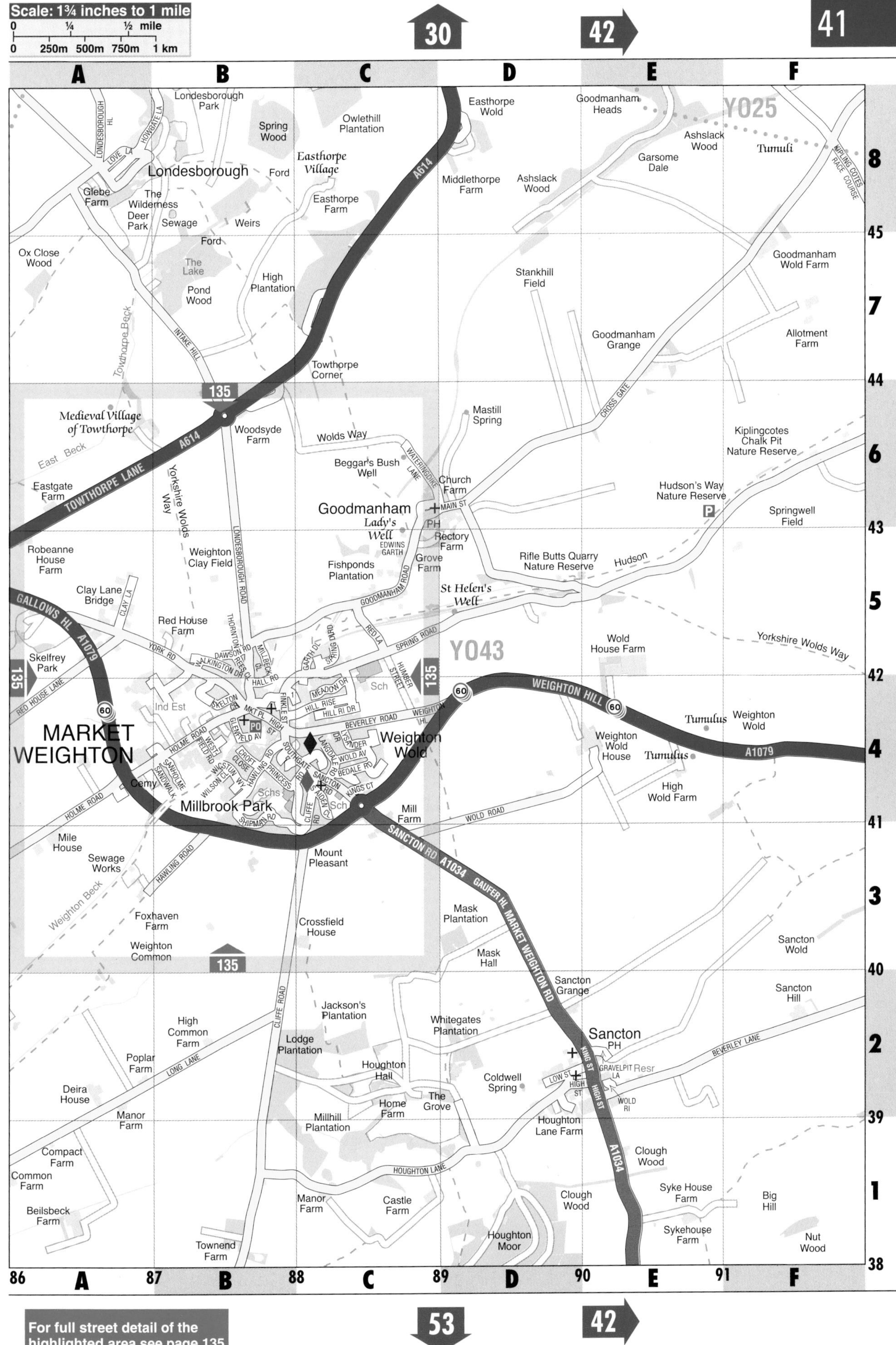
Scale: 1¾ inches to 1 mile
0 ¼ ½ mile
0 250m 500m 750m 1 km
30
42
A B C D E F
Londesborough Park
Spring Wood
Owlethill Plantation
Easthorpe Wold
Goodmanham Heads
YO25
Ashslack Wood
Tumuli
Garsome Dale
LONDESBOROUGH HL
HOWGATE LA
LOVE LA
Londesborough
Ford
Easthorpe Village
A614
Middlethorpe Farm
Ashslack Wood
KIPLING COTES RACE COURSE
Glebe Farm
The Wilderness
Deer Park
Sewage
Weirs
Easthorpe Farm
Ford
Ox Close Wood
The Lake
High Plantation
Pond Wood
Stankhill Field
Goodmanham Wold Farm
Towthorpe Beck
INTAKE HILL
Goodmanham Grange
Allotment Farm
Towthorpe Corner
135
Mastill Spring
CROSS GATE
Medieval Village of Towthorpe
Woodsyde Farm
Wolds Way
Kiplingcotes Chalk Pit Nature Reserve
East Beck
A614
Beggar's Bush Well
WATERINGDIKE LANE
Church Farm
Hudson's Way Nature Reserve
Eastgate Farm
TOWTHORPE LANE
Yorkshire Wolds Way
Goodmanham
MAIN ST
PH
Springwell Field
Lady's Well
Rectory Farm
Robeanne House Farm
Weighton Clay Field
LONDESBOROUGH ROAD
EDWINS GARTH
Grove Farm
Fishponds Plantation
Rifle Butts Quarry Nature Reserve
Hudson
Clay Lane Bridge
CLAY LA
GOODMANHAM ROAD
St Helen's Well
GALLOWS HL
A1079
Red House Farm
THORNTON
RED LA
SPRING ROAD
YO43
Wold House Farm
Yorkshire Wolds Way
Skelfrey Park
YORK RD
DAWSON RD
MILLBECK CL
GARTH CL
SPRING GDNS
WALKINGTON DR
REESCL
HUMBER STREET
135
RED HOUSE LANE
HALL RD
MEADOW DR
Sch
WEIGHTON HILL
Ind Est
KELTON
MKT PL
FINKLE ST
HILL RISE
HILL RI DR
60
Tumulus
Weighton Wold
MARKET WEIGHTON
PO
HIGH ST
BEVERLEY ROAD
WEIGHTON HL
GLENFIELD AV
LYSANDER DR
Weighton Wold
Weighton Wold House
Tumulus
HOLME ROAD
WESTFIELD RD
CROFT CLOSE
SOUTHGATE
LANGDALE RD
WOLD AV
BEDALE RD
A1079
SANDHOLME
SANDWALK
WIGSTUN WY
HAWLING RD
PRINCESS RD
SANCTON RD
KINGS CT
High Wold Farm
Cemy
WILSON CL
Schs
CLIFFE RD
SAXDEN CL
Sch
HOLME ROAD
Millbrook Park
SHIPMAN RD
Mill Farm
WOLD ROAD
Mile House
SANCTON RD
A1034
Mount Pleasant
Sewage Works
HAWLING ROAD
GAUFER HL
Weighton Beck
Mask Plantation
Foxhaven Farm
Crossfield House
MARKET WEIGHTON RD
Sancton Wold
Weighton Common
Mask Hall
135
Sancton Grange
Sancton Hill
Jackson's Plantation
CLIFFE ROAD
High Common Farm
Whitegates Plantation
Sancton
PH
Lodge Plantation
BEVERLEY LANE
Poplar Farm
LONG LANE
Houghton Hall
Coldwell Spring
LOW ST
HIGH ST
KING ST
GRAVELPIT LA
Resr
WOLD RI
Deira House
The Grove
Home Farm
HIGH ST
Manor Farm
Millhill Plantation
Houghton Lane Farm
Compact Farm
A1034
Clough Wood
HOUGHTON LANE
Common Farm
Syke House Farm
Big Hill
Manor Farm
Castle Farm
Clough Wood
Beilsbeck Farm
Sykehouse Farm
Houghton Moor
Nut Wood
Townend Farm
8 45 7 44 6 43 5 42 4 41 3 40 2 39 1 38
86 87 88 89 90 91
53
42
For full street detail of the highlighted area see page 135.

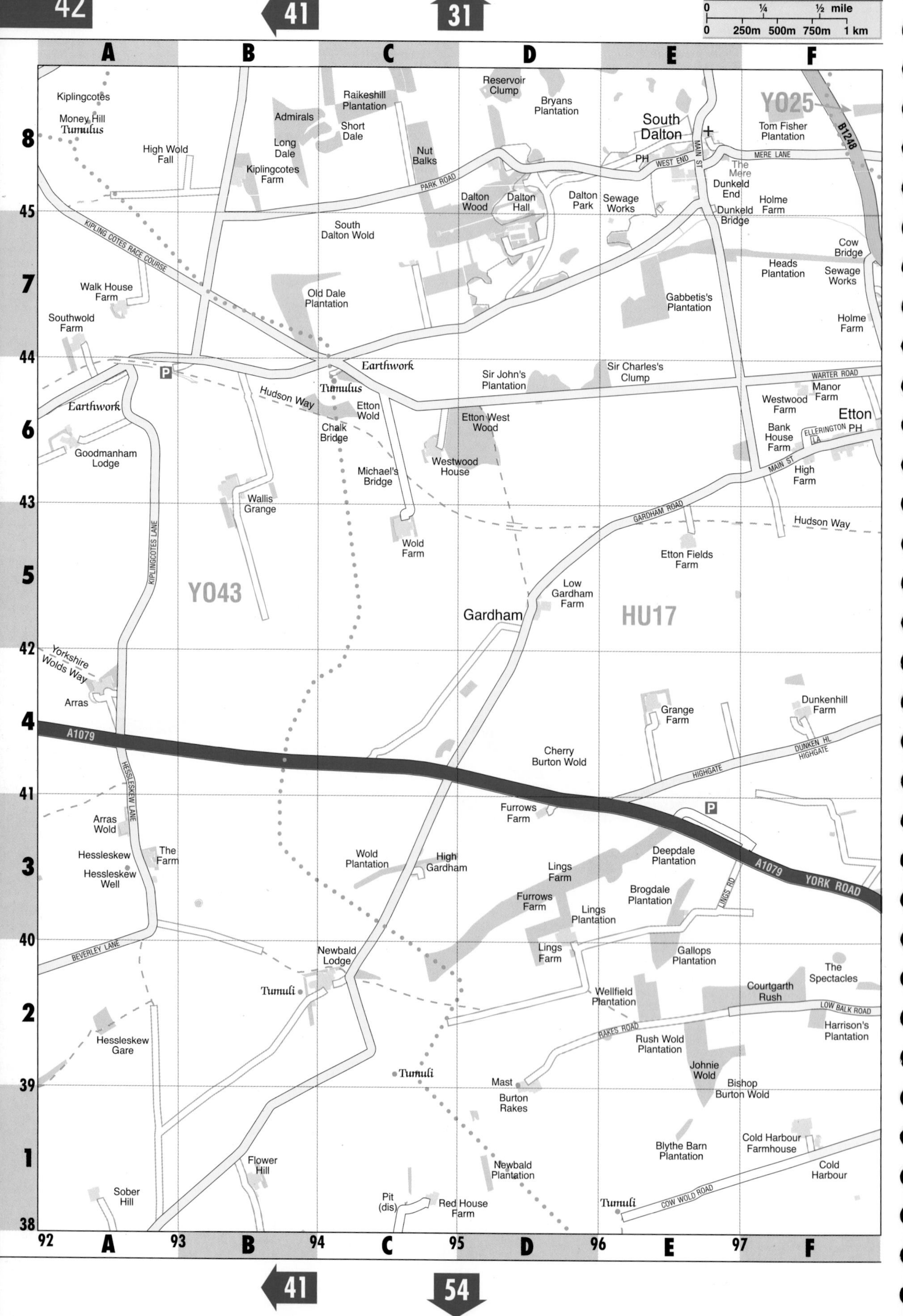

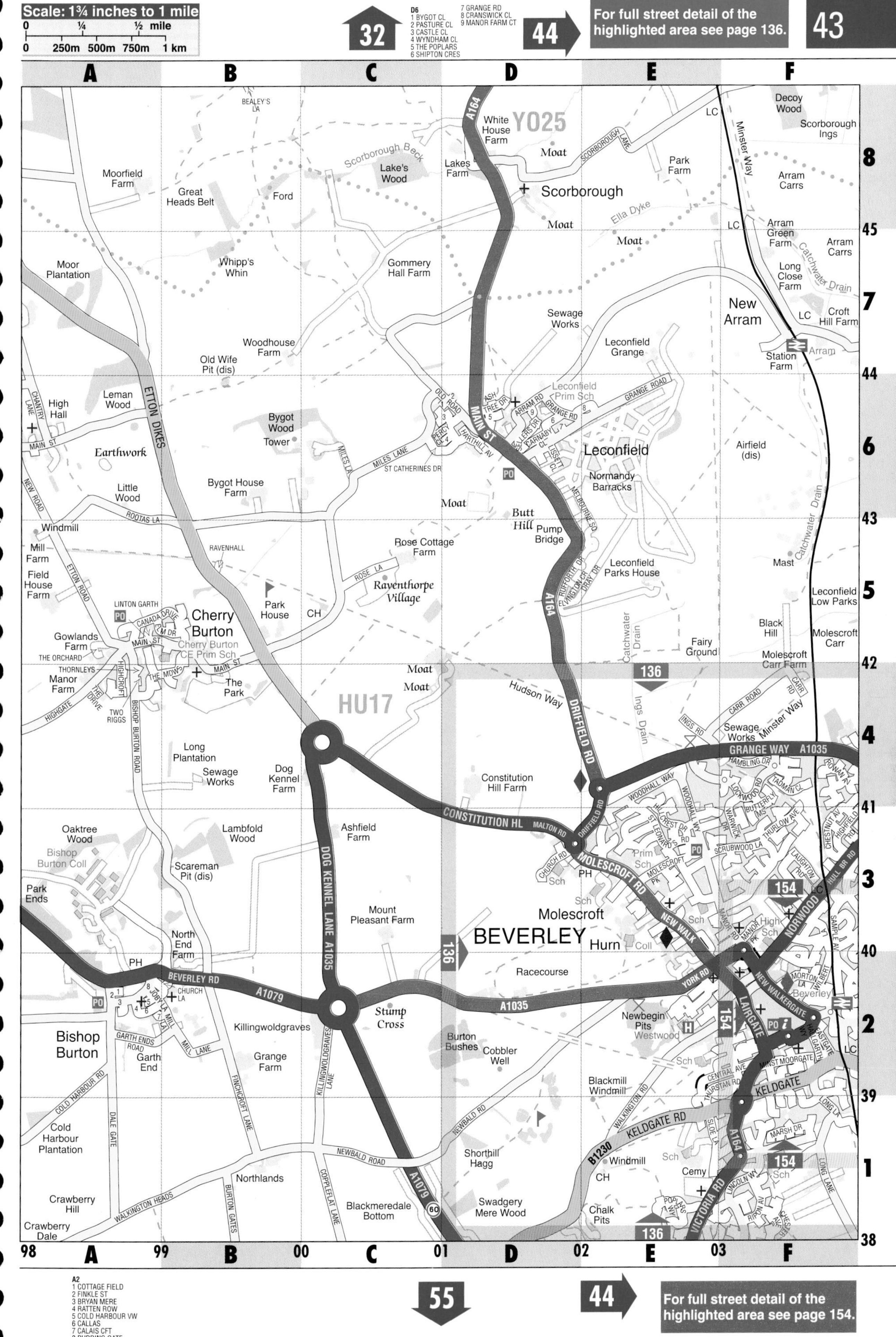

For full street detail of the highlighted area see page 136.

D6
1 BYGOT CL
2 PASTURE CL
3 CASTLE CL
4 WYNDHAM CL
5 THE POPLARS
6 SHIPTON CRES

7 GRANGE RD
8 CRANSWICK CL
9 MANOR FARM CT

A2
1 COTTAGE FIELD
2 FINKLE ST
3 BRYAN MERE
4 RATTEN ROW
5 COLD HARBOUR VW
6 CALLAS
7 CALAIS CFT
8 PUDDING GATE

For full street detail of the highlighted area see page 154.

43   33

Scale: 1¾ inches to 1 mile

0   ¼   ½ mile
0   250m   500m   750m   1 km

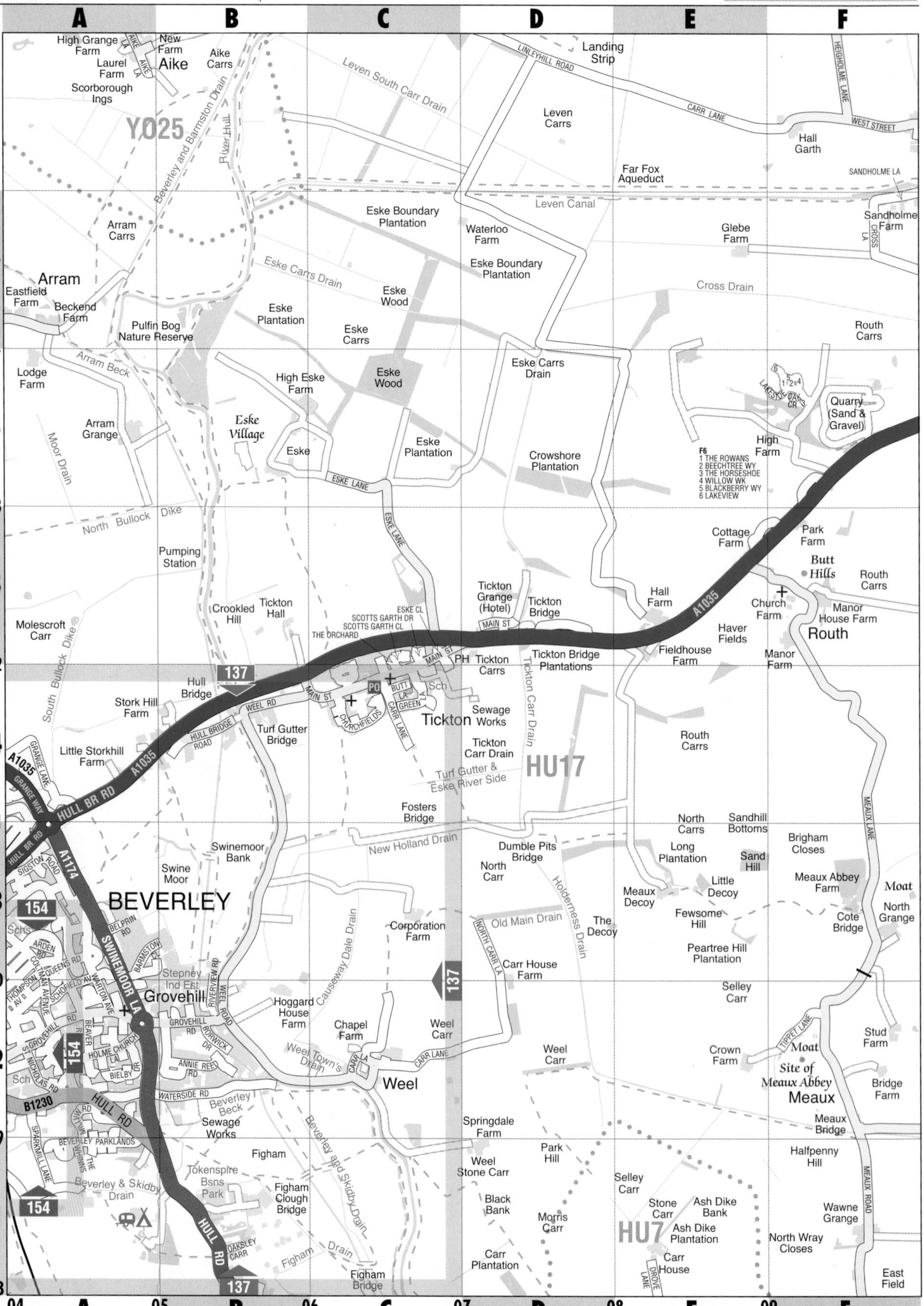

A   B   C   D   E   F

High Grange Farm
Laurel Farm
New Farm
Aike
Aike Carrs
Scorborough Ings

Landing Strip

LINLEYHILL ROAD

HEIGHOLME LANE

CARR LANE

WEST STREET

Hall Garth

SANDHOLME LA

Leven South Carr Drain

Leven Carrs

Beverley and Barmston Drain

River Hull

YO25

Far Fox Aqueduct

Leven Canal

Glebe Farm

Sandholme Farm

Arram Carrs

Eske Boundary Plantation

Waterloo Farm

CROSS LA

8

45

Arram

Eastfield Farm
Beckend Farm

Eske Plantation

Eske Boundary Plantation

Cross Drain

Routh Carrs

Eske Carrs Drain

Eske Wood

Pulfin Bog Nature Reserve

7

44

Lodge Farm

Arram Beck

Arram Grange

High Eske Farm

Eske Village

Eske

Eske Wood

Eske Carrs

Eske Plantation

Eske Carrs Drain

LAKESIDE OAKS CR

Quarry (Sand & Gravel)

High Farm

Cottage Farm

Park Farm

F6
1 THE ROWANS
2 BEECHTREE WY
3 THE HORSESHOE
4 WILLOW WK
5 BLACKBERRY WY
6 LAKEVIEW

6

43

Moor Drain

North Bullock Dike

Eske Plantation

ESKE LANE

Crowshore Plantation

Butt Hills

Routh Carrs

5

Molescroft Carr

South Bullock Dike

Pumping Station

Crookled Hill

Tickton Hall

ESKE LANE

Tickton Grange (Hotel)

Tickton Bridge

Hall Farm

A1035

Church Farm

Manor House Farm

Routh

42

Stork Hill Farm

Hull Bridge

137

WEEL RD

SCOTTS GARTH DR
SCOTTS GARTH CL
THE ORCHARD

ESKE CL

MAIN ST

MAIN ST

PH

Tickton Carrs

Tickton Bridge Plantations

Tickton Carr Drain

Fieldhouse Farm

Haver Fields

Manor Farm

Little Storkhill Farm

A1035

HULL BRIDGE ROAD

Turf Gutter Bridge

CHURCHFIELDS

PO

BUTT LA

CARR LANE

BUTT GREEN

Sch

Tickton

Sewage Works

Routh Carrs

4

A1035

GRANGE LANE
GRANGE WAY
HULL BR RD
SIGSTON RD

HULL BR RD

A1174

MAIN ST

Tickton Carr Drain

Turf Gutter & Eske River Side

HU17

North Carrs

Sandhill Bottoms

Brigham Closes

41

154

BEVERLEY

Swine Moor

Swinemoor Bank

Fosters Bridge

New Holland Drain

Dumble Pits Bridge

North Carr

Long Plantation

Sand Hill

Meaux Abbey Farm

Moat

North Grange

3

154

SWINEMOOR LA

Grovehill

BELPRIN RD

BARMSTON

STEPNEY
Ind Est
RIVERVIEW RD
TEEM

Corporation Farm

Holderness Drain

Old Main Drain

The Decoy

Meaux Decoy

Little Decoy

Fewsome Hill

Cote Bridge

40

THOMPSON RD
BEAVER AV 8
COTTAM AVENUE
QUEENS RD

GROVEHILL RD
BERWICK
DR

Hoggard House Farm

Chapel Farm

NORTH CARR LA

Carr House Farm

137

Peartree Hill Plantation

Selley Carr

LIPPET LANE

MEAUX LANE

Stud Farm

2

154

SCHOLAST RD
ARDEN
GROVEHILL RD
HOLME CHURCH LA
NICHOLAS RD

ANNIE REED RD
BIELBY DR

CARR LA

Weel Town's Drain

Weel Carr

Causeway Dale Drain

Weel

Weel Carr

CARR LANE

Crown Farm

Moat

Site of Meaux Abbey

Meaux

Bridge Farm

39

B1230

HULL RD
WATERSIDE RD

BEVERLEY BECK

Beverley Beck

Sewage Works

Figham

Beverley and Skidby Drain

Springdale Farm

Weel Stone Carr

Park Hill

Meaux Bridge

Halfpenny Hill

MEAUX ROAD

1

154

SPARRMILL LANE
THE NELLONS
BEVERLEY PARKLANDS

Beverley & Skidby Drain

Tokenspire Bsns Park

Figham Clough Bridge

Figham Drain

HULL RD

OAKSLEY CARR

137

Figham Bridge

Black Bank

Morris Carr

Selley Carr

Stone Carr

Ash Dike Bank

Ash Dike Plantation

Carr House

ASH DIKE LANE

HU7

Wawne Grange

North Wray Closes

East Field

38

04   A   05   B   06   C   07   D   08   E   09   F

For full street detail of the highlighted area see page 154.

For full street detail of the highlighted area see page 137.

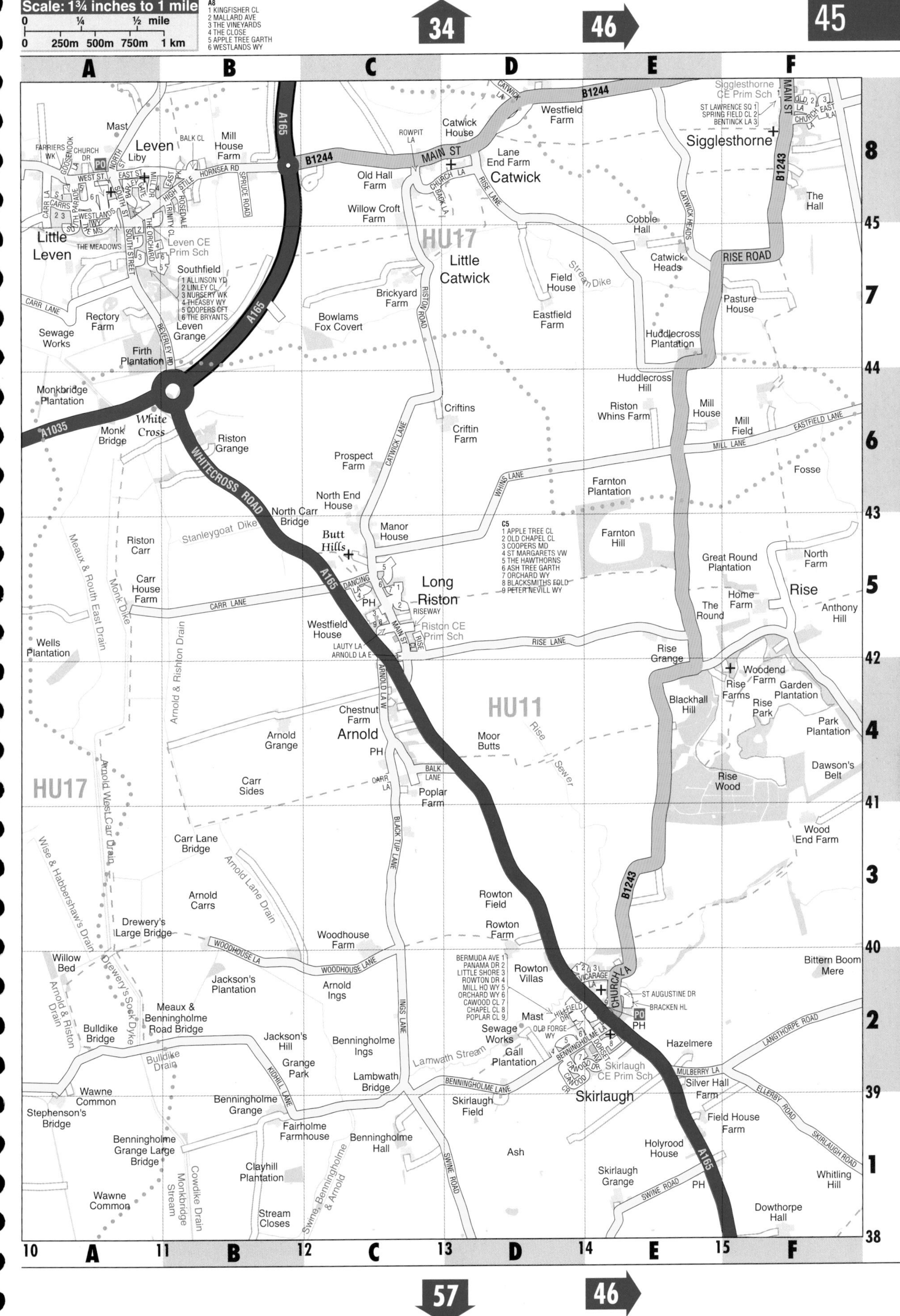
Scale: 1¾ inches to 1 mile
A8
1 KINGFISHER CL
2 MALLARD AVE
3 THE VINEYARDS
4 THE CLOSE
5 APPLE TREE GARTH
6 WESTLANDS WY
34
46
Leven
Little Leven
Mill House Farm
Southfield
1 ALLINSON YD
2 LINLEY CL
3 NURSERY WK
4 THEASBY WY
5 COOPERS CFT
6 THE BRYANTS
Rectory Farm
Sewage Works
Leven Grange
Firth Plantation
Leven CE Prim Sch
Catwick House
Old Hall Farm
Willow Croft Farm
Lane End Farm
Catwick
Westfield Farm
Little Catwick
Brickyard Farm
Bowlams Fox Covert
Field House
Eastfield Farm
Cobble Hall
Catwick Heads
Huddlecross Plantation
Pasture House
Sigglesthorne CE Prim Sch
ST LAWRENCE SQ 1
SPRING FIELD CL 2
BENTINCK LA 3
Sigglesthorne
The Hall
RISE ROAD
Monkbridge Plantation
White Cross
Monk Bridge
Riston Grange
Criftins
Criftin Farm
Prospect Farm
North End House
Huddlecross Hill
Riston Whins Farm
Mill House
Mill Field
Fosse
Farnton Plantation
Farnton Hill
North Carr Bridge
Manor House
Butt Hills
Riston Carr
Carr House Farm
Long Riston
Riston CE Prim Sch
Westfield House
C5
1 APPLE TREE CL
2 OLD CHAPEL CL
3 COOPERS MD
4 ST MARGARETS VW
5 THE HAWTHORNS
6 ASH TREE GARTH
7 ORCHARD WY
8 BLACKSMITHS FOLD
9 PETER NEVILL WY
Great Round Plantation
North Farm
Rise
Home Farm
The Round
Anthony Hill
Wells Plantation
Rise Grange
Woodend Farm
Rise Farms
Garden Plantation
Blackhall Hill
Rise Park
Park Plantation
Chestnut Farm
Arnold
Arnold Grange
Moor Butts
Dawson's Belt
Rise Wood
Carr Sides
Poplar Farm
Wood End Farm
Carr Lane Bridge
Arnold Carrs
Drewery's Large Bridge
Rowton Field
Rowton Farm
Woodhouse Farm
Willow Bed
Jackson's Plantation
Arnold Ings
BERMUDA AVE 1
PANAMA DR 2
LITTLE SHORE 3
ROWTON DR 4
MILL HO WY 5
ORCHARD WY 6
CAWOOD CL 7
CHAPEL CL 8
POPLAR CL 9
Rowton Villas
Bittern Boom Mere
Meaux & Benningholme Road Bridge
Bulldike Bridge
Jackson's Hill
Benningholme Ings
Sewage Works
Mast
Gall Plantation
Hazelmere
ST AUGUSTINE DR
BRACKEN HL
Grange Park
Lambwath Bridge
Skirlaugh CE Prim Sch
Skirlaugh
Silver Hall Farm
Wawne Common
Stephenson's Bridge
Benningholme Grange
Skirlaugh Field
Field House Farm
Fairholme Farmhouse
Benningholme Hall
Benningholme Grange Large Bridge
Ash
Holyrood House
Clayhill Plantation
Skirlaugh Grange
Whitling Hill
Wawne Common
Stream Closes
Dowthorpe Hall
HU17
HU11
A165
A1035
B1244
B1243
WHITECROSS ROAD
57
46

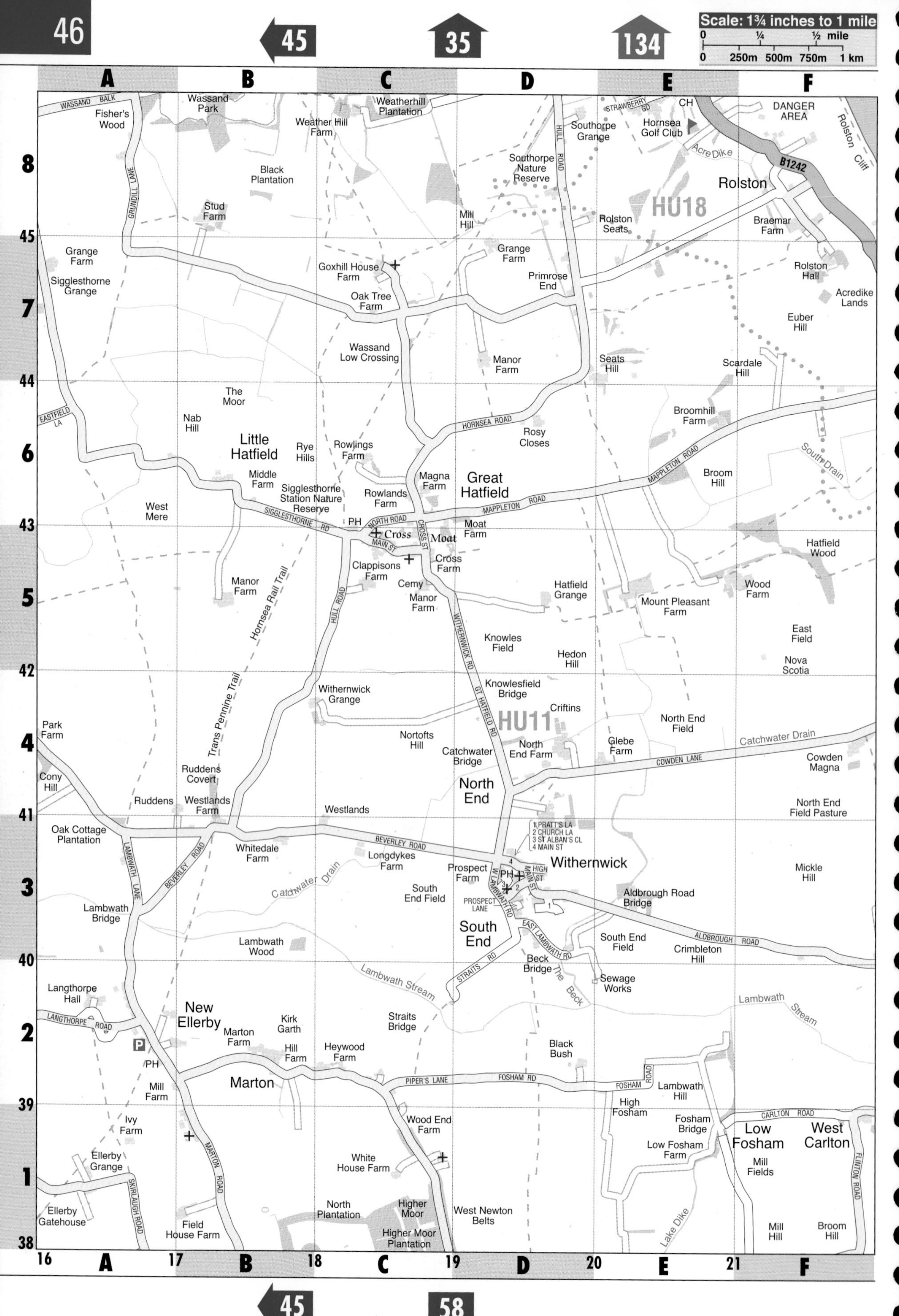

45
35
134

Scale: 1¾ inches to 1 mile

0   ¼   ½ mile
0   250m   500m   750m   1 km

8
45
7
44
6
43
5
42
4
41
3
40
2
39
1
38

A   B   C   D   E   F

WASSAND BALK
Fisher's Wood
Wassand Park
Weather Hill Farm
Weatherhill Plantation
STRAWBERRY GD
CH
DANGER AREA
Rolston Cliff

Southorpe Grange
Hornsea Golf Club
Acre Dike
B1242
Black Plantation
Southorpe Nature Reserve
HULL ROAD
Rolston
HU18

Stud Farm
Grange Farm
Sigglesthorne Grange
Goxhill House Farm
Oak Tree Farm
Grange Farm
Primrose End
Rolston Seats
Braemar Farm
Rolston Hall
Acredike Lands

EASTFIELD LA
Wassand Low Crossing
Manor Farm
Seats Hill
Euber Hill
Scardale Hill

The Moor
Nab Hill
Little Hatfield
Rye Hills
Rowlings Farm
HORNSEA ROAD
Rosy Closes
Broomhill Farm
South Drain
Broom Hill

Middle Farm
Sigglesthorne Station Nature Reserve
Rowlands Farm
Magna Farm
Great Hatfield
MAPPLETON ROAD
West Mere
SIGGLESTHORNE RD
NORTH ROAD
PH
Cross
MAIN ST
CROSS ST
Moat Farm
MAPPLETON ROAD
Hatfield Wood

Manor Farm
HULL ROAD
Clappisons Farm
Cemy
Manor Farm
Cross Farm
Moat
Hatfield Grange
Mount Pleasant Farm
Wood Farm
Hornsea Rail Trail
WITHERNWICK RD
Knowles Field
Hedon Hill
East Field
Nova Scotia

Trans Pennine Trail
Withernwick Grange
Nortofts Hill
Knowlesfield Bridge
Criftins
HU11
North End Field
Catchwater Drain

Park Farm
Ruddens Covert
Catchwater Bridge
GT HATFIELD RD
North End Farm
Glebe Farm
COWDEN LANE
Cowden Magna

Cony Hill
Ruddens
Westlands Farm
Westlands
North End
North End Field Pasture

Oak Cottage Plantation
BEVERLEY ROAD
Longdykes Farm
1 PRATT'S LA
2 CHURCH LA
3 ST ALBAN'S CL
4 MAIN ST
Withernwick
Mickle Hill

LAMBWATH LANE
BEVERLEY ROAD
Whitedale Farm
Prospect Farm
HIGH MAIN ST
PH
Aldbrough Road Bridge

Lambwath Bridge
Catchwater Drain
South End Field
PROSPECT LANE
South End
EAST LAMBWATH RD
ALDBROUGH ROAD
Crimbleton Hill

Lambwath Wood
Lambwath Stream
STRAITS RD
Beck Bridge
The Beck
South End Field
Sewage Works
Lambwath Stream

Langthorpe Hall
New Ellerby
Marton Farm
Kirk Garth
Hill Farm
Straits Bridge
Black Bush
ROAD
Lambwath Hill

LANGTHORPE ROAD
P
PH
Heywood Farm
PIPER'S LANE
FOSHAM RD
FOSHAM ROAD
High Fosham
CARLTON ROAD
Low Fosham
West Carlton

Mill Farm
Marton
MARTON ROAD
Wood End Farm
Fosham Bridge
Mill Fields
FLINTON ROAD

Ivy Farm
SKIRLAUGH ROAD
Low Fosham Farm
Mill Hill
Broom Hill

Ellerby Grange
White House Farm
Lake Dike

Ellerby Gatehouse
Field House Farm
North Plantation
Higher Moor
Higher Moor Plantation
West Newton Belts

16   A   17   B   18   C   19   D   20   E   21   F

45
58

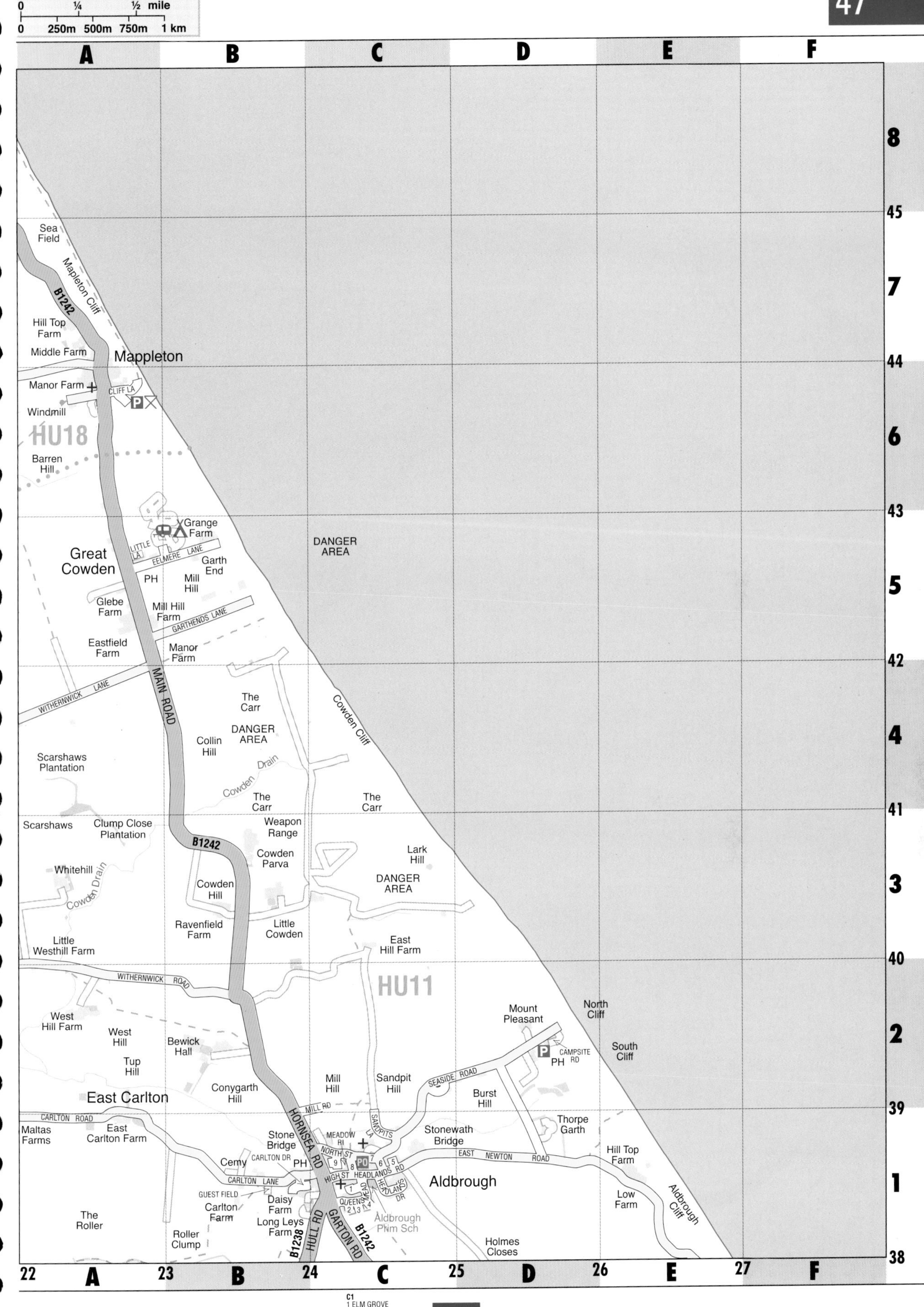

Scale: 1¾ inches to 1 mile

0   ¼   ½   mile
0 250m 500m 750m 1 km

A   B   C   D   E   F

8

45

7

44

6

43

5

42

4

41

3

40

2

39

1

38

Sea Field

B1242

Mappleton Cliff

Hill Top Farm

Middle Farm

Mappleton

Manor Farm

CLIFF LA

Windmill

HU18

Barren Hill

Grange Farm

Great Cowden

LITTLE LA

EELMERE LANE

Garth End

PH

Mill Hill

DANGER AREA

Glebe Farm

Mill Hill Farm

GARTHENDS LANE

Eastfield Farm

Manor Farm

WITHERNWICK LANE

MAIN ROAD

The Carr

DANGER AREA

Collin Hill

Cowden Drain

Cowden Cliff

Scarshaws Plantation

Cowden Drain

The Carr

The Carr

Scarshaws

Clump Close Plantation

B1242

Weapon Range

Cowden Parva

Lark Hill

DANGER AREA

Whitehill

Cowden Drain

Cowden Hill

Ravenfield Farm

Little Cowden

East Hill Farm

Little Westhill Farm

WITHERNWICK ROAD

HU11

Mount Pleasant

North Cliff

West Hill Farm

West Hill

Bewick Hall

CAMPSITE RD

PH

South Cliff

Tup Hill

Conygarth Hill

Mill Hill

Sandpit Hill

SEASIDE ROAD

Burst Hill

Thorpe Garth

East Carlton

Mill RD

SANDPITS LA

Stonewath Bridge

EAST NEWTON ROAD

Hill Top Farm

CARLTON ROAD

Maltas Farms

East Carlton Farm

HORNSEA RD

Stone Bridge

MEADOW RD

NORTH ST

CARLTON DR

PH

Cemy

PO

HEADLANDS RD

Aldbrough

Low Farm

CARLTON LANE

HIGH ST

QUEENS

Aldbrough Cliff

GUEST FIELD

Carlton Farm

Daisy Farm

The Roller

B1238

HULL RD

Long Leys Farm

GARTON RD

B1242

Aldbrough Prim Sch

Holmes Closes

Roller Clump

22   A   23   B   24   C   25   D   26   E   27   F   38

C1
1 ELM GROVE
2 CEDAR GROVE
3 WILLOW GROVE
4 ASH GROVE
5 WENTWORTH GROVE
6 NOTTINGHAM RD
7 CHURCH ST
8 CROSS ST
9 CASTLE PARK

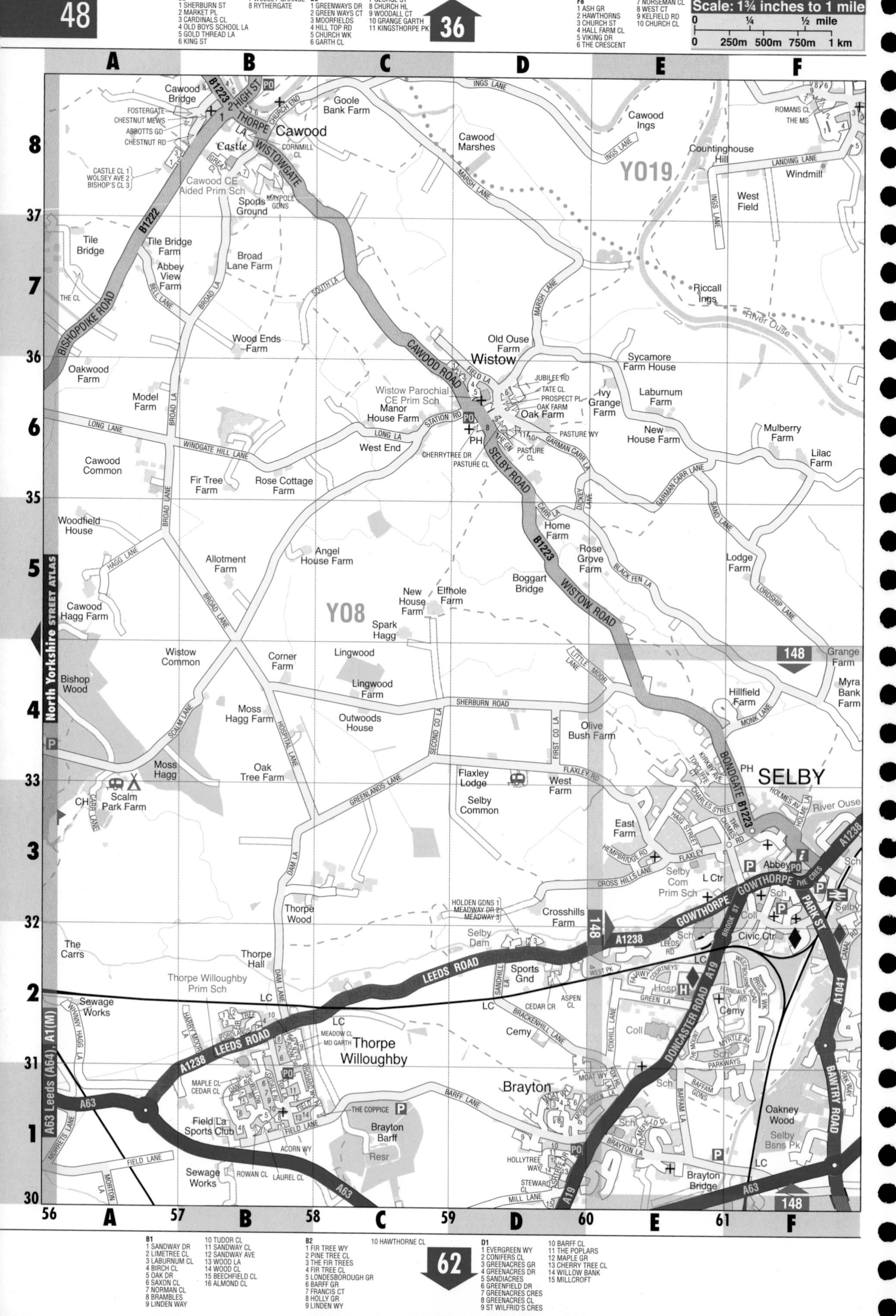
B8
1 SHERBURN ST
2 MARKET PL
3 CARDINALS CL
4 OLD BOYS SCHOOL LA
5 GOLD THREAD LA
6 KING ST
7 WOLSEY GRANGE
8 RYTHERGATE
D6
1 GREENWAYS DR
2 GREEN WAYS CT
3 MOORFIELDS
4 HILL TOP RD
5 CHURCH WK
6 GARTH CL
7 GEORGE ST
8 CHURCH HL
9 WOODALL CT
10 GRANGE GARTH
11 KINGSTHORPE PK
36
F8
1 ASH GR
2 HAWTHORNS
3 CHURCH ST
4 HALL FARM CL
5 VIKING DR
6 THE CRESCENT
7 NORSEMAN CL
8 WEST CT
9 KELFIELD RD
10 CHURCH CL
Scale: 1¾ inches to 1 mile
0 ¼ ½ mile
0 250m 500m 750m 1 km
A B C D E F
Cawood Bridge
Cawood
Castle
Goole Bank Farm
Cawood Marshes
Cawood Ings
Countinghouse Hill
YO19
West Field
Windmill
LANDING LANE
INGS LANE
MARSH LANE
Cawood CE Aided Prim Sch
Sports Ground
Tile Bridge
Tile Bridge Farm
Abbey View Farm
Broad Lane Farm
BISHOPDIKE ROAD
B1222
B1223
Riccall Ings
River Ouse
Wood Ends Farm
Old Ouse Farm
Wistow
Sycamore Farm House
Oakwood Farm
Model Farm
Wistow Parochial CE Prim Sch
Manor House Farm
Oak Farm
Ivy Grange Farm
Laburnum Farm
New House Farm
Mulberry Farm
Lilac Farm
CAWOOD ROAD
SELBY ROAD
LONG LANE
WINDGATE HILL LANE
West End
Cawood Common
Fir Tree Farm
Rose Cottage Farm
Home Farm
Rose Grove Farm
Woodfield House
Allotment Farm
Angel House Farm
Boggart Bridge
Lodge Farm
WISTOW ROAD
Cawood Hagg Farm
YO8
New House Farm
Elfhole Farm
Spark Hagg
Wistow Common
Corner Farm
Lingwood
Lingwood Farm
Bishop Wood
148
Grange Farm
Hillfield Farm
Myra Bank Farm
Moss Hagg Farm
Outwoods House
SHERBURN ROAD
Olive Bush Farm
Moss Hagg
Oak Tree Farm
Flaxley Lodge
West Farm
SELBY
Scalm Park Farm
Selby Common
East Farm
River Ouse
Abbey
Selby Com Prim Sch
L Ctr
GOWTHORPE
Thorpe Wood
Crosshills Farm
Selby Dam
Civic Ctr
The Carrs
Thorpe Hall
A1238
LEEDS ROAD
Sports Gnd
Thorpe Willoughby Prim Sch
Sewage Works
Hosp
Cemy
Coll
Thorpe Willoughby
Brayton
A63
Field La Sports Club
Brayton Barff
Resr
Oakney Wood
Selby Bsns Pk
Sewage Works
Brayton Bridge
A19
A1041
BAWTRY ROAD
DONCASTER ROAD
North Yorkshire STREET ATLAS
56 A 57 B 58 C 59 D 60 E 61 F
B1
1 SANDWAY DR
2 LIMETREE CL
3 LABURNUM CL
4 BIRCH CL
5 OAK DR
6 SAXON CL
7 NORMAN CL
8 BRAMBLES
9 LINDEN WAY
10 TUDOR CL
11 SANDWAY CL
12 SANDWAY AVE
13 WOOD LA
14 WOOD CL
15 BEECHFIELD CL
16 ALMOND CL
B2
1 FIR TREE WY
2 PINE TREE CL
3 THE FIR TREES
4 FIR TREE CL
5 LONDESBOROUGH GR
6 BARFF GR
7 FRANCIS CT
8 HOLLY GR
9 LINDEN WY
10 HAWTHORNE CL
62
D1
1 EVERGREEN WY
2 CONIFERS CL
3 GREENACRES GR
4 GREENACRES DR
5 SANDIACRES
6 GREENFIELD DR
7 GREENACRES CRES
8 GREENACRES CL
9 ST WILFRID'S CRES
10 BARFF CL
11 THE POPLARS
12 MAPLE GR
13 CHERRY TREE CL
14 WILLOW BANK
15 MILLCROFT

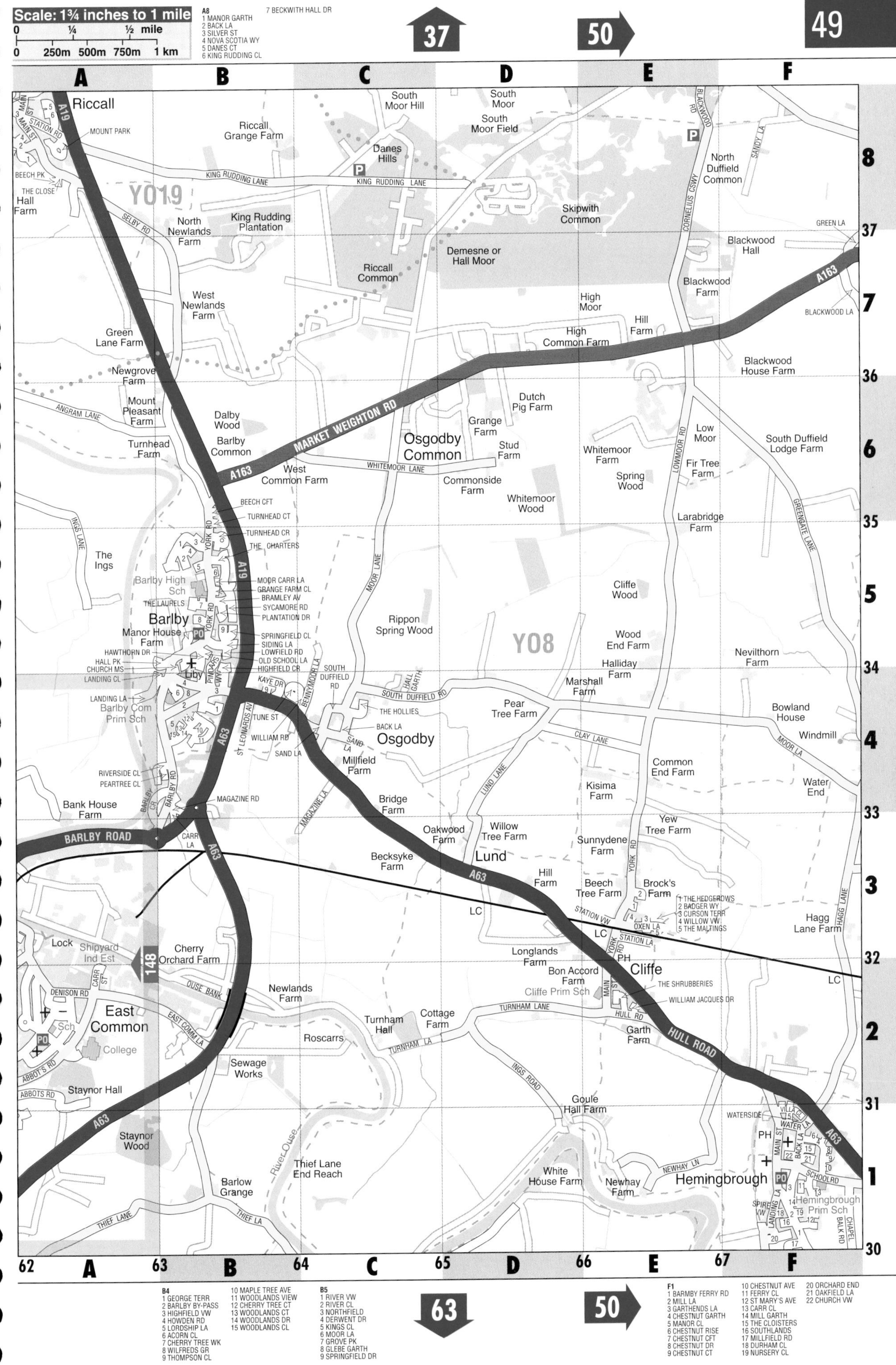

Scale: 1¾ inches to 1 mile
0 ¼ ½ mile
0 250m 500m 750m 1 km
A8
1 MANOR GARTH
2 BACK LA
3 SILVER ST
4 NOVA SCOTIA WY
5 DANES CT
6 KING RUDDING CL
7 BECKWITH HALL DR
37
50
49
A B C D E F
8 37 7 36 6 35 5 34 4 33 3 32 2 31 1 30
Riccall
MAIN ST
STATION RD
MOUNT PARK
BEECH PK
THE CLOSE
Hall Farm
A19
Riccall Grange Farm
South Moor Hill
South Moor
South Moor Field
Danes Hills
KING RUDDING LANE
YO19
SELBY RD
North Newlands Farm
King Rudding Plantation
Skipwith Common
BLACKWOOD RD
North Duffield Common
SANDY LA
CORNELIUS CSWY
GREEN LA
Blackwood Hall
Demesne or Hall Moor
Riccall Common
West Newlands Farm
Blackwood Farm
A163
BLACKWOOD LA
High Moor
Hill Farm
High Common Farm
Green Lane Farm
Newgrove Farm
Mount Pleasant Farm
Blackwood House Farm
ANGRAM LANE
Dalby Wood
Dutch Pig Farm
Grange Farm
Low Moor
South Duffield Lodge Farm
Turnhead Farm
Barlby Common
MARKET WEIGHTON RD
Osgodby Common
Stud Farm
Whitemoor Farm
LOWMOOR RD
Fir Tree Farm
West Common Farm
WHITEMOOR LANE
Commonside Farm
Spring Wood
Whitemoor Wood
BEECH CFT
TURNHEAD CT
TURNHEAD CR
THE CHARTERS
INGS LANE
Larabridge Farm
GREENGATE LANE
The Ings
YORK RD
Barlby High Sch
MOOR CARR LA
GRANGE FARM CL
BRAMLEY AV
SYCAMORE RD
PLANTATION DR
MOOR LANE
Cliffe Wood
THE LAURELS
Barlby
Manor House Farm
Rippon Spring Wood
YO8
SPRINGFIELD CL
SIDING LA
LOWFIELD RD
OLD SCHOOL LA
HIGHFIELD CR
Wood End Farm
HAWTHORN DR
HALL PK
CHURCH MS
LANDING CL
Liby
PINDARS WY
BENNYMOOR LA
SOUTH DUFFIELD RD
HALL GARTH
Halliday Farm
Nevilthorn Farm
Marshall Farm
KAYE DR
LANDING LA
Barlby Com Prim Sch
Pear Tree Farm
Bowland House
THE HOLLIES
TUNE ST
BACK LA
Osgodby
CLAY LANE
Windmill
WILLIAM RD
SAND LA
ST LEONARDS AV
MOOR LA
Millfield Farm
Common End Farm
Water End
RIVERSIDE CL
PEARTREE CL
LUND LANE
Kisima Farm
Bank House Farm
BARLBY CR
BARLBY RD
MAGAZINE RD
Bridge Farm
MAGAZINE LA
Yew Tree Farm
BARLBY ROAD
CARR LA
Oakwood Farm
Willow Tree Farm
Lund
Sunnydene Farm
A63
Becksyke Farm
Hill Farm
YORK RD
Beech Tree Farm
Brock's Farm
1 THE HEDGEROWS
2 BADGER WY
3 CURSON TERR
4 WILLOW VW
5 THE MALTINGS
HAGG LANE
LC
STATION VW
OXEN LA
STATION LA
Hagg Lane Farm
Lock
Shipyard Ind Est
148
Cherry Orchard Farm
Longlands Farm
PH
Cliffe
DENISON RD
CARR ST
OUSE BANK
Bon Accord Farm
Cliffe Prim Sch
THE SHRUBBERIES
WILLIAM JACQUES DR
Newlands Farm
East Common
Sch
EAST COMM LA
TURNHAM LANE
PO
College
Turnham Hall
Cottage Farm
HULL RD
Garth Farm
HULL ROAD
Roscarrs
TURNHAM LA
ABBOT'S RD
Sewage Works
INGS ROAD
ABBOTS RD
Staynor Hall
Goule Hall Farm
WATERSIDE
VILLA CL
WATER LA
Staynor Wood
River Ouse
Thief Lane End Reach
White House Farm
NEWHAY LN
Newhay Farm
Hemingbrough
SCHOOL RD
Barlow Grange
Hemingbrough Prim Sch
SPIRE VW
LANDING LA
MAIN ST
BACK LA
BALK RD
CHAPEL
THIEF LANE
THIEF LA
62 63 64 65 66 67
B4
1 GEORGE TERR
2 BARLBY BY-PASS
3 HIGHFIELD VW
4 HOWDEN RD
5 LORDSHIP LA
6 ACORN CL
7 CHERRY TREE WK
8 WILFREDS GR
9 THOMPSON CL
10 MAPLE TREE AVE
11 WOODLANDS VIEW
12 CHERRY TREE CT
13 WOODLANDS CT
14 WOODLANDS DR
15 WOODLANDS CL
B5
1 RIVER VW
2 RIVER CL
3 NORTHFIELD
4 DERWENT DR
5 KINGS CL
6 MOOR LA
7 GROVE PK
8 GLEBE GARTH
9 SPRINGFIELD DR
63
50
F1
1 BARMBY FERRY RD
2 MILL LA
3 GARTHENDS LA
4 CHESTNUT GARTH
5 MANOR CL
6 CHESTNUT RISE
7 CHESTNUT CFT
8 CHESTNUT DR
9 CHESTNUT CT
10 CHESTNUT AVE
11 FERRY CL
12 ST MARY'S AVE
13 CARR CL
14 MILL GARTH
15 THE CLOISTERS
16 SOUTHLANDS
17 MILLFIELD RD
18 DURHAM CL
19 NURSERY CL
20 ORCHARD END
21 OAKFIELD LA
22 CHURCH VW

A7
1 WILLOW DR
2 OAK RD
3 WESTFIELD RD
4 GARTH AVE
5 MANOR DR
6 MANOR CL

49
38

D7
1 MEADOWFIELD
2 VICARAGE CL
3 STAITHE ST
4 CHURCH CL
5 HONEY POT
6 MANOR CT

Scale: 1¾ inches to 1 mile

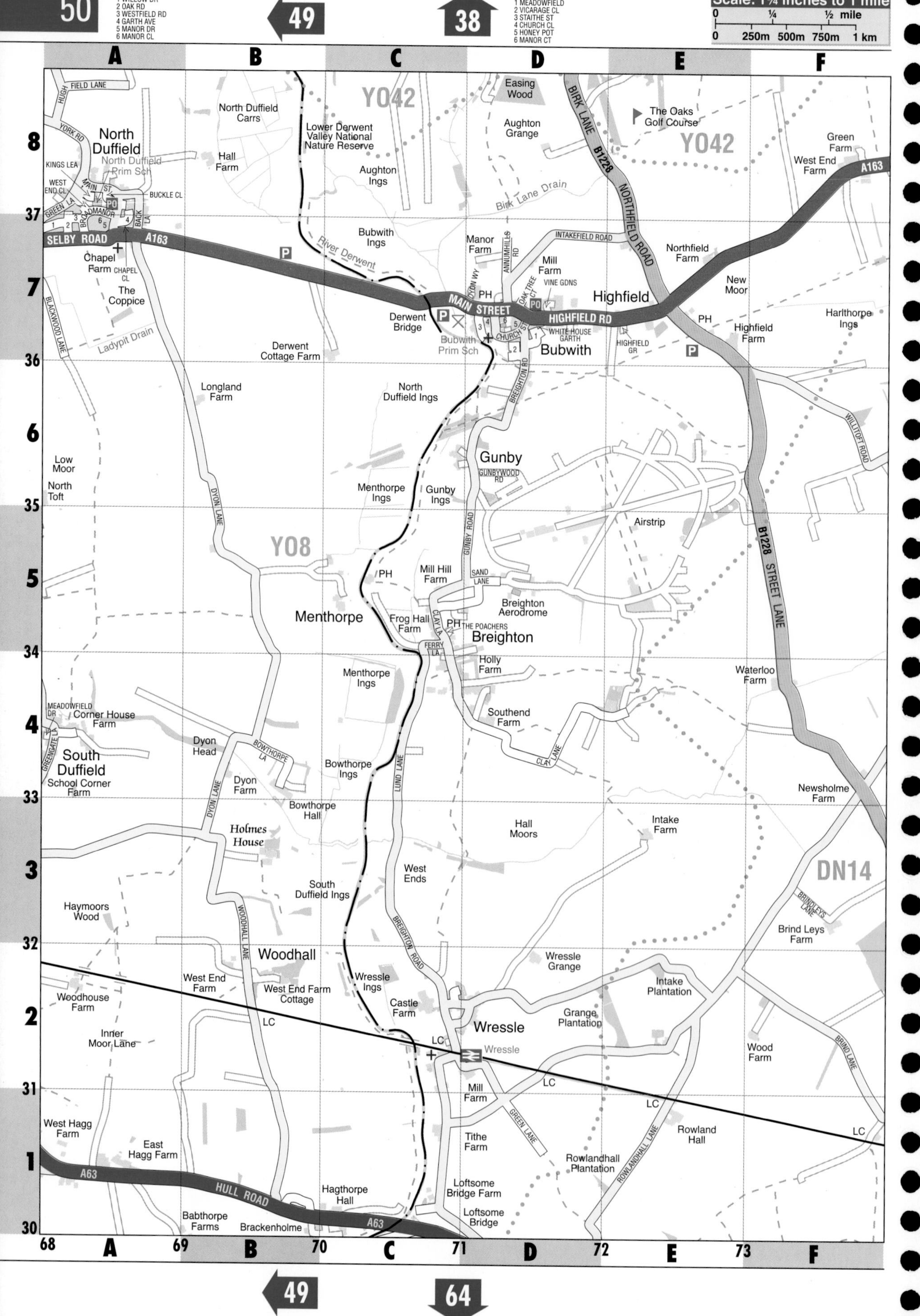

49
64

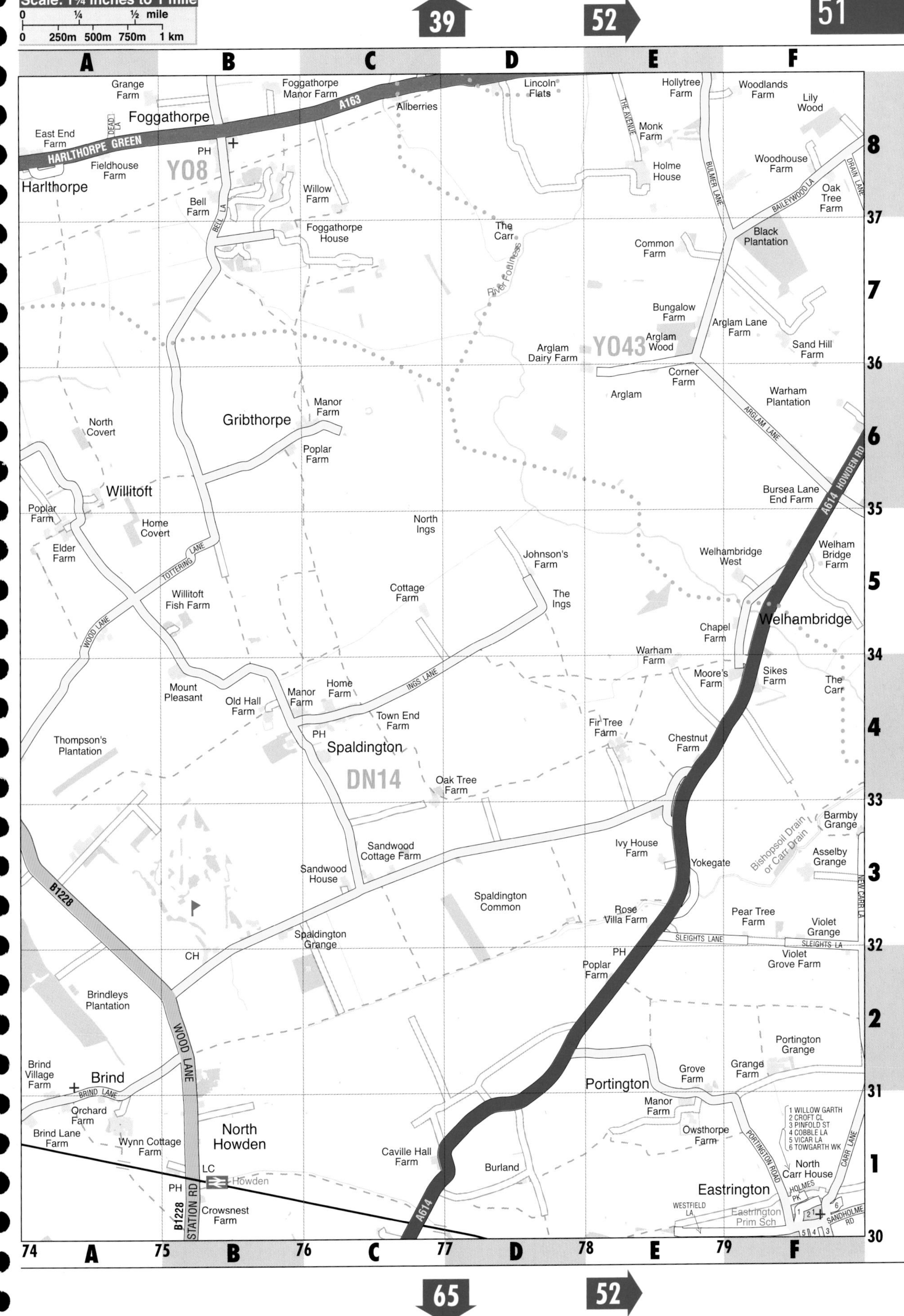

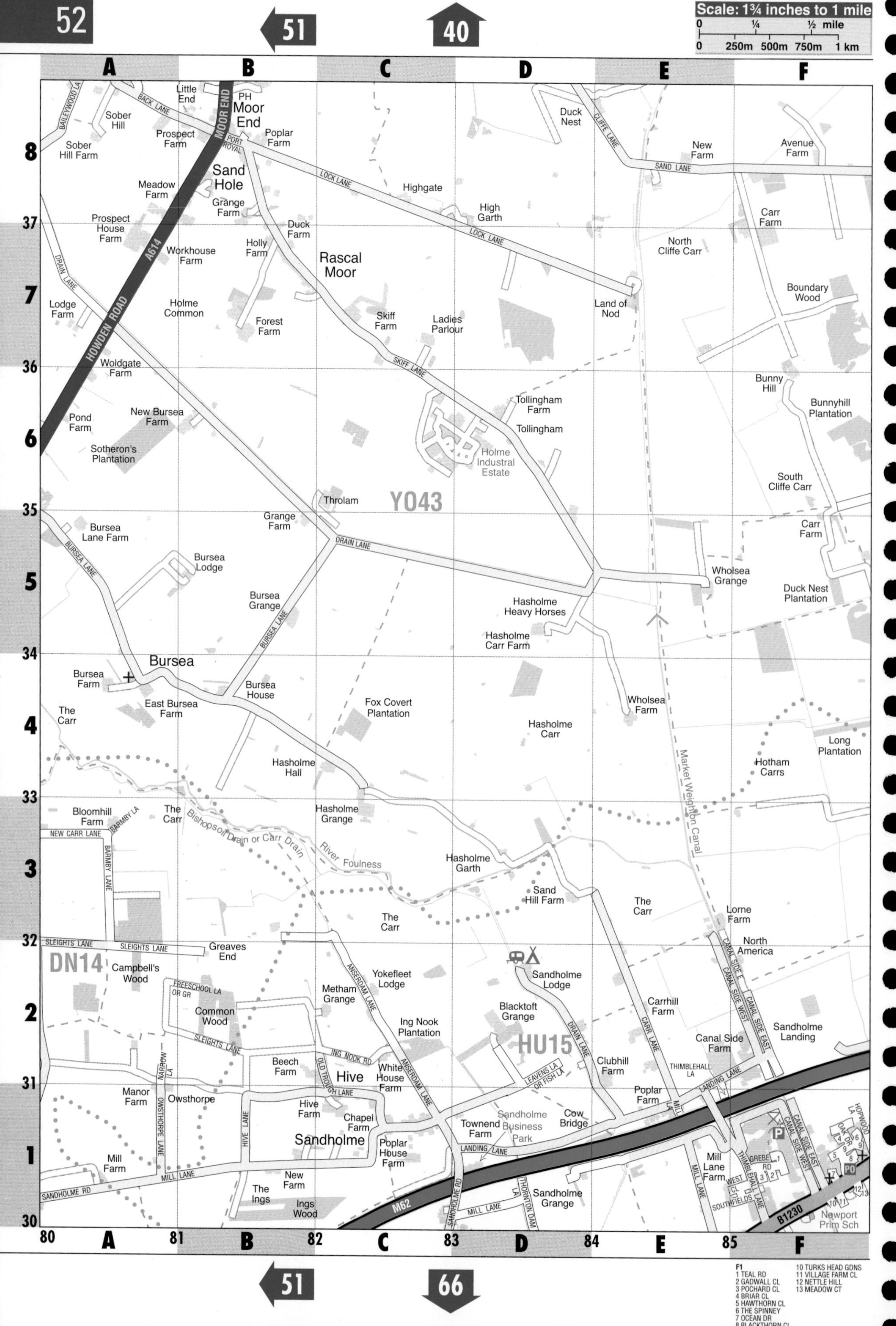

52
51
40
Scale: 1¾ inches to 1 mile
0 ¼ ½ mile
0 250m 500m 750m 1 km
A B C D E F
8 37 7 36 6 35 5 34 4 33 3 32 2 31 1 30
80 81 82 83 84 85
BAILEYWOOD LA
Sober Hill
Sober Hill Farm
BACK LANE
Little End
PH
Moor End
MOOR END
PORT ROYAL
Prospect Farm
Poplar Farm
Sand Hole
Meadow Farm
Grange Farm
LOCK LANE
Highgate
Duck Nest
CLIFFE LANE
SAND LANE
New Farm
Avenue Farm
Prospect House Farm
Duck Farm
High Garth
Carr Farm
Holly Farm
Workhouse Farm
A614
Rascal Moor
North Cliffe Carr
DRAIN LANE
Lodge Farm
Holme Common
Forest Farm
Skiff Farm
Ladies Parlour
Land of Nod
Boundary Wood
HOWDEN ROAD
SKIFF LANE
Woldgate Farm
Bunny Hill
Bunnyhill Plantation
Tollingham Farm
Pond Farm
New Bursea Farm
Tollingham
Holme Industral Estate
Sotheron's Plantation
South Cliffe Carr
Throlam
YO43
Grange Farm
Bursea Lane Farm
Carr Farm
BURSEA LANE
Bursea Lodge
Wholsea Grange
Duck Nest Plantation
Bursea Grange
Hasholme Heavy Horses
Hasholme Carr Farm
Bursea
Bursea Farm
Bursea House
East Bursea Farm
The Carr
Fox Covert Plantation
Wholsea Farm
Hasholme Carr
Long Plantation
Hasholme Hall
Hotham Carrs
Market Weighton Canal
Bloomhill Farm
BARMBY LA
The Carr
Hasholme Grange
NEW CARR LANE
BARMBY LANE
Bishopsoil Drain or Carr Drain
River Foulness
Hasholme Garth
Sand Hill Farm
The Carr
The Carr
Lorne Farm
SLEIGHTS LANE
Greaves End
North America
DN14
Campbell's Wood
Yokefleet Lodge
Sandholme Lodge
CANAL SIDE
FREESCHOOL LA OR GR
Metham Grange
ANSERDAM LANE
Carrhill Farm
CANAL SIDE WEST
CANAL SIDE EAST
Common Wood
Ing Nook Plantation
Blacktoft Grange
CARR LANE
Sandholme Landing
SLEIGHTS LANE
HU15
DRAIN LANE
Canal Side Farm
NARROW LA
ING NOOK RD
Beech Farm
White House Farm
Clubhill Farm
THIMBLEHALL LA
OLD TROUGH LANE
Hive
LEAVENS LA
OR FISH LA
LANDING LANE
Manor Farm
Owsthorpe
Poplar Farm
OWSTHORPE LANE
HIVE LANE
Hive Farm
Chapel Farm
Sandholme Business Park
Cow Bridge
Townend Farm
HOPWOOD LA
Sandholme
Poplar House Farm
LANDING LANE
Mill Farm
Mill Lane Farm
GREBE RD
CANAL SIDE WEST
MILL LANE
New Farm
SANDHOLME RD
THORNTON DAM LA
Sandholme Grange
MILL LANE
WEST CL
THIMBLEHALL LANE
SANDHOLME RD
The Ings
Ings Wood
M62
MILL LANE
SOUTHFIELDS
B1230
Newport Prim Sch
F1
1 TEAL RD
2 GADWALL CL
3 POCHARD CL
4 BRIAR CL
5 HAWTHORN CL
6 THE SPINNEY
7 OCEAN DR
8 BLACKTHORN CL
9 MEADOW LA
10 TURKS HEAD GDNS
11 VILLAGE FARM CL
12 NETTLE HILL
13 MEADOW CT
51
66

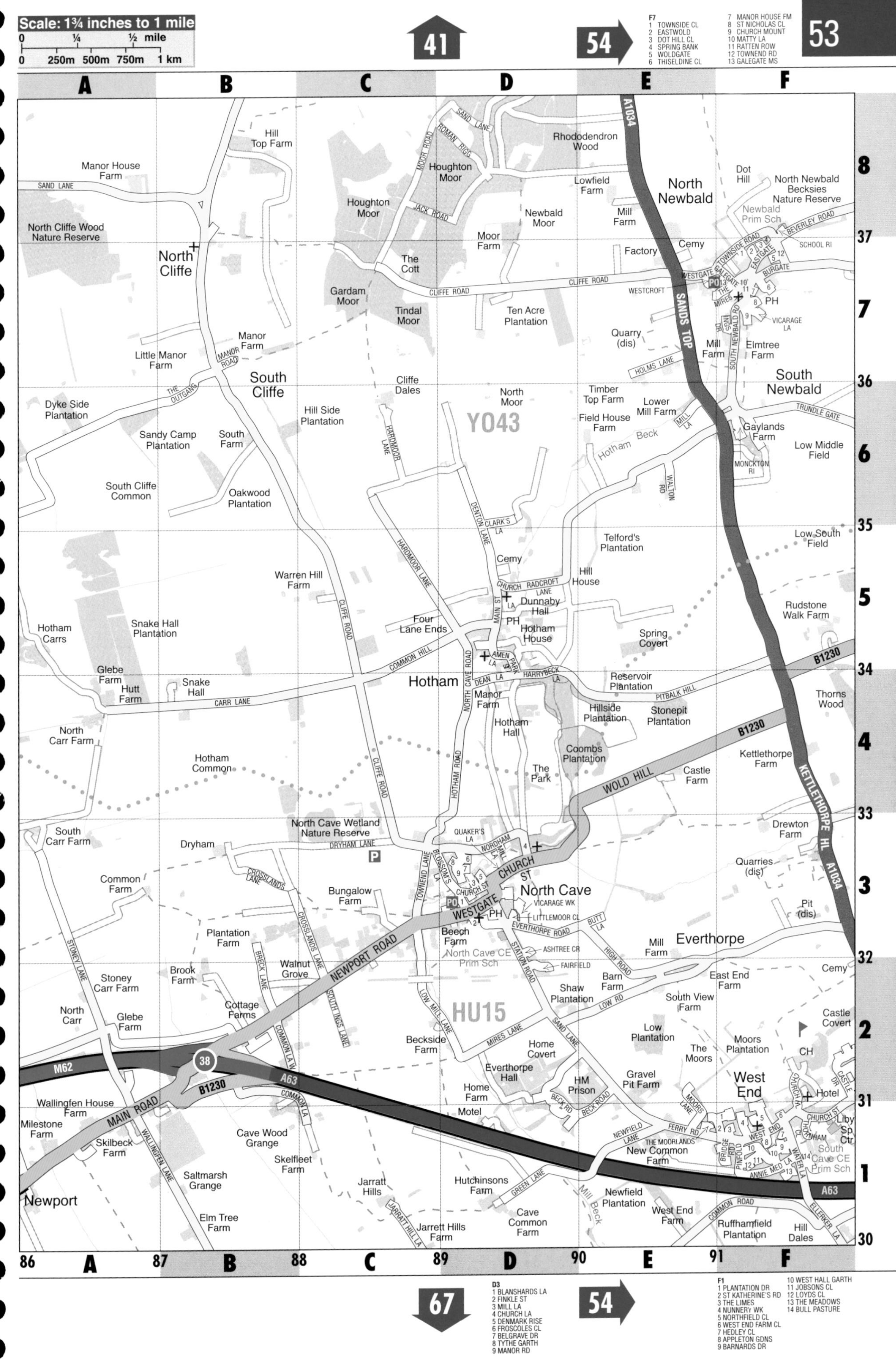

F7
1 TOWNSIDE CL
2 EASTWOLD
3 DOT HILL CL
4 SPRING BANK
5 WOLDGATE
6 THISELDINE CL

7 MANOR HOUSE FM
8 ST.NICHOLAS CL
9 CHURCH MOUNT
10 MATTY LA
11 RATTEN ROW
12 TOWNEND RD
13 GALEGATE MS

A B C D E F

8
37
7
36
6
35
5
34
4
33
3
32
2
31
1
30

Manor House Farm
North Cliffe Wood Nature Reserve
SAND LANE
North Cliffe
Little Manor Farm
Manor Farm
MANOR ROAD
THE OUTGANG
South Cliffe
Dyke Side Plantation
Sandy Camp Plantation
South Farm
Hill Side Plantation
South Cliffe Common
Oakwood Plantation
HARDMOOR LANE
CLIFFE ROAD
DENTON LANE
CLARK'S LA
Cemy
Warren Hill Farm
COMMON HILL
Four Lane Ends
CHURCH LANE
RADCROFT LANE
Cemy
MAIN ST
AMEN LA
PARK LA
DEAN LA
HARRYBECK LA
Dunnaby Hall
Hotham House
Hotham
PH
Manor Farm
Hotham Hall
Hill House
Hill Top Farm
Houghton Moor
Houghton Moor
ROMAN RIGG
SAND LANE
MOOR ROAD
JACK ROAD
The Cott
Gardam Moor
Tindal Moor
Cliffe Dales
Moor Farm
CLIFFE ROAD
CLIFFE ROAD
Ten Acre Plantation
Newbald Moor
North Moor
YO43
Hotham Beck
Rhododendron Wood
Lowfield Farm
Mill Farm
Factory
Cemy
WESTGATE
North Newbald
Dot Hill
North Newbald Becksies Nature Reserve
Newbald Prim Sch
BEVERLEY ROAD
SCHOOL RI
TOWNSIDE ROAD
EASTGATE
BURGATE
WESTCROFT
THE MIRES
SOUTH NEWBALD
PO
PH
VICARAGE LA
SANDS TOP
South Newbald
Mill Farm
Elmtree Farm
Quarry (dis)
HOLMS LANE
Timber Top Farm
Field House Farm
Lower Mill Farm
MILL LA
WALTON RD
Gaylands Farm
MONCKTON RI
Low Middle Field
TRUNDLE GATE
Telford's Plantation
Low South Field
Rudstone Walk Farm
B1230
Hotham Carrs
Snake Hall Plantation
Glebe Farm
Hutt Farm
Snake Hall
CARR LANE
North Carr Farm
Hotham Common
CLIFFE ROAD
HOTHAM ROAD
NORTH CAVE ROAD
Reservoir Plantation
PITBALK HILL
Hillside Plantation
Stonepit Plantation
Coombs Plantation
The Park
Castle Farm
WOLD HILL
Kettlethorpe Farm
B1230
B1230
Thorns Wood
KETTLETHORPE HL
A1034
Drewton Farm
Quarries (dis)
South Carr Farm
Dryham
North Cave Wetland Nature Reserve
DRYHAM LANE
P
QUAKER'S LA
BLOSSOM'S LA
NORDHAM
CHURCH ST
North Cave
VICARAGE WK
LITTLEMOOR CL
EVERTHORPE ROAD
BUTT LA
Everthorpe
Pit (dis)
Common Farm
CROSSLANDS LANE
Bungalow Farm
TOWNEND LANE
CHURCH ST
PO
WESTGATE
PH
Beech Farm
North Cave CE Prim Sch
ASHTREE CR
FAIRFIELD
Mill Farm
Cemy
Plantation Farm
BRICK LANE
Walnut Grove
LOW RD
Shaw Plantation
Barn Farm
South View Farm
East End Farm
Castle Covert
CH
Stoney Carr Farm
Brook Farm
Cottage Farms
CROSSLANDS LANE
SOUTH INGS LANE
COMMON LANE
LOW MILL LANE
STATION ROAD
HIGH RD
Beckside Farm
Home Covert
SAND LANE
MIRES LANE
Low Plantation
The Moors
Moors Plantation
West End
Hotel
North Carr
Glebe Farm
STONEY LANE
M62
38
B1230
A63
Home Farm
Everthorpe Hall
HM Prison
Gravel Pit Farm
The Moors
CASTLE RD
CHURCH LA
Liby Sp. Ctr
South Cave CE Prim Sch
Wallingfen House Farm
Milestone Farm
Skilbeck Farm
MAIN ROAD
WALLINGFEN LANE
B1230
COMMON LA
Motel
Home Farm
BECK RD
BECK RD
New Common Farm
FERRY RD
WEST END
PINFOLD
THE MOORLANDS
NEWFIELD LANE
ANNIE MED LA
WATER LA
CHURCH ST
Newport
Cave Wood Grange
Saltmarsh Grange
Skelfleet Farm
Elm Tree Farm
Jarratt Hills
Jarrett Hills Farm
LAGBATT HILL LA
Cave Common Farm
Hutchinsons Farm
GREEN LANE
Mill Beck
Newfield Plantation
West End Farm
Ruffhamfield Plantation
COMMON ROAD
ELLERKER RD
A63
Hill Dales
HU15

D3
1 BLANSHARDS LA
2 FINKLE ST
3 MILL LA
4 CHURCH LA
5 DENMARK RISE
6 FROSCOLES CL
7 BELGRAVE DR
8 TYTHE GARTH
9 MANOR RD

67

54

F1
1 PLANTATION DR
2 ST KATHERINE'S RD
3 THE LIMES
4 NUNNERY WK
5 NORTHFIELD CL
6 WEST END FARM CL
7 HEDLEY CL
8 APPLETON GDNS
9 BARNARDS DR

10 WEST HALL GARTH
11 JOBSONS CL
12 LOYDS CL
13 THE MEADOWS
14 BULL PASTURE

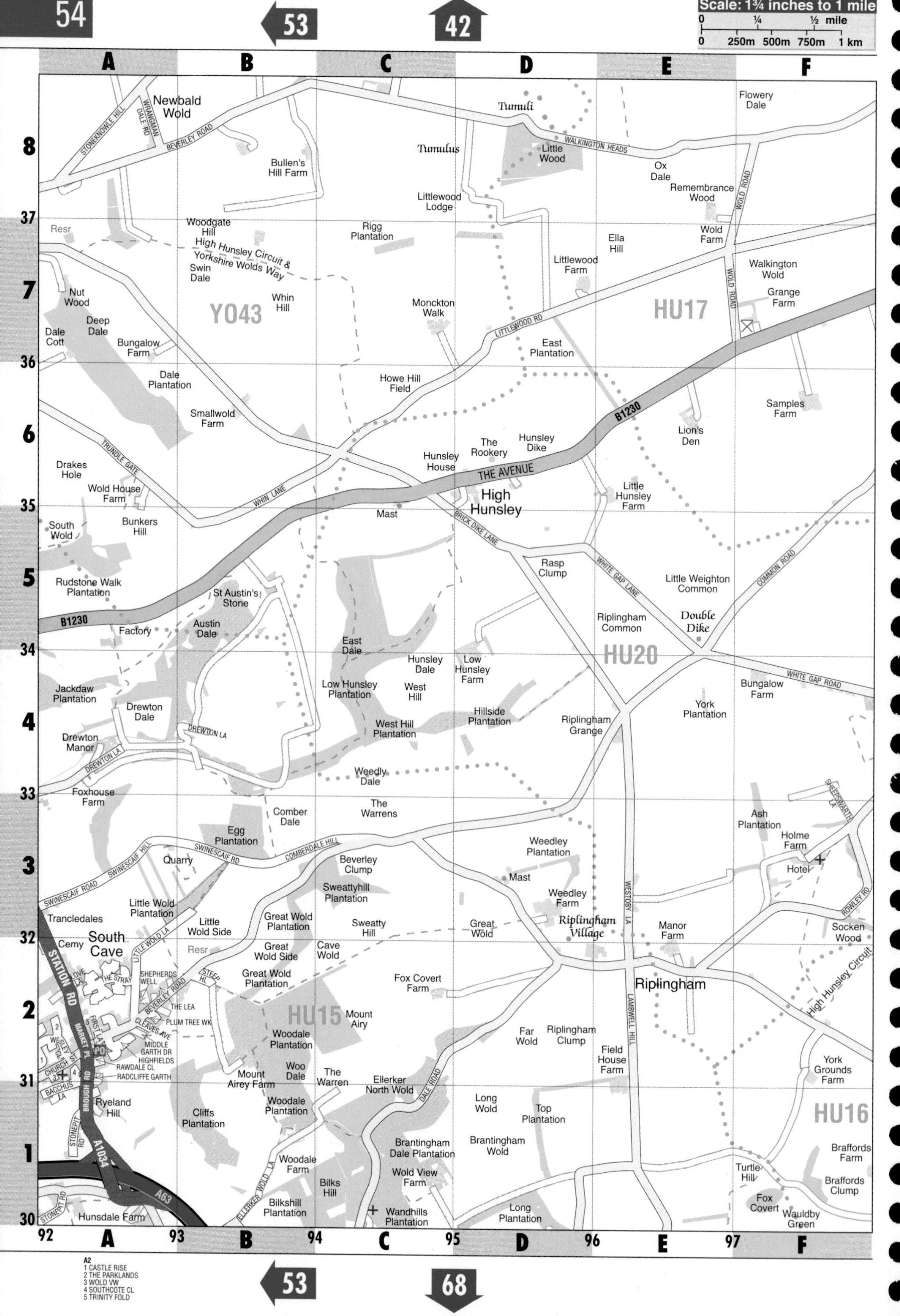

A · B · C · D · E · F

8

Newbald Wold

Tumuli

Tumulus

Little Wood

Flowery Dale

Bullen's Hill Farm

Walkington Heads

Ox Dale

Remembrance Wood

37

Resr

Woodgate Hill

High Hunsley Circuit & Yorkshire Wolds Way

Swin Dale

Littlewood Lodge

Rigg Plantation

Ella Hill

Wold Farm

Wold Road

7

Nut Wood

Deep Dale

YO43

Whin Hill

Monckton Walk

Littlewood Farm

HU17

Walkington Wold

Grange Farm

36

Dale Cott

Bungalow Farm

Dale Plantation

Littlewood Rd

East Plantation

6

Smallwold Farm

Howe Hill Field

Hunsley House

The Rookery

Hunsley Dike

B1230

Lion's Den

Samples Farm

Drakes Hole

Trundle Gate

Wold House Farm

THE AVENUE

Little Hunsley Farm

35

South Wold

Bunkers Hill

Whin Lane

Mast

High Hunsley

Brick Dike Lane

5

Rudstone Walk Plantation

St Austin's Stone

Rasp Clump

White Gap Lane

Little Weighton Common

Common Road

B1230

Factory

Austin Dale

Riplingham Common

Double Dike

34

Jackdaw Plantation

Drewton Dale

East Dale

Hunsley Dale

Low Hunsley Farm

HU20

White Gap Road

Bungalow Farm

4

Drewton Manor

Drewton La

Low Hunsley Plantation

West Hill

Hillside Plantation

Riplingham Grange

York Plantation

Drewton La

West Hill Plantation

33

Foxhouse Farm

Comber Dale

The Warrens

Weedly Dale

Weedley Plantation

Ash Plantation

Holme Farm

3

Egg Plantation

Quarry

Swinescaif Rd

Comberdale Hill

Beverley Clump

Mast

Weedley Farm

Hotel

Swinescaif Hill

Sweattyhill Plantation

Westory La

Rowley Rd

32

Trancledales

Swinescaif Road

Little Wold Plantation

Little Wold Side

Great Wold Plantation

Sweatty Hill

Great Wold

Riplingham Village

Manor Farm

Socken Wood

Cemy

South Cave

Little Wold La

Resr

Great Wold Side

Cave Wold

High Hunsley Circuit

2

Shepherds Well

Beverley Road

Steep Hil

Great Wold Plantation

HU15

Woodale Plantation

Mount Airy

Fox Covert Farm

Riplingham

Field House Farm

York Grounds Farm

THE STRAY

THE LEA

PLUM TREE WK

CLEAVES AVE

MIDDLE GARTH DR

HIGHFIELDS

Lambwell Hill

HU16

31

Station Rd

Market Pl

Bridge Rd

Church St

Bacchus La

RAWDALE CL

RADCLIFFE GARTH

Ryeland Hill

Mount Airey Farm

Woodale Plantation

Woo Dale

The Warren

Ellerker North Wold

Dale Road

Far Wold

Riplingham Clump

Brafords Farm

1

A1034

Hunsdale Farm

Cliffs Plantation

Woodale Farm

Bilks Hill

Brantingham Dale Plantation

Wold View Farm

Brantingham Wold

Long Wold

Top Plantation

Turtle Hill

Brafords Clump

30

Stoneply Rd

A63

Ellerker Holme La

Bilkshill Plantation

Wandhills Plantation

Long Plantation

Fox Covert

Wauldby Green

92 · A · 93 · B · 94 · C · 95 · D · 96 · E · 97 · F

A2
1 CASTLE RISE
2 THE PARKLANDS
3 WOLD VW
4 SOUTHCOTE CL
5 TRINITY FOLD

Scale: 1¾ inches to 1 mile
0 ¼ ½ mile
0 250m 500m 750m 1 km

B7
1 LAWSON CL
2 FERGUSON RD
3 ALL HALLOWS RD
4 WEST MILL RISE
5 TAYLORS CL

B8
1 WESTFIELD GARTH
2 MIDDLEHOWE GN
3 BIRCH LEA
4 SAUNDERS CFT

C8
1 AUTHERD GARTH
2 WAUDBY CL
3 MEADOW WY
4 SHERWOOD CL

D8
1 SPEEDWELL LA
2 THE HAVEN
3 HAYWARD CL
4 NIGHTINGALE CL
5 HUZZARD CL
6 ORIEL CL
7 ASH DENE
8 MEGSON WAY

43 136 56

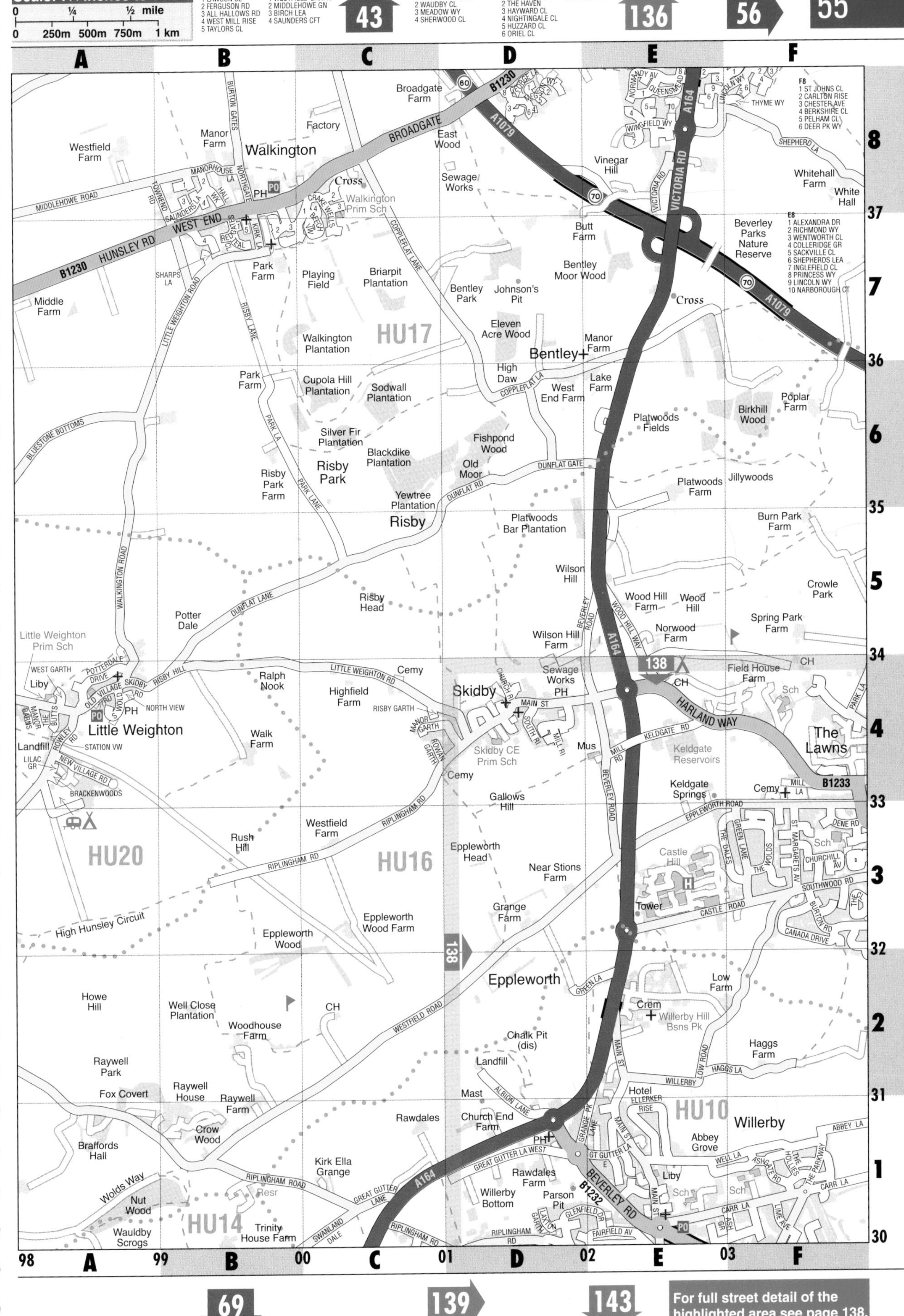

69 139 143

For full street detail of the highlighted area see page 138.

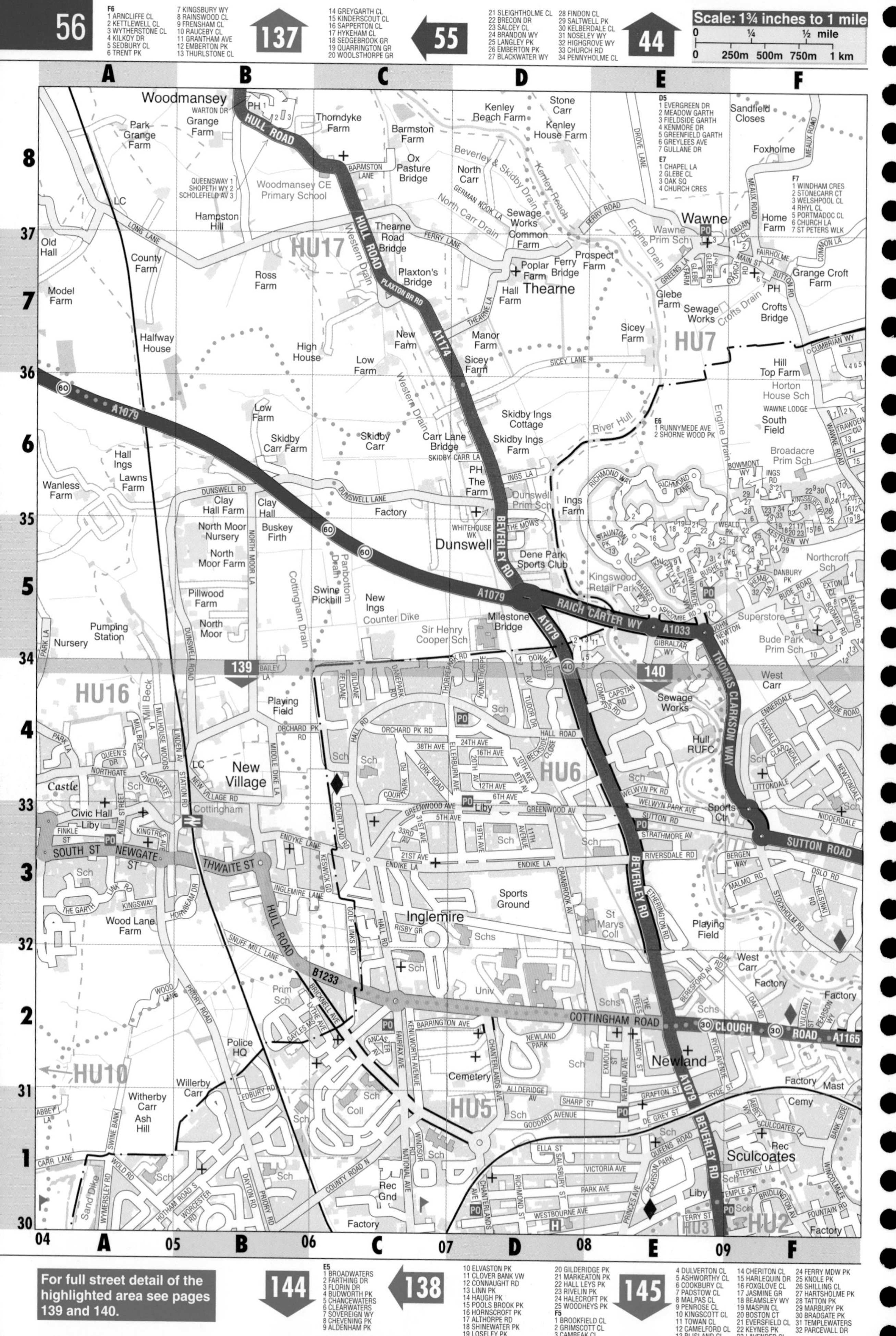

56
F6
1 ARNCLIFFE CL
2 KETTLEWELL CL
3 WYTHERSTONE CL
4 KILKOY DR
5 SEDBURY CL
6 TRENT PK
7 KINGSBURY WY
8 RAINSWOOD CL
9 FRENSHAM CL
10 RAUCEBY CL
11 GRANTHAM AVE
12 EMBERTON PK
13 THURLSTONE CL
137
14 GREYGARTH CL
15 KINDERSCOUT CL
16 SAPPERTON CL
17 HYKEHAM CL
18 SEDGEBROOK GR
19 QUARRINGTON GR
20 WOOLSTHORPE GR
55
21 SLEIGHTHOLME CL
22 BRECON DR
23 SALCEY CL
24 BRANDON WY
25 LANGLEY PK
26 EMBERTON PK
27 BLACKWATER WY
28 FINDON CL
29 SALTWELL PK
30 KELBERDALE CL
31 NOSELEY WY
32 HIGHGROVE WY
33 CHURCH RD
34 PENNYHOLME CL
44
Scale: 1¾ inches to 1 mile
0 ¼ ½ mile
0 250m 500m 750m 1 km
A B C D E F
D5
1 EVERGREEN DR
2 MEADOW GARTH
3 FIELDSIDE GARTH
4 KENMORE DR
5 GREENFIELD GARTH
6 GREYLEES AVE
7 GULLANE DR
E7
1 CHAPEL LA
2 GLEBE CL
3 OAK SQ
4 CHURCH CRES
F7
1 WINDHAM CRES
2 STONECARR CT
3 WELSHPOOL CL
4 RHYL CL
5 PORTMADOC CL
6 CHURCH LA
7 ST PETERS WLK
E6
1 RUNNYMEDE AVE
2 SHORNE WOOD PK
Woodmansey
Park Grange Farm
Grange Farm
HULL ROAD
Thorndyke Farm
Barmston Farm
Kenley Beach Farm
Stone Carr
Kenley House Farm
Sandfield Closes
Foxholme
Ox Pasture Bridge
North Carr
Woodmansey CE Primary School
Hampston Hill
Old Hall
County Farm
HU17
Thearne Road Bridge
Sewage Works
Common Farm
Wawne
Wawne Prim Sch
Home Farm
Poplar Farm
Ferry Bridge
Prospect Farm
Plaxton's Bridge
Grange Croft Farm
Model Farm
Ross Farm
Hall Farm
Thearne
Glebe Farm
Sewage Works
Crofts Bridge
Halfway House
High House
New Farm
Manor Farm
Sicey Farm
Sicey Farm
HU7
Low Farm
Hill Top Farm
Horton House Sch
South Field
A1079
A1174
Low Farm
Skidby Carr Farm
Skidby Carr
Carr Lane Bridge
Skidby Ings Cottage
Skidby Ings Farm
River Hull
Hall Ings
Lawns Farm
Wanless Farm
PH The Farm
Broadacre Prim Sch
Clay Hall Farm
Clay Hall
North Moor Nursery
Buskey Firth
Factory
Dunswell Prim Sch
Ings Farm
North Moor Farm
Dunswell
Dene Park Sports Club
Northcroft Sch
Pillwood Farm
Swine Pickhill
New Ings
Counter Dike
Kingswood Retail Park
RAICH CARTER WY
A1033
Pumping Station
North Moor
Nursery
Sir Henry Cooper Sch
Milestone Bridge
Superstore
Bude Park Prim Sch
139
140
HU16
Playing Field
West Carr
Sewage Works
Hull RUFC
New Village
HU6
THOMAS CLARKSON WAY
Castle
Civic Hall
Cottingham
SOUTH ST
NEWGATE ST
THWAITE ST
HULL ROAD
SUTTON ROAD
Sports Ctr
Sports Ground
Inglemire
St Marys Coll
Playing Field
Wood Lane Farm
West Carr
Factory
BEVERLEY RD
B1233
COTTINGHAM ROAD
CLOUGH ROAD
A1165
Univ
Factory
Police HQ
HU10
Willerby Carr
Witherby Carr
Ash Hill
Cemetery
Newland
Mast
Factory
Cemy
Coll
HU5
Rec Gnd
Sculcoates
Factory
HU3
HU2
Factory
04 A 05 B 06 C 07 D 08 E 09 F
For full street detail of the highlighted area see pages 139 and 140.
144
E5
1 BROADWATERS
2 FARTHING DR
3 FLORIN DR
4 BUDWORTH PK
5 CHANCEWATERS
6 CLEARWATERS
7 SOVEREIGN WY
8 CHEVENING PK
9 ALDENHAM PK
138
10 ELVASTON PK
11 CLOVER BANK VW
12 CONNAUGHT RD
13 LINN PK
14 HAUGH PK
15 POOLS BROOK PK
16 HORNSCROFT PK
17 ALTHORPE RD
18 SHINEWATER PK
19 LOSELEY PK
20 GILDERIDGE PK
21 MARKEATON PK
22 HALL LEYS PK
23 RIVELIN PK
24 HALECROFT PK
25 WOODHEYS PK
F5
1 BROOKFIELD CL
2 GRIMSCOTT CL
3 CAMBEAK CL
145
4 DULVERTON CL
5 ASHWORTHY CL
6 COOKBURY CL
7 PADSTOW CL
8 MALPAS CL
9 PENROSE CL
10 KINGSCOTT CL
11 TOWAN CL
12 CAMELFORD CL
13 BLISLAND CL
14 CHERITON CL
15 HARLEQUIN DR
16 FOXGLOVE CL
17 JASMINE GR
18 BEAMSLEY WY
19 MASPIN CL
20 BOSTON CT
21 EVERSFIELD CL
22 KEYNES PK
23 LAVENDER CL
24 FERRY MDW PK
25 KNOLE PK
26 SHILLING CL
27 HARTSHOLME PK
28 TATTON PK
29 MARBURY PK
30 BRADGATE PK
31 TEMPLEWATERS
32 PARCEVALL DR

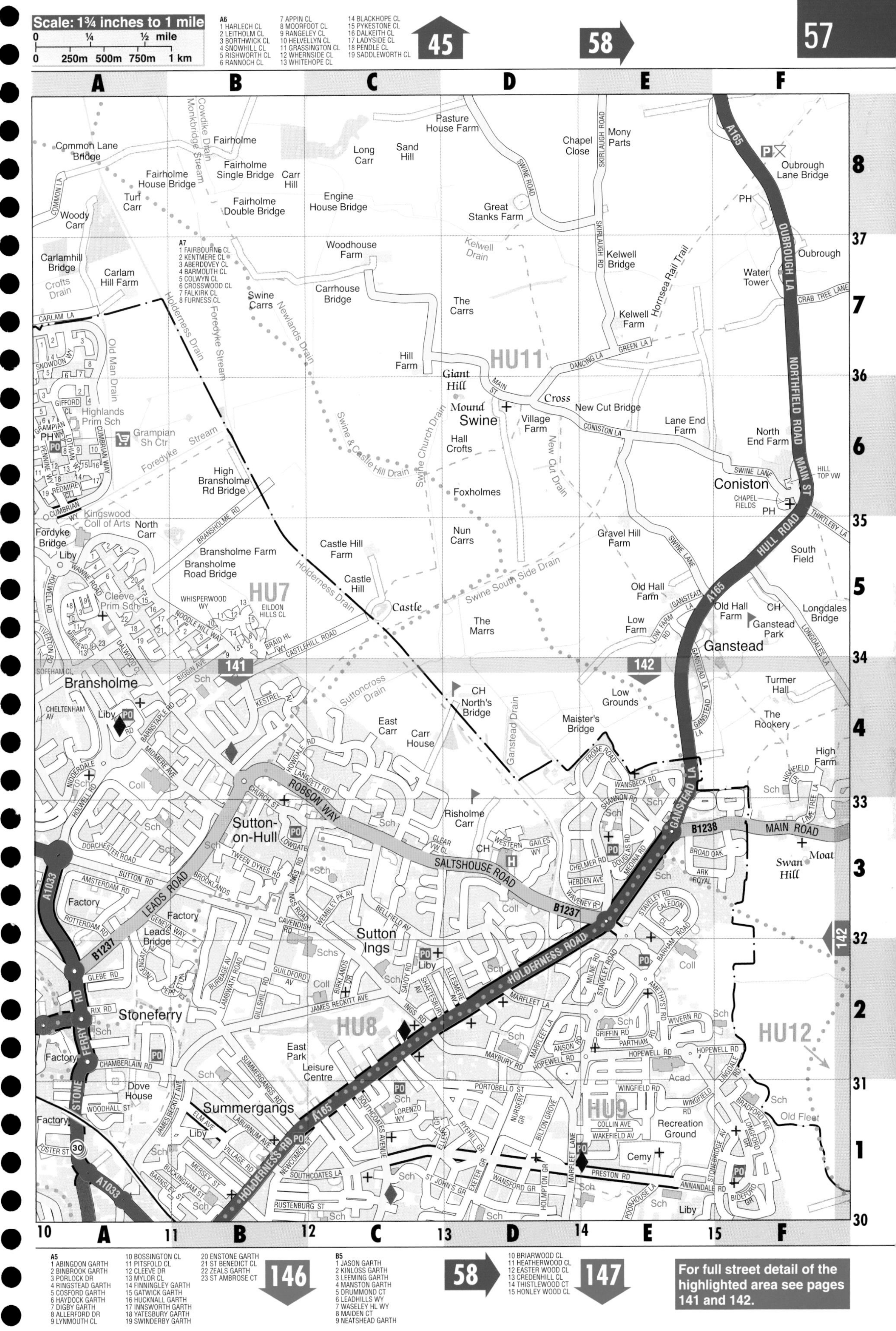

57
Scale: 1¾ inches to 1 mile
0 ¼ ½ mile
0 250m 500m 750m 1 km
A6
1 HARLECH CL
2 LEITHOLM CL
3 BORTHWICK CL
4 SNOWHILL CL
5 RISHWORTH CL
6 RANNOCH CL
7 APPIN CL
8 MOORFOOT CL
9 RANGELEY CL
10 HELVELLYN CL
11 GRASSINGTON CL
12 WHERNSIDE CL
13 WHITEHOPE CL
14 BLACKHOPE CL
15 PYKESTONE CL
16 DALKEITH CL
17 LADYSIDE CL
18 PENDLE CL
19 SADDLEWORTH CL
45
58
A B C D E F
Common Lane Bridge
Cowdike Drain
Monkbridge Stream
Fairholme
Fairholme Single Bridge
Fairholme House Bridge
Fairholme Double Bridge
Carr Hill
Turf Carr
Woody Carr
Long Carr
Sand Hill
Engine House Bridge
Pasture House Farm
Swine Road
Chapel Close
Skirlaugh Road
Mony Parts
Oubrough Lane Bridge
Great Stanks Farm
Kelwell Drain
Kelwell Bridge
Oubrough
Oubrough La
Water Tower
Crab Tree Lane
Carlamhill Bridge
Crofts Drain
Carlam Hill Farm
A7
1 FAIRBOURNE CL
2 KENTMERE CL
3 ABERDOVEY CL
4 BARMOUTH CL
5 COLWYN CL
6 CROSSWOOD CL
7 FALKIRK CL
8 FURNESS CL
Woodhouse Farm
Carrhouse Bridge
Swine Carrs
Newlands Drain
Holderness Drain
Foredyke Stream
The Carrs
Kelwell Farm
Hornsea Rail Trail
Carlam La
Snowdon Wy
Old Man Drain
Hill Farm
Giant Hill
HU11
Dancing La
Green La
Northfield Road
Main St
Mound
Swine
Cross
New Cut Bridge
Gifford Cl
Highlands Prim Sch
Grampian Wy
Grampian Sh Ctr
Foredyke Stream
Swine & Castle Hill Drain
Swine Church Drain
Village Farm
Hall Crofts
Coniston La
Lane End Farm
North End Farm
New Cut Drain
Pennine Wy
Lothian Wy
Cumbrian Way
Redmire Cl
High Bransholme Rd Bridge
Swine Lane
Hill Top Vw
Coniston
Chapel Fields
Foxholmes
Cumbrian Wy
Kingswood Coll of Arts
North Carr
Bransholme Rd
Fordyke Bridge
Nun Carrs
Gravel Hill Farm
Thirtleby La
Hull Road
South Field
Liby
Wawne Road
Castle Hill Farm
Bransholme Farm
Bransholme Road Bridge
Castle Hill
Swine South Side Drain
Old Hall Farm
Howell Rd
Cleeve Prim Sch
HU7
Whisperwood Wy
Eildon Hills Cl
Castle
Ganstead La
Old Hall Farm
CH
Longdales Bridge
Tiverton Rd
Noodle Hill Way
Braid Hl Wy
Castlehill Road
The Marrs
Low Farm
Low Farm Rd
Ganstead Park
Longdales La
Dalwood Cl
Ganstead
Sofeham Cl
Biggin Ave
141
142
Bransholme
Sch
Kestrel Av
Suttoncross Drain
CH
North's Bridge
Low Grounds
Turmer Hall
Cheltenham Av
Liby
PO
Barnstaple Rd
East Carr
Carr House
Ganstead Drain
Maister's Bridge
The Rookery
Midmere Ave
Howdale Rd
Lansbett Rd
Frome Road
Wansbeck Rd
High Farm
Highfield Cr
Nidderdale
Coll
Church St
Robson Way
Risholme Carr
Shannon Rd
Ganstead La
Sch
Lime Tree La
Howell Rd
Sutton-on-Hull
Clear Vw Cl
Western Gailes Wy
Douglas Rd
Medina Rd
B1238
Main Road
Dorchester Road
Lowgate
Tween Dykes Rd
Saltshouse Road
CH
H
Chelmer Rd
Broad Oak
Swan Hill
Moat
Sutton Rd
A1033
Amsterdam Rd
Ings Rd
Brooklands
Wembley Pk Av
Coll
Hebden Ave
Waveney Rd
Ark Royal
Factory
Leads Road
Ings Road
Bellfield Av
B1237
Staveley Rd
Caledon Cl
Rotterdam Rd
Factory
Geneva Way
Cavendish Rd
Sutton Ings
Barham Road
Leads Bridge
Schs
Holderness Road
Milne Rd
Staveley Road
Coll
Glebe Rd
Burbage Av
Lambwath Road
Guildford Av
Birklands Dr
Savoy Rd
Shaftesbury Av
Ellesmere Av
Amethyst Rd
Rix Rd
Ferry Rd
Stoneferry
Gillshill Rd
James Reckitt Ave
Marfleet La
Wivern Rd
HU8
Griffin Rd
Parthian Rd
HU12
Factory
East Park
Maybury Rd
Anson Rd
Hopewell Rd
Chamberlain Rd
Leisure Centre
Hopewell Rd
Acad
Stone Ferry
Dove House
Summergangs Rd
Portobello St
Wingfield Rd
Lingdale Rd
Woodhall St
James Reckitt Ave
Summergangs
Southcoates Avenue
Lorenzo Wy
Nursery Gr
Bilton Grove
HU9
Collin Ave
Wakefield Av
Recreation Ground
Bradford Ave
Longford Gr
Old Fleet
Factory
Elm Ave
Laburnum Ave
Liby
A165
Ryehill Gr
Marfleet Lane
Cemy
Stonebridge Av
Foster St
30
Village Rd
Mersey St
Buckingham St
Barnsley St
A1033
Southcoates La
St John's Gr
Exeter Gr
Wansford Gr
Holmpton Gr
Preston Rd
Annandale Rd
Bideford Gr
Newcomen St
Rustenburg St
Poorhouse La
Liby
10 A 11 B 12 C 13 D 14 E 15 F
8 37 7 36 6 35 5 34 4 33 3 32 2 31 1 30
A5
1 ABINGDON GARTH
2 BINBROOK GARTH
3 PORLOCK DR
4 RINGSTEAD GARTH
5 COSFORD GARTH
6 HAYDOCK GARTH
7 DIGBY GARTH
8 ALLERFORD DR
9 LYNMOUTH CL
10 BOSSINGTON CL
11 PITSFOLD CL
12 CLEEVE DR
13 MYLOR CL
14 FINNINGLEY GARTH
15 GATWICK GARTH
16 HUCKNALL GARTH
17 INNSWORTH GARTH
18 YATESBURY GARTH
19 SWINDERBY GARTH
20 ENSTONE GARTH
21 ST BENEDICT CL
22 ZEALS GARTH
23 ST AMBROSE CT
146
B5
1 JASON GARTH
2 KINLOSS GARTH
3 LEEMING GARTH
4 MANSTON GARTH
5 DRUMMOND CT
6 LEADHILLS WY
7 WASELEY HL WY
8 MAIDEN CT
9 NEATSHEAD GARTH
58
10 BRIARWOOD CL
11 HEATHERWOOD CL
12 EASTER WOOD CL
13 CREDENHILL CL
14 THISTLEWOOD CT
15 HONLEY WOOD CL
147
For full street detail of the highlighted area see pages 141 and 142.

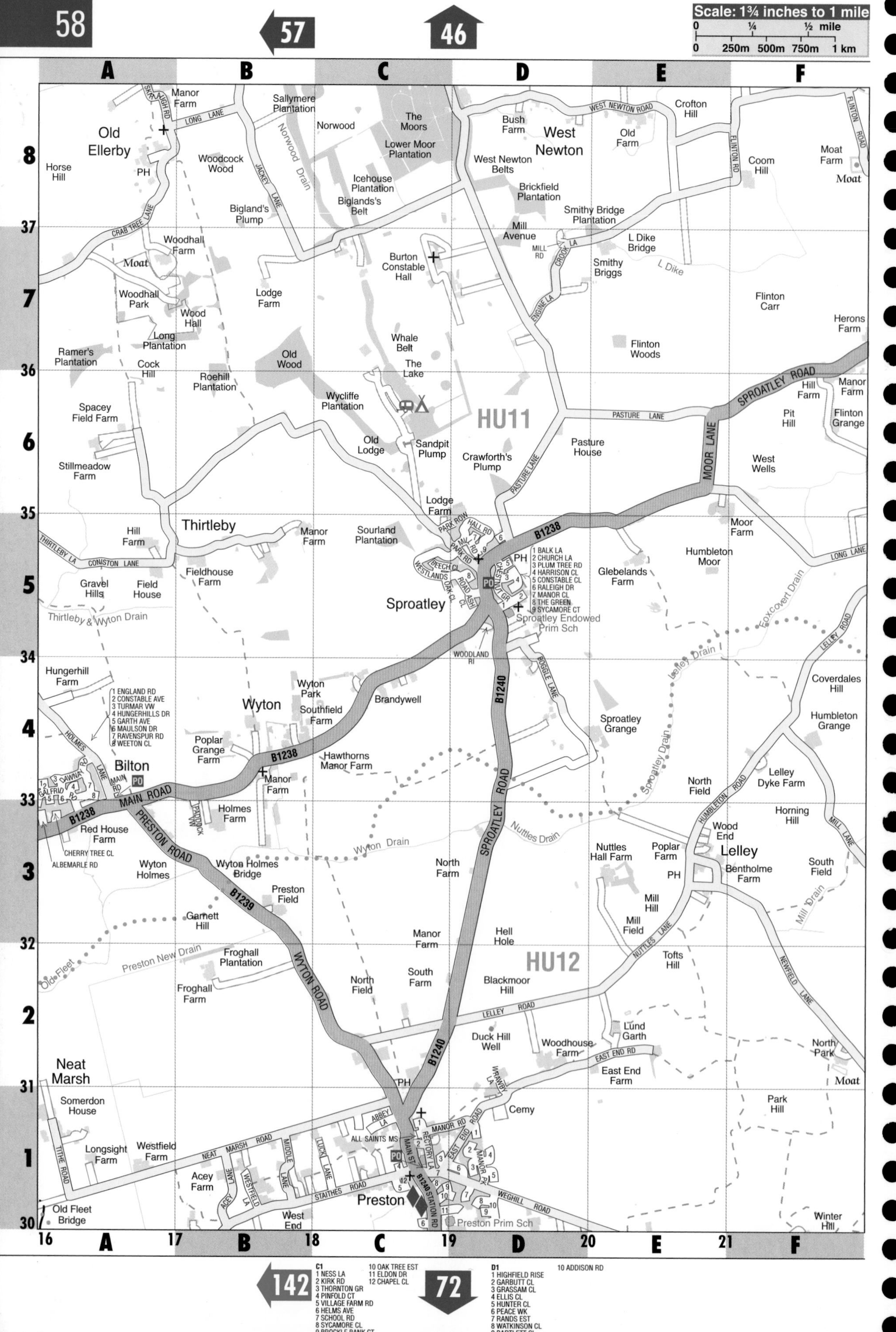

C1
1 NESS LA
2 KIRK RD
3 THORNTON GR
4 PINFOLD CT
5 VILLAGE FARM RD
6 HELMS AVE
7 SCHOOL RD
8 SYCAMORE CL
9 BROCKLE BANK CT
10 OAK TREE EST
11 ELDON DR
12 CHAPEL CL

D1
1 HIGHFIELD RISE
2 GARBUTT CL
3 GRASSAM CL
4 ELLIS CL
5 HUNTER CL
6 PEACE WK
7 RANDS EST
8 WATKINSON CL
9 BARTLETT CL
10 ADDISON RD

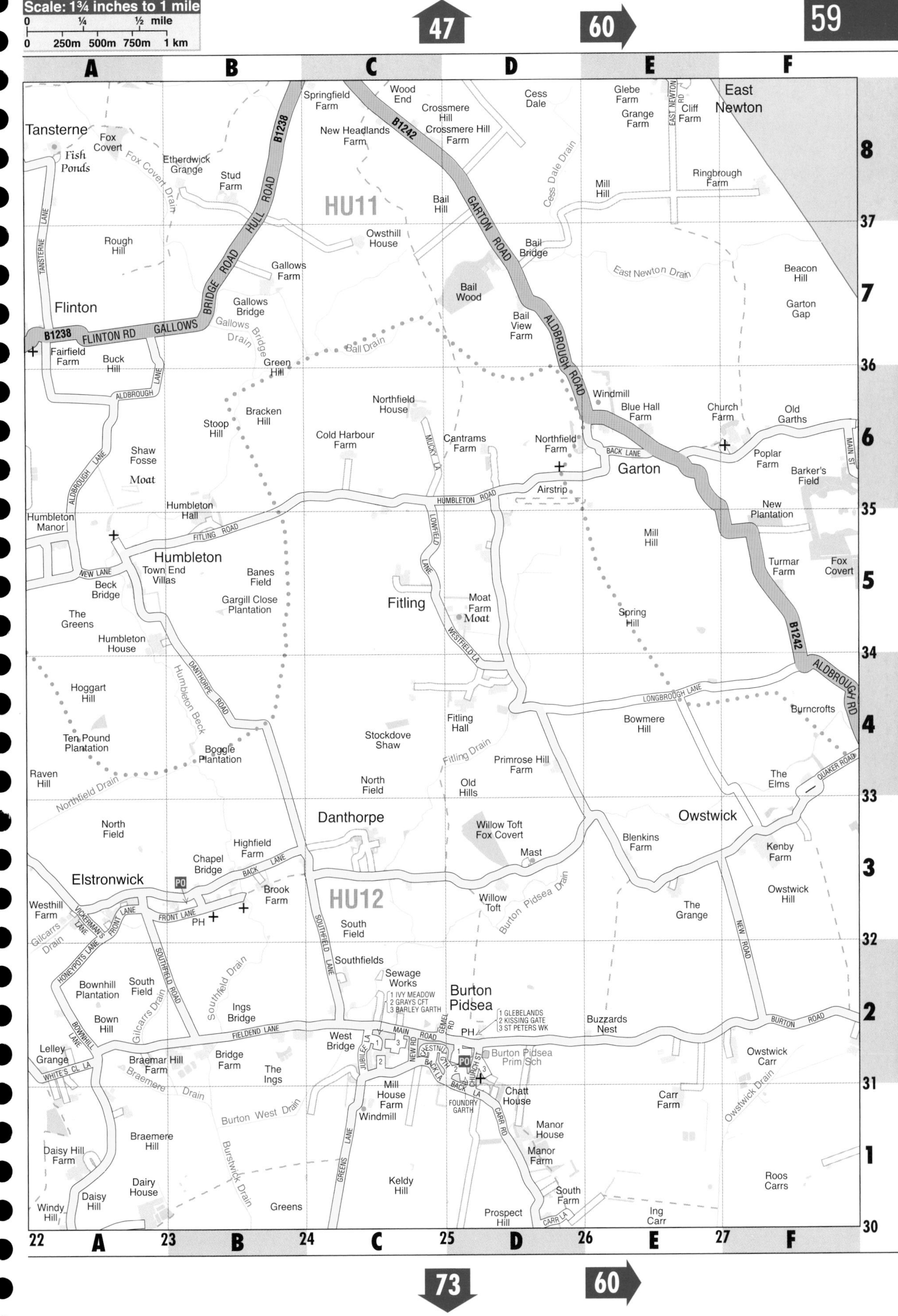

Scale: 1¾ inches to 1 mile
47
60
Tansterne
Fox Covert
Fish Ponds
Etherdwick Grange
Stud Farm
Springfield Farm
Wood End
Crossmere Hill
Crossmere Hill Farm
New Headlands Farm
Cess Dale
Glebe Farm
Grange Farm
Cliff Farm
East Newton
HU11
Owsthill House
Bail Hill
Mill Hill
Ringbrough Farm
Rough Hill
Gallows Farm
Bail Bridge
East Newton Drain
Beacon Hill
Bail Wood
Garton Gap
Flinton
Gallows Bridge
Bail View Farm
Fairfield Farm
Buck Hill
Green Hill
Ball Drain
Windmill
Blue Hall Farm
Church Farm
Old Garths
Northfield House
Bracken Hill
Stoop Hill
Cold Harbour Farm
Cantrams Farm
Northfield Farm
Garton
Poplar Farm
Barker's Field
Shaw Fosse
Moat
Airstrip
New Plantation
Humbleton Hall
Humbleton Manor
Mill Hill
Humbleton
Town End Villas
Banes Field
Turmar Farm
Fox Covert
Beck Bridge
Gargill Close Plantation
Fitling
Moat Farm
Spring Hill
The Greens
Humbleton House
Hoggart Hill
Fitling Hall
Bowmere Hill
Burncrofts
Ten Pound Plantation
Stockdove Shaw
Boggle Plantation
Primrose Hill Farm
Raven Hill
North Field
Old Hills
The Elms
Northfield Drain
North Field
Danthorpe
Willow Toft Fox Covert
Owstwick
Highfield Farm
Mast
Blenkins Farm
Kenby Farm
Chapel Bridge
Elstronwick
Brook Farm
HU12
Willow Toft
The Grange
Owstwick Hill
Westhill Farm
South Field
Southfields
Bownhill Plantation
South Field
Sewage Works
1 IVY MEADOW
2 GRAYS CFT
3 BARLEY GARTH
Burton Pidsea
1 GLEBELANDS
2 KISSING GATE
3 ST PETERS WK
Ings Bridge
Bown Hill
Buzzards Nest
West Bridge
Lelley Grange
Braemar Hill Farm
Bridge Farm
The Ings
Burton Pidsea Prim Sch
Owstwick Carr
Mill House Farm
Chatt House
Carr Farm
Windmill
Manor House
Braemere Hill
Daisy Hill Farm
Manor Farm
Roos Carrs
Dairy House
Keldy Hill
South Farm
Daisy Hill
Windy Hill
Greens
Prospect Hill
Ing Carr
73
60

A   B   C   D   E   F

8

37

7

36

Great Parks
The Mount
Moat
Moat Farm

6

Sewage Works

35

Grimston Garth

Grimston Park

Bracken Hill

5

HU11

Norwood Plantation

34

Admiral Storr's Tower

Glebe Farm

Tunstall Pastures

TOWER ROAD
Mayfield Farm
Mount Farm
+ Hilston
Pit (dis)

4

QUAKER RD

HOGSEA LANE

Gills Mere

33

B1242

The Furze

Roos Furze

East Furze

Monkwith

ALDBROUGH ROAD

North End Farm

Mill Hill

PASTURES LANE

3

West Furze

Glebe Farm

HU12

RECTORY LA

Church Farm

32

Furze Road

Furze Farm

Westhill Farm
Town Farm

+

Manor Farm

SEASIDE LANE

Elmtree Farm

Carr Farm

Tunstall

Kiln House

SEASIDE LANE

2

BURTON ROAD

Poplar Farm

ROSTUN ROAD

Kiln Well

KILNHOUSE LA

PH

NORTH END RD

Cliff Farm

North End Villas

PINFOLD LA

North End

East Field

Tunstall Hall

Sewage Works

31

Hill Top Farm

Cote Farm

Roos CE Prim Sch

MAIN ST

1 HINCH GARTH
2 BEECHWOOD VWS
3 PILMAR LA
4 BECKSIDE MANOR

SOUTHFIELD LANE

Round Close Plantation

Tunstall Drain

RECTORY RD

GREENACRES
PK

1

Roos

PH

PILMAR LANE

B1242

INGLEPOOL CORNER

HU19

Redhouse Farm

SOUTH END ELM RD
SOUTH PK GARTH

EASTFIELD EST

HODGSON LA

CHESTNUT GARTH

CAMP END LA

Tedder Hill

Cherry Hill

WITHERNSEA RD

Broom Hill

THIRTLE BR LA

Thirtle Bridge

30

Burnham Carrs

Butcher Bridge

Renish

28   A   29   B   30   C   31   D   32   E   33   F

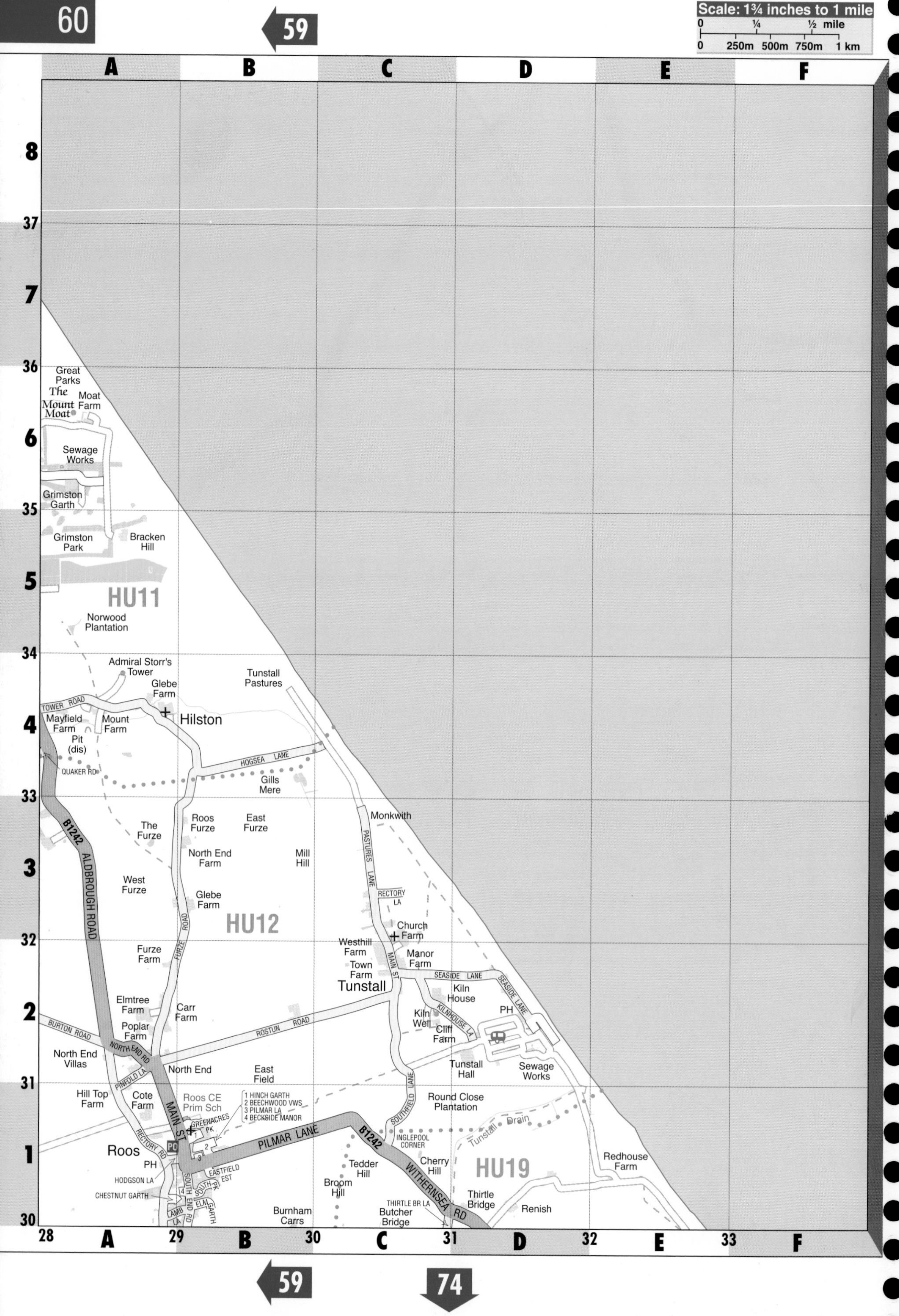

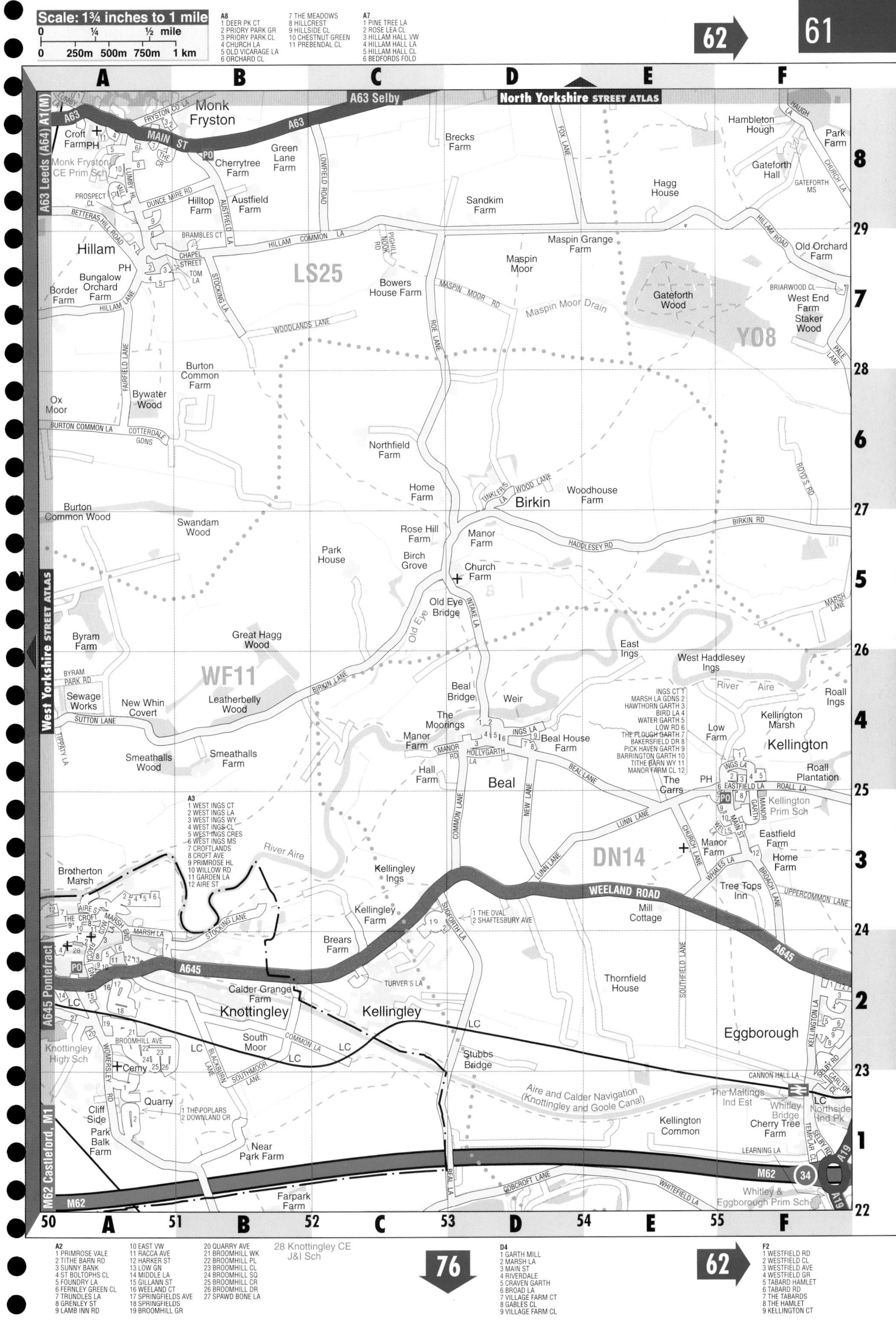

Scale: 1¾ inches to 1 mile

0   ¼   ½ mile

0   250m 500m 750m 1 km

A8
1 DEER PK CT
2 PRIORY PARK GR
3 PRIORY PARK CL
4 CHURCH LA
5 OLD VICARAGE LA
6 ORCHARD CL

7 THE MEADOWS
8 HILLCREST
9 HILLSIDE CL
10 CHESTNUT GREEN
11 PREBENDAL CL

A7
1 PINE TREE LA
2 ROSE LEA CL
3 HILLAM HALL VW
4 HILLAM HALL CL
5 HILLAM HALL CL
6 BEDFORDS FOLD

North Yorkshire STREET ATLAS

West Yorkshire STREET ATLAS

A3
1 WEST INGS CT
2 WEST INGS LA
3 WEST INGS WY
4 WEST INGS CL
5 WEST INGS CRES
6 WEST INGS MS
7 CROFTLANDS
8 CROFT AVE
9 PRIMROSE HL
10 WILLOW RD
11 GARDEN LA
12 AIRE ST

INGS CT 1
MARSH LA GDNS 2
HAWTHORN GARTH 3
BIRD LA 4
WATER GARTH 5
LOW RD 6
THE PLOUGH GARTH 7
BAKERSFIELD DR 8
PICK HAVEN GARTH 9
BARRINGTON GARTH 10
TITHE BARN WY 11
MANOR FARM CL 12

1 THE OVAL
2 SHAFTESBURY AVE

A2
1 PRIMROSE VALE
2 TITHE BARN RD
3 SUNNY BANK
4 ST BOLTOPHS CL
5 FOUNDRY LA
6 FERNLEY GREEN CL
7 TRUNDLES LA
8 GRENLEY ST
9 LAMB INN RD

10 EAST VW
11 RACCA AVE
12 HARKER ST
13 LOW GN
14 MIDDLE LA
15 GILLANN ST
16 WEELAND CT
17 SPRINGFIELDS AVE
18 SPRINGFIELDS
19 BROOMHILL GR

20 QUARRY AVE
21 BROOMHILL WK
22 BROOMHILL PL
23 BROOMHILL CL
24 BROOMHILL SQ
25 BROOMHILL CR
26 BROOMHILL DR
27 SPAWD BONE LA

28 Knottingley CE
J&I Sch

D4
1 GARTH MILL
2 MARSH LA
3 MAIN ST
4 RIVERDALE
5 CRAVEN GARTH
6 BROAD LA
7 VILLAGE FARM CT
8 GABLES CL
9 VILLAGE FARM CL

F2
1 WESTFIELD RD
2 WESTFIELD CL
3 WESTFIELD AVE
4 WESTFIELD GR
5 TABARD HAMLET
6 TABARD RD
7 THE TABARDS
8 THE HAMLET
9 KELLINGTON CT

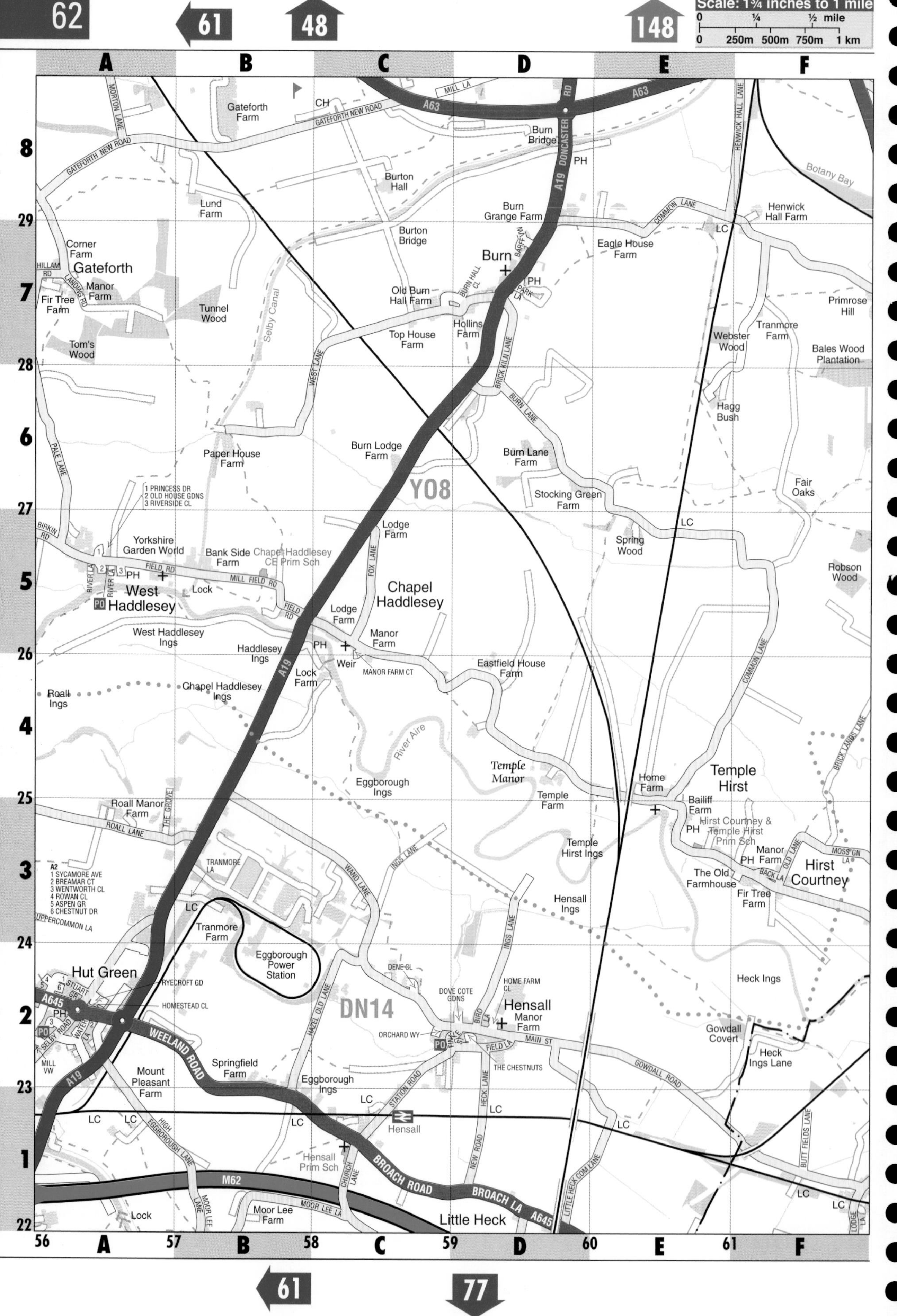
61
48
148
Scale: 1¾ inches to 1 mile
0 ¼ ½ mile
0 250m 500m 750m 1 km
A B C D E F
Gateforth Farm
CH
Burn Bridge
Burton Hall
Lund Farm
Burn Grange Farm
Henwick Hall Farm
Botany Bay
Corner Farm
Gateforth
Burton Bridge
Eagle House Farm
Burn
Manor Farm
Fir Tree Farm
Old Burn Hall Farm
Tunnel Wood
Selby Canal
Hollins Farm
Top House Farm
Webster Wood
Tranmore Farm
Primrose Hill
Tom's Wood
Bales Wood Plantation
Hagg Bush
Paper House Farm
Burn Lodge Farm
Burn Lane Farm
YO8
Stocking Green Farm
Fair Oaks
Lodge Farm
Spring Wood
Yorkshire Garden World
Bank Side Farm
Chapel Haddlesey CE Prim Sch
Robson Wood
West Haddlesey
Lock
Chapel Haddlesey
Lodge Farm
Manor Farm
West Haddlesey Ings
Haddlesey Ings
Weir
Lock Farm
Eastfield House Farm
Roall Ings
Chapel Haddlesey Ings
River Aire
Temple Manor
Eggborough Ings
Home Farm
Temple Hirst
Temple Farm
Bailiff Farm
Roall Manor Farm
Hirst Courtney & Temple Hirst Prim Sch
Temple Hirst Ings
Manor Farm
Hirst Courtney
The Old Farmhouse
Fir Tree Farm
Hensall Ings
Tranmore Farm
Eggborough Power Station
Heck Ings
Hut Green
DN14
Hensall
Manor Farm
Gowdall Covert
Heck Ings Lane
Mount Pleasant Farm
Springfield Farm
Eggborough Ings
Hensall
Hensall Prim Sch
Moor Lee Farm
Lock
Little Heck
1 PRINCESS DR
2 OLD HOUSE GDNS
3 RIVERSIDE CL
A2
1 SYCAMORE AVE
2 BREAMAR CT
3 WENTWORTH CL
4 ROWAN CL
5 ASPEN GR
6 CHESTNUT DR
A63
A19
A645
M62
DONCASTER RD
GATEFORTH NEW ROAD
MILL LA
COMMON LANE
HENWICK HALL LANE
MORTON LANE
WEST LANE
BRICK KILN LANE
BURN LANE
PALE LANE
FOX LANE
FIELD RD
MILL FIELD RD
ROALL LANE
THE GROVE
WAND LANE
INGS LANE
UPPERCOMMON LA
WEELAND ROAD
HAZEL OLD LANE
STATION ROAD
HECK LANE
NEW ROAD
MAIN ST
GOWDALL ROAD
BROACH ROAD
BROACH LA
CHURCH LANE
MOOR LEE LANE
HIGH EGGBOROUGH LANE
LITTLE HECK COM LANE
BUTT FIELDS LANE
BACK LA
OLD LANE
MOSS GN LA
BRICK LANDS LANE
LODGE LA
RYECROFT GD
HOMESTEAD CL
HOME FARM CL
DOVE COTE GDNS
ORCHARD WY
THE CHESTNUTS
MANOR FARM CT
TRANMORE LA
8 29 7 28 6 27 5 26 4 25 3 24 2 23 1 22
56 57 58 59 60 61
61
77

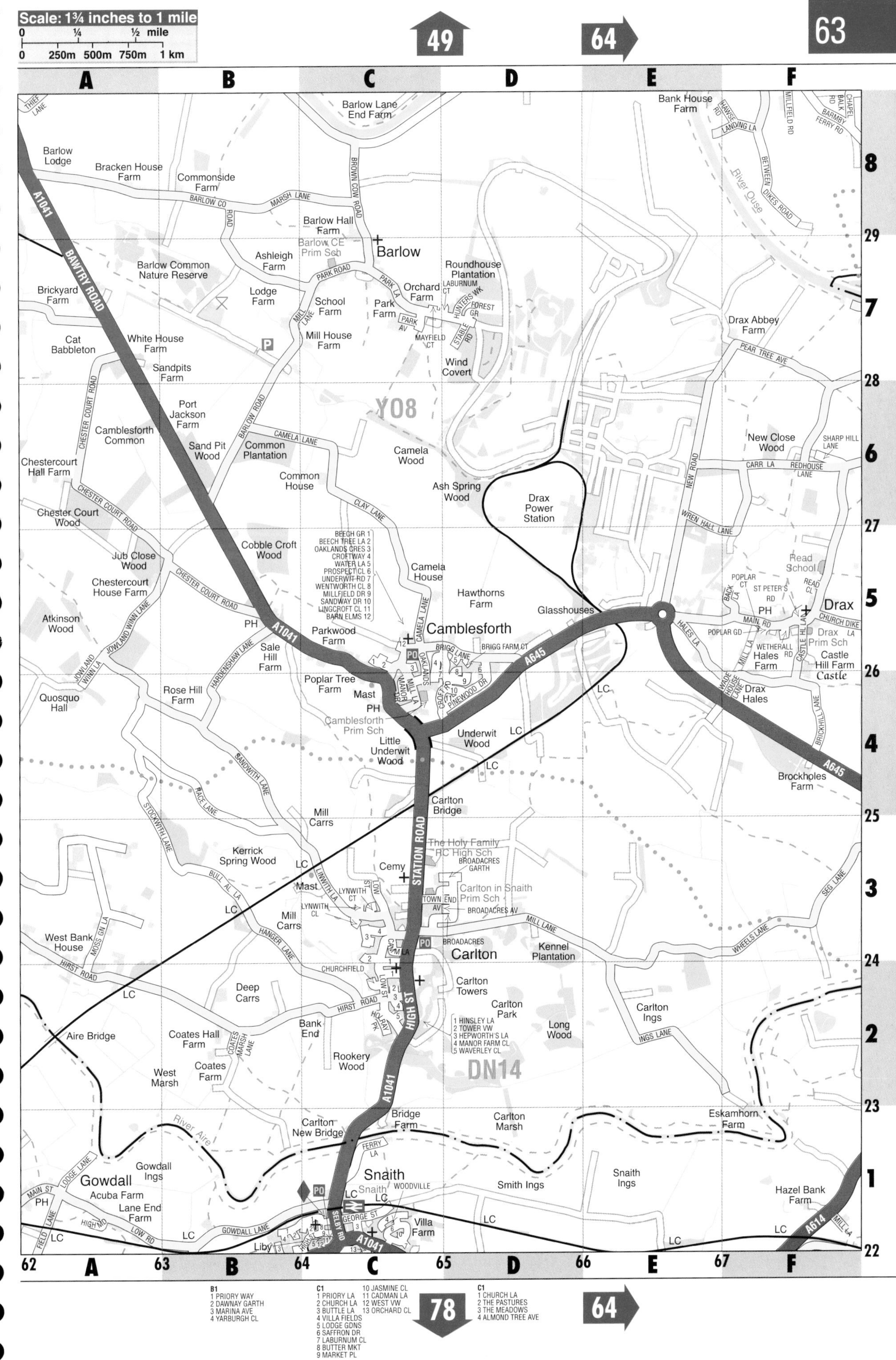

B1
1 PRIORY WAY
2 DAWNAY GARTH
3 MARINA AVE
4 YARBURGH CL

C1
1 PRIORY LA
2 CHURCH LA
3 BUTTLE LA
4 VILLA FIELDS
5 LODGE GDNS
6 SAFFRON DR
7 LABURNUM CL
8 BUTTER MKT
9 MARKET PL
10 JASMINE CL
11 CADMAN LA
12 WEST VW
13 ORCHARD CL

C1
1 CHURCH LA
2 THE PASTURES
3 THE MEADOWS
4 ALMOND TREE AVE

Scale: 1¾ inches to 1 mile

0   ¼   ½   mile
0 250m 500m 750m 1 km

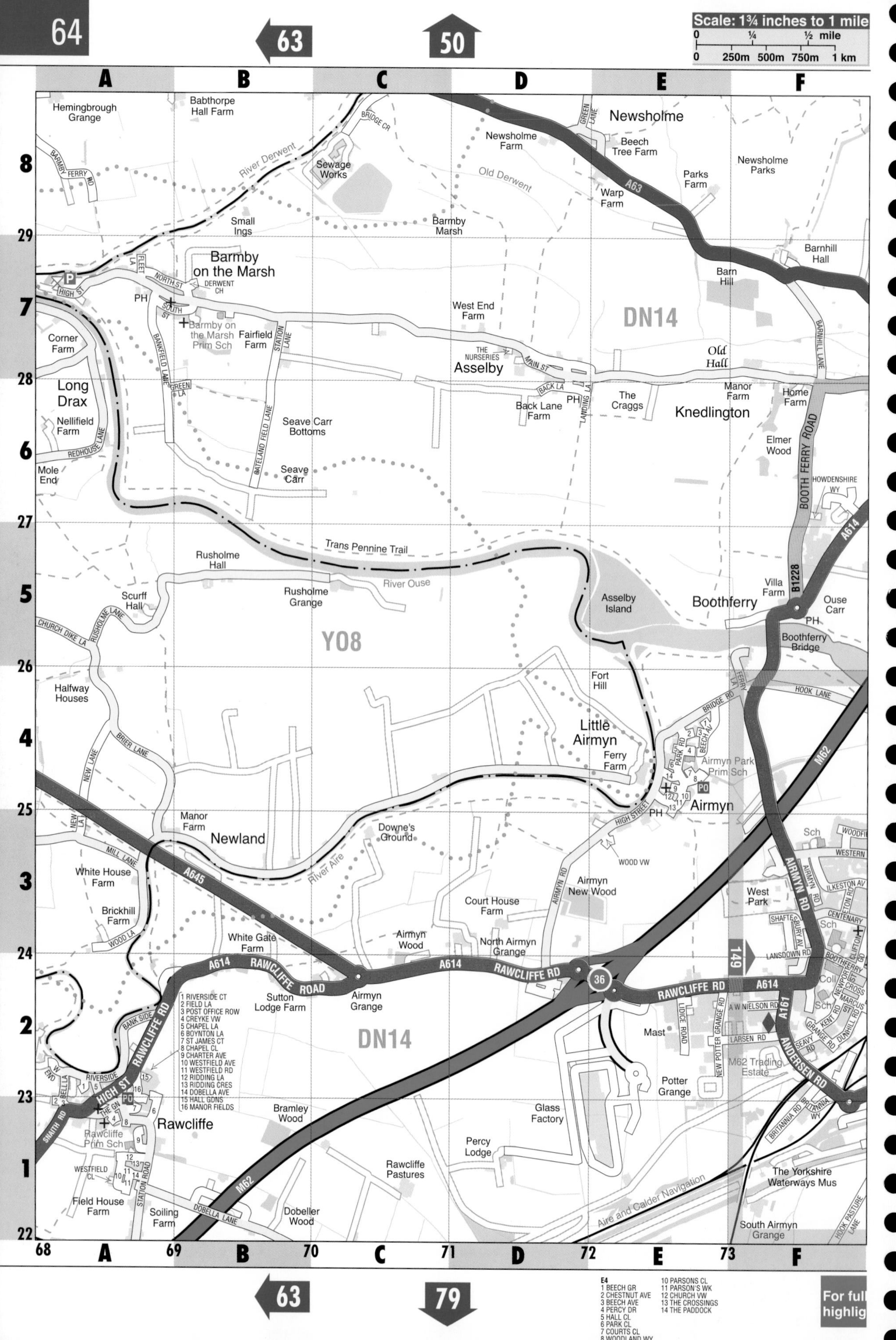

A   B   C   D   E   F

8   Hemingbrough Grange   Babthorpe Hall Farm   River Derwent   Sewage Works   Old Derwent   Newsholme   Newsholme Farm   Beech Tree Farm   Parks Farm   Newsholme Parks

29   Small Ings   Barmby Marsh   Warp Farm   A63   Barn Hill   Barnhill Hall

7   Barmby on the Marsh   FLEET LA   NORTH ST   P   PH   SOUTH ST   Barmby on the Marsh Prim Sch   DERWENT CH   Fairfield Farm   STATION LANE   West End Farm   DN14   Old Hall   BARNHILL LANE

28   Corner Farm   HIGH ST   BANKFIELD LANE   GREEN LA   THE NURSERIES   Asselby   MAIN ST   BACK LA   LANDING LA   PH   The Craggs   Manor Farm   Knedlington   Home Farm   BOOTH FERRY ROAD

6   Long Drax   Nellifield Farm   REDHOUSE LANE   OWTELAND FIELD LANE   Seave Carr Bottoms   Back Lane Farm   Elmer Wood   HOWDENSHIRE WY   A614

Mole End   Seave Carr

27   Trans Pennine Trail   Ouse Carr   B1228

5   Scurff Hall   Rusholme Hall   RUSHOLME LANE   Rusholme Grange   River Ouse   Asselby Island   Villa Farm   Boothferry   Ouse Carr   PH   Boothferry Bridge

CHURCH DIKE LA   YO8

26   Halfway Houses   Fort Hill   FERRY RD   HOOK LANE

4   NEW LANE   BRIER LANE   Little Airmyn   Ferry Farm   BRIDGE RD   Airmyn Park Prim Sch   PO   M62

25   NEW LA   Manor Farm   Newland   Downe's Ground   PARK RD   BEECH WY   HIGH STREET   PH   Airmyn   WOODFI   Sch   WESTERN

3   MILL LANE   White House Farm   A645   River Aire   WOOD VW   AIRMYN RD   Airmyn New Wood   West Park   AIRMYN RD   ILKESTON AV   Sch   CENTENARY

Brickhill Farm   WOOD LA   Court House Farm   Airmyn Wood   SHAFTE   BOOTHFERRY   Sch

24   White Gate Farm   A614   North Airmyn Grange   LANSDOWN RD   149   A614   A161   Coll

2   RAWCLIFFE ROAD   Sutton Lodge Farm   Airmyn Grange   A614 RAWCLIFFE RD   36   RAWCLIFFE RD   NEW POTTER GRANGE RD   LODGE ROAD   LARSEN RD   Mast   A W Nielson Rd   MARCUS

1 RIVERSIDE CT   BANK SIDE   RAWCLIFFE RD   DN14   1 Potter Grange   M62 Trading Estate   BRITANNIA RD   ANDERSEN RD
2 FIELD LA
3 POST OFFICE ROW
4 CREYKE VW
5 CHAPEL LA
6 BOYNTON LA
7 ST JAMES CT
8 CHAPEL CL
9 CHARTER AVE
10 WESTFIELD AVE
11 WESTFIELD RD
12 RIDDING LA
13 RIDDING CRES
14 DOBELLA AVE
15 HALL GDNS
16 MANOR FIELDS

23   RIVERSIDE   THE GN   PO   Glass Factory   Bramley Wood

SMITH RD   HIGH ST   Rawcliffe Prim Sch   Rawcliffe   Percy Lodge

1   WESTFIELD CL   Field House Farm   STATION ROAD   M62   Soiling Farm   DOBELLA LANE   Dobeller Wood   Rawcliffe Pastures   The Yorkshire Waterways Mus   HOOK PASTURE LANE

22   Aire and Calder Navigation   South Airmyn Grange

68   A   69   B   70   C   71   D   72   E   73   F

E4
1 BEECH GR
2 CHESTNUT AVE
3 BEECH AVE
4 PERCY DR
5 HALL CL
6 PARK CL
7 COURTS CL
8 WOODLAND WY
9 ST DAVID'S VW
10 PARSONS CL
11 PARSON'S WK
12 CHURCH VW
13 THE CROSSINGS
14 THE PADDOCK

For full highlig

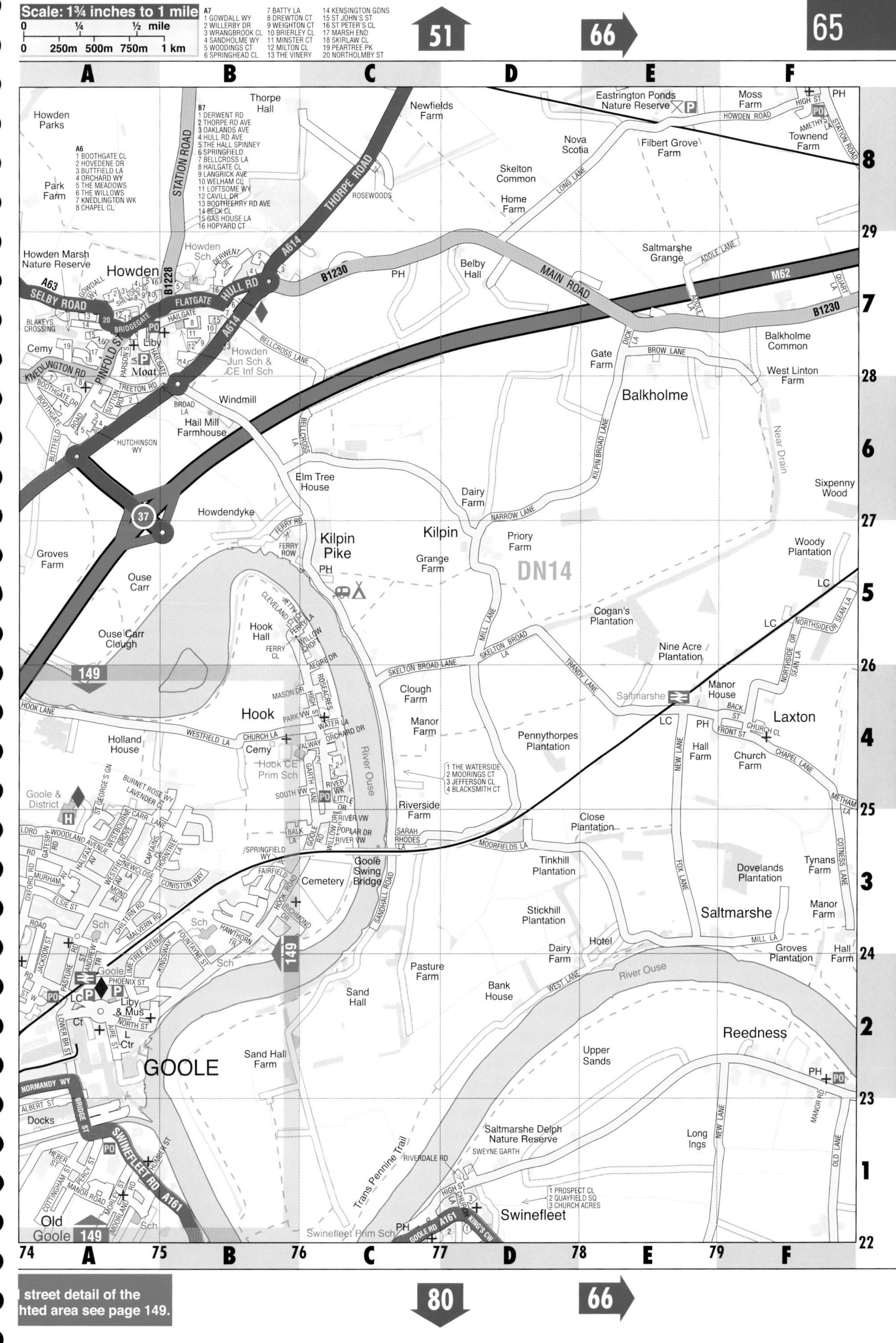

65
Scale: 1¾ inches to 1 mile
0 ¼ ½ mile
0 250m 500m 750m 1 km
A7
1 GOWDALL WY
2 WILLERBY DR
3 WRANGBROOK CL
4 SANDHOLME WY
5 WOODINGS CT
6 SPRINGHEAD CL
7 BATTY LA
8 DREWTON CT
9 WEIGHTON CT
10 BRIERLEY CL
11 MINSTER CT
12 MILTON CL
13 THE VINERY
14 KENSINGTON GDNS
15 ST JOHN'S ST
16 ST PETER'S CL
17 MARSH END
18 SKIRLAW CL
19 PEARTREE PK
20 NORTHOLMBY ST
51
66
A
B
C
D
E
F
Howden Parks
A6
1 BOOTHGATE CL
2 HOVEDENE DR
3 BUTTFIELD LA
4 ORCHARD WY
5 THE MEADOWS
6 THE WILLOWS
7 KNEDLINGTON WK
8 CHAPEL CL
Park Farm
STATION ROAD
B7
1 DERWENT RD
2 THORPE RD AVE
3 OAKLANDS AVE
4 HULL RD AVE
5 THE HALL SPINNEY
6 SPRINGFIELD
7 BELLCROSS LA
8 HAILGATE CL
9 LANGRICK AVE
10 WELHAM CL
11 LOFTSOME WY
12 CAVILL DR
13 BOOTHFERRY RD AVE
14 BECK CL
15 GAS HOUSE LA
16 HOPYARD CT
Thorpe Hall
THORPE ROAD
ROSEWOODS
Newfields Farm
Eastrington Ponds Nature Reserve
Moss Farm
HIGH ST
PH
HOWDEN ROAD
Townend Farm
STATION ROAD
Nova Scotia
Filbert Grove Farm
Skelton Common
LONG LANE
Home Farm
8
29
Howden Marsh Nature Reserve
Howden
Howden Sch
A63
SELBY ROAD
B1228
HULL RD
A614
B1230
PH
Belby Hall
MAIN ROAD
Saltmarshe Grange
ADDLE LANE
M62
B1230
7
BLAKEYS CROSSING
BRIDGEGATE
FLATGATE
HAILGATE
Cemy
PINFOLD ST
Liby
Moat
Howden Jun Sch & CE Inf Sch
BELLCROSS LANE
DICK LA
BROW LANE
Gate Farm
Balkholme Common
West Linton Farm
28
KNEDLINGTON RD
TREETON RD
BROAD LA
Windmill
Hail Mill Farmhouse
HUTCHINSON WY
BUTTFIELD
Balkholme
KILPIN BROAD LANE
Near Drain
BELLCROSS LA
6
Elm Tree House
Dairy Farm
Sixpenny Wood
37
Howdendyke
FERRY RD
FERRY ROW
NARROW LANE
Kilpin Pike
Kilpin
Priory Farm
27
Groves Farm
PH
Grange Farm
DN14
Woody Plantation
Ouse Carr
LC
5
Hook Hall
Cogan's Plantation
MILL LANE
Ouse Carr Clough
FERRY CL
SKELTON BROAD LA
LC
NORTHSIDE OR SEAN LA
Nine Acre Plantation
149
SKELTON BROAD LANE
TRANDY LANE
26
HOOK LANE
MASON DR
Hook
HIGH ST
Clough Farm
Saltmarshe
Manor House
BACK ST
Laxton
WESTFIELD LA
CHURCH LA
WATER LA
ORCHARD DR
Manor Farm
LC
PH
FRONT ST
CHURCH CL
Holland House
Cemy
Pennythorpes Plantation
Hall Farm
Church Farm
CHAPEL LANE
4
Hook CE Prim Sch
River Ouse
1 THE WATERSIDE
2 MOORINGS CT
3 JEFFERSON CL
4 BLACKSMITH CT
NEW LANE
Goole & District
SOUTH VW
Riverside Farm
METHAM LA
25
H
SARAH RHODES LA
Close Plantation
MOORFIELDS LA
WOODLAND AVENUE
SPRINGFIELD WY
Goole Swing Bridge
Tinkhill Plantation
Dovelands Plantation
Tynans Farm
COTNESS LANE
FOX LANE
Cemetery
CONISTON WAY
HOOK ROAD
SANDHALL ROAD
3
ELSIE ST
Sch
Sch
Stickhill Plantation
Saltmarshe
Manor Farm
Hotel
MILL LA
Groves Plantation
Hall Farm
24
149
Dairy Farm
Goole
PHOENIX ST
Sch
Pasture Farm
WEST LANE
River Ouse
Bank House
Sand Hall
LC
Liby & Mus
NORTH ST
Ct
L Ctr
2
Reedness
Upper Sands
GOOLE
Sand Hall Farm
PH
NORMANDY WY
ALBERT ST
BRIDGE ST
23
Docks
MANOR RD
SWINEFLEET RD
A161
Saltmarshe Delph Nature Reserve
SWEYNE GARTH
Long Ings
NEW LANE
OLD LANE
Trans Pennine Trail
RIVERDALE RD
1
MANOR ROAD
HIGH ST
1 PROSPECT CL
2 QUAYFIELD SQ
3 CHURCH ACRES
Old Goole
149
PH
A161
Swinefleet Prim Sch
Swinefleet
22
74
75
76
77
78
79
street detail of the
hted area see page 149.
80
66

65
52

D8
1 SANDHOLME CL
2 THE PEPPERCORNS
3 VICTORIA DR
4 ST STEPHEN'S CRES
5 HANSARD CRES
6 HANSARD DR
7 WILLOW GN
8 CHAPEL MEADOWS
9 BISHOP CT
10 MANOR DR
11 CHAPEL GARTH
12 WESTBROOK RD
13 THE PADDOCK
14 SYCAMORE CL
15 CHESTNUT DR
16 CHERRY CT
17 LABURNUM WK
18 CLAYTONS FOLD
19 LINDEN CL
20 THE ACORNS

Scale: 1¾ inches to 1 mile
0 ¼ ½ mile
0 250m 500m 750m 1 km

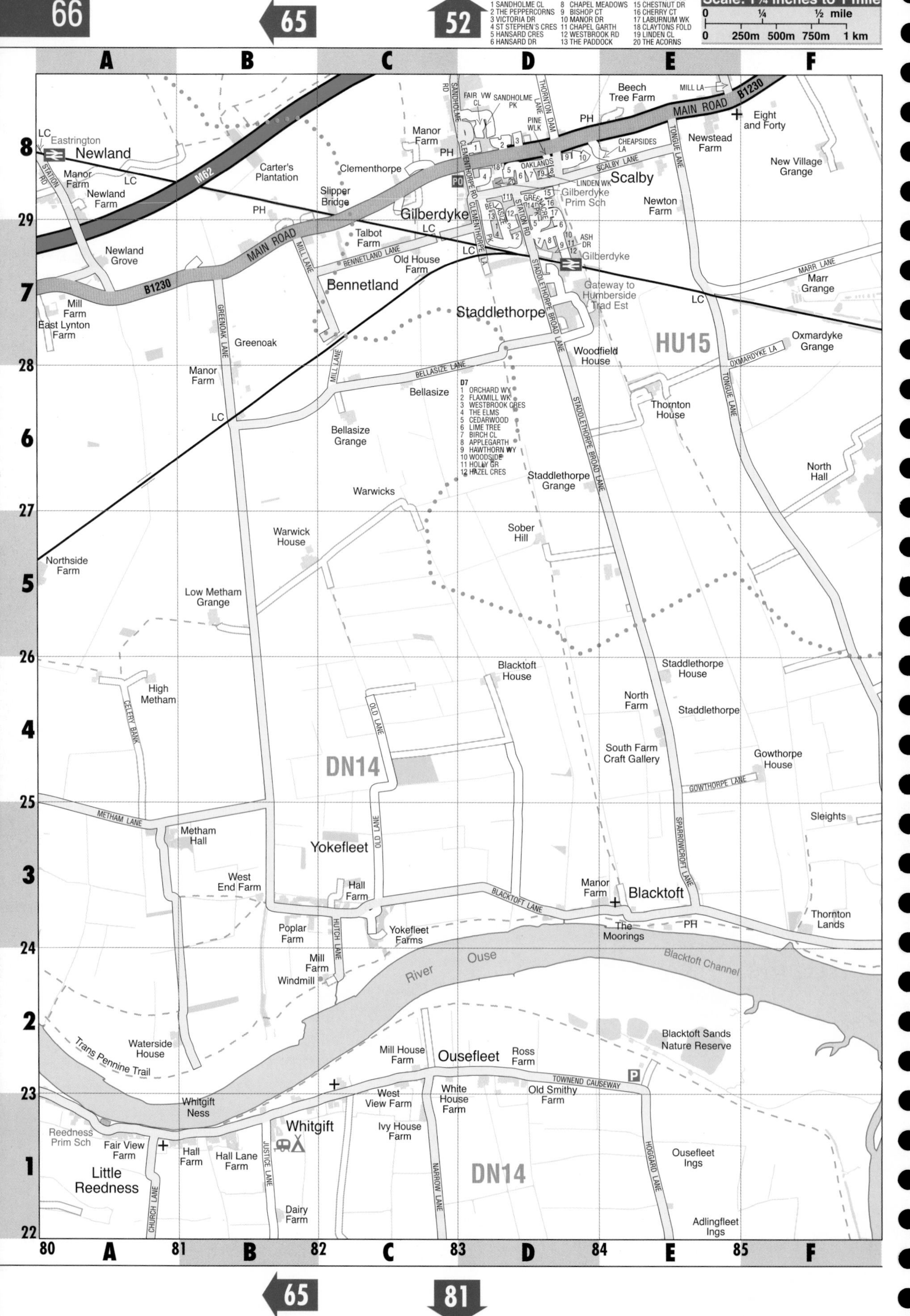

65
81

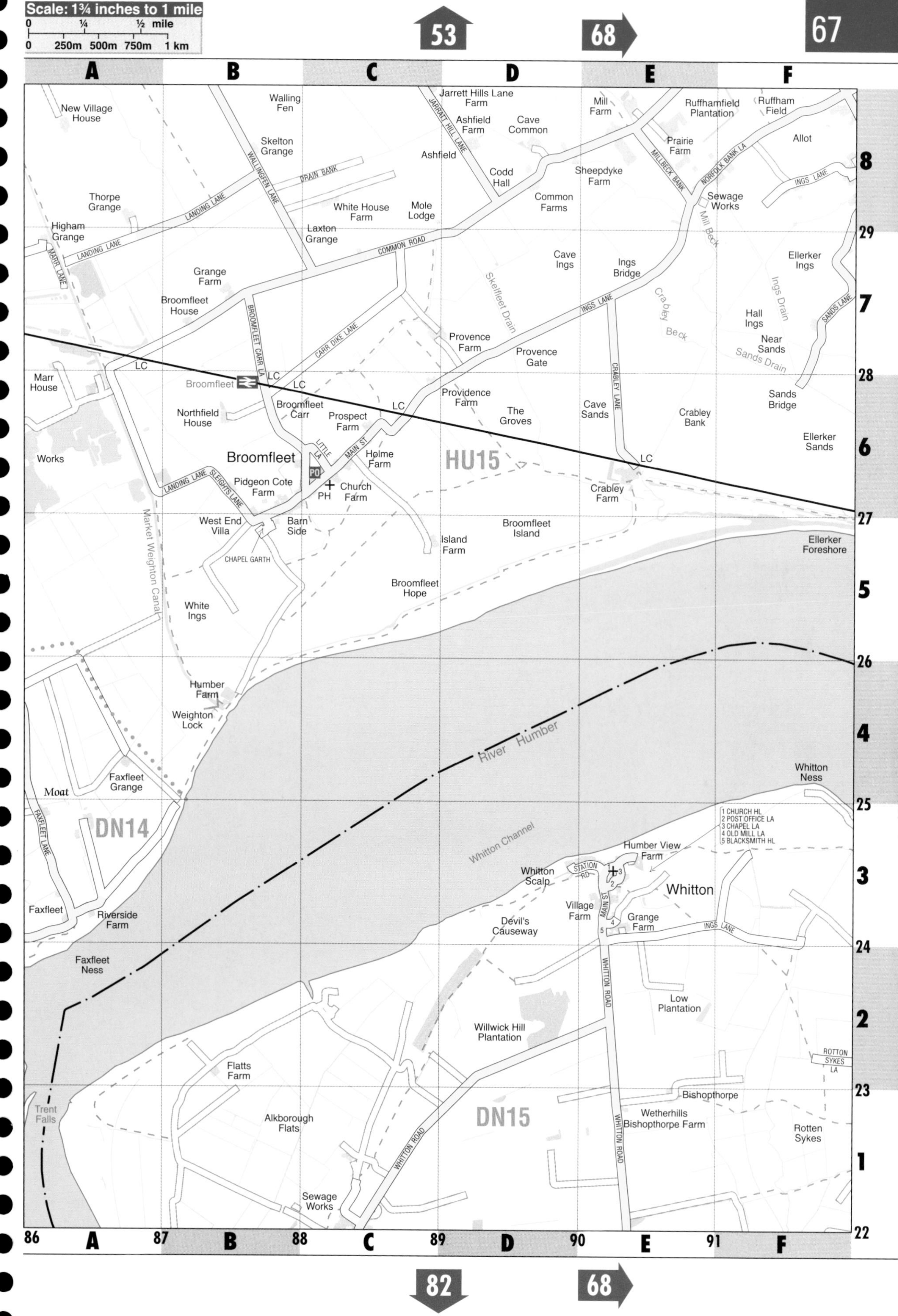
Scale: 1¾ inches to 1 mile
53
68
82
68
Broomfleet
Whitton
HU15
DN14
DN15
River Humber
Whitton Channel
New Village House
Walling Fen
Skelton Grange
Jarrett Hills Lane Farm
Ashfield Farm
Cave Common
Ashfield
Codd Hall
Mill Farm
Ruffhamfield Plantation
Ruffham Field
Prairie Farm
Allot
Sheepdyke Farm
Sewage Works
Thorpe Grange
Higham Grange
White House Farm
Mole Lodge
Laxton Grange
Common Farms
Cave Ings
Ings Bridge
Ellerker Ings
Grange Farm
Broomfleet House
Provence Farm
Provence Gate
Hall Ings
Near Sands
Marr House
Northfield House
Broomfleet Carr
Prospect Farm
Providence Farm
The Groves
Cave Sands
Crabley Bank
Sands Bridge
Ellerker Sands
Works
Holme Farm
Pidgeon Cote Farm
Church Farm
Crabley Farm
West End Villa
Barn Side
Island Farm
Broomfleet Island
Ellerker Foreshore
Broomfleet Hope
White Ings
Humber Farm
Weighton Lock
Moat
Faxfleet Grange
Whitton Ness
Humber View Farm
Whitton Scalp
Village Farm
Grange Farm
Devil's Causeway
Faxfleet
Riverside Farm
Faxfleet Ness
Low Plantation
Willwick Hill Plantation
Flatts Farm
Bishopthorpe
Wetherhills Bishopthorpe Farm
Alkborough Flats
Rotten Sykes
Trent Falls
Sewage Works
1 CHURCH HL
2 POST OFFICE LA
3 CHAPEL LA
4 OLD MILL LA
5 BLACKSMITH HL

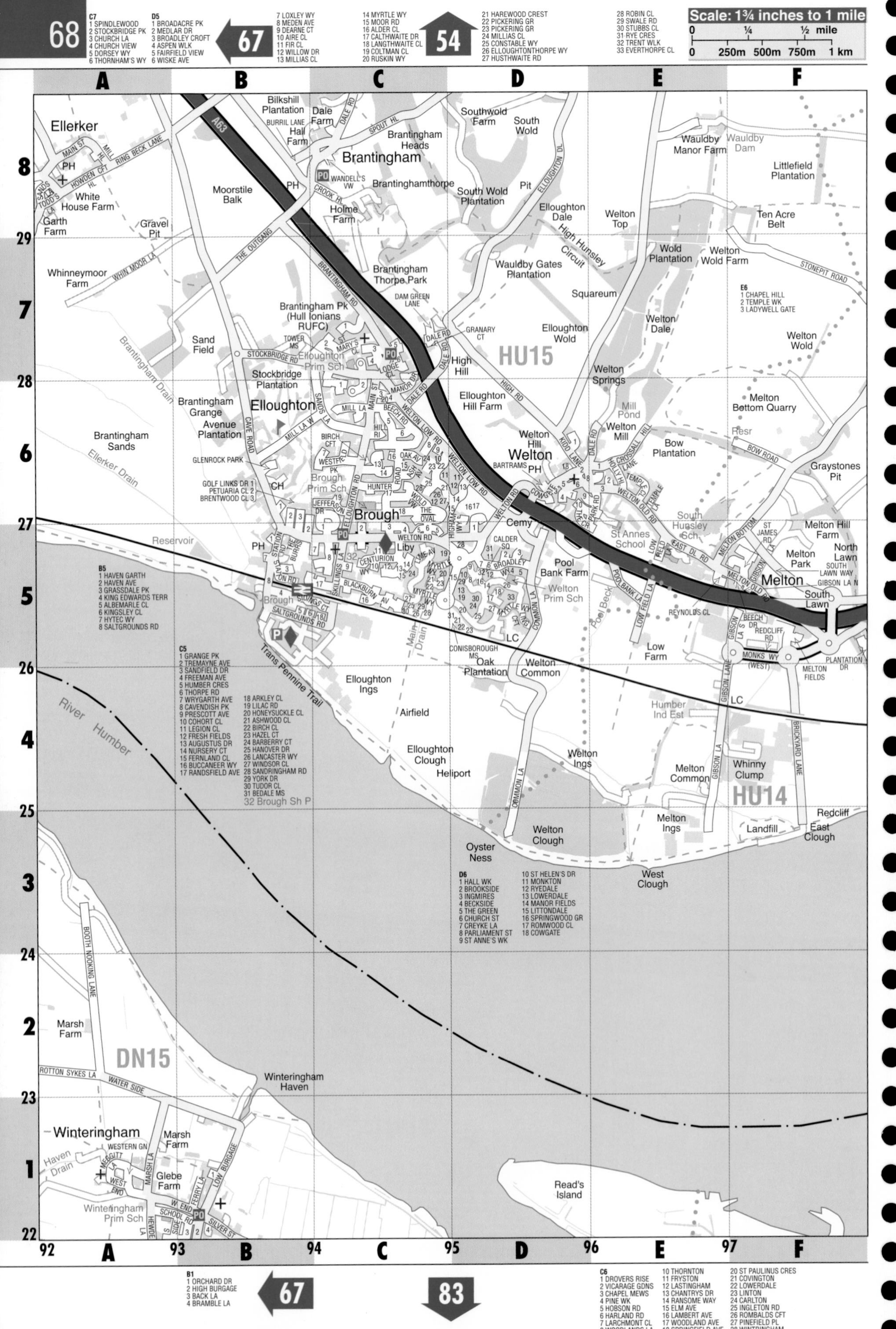

68
C7
1 SPINDLEWOOD
2 STOCKBRIDGE PK
3 CHURCH LA
4 CHURCH VIEW
5 DORSEY WY
6 THORNHAM'S WY
D5
1 BROADACRE PK
2 MEDLAR DR
3 BROADLEY CROFT
4 ASPEN WLK
5 FAIRFIELD VIEW
6 WISKE AVE
67
7 LOXLEY WY
8 MEDEN AVE
9 DEARNE CT
10 AIRE CL
11 FIR CL
12 WILLOW DR
13 MILLIAS CL
14 MYRTLE WY
15 MOOR RD
16 ALDER CL
17 CALTHWAITE DR
18 LANGTHWAITE CL
19 COLTMAN CL
20 RUSKIN WY
54
21 HAREWOOD CREST
22 PICKERING GR
23 PICKERING GR
24 MILLIAS CL
25 CONSTABLE WY
26 ELLOUGHTONTHORPE WY
27 HUSTHWAITE RD
28 ROBIN CL
29 SWALE RD
30 STUBBS CL
31 RYE CRES
32 TRENT WLK
33 EVERTHORPE CL
Scale: 1¾ inches to 1 mile
0 ¼ ½ mile
0 250m 500m 750m 1 km
A B C D E F
Ellerker
Bilkshill Plantation
Dale Farm
Hall Farm
Brantingham
Brantingham Heads
Southwold Farm
South Wold
Wauldby Manor Farm
Wauldby Dam
Littlefield Plantation
White House Farm
Garth Farm
Moorstile Balk
Gravel Pit
Brantinghamthorpe
Holme Farm
South Wold Plantation
Pit
Elloughton Dale
Welton Top
Ten Acre Belt
High Hunsley Circuit
Wold Plantation
Welton Wold Farm
Whinneymoor Farm
Brantingham Thorpe Park
Wauldby Gates Plantation
Squareum
STONEPIT ROAD
E6
1 CHAPEL HILL
2 TEMPLE WK
3 LADYWELL GATE
Brantingham Pk (Hull Ionians RUFC)
Welton Dale
Elloughton Wold
Welton Wold
Sand Field
Brantingham Drain
Elloughton Prim Sch
Stockbridge Plantation
High Hill
HU15
Welton Springs
Brantingham Grange
Elloughton
Elloughton Hill Farm
Mill Pond
Melton Bottom Quarry
Avenue Plantation
Brantingham Sands
Welton Hill
Welton Mill
Bow Plantation
Resr
Welton
Graystones Pit
Ellerker Drain
Brough Prim Sch
Brough
South Hunsley Sch
Melton Hill Farm
Cemy
St Annes School
Reservoir
Liby
Pool Bank Farm
Melton Park
North Lawn
Welton Prim Sch
Melton
South Lawn
B5
1 HAVEN GARTH
2 HAVEN AVE
3 GRASSDALE PK
4 KING EDWARDS TERR
5 ALBEMARLE CL
6 KINGSLEY CL
7 HYTEC WY
8 SALTGROUNDS RD
Brough
Poo Beck
Main Drain
Low Farm
C5
1 GRANGE PK
2 TREMAYNE AVE
3 SANDFIELD DR
4 FREEMAN AVE
5 HUMBER CRES
6 THORPE RD
7 WRYGARTH AVE
8 CAVENDISH PK
9 PRESCOTT AVE
10 COHORT CL
11 LEGION CL
12 FRESH FIELDS
13 AUGUSTUS DR
14 NURSERY CT
15 FERNLAND CL
16 BUCCANEER WY
17 RANDSFIELD AVE
18 ARKLEY CL
19 LILAC RD
20 HONEYSUCKLE CL
21 ASHWOOD CL
22 BIRCH CL
23 HAZEL CT
24 BARBERRY CT
25 HANOVER DR
26 LANCASTER WY
27 WINDSOR CL
28 SANDRINGHAM RD
29 YORK DR
30 TUDOR CL
31 BEDALE MS
32 Brough Sh P
Trans Pennine Trail
Oak Plantation
Welton Common
Elloughton Ings
River Humber
Airfield
Humber Ind Est
Elloughton Clough
Heliport
Welton Ings
Melton Common
Whinny Clump
HU14
Redcliff
East Clough
Welton Clough
Melton Ings
Landfill
Oyster Ness
West Clough
D6
1 HALL WK
2 BROOKSIDE
3 INGMIRES
4 BECKSIDE
5 THE GREEN
6 CHURCH ST
7 CREYKE LA
8 PARLIAMENT ST
9 ST ANNE'S WK
10 ST HELEN'S DR
11 MONKTON
12 RYEDALE
13 LOWERDALE
14 MANOR FIELDS
15 LITTONDALE
16 SPRINGWOOD GR
17 ROMWOOD CL
18 COWGATE
BOOTH NOOKING LANE
Marsh Farm
DN15
Winteringham Haven
ROTTON SYKES LA
WATER SIDE
Winteringham
Marsh Farm
Haven Drain
Glebe Farm
Read's Island
Winteringham Prim Sch
92 93 94 95 96 97
B1
1 ORCHARD DR
2 HIGH BURGAGE
3 BACK LA
4 BRAMBLE LA
67
83
C6
1 DROVERS RISE
2 VICARAGE GDNS
3 CHAPEL MEWS
4 PINE WK
5 HOBSON RD
6 HARLAND RD
7 LARCHMONT CL
8 WOODLANDS LA
9 PLOVER DR
10 THORNTON
11 FRYSTON
12 LASTINGHAM
13 CHANTRYS DR
14 RANSOME WAY
15 ELM AVE
16 LAMBERT AVE
17 WOODLAND AVE
18 SPRINGFIELD AVE
19 ATKINSON DR
20 ST PAULINUS CRES
21 COVINGTON
22 LOWERDALE
23 LINTON
24 CARLTON
25 INGLETON RD
26 ROMBALDS CFT
27 PINEFIELD PL
28 WINTRINGHAM

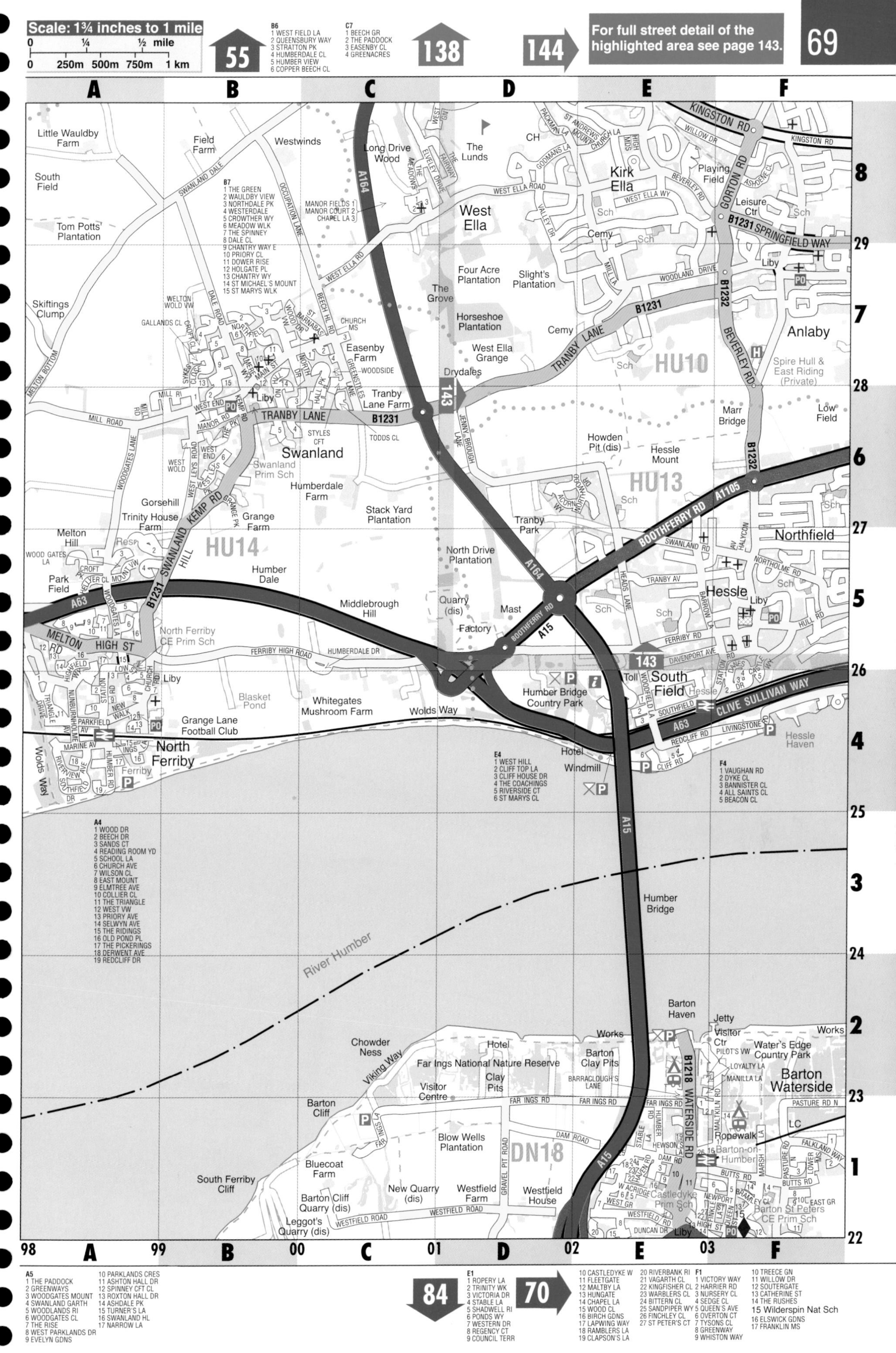

Scale: 1¾ inches to 1 mile
0 ¼ ½ mile
0 250m 500m 750m 1 km
55
B6
1 WEST FIELD LA
2 QUEENSBURY WAY
3 STRATTON PK
4 HUMBERDALE CL
5 HUMBER VIEW
6 COPPER BEECH CL
C7
1 BEECH GR
2 THE PADDOCK
3 EASENBY CL
4 GREENACRES
138
144
For full street detail of the highlighted area see page 143.
69
A B C D E F
Little Wauldby Farm
Field Farm
Westwinds
Long Drive Wood
The Lunds
CH
KINGSTON RD
South Field
Kirk Ella
Playing Field
B7
1 THE GREEN
2 WAULDBY VIEW
3 NORTHDALE PK
4 WESTERDALE
5 CROWTHER WY
6 MEADOW WLK
7 THE SPINNEY
8 DALE CL
9 CHANTRY WAY E
10 PRIORY CL
11 DOWER RISE
12 HOLGATE PL
13 CHANTRY WY
14 ST MICHAEL'S MOUNT
15 ST MARYS WLK
MANOR FIELDS 1
MANOR COURT 2
CHAPEL LA 3
West Ella
Leisure Ctr
Tom Potts' Plantation
B1231 SPRINGFIELD WAY
Four Acre Plantation
Slight's Plantation
Liby
Skiftings Clump
The Grove
Horseshoe Plantation
Cemy
B1231
Anlaby
Easenby Farm
West Ella Grange
HU10
Spire Hull & East Riding (Private)
Drydales
Tranby Lane Farm
TRANBY LANE
B1231
Marr Bridge
Low Field
Swanland
Howden Pit (dis)
Hesle Mount
Swanland Prim Sch
Humberdale Farm
HU13
Gorsehill
Trinity House Farm
Grange Farm
Stack Yard Plantation
Tranby Park
Northfield
Melton Hill
HU14
North Drive Plantation
Humber Dale
BOOTHFERRY RD A1105
Park Field
A63
Middlebrough Hill
Quarry (dis)
Mast
Hesle
Factory
North Ferriby CE Prim Sch
143
South Field
Liby
Blasket Pond
Whitegates Mushroom Farm
Humber Bridge Country Park
Wolds Way
CLIVE SULLIVAN WAY
Grange Lane Football Club
North Ferriby
Hotel
Windmill
Hessle Haven
E4
1 WEST HILL
2 CLIFF TOP LA
3 CLIFF HOUSE DR
4 THE COACHINGS
5 RIVERSIDE CT
6 ST MARYS CL
F4
1 VAUGHAN RD
2 DYKE CL
3 BANNISTER CL
4 ALL SAINTS CL
5 BEACON CL
A4
1 WOOD DR
2 BEECH DR
3 SANDS CT
4 READING ROOM YD
5 SCHOOL LA
6 CHURCH AVE
7 WILSON CL
8 EAST MOUNT
9 ELMTREE AVE
10 COLLIER CL
11 THE TRIANGLE
12 WEST VW
13 PRIORY AVE
14 SELWYN AVE
15 THE RIDINGS
16 OLD POND PL
17 THE PICKERINGS
18 DERWENT AVE
19 REDCLIFF DR
Humber Bridge
River Humber
Barton Haven
Jetty
Visitor Ctr
Works
Chowder Ness
Hotel
Barton Clay Pits
Water's Edge Country Park
Far Ings National Nature Reserve
Clay Pits
Barton Waterside
Visitor Centre
Barton Cliff
Blow Wells Plantation
DN18
Ropewalk
Barton-on-Humber
Bluecoat Farm
South Ferriby Cliff
New Quarry (dis)
Westfield Farm
Westfield House
Castledyke Prim Sch
Barton Cliff Quarry (dis)
Leggot's Quarry (dis)
Barton St Peters CE Prim Sch
8 29 7 28 6 27 5 26 4 25 3 24 2 23 1 22
98 99 00 01 02 03
A5
1 THE PADDOCK
2 GREENWAYS
3 WOODGATES MOUNT
4 SWANLAND GARTH
5 WOODLANDS RI
6 WOODGATES CL
7 THE RISE
8 WEST PARKLANDS DR
9 EVELYN GDNS
10 PARKLANDS CRES
11 ASHTON HALL DR
12 SPINNEY CFT CL
13 ROXTON HALL DR
14 ASHDALE PK
15 TURNER'S LA
16 SWANLAND HL
17 NARROW LA
84
E1
1 ROPERY LA
2 TRINITY WK
3 VICTORIA DR
4 STABLE LA
5 SHADWELL RI
6 PONDS WY
7 WESTERN DR
8 REGENCY CT
9 COUNCIL TERR
70
10 CASTLEDYKE W
11 FLEETGATE
12 MALTBY LA
13 HUNGATE
14 CHAPEL LA
15 WOOD CL
16 BIRCH GDNS
17 LAPWING WAY
18 RAMBLERS LA
19 CLAPSON'S LA
20 RIVERBANK RI
21 VAGARTH CL
22 KINGFISHER CL
23 WARBLERS CL
24 BITTERN CL
25 SANDPIPER WY
26 FINCHLEY CL
27 ST PETER'S CT
F1
1 VICTORY WAY
2 HARRIER RD
3 NURSERY CL
4 SEDGE CL
5 QUEEN'S AVE
6 OVERTON CT
7 TYSONS CL
8 GREENWAY
9 WHISTON WAY
10 TREECE GN
11 WILLOW DR
12 SOUTERGATE
13 CATHERINE ST
14 THE RUSHES
15 Wilderspin Nat Sch
16 ELSWICK GDNS
17 FRANKLIN MS

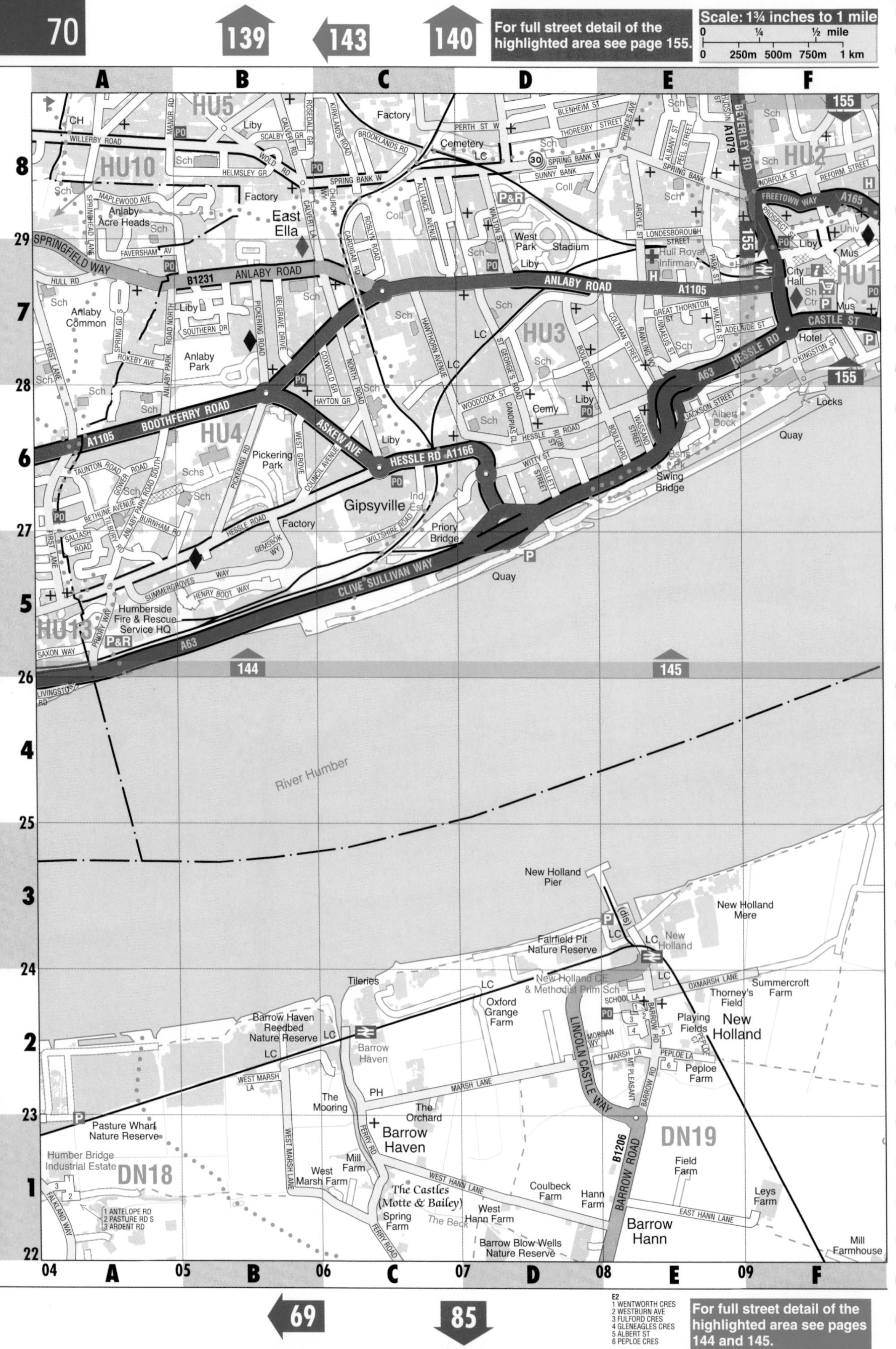

↑ 139   ← 143   ↑ 140

For full street detail of the highlighted area see page 155.

Scale: 1¾ inches to 1 mile

0   ¼   ½   mile
0   250m   500m   750m   1 km

155

A · B · C · D · E · F

CH
WILLERBY ROAD
MANOR RD
HU5
Liby
PO
SCALBY LA
ROSEDALE GR
KIRKLANDS ROAD
BROOKLANDS RD
Factory
CALVERT RD
PERTH ST W
BLENHEIM ST
THORESBY STREET
PRINCES AVE
HUDSON ST
ALBANY ST
Sch
HU2
Sch
Cemetery
Coll
PEEL STREET
ALBANY STREET
REFORM STREET
BEVERLEY RD A1079
NORFOLK ST
H
PROSPECT ST
FREETOWN WAY
A165
8
HU10
CALVERT LA
HELMSLEY GR
Factory
CHURCH
Sch
30
SPRING BANK W
SPRING BANK
Coll
SUNNY BANK
WALTON ST
ARGYLE ST
LONDESBOROUGH STREET
PARK AVE
Univ
Mus
HU1
Sch
MAPLEWOOD AVE
Anlaby
Acre Heads
Sch
East
Ella
ROSLYN ROAD
CARDIGAN RD
ALLIANCE AVENUE
West
Park
Stadium
Sch
Liby
Hull Royal
Infirmary
GREAT THORNTON
Hull
City
Hall
i
Sh
Ctr
Mus
29
SPRINGFIELD WAY
FAVERSHAM AV
PO
Liby
Coll
P&R
Liby
Sch
PO
P
P
HULL RD
B1231
ANLABY ROAD
BELGRAVE DRIVE
PICKERING ROAD
ANLABY ROAD
A1105
CASTLE ST
155
7
Sch
Anlaby
Common
Liby
SOUTHERN DR
HAWTHORN AVENUE
NORTH ROAD
ST GEORGE'S ROAD
Sch
HU3
LC
COLTMAN STREET
RAWLING WY
WALKER ST
ADELAIDE ST
Hotel
KINGSTON ST
P
ROAD NORTH
ROKEBY AVE
Anlaby
Park
CONWAY GR
Sch
LC
LC
CANOPUS CL
BOULEVARD
GREAT UNION ST
HESSLE RD
Locks
28
PO
HAYTON GR
WOODCOCK ST
Cemy
Liby
PO
A63
JACKSON STREET
Albert
Dock
155
6
A1105
BOOTHFERRY ROAD
HU4
ASKEW AVE
WEST GROVE
COUNCIL AVENUE
HESSLE RD A1166
Liby
RUGBY STREET
WASSAND
Bsns
Pk
Swing
Bridge
Quay
TAUNTON ROAD
GONER ROAD
Pickering
Park
PO
WITTY ST
GILLETT STREET
HU13
BETHUNE AVENUE
ANLABY PARK ROAD SOUTH
TILBURY ROAD
Schs
Sch
Gipsyville
Ind
Est
Priory
Bridge
27
PO
SALTASH
ROAD
BURNHAM RD
GEMSBOK WY
Factory
WILTSHIRE ROAD
P
Quay
FIRST LANE
HESSLE ROAD
SUMMERGROVES WAY
HENRY BOOT WAY
CLIVE SULLIVAN WAY
5
SAXON WAY
Humberside
Fire & Rescue
Service HQ
P&R
A63
26
LIVINGSTONE
RD

144   145

4

River Humber

25

3
New Holland
Pier
New Holland
Mere
P (dis)
LC
24
Fairfield Pit
Nature Reserve
LC
New
Holland
LC
OXMARSH LANE
Summercroft
Farm
Tileries
LC
New Holland CE
& Methodist Prim Sch
SCHOOL LA
Thorney's
Field
New
Holland
2
Barrow Haven
Reedbed
Nature Reserve
LC
LC
Oxford
Grange
Farm
MORDAN WY
Playing
Fields
PEPLOE LA
Peploe
Farm
WEST MARSH LA
Barrow
Haven
MARSH LA
MT PLEASANT
LINCOLN CASTLE WAY
23
P
Pasture Wharf
Nature Reserve
The
Mooring
PH
The
Orchard
MARSH LANE
Coulbeck
Farm
BARROW ROAD
B1206
DN19
Field
Farm
1
Humber Bridge
Industrial Estate
DN18
WEST MARSH LANE
West
Marsh Farm
Mill
Farm
West
Hann
Farm
WEST HANN LANE
Hann
Farm
EAST HANN LANE
Leys
Farm
FALKLAND WAY
3
2
1
1 ANTELOPE RD
2 PASTURE RD S
3 ARDENT RD
FERRY ROAD
The Castles
(Motte & Bailey)
The Beck
Spring
Farm
Barrow Blow Wells
Nature Reserve
Barrow
Hann
Mill
Farmhouse
22

04 · A · 05 · B · 06 · C · 07 · D · 08 · E · 09 · F

← 69   85

E2
1 WENTWORTH CRES
2 WESTBURN AVE
3 FULFORD CRES
4 GLENEAGLES CRES
5 ALBERT ST
6 PEPLOE CRES

For full street detail of the highlighted area see pages 144 and 145.

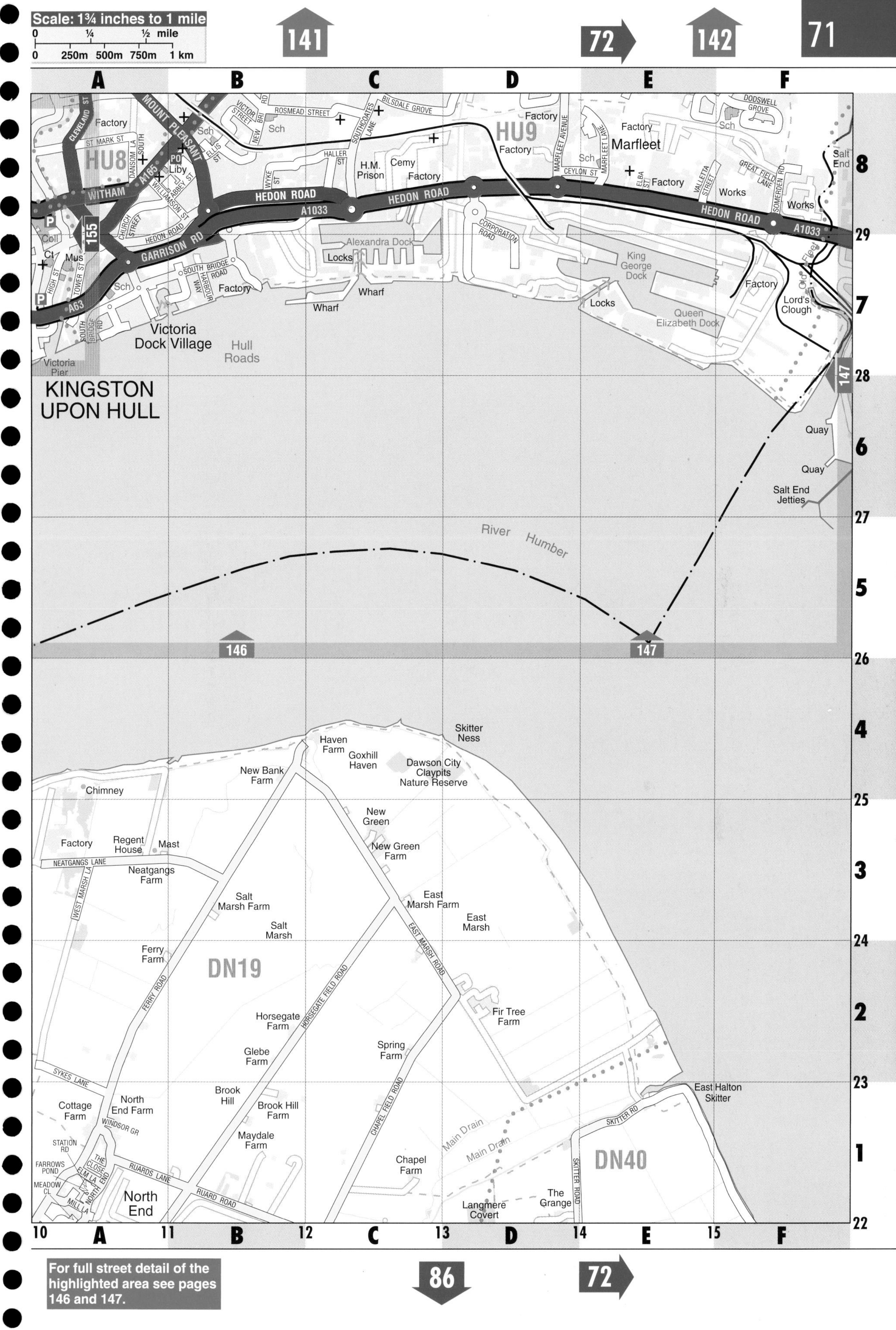

A   B   C   D   E   F

Cleveland St
St Mark St   Factory
HU8
A165   MOUNT PLEASANT
WITHAM
DANSOM LA SOUTH   Sch
PO   Liby
ABBEY ST   WILLIAMSON ST
P   155   CHURCH STREET   HEDON ROAD   GARRISON RD
Coll
Ct   Mus
High St   A63   Sch
TOWER ST   SOUTH BRIDGE   HARBOUR WAY   Factory
P   A63   SOUTH BRIDGE ROAD

Victoria
Dock Village

Victoria
Pier

VICTORIA STREET   NEW BRI   Sch
ROSMEAD STREET
WYKE ST   HALLER ST   H.M. Prison   Cemy   Factory
BILSDALE GROVE
SOUTHCOATES LANE
HEDON ROAD   HEDON ROAD
A1033

Alexandra Dock
Locks
Wharf   Wharf

Hull
Roads

CORPORATION ROAD

Factory
Factory
HU9
MARFLEET AVENUE   MARFLEET LANE   CEYLON ST   Sch   Factory
ELBA ST   Factory   Marfleet
GREAT FIELD LANE   VALLETTA ST
Works
Works
HEDON ROAD   A1033
DODSWELL GROVE   Sch

Salt
End

King
George
Dock
Locks
Queen
Elizabeth Dock
Factory

Lord's
Clough

SOMERDEN RD   147

Quay

Quay

Salt End
Jetties

KINGSTON
UPON HULL

River   Humber

146   147

Skitter
Ness
Haven
Farm   Goxhill
Haven   Dawson City
Claypits
Nature Reserve
New Bank
Farm
Chimney
New
Green
New Green
Farm
Factory   Regent
House   Mast
NEATGANGS LANE
Neatgangs
Farm
WEST MARSH LA   Salt
Marsh Farm   East
Marsh Farm   East
Marsh
Salt
Marsh   EAST MARSH ROAD
DN19
Ferry
Farm
FERRY ROAD   HORSEGATE FIELD ROAD   Fir Tree
Farm
Horsegate
Farm
Glebe
Farm   Spring
Farm   CHAPEL FIELD ROAD
SYKES LANE   Brook
Hill   Brook Hill
Farm
North
End Farm   WINDSOR GR
Cottage
Farm   Maydale
Farm   East Halton
Skitter
STATION RD   RUARDS LANE
FARROWS
POND   THE CLOSE   ELM LA END   NORTH LA END
MEADOW CL   MILL LA
North
End   RUARD ROAD   Chapel
Farm   Main Drain   SKITTER RD
Main Drain   SKITTER ROAD
DN40
Langmere
Covert   The
Grange

10   A   11   B   12   C   13   D   14   E   15   F   22

8
29
7
28
6
27
5
26
4
25
3
24
2
23
1

**For full street detail of the
highlighted area see pages
146 and 147.**

86   72 ▶

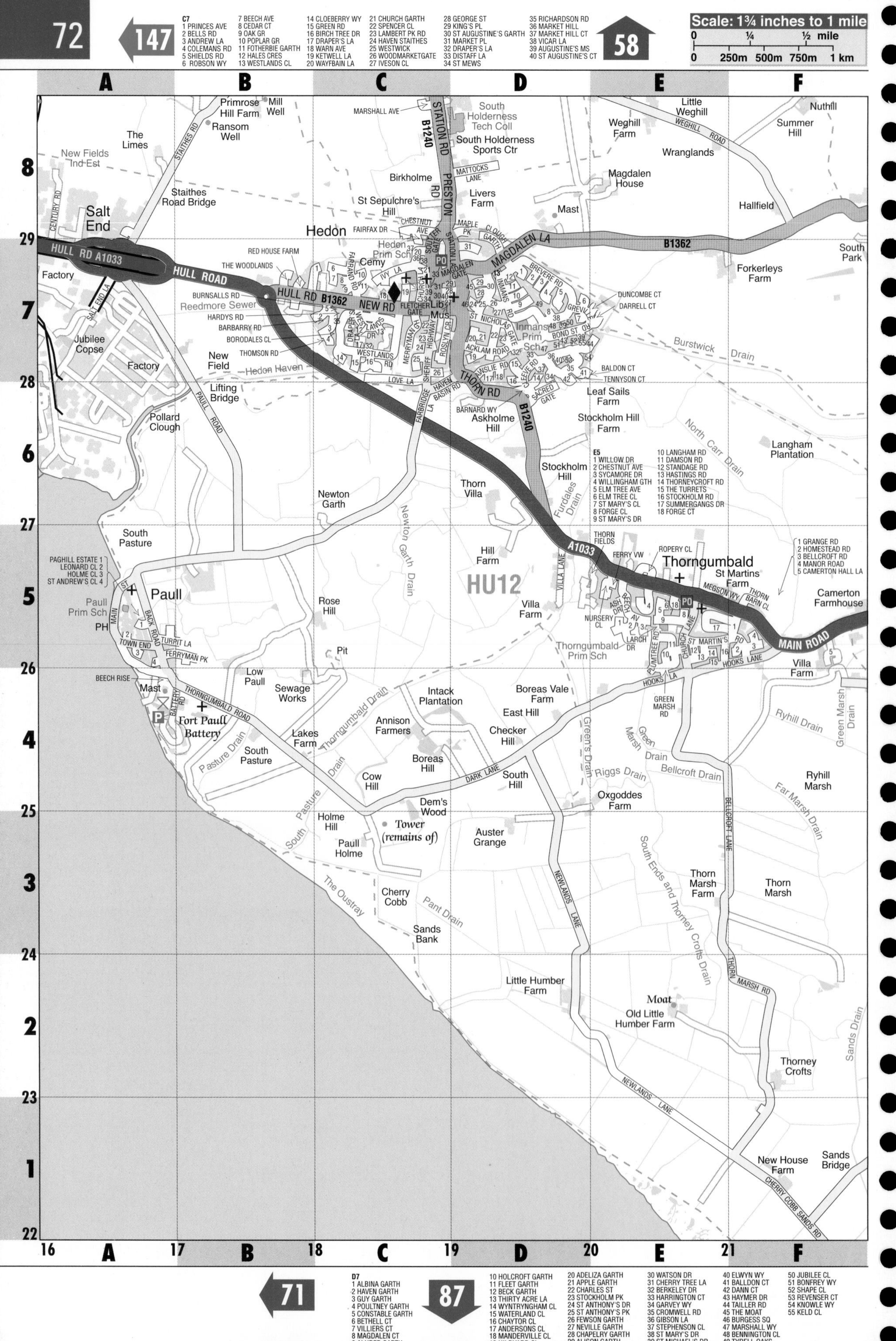

Scale: 1¾ inches to 1 mile

E5
1 WILLOW DR
2 CHESTNUT AVE
3 SYCAMORE DR
4 WILLINGHAM GTH
5 ELM TREE AVE
6 ELM TREE CL
7 ST MARY'S CL
8 FORGE CL
9 ST MARY'S CT
10 LANGHAM DR
11 DAMSON RD
12 STANDAGE RD
13 HASTINGS RD
14 THORNEYCROFT RD
15 THE TURRETS
16 STOCKHOLM RD
17 SUMMERGANGS DR
18 FORGE CT

1 GRANGE RD
2 HOMESTEAD RD
3 BELLCROFT RD
4 MANOR ROAD
5 CAMERTON HALL LA

PAGHILL ESTATE 1
LEONARD CL 2
HOLME CL 3
ST ANDREW'S CL 4

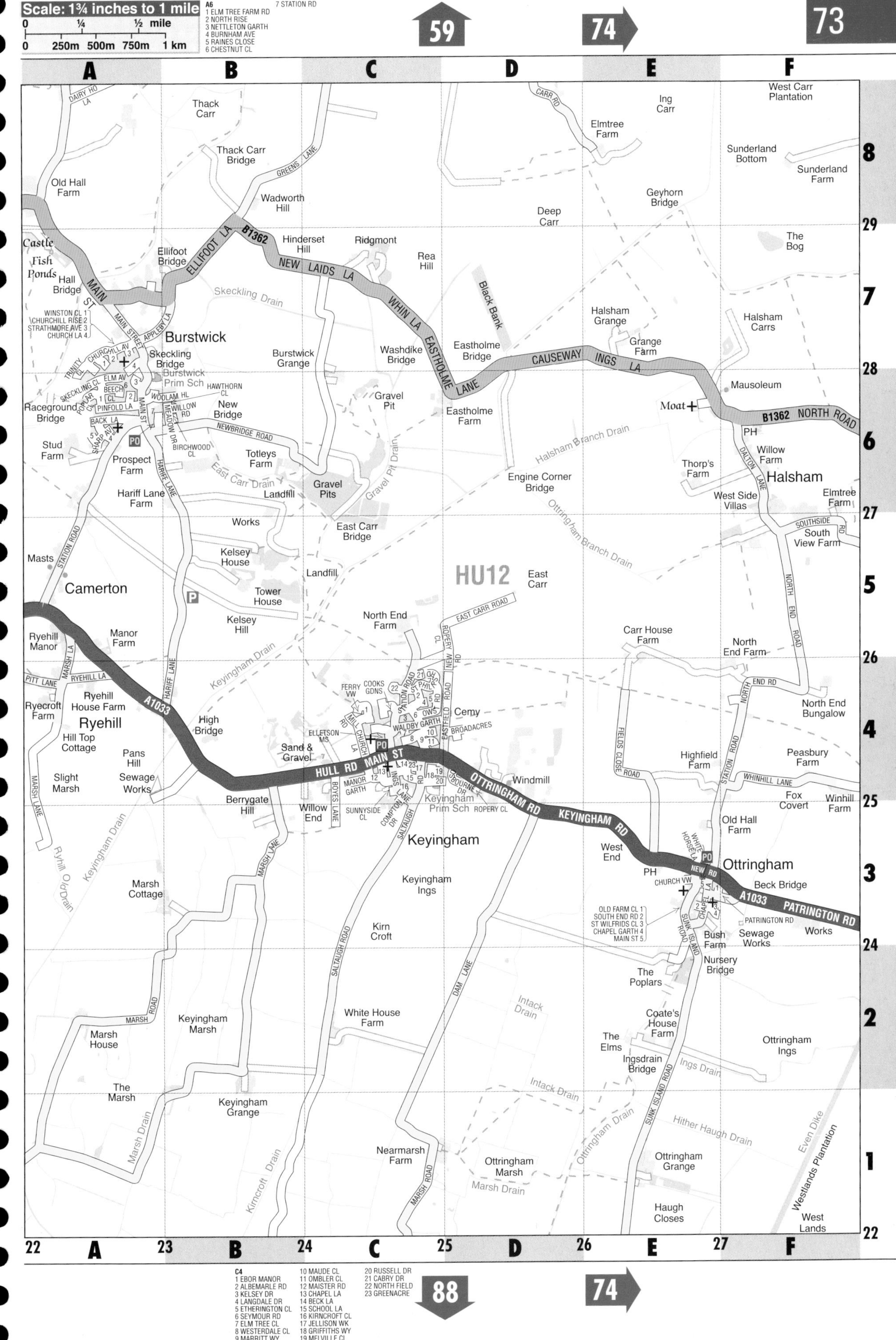
Scale: 1¾ inches to 1 mile
0 ¼ ½ mile
0 250m 500m 750m 1 km
A6
1 ELM TREE FARM RD
2 NORTH RISE
3 NETTLETON GARTH
4 BURNHAM AVE
5 RAINES CLOSE
6 CHESTNUT CL
7 STATION RD
59
74
A
B
C
D
E
F
Thack Carr
Ing Carr
West Carr Plantation
Elmtree Farm
Thack Carr Bridge
Sunderland Bottom
Sunderland Farm
Old Hall Farm
Wadworth Hill
Geyhorn Bridge
Deep Carr
The Bog
Castle Fish Ponds
Hall Bridge
Ellifoot Bridge
ELLIFOOT LA
B1362
Hinderset Hill
Ridgmont
Rea Hill
NEW LAIDS LA
Black Bank
Skeckling Drain
WINSTON CL 1
CHURCHILL RISE 2
STRATHMORE AVE 3
CHURCH LA 4
Burstwick
Skeckling Bridge
Burstwick Prim Sch
Burstwick Grange
Washdike Bridge
WHIN LA
EASTHOLME LANE
Eastholme Bridge
CAUSEWAY
INGS LA
Halsham Grange
Grange Farm
Halsham Carrs
Mausoleum
Moat
B1362 NORTH ROAD
HAWTHORN CL
New Bridge
NEWBRIDGE ROAD
Raceground Bridge
Stud Farm
Prospect Farm
Gravel Pit
Eastholme Farm
Halsham Branch Drain
PH
Willow Farm
Thorp's Farm
Halsham
Totleys Farm
East Carr Drain
Gravel Pit Drain
Gravel Pits
Landfill
Engine Corner Bridge
Hariff Lane Farm
HARIFF LANE
West Side Villas
Elmtree Farm
Works
East Carr Bridge
Ottringham Branch Drain
SOUTHSIDE RD
South View Farm
Masts
STATION ROAD
Kelsey House
Landfill
Camerton
HU12
East Carr
Tower House
NORTH END ROAD
EAST CARR ROAD
Ryehill Manor
Manor Farm
Kelsey Hill
North End Farm
Carr House Farm
North End Farm
Keyingham Drain
PITT LANE
RYEHILL LA
MARSH LA
Ryehill House Farm
Ryecroft Farm
Ryehill
A1033
High Bridge
Cemy
BROADACRES
North End Bungalow
Hill Top Cottage
Pans Hill
Sand & Gravel
ELLETSON MS
HULL RD
MAIN ST
FIELDS CLOSE ROAD
Highfield Farm
Peasbury Farm
Slight Marsh
Sewage Works
Berrygate Hill
Willow End
BOYES LANE
Windmill
WHINHILL LANE
Fox Covert
Winhill Farm
MARSH LANE
MANOR GARTH
SUNNYSIDE CL
Keyingham Prim Sch
OTTRINGHAM RD
KEYINGHAM RD
ROPERY CL
Old Hall Farm
Keyingham
West End
Ryehill Old Drain
Keyingham Drain
MARSH LANE
SALTAUGH
PH
Ottringham
CHURCH VW
NEW RD
Beck Bridge
Marsh Cottage
Keyingham Ings
A1033 PATRINGTON RD
OLD FARM CL 1
SOUTH END RD 2
ST WILFRIDS CL 3
CHAPEL GARTH 4
MAIN ST 5
PATRINGTON RD
Kirn Croft
Bush Farm
Sewage Works
Works
SALTAUGH ROAD
Nursery Bridge
DAM LANE
The Poplars
Intack Drain
MARSH ROAD
Keyingham Marsh
White House Farm
Coate's House Farm
Marsh House
The Elms
Ottringham Ings
Ingsdrain Bridge
Ings Drain
The Marsh
Intack Drain
Keyingham Grange
Marsh Drain
Ottringham Drain
SUNK ISLAND ROAD
Hither Haugh Drain
Even Dike
Westlands Plantation
Nearmarsh Farm
Ottringham Marsh
Ottringham Grange
Kirncroft Drain
Marsh Drain
Haugh Closes
West Lands
22
23
24
25
26
27
C4
1 EBOR MANOR
2 ALBEMARLE RD
3 KELSEY DR
4 LANGDALE DR
5 ETHERINGTON CL
6 SEYMOUR RD
7 ELM TREE CL
8 WESTERDALE CL
9 MARRITT WY
10 MAUDE CL
11 OMBLER CL
12 MAISTER RD
13 CHAPEL LA
14 BECK LA
15 SCHOOL LA
16 KIRNCROFT CL
17 JELLISON WK
18 GRIFFITHS WY
19 MELVILLE CL
20 RUSSELL DR
21 CABRY DR
22 NORTH FIELD
23 GREENACRE
88
74

73
60

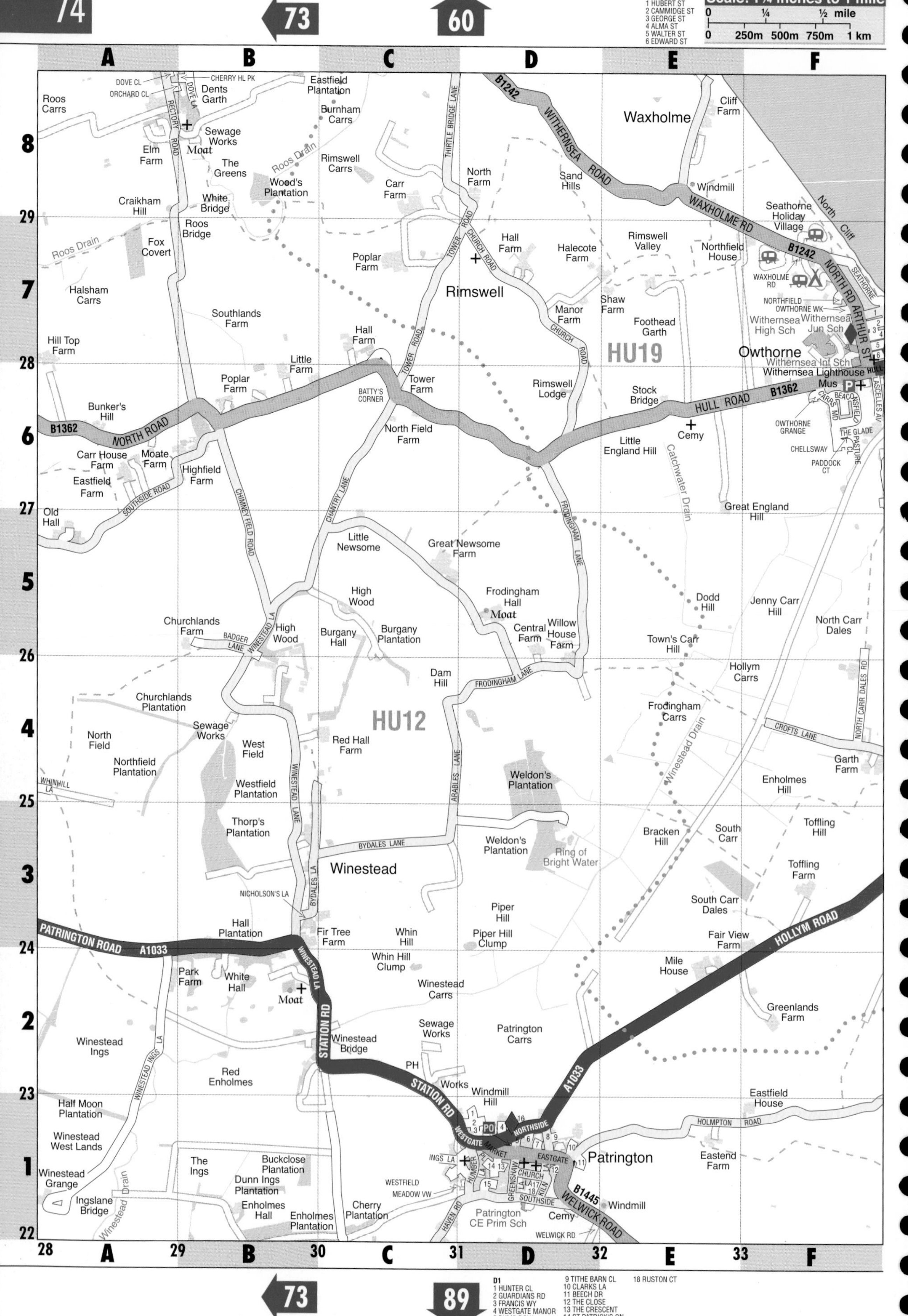

73
89

D1
1 HUNTER CL
2 GUARDIANS RD
3 FRANCIS WY
4 WESTGATE MANOR
5 PUMP ROW
6 NORTHSIDE CT
7 CHURCH VW
8 TITHE BARN LA
9 TITHE BARN CL
10 CLARKS LA
11 BEECH DR
12 THE CLOSE
13 THE CRESCENT
14 ST PATRICK'S GN
15 SAFFRON GARTH
16 CROMWELL CL
17 RUSTON TERR
18 RUSTON CT

Scale: 1¾ inches to 1 mile

0 ¼ ½ mile
0 250m 500m 750m 1 km

A B C D E F

8
29
7
28
6
27
5
26
4
25
3
24
2
23
1
22

WITHERNSEA

Liby Withernsea Community

YOUNG ST
SEASIDE RD

PO
P H P
IRB Sta

A6
1 JAMES CL
2 RAILWAY CRES
3 ROBERT CL
4 PIGGY LA
5 STATION RD
6 ST NICHOLAS PK
7 SCOTT GDNS
8 THE CLOSE
9 CHERRY TREE AVE
10 FRANCIS AVE
11 WHITETHORN AVE
12 VICTORIA AVE
13 WESTFIELD RISE
14 MEMORIAL AVE
15 THE PROMENADE
16 KAY KENDALL CT
17 KING ST
18 HIGH BRIGHTON ST
19 CHEVERTON AVE
20 Pavilion L Ctr
21 RUGBY CL
22 TRINITY FIELDS
23 THE OLD WOODYARD

CH

Withernsea
Golf Club

HAZEL AVE 1
CHESTNUT AVE 2
HOLMPTON RD 3
TURNER RD 4
NEWSHAM GDNS 5
CHESTNUT GR 6

First
Farm

Holiday
Chalets

COLLEYS
KENWOOD

Red
House

Valley
Farm
Smook
Hills
SMOOK HILLS RD
(PEARCY LANE)
Intack
Farm

HOLMPTON ROAD

Sewage
Works

Hollym

Nevilles
Farm

NORTHSIDE
VICAR
ROAD
PH
CHURCH
LA
IM LANE
SOUTH CARR
DALES RD
SOUTH LEYS ROAD
NORTH LEYS ROAD

Bowmer
Hill

Eastfield
Farm

Manor
Farm

SOUTH
LEYS
ROAD

North
Leys

The
Runnell

South
Leys

WITHERNSEA ROAD

HU19

Scarborough
Hill

Nevills Drain

HOOKS LANE

Intack
Plantation

SEASIDE
ROAD
TAYLORS CL
SCHOOL LANE

Cliff House
Farm

Holmpton

Brick Close
Plantation

MAIN ROAD

West
Farm
Manor
Farm
PH

Cow Close
Plantation

Mill
Hill

Old
Hive

WAKEFIELD LANE
PATRINGTON ROAD

Old Hive Dike

Little
Plowland

Trinity House
Farm

RYSOME LANE

RAF
Holmpton &
Underground
Bunker

OLD NEWTON ROAD

Long Close
Plantation

HU12

NORTHFIELD LANE

Parker's Close
Plantation

Woods
Plantation

Black
Dike

Grass North
Field

Beacon
Hill

North
Farm

Rysome
Garth

WEETON N
LA

Balk
Hill

Cliff
Farm

Water
Tower

Model
Farm

34 A 35 B 36 C 37 D 38 E 39 F

61

Scale: 1¾ inches to 1 mile

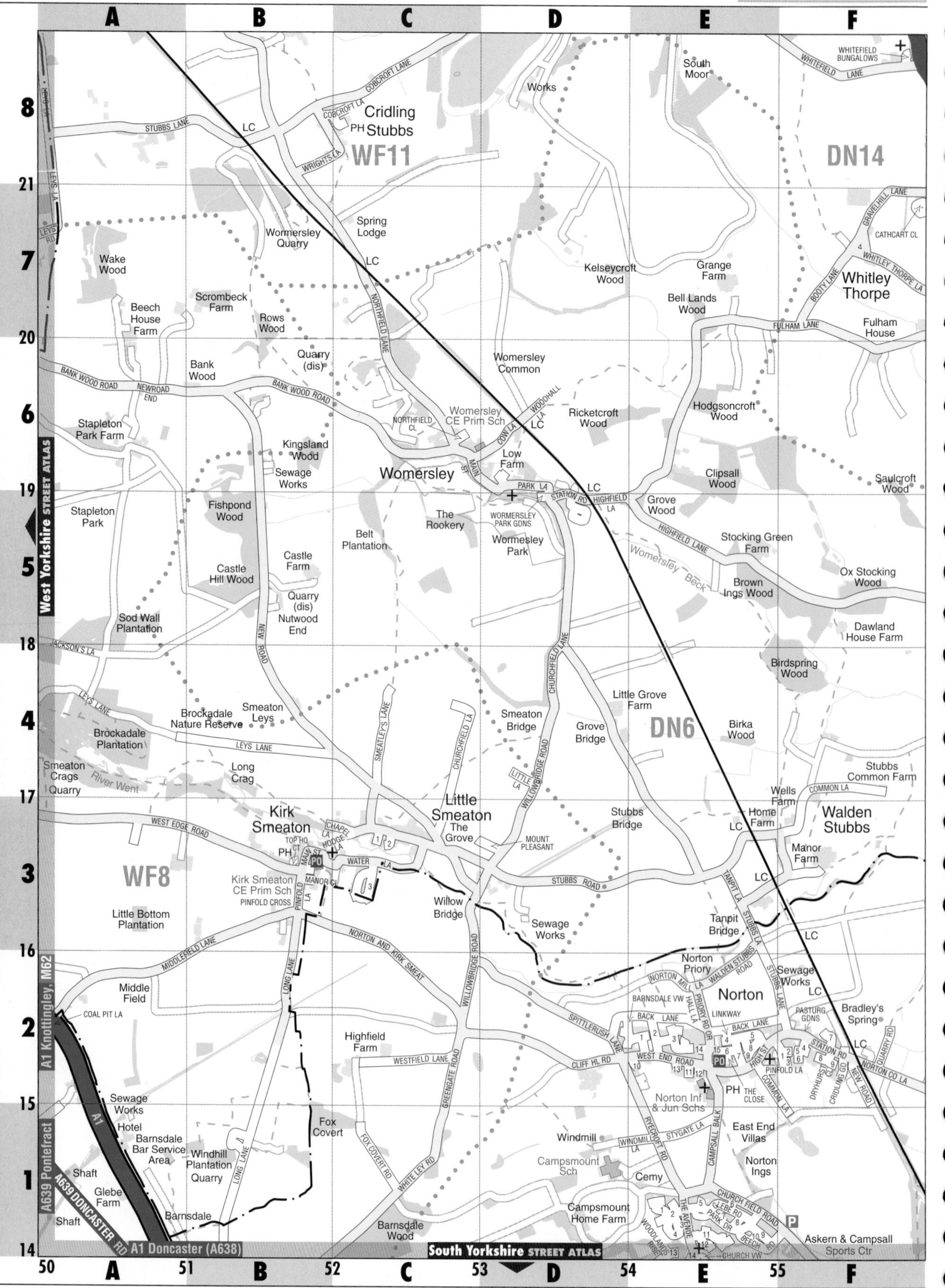

West Yorkshire STREET ATLAS

South Yorkshire STREET ATLAS

C3
1 WENTDALE
2 STAN VALLEY
3 SPRINGFIELD CRES

E1
1 TENNYSON AVE
2 SHAKESPEARE AVE
3 BYRON AVE
4 WORDSWORTH AVE
5 WELLINGTONIA DR
6 LANGLEYS RD
7 EAST VW
8 GRANGE RD
9 WILLOW RD

10 VAUGHAN RD
11 CAMPSALL PK RD
12 CAMPSALL HALL RD
13 SHERWOOD CL
14 HIGH ST

E2
1 BROC-O-BANK
2 NEWTHORPE RD
3 FORRESTER'S CL
4 TRAFFORD RD
5 ARUNDEL RD
6 ADELAIDE RD
7 HEADINGLEY RD
8 ORCHARD DR
9 ORCHARD CL

10 RYECROFT AVE
11 FIR TREE DR
12 MANOR CL
13 WINDMILL MD
14 KIPLIN DR
15 LANGOLD DR

F2
1 LYNDHURST DR
2 LYNDHURST CL
3 LYNDHURST RISE
4 ASHBURNHAM CL
5 ASHBURNHAM WK
6 DENVER RD
7 MANOR GARTH
8 SWAN SYKE DR
9 DRYHURST CL

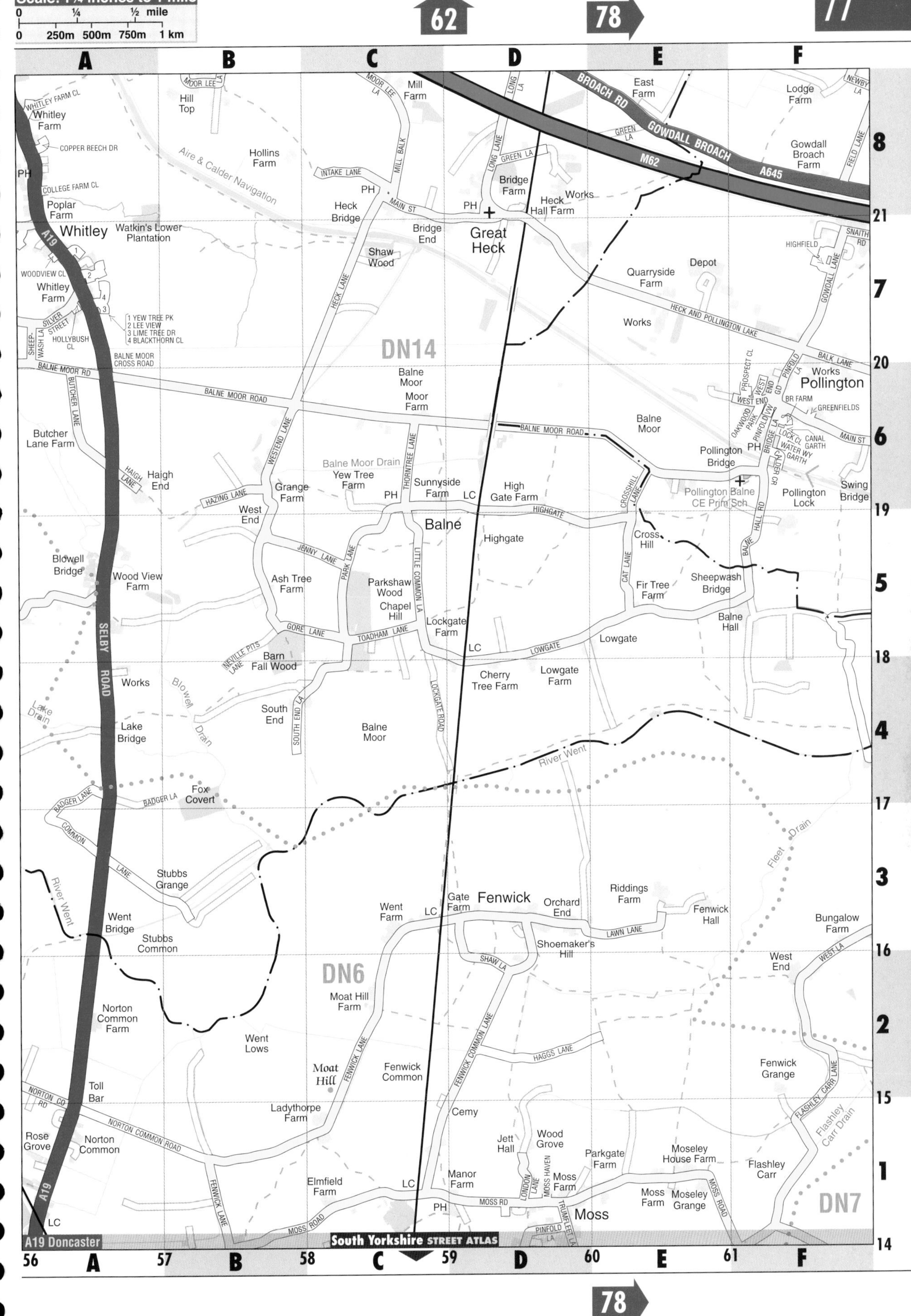

A   B   C   D   E   F

8
21
7
DN14
20
6
19
5
18
4
17
3
16
2
15
1
14

Whitley Farm CL
Whitley Farm
COPPER BEECH DR
Hill Top
Moor Lee LA
Mill Farm
Mill BALK
Moor Lee LA
Long LA
Long Lane
Green LA
Green La
BROACH RD
East Farm
GOWDALL BROACH
Lodge Farm
NEWBY LA

Hollins Farm
Aire & Calder Navigation
INTAKE LANE
PH
Heck Bridge
Main St
Bridge Farm
PH
Heck Hall Farm
Works
M62
A645
Gowdall Broach Farm
FIELD LA

College Farm CL
PH
Poplar Farm
Watkin's Lower Plantation
Heck LANE
Shaw Wood
Bridge End
Great Heck
Quarryside Farm
Depot
HIGHFIELD
SNAITH RD

Whitley
A19
Whitley Farm
WOODVIEW CL
1 YEW TREE PK
2 LEE VIEW
3 LIME TREE DR
4 BLACKTHORN CL
SILVER STREET
SHEEP WASH LA
HOLLYBUSH CL
Works
HECK AND POLLINGTON LAKE
GOWDALL LANE

BALNE MOOR CROSS ROAD
Balne Moor Road
Balne Moor Farm
WESTEND LANE
THORNTREE LANE
Balne Moor Road
Balne Moor
Works
Pollington
PROSPECT CL
WEST END
OAKWOOD PARK
PINFOLD
BALK LANE
Main St
Greenfields
BR FARM

Butcher Lane Farm
BUTCHER LANE
Haigh End
HAIGH LANE
HAZING LANE
West End
Grange Farm
Yew Tree Farm
PH
Sunnyside Farm
LC
High Gate Farm
HIGHGATE
Balne Moor
Pollington Bridge
PH
Pollington Balne CE Prim Sch
Pollington Lock
Swing Bridge
LOCK CL
WATER WY GARTH
CANAL GARTH
BRIDGE LA
BALNE HALL RD

Balne Moor Drain
Blowell Bridge
Wood View Farm
JENNY LANE
PARK LANE
Ash Tree Farm
LITTLE COMMON LA
Balne
Highgate
HIGHGATE
CAT LANE
Cross Hill
Fir Tree Farm
Sheepwash Bridge
CROSSHILL LANE
Balne Hall

Works
Blowell Drain
GORE LANE
Parkshaw Wood
Chapel Hill
TOADHAM LANE
Lockgate Farm
LC
LOWGATE
Lowgate
Lowgate
Lake Drain
NEVILLE PITS LANE
SOUTH END LA
Barn Fall Wood
South End
Balne Moor
Cherry Tree Farm
Lowgate Farm
LOCKGATE ROAD
Lake Bridge
River Went
Fleet Drain

BADGER LANE
BADGER LA
Fox Covert
COMMON LANE
Stubbs Grange
Went Farm
LC
Gate Farm
Fenwick
Orchard End
Riddings Farm
Fenwick Hall
LAWN LANE
Bungalow Farm
West End
WEST LA

Went Bridge
Stubbs Common
DN6
Shoemaker's Hill
SHAW LA
FENWICK COMMON LANE

Norton Common Farm
Went Lows
Moat Hill Farm
FENWICK LANE
Fenwick Common
Moat Hill
HAGGS LANE
Fenwick Grange
FLASHLEY CARR LANE
Flashley Carr Drain

Toll Bar
NORTON CO RD
NORTON COMMON ROAD
FENWICK LANE
Ladythorpe Farm
Cemy
Jett Hall
Wood Grove
MOSS HAVEN
Parkgate Farm
Moseley House Farm
Flashley Carr
DN7

Rose Grove
Norton Common
A19
LC
Elmfield Farm
LC
Manor Farm
PH
MOSS RD
LONDON LANE
Moss Hall
Moss
Moss Farm
Moseley Grange
MOSS ROAD
TRUMPFLEET LA
PINFOLD LA

Moss Road
A19 Doncaster

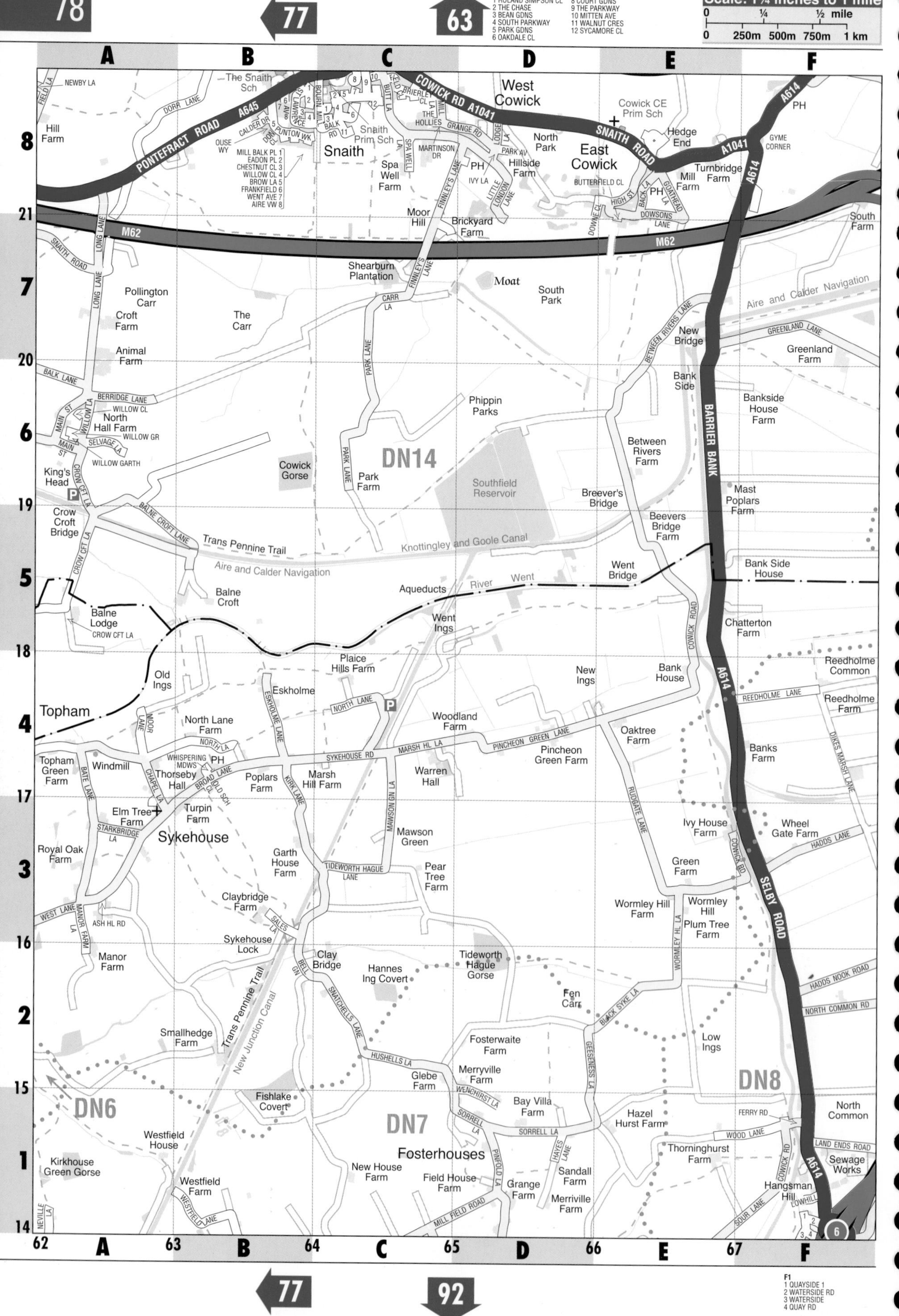

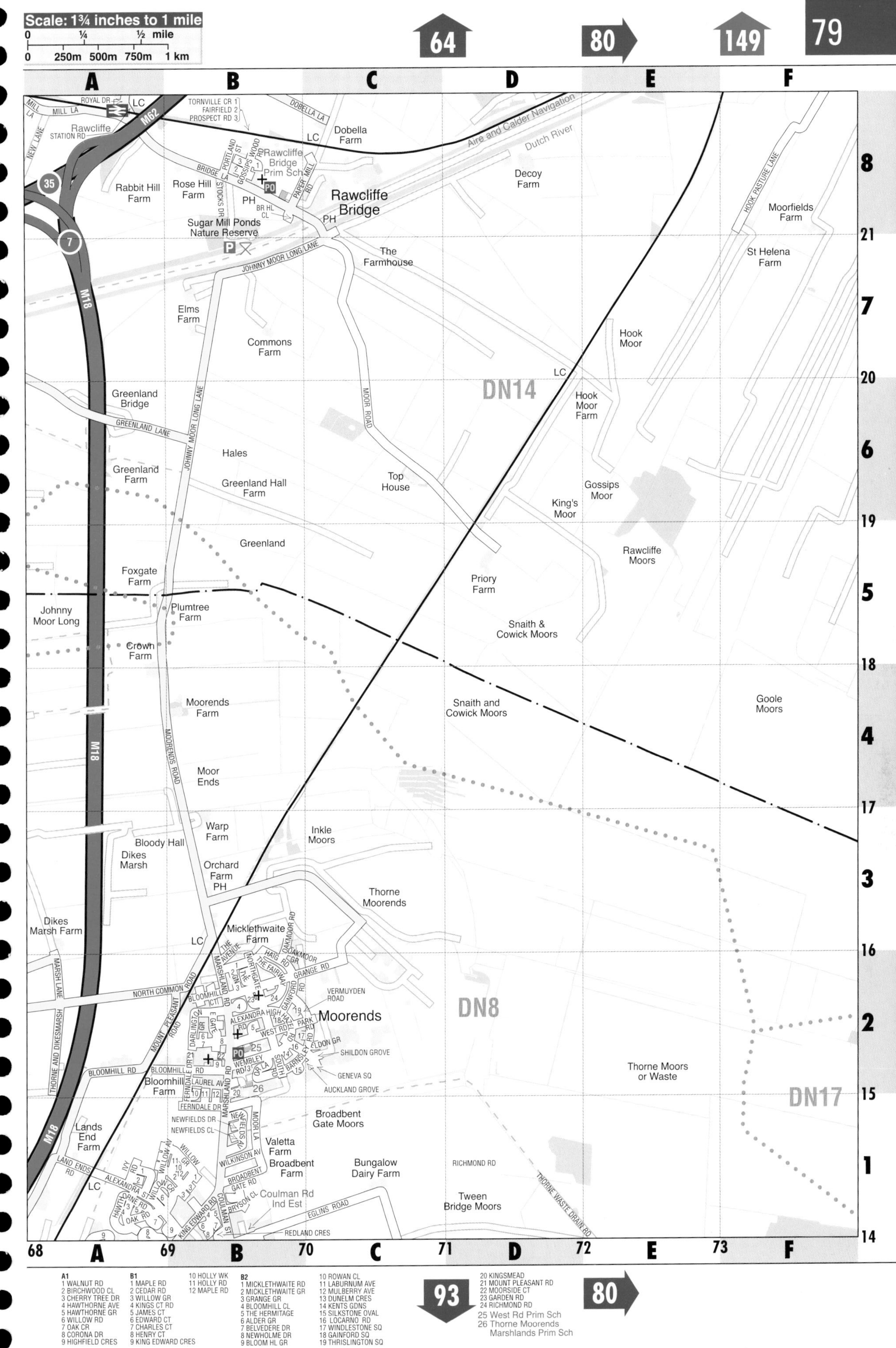

A · B · C · D · E · F

DN14

DN8

DN17

Rawcliffe Bridge

Moorends

149 79 65

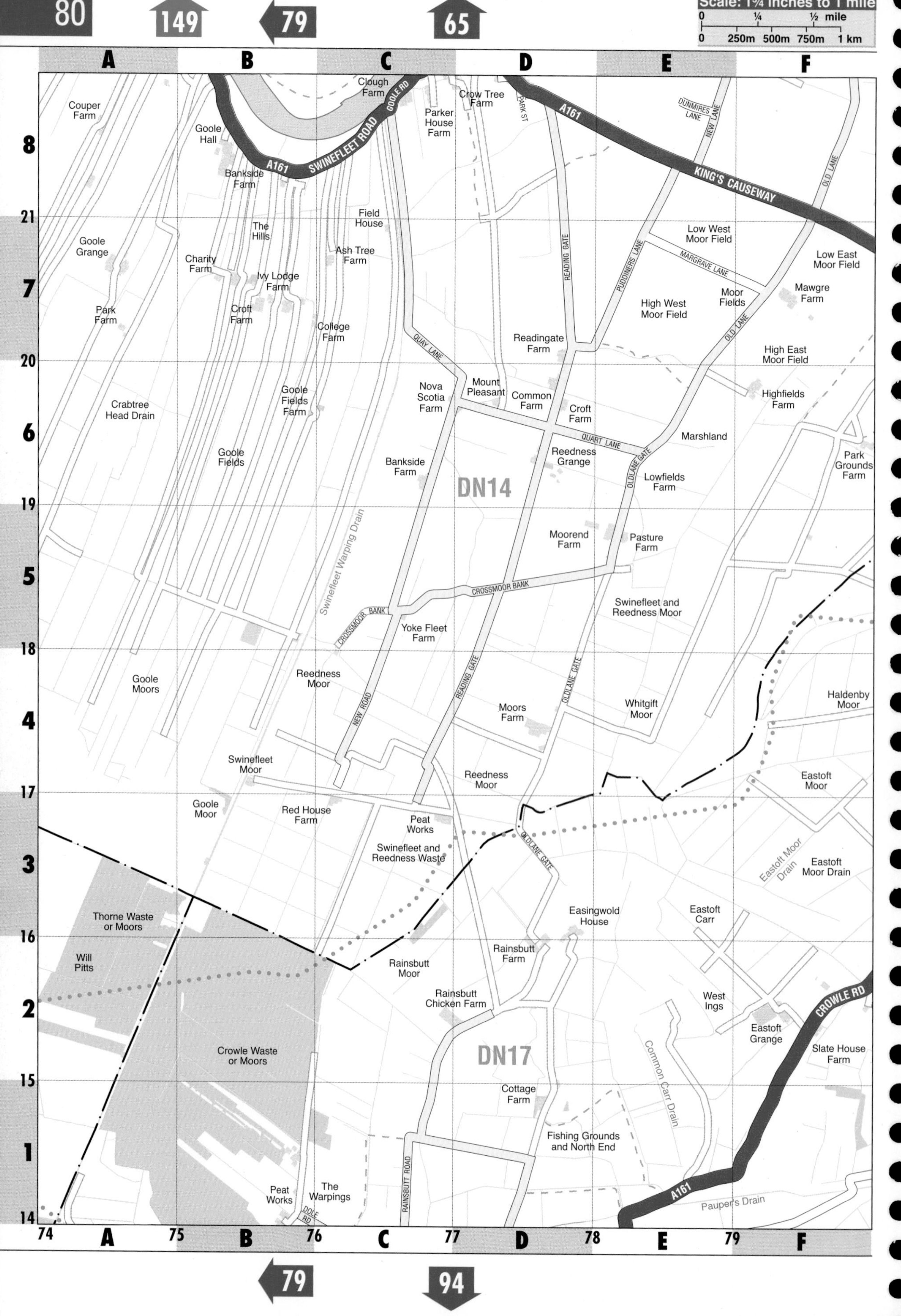
Scale: 1¾ inches to 1 mile
0 ¼ ½ mile
0 250m 500m 750m 1 km
A B C D E F
Couper Farm
Goole Hall
Clough Farm
GOOLE RD
SWINEFLEET ROAD
A161
Parker House Farm
Crow Tree Farm
PARK ST
DUNMIRES LANE
NEW LANE
KING'S CAUSEWAY
OLD LANE
Bankside Farm
Field House
The Hills
Goole Grange
Charity Farm
Ash Tree Farm
Ivy Lodge Farm
READING GATE
PUDDINERS LANE
Low West Moor Field
MARGRAVE LANE
Low East Moor Field
Croft Farm
Park Farm
College Farm
High West Moor Field
Moor Fields
Mawgre Farm
Readingate Farm
High East Moor Field
QUAY LANE
Nova Scotia Farm
Mount Pleasant
Common Farm
Croft Farm
Highfields Farm
Crabtree Head Drain
Goole Fields Farm
QUART LANE
Marshland
Goole Fields
Bankside Farm
Reedness Grange
OLDLANE GATE
Lowfields Farm
Park Grounds Farm
DN14
Moorend Farm
Pasture Farm
Swinefleet Warping Drain
CROSSMOOR BANK
Swinefleet and Reedness Moor
Yoke Fleet Farm
Goole Moors
Reedness Moor
NEW ROAD
Moors Farm
Whitgift Moor
Haldenby Moor
Swinefleet Moor
Reedness Moor
Eastoft Moor
Goole Moor
Red House Farm
Peat Works
Swinefleet and Reedness Waste
Eastoft Moor Drain
Eastoft Moor Drain
Thorne Waste or Moors
Easingwold House
Eastoft Carr
Will Pitts
Rainsbutt Moor
Rainsbutt Farm
Rainsbutt Chicken Farm
West Ings
Eastoft Grange
CROWLE RD
Crowle Waste or Moors
DN17
Slate House Farm
Common Carr Drain
Cottage Farm
Fishing Grounds and North End
RAINSBUTT ROAD
Peat Works
The Warpings
DOLE RD
Pauper's Drain
8 21 7 20 6 19 5 18 4 17 3 16 2 15 1 14
74 75 76 77 78 79

79 94

A   B   C   D   E   F

8
21
7
20
6
19
5
18
4
17
3
16
2
15
1
14

New Brakes Farm

Black Plantation

Stripe Close Plantation

DN14

Adlingfleet Ings

East View Farm

Garthorpe Grange

Manor Farm

Adlingfleet

COW LANE

Swarth Ends

A161

CHURCH LANE

JUSTICE LA

NARROW LANE

Adlingfleet Drain

HOGGARD LANE

MANOR RD

GRANGE ROAD

GARTHORPE ROAD

Pasture Farm

Bracken Hill

COW LANE

COMMON LANE

SANDHILL RD

PASTURE LANE

Nessfield House

White House Farm

Garthorpe

Fockerby

NESS LANE

STATION RD

WEST END

Adlingfleet HIGH ST

ISLAND ROAD

CROSS ST

BACK LANE

Manor Farm

SHORE ROAD

LUDDINGTON RD

MARGRAVE LA

Ousefleet Moor

Adlingfleet Moor

Sand House Farm

Mast

Sand Hill

WHINS GATE

Adlingfleet Grange

Haldenby Hall Farm

Waterton Hall

Haldenby Farm

Boltgate

Haldenby Common

Haldenby Grange

FIELD LANE

Eastoft Moor Drain

Haldenby Park

Windmill

Great Woods

White House Farm

MILL HIGH RD

GARTHORPE ROAD

CHURCH LA

CARR LANE

DN17

Luddington & Garthorpe Prim Sch

Luddington

PH

JACKLIN LA

BRITTON CL

HALKON CL

Elm Tree Farm

Eastoft CE Prim Sch

A161

YORKSHIRESIDE

HIGH ST

HALL CT

PO

THE OLD MOORINGS

Eastoft

MEREDYKE ROAD

B1392

Mere Dyke

RIVER TRENT

Corner Farm

SAMPSON ST

B1392

DOMVILLE RD

STRICKLAND RD

PADEMOOR TR

EASTOFT ROAD

Haldenby Ness

High Bridge

OX PASTURE LANE

Waterton Hall Farm

Livthorpe Kennels

Flixborough Grange

DN15

WASTINGHALL LANE

Luddington Carr Ings Drain

Carr House

CARR LANE

Pauper's Drain

Pasture Farm

PASTURE LA

NORTHFIELD LANE

Industrial Estate

SECOND AV

Rose Cottage Farm

Leam Farm

Pademoor

Poplar Farm

PASTURE LANE

MIDDLE LANE

Amcotts

PH

CHURCH ST

B1392

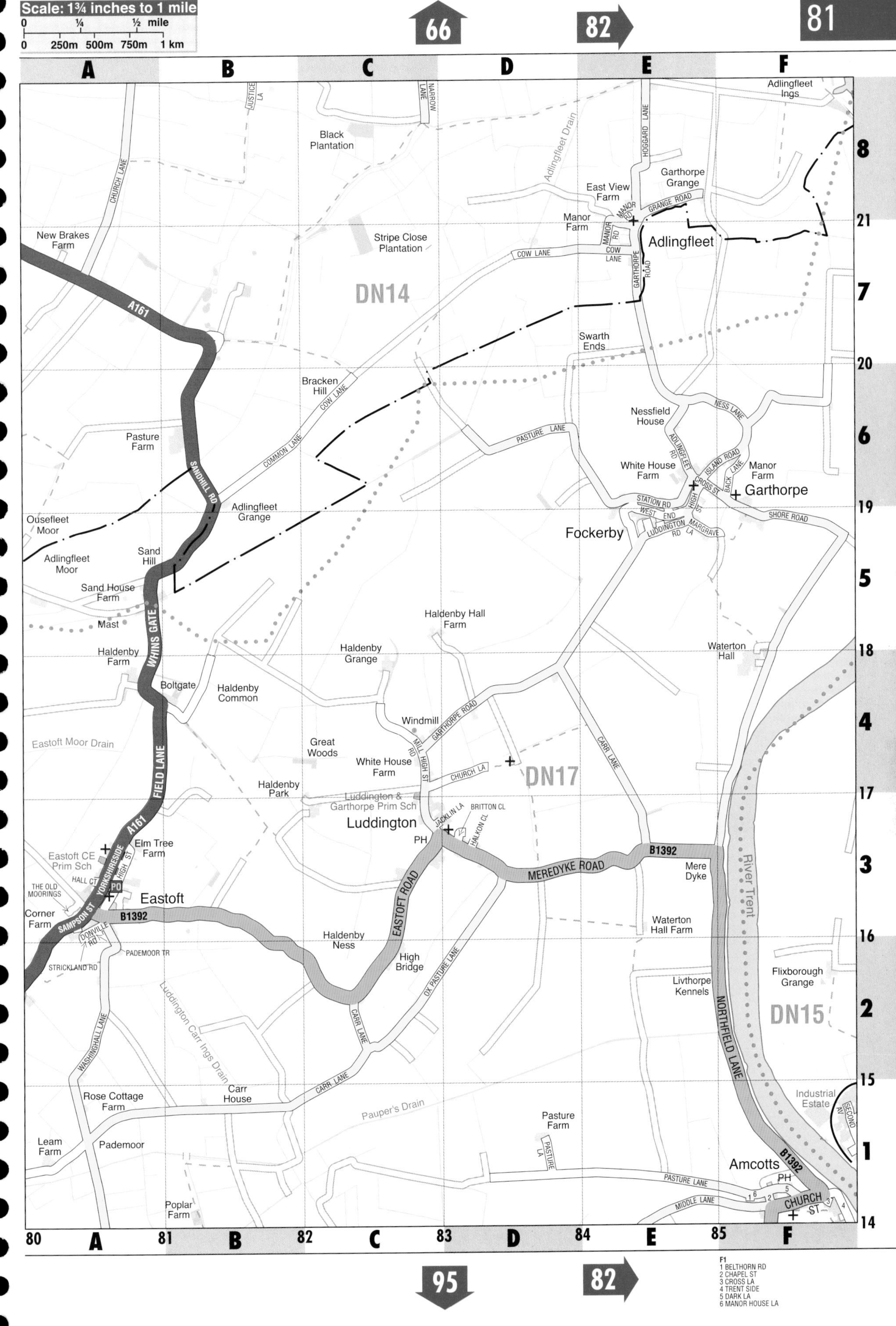

F1
1 BELTHORN RD
2 CHAPEL ST
3 CROSS LA
4 TRENT SIDE
5 DARK LA
6 MANOR HOUSE LA

81
67

Scale: 1¾ inches to 1 mile

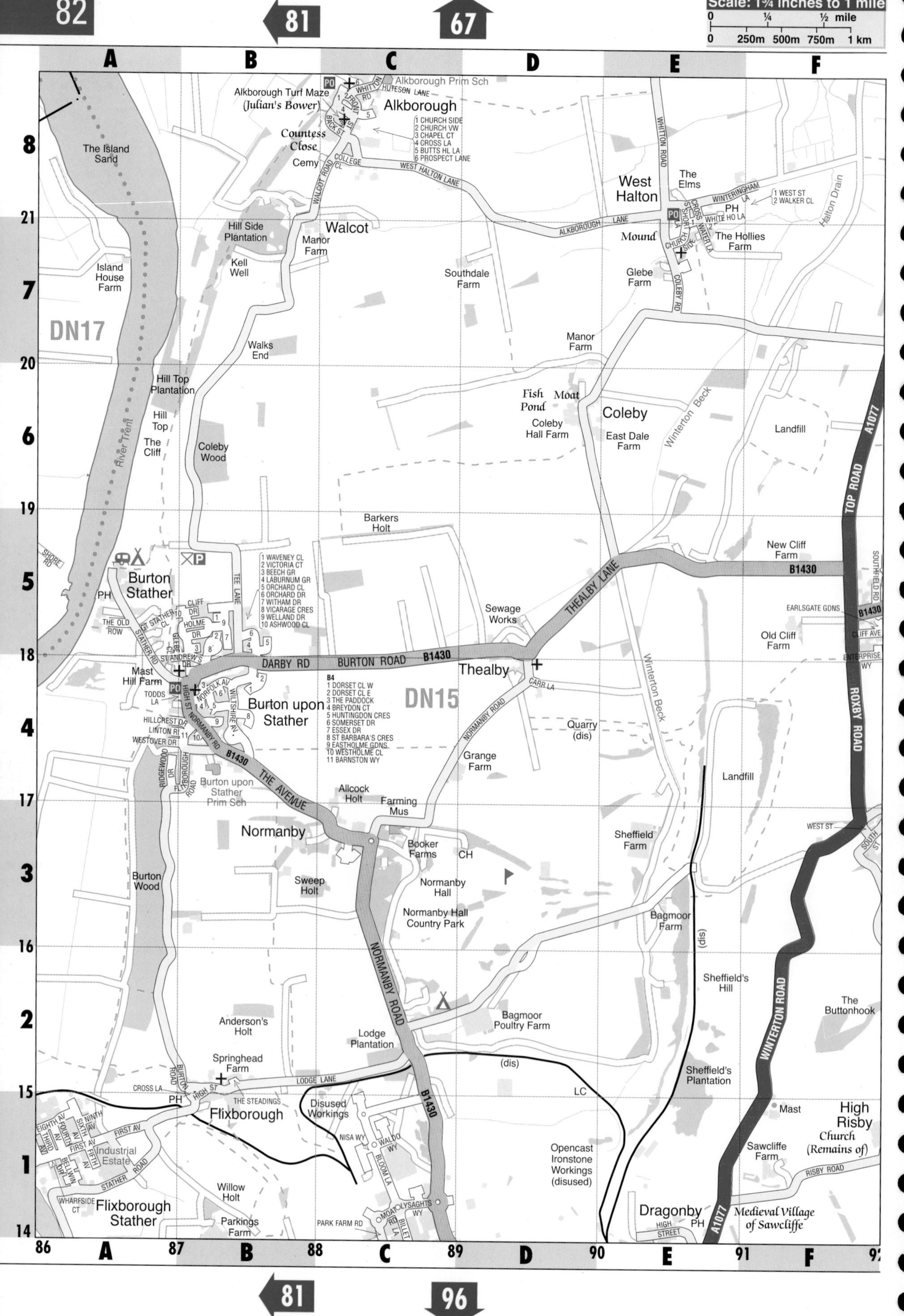
Alkborough
Alkborough Turf Maze
(Julian's Bower)
Alkborough Prim Sch
Countess Close
Cemy
1 CHURCH SIDE
2 CHURCH VW
3 CHAPEL CT
4 CROSS LA
5 BUTTS HL LA
6 PROSPECT LANE
WEST HALTON LANE
WALCOT ROAD
Walcot
Manor Farm
Hill Side Plantation
Kell Well
The Island Sand
Island House Farm
DN17
Walks End
Hill Top Plantation
Hill Top
The Cliff
River Trent
Coleby Wood
West Halton
The Elms
WINTERINGHAM LA
1 WEST ST
2 WALKER CL
PH
Mound
The Hollies Farm
Glebe Farm
ALKBOROUGH LANE
WHITTON ROAD
COLEBY RD
Southdale Farm
Manor Farm
Halton Drain
Fish Pond
Moat
Coleby
Coleby Hall Farm
East Dale Farm
Winterton Beck
Landfill
TOP ROAD
A1077
Barkers Holt
New Cliff Farm
B1430
Burton Stather
PH
1 WAVENEY CL
2 VICTORIA CT
3 BEECH GR
4 LABURNUM GR
5 ORCHARD CL
6 ORCHARD DR
7 WITHAM DR
8 VICARAGE CRES
9 WELLAND DR
10 ASHWOOD CL
TEE LANE
THEALBY LANE
Sewage Works
EARLSGATE GDNS
Old Cliff Farm
THE OLD ROW
Mast Hill Farm
DARBY RD
BURTON ROAD
B1430
Thealby
CARR LA
Burton upon Stather
DN15
B4
1 DORSET CL W
2 DORSET CL E
3 THE PADDOCK
4 BREYDON CT
5 HUNTINGDON CRES
6 SOMERSET DR
7 ESSEX DR
8 ST BARBARA'S CRES
9 EASTHOLME GDNS
10 WESTHOLME CL
11 BARNSTON WY
NORMANBY ROAD
Quarry (dis)
Grange Farm
Landfill
ROXBY ROAD
HILLCREST DR
LINTON RI
WESTOVER DR
THE AVENUE
Burton upon Stather Prim Sch
Allcock Holt
Farming Mus
Normanby
Booker Farms
CH
Sheffield Farm
WEST ST
Burton Wood
Sweep Holt
Normanby Hall
Normanby Hall Country Park
Bagmoor Farm
(dis)
Sheffield's Hill
WINTERTON ROAD
The Buttonhook
Anderson's Holt
Lodge Plantation
Bagmoor Poultry Farm
Springhead Farm
(dis)
LODGE LANE
Sheffield's Plantation
CROSS LA
PH
Flixborough
THE STEADINGS
Disused Workings
LC
Mast
High Risby
Church (Remains of)
Industrial Estate
STATHER ROAD
Opencast Ironstone Workings (disused)
Sawcliffe Farm
RISBY ROAD
Willow Holt
Flixborough Stather
Parkings Farm
PARK FARM RD
Dragonby
PH
HIGH STREET
Medieval Village of Sawcliffe

81
96

Scale: 1¾ inches to 1 mile
0 ¼ ½ mile
0 250m 500m 750m 1 km

A5
1 FARNDALE WY
2 NORTHLANDS AVE
3 FOWLER CT
4 BOYNTON CRES
5 HILLSMERE GR
6 BOSTON CL
7 WATERLOW DR
8 PLYMOUTH CL
9 LEEK HILL
10 WESTWINDS RD
11 MALKINSON CL
12 HAWTHORNE CL
13 BLANKNEY CT
14 MARKET ST
15 QUEEN ST
16 CHURCH SIDE
17 SAFFRE CL

68
84

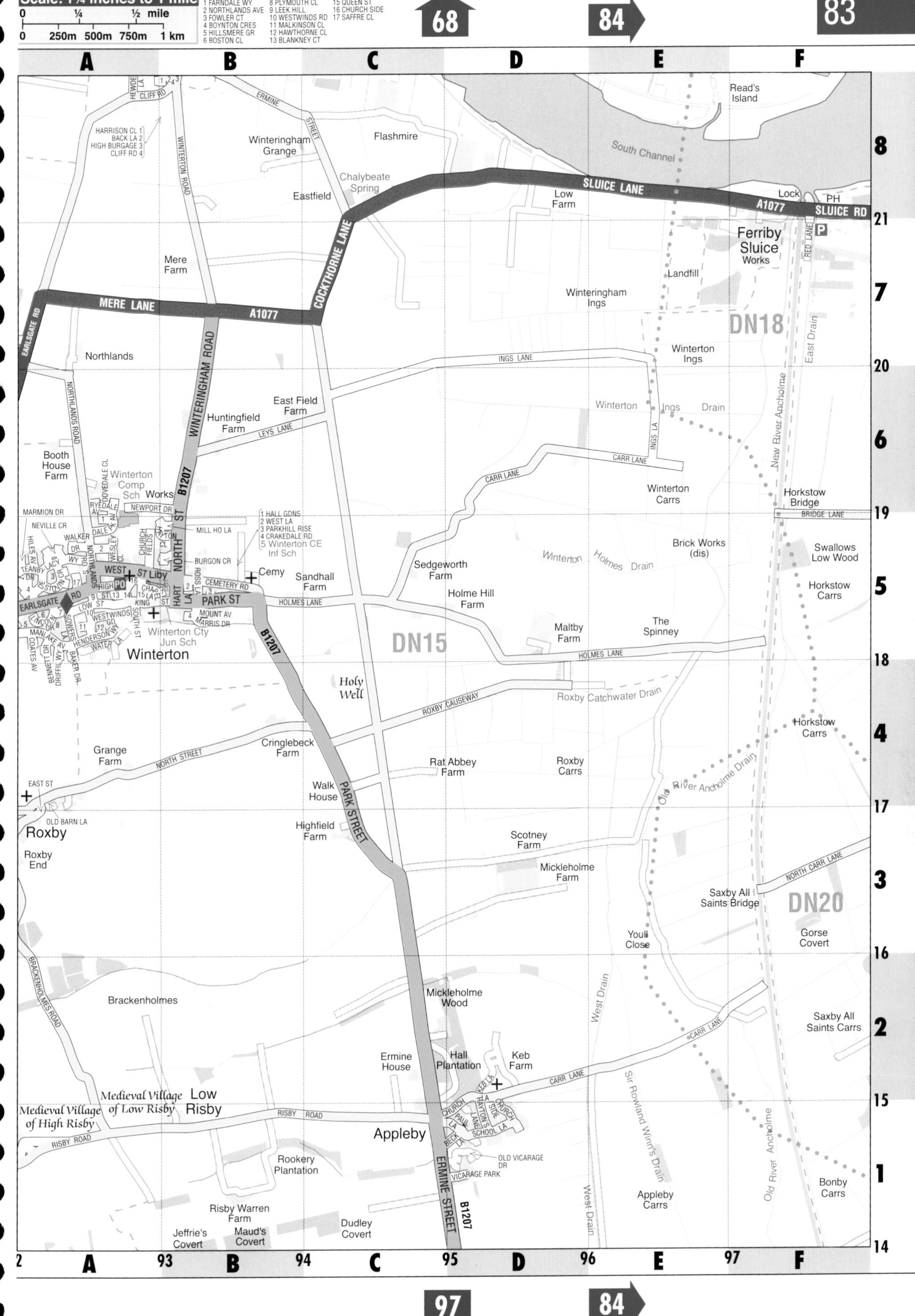

97
84

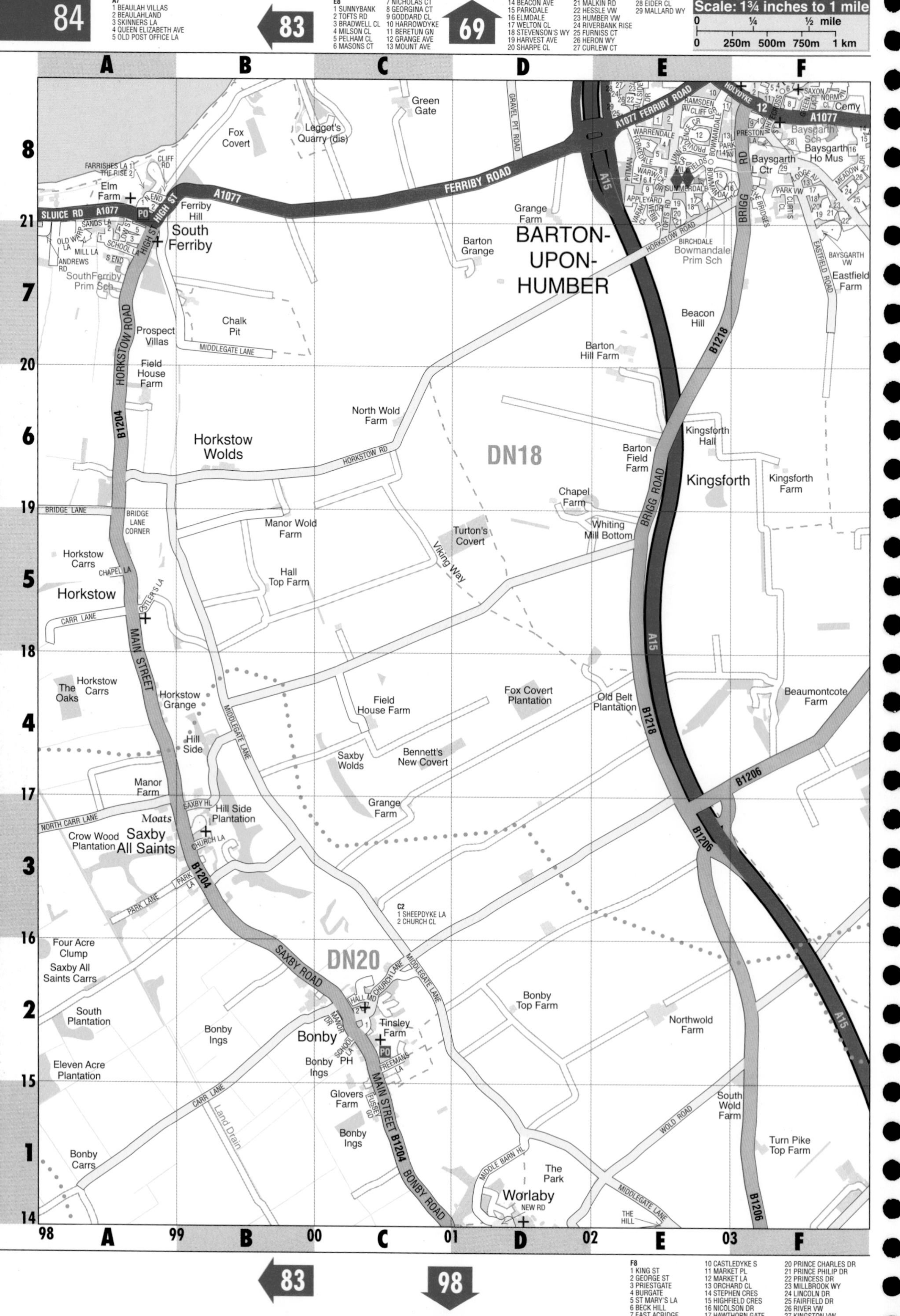

83

69

A7
1 BEAULAH VILLAS
2 BEAULAHLAND
3 SKINNERS LA
4 QUEEN ELIZABETH AVE
5 OLD POST OFFICE LA

E8
1 SUNNYBANK
2 TOFTS RD
3 BRADWELL CL
4 MILSON CL
5 PELHAM CL
6 MASONS CT

7 NICHOLAS CT
8 GEORGINA CT
9 GODDARD CL
10 HARROWDYKE
11 BERETUN GN
12 GRANGE AVE
13 MOUNT AVE

14 BEACON AVE
15 PARKDALE
16 ELMDALE
17 WELTON CL
18 STEVENSON'S WY
19 HARVEST AVE
20 SHARPE CL

21 MALKIN RD
22 HESSLE VW
23 HUMBER VW
24 RIVERBANK RISE
25 FURNISS CT
26 HERON WY
27 CURLEW CT

28 EIDER CL
29 MALLARD WY

Scale: 1¾ inches to 1 mile
0   ¼   ½   mile
0 250m 500m 750m 1 km

Map grid references (left, top to bottom): 8, 21, 7, 20, 6, 19, 5, 18, 4, 17, 3, 16, 2, 15, 1, 14

Column letters (top and bottom): A, B, C, D, E, F

Bottom grid numbers: 98, 99, 00, 01, 02, 03

Green Gate

Fox Covert

Leggot's Quarry (dis)

FARRISHES LA
THE RISE
Elm Farm
CLIFF RD

SLUICE RD   A1077   FERRIBY ROAD

Ferriby Hill

South Ferriby

SouthFerriby Prim Sch

HORKSTOW ROAD   B1204

Prospect Villas

Chalk Pit

MIDDLEGATE LANE

Field House Farm

North Wold Farm

Horkstow Wolds

HORKSTOW RD

DN18

BARTON-UPON-HUMBER

A1077 FERRIBY ROAD

A15

Grange Farm

Barton Grange

Barton Hill Farm

Bowmandale Prim Sch

Baysgarth Sch

Baysgarth Ho Mus

Eastfield Farm

Beacon Hill

B1218

Kingsforth Hall

Barton Field Farm

Kingsforth

Kingsforth Farm

BRIGG GATE

BRIDGE LANE

BRIDGE LANE CORNER

Horkstow Carrs

CHAPEL LA

Horkstow

CARR LANE

The Oaks

Horkstow Carrs

MAIN STREET

OSTLER'S LA

MIDDLEGATE LANE

Manor Wold Farm

Hall Top Farm

Viking Way

Turton's Covert

Chapel Farm

Whiting Mill Bottom

Field House Farm

Fox Covert Plantation

Old Belt Plantation

Saxby Wolds

Bennett's New Covert

Horkstow Grange

Hill Side

Manor Farm

NORTH CARR LANE

Crow Wood Plantation

Moats

Saxby All Saints

Hill Side Plantation

CHURCH LA

SAXBY HL

Grange Farm

B1206

Beaumontcote Farm

B1204

PARK LANE   PARK LA

SAXBY ROAD

DN20

C2
1 SHEEPDYKE LA
2 CHURCH CL

Four Acre Clump

Saxby All Saints Carrs

South Plantation

Bonby Ings

Bonby

MANOR RD

SCHOOL LA

HALL RD

CHURCH LANE

MIDDLEGATE LANE

Tinsley Farm

Bonby Top Farm

Northwold Farm

Eleven Acre Plantation

CARR LANE

Land Drain

Bonby PH

Bonby Ings

ELSEY RD

FREEMANS LA

Glovers Farm

MAIN STREET   B1204

Bonby Ings

Bonby Carrs

MIDDLE BARN HL

BONBY ROAD

The Park

Worlaby

NEW RD

South Wold Farm

WOLD ROAD

MIDDLEGATE LANE

B1206

THE HILL

Turn Pike Top Farm

A15

83

98

F8
1 KING ST
2 GEORGE ST
3 PRIESTGATE
4 BURGATE
5 ST MARY'S LA
6 BECK HILL
7 EAST ACRIDGE
8 CHURCH VW
9 CASTLE CT

10 CASTLEDYKE S
11 MARKET PL
12 MARKET LA
13 ORCHARD CL
14 STEPHEN CRES
15 HIGHFIELD CRES
16 NICOLSON DR
17 HAWTHORN GATE
18 RAVENDALE
19 QUEEN ELIZABETH WY

20 PRINCE CHARLES DR
21 PRINCE PHILIP DR
22 PRINCESS DR
23 MILLBROOK WY
24 LINCOLN DR
25 FAIRFIELD DR
26 RIVER VW
27 KINGSTON VW
28 NIGHTINGALE CL
29 STOWGARTH

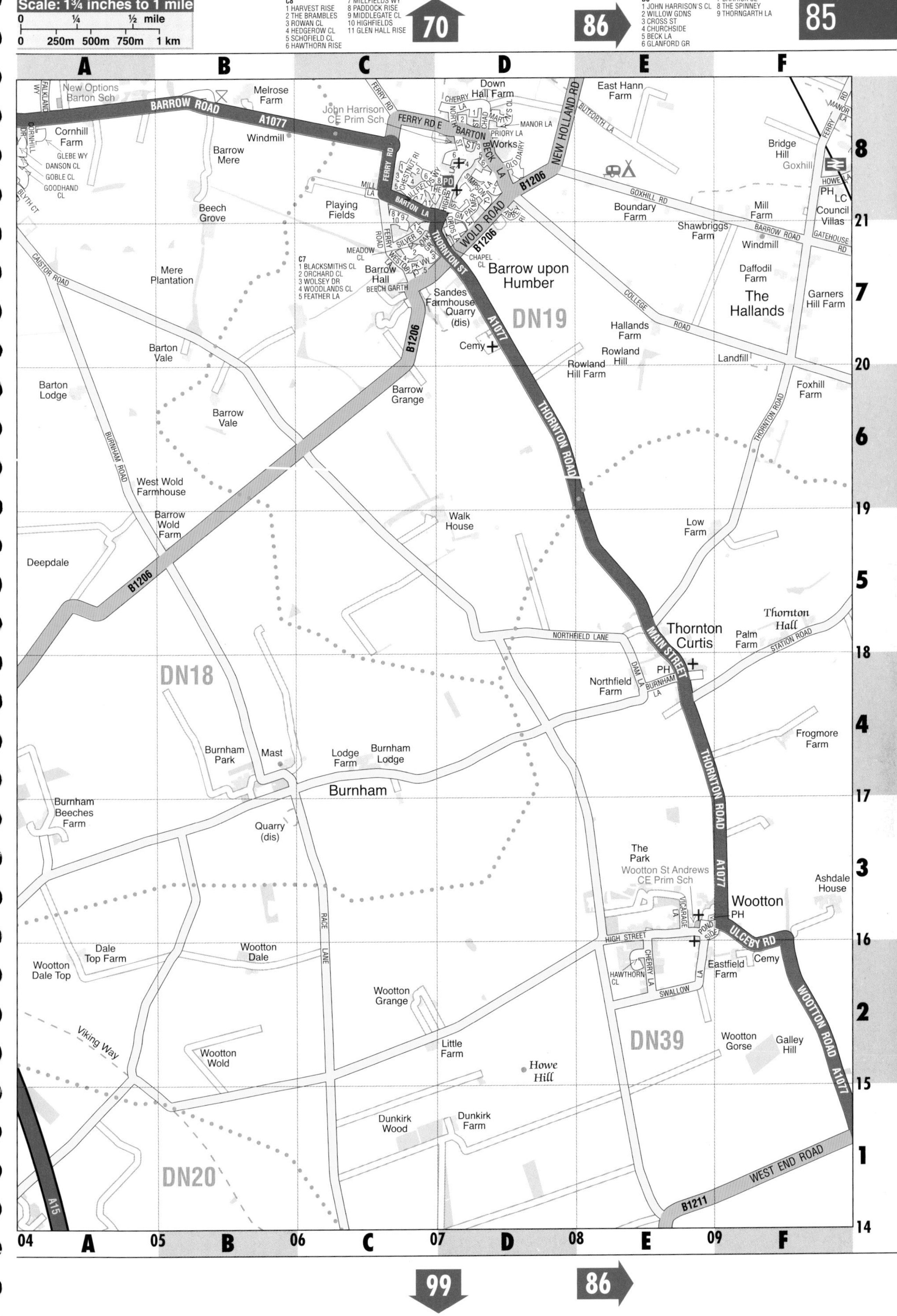
Scale: 1¾ inches to 1 mile
0 ¼ ½ mile
0 250m 500m 750m 1 km
C8
1 HARVEST RISE
2 THE BRAMBLES
3 ROWAN CL
4 HEDGEROW CL
5 SCHOFIELD CL
6 HAWTHORN RISE
7 MILLFIELDS WY
8 PADDOCK RISE
9 MIDDLEGATE CL
10 HIGHFIELDS
11 GLEN HALL RISE
70
86
D8
1 JOHN HARRISON'S CL
2 WILLOW GDNS
3 CROSS ST
4 CHURCHSIDE
5 BECK LA
6 GLANFORD GR
7 BARRICK CL
8 THE SPINNEY
9 THORNGARTH LA
A B C D E F
New Options Barton Sch
Melrose Farm
Down Hall Farm
East Hann Farm
BARROW ROAD A1077
John Harrison CE Prim Sch
FERRY RD E
Cornhill Farm
GLEBE WY
DANSON CL
GOBLE CL
GOODHAND CL
Windmill
Barrow Mere
Works
MANOR LA
NEW HOLLAND RD
BUTFORTH LA
Bridge Hill
Goxhill
B1206
GOXHILL RD
Playing Fields
Beech Grove
BARTON LA
WOLD ROAD
Boundary Farm
Shawbriggs Farm
Mill Farm
Council Villas
Windmill
BARROW ROAD
GATEHOUSE RD
MEADOW CL
C7
1 BLACKSMITHS CL
2 ORCHARD CL
3 WOLSEY DR
4 WOODLANDS CL
5 FEATHER LA
Barrow Hall
BEECH GARTH
CHAPEL CL
THORNTON ST
Barrow upon Humber
Daffodil Farm
The Hallands
Garners Hill Farm
CAISTOR ROAD
Mere Plantation
Sandes Farmhouse
Quarry (dis)
DN19
COLLEGE ROAD
Hallands Farm
Barton Vale
Cemy
Rowland Hill
Rowland Hill Farm
Landfill
Barton Lodge
Barrow Grange
Foxhill Farm
Barrow Vale
THORNTON ROAD
BURNHAM ROAD
West Wold Farmhouse
Barrow Wold Farm
Walk House
Low Farm
Deepdale
Thornton Curtis
Thornton Hall
Palm Farm
STATION ROAD
NORTHFIELD LANE
MAIN STREET
DN18
Northfield Farm
DAM LA
BURNHAM LA
PH
Frogmore Farm
Burnham Park
Mast
Lodge Farm
Burnham Lodge
Burnham
Burnham Beeches Farm
Quarry (dis)
The Park
Wootton St Andrews CE Prim Sch
Ashdale House
Wootton
VICARAGE LA
POND SIDE
HIGH STREET
ULCEBY RD
RACE LANE
Dale Top Farm
Wootton Dale
Wootton Dale Top
HAWTHORN CL
CHERRY LA
SWALLOW LA
Eastfield Farm
Wootton Grange
Viking Way
WOOTTON ROAD
Wootton Wold
Little Farm
Howe Hill
DN39
Wootton Gorse
Galley Hill
Dunkirk Wood
Dunkirk Farm
DN20
A15
WEST END ROAD
B1211
04 05 06 07 08 09
8 21 7 20 6 19 5 18 4 17 3 16 2 15 1 14
99
86

A8
1 STOTHARDS LA
2 GREENGATE LA
3 PIDGEON COTE LA
4 WESTFIELD RD
5 CHURCH ST
6 CHESTNUT WY
7 ROWEN CT
8 JASMINE CT
9 THE BRIDLES
10 BRIAR CT
11 ROSBROOK WY
12 ST JOHNS CL

85
71

Scale: 1¾ inches to 1 mile
0 ¼ ½ mile
0 250m 500m 750m 1 km

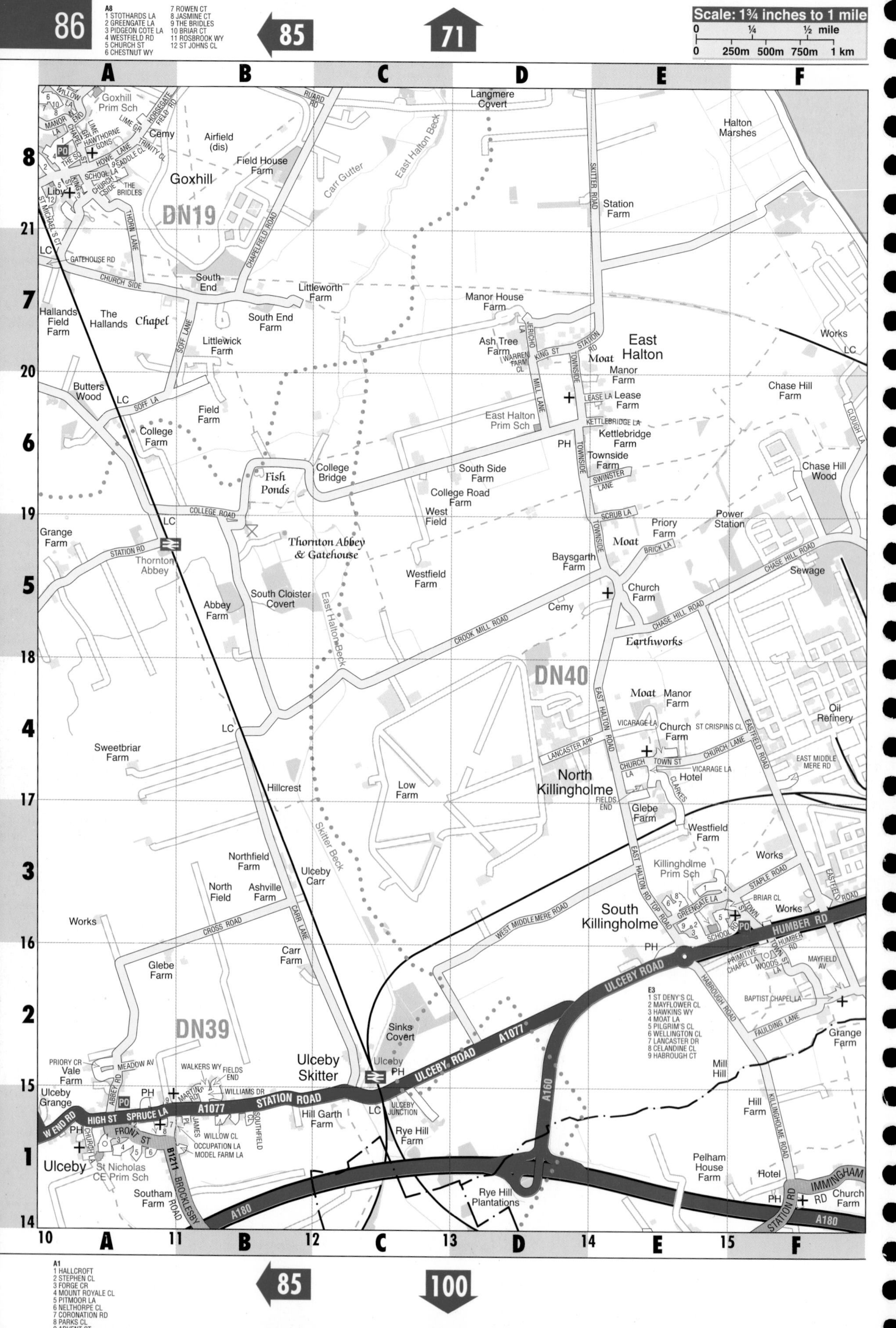

A1
1 HALLCROFT
2 STEPHEN CL
3 FORGE CR
4 MOUNT ROYALE CL
5 PITMOOR LA
6 NELTHORPE CL
7 CORONATION RD
8 PARKS CL
9 ADVENT CT

85
100

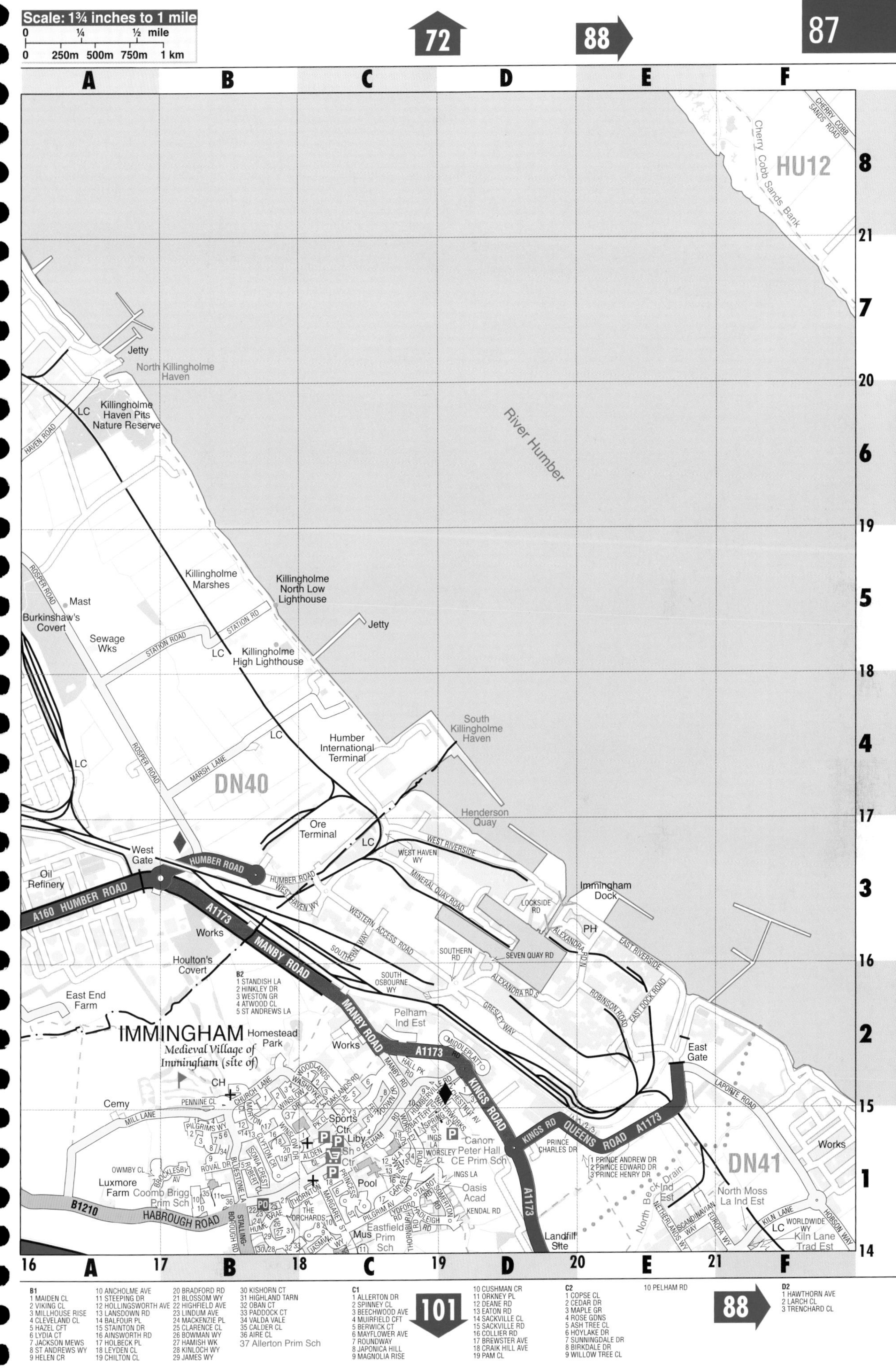

A B C D E F

HU12

8

21

7

20

Jetty

North Killingholme
Haven

LC

Killingholme
Haven Pits
Nature Reserve

6

River Humber

19

Killingholme
Marshes

Killingholme
North Low
Lighthouse

5

Jetty

Burkinshaw's
Covert

Mast

Sewage
Wks

STATION ROAD

STATION RD

LC

Killingholme
High Lighthouse

ROSPER ROAD

18

LC

South
Killingholme
Haven

4

ROSPER ROAD

MARSH LANE

LC

DN40

Humber
International
Terminal

17

LC

Oil
Refinery

West
Gate

HUMBER ROAD

Ore
Terminal

LC

Henderson
Quay

WEST RIVERSIDE

WEST HAVEN
WY

A160 HUMBER ROAD

A1173

HUMBER ROAD

WEST HAVEN WY

Humber Road

MINERAL QUAY ROAD

LOCKSIDE
RD

Immingham
Dock

3

Works

MANBY ROAD

WESTERN ACCESS ROAD

SOUTHERN WAY

SEVEN QUAY RD

ALEXANDRA RD N

PH

EAST RIVERSIDE

Houlton's
Covert

B2
1 STANDISH LA
2 HINKLEY DR
3 WESTON GR
4 ATWOOD CL
5 ST ANDREWS LA

SOUTH
OSBOURNE
WY

SOUTHERN
RD

ALEXANDRA RD S

ROBINSON ROAD

EAST DOCK ROAD

16

East End
Farm

MANBY ROAD

A1173

Pelham
Ind Est

GRESLEY WAY

East
Gate

LAPONTE ROAD

2

IMMINGHAM

Homestead
Park

Medieval Village of
Immingham (site of)

CH

Works

HALL PK

MIDDLE PLATO

KINGS ROAD

DN41

Works

15

Cemy

PENNINE CL

CHURCH LANE

Sports
Ctr

Libry

P

Canon
Peter Hall
CE Prim Sch

KINGS RD   QUEENS ROAD   A1173

PRINCE
CHARLES DR

1 PRINCE ANDREW DR
2 PRINCE EDWARD DR
3 PRINCE HENRY DR

MILL LANE

PILGRIMS WY

P
P

Sh
Ctr

P

Pool

INGS LA

Oasis
Acad

North Moss
La Ind Est

1

Luxmore
Farm

Coomb Brigg
Prim Sch

OWMBY CL

THE
ORCHARDS

THORNTON

Eastfield
Prim Sch

Mus

A1173

Landfill
Site

North Beck Drain

NETHERLANDS WY

SCANDINAVIAN
WY

EUROPA WY

KILN LANE

WORLDWIDE
WY

Kiln Lane
Trad Est

LC

Works

B1210

HABROUGH ROAD

STALLING-
BOROUGH RD

KENDAL RD

14

16   A   17   B   18   C   19   D   20   E   21   F   14

B1
1 MAIDEN CL
2 VIKING CL
3 MILLHOUSE RISE
4 CLEVELAND CL
5 HAZEL CFT
6 LYDIA CT
7 JACKSON MEWS
8 ST ANDREWS WY
9 HELEN CR
10 ANCHOLME AVE
11 STEEPING DR
12 HOLLINGSWORTH AVE
13 LANSDOWN RD
14 BALFOUR PL
15 STAINTON DR
16 AINSWORTH RD
17 HOLBECK PL
18 LEYDEN CL
19 CHILTON CL
20 BRADFORD RD
21 BLOSSOM WY
22 HIGHFIELD AVE
23 LINDUM AVE
24 MACKENZIE PL
25 CLARENCE CL
26 BOWMAN WY
27 HAMISH WK
28 KINLOCH WY
29 JAMES WY
30 KISHORN CT
31 HIGHLAND TARN
32 OBAN CT
33 PADDOCK CL
34 VALDA VALE
35 CALDER CL
36 AIRE CL
37 Allerton Prim Sch

C1
1 ALLERTON DR
2 SPINNEY CL
3 BEECHWOOD AVE
4 MUIRFIELD CFT
5 BERWICK CT
6 MAYFLOWER AVE
7 ROUNDWAY
8 JAPONICA HILL
9 MAGNOLIA RISE
10 CUSHMAN CR
11 ORKNEY PL
12 DEANE RD
13 EATON RD
14 SACKVILLE CL
15 SACKVILLE RD
16 COLLIER RD
17 BREWSTER AVE
18 CRAIK HILL AVE
19 PAM CL

C2
1 COPSE CL
2 CEDAR DR
3 MAPLE GR
4 ROSE GDNS
5 ASH TREE CL
6 HOYLAKE DR
7 SUNNINGDALE DR
8 BIRKDALE DR
9 WILLOW TREE CL

10 PELHAM RD

D2
1 HAWTHORN AVE
2 LARCH CL
3 TRENCHARD CL

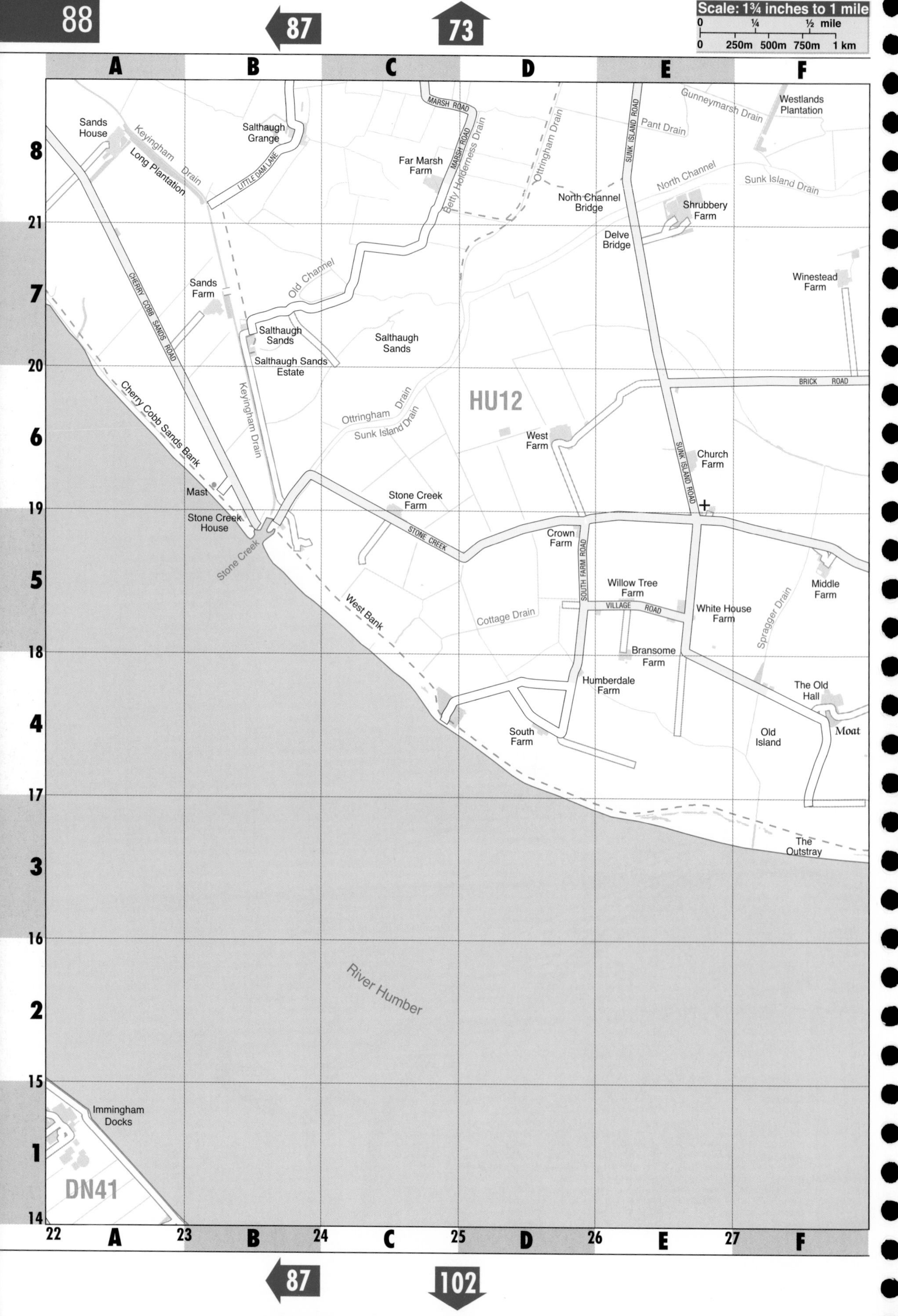

A   B   C   D   E   F

Sands
House

Keyingham Drain

Long Plantation

Salthaugh
Grange

LITTLE DAM LANE

MARSH ROAD

Far Marsh
Farm

Betty Holderness Drain

MARSH ROAD

Ottringham Drain

North Channel
Bridge

Pant Drain

SUNK ISLAND ROAD

Gunneymarsh Drain

Westlands
Plantation

North Channel

Sunk Island Drain

Shrubbery
Farm

8

21

7

20

6

19

5

18

4

17

3

16

2

15

1

14

Delve
Bridge

Winestead
Farm

Sands
Farm

Old Channel

Salthaugh
Sands

Salthaugh
Sands

CHERRY COBB SANDS ROAD

Keyingham Drain

Salthaugh Sands
Estate

Ottringham Drain

Sunk Island Drain

HU12

BRICK   ROAD

Cherry Cobb Sands Bank

Mast

Stone Creek
House

Stone Creek

West Farm

West
Farm

SUNK ISLAND ROAD

Church
Farm

+

Stone Creek
Farm

STONE CREEK

Crown
Farm

SOUTH FARM ROAD

Middle
Farm

Spragger Drain

West Bank

Cottage Drain

Willow Tree
Farm

VILLAGE   ROAD

White House
Farm

Bransome
Farm

The Old
Hall

Humberdale
Farm

South
Farm

Old
Island

Moat

The
Outstray

River Humber

Immingham
Docks

DN41

22   A   23   B   24   C   25   D   26   E   27   F

Scale: 1¾ inches to 1 mile

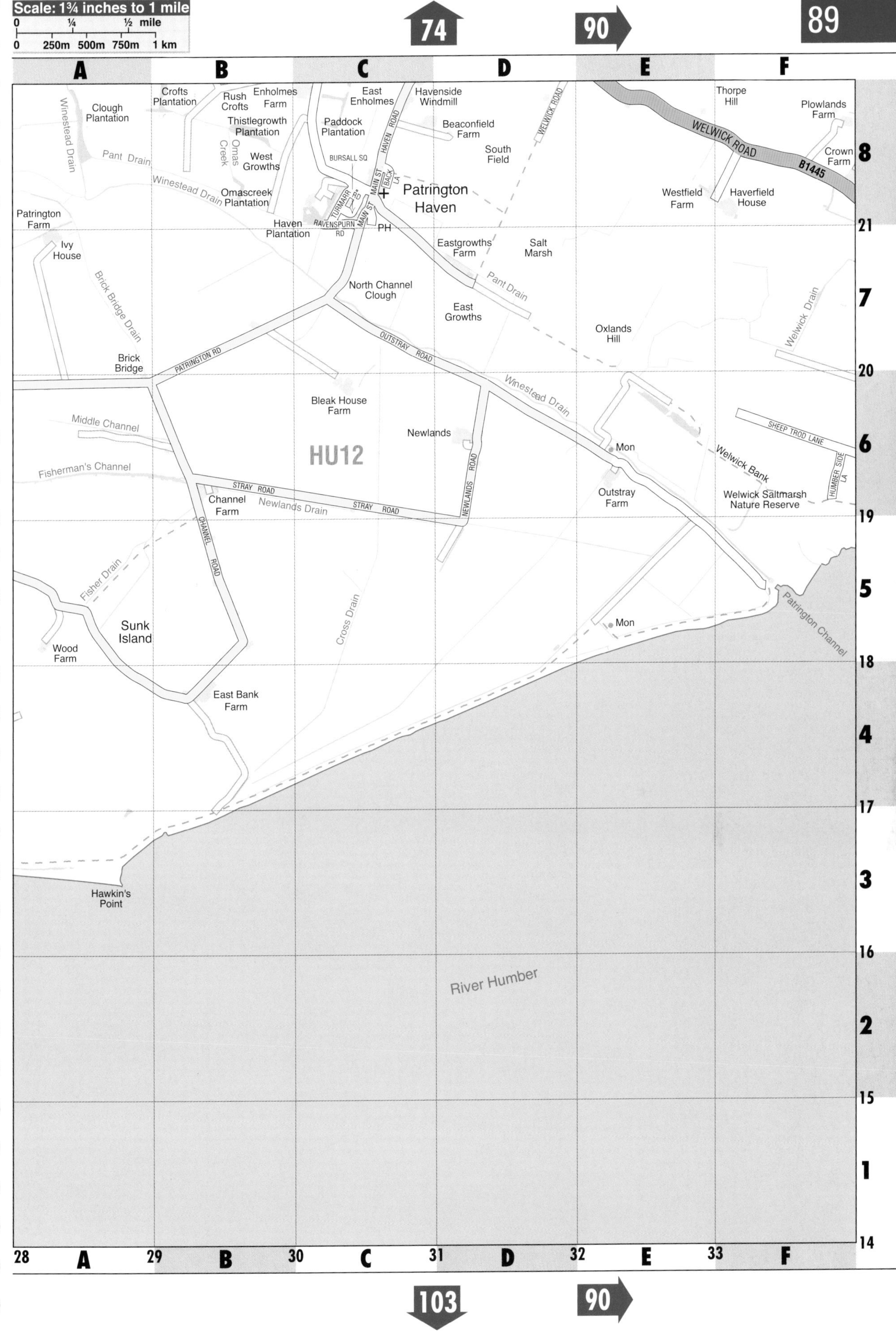

74
90
A
B
C
D
E
F
Clough Plantation
Crofts Plantation
Rush Crofts
Enholmes Farm
East Enholmes
Havenside Windmill
Thistlegrowth Plantation
Paddock Plantation
Beaconfield Farm
South Field
Thorpe Hill
Plowlands Farm
WELWICK ROAD
B1445
Crown Farm
Westfield Farm
Haverfield House
Winestead Drain
Pant Drain
Omas Creek
West Growths
BURSALL SQ
HAVEN ROAD
BACK LA
MAIN ST
TURMARR RD
Patrington Haven
Omascreek Plantation
Haven Plantation
RAVENSPURN RD
PH
Patrington Farm
Ivy House
Eastgrowths Farm
Salt Marsh
North Channel Clough
Brick Bridge Drain
East Growths
Oxlands Hill
Welwick Drain
Brick Bridge
PATRINGTON RD
OUTSTRAY ROAD
Bleak House Farm
Newlands
HU12
Middle Channel
Fisherman's Channel
SHEEP TROD LANE
Mon
Welwick Bank
HUMBER SIDE LA
Welwick Saltmarsh Nature Reserve
Outstray Farm
STRAY ROAD
Channel Farm
Newlands Drain
NEWLANDS ROAD
CHANNEL ROAD
Fisher Drain
Sunk Island
Wood Farm
Cross Drain
Patrington Channel
East Bank Farm
Hawkin's Point
River Humber
WELWICK ROAD
8
21
7
20
6
19
5
18
4
17
3
16
2
15
1
14
28
29
30
31
32
33
103
90

89

75

Scale: 1¾ inches to 1 mile

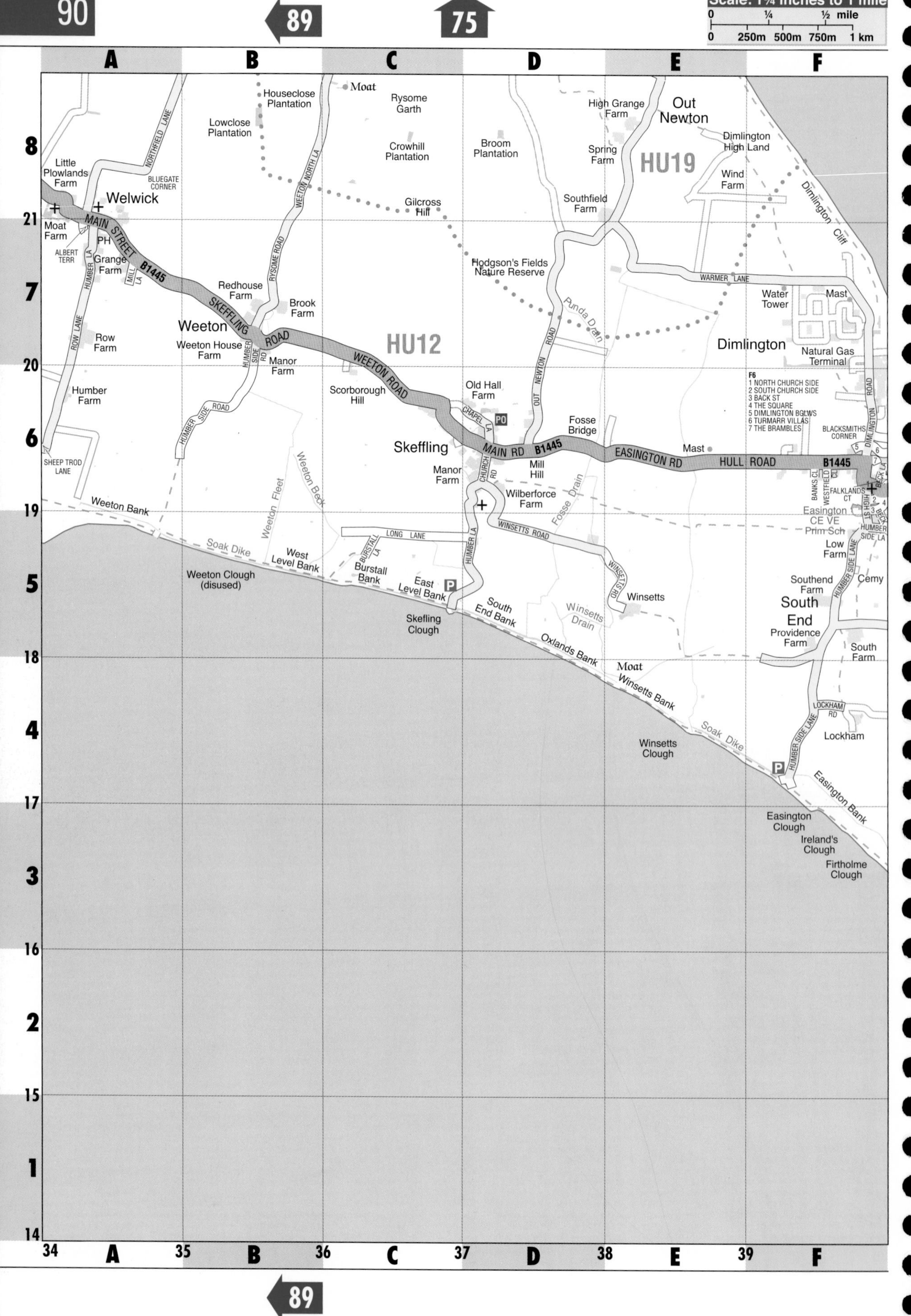

Welwick
Weeton
Skeffling
Out Newton
Dimlington
South End
HU12
HU19
Little Plowlands Farm
Moat Farm
Grange Farm
Row Farm
Humber Farm
Houseclose Plantation
Lowclose Plantation
Rysome Garth
Crowhill Plantation
Broom Plantation
Gilcross Hill
Hodgson's Fields Nature Reserve
Redhouse Farm
Brook Farm
Weeton House Farm
Manor Farm
Scorborough Hill
Old Hall Farm
Mill Hill
Wilberforce Farm
Fosse Bridge
High Grange Farm
Spring Farm
Southfield Farm
Dimlington High Land
Wind Farm
Water Tower
Mast
Natural Gas Terminal
MAIN STREET
SKEFFLING ROAD
WEETON ROAD
MAIN RD
EASINGTON RD
HULL ROAD
WARMER LANE
B1445
Weeton Bank
Soak Dike
West Level Bank
Weeton Clough (disused)
Burstall Bank
East Level Bank
Skefling Clough
South End Bank
Oxlands Bank
Winsetts Bank
Winsetts
Winsetts Clough
Easington Bank
Easington Clough
Ireland's Clough
Firtholme Clough
Lockham
South Farm
Southend Farm
Providence Farm
Low Farm
Easington CE VE Prim Sch
Dimlington Cliff
F6
1 NORTH CHURCH SIDE
2 SOUTH CHURCH SIDE
3 BACK ST
4 THE SQUARE
5 DIMLINGTON BGLWS
6 TURMARR VILLAS
7 THE BRAMBLES

89

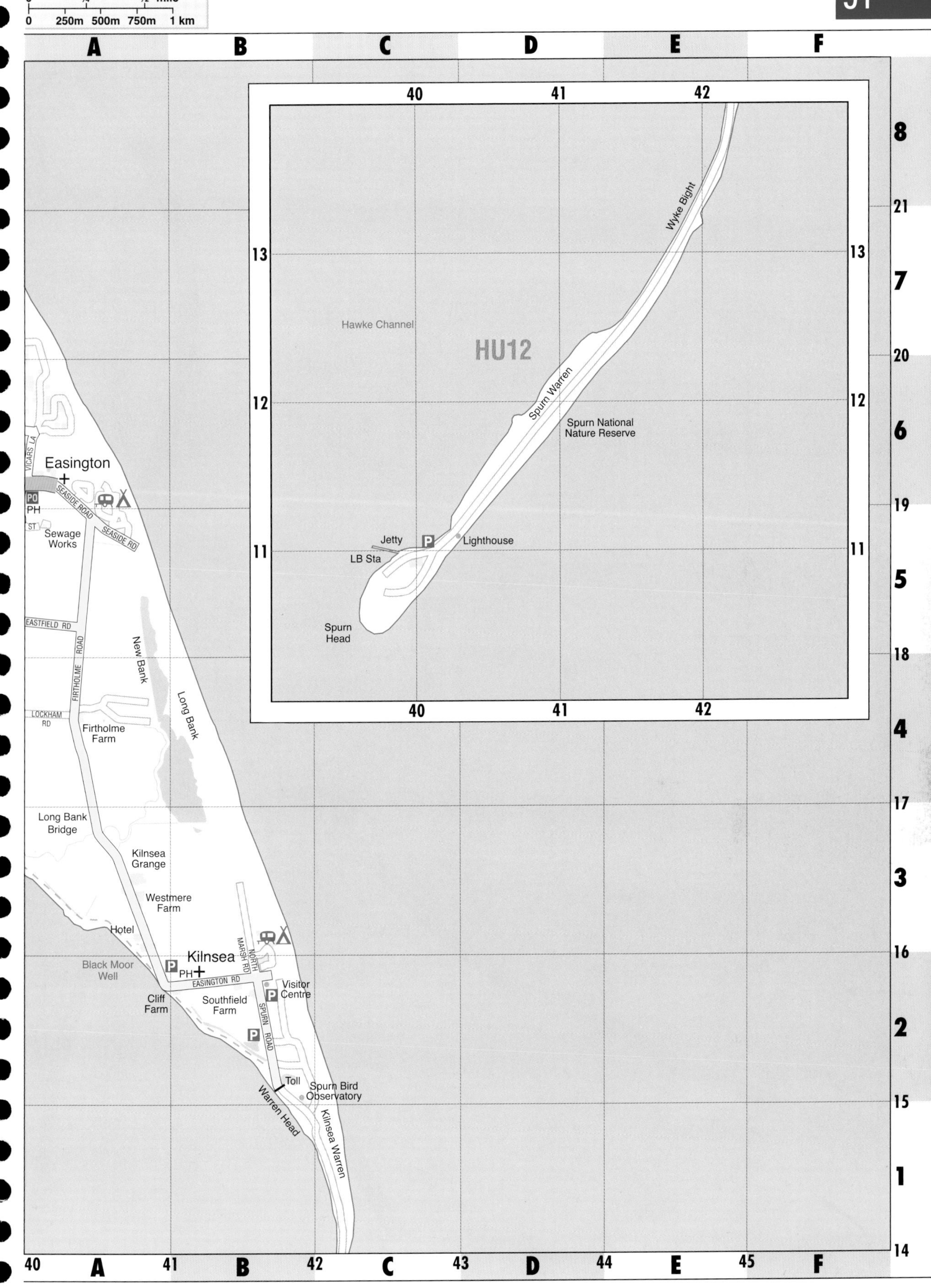

Scale: 1¾ inches to 1 mile

0   ¼   ½   mile
0   250m   500m   750m   1 km

HU12

Hawke Channel

Wyke Bight

Spurn Warren

Spurn National
Nature Reserve

Jetty
LB Sta
P
Lighthouse

Spurn
Head

Easington

PO
PH
ST
Sewage
Works

VICARS LA
SEASIDE ROAD
SEASIDE RD

EASTFIELD RD

FIRTHOLME ROAD

LOCKHAM
RD

Firtholme
Farm

New Bank

Long Bank

Long Bank
Bridge

Kilnsea
Grange

Westmere
Farm

Hotel

Black Moor
Well

Kilnsea

P
PH

EASINGTON RD

NORTH MARSH RD

SPURN ROAD

Cliff
Farm

Southfield
Farm

P

Visitor
Centre

P

Toll

Spurn Bird
Observatory

Warren Head

Kilnsea Warren

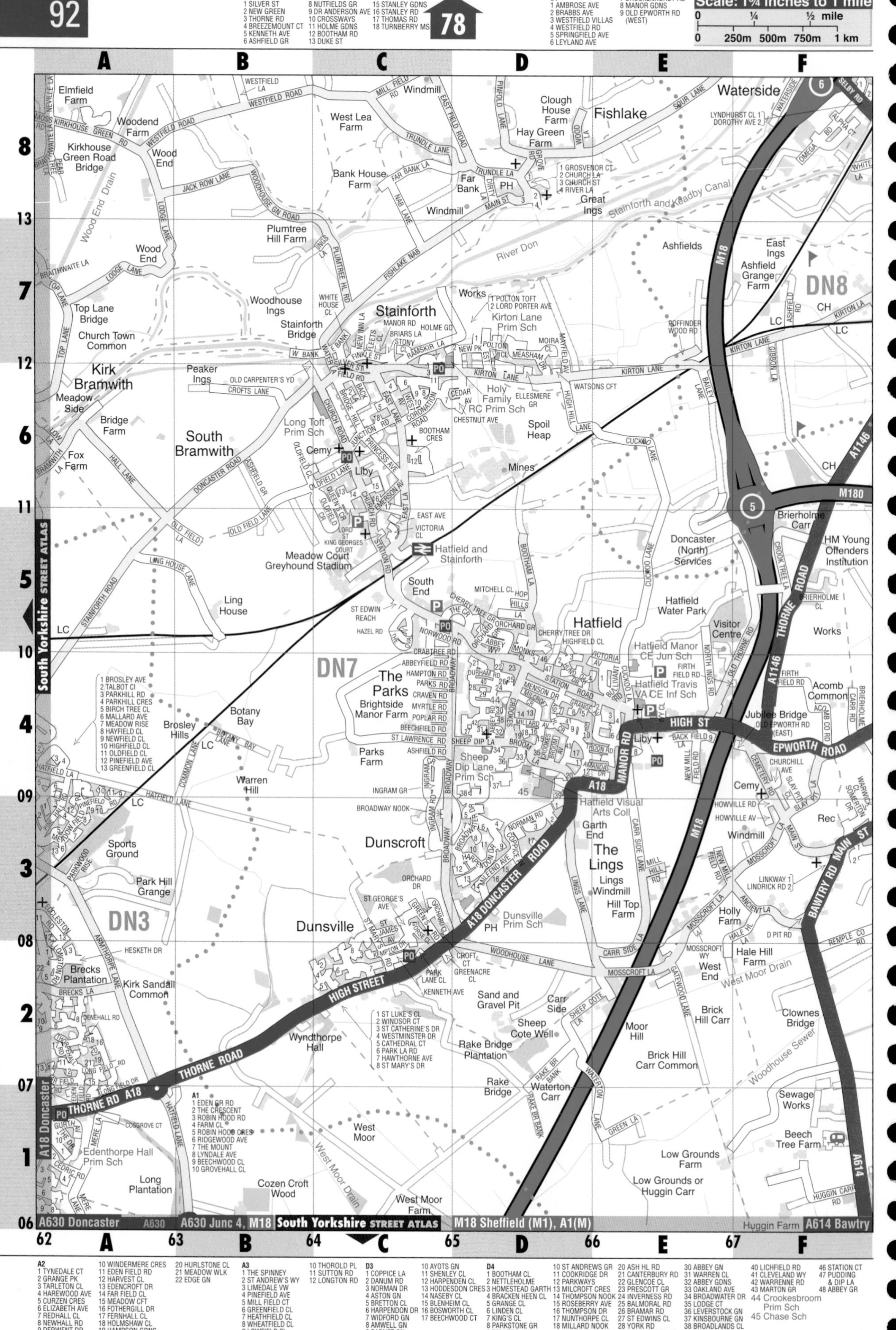
C6
1 SILVER ST
2 NEW GREEN
3 THORNE RD
4 BREEZEMOUNT CT
5 KENNETH AVE
6 ASHFIELD GR
7 BEECH CRES
8 NUTFIELDS GR
9 DR ANDERSON AVE
10 CROSSWAYS
11 HOLME GDNS
12 BOOTHAM RD
13 DUKE ST
14 KINGSWAY
15 STANLEY GDNS
16 STANLEY RD
17 THOMAS RD
18 TURNBERRY MS
78
E4
1 AMBROSE AVE
2 BRABBS AVE
3 WESTFIELD VILLAS
4 WESTFIELD RD
5 SPRINGFIELD AVE
6 LEYLAND AVE
7 BROCKENHURST RD
8 MANOR GDNS
9 OLD EPWORTH RD (WEST)
Scale: 1¾ inches to 1 mile
0 ¼ ½ mile
0 250m 500m 750m 1 km
A B C D E F
8 13 7 12 6 11 5 10 4 09 3 08 2 07 1 06
62 63 64 65 66 67
Elmfield Farm
Woodend Farm
Kirkhouse Green Road Bridge
Wood End
Windmill
West Lea Farm
Clough House Farm
Fishlake
Hay Green Farm
Waterside
Bank House Farm
Far Bank
Great Ings
Stainforth and Keadby Canal
River Don
Plumtree Hill Farm
Wood End
Ashfields
East Ings
Ashfield Grange Farm
DN8
Woodhouse Ings
Stainforth Bridge
Stainforth
Works
Kirton Lane Prim Sch
Top Lane Bridge
Church Town Common
Kirk Bramwith
Peaker Ings
Meadow Side
Bridge Farm
South Bramwith
Long Toft Prim Sch
Holy Family RC Prim Sch
Spoil Heap
Fox Farm
Mines
Brierholme Carr
Doncaster (North) Services
HM Young Offenders Institution
Hatfield and Stainforth
Meadow Court Greyhound Stadium
South End
Ling House
Hatfield Water Park
Hatfield
Visitor Centre
Works
DN7
The Parks
Brightside Manor Farm
Hatfield Manor CE Jun Sch
Hatfield Travis VA CE Inf Sch
Acomb Common
Botany Bay
Brosley Hills
Jubilee Bridge
Parks Farm
Sheep Dip Lane Prim Sch
Warren Hill
Cemy
Rec
Hatfield Visual Arts Coll
Garth End
Windmill
Sports Ground
Dunscroft
The Lings
Lings Windmill
Park Hill Grange
Hill Top Farm
DN3
Dunsville
Dunsville Prim Sch
Holly Farm
Hale Hill Farm
Bracks Plantation
West End
West Moor Drain
Kirk Sandall Common
Sand and Gravel Pit
Carr Side
Brick Hill Carr
Clownes Bridge
Wyndthorpe Hall
Sheep Cote Well
Moor Hill
Rake Bridge Plantation
Brick Hill Carr Common
Woodhouse Sewer
Rake Bridge
Waterton Carr
Sewage Works
West Moor
Edenthorpe Hall Prim Sch
Beech Tree Farm
Long Plantation
Low Grounds Farm
Low Grounds or Huggin Carr
Cozen Croft Wood
West Moor Farm
HIGH STREET
THORNE ROAD
A18 DONCASTER ROAD
HIGH ST
EPWORTH ROAD
BAWTRY RD MAIN ST
THORNE ROAD
M18
M180
A1146
A614
South Yorkshire STREET ATLAS
A18 Doncaster
A630 Doncaster
A630 Junc 4, M18
South Yorkshire STREET ATLAS
M18 Sheffield (M1), A1(M)
Huggin Farm
A614 Bawtry
A2
1 TYNEDALE CT
2 GRANGE PK
3 TARLETON CL
4 HAREWOOD AVE
5 CURZEN CRES
6 ELIZABETH AVE
7 REDHALL CL
8 NEWHALL RD
9 DERWENT DR
10 WINDERMERE CRES
11 EDEN FIELD RD
12 HARVEST CL
13 EDENCROFT DR
14 FAR FIELD CL
15 MEADOW CFT
16 FOTHERGILL DR
17 FERNHALL CL
18 HOLMSHAW CL
19 HAMPSON GDNS
20 HURLSTONE CL
21 MEADOW WLK
22 EDGE GN
A3
1 THE SPINNEY
2 ST ANDREW'S WY
3 LIMEDALE VW
4 PINEFIELD AVE
5 MILL FIELD CT
6 GREENFIELD CL
7 HEATHFIELD CL
8 WHEATFIELD CL
9 LOWFIELD CL
10 THOROLD PL
11 SUTTON RD
12 LONGTON RD
D3
1 COPPICE LA
2 DANUM RD
3 NORMAN DR
4 ASTON GN
5 BRETTON CL
6 HARPENDON DR
7 WIDFORD GN
8 AMWELL GN
9 BARNET GN
10 AYOTS GN
11 SHENLEY CL
12 HARPENDEN CL
13 HODDESDON CRES
14 NASEBY CL
15 BLENHEIM CL
16 BOSWORTH CL
17 BEECHWOOD CT
D4
1 BOOTHAM CL
2 NETTLEHOLME
3 HOMESTEAD GARTH
4 BRACKEN HEEN CL
5 GRANGE CL
6 LINDEN CL
7 KING'S CL
8 PARKSTONE GR
9 TOLLESBY LA
10 ST ANDREWS GR
11 CONCRIDGE DR
12 PARKWAYS
13 MILCROFT CRES
14 THOMPSON NOOK
15 ROSEBERRY AVE
16 THOMPSON DR
17 NUNTHORPE CL
18 MILLARD NOOK
19 WHITE HO CL
20 ASH HL RD
21 CANTERBURY RD
22 GLENCOE CL
23 PRESCOTT GR
24 INVERNESS RD
25 BALMORAL RD
26 BRAMAR RD
27 ST EDWINS CL
28 YORK RD
29 WINCHESTER RD
30 ABBEY GN
31 WARREN CL
32 ABBEY GDNS
33 OAKLAND AVE
34 BROADWATER DR
35 LODGE CT
36 LEVERSTOCK GN
37 KINSBOURNE GN
38 BROADLANDS CL
39 COPPICE GR
40 LICHFIELD RD
41 CLEVELAND WY
42 WARRENNE RD
43 MARTON GR
44 Crookesbroom Prim Sch
45 Chase Sch
46 STATION CT
47 PUDDING & DIP LA
48 ABBEY GR

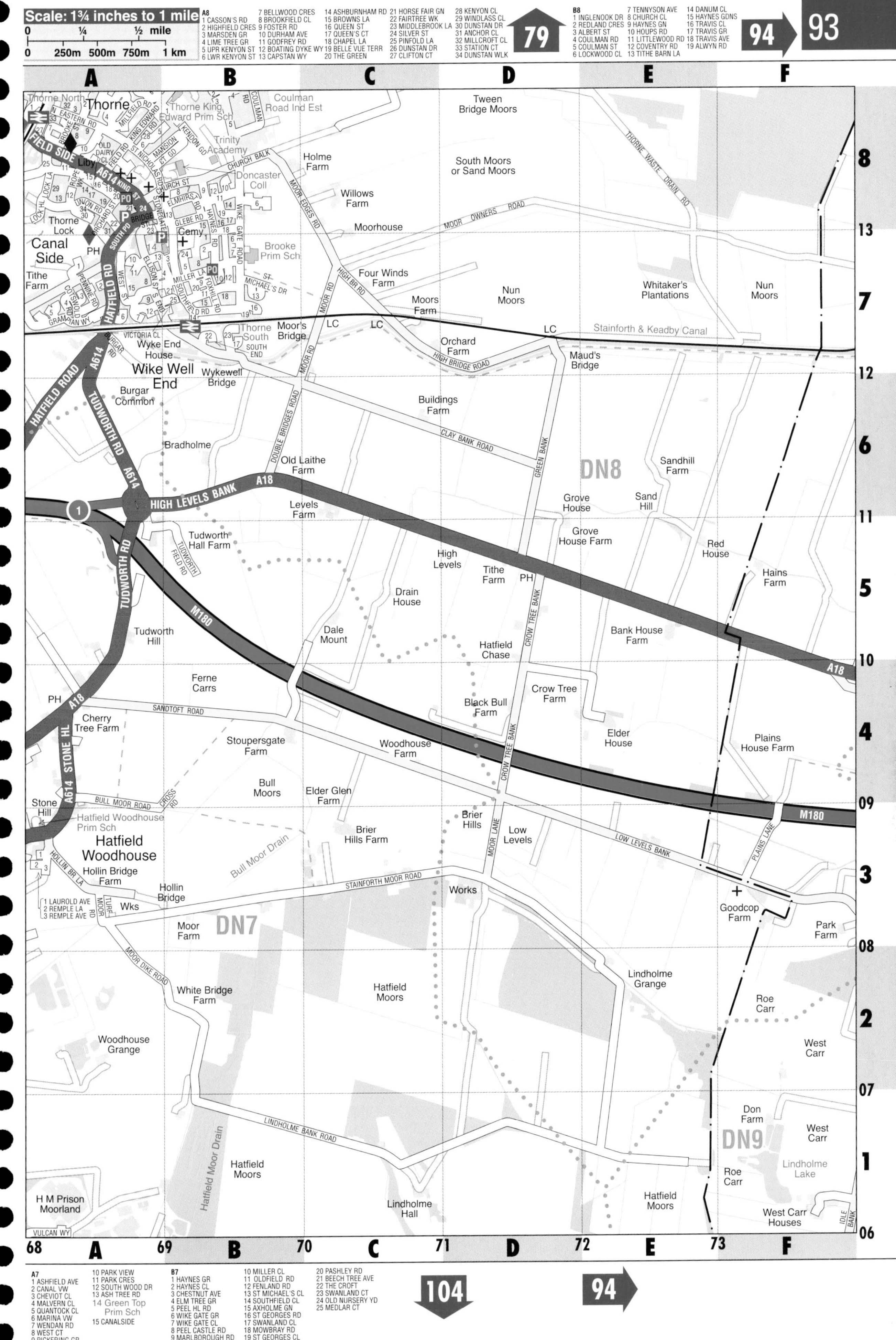

A8
1 CASSON'S RD
2 HIGHFIELD CRES
3 MARSDEN GN
4 LIME TREE GR
5 UPR KENYON ST
6 LWR KENYON ST
7 BELLWOOD CRES
8 BROOKFIELD CL
9 FOSTER RD
10 DURHAM AVE
11 GODFREY RD
12 BOATING DYKE WY
13 CAPSTAN WY
14 ASHBURNHAM RD
15 BROWNS LA
16 QUEEN ST
17 QUEEN'S CT
18 CHAPEL LA
19 BELLE VUE TERR
20 THE GREEN
21 HORSE FAIR GN
22 FAIRTREE WK
23 MIDDLEBROOK LA
24 SILVER ST
25 PINFOLD LA
26 DUNSTAN DR
27 CLIFTON CT
28 KENYON CL
29 WINDLASS CL
30 DUNSTAN DR
31 ANCHOR CL
32 MILLCROFT CL
33 STATION CT
34 DUNSTAN WLK

B8
1 INGLENOOK DR
2 REDLAND CRES
3 ALBERT ST
4 COULMAN RD
5 COULMAN ST
6 LOCKWOOD CL
7 TENNYSON AVE
8 CHURCH CL
9 HAYNES GN
10 HOUPS RD
11 LITTLEWOOD RD
12 COVENTRY RD
13 TITHE BARN LA
14 DANUM CL
15 HAYNES GDNS
16 TRAVIS CL
17 TRAVIS GR
18 TRAVIS AVE
19 ALWYN RD

79 94 93

Thorne North
Thorne
Coulman
Road Ind Est
Tween
Bridge Moors
Thorne King
Edward Prim Sch
Trinity
Academy
Holme
Farm
South Moors
or Sand Moors
Doncaster
Coll
Willows
Farm
Moorhouse
MOOR OWNERS ROAD
Canal
Side
Thorne
Lock
Cemy
Brooke
Prim Sch
Four Winds
Farm
Nun
Moors
Whitaker's
Plantations
Nun
Moors
Tithe
Farm
Moors
Farm
Orchard
Farm
LC
LC
LC
Stainforth & Keadby Canal
Moor's
Bridge
Victoria Cl
Wyke End
House
Thorne
South
SOUTH
END
Maud's
Bridge
Wike Well
End
Wykewell
Bridge
HIGH BRIDGE ROAD
Burgar
Common
Buildings
Farm
Bradholme
CLAY BANK ROAD
DN8
Old Laithe
Farm
Sandhill
Farm
HIGH LEVELS BANK A18
Levels
Farm
Grove
House
Sand
Hill
Tudworth
Hall Farm
High
Levels
Grove
House Farm
Red
House
Tudworth
Hill
Drain
House
Tithe
Farm
PH
Hains
Farm
Dale
Mount
Bank House
Farm
A18
Ferne
Carrs
Hatfield
Chase
PH A18
Cherry
Tree Farm
Stoupersgate
Farm
Woodhouse
Farm
Black Bull
Farm
Crow Tree
Farm
Elder
House
Plains
House Farm
M180
Bull
Moors
Elder Glen
Farm
Brier
Hills
Low
Levels
Stone
Hill
Hatfield Woodhouse
Prim Sch
Brier
Hills Farm
LOW LEVELS BANK
M180
**Hatfield
Woodhouse**
Hollin Bridge
Farm
STAINFORTH MOOR ROAD
Works
Goodcop
Farm
Park
Farm
Hollin
Bridge
Wks
Moor
Farm
DN7
Lindholme
Grange
Roe
Carr
White Bridge
Farm
Hatfield
Moors
Don
Farm
West
Carr
Woodhouse
Grange
LINDHOLME BANK ROAD
DN9
West
Carr
Roe
Carr
Lindholme
Lake
H M Prison
Moorland
Hatfield
Moors
Lindholme
Hall
Hatfield
Moors
West Carr
Houses

104 94

A7
1 ASHFIELD AVE
2 CANAL VW
3 CHEVIOT CL
4 MALVERN CL
5 QUANTOCK CL
6 MARINA VW
7 WENDAN RD
8 WEST CT
9 PICKERING GR
10 PARK VIEW
11 PARK CRES
12 SOUTH WOOD DR
13 ASH TREE RD
14 Green Top
Prim Sch
15 CANALSIDE

B7
1 HAYNES GR
2 HAYNES CL
3 CHESTNUT AVE
4 ELM TREE GR
5 PEEL HL RD
6 WIKE GATE GR
7 WIKE GATE CL
8 PEEL CASTLE RD
9 MARLBOROUGH RD
10 MILLER CL
11 OLDFIELD RD
12 FENLAND RD
13 ST MICHAEL'S CL
14 SOUTHFIELD CL
15 AXHOLME GN
16 ST GEORGES RD
17 SWANLAND CL
18 MOWBRAY RD
19 ST GEORGES CL
20 PASHLEY RD
21 BEECH TREE AVE
22 THE CROFT
23 SWANLAND CT
24 OLD NURSERY YD
25 MEDLAR CT

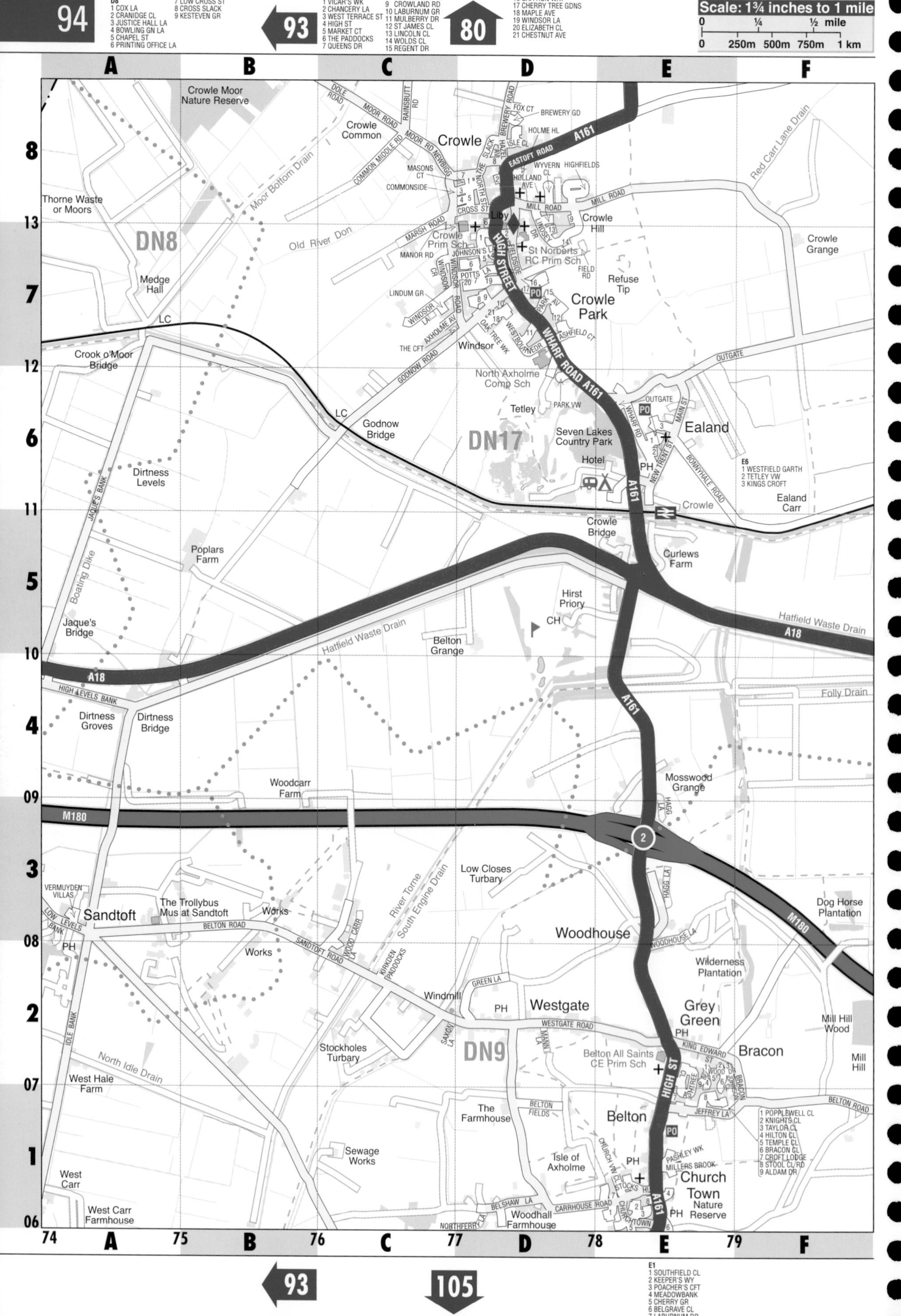

94

D8
1 COX LA
2 CRANIDGE CL
3 JUSTICE HALL LA
4 BOWLING GN LA
5 CHAPEL ST
6 PRINTING OFFICE LA

7 LOW CROSS ST
8 CROSS SLACK
9 KESTEVEN GR

D7
1 VICAR'S WK
2 CHANCERY LA
3 WEST TERRACE ST
4 HIGH ST
5 MARKET CT
6 THE PADDOCKS
7 QUEENS DR

8 SOUTHFIELD RD
9 CROWLAND RD
10 LABURNUM GR
11 MULBERRY DR
12 ST JAMES CL
13 LINCOLN CL
14 WOLDS CL
15 REGENT DR

16 SAFFRON WAY
17 CHERRY TREE GDNS
18 MAPLE AVE
19 WINDSOR LA
20 ELIZABETH CL
21 CHESTNUT AVE

93

80

Scale: 1¾ inches to 1 mile

0 ¼ ½ mile
0 250m 500m 750m 1 km

E6
1 WESTFIELD GARTH
2 TETLEY VW
3 KINGS CROFT

E1
1 SOUTHFIELD CL
2 KEEPER'S WY
3 POACHER'S CFT
4 MEADOWBANK
5 CHERRY GR
6 BELGRAVE CL
7 LABURNUM DR
8 ORCHARD GR

1 POPPLEWELL CL
2 KNIGHTS CL
3 TAYLOR CL
4 HILTON CL
5 TEMPLE CL
6 BRACON CL
7 CROFT LODGE
8 STOOL CL/RD
9 ALDAM DR

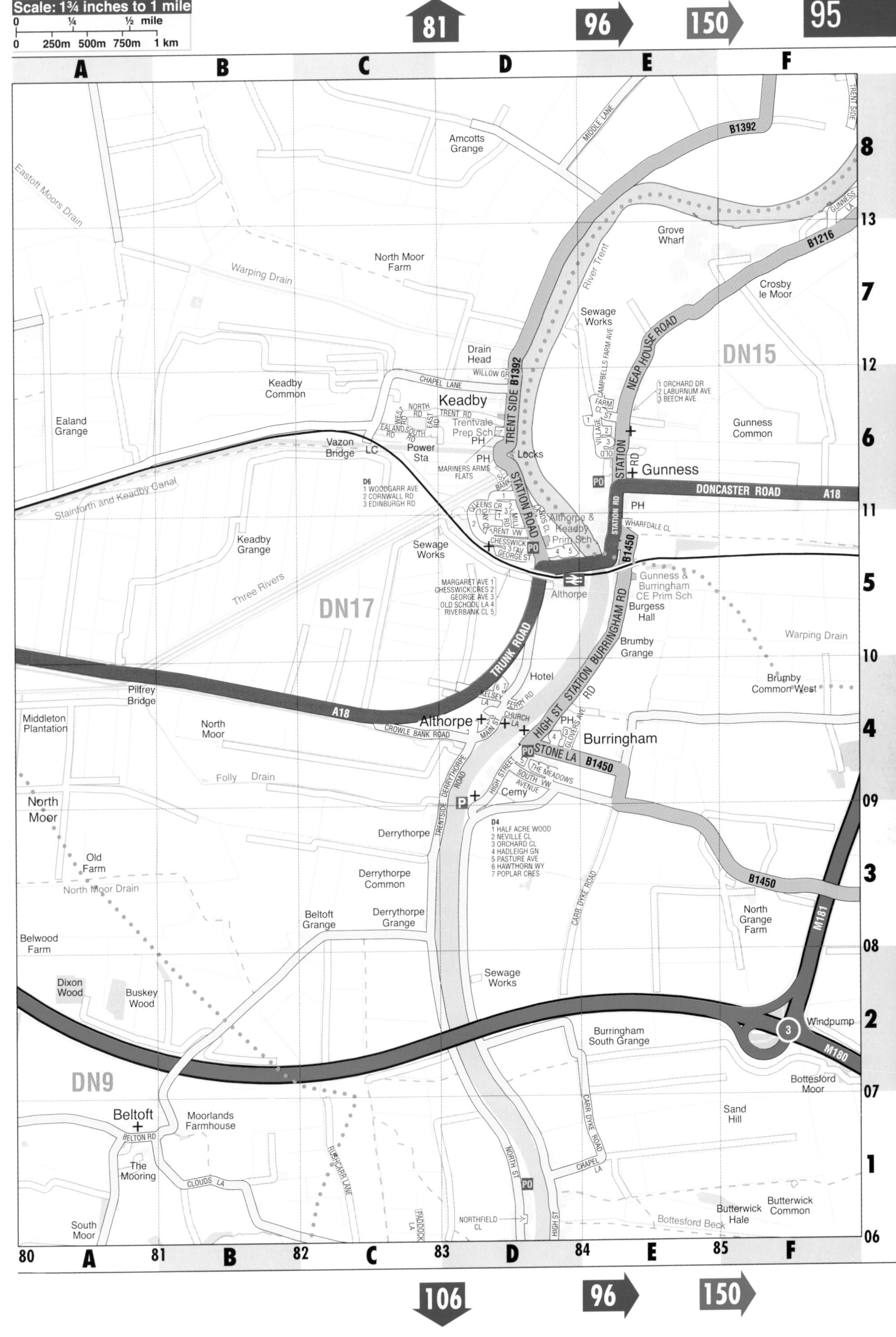
Scale: 1¾ inches to 1 mile
81
96
150
Keadby
Gunness
Althorpe
Burringham
Beltoft
DN17
DN15
DN9
DONCASTER ROAD
A18
TRUNK ROAD
B1392
B1216
B1450
M181
M180
Amcotts Grange
North Moor Farm
Grove Wharf
Crosby le Moor
Sewage Works
Drain Head
Keadby Common
Ealand Grange
Vazon Bridge
Power Sta
Locks
Gunness Common
Keadby Grange
Three Rivers
Warping Drain
Stainforth and Keadby Canal
Eastoft Moors Drain
River Trent
Pilfrey Bridge
Middleton Plantation
North Moor
Folly Drain
Old Farm
North Moor Drain
Belwood Farm
Dixon Wood
Buskey Wood
Derrythorpe
Derrythorpe Common
Derrythorpe Grange
Beltoft Grange
Burgess Hall
Brumby Grange
Brumby Common West
North Grange Farm
Windpump
Burringham South Grange
Bottesford Moor
Sand Hill
Moorlands Farmhouse
The Mooring
South Moor
Butterwick Hale
Butterwick Common
Bottesford Beck
Gunness & Burringham CE Prim Sch
Althorpe & Keadby Prim Sch
Trentvale Prep Sch
D6 1 WOODGARR AVE 2 CORNWALL RD 3 EDINBURGH RD
1 ORCHARD DR 2 LABURNUM AVE 3 BEECH AVE
D4 1 HALF ACRE WOOD 2 NEVILLE CL 3 ORCHARD CL 4 HADLEIGH GN 5 PASTURE AVE 6 HAWTHORN WY 7 POPLAR CRES
MARGARET AVE 1 CHESSWICK CRES 2 GEORGE AVE 3 OLD SCHOOL LA 4 RIVERBANK CL 5
106
96
150

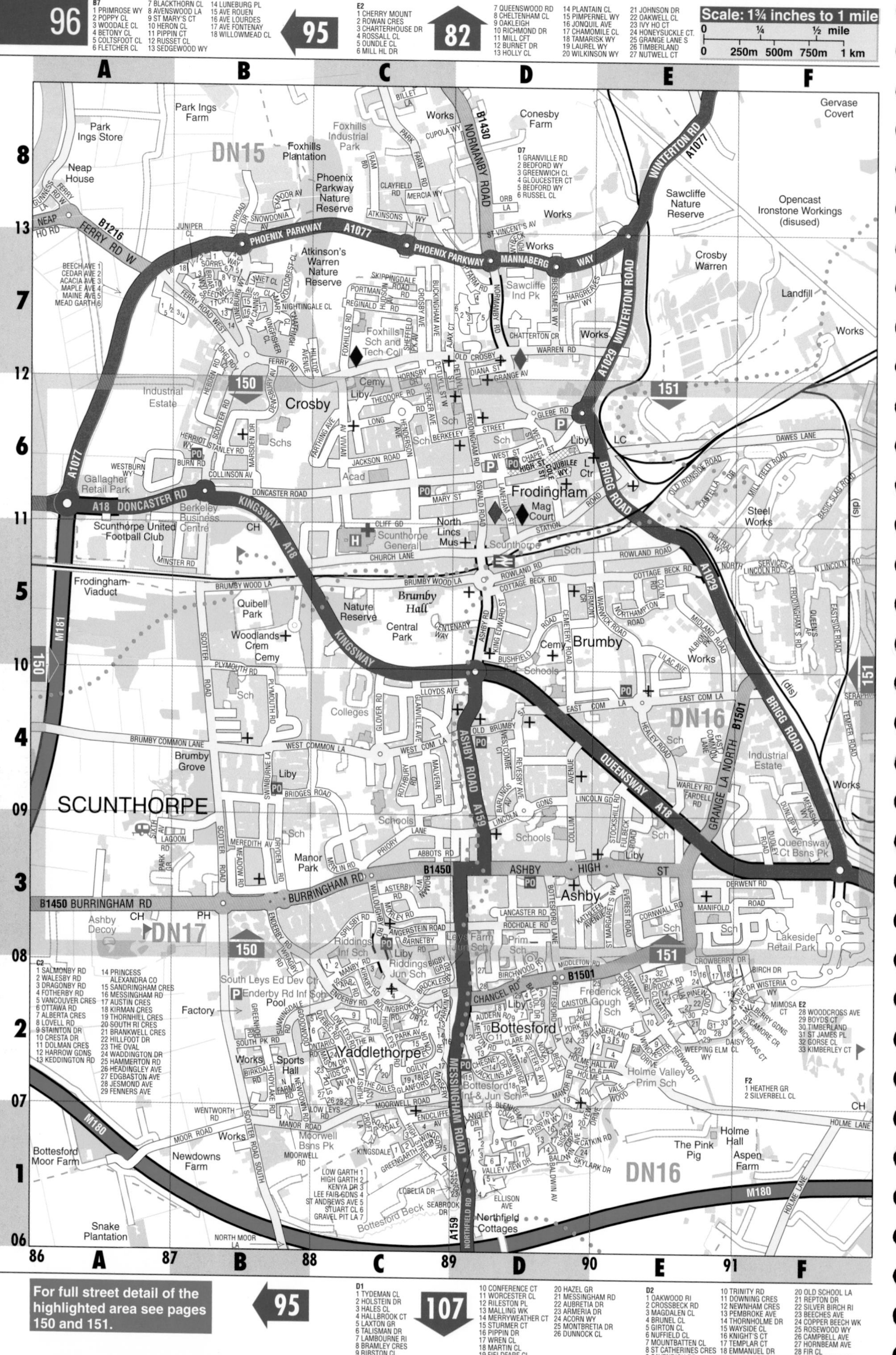

96
B7
1 PRIMROSE WY
2 POPPY CL
3 WOODALE CL
4 BETONY CL
5 COLTSFOOT CL
6 FLETCHER CL
7 BLACKTHORN CL
8 AVENSWOOD LA
9 ST MARY'S CT
10 HERON CL
11 PIPPIN CT
12 RUSSET CL
13 SEDGEWOOD WY
14 LUNEBURG PL
15 AVE ROUEN
16 AVE LOURDES
17 AVE FONTENAY
18 WILLOWMEAD CL
95
E2
1 CHERRY MOUNT
2 ROWAN CRES
3 CHARTERHOUSE DR
4 ROSSALL CL
5 OUNDLE CL
6 MILL HL DR
82
7 QUEENSWOOD RD
8 CHELTENHAM CL
9 OAKLEIGH
10 RICHMOND DR
11 MILL CFT
12 BURNET DR
13 HOLLY CL
14 PLANTAIN CL
15 PIMPERNEL WY
16 JONQUIL AVE
17 CHAMOMILE CL
18 TAMARISK WY
19 LAUREL WY
20 WILKINSON WY
21 JOHNSON DR
22 OAKWELL CL
23 IVY HO CT
24 HONEYSUCKLE CT.
25 GRANGE LANE S
26 TIMBERLAND
27 NUTWELL CT
Scale: 1¾ inches to 1 mile
0 ¼ ½ mile
0 250m 500m 750m 1 km
A B C D E F
Park Ings Farm
Park Ings Store
Neap House
DN15
Foxhills Plantation
Foxhills Industrial Park
Phoenix Parkway Nature Reserve
Works
Conesby Farm
NORMANBY ROAD
B1430
D7
1 GRANVILLE RD
2 BEDFORD WY
3 GREENWICH CL
4 GLOUCESTER CT
5 BEDFORD WY
6 RUSSEL CL
WINTERTON RD
A1077
Gervase Covert
Sawcliffe Nature Reserve
Opencast Ironstone Workings (disused)
PHOENIX PARKWAY
A1077
MANNABERG WAY
Atkinson's Warren Nature Reserve
Crosby Warren
Sawcliffe Ind Pk
Landfill
WINTERTON ROAD
A1029
BEECH AVE 1
CEDAR AVE 2
ACACIA AVE 3
MAPLE AVE 4
MAINE AVE 5
MEAD GARTH 6
B1216 FERRY RD W
Foxhills Sch and Tech Coll
150
151
Industrial Estate
Crosby
Schs
Cemy
Liby
Sch
Frodingham
Mag Court
DAWES LANE
BRIGG ROAD
A18 DONCASTER RD
Gallagher Retail Park
Berkeley Business Centre
Scunthorpe United Football Club
KINGSWAY
A18
Scunthorpe General
North Lincs Mus
Scunthorpe
Steel Works
Frodingham Viaduct
M181
Quibell Park
Woodlands Crem
Cemy
Nature Reserve
Brumby Hall
Central Park
Brumby
Works
Colleges
DN16
QUEENSWAY
A18
ASHBY ROAD
A159
Brumby Grove
SCUNTHORPE
Industrial Estate
Queensway Ct Bsns Pk
Manor Park
Schools
B1450 BURRINGHAM RD
Ashby
Ashby Decoy
DN17
Lakeside Retail Park
C2
1 SALMONBY RD
2 WALESBY RD
3 DRAGONBY RD
4 FOTHERBY RD
5 VANCOUVER CRES
6 OTTAWA RD
7 ALBERTA CRES
8 LOVELL RD
9 STAINTON DR
10 CRESTA DR
11 DOLMAN CRES
12 HARROW GDNS
13 KEDDINGTON RD
14 PRINCESS ALEXANDRA CO
15 SANDRINGHAM CRES
16 MESSINGHAM RD
17 AUSTIN CRES
18 KIRMAN CRES
19 THORNHILL CRES
20 SOUTH RI CRES
21 BRANKWELL CRES
22 HILLFOOT DR
23 THE OVAL
24 WADDINGTON DR
25 HAMMERTON RD
26 HEADINGLEY AVE
27 EDGBASTON AVE
28 JESMOND AVE
29 FENNERS AVE
South Leys Ed Dev Ctr
Enderby Rd Inf Sch
Riddings Inf Sch
Riddings Jun Sch
Factory
Pool
B1501
Frederick Gough Sch
Bottesford
Yaddlethorpe
Sports Hall
MESSINGHAM ROAD
Holme Valley Prim Sch
E2
28 WOODCROSS AVE
29 BOYDS CT
30 TIMBERLAND
31 ST JAMES PL
32 GORSE CL
33 KIMBERLEY CT
F2
1 HEATHER GR
2 SILVERBELL CL
M180
Bottesford Moor Farm
Newdowns Farm
Moorwell Bsns Pk
LOW GARTH 1
HIGH GARTH 2
KENYA DR 3
LEE FAIR GDNS 4
ST ANDREWS AVE 5
STUART CL 6
GRAVEL PIT LA 7
Bottesford Beck
Northfield Cottages
The Pink Pig
Holme Hall
Aspen Farm
DN16
Snake Plantation
86 87 88 89 90 91
For full street detail of the highlighted area see pages 150 and 151.
95
D1
1 TYDEMAN CL
2 HOLSTEIN DR
3 HALES CL
4 HALLBROOK CT
5 LAXTON GR
6 TALISMAN DR
7 LAMBOURNE RI
8 BRAMLEY CRES
9 RIBSTON CL
107
10 CONFERENCE CT
11 WORCESTER CL
12 RILESTON PL
13 MALLING WK
14 MERRYWEATHER CT
15 STURMER CT
16 PIPPIN DR
17 WREN CL
18 MARTIN CL
19 FIELDFARE CL
20 HAZEL GR
21 MESSINGHAM RD
22 AUBRETIA DR
23 ARMERIA DR
24 ACORN WY
25 MONTBRETIA DR
26 DUNNOCK CL
D2
1 OAKWOOD RI
2 CROSSBECK RD
3 MAGDALEN CL
4 BRUNEL CL
5 GIRTON CL
6 NUFFIELD CL
7 MOUNTBATTEN CL
8 ST CATHERINES CRES
9 CAVENDISH RD
10 TRINITY RD
11 DOWNING CRES
12 NEWNHAM CRES
13 PEMBROKE AVE
14 THORNHOLME DR
15 WAYSIDE CL
16 KNIGHT'S CT
17 TEMPLAR CT
18 EMMANUEL DR
19 CHURCH LA
20 OLD SCHOOL LA
21 REPTON DR
22 SILVER BIRCH RI
23 BEECHES AVE
24 COPPER BEECH WK
25 ROSEWOOD WY
26 CAMPBELL AVE
27 HORNBEAM AVE
28 FIR CL
29 PETERHOUSE CT

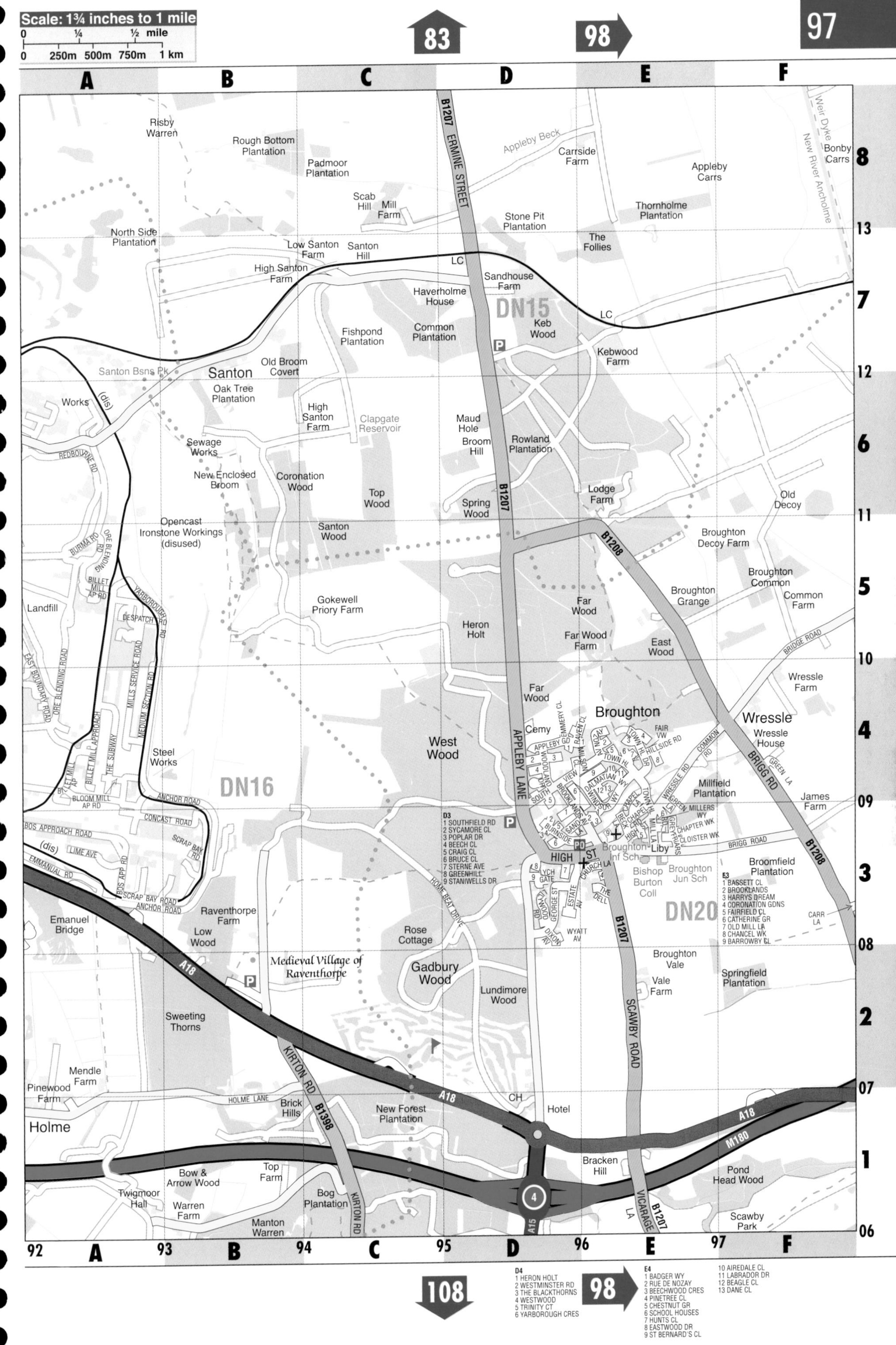

83 ▲   98 ▶

A   B   C   D   E   F

8
13
7
12
6
11
5
10
4
09
3
08
2
07
1
06

Risby Warren

Rough Bottom Plantation

Padmoor Plantation

Scab Hill

Mill Farm

North Side Plantation

Low Santon Farm

Santon Hill

High Santon Farm

Santon

Oak Tree Plantation

Old Broom Covert

Santon Bsns Pk

Works

(dis)

REDBOURNE RD

Sewage Works

New Enclosed Broom

High Santon Farm

Clapgate Reservoir

Coronation Wood

Top Wood

Fishpond Plantation

Common Plantation

Haverholme House

Sandhouse Farm

Keb Wood

Kebwood Farm

DN15

LC

LC

Appleby Beck

Carrside Farm

Stone Pit Plantation

Appleby Carrs

Thornholme Plantation

The Follies

Bonby Carrs

Weir Dyke

New River Ancholme

Maud Hole

Broom Hill

Spring Wood

Rowland Plantation

Lodge Farm

Old Decoy

Broughton Decoy Farm

Broughton Common

Common Farm

BURMA RD

ORE BLENDING RD

BILLET MILL AP RD

Landfill

Opencast Ironstone Workings (disused)

Gokewell Priory Farm

Santon Wood

Heron Holt

Far Wood

Far Wood Farm

East Wood

Broughton Grange

Wressle Farm

Wressle

YARBOROUGH RD

DESPATCH RD

MILLS SERVICE ROAD

MEDIUM SERVICE RD

THE SUBWAY

Steel Works

West Wood

Far Wood

Broughton

Wressle House

Wressle James Farm

GREEN LA

BRIGG RD

B1208

DN16

ANCHOR ROAD

CONCAST ROAD

BLOOM MILL AP RD

Scrap Bay Rd

LIME AVE

(dis)

BOS APPROACH ROAD

Cemy

APPLEBY LANE

D3
1 SOUTHFIELD RD
2 SYCAMORE CL
3 POPLAR DR
4 BEECH CL
5 CRAIG CL
6 BRUCE CL
7 STERNE AVE
8 GREENHILL
9 STANIWELLS DR

Millfield Plantation

Broomfield Plantation

CARR LA

E3
1 BASSETT CL
2 BROOKLANDS
3 HARRYS DREAM
4 CORONATION GDNS
5 FAIRFIELD CL
6 CATHERINE GR
7 OLD MILL LA
8 CHANCEL WK
9 BARROWBY CL

DN20

HIGH ST

Broughton Inf Sch

Broughton Jun Sch

Bishop Burton Coll

Liby

BRIGG ROAD

B1207

Emmanuel Bridge

EMMANUEL RD

A18

Raventhorpe Farm

Low Wood

HOLME BEAT DRIVE

Rose Cottage

Medieval Village of Raventhorpe

Gadbury Wood

Lundimore Wood

Broughton Vale

Vale Farm

Springfield Plantation

SCAWBY ROAD

Sweeting Thorns

KIRTON RD

B1398

HOLME LANE

Brick Hills

New Forest Plantation

A18

CH

Hotel

Bracken Hill

A18

M180

Pond Head Wood

VICARAGE LA

B1207

Scawby Park

Pinewood Farm

Mendle Farm

Holme

Twigmoor Hall

Warren Farm

Bow & Arrow Wood

Top Farm

Bog Plantation

Manton Warren

KIRTON RD

A15

4

92   93   94   95   96   97

D4
1 HERON HOLT
2 WESTMINSTER RD
3 THE BLACKTHORNS
4 WESTWOOD
5 TRINITY CT
6 YARBOROUGH CRES

E4
1 BADGER WY
2 RUE DE NOZAY
3 BEECHWOOD CRES
4 PINETREE CL
5 CHESTNUT GR
6 SCHOOL HOUSES
7 HUNTS CL
8 EASTWOOD DR
9 ST BERNARD'S CL

10 AIREDALE CL
11 LABRADOR DR
12 BEAGLE CL
13 DANE CL

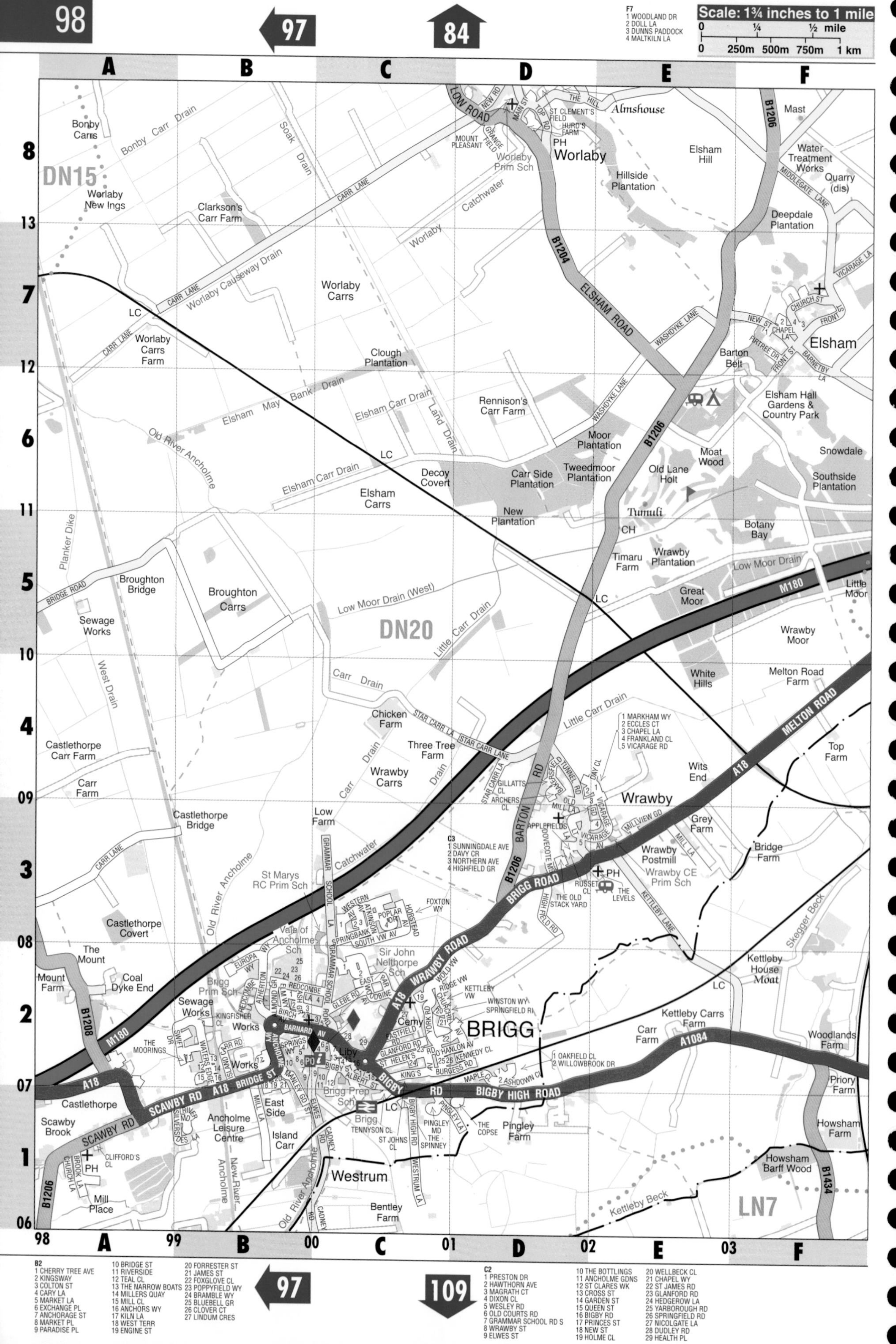

F7
1 WOODLAND DR
2 DOLL LA
3 DUNNS PADDOCK
4 MALTKILN LA

DN15

Bonby Carrs

Worlaby New Ings

Bonby Carr Drain

Clarkson's Carr Farm

Soak Drain

Carr Lane

Worlaby Causeway Drain

Worlaby Carrs

Carr Lane

Worlaby Carrs Farm

LC

Clough Plantation

Worlaby Catchwater

Low Road

St Clement's Field
Hurd's Farm
PH
Worlaby Prim Sch
Worlaby

The Hill
St Clement's
Mount Pleasant
Grange Field
Mill La

Almshouse

Hillside Plantation

Elsham Hill

Water Treatment Works

Quarry (dis)

Mast

B1206

Middlegate Lane

Vicarage La

Deepdale Plantation

Church St
New St
Chapel La
Firthie Dr
Front St
Barnetby
Elsham

Barton Belt

Elsham Hall Gardens & Country Park

DN20

Elsham May Bank Drain

Old River Ancholme

Planker Dike

Elsham Carr Drain

Land Drain

Elsham Carr Drain

LC

Decoy Covert

Elsham Carrs

Rennison's Carr Farm

Carr Side Plantation

New Plantation

Washdyke Lane

Moor Plantation

Tweedmoor Plantation

B1206

B1204
Elsham Road

Old Lane Holt

Tumuli

Moat Wood

Snowdale

Southside Plantation

Botany Bay

CH

Wrawby Plantation

Timaru Farm

LC

Low Moor Drain

M180

Great Moor

White Hills

Wrawby Moor

Little Moor

Broughton Bridge

Broughton Carrs

Low Moor Drain (West)

Little Carr Drain

West Drain

Sewage Works

Castlethorpe Carr Farm

Carr Farm

Castlethorpe Bridge

Old River Ancholme

Carr Drain

Chicken Farm

Three Tree Farm

Wrawby Carrs

Little Carr Drain

Star Carr La
Star Carr Lane

Low Farm

Carr Drain

Catchwater

Carr Drain

1 MARKHAM WY
2 ECCLES CT
3 CHAPEL LA
4 FRANKLAND CL
5 VICARAGE RD

Wits End

Wrawby

Grey Farm

Melton Road Farm

A18
Melton Road

Top Farm

Bridge Farm

St Marys RC Prim Sch

Castlethorpe Covert

C3
1 SUNNINGDALE AVE
2 DAVY CR
3 NORTHERN AVE
4 HIGHFIELD GR

Grammar School La

Barton Rd

B1206

Brigg Road

Old Mill La
Dunne Rd
Davy Cl

Gillatts Cl
Archers Cl

Applefields

Vicarage

Maltview Gd

Wrawby Postmill
Wrawby CE Prim Sch

PH
Russet La
The Levels

Kettleby Lane

Skegger Beck

Kettleby House Moat

B1208

M180

The Mount

Mount Farm

Coal Dyke End

The Moorings

Brigg Prim Sch

Vale of Ancholme Sch

Western Atkinson Springbank Poplar
Elm
Redcombe La
Grammar School Rd

Sir John Nelthorpe Sch

Wrawby Road

Foxton Wy

Ridge Vw
Kettleby Vw
Winston Wy
Springfield Ri

Wrawby Road

1 OAKFIELD CL
2 WILLOWBROOK DR

Carr Farm

Kettleby Carrs Farm

A1084

Woodlands Farm

Sewage Works

Works

Kingfisher Cl

Barnard Av

BRIGG

Cerny

Euro Wy

Atherton

Elm
Birch

Clover
Glanford Rd

Hanlon Av
Kennedy Cl
Burgess Rd

Bigby
King's

A18

Scawby Rd

Bridge St

Waters Edge

PO
Liby

Bigby

Ashdown Cl

Bigby Rd

Maple

A1084

Priory Farm

Castlethorpe

Scawby Brook

B1206

Mill Place

Clifford's Cl
PH
Brook La

Scawby Rd

Anchome Leisure Centre

East Side

Island Carr

New River Ancholme

Cadney Rd

Brigg Prep Sch

Brigg

Tennyson Cl
St Johns Cl

LC

Westrum

Bentley Farm

Pingley La
The Spinney

Westrum La

The Copse

Pingley Farm

Pingley MD

Kettleby Beck

Howsham Farm

LN7

Howsham Barff Wood

B1434

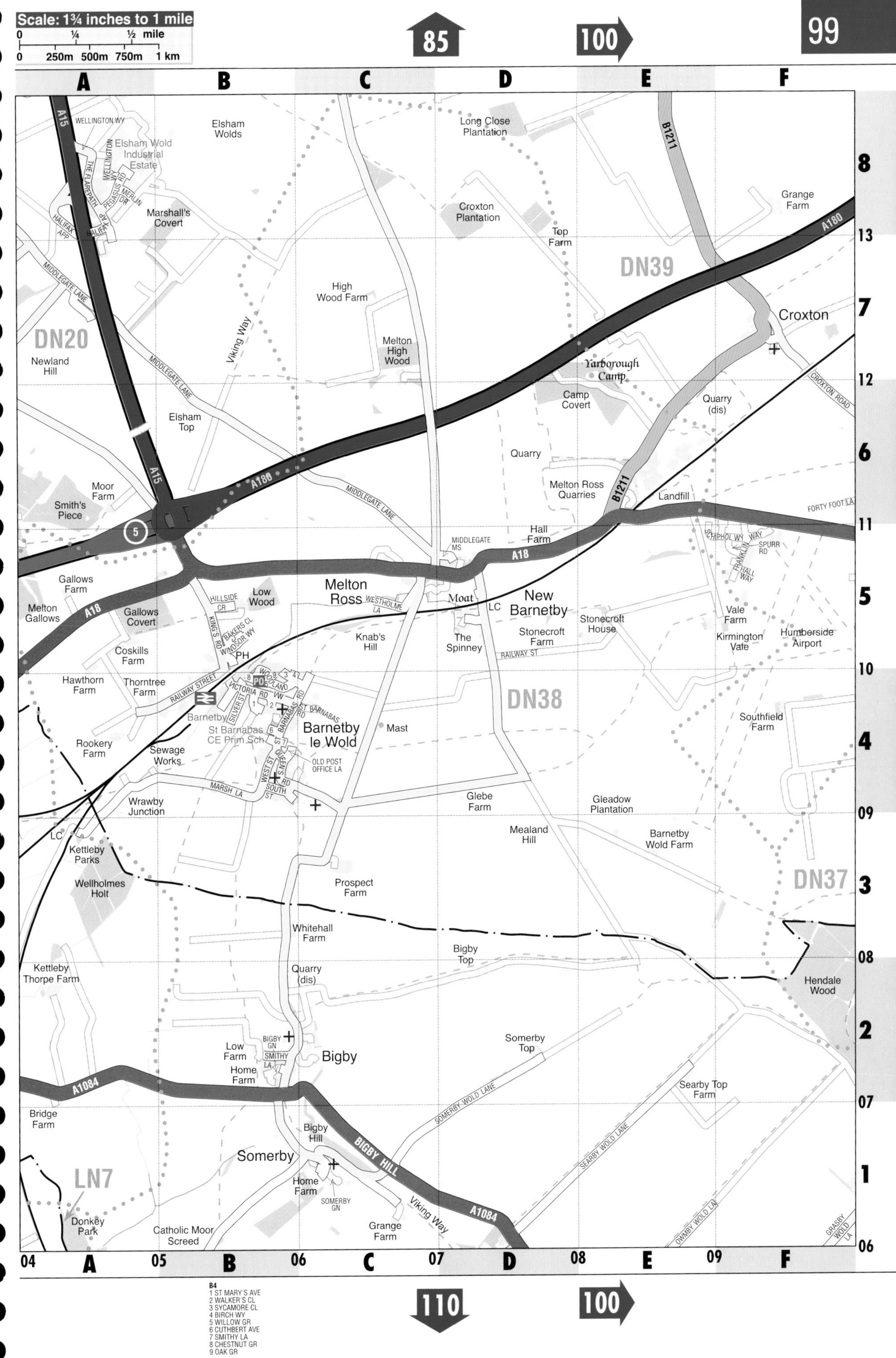

Scale: 1¾ inches to 1 mile

0 ¼ ½ mile
0 250m 500m 750m 1 km

A   B   C   D   E   F

WELLINGTON WY
A15
Elsham Wold Industrial Estate
THE FLAT
WELLINGTON
PEGASUS CL
MERLIN CL
SPITFIRE
HALIFAX APP
HALIFAX
Marshall's Covert
Elsham Wolds
Long Close Plantation
Grange Farm
8

MIDDLEGATE LANE
Viking Way
DN39
A180
Croxton
13

DN20
Newland Hill
High Wood Farm
Croxton Plantation
Top Farm
B1211
7

Elsham Top
Melton High Wood
Yarborough Camp
CROXTON ROAD
12

A15
A180
MIDDLEGATE LANE
Camp Covert
Quarry (dis)
6

Moor Farm
Smith's Piece
Quarry
Melton Ross Quarries
B1211
Landfill
FORTY FOOT LA
11

5
Gallows Farm
A18
Melton Gallows
Gallows Covert
Coskills Farm
HILLSIDE CR
Low Wood
KING'S RD
BAKERS CL
WINDSOR WY
PH
Melton Ross
WESTHOLME LA
MIDDLEGATE MS
A18
Moat
LC
New Barnetby
Hall Farm
Stonecroft House
FRANKLIN WAY
PHIPHOL WY
SPURR RD
HALL WAY
Vale Farm
Kirmington Vate
Humberside Airport
5

Hawthorn Farm
Thorntree Farm
RAILWAY STREET
VICTORIA RD
SILVER ST
ST BARNABAS
Knab's Hill
The Spinney
Stonecroft Farm
RAILWAY ST
DN38
10

Rookery Farm
Sewage Works
Barnetby
St Barnabas CE Prim Sch
POD
WO
ST
W
Barnetby le Wold
Mast
Southfield Farm
4

Wrawby Junction
MARSH LA
SOUTH ST
WEST ST
OLD POST OFFICE LA
Glebe Farm
Gleadow Plantation
Barnetby Wold Farm
09

LC
Kettleby Parks
Wellholmes Holt
Mealand Hill
DN37
3

Kettleby Thorpe Farm
Prospect Farm
Whitehall Farm
Bigby Top
Hendale Wood
08

Quarry (dis)
Somerby Top
2

A1084
Low Farm
Home Farm
BIGBY GN
SMITHY LA
Bigby
Searby Top Farm
07

Bridge Farm
Bigby Hill
Somerby
SOMERBY GN
Home Farm
BIGBY HILL
Viking Way
A1084
SOMERBY WOLD LANE
SEARBY WOLD LANE
1

LN7
Donkey Park
Catholic Moor Screed
Grange Farm
GRASBY WOLD LA
ORMSBY WOLD LA
06

04   A   05   B   06   C   07   D   08   E   09   F   06

B4
1 ST MARY'S AVE
2 WALKER'S CL
3 SYCAMORE CL
4 BIRCH WY
5 WILLOW GR
6 CUTHBERT AVE
7 SMITHY LA
8 CHESTNUT GR
9 OAK GR

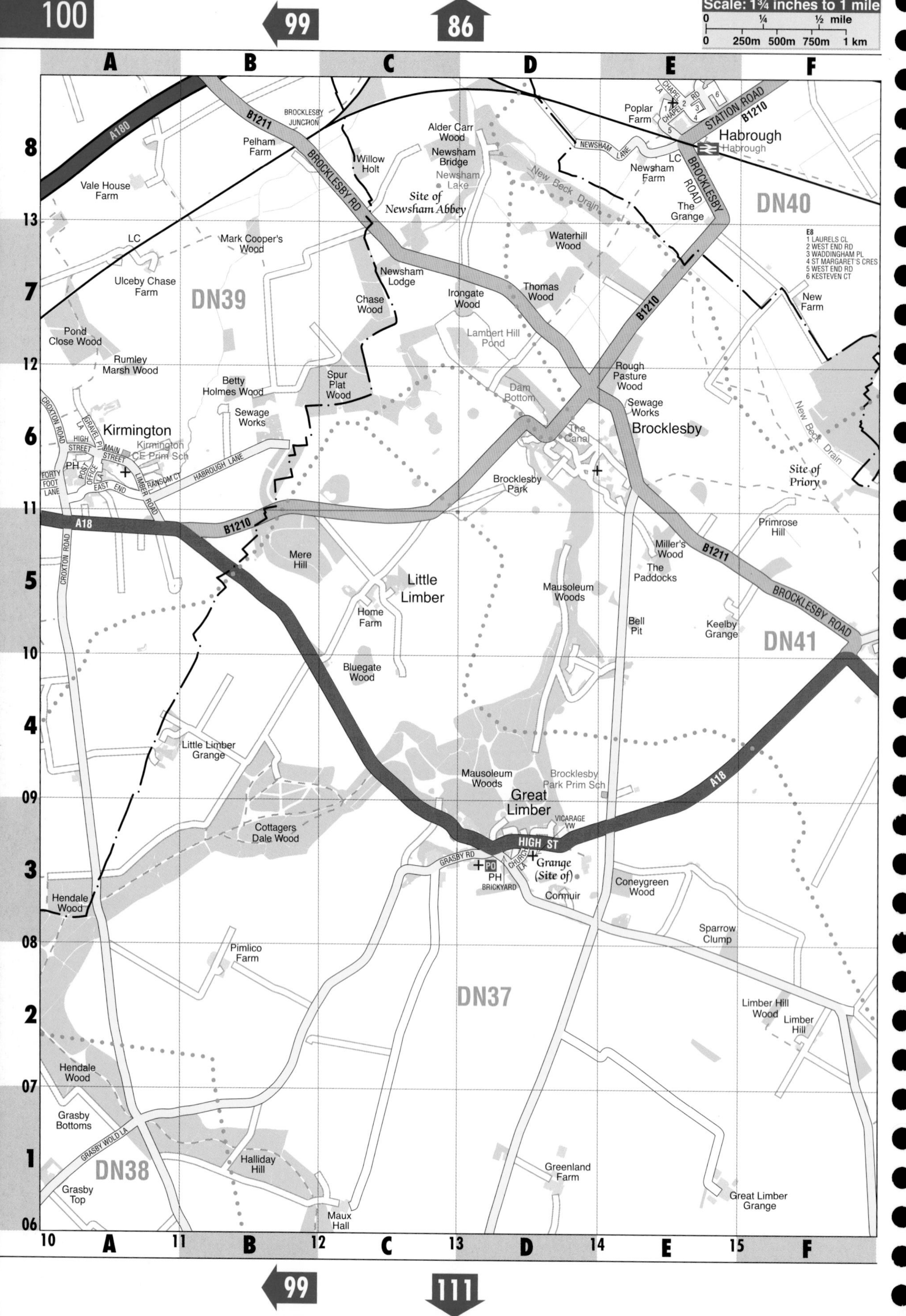

99
86

Scale: 1¾ inches to 1 mile

0   ¼   ½   mile
0 250m 500m 750m 1 km

A   B   C   D   E   F

A180

B1211

BROCKLESBY JUNCTION

Pelham Farm

Willow Holt

Alder Carr Wood

Newsham Bridge

Newsham Lake

Site of Newsham Abbey

Poplar Farm

CHAPEL RD

STATION ROAD

B1210

Habrough

Habrough

LC

8

Vale House Farm

Mark Cooper's Wood

BROCKLESBY RD

Newsham Lodge

Chase Wood

Newsham Farm

The Grange

Waterhill Wood

DN40

13

LC

DN39

Ulceby Chase Farm

E8
1 LAURELS CL
2 WEST END RD
3 WADDINGHAM PL
4 ST MARGARET'S CRES
5 WEST END RD
6 KESTEVEN CT

7

Irongate Wood

Thomas Wood

B1210

New Farm

Pond Close Wood

Rumley Marsh Wood

Lambert Hill Pond

Rough Pasture Wood

12

Betty Holmes Wood

Spur Plat Wood

Dam Bottom

Sewage Works

New Beck Drain

6

Kirmington

Sewage Works

Kirmington CE Prim Sch

The Canal

Brocklesby

Site of Priory

CROXTON ROAD

GRAVEL LA

HIGH STREET

MAIN ST

RANSOM CT

HABROUGH LANE

Brocklesby Park

Primrose Hill

11

PH
POST OFFICE
FORTY FOOT LANE
EAST END
LIMBER ROAD

A18

B1210

Mere Hill

Miller's Wood

The Paddocks

B1211

BROCKLESBY ROAD

5

Little Limber

Home Farm

Mausoleum Woods

Bell Pit

Keelby Grange

DN41

Bluegate Wood

10

4

Little Limber Grange

Cottagers Dale Wood

Mausoleum Woods

Great Limber

Brocklesby Park Prim Sch

A18

09

VICARAGE VW

3

Hendale Wood

HIGH ST

GRASBY RD

CHURCH LA

PO
PH
BRICKYARD

Grange (Site of)

Cornuir

Coneygreen Wood

Sparrow Clump

08

Pimlico Farm

DN37

Limber Hill Wood

Limber Hill

2

Hendale Wood

07

Grasby Bottoms

GRASBY WOLD LA

Halliday Hill

Greenland Farm

1

DN38

Grasby Top

Maux Hall

Great Limber Grange

06

10   A   11   B   12   C   13   D   14   E   15   F

99
111

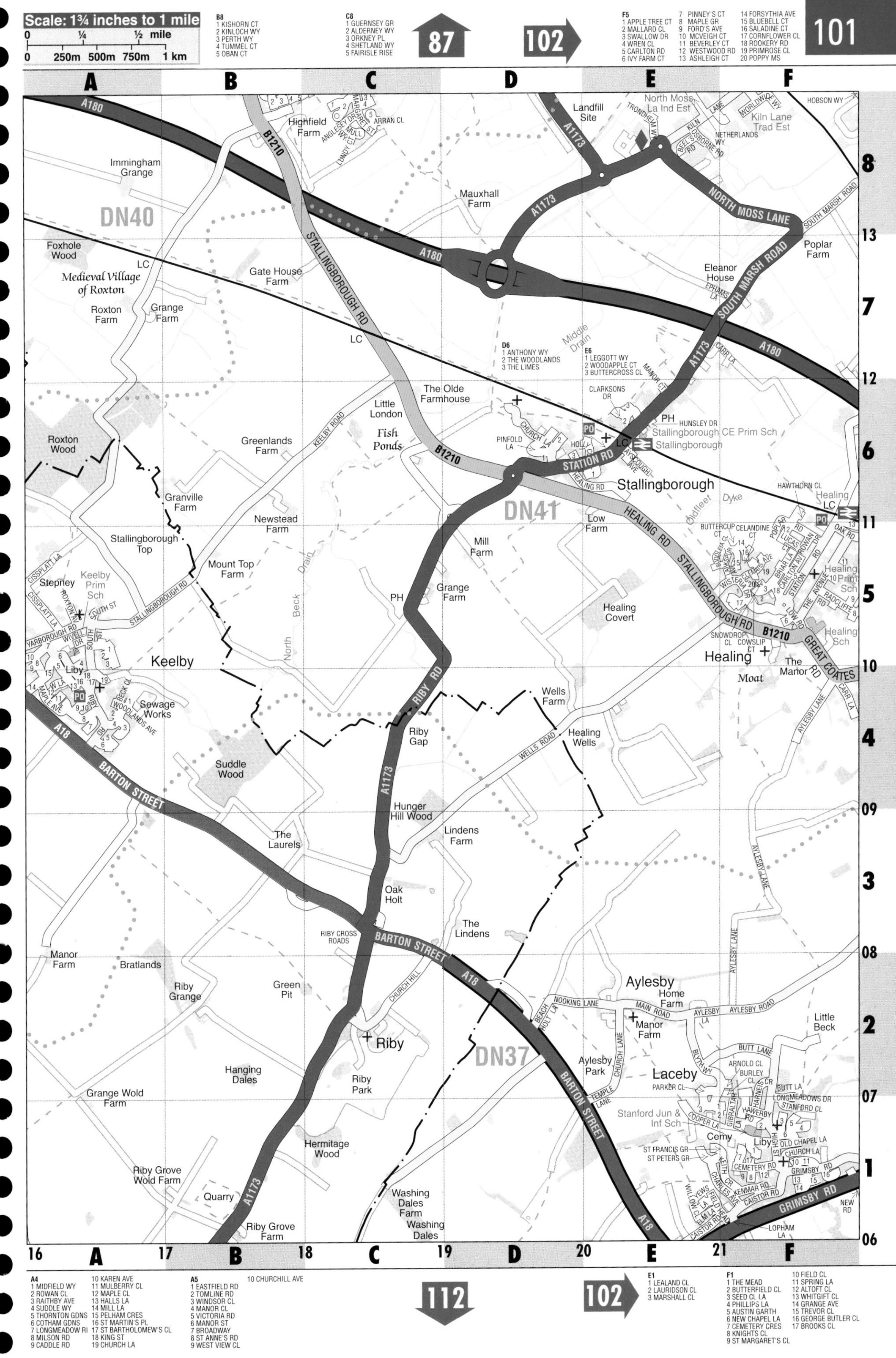

Scale: 1¾ inches to 1 mile
0 ¼ ½ mile
0 250m 500m 750m 1 km
B8
1 KISHORN CT
2 KINLOCH WY
3 PERTH WY
4 TUMMEL CT
5 OBAN CT
C8
1 GUERNSEY GR
2 ALDERNEY WY
3 ORKNEY PL
4 SHETLAND WY
5 FAIRISLE RISE
87
102
F5
1 APPLE TREE CT
2 MALLARD CL
3 SWALLOW DR
4 WREN CL
5 CARLTON RD
6 IVY FARM CT
7 PINNEY'S CT
8 MAPLE GR
9 FORD'S AVE
10 MCVEIGH CT
11 BEVERLEY CT
12 WESTWOOD RD
13 ASHLEIGH CT
14 FORSYTHIA AVE
15 BLUEBELL CT
16 SALADINE CT
17 CORNFLOWER CL
18 ROOKERY RD
19 PRIMROSE CL
20 POPPY MS
101
A B C D E F
Immingham Grange
DN40
Foxhole Wood
Medieval Village of Roxton
Roxton Farm
Grange Farm
Gate House Farm
Highfield Farm
Mauxhall Farm
Landfill Site
North Moss La Ind Est
Kiln Lane Trad Est
NORTH MOSS LANE
SOUTH MARSH ROAD
Poplar Farm
Eleanor House
A180
A1173
B1210
STALLINGBOROUGH RD
D6
1 ANTHONY WY
2 THE WOODLANDS
3 THE LIMES
E6
1 LEGGOTT WY
2 WOODAPPLE CT
3 BUTTERCROSS CL
Middle Drain
Roxton Wood
Little London
The Olde Farmhouse
Fish Ponds
Greenlands Farm
Granville Farm
Newstead Farm
Stallingborough Top
Mount Top Farm
Stallingborough CE Prim Sch
Stallingborough
STATION RD
HEALING RD
DN41
Low Farm
Mill Farm
Grange Farm
Healing Covert
Oldfleet Dyke
Healing
Stepney
Keelby Prim Sch
Keelby
Sewage Works
North Beck Drain
Wells Farm
Healing Wells
Riby Gap
RIBY RD
WELLS ROAD
Suddle Wood
BARTON STREET
A18
Hunger Hill Wood
Lindens Farm
The Laurels
Oak Holt
The Lindens
RIBY CROSS ROADS
Manor Farm
Bratlands
Riby Grange
Green Pit
Aylesby
Home Farm
Manor Farm
Little Beck
Riby
Riby Park
Hanging Dales
Aylesby Park
DN37
Laceby
Stanford Jun & Inf Sch
Grange Wold Farm
Hermitage Wood
Riby Grove Wold Farm
Quarry
Washing Dales Farm
Washing Dales
Riby Grove Farm
GRIMSBY RD
AYLESBY LANE
8 13 7 12 6 11 5 10 4 09 3 08 2 07 1 06
16 17 18 19 20 21
A4
1 MIDFIELD WY
2 ROWAN CL
3 RAITHBY AVE
4 SUDDLE WY
5 THORNTON GDNS
6 COTHAM GDNS
7 LONGMEADOW RI
8 MILSON RD
9 CADDLE RD
10 KAREN AVE
11 MULBERRY CL
12 MAPLE CL
13 HALLS LA
14 MILL LA
15 PELHAM CRES
16 ST MARTIN'S PL
17 ST BARTHOLOMEW'S CL
18 KING ST
19 CHURCH LA
A5
1 EASTFIELD RD
2 TOMLINE RD
3 WINDSOR CL
4 MANOR CL
5 VICTORIA RD
6 MANOR ST
7 BROADWAY
8 ST ANNE'S RD
9 WEST VIEW CL
10 CHURCHILL AVE
112
102
E1
1 LEALAND CL
2 LAURIDSON CL
3 MARSHALL CL
F1
1 THE MEAD
2 BUTTERFIELD CL
3 SEED CL LA
4 PHILLIPS LA
5 AUSTIN GARTH
6 NEW CHAPEL LA
7 CEMETERY CRES
8 KNIGHTS CL
9 ST MARGARET'S CL
10 FIELD CL
11 SPRING LA
12 ALTOFT CL
13 WHITGIFT CL
14 GRANGE AVE
15 TREVOR CL
16 GEORGE BUTLER CL
17 BROOKS CL

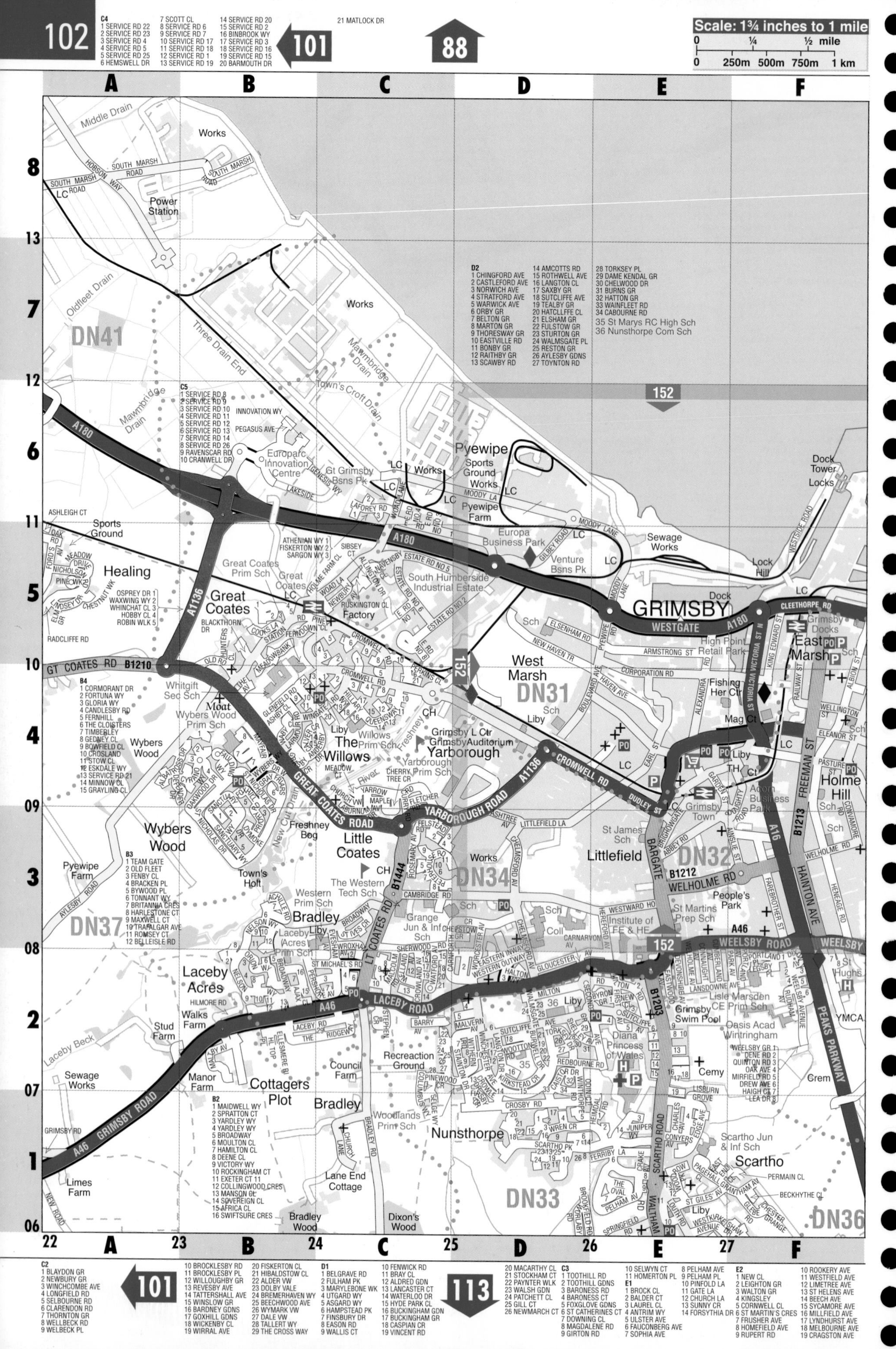
C4
1 SERVICE RD 22
2 SERVICE RD 23
3 SERVICE RD 4
4 SERVICE RD 5
5 SERVICE RD 25
6 HEMSWELL DR
7 SCOTT CL
8 SERVICE RD 6
9 SERVICE RD 7
10 SERVICE RD 17
11 SERVICE RD 18
12 SERVICE RD 1
13 SERVICE RD 19
14 SERVICE RD 20
15 SERVICE RD 2
16 BINBROOK WY
17 SERVICE RD 3
18 SERVICE RD 16
19 SERVICE RD 15
20 BARMOUTH DR
21 MATLOCK DR
101
88
Scale: 1¾ inches to 1 mile
0 ¼ ½ mile
0 250m 500m 750m 1 km
A B C D E F
Middle Drain
Works
SOUTH MARSH ROAD
HOBSON WAY
SOUTH MARSH ROAD
LC
Power Station
Oldfleet Drain
DN41
Three Drain End
Works
Mawmbridge Drain
Town's Croft Drain
D2
1 CHINGFORD AVE
2 CASTLEFORD AVE
3 NORWICH AVE
4 STRATFORD AVE
5 WARWICK AVE
6 ORBY GR
7 BELTON GR
8 MARTON GR
9 THORESWAY GR
10 EASTVILLE RD
11 BONBY GR
12 RAITHBY GR
13 SCAWBY RD
14 AMCOTTS RD
15 ROTHWELL AVE
16 LANGTON CL
17 SAXBY GR
18 SUTCLIFFE AVE
19 TEALBY GR
20 HATCLLFFE CL
21 ELSHAM GR
22 FULSTOW GR
23 STURTON GR
24 WALMSGATE PL
25 RESTON GR
26 AYLESBY GDNS
27 TOYNTON RD
28 TORKSEY PL
29 DAME KENDAL GR
30 CHELWOOD DR
31 BURNS GR
32 HATTON GR
33 WAINFLEET RD
34 CABOURNE RD
35 St Marys RC High Sch
36 Nunsthorpe Com Sch
152
C5
1 SERVICE RD 8
2 SERVICE RD 9
3 SERVICE RD 10
4 SERVICE RD 11
5 SERVICE RD 12
6 SERVICE RD 13
7 SERVICE RD 14
8 SERVICE RD 26
9 RAVENSCAR RD
10 CRANWELL DR
INNOVATION WY
PEGASUS AVE
Europarc Innovation Centre
GENESIS WY
LAKESIDE
Gt Grimsby Bsns Pk
A180
Pyewipe Sports Ground Works
Pyewipe Farm
MOODY LANE
Dock Tower
Locks
ASHLEIGH CT
Sports Ground
Healing
ATHENIAN WY 1
FISKERTON WY 2
SARGON WY 3
SIBSEY CT
Europa Business Park
GILBEY ROAD
Venture Bsns Pk
Sewage Works
Lock Hill
WESTSIDE ROAD
Great Coates Prim Sch
Great Coates
South Humberside Industrial Estate
OSPREY DR 1
WAXWING WY 2
WHINCHAT CL 3
HOBBY CL 4
ROBIN WLK 5
Great Coates
A1136
BLACKTHORN DR
Factory
RUSKINGTON CL
GRIMSBY
WESTGATE
Dock
CLEETHORPE RD
Grimsby Docks
East Marsh
High Point Retail Park
RADCLIFFE RD
ARMSTRONG ST
CORPORATION RD
West Marsh
DN31
GT COATES RD B1210
B4
1 CORMORANT DR
2 FORTUNA WY
3 GLORIA WY
4 CANDLESBY RD
5 FERNHILL
6 THE CLOISTERS
7 TIMBERLEY
8 GEDNEY CL
9 BOWFIELD CL
10 CROSLAND
11 STOW CL
12 ESKDALE WY
13 SERVICE RD 21
14 MINNOW CL
15 GRAYLING CL
Whitgift Sec Sch
Moat
Wybers Wood Prim Sch
Wybers Wood
Liby
The Willows
Willows Prim Sch
Grimsby L Ctr
Grimsby Auditorium
Yarborough
Yarborough Prim Sch
CROMWELL RD
DUDLEY ST
Fishing Her Ctr
Mag Ct
Liby
Holme Hill
FREEMAN ST
GREAT COATES ROAD
YARBOROUGH ROAD
Wybers Wood
Freshney Bog
Little Coates
Works
DN34
Littlefield
St James Sch
BARGATE
DN32
Grimsby Town
Acorn Business Park
B1213
A16
Pyewipe Farm
B3
1 TEAM GATE
2 OLD FLEET
3 FENBY CL
4 BRACKEN PL
5 BYWOOD PL
6 TONNANT WY
7 BRITANNIA CRES
8 HARLESTONE CT
9 MAXWELL CT
10 TRAFALGAR AVE
11 ROMSEY CT
12 BELLEISLE RD
Town's Holt
The Western Tech Sch
Western Prim Sch
B1444
Bradley
Laceby Acres Prim Sch
Grange Jun & Inf Sch
DN37
B1212
WELHOLME RD
People's Park
St Martins Prep Sch
Institute of FE & HE
WEELSBY ROAD
A46
HAINTON AVE
Laceby Acres
HILMORE RD
LACEBY ROAD
Liby
Grimsby Swim Pool
Lisle Marsden CE Prim Sch
Oasis Acad Wintringham
YMCA
Walks Farm
Stud Farm
Laceby Beck
Sewage Works
Manor Farm
Cottagers Plot
Council Farm
Recreaction Ground
Diana Princess of Wales
Cemy
Grem
PEAKS PARKWAY
B1203
B2
1 MAIDWELL WY
2 SPRATTON CT
3 YARDLEY WY
4 YARDLEY WY
5 BROADWAY
6 MOULTON CL
7 HAMILTON CL
8 DEENE CL
9 VICTORY WY
10 ROCKINGHAM CT
11 EXETER CT 11
12 COLLINGWOOD CRES
13 MANSON CL
14 SOVEREIGN CL
15 AFRICA CL
16 SWIFTSURE CRES
Bradley
Woodlands Prim Sch
Nunsthorpe
SCARTHO ROAD
Scartho Jun & Inf Sch
Scartho
PERMAIN CL
BECKHYTHE CL
GRIMSBY RD
A46 GRIMSBY ROAD
Limes Farm
Lane End Cottage
DN33
Liby
DN36
NEW ROAD
Bradley Wood
Dixon's Wood
WALTHAM
22 A 23 B 24 C 25 D 26 E 27 F
C2
1 BLAYDON GR
2 NEWBURY GR
3 WINCHCOMBE AVE
4 LONGFIELD RD
5 SELBOURNE RD
6 CLARENDON RD
7 THORNTON GR
8 WELLBECK RD
9 WELBECK PL
10 BROCKLESBY RD
11 BROCKLESBY PL
12 WILLOUGHBY GR
13 REVESBY AVE
14 TATTERSHALL AVE
15 WINSLOW GR
16 BARDNEY GDNS
17 GOXHILL GDNS
18 WICKENBY CL
19 WIRRAL AVE
20 FISKERTON CL
21 HIBALDSTOW CL
22 ALDER VW
23 DOLBY VALE
24 BREMERHAVEN WY
25 BEECHWOOD AVE
26 WYMARK VW
27 DALE VW
28 TALLERT WY
29 THE CROSS WAY
D1
1 BELGRAVE RD
2 FULHAM PK
3 MARYLEBONE WK
4 UTGARD WY
5 ASGARD WY
6 HAMPSTEAD PK
7 FINSBURY DR
8 EASON RD
9 WALLIS CT
10 FENWICK RD
11 BRAY CL
12 ALDRED GDN
13 LANCASTER CT
14 WATERLOO DR
15 HYDE PARK CL
16 BUCKINGHAM GDN
17 BUCKINGHAM GR
18 CASPIAN CR
19 VINCENT RD
20 MACARTHY CL
21 STOCKHAM CT
22 PAYNTER WLK
23 WALSH GDN
24 PATCHETT CL
25 GILL CT
26 NEWMARCH CT
C3
1 TOOTHILL RD
2 TOOTHILL GDNS
3 BARONESS RD
4 BARONESS CT
5 FOXGLOVE GDNS
6 ST CATHERINES CT
7 DOWNING CL
8 MAGDALENE RD
9 GIRTON RD
10 SELWYN CT
11 HOMERTON PL
E1
1 BROCK CL
2 BALDER CT
3 LAUREL CL
4 ANTRIM WY
5 ULSTER AVE
6 FAUCONBERG AVE
7 SOPHIA AVE
8 PELHAM AVE
9 PELHAM PL
10 PINFOLD LA
11 GATE LA
12 CHURCH LA
13 SUNNY CR
14 FORSYTHIA DR
E2
1 NEW CL
2 LEIGHTON GR
3 WALTON GR
4 KINGSLEY
5 CORNWELL CL
6 ST MARTIN'S CRES
7 FRUSHER AVE
8 HOMEFIELD AVE
9 RUPERT RD
10 ROOKERY AVE
11 WESTFIELD AVE
12 LIMETREE AVE
13 ST HELENS AVE
14 BEECH AVE
15 SYCAMORE AVE
16 MILLFIELD AVE
17 LYNDHURST AVE
18 MELBOURNE AVE
19 CRAGSTON AVE
101
113

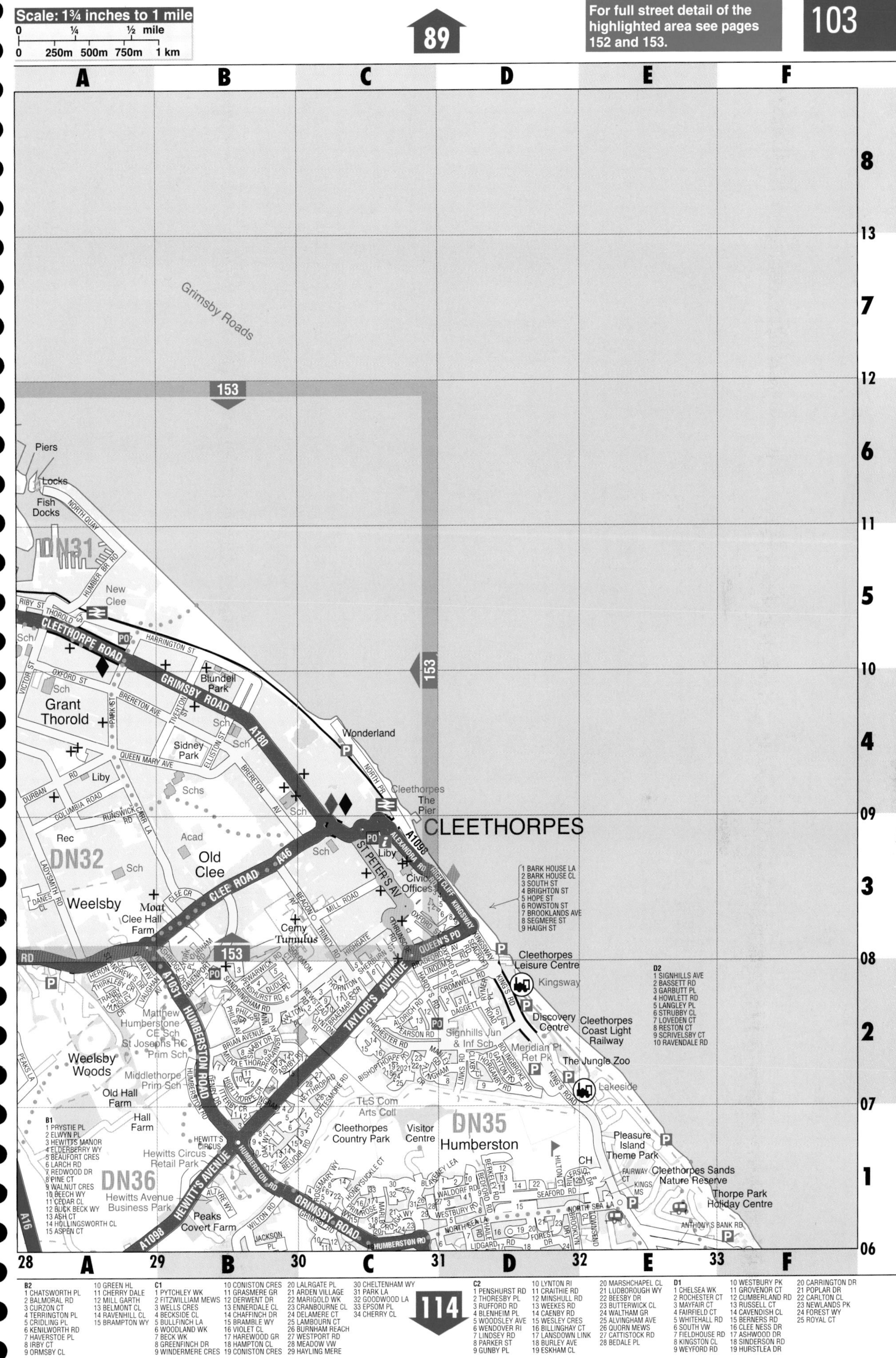

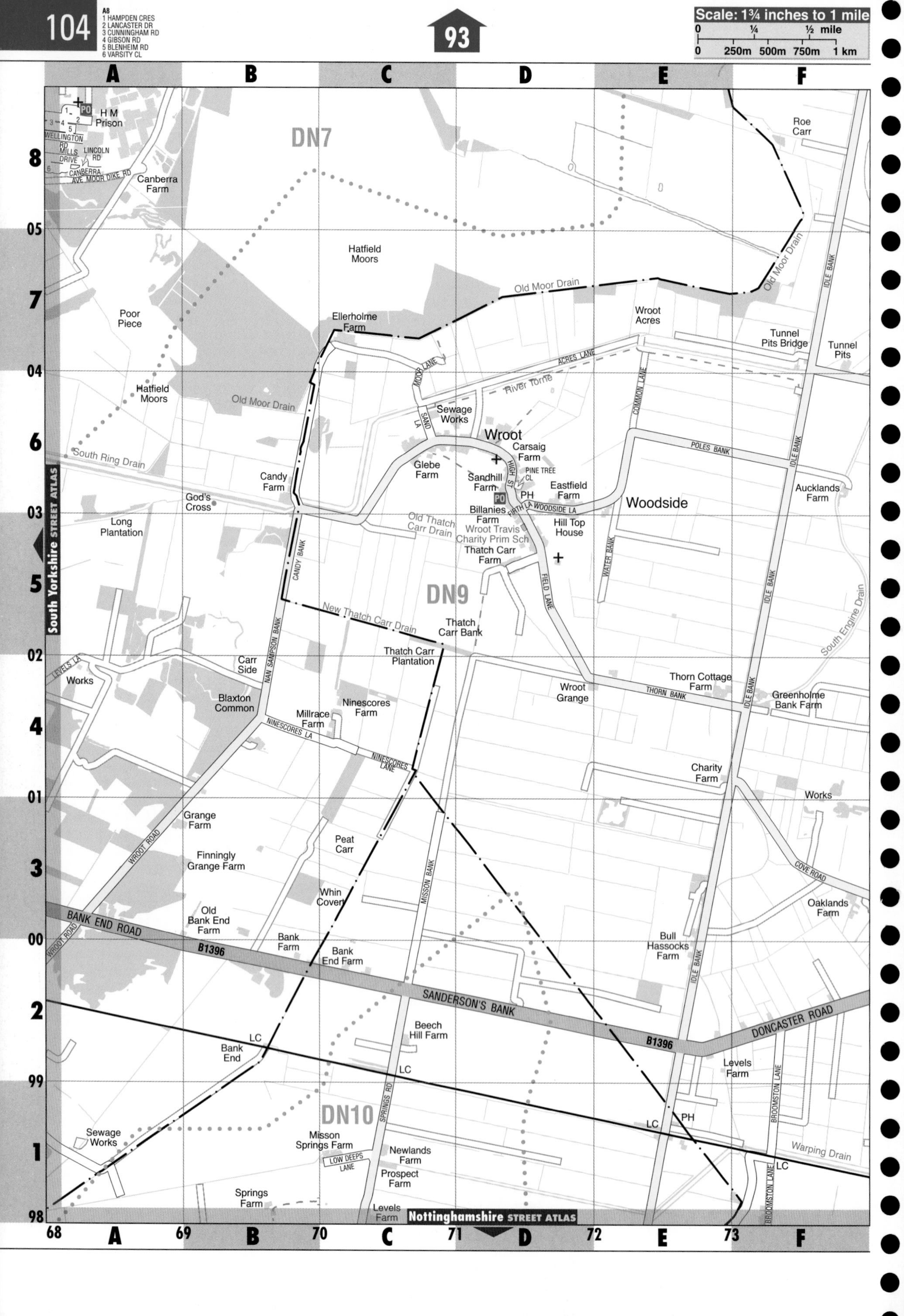

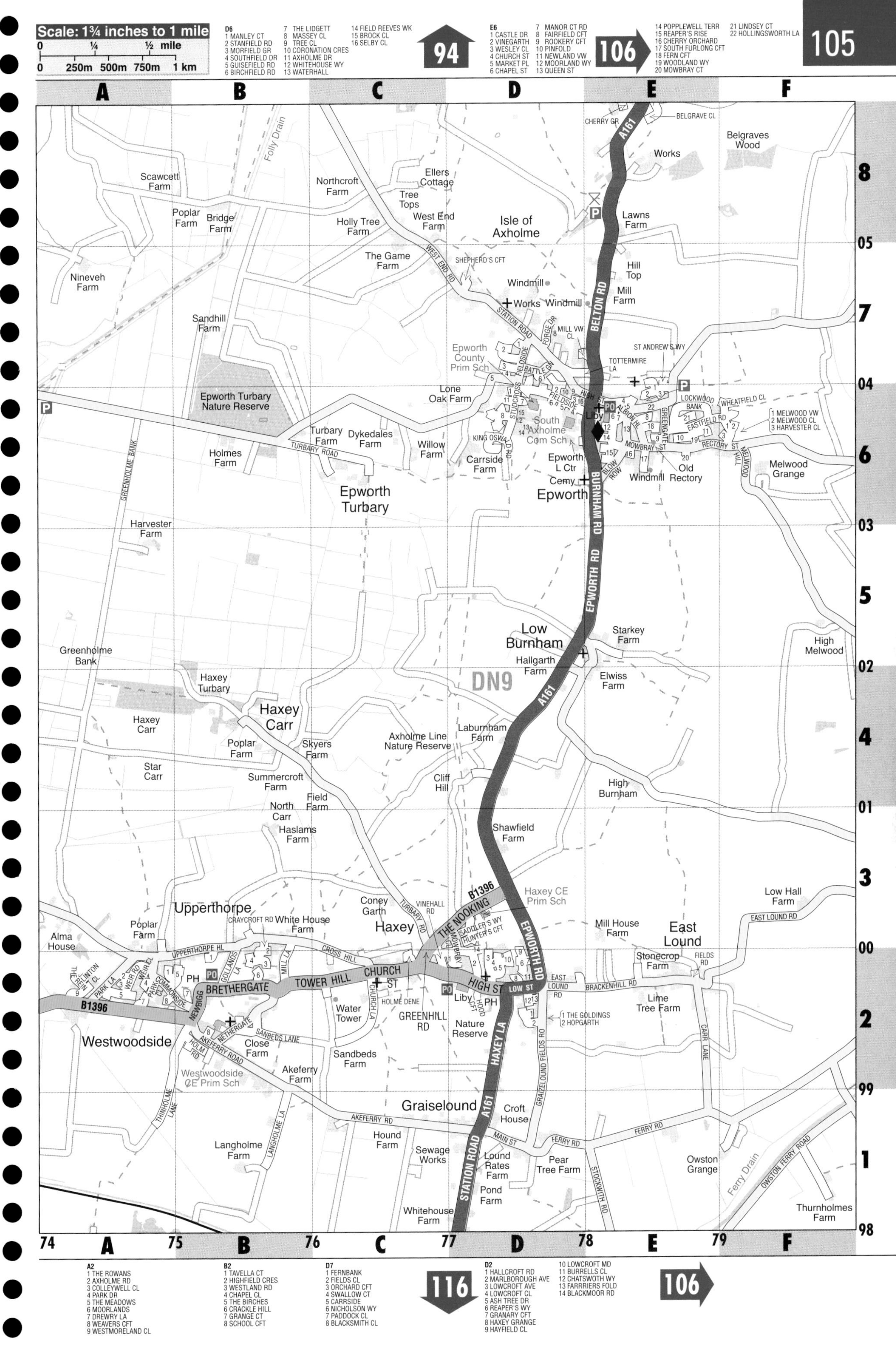

D6
1 MANLEY CT
2 STANFIELD RD
3 MORFIELD GR
4 SOUTHFIELD DR
5 GUISEFIELD RD
6 BIRCHFIELD RD
7 THE LIDGETT
8 MASSEY CL
9 TREE CL
10 CORONATION CRES
11 AXHOLME DR
12 WHITEHOUSE WY
13 WATERHALL
14 FIELD REEVES WK
15 BROCK CL
16 SELBY CL

94

E6
1 CASTLE DR
2 VINEGARTH
3 WESLEY CL
4 CHURCH ST
5 MARKET PL
6 CHAPEL ST
7 MANOR CT RD
8 FAIRFIELD CFT
9 ROOKERY CFT
10 PINFOLD
11 NEWLAND VW
12 MOORLAND WY
13 QUEEN ST

106

14 POPPLEWELL TERR
15 REAPER'S RISE
16 CHERRY ORCHARD
17 SOUTH FURLONG CFT
18 FERN CFT
19 WOODLAND WY
20 MOWBRAY CT
21 LINDSEY CT
22 HOLLINGSWORTH LA

Map Labels

Folly Drain

CHERRY GR
BELGRAVE CL

A161

Works

Belgraves Wood

Scawcett Farm

Poplar Farm

Bridge Farm

Northcroft Farm

Tree Tops

West End Farm

Isle of Axholme

BELTON RD

Lawns Farm

8

05

Nineveh Farm

Holly Tree Farm

The Game Farm

WEST END RD

SHEPHERD'S CFT

Windmill

Works Windmill

MILL VW CL

Hill Top

Mill Farm

ST ANDREW'S WY

7

Sandhill Farm

STATION ROAD

Epworth County Prim Sch

FIELDSIDE

FORGE LA

HIGH ST

TOTTERMIRE LA

04

P

Epworth Turbary Nature Reserve

Lone Oak Farm

BATTLE LA

STUDCROFT

ALBION RD

PO Liby

GREENGATE

MOWBRAY ST

LOCKWOOD BANK

WHEATFIELD CL

EASTFIELD RD

RECTORY ST

MELWOOD HILL

1 MELWOOD VW
2 MELWOOD CL
3 HARVESTER CL

Turbary Farm

Dykedales Farm

Willow Farm

TURBARY ROAD

South Axholme Com Sch

KING OSWA

Old Rectory

Melwood Grange

6

Holmes Farm

Carrside Farm

Epworth L Ctr

Cemy

BURNHAM RD

EPWORTH RD

BLOW ROW

Windmill

Harvester Farm

Epworth Turbary

Epworth

03

Low Burnham

Starkey Farm

High Melwood

5

02

Greenholme Bank

GREENHOLME BANK

Haxey Turbary

Haxey Carr

DN9

Hallgarth Farm

A161

Elwiss Farm

Laburnham Farm

4

Axholme Line Nature Reserve

High Burnham

Star Carr

Poplar Farm

Skyers Farm

Summercroft Farm

Field Farm

Cliff Hill

01

North Carr

Haslams Farm

Shawfield Farm

Low Hall Farm

3

Coney Garth

VINEHALL RD

B1396

Haxey CE Prim Sch

EAST LOUND RD

Upperthorpe

CRAYCROFT RD

White House Farm

Haxey

TURBARY RD

THE NOOKING

Mill House Farm

East Lound

Stonecrop Farm

FIELDS RD

00

Alma House

Poplar Farm

UPPERTHORPE HL

GOLLANDS

CROSS HILL

CHURCH ST

SADDLER'S WY

HUNTER'S CFT

MOWBRAY

HIGH ST

LOW ST

EPWORTH RD

EAST LOUND RD

BRACKENHILL RD

Lime Tree Farm

CARR LANE

2

THE BELTON CL

PARK LA

NEWBIGG

PARK COMMON

WEIR RD

PH

BRETHERGATE

TOWER HILL

Water Tower

HOLME DENE

GREENHILL RD

PO

Liby

PH

HAXEY LA

1 THE GOLDINGS
2 HOPGARTH

B1396

Westwoodside

NETHERGATE

HOLM RD

SANBEDS LANE

Close Farm

Sandbeds Farm

Nature Reserve

MAIN ST

99

THORNHOLME LANE

LANGHOLME LA

AKEFERRY ROAD

Akeferry Farm

Westwoodside CE Prim Sch

Graiselound

Croft House

GRAIZELOUND FIELDS RD

STOCKWITH RD

FERRY RD

Owston Grange

Ferry Drain

OWSTON FERRY ROAD

Langholme Farm

AKEFERRY RD

Hound Farm

Sewage Works

STATION ROAD

A161

Lound Rates Farm

Pond Farm

Pear Tree Farm

FERRY RD

1

Whitehouse Farm

Thurnholmes Farm

98

A2
1 THE ROWANS
2 AXHOLME RD
3 COLLEYWELL CL
4 PARK DR
5 THE MEADOWS
6 MOORLANDS
7 DREWRY LA
8 WEAVERS CFT
9 WESTMORELAND CL

B2
1 TAVELLA CT
2 HIGHFIELD CRES
3 WESTLAND RD
4 CHAPEL CL
5 THE BIRCHES
6 CRACKLE HILL
7 GRANGE CT
8 SCHOOL CFT

D7
1 FERNBANK
2 FIELDS CL
3 ORCHARD CFT
4 SWALLOW CT
5 CARRSIDE
6 NICHOLSON WY
7 PADDOCK CL
8 BLACKSMITH CL

116

D2
1 HALLCROFT RD
2 MARLBOROUGH AVE
3 LOWCROFT AVE
4 LOWCROFT CL
5 ASH TREE DR
6 REAPER'S WY
7 GRANARY CFT
8 HAXEY GRANGE
9 HAYFIELD CL
10 LOWCROFT MD
11 BURRELLS CL
12 CHATSWORTH WY
13 FARRIERS FOLD
14 BLACKMOOR RD

106

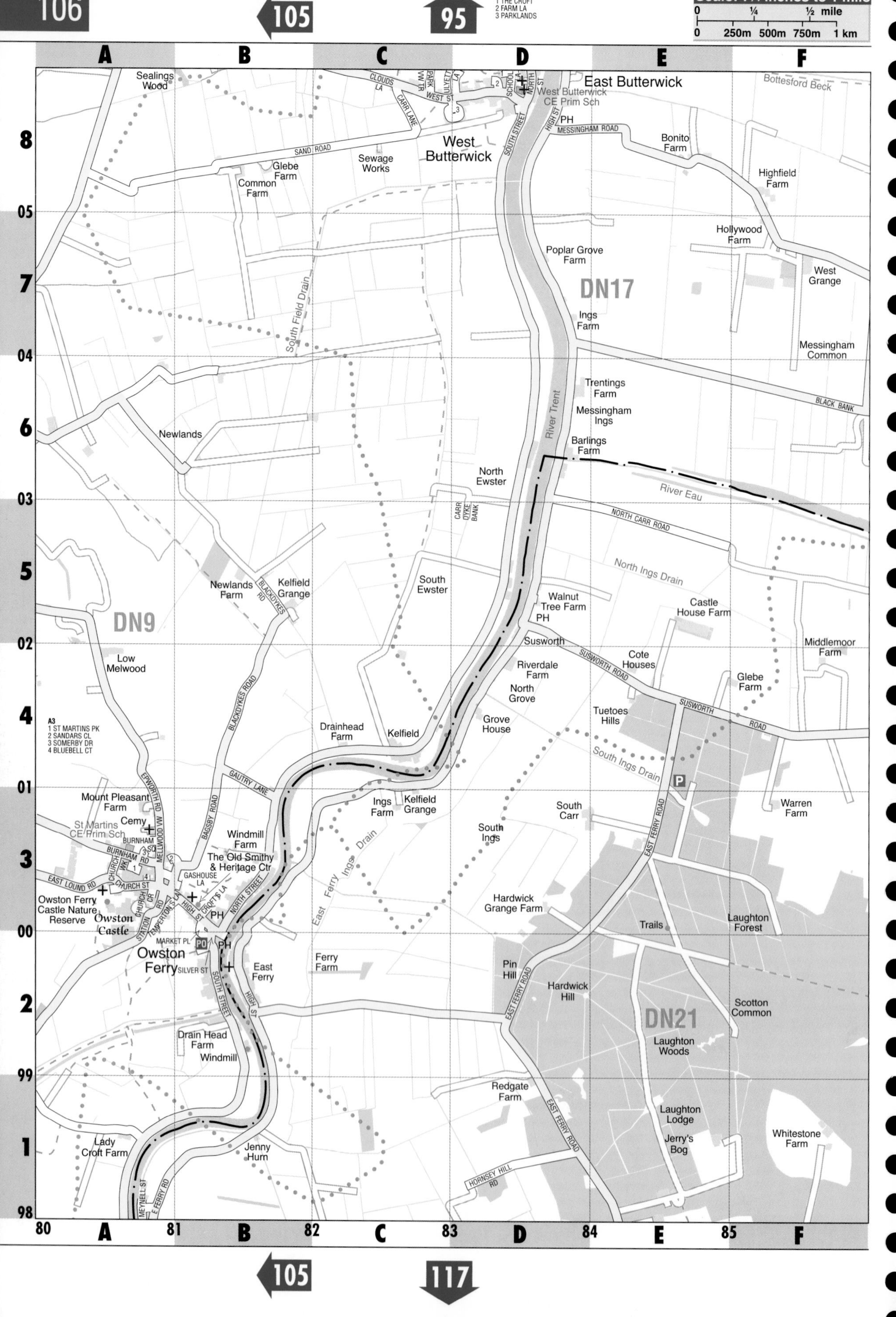

106

105

95

D8
1 THE CROFT
2 FARM LA
3 PARKLANDS

Scale: 1¾ inches to 1 mile
0   ¼   ½   mile
0   250m 500m 750m   1 km

East Butterwick

Bottesford Beck

West Butterwick
CE Prim Sch

PH

Bonito
Farm

Sealings
Wood

SAND ROAD

CLOUDS LA

CARR LANE

WEST ST

PARK
VW TR

ULVETT LA

SOUTH STREET

SCHOOL

HIGH ST

NORTH

West Butterwick

MESSINGHAM ROAD

Highfield
Farm

Glebe
Farm

Common
Farm

Sewage
Works

Hollywood
Farm

West
Grange

DN17

05

7

Poplar Grove
Farm

04

Ings
Farm

Messingham
Common

South Field Drain

Trentings
Farm

BLACK BANK

6

03

Newlands

River Trent

Messingham
Ings

Barlings
Farm

River Eau

North
Ewster

CARR
DYKE
BANK

NORTH CARR ROAD

DN9

Newlands
Farm

Kelfield
Grange

BLACKMORES RD

South
Ewster

North Ings Drain

5

02

Low
Melwood

Walnut
Tree Farm
PH

Castle
House Farm

Middlemoor
Farm

Susworth

4

A3
1 ST MARTINS PK
2 SANDARS CL
3 SOMERBY DR
4 BLUEBELL CT

Drainhead
Farm

Kelfield

Riverdale
Farm

North
Grove

SUSWORTH ROAD

Cote
Houses

Glebe
Farm

SUSWORTH
ROAD

Grove
House

Tuetoes
Hills

01

Mount Pleasant
Farm

GAUTRY LANE

Ings
Farm

Kelfield
Grange

South
Ings Drain

P

Warren
Farm

St Martins
CE Prim Sch

Cemy

BURNHAM
RD

BAGSBY ROAD

Windmill
Farm

South
Carr

EAST FERRY ROAD

3

Owston Ferry
Castle Nature
Reserve

EAST LOUND RD

CHURCH ST

STATION RD

HIGH ST

BURNHAM

The Old Smithy
& Heritage Ctr

GASHOUSE
LA

CROFT LA

NORTH STREET

East Ferry Ings Drain

South
Ings

Hardwick
Grange Farm

Trails

Laughton
Forest

Owston
Castle

PH

00

Owston
Ferry

MARKET PL

PO

PH

East Ferry

Ferry
Farm

Pin
Hill

Hardwick
Hill

SILVER ST

SOUTH STREET

HIGH ST

EAST FERRY ROAD

DN21

Scotton
Common

2

Drain Head
Farm

Laughton
Woods

Windmill

99

MEXBELL LA

E FERRY RD

Redgate
Farm

Laughton
Lodge

Whitestone
Farm

1

Lady
Croft Farm

Jenny
Hurn

Jerry's
Bog

HORNSEY HILL
RD

98

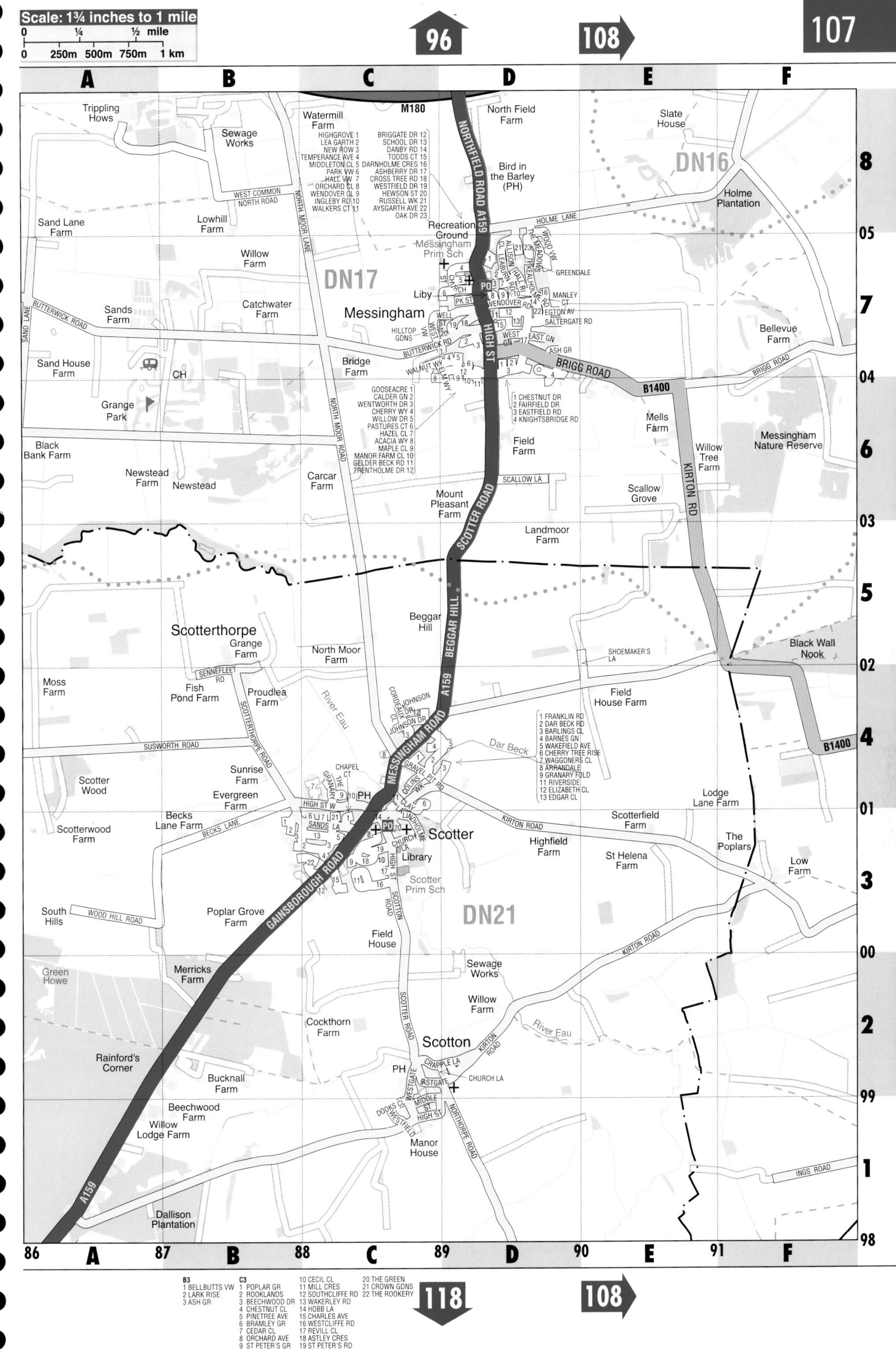
Scale: 1¾ inches to 1 mile
0 ¼ ½ mile
0 250m 500m 750m 1 km
96
108
A B C D E F
M180
Trippling Hows
Sewage Works
Watermill Farm
North Field Farm
Slate House
DN16
Bird in the Barley (PH)
Holme Plantation
HIGHGROVE 1
LEA GARTH 2
NEW ROW 3
TEMPERANCE AVE 4
MIDDLETON CL 5
PARK VW 6
HALL VW 7
ORCHARD CL 8
WENDOVER CL 9
INGLEBY RD 10
WALKERS CT 11
BRIGGATE DR 12
SCHOOL DR 13
DANBY RD 14
TODDS CT 15
DARNHOLME CRES 16
ASHBERRY DR 17
CROSS TREE RD 18
WESTFIELD DR 19
HEWSON ST 20
RUSSELL WK 21
AYSGARTH AVE 22
OAK DR 23
WEST COMMON
NORTH ROAD
NORTH MOOR LANE
NORTHFIELD ROAD A159
HOLME LANE
Sand Lane Farm
Lowhill Farm
Recreation Ground
Messingham Prim Sch
Willow Farm
DN17
GREENDALE
Liby
PO
MANLEY CT
EGTON AV
SALTERGATE RD
Catchwater Farm
Sands Farm
Messingham
BUTTERWICK ROAD
SAND LANE
HILLTOP GDNS
WELL ST
WEST GN
EAST GN
ASH GR
HIGH ST
Bellevue Farm
BRIGG ROAD
Sand House Farm
CH
Bridge Farm
BUTTERWICK RD
WALNUT WY
ELM WY
B1400
Grange Park
GOOSEACRE 1
CALDER GN 2
WENTWORTH DR 3
CHERRY WY 4
WILLOW DR 5
PASTURES CT 6
HAZEL CL 7
ACACIA WY 8
MAPLE CL 9
MANOR FARM CL 10
GELDER BECK RD 11
TRENTHOLME DR 12
1 CHESTNUT DR
2 FAIRFIELD DR
3 EASTFIELD RD
4 KNIGHTSBRIDGE RD
Mells Farm
Black Bank Farm
Willow Tree Farm
Messingham Nature Reserve
Field Farm
KIRTON RD
Newstead Farm
Newstead
Carcar Farm
SCALLOW LA
Scallow Grove
Mount Pleasant Farm
SCOTTER ROAD
Landmoor Farm
Beggar Hill
BEGGAR HILL
Scotterthorpe
Grange Farm
North Moor Farm
SHOEMAKER'S LA
Black Wall Nook
Moss Farm
SENNEFLEET RD
Fish Pond Farm
Proudlea Farm
River Eau
Field House Farm
JOHNSON DR
CORDEAUX CL
1 FRANKLIN RD
2 DAR BECK RD
3 BARLINGS CL
4 BARNES GN
5 WAKEFIELD AVE
6 CHERRY TREE RISE
7 WAGGONERS CL
8 ARRANDALE
9 GRANARY FOLD
11 RIVERSIDE
12 ELIZABETH CL
13 EDGAR CL
SUSWORTH ROAD
SCOTTERTHORPE ROAD
Dar Beck
MESSINGHAM ROAD
GRAVEL PIT RD
Sunrise Farm
Scotter Wood
CHAPEL CT
THE GRANARY
PH
Evergreen Farm
HIGH ST W
Lodge Lane Farm
Becks Lane Farm
BECKS LANE
SANDS LA
CHURCH LA
Scotter
KIRTON ROAD
Scotterfield Farm
Scotterwood Farm
Library
Highfield Farm
St Helena Farm
The Poplars
Low Farm
GAINSBOROUGH ROAD
Scotter Prim Sch
South Hills
WOOD HILL ROAD
Poplar Grove Farm
SCOTTON ROAD
DN21
Field House
Green Howe
Merricks Farm
Sewage Works
KIRTON ROAD
Willow Farm
SCOTTER ROAD
Cockthorn Farm
River Eau
Scotton
KIRTON ROAD
Rainford's Corner
CRAPPLE LA
PH
CHURCH LA
Bucknall Farm
WESTGATE
EASTGATE
MIDDLE ST
HIGH ST
DOOKS CL
WESTFIELD
NORTHORPE ROAD
Beechwood Farm
Willow Lodge Farm
Manor House
INGS ROAD
A159
Dallison Plantation
8 05 7 04 6 03 5 02 4 01 3 00 2 99 1 98
86 A 87 B 88 C 89 D 90 E 91 F
B3
1 BELLBUTTS VW
2 LARK RISE
3 ASH GR
C3
1 POPLAR GR
2 ROOKLANDS
3 BEECHWOOD DR
4 CHESTNUT CL
5 PINETREE AVE
6 BRAMLEY GR
7 CEDAR CL
8 ORCHARD AVE
9 ST PETER'S GR
10 CECIL CL
11 MILL CRES
12 SOUTHCLIFFE RD
13 WAKERLEY RD
14 HOBB LA
15 CHARLES AVE
16 WESTCLIFFE RD
17 REVILL CL
18 ASTLEY CRES
19 ST PETER'S RD
20 THE GREEN
21 CROWN GDNS
22 THE ROOKERY
118
108

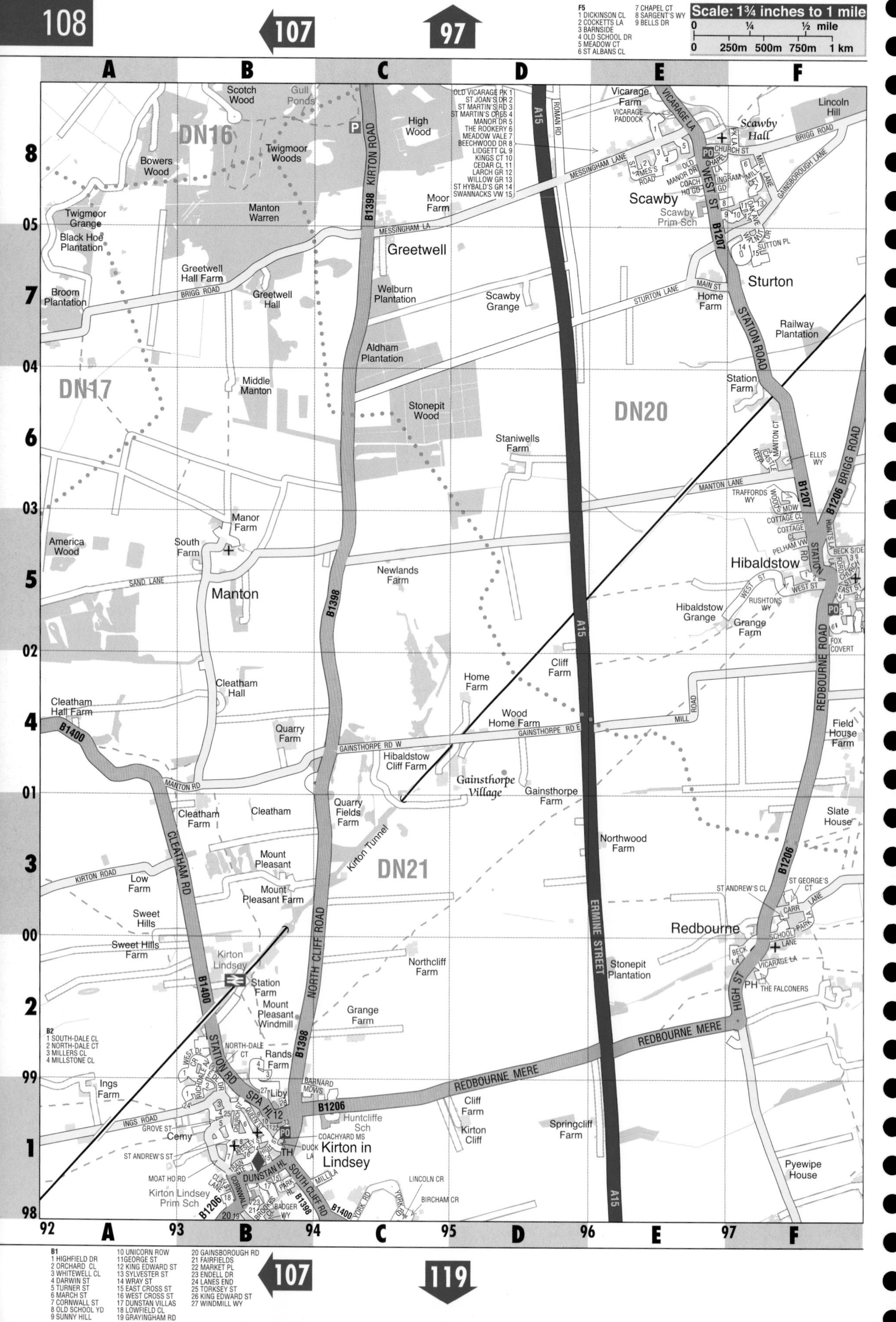

107

119

Scale: 1¾ inches to 1 mile

0 ¼ ½ mile
0 250m 500m 750m 1 km

F5
1 DICKINSON CL
2 COCKETTS LA
3 BARNSIDE
4 OLD SCHOOL DR
5 MEADOW CT
6 ST ALBANS CL
7 CHAPEL CT
8 SARGENT'S WY
9 BELLS DR

OLD VICARAGE PK 1
ST JOAN'S DR 2
ST MARTIN'S RD 3
ST MARTIN'S CRES 4
MANOR DR 5
THE ROOKERY 6
MEADOW VALE 7
BEECHWOOD DR 8
LIDGETT CL 9
KINGS CT 10
CEDAR CL 11
LARCH GR 12
WILLOW GR 13
ST HYBALD'S GR 14
SWANNACKS VW 15

B2
1 SOUTH-DALE CL
2 NORTH-DALE CT
3 MILLERS CL
4 MILLSTONE CL

B1
1 HIGHFIELD DR
2 ORCHARD CL
3 WHITEWELL CL
4 DARWIN ST
5 TURNER ST
6 MARCH ST
7 CORNWALL ST
8 OLD SCHOOL YD
9 SUNNY HILL
10 UNICORN ROW
11 GEORGE ST
12 KING EDWARD ST
13 SYLVESTER ST
14 WRAY ST
15 EAST CROSS ST
16 WEST CROSS ST
17 DUNSTAN VILLAS
18 LOWFIELD CL
19 GRAYINGHAM RD
20 GAINSBOROUGH RD
21 FAIRFIELDS
22 MARKET PL
23 ENDELL DR
24 LANES END
25 TORKSEY ST
26 KING EDWARD WY
27 WINDMILL WY

DN16

DN17

DN20

DN21

Scotch Wood

Gull Ponds

Bowers Wood

High Wood

Twigmoor Woods

Manton Warren

Moor Farm

Twigmoor Grange

Black Hoe Plantation

Broom Plantation

Greetwell Hall Farm

Greetwell Hall

Greetwell

Welburn Plantation

Scawby Grange

Vicarage Farm

VICARAGE PADDOCK

Scawby

Scawby Prim Sch

Scawby Hall

Lincoln Hill

Sturton

Home Farm

Railway Plantation

Aldham Plantation

Middle Manton

Stonepit Wood

Staniwells Farm

Station Farm

Manor Farm

South Farm

America Wood

Manton

SAND LANE

Newlands Farm

Manton Lane

TRAFFORDS WY

COTTAGE CT

Hibaldstow

Hibaldstow Grange

Grange Farm

Fox Covert

ELLIS WY

Cleatham Hall

Cleatham Hall Farm

Quarry Farm

Home Farm

Wood Home Farm

Cliff Farm

Cliff Farm

GAINSTHORPE RD W

GAINSTHORPE RD E

Hibaldstow Cliff Farm

Gainsthorpe Village

Gainsthorpe Farm

MILL ROAD

Field House Farm

Slate House

Cleatham Farm

Cleatham

Quarry Fields Farm

Kirton Tunnel

Mount Pleasant

Mount Pleasant Farm

Northwood Farm

ST ANDREW'S CL

ST GEORGE'S CT

Redbourne

Low Farm

KIRTON ROAD

Sweet Hills

Sweet Hills Farm

Kirton Lindsey

Station Farm

Mount Pleasant Windmill

Northcliff Farm

Grange Farm

Stonepit Plantation

THE FALCONERS

PH

Ings Farm

INGS ROAD

GROVE ST

Cemy

ST ANDREW'S ST

MOAT HO RD

Kirton Lindsey Prim Sch

NORTH-DALE CT

Rands Farm

Liby

BARNARD MDWS

Huntcliffe Sch

COACHYARD MS

DUCK LA

Kirton in Lindsey

Cliff Farm

Kirton Cliff

Springcliff Farm

REDBOURNE MERE

REDBOURNE MERE

LINCOLN CR

BIRCHAM CR

Pyewipe House

ERMINE STREET

A15

ROMAN RD

B1398

KIRTON ROAD

B1207

STATION ROAD

BRIGG ROAD

GAINSBROUGH LANE

MILL LANE

MESSINGHAM LA

BRIGG ROAD

STURTON LANE

MAIN ST

WEST ST

B1206

B1207

HUNT'S LA

BRIGG ROAD

B1206

REDBOURNE ROAD

B1400

MANTON RD

CLEATHAM RD

B1400

NORTH CLIFF ROAD

B1398

STATION RD

SPA HILL

HIGH ST

SCHOOL LA

VICARAGE LA

CLAY LANE

DUNSTAN HILL

SOUTH CLIFF RD

MILL LA

YORK RD

B1206

8

05

7

04

6

03

5

02

4

01

3

00

2

99

1

98

92 93 94 95 96 97

A B C D E F

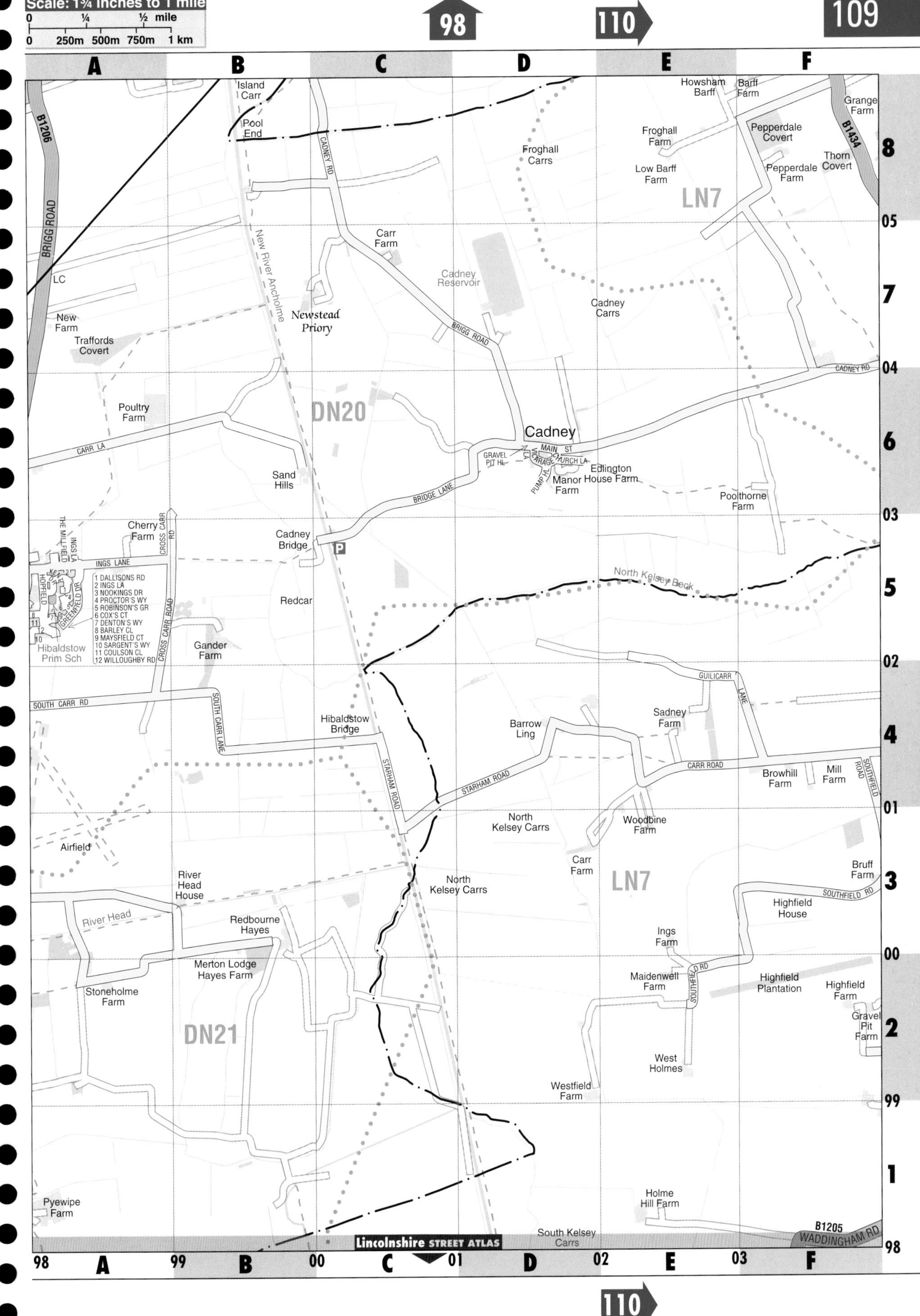

Scale: 1¾ inches to 1 mile
0 ¼ ½ mile
0 250m 500m 750m 1 km
98
110
A B C D E F
Island Carr
Pool End
B1206
BRIGG ROAD
CADNEY RD
New River Ancholme
Carr Farm
LC
New Farm
Traffords Covert
Newstead Priory
Cadney Reservoir
BRIGG ROAD
Froghall Carrs
Howsham Barff
Barff Farm
Grange Farm
Froghall Farm
Low Barff Farm
Pepperdale Covert
B1434
Pepperdale Farm
Thorn Covert
LN7
Cadney Carrs
CADNEY RD
Poultry Farm
DN20
CARR LA
Cadney
MAIN ST
GRAVEL PIT HL
VICARAGE
CHURCH LA
PUMP HL
Edlington House Farm
Manor Farm
Sand Hills
BRIDGE LANE
Poolthorne Farm
Cherry Farm
THE MILLFIELD
INGS LA
CROSS CARR RD
Cadney Bridge
P
INGS LANE
North Kelsey Beck
HOPFIELD
GREENFIELD DR
1 DALLISONS RD
2 INGS LA
3 NOOKINGS DR
4 PROCTOR'S WY
5 ROBINSON'S GR
6 COX'S CT
7 DENTON'S WY
8 BARLEY CL
9 MAYSFIELD CT
10 SARGENT'S WY
11 COULSON CL
12 WILLOUGHBY RD
Redcar
CROSS CARR ROAD
Hibaldstow Prim Sch
Gander Farm
GUILICARR LANE
SOUTH CARR RD
SOUTH CARR LANE
Hibaldstow Bridge
Barrow Ling
Sadney Farm
STARHAM ROAD
CARR ROAD
Browhill Farm
Mill Farm
SOUTHFIELD ROAD
North Kelsey Carrs
Woodbine Farm
Airfield
Carr Farm
LN7
Bruff Farm
River Head House
North Kelsey Carrs
SOUTHFIELD RD
Highfield House
River Head
Redbourne Hayes
Ings Farm
Merton Lodge Hayes Farm
Maidenwell Farm
SOUTHFIELD RD
Highfield Plantation
Highfield Farm
Stoneholme Farm
Gravel Pit Farm
DN21
West Holmes
Westfield Farm
Holme Hill Farm
Pyewipe Farm
South Kelsey Carrs
B1205
WADDINGHAM RD
8
05
7
04
6
03
5
02
4
01
3
00
2
99
1
98
98 A 99 B 00 C 01 D 02 E 03 F

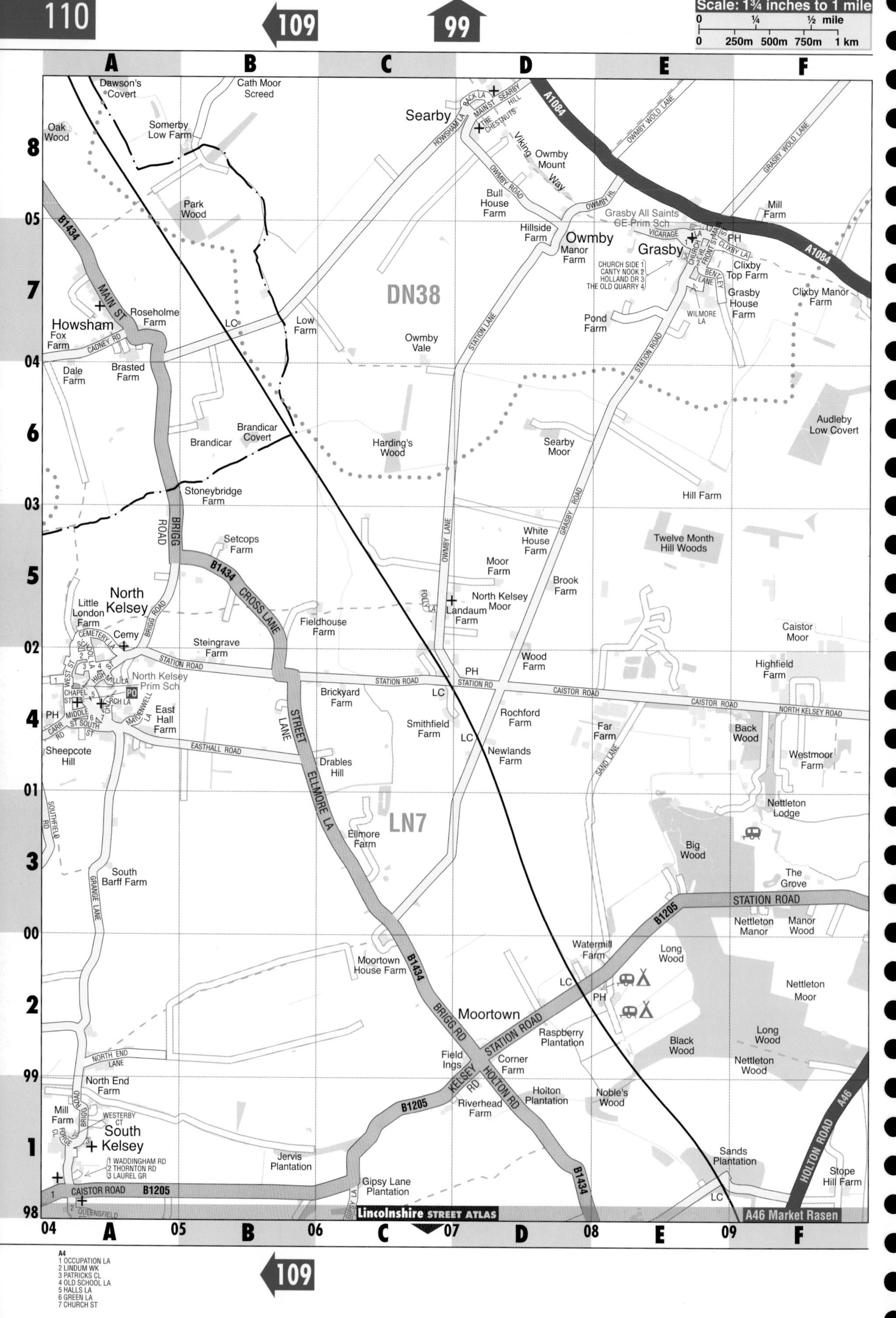

110

◀ 109

▲ 99

Scale: 1¾ inches to 1 mile

0   ¼   ½   mile
0 250m 500m 750m 1 km

Dawson's Covert
Cath Moor Screed
Oak Wood
Somerby Low Farm
Searby
BACK LA
HOWSHAM LA
THE CHESTNUTS
MAIN ST
SEARBY HILL
A1084
OWMBY WOLD LANE
GRASBY WOLD LANE
Mill Farm

Park Wood
Owmby Mount
OWMBY ROAD
Viking Way
Bull House Farm
OWMBY HILL
Grasby All Saints CE Prim Sch
VICARAGE
PH
A1084

8
05
Hillside Farm
Owmby
Grasby
Clixby Manor Farm
B1434
MAIN ST
Manor Farm
CHURCH SIDE 1
CANTY NOOK 2
HOLLAND DR 3
THE OLD QUARRY 4
FRONT ST
CLIXBY LA
Clixby Top Farm
7
Howsham
DN38
Grasby House Farm
Fox Farm
CADNET RD
Roseholme Farm
LC
Low Farm
Owmby Vale
WILMORE LA
BENTLEY LA

04
Dale Farm
Brasted Farm
Pond Farm
STATION LANE

6
Brandicar Covert
Brandicar
Harding's Wood
Searby Moor
Audleby Low Covert

03
Stoneybridge Farm
BRIGG ROAD
White House Farm
Hill Farm
GRASBY ROAD

5
Setcops Farm
CROSS LANE
Moor Farm
Twelve Month Hill Woods
Little London Farm
North Kelsey
BRIGG ROAD
Fieldhouse Farm
North Kelsey Moor
Landaum Farm
FOLLY LA
Brook Farm
Caistor Moor

02
Cemy
CEMETERY LA
Steingrave Farm
STATION ROAD
Wood Farm
PH
STATION RD
Highfield Farm
SCHOOL LA
North Kelsey Prim Sch
Brickyard Farm
STATION ROAD
LC
CAISTOR ROAD
CAISTOR ROAD
NORTH KELSEY ROAD
WEST ST
HIGH ST
VILLA LA
PO
Rochford Farm
SAND LANE
Back Wood

4
CHAPEL ST
CARR RD
MIDDLE ST SOUTH
CHURCH LA
MATTENWELL
East Hall Farm
EASTHALL ROAD
Smithfield Farm
Far Farm
Westmoor Farm
PH

Sheepcote Hill
STREET LANE
Drables Hill
Newlands Farm
LC

01
ELMORE LA
Nettleton Lodge

3
SOUTHFIELD RD
LN7
Elmore Farm
Big Wood
The Grove

South Barff Farm
GRANGE LANE
B1205
STATION ROAD

00
Moortown House Farm
Watermill Farm
Nettleton Manor
Manor Wood
B1434
Long Wood

2
NORTH END LANE
BRIGG RD
STATION ROAD
Moortown
LC
PH
Nettleton Moor
Black Wood
Raspberry Plantation
Long Wood
Nettleton Wood

99
North End Farm
Field Ings
KELSEY RD
Corner Farm
HOLTON RD
Noble's Wood

Mill Farm
FORGE CL
WESTERBY CT
Riverhead Farm
Holton Plantation
A46
South Kelsey
B1205
HOLTON ROAD

1
1 WADDINGHAM RD
2 THORNTON RD
3 LAUREL GR
Jervis Plantation
Sands Plantation
Stope Hill Farm
B1434
QUEENSFIELD
CAISTOR ROAD
B1205
Gipsy Lane Plantation
GIPSY LA
LC
A46 Market Rasen

98

04   A   05   B   06   C   07   D   08   E   09   F

A4
1 OCCUPATION LA
2 LINDUM WK
3 PATRICKS CL
4 OLD SCHOOL LA
5 HALLS LA
6 GREEN LA
7 CHURCH ST

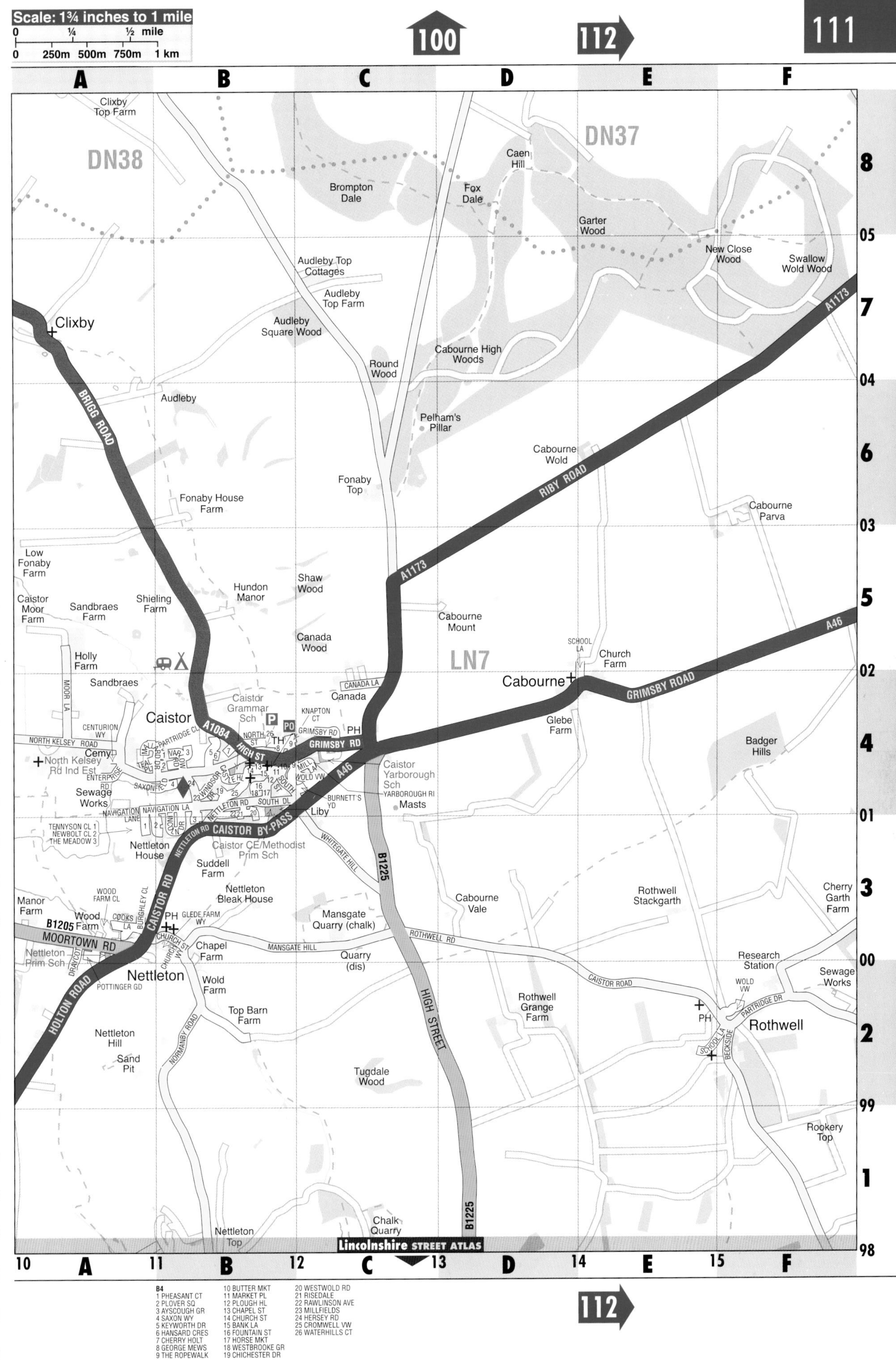

DN38

DN37

Clixby Top Farm

Caen Hill

Brompton Dale

Fox Dale

Garter Wood

New Close Wood

Swallow Wold Wood

05

8

Clixby

Audleby Top Cottages

Audleby Square Wood

Audleby Top Farm

Cabourne High Woods

A1173

7

04

BRIGG ROAD

Audleby

Round Wood

Pelham's Pillar

Cabourne Wold

RIBY ROAD

Cabourne Parva

6

03

Fonaby House Farm

Fonaby Top

Low Fonaby Farm

Caistor Moor Farm

Sandbraes Farm

Shieling Farm

Hundon Manor

Shaw Wood

A1173

Cabourne Mount

LN7

Cabourne Parva

A46

5

02

Holly Farm

Sandbraes

Canada Wood

CANADA LA

Canada

SCHOOL LA

Church Farm

Cabourne

GRIMSBY ROAD

Badger Hills

Caistor

Caistor Grammar Sch

KNAPTON CT

Glebe Farm

4

North Kelsey Rd Ind Est

Cemy

CENTURION WY

PARTRIDGE CO

NORTH KELSEY ROAD

HIGH ST

A1084

P

PO

NO. 26

TH

GRIMSBY RD

PH

GRIMSBY RD

MILL LA

WOLD VW

A46

Caistor Yarborough Sch

YARBOROUGH RI

Cabourne Vale

Sewage Works

ENTERPRISE RD

SAXON FIELD

WINDSOR DR

SOUTH DL

NETTLETON RD

BURNETT'S YD

Masts

01

TENNYSON CL 1
NEWBOLT CL 2
THE MEADOW 3

NAVIGATION LANE

NAVIGATION LA

Nettleton House

CAISTOR BY-PASS

NETTLETON RD

Liby

WHITEGATE HILL

B1225

3

Manor Farm

WOOD FARM CL

COOKS LA

BURGHLEY CL

CAISTOR RD

PH

GLEDE FARM WY

Suddell Farm

Caistor CE/Methodist Prim Sch

Nettleton Bleak House

Mansgate Quarry (chalk)

ROTHWELL RD

Rothwell Stackgarth

Cherry Garth Farm

B1205

Wood Farm

Nettleton Prim Sch

POTTINGER GD

DRAGOTT RD

MOORTOWN RD

CHURCH ST

CHURCH ST WY

Chapel Farm

MANSGATE HILL

Quarry (dis)

Research Station

WOLD VW

Sewage Works

00

HOLTON ROAD

Nettleton

Wold Farm

NORMANBY ROAD

Top Barn Farm

HIGH STREET

Rothwell Grange Farm

CAISTOR ROAD

PH

SCHOOL LA

BECKSIDE

PARTRIDGE DR

Rothwell

2

Nettleton Hill

Sand Pit

Tugdale Wood

99

Rookery Top

1

Nettleton Top

Chalk Quarry

B1225

111
101

Scale: 1¾ inches to 1 mile

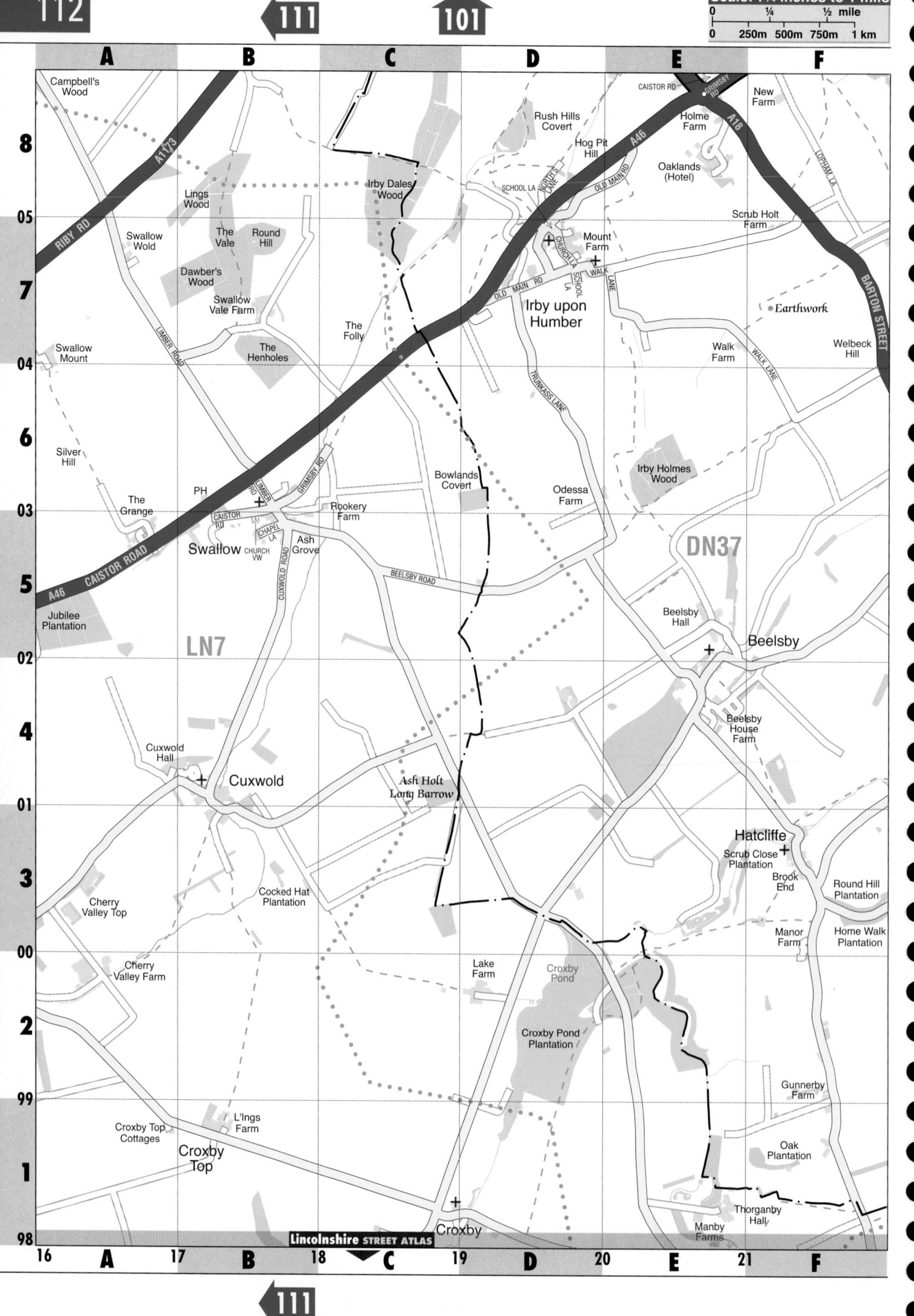
Campbell's Wood
Lings Wood
Irby Dales Wood
Rush Hills Covert
Hog Pit Hill
CAISTOR RD
GRIMSBY RD
New Farm
Holme Farm
A18
Oaklands (Hotel)
LOPHAM LA
A1173
RIBY RD
Swallow Wold
The Vale
Round Hill
Dawber's Wood
Swallow Vale Farm
SCHOOL LA
NORTH'S LANE
OLD MAIN RD
A46
Mount Farm
CHURCH LA
SCHOOL LA
WALK LANE
Scrub Holt Farm
BARTON STREET
Earthwork
Irby upon Humber
Swallow Mount
LIMBER ROAD
The Henholes
The Folly
Walk Farm
WALK LANE
Welbeck Hill
TRUNKASS LANE
Silver Hill
Bowlands Covert
Irby Holmes Wood
Odessa Farm
The Grange
PH
LIMBER RD
GRIMSBY RD
Rookery Farm
CAISTOR RD
CHAPEL LA
Swallow
CHURCH VW
CUXWOLD ROAD
Ash Grove
DN37
CAISTOR ROAD
BEELSBY ROAD
Jubilee Plantation
LN7
Beelsby Hall
Beelsby
Beelsby House Farm
Cuxwold Hall
Cuxwold
Ash Holt Long Barrow
Hatcliffe
Scrub Close Plantation
Brook End
Round Hill Plantation
Cocked Hat Plantation
Cherry Valley Top
Manor Farm
Home Walk Plantation
Lake Farm
Croxby Pond
Cherry Valley Farm
Croxby Pond Plantation
Gunnerby Farm
L'Ings Farm
Croxby Top Cottages
Croxby Top
Oak Plantation
Thorganby Hall
Croxby
Manby Farms
A B C D E F
8 7 6 5 4 3 2 1
05 04 03 02 01 00 99 98
16 17 18 19 20 21

111

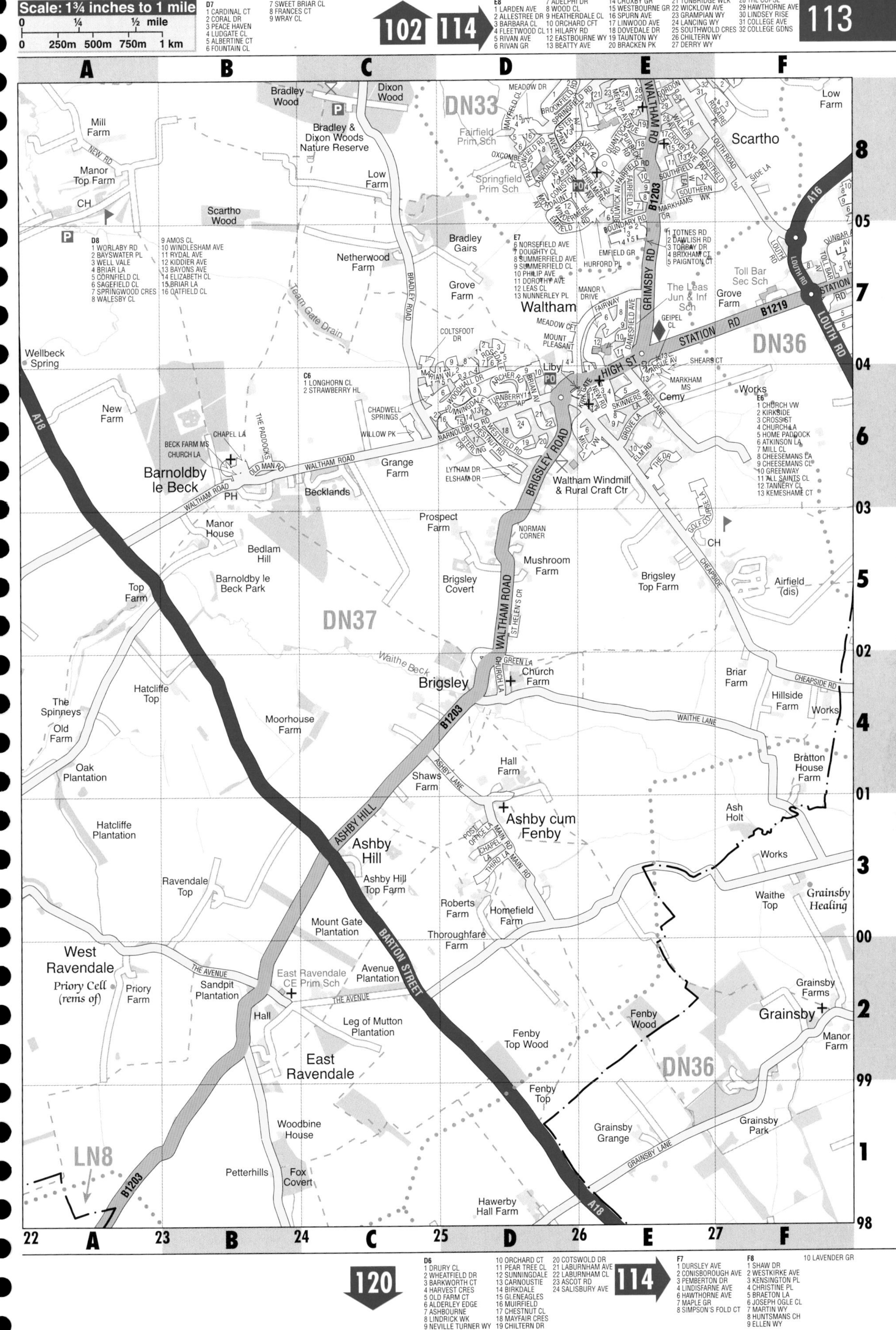

Scale: 1¾ inches to 1 mile

0 ¼ ½ mile
0 250m 500m 750m 1 km

102 114

D7
1 CARDINAL CT
2 CORAL DR
3 PEACE HAVEN
4 LUDGATE CL
5 ALBERTINE CT
6 FOUNTAIN CL

7 SWEET BRIAR CL
8 FRANCES CT
9 WRAY CL

E8
1 LARDEN AVE
2 ALLESTREE DR
3 BARBARA CL
4 FLEETWOOD CL
5 RIVAN AVE
6 RIVAN GR

7 ADELPHI DR
8 WOOD CL
9 HEATHERDALE CL
10 ORCHARD CFT
11 HILARY RD
12 EASTBOURNE WY
13 BEATTY AVE

14 CROXBY GR
15 WESTBOURNE GR
16 SPURN AVE
17 LINWOOD AVE
18 DOVEDALE CL
19 TAUNTON WY
20 BRACKEN PK

21 TONBRIDGE WLK
22 WICKLOW AVE
23 GRAMPIAN WY
24 LANCING WY
25 SOUTHWOLD CRES
26 CHILTERN WY
27 DERRY CL

28 THE COPSE
29 HAWTHORNE AVE
30 LINDSEY RISE
31 COLLEGE AVE
32 COLLEGE GDNS

D8
1 WORLABY RD
2 BAYSWATER PL
3 WELL VALE
4 BRIAR LA
5 CORNFIELD CL
6 SAGEFIELD CL
7 SPRINGWOOD CRES
8 WALESBY CL

9 AMOS CL
10 WINDLESHAM AVE
11 RYDAL AVE
12 KIDDIER AVE
13 BAYONS AVE
14 ELIZABETH CL
15 BRIAR LA
16 OATFIELD CL

C6
1 LONGHORN CL
2 STRAWBERRY HL

E7
1 NORSEFIELD AVE
2 DOUGHTY CL
3 SUMMERFIELD AVE
4 SUMMERFIELD CL
5 PHILIP AVE
6 DOROTHY AVE
7 LEAS CL
8 NUNNERLEY PL

E6
1 CHURCH VW
2 KIRKSIDE
3 CROSS ST
4 CHURCH LA
5 HOME PADDOCK
6 ATKINSON LA
7 MILL CL
8 CHEESEMANS LA
9 CHEESEMANS CL
10 GREENWAY
11 ALL SAINTS CL
12 TANNERY CL
13 KEMESHAME CT

120 114

D6
1 DRURY CL
2 WHEATFIELD DR
3 BARKWORTH CT
4 HARVEST CRES
5 OLD FARM CT
6 ALDERLEY EDGE
7 ASHBOURNE
8 LINDRICK WK
9 NEVILLE TURNER WY

10 ORCHARD CT
11 PEAR TREE CL
12 SUNNINGDALE
13 CARNOUSTIE
14 BIRKDALE
15 GLENEAGLES
16 MUIRFIELD
17 CHESTNUT CL
18 MAYFAIR CRES
19 CHILTERN DR

20 COTSWOLD DR
21 LABURNHAM AVE
22 LABURNHAM CL
23 ASCOT RD
24 SALISBURY AVE

F7
1 DURSLEY AVE
2 CONISBOROUGH AVE
3 PEMBERTON DR
4 LINDISFARNE AVE
5 HAWTHORNE AVE
6 MAPLE GR
7 SIMPSON'S FOLD CT

F8
1 SHAW DR
2 WESTKIRKE AVE
3 KENSINGTON PL
4 CHRISTINE PL
5 BRAETON LA
6 JOSEPH OGLE CL
7 MARTIN WY
8 HUNTSMANS CH
9 ELLEN WY

10 LAVENDER GR

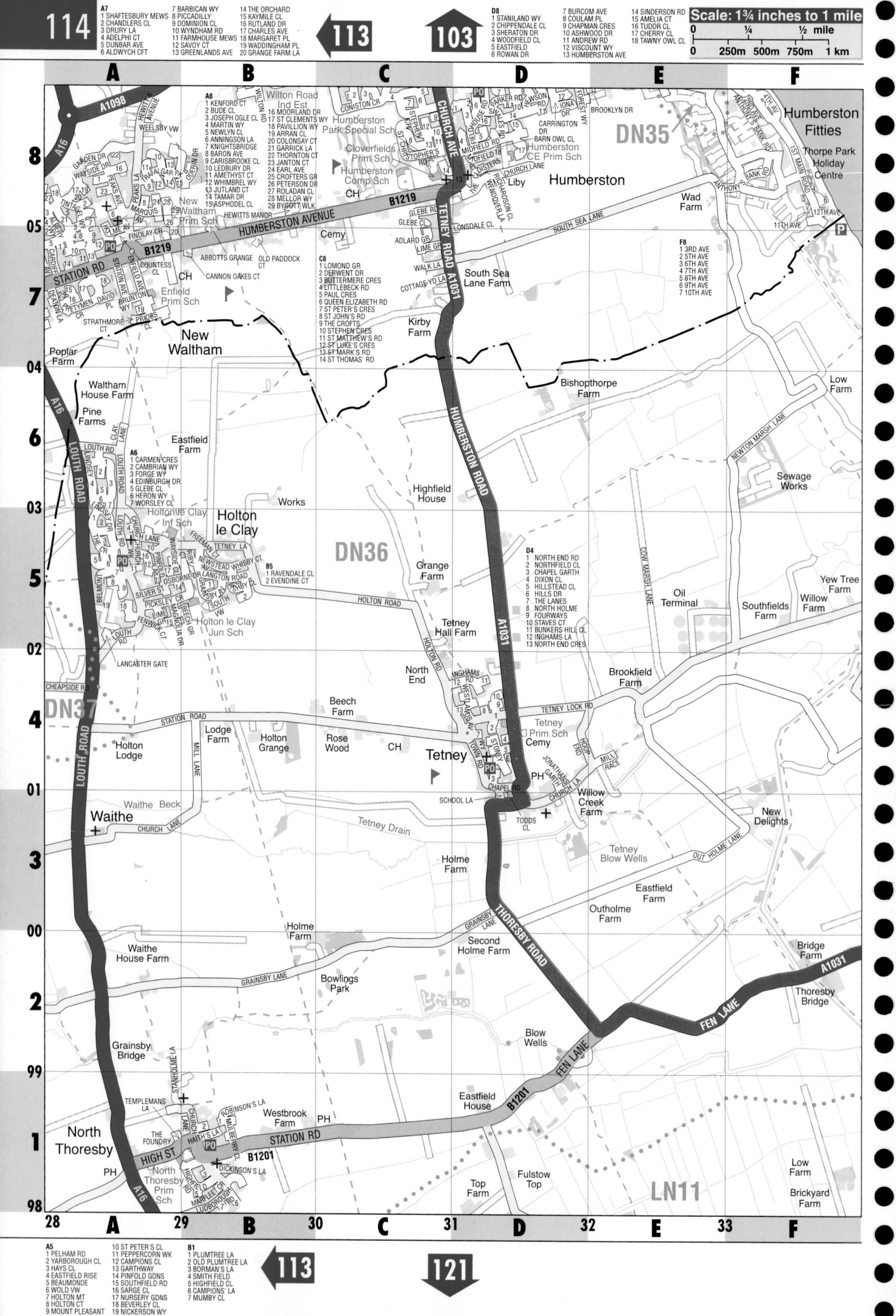
114
A7
1 SHAFTESBURY MEWS
2 CHANDLERS CL
3 DRURY LA
4 ADELPHI CT
5 DUNBAR AVE
6 ALDWYCH CFT
7 BARBICAN WY
8 PICCADILLY
9 DOMINION CL
10 WYNDHAM RD
11 FARMHOUSE MEWS
12 SAVOY CT
13 GREENLANDS AVE
14 THE ORCHARD
15 KAYMILE CL
16 RUTLAND DR
17 CHARLES AVE
18 MARGARET PL
19 WADDINGHAM PL
20 GRANGE FARM LA
113
103
D8
1 STANILAND WY
2 CHIPPENDALE CL
3 SHERATON DR
4 WOODFIELD CL
5 EASTFIELD
6 ROWAN DR
7 BURCOM AVE
8 COULAM PL
9 CHAPMAN CRES
10 ASHWOOD DR
11 ANDREW RD
12 VISCOUNT WY
13 HUMBERSTON AVE
14 SINDERSON RD
15 AMELIA CT
16 TUDOR CL
17 CHERRY CL
18 TAWNY OWL CL
Scale: 1¾ inches to 1 mile
0 ¼ ½ mile
0 250m 500m 750m 1 km
A B C D E F
8 05 7 04 6 03 5 02 4 01 3 00 2 99 1 98
28 29 30 31 32 33
A8
1 KENFORD CT
2 BUDE CL
3 JOSEPH OGLE CL
4 MARTIN WY
5 NEWLYN CL
6 ANNINGSON LA
7 KNIGHTSBRIDGE
8 BARON AVE
9 CARISBROOKE CL
10 LEDBURY DR
11 AMETHYST CT
12 WHIMBREL WY
13 JUTLAND CT
14 TAMAR DR
15 ASPHODEL CL
16 MOORLAND DR
17 ST CLEMENTS WY
18 PAVILLION WY
19 ARRAN CL
20 COLONSAY CT
21 GARRICK LA
22 THORNTON CT
23 JANTON CT
24 EARL AVE
25 CROFTERS GR
26 PETERSON DR
27 ROLADAN CL
28 MELLOR WY
29 BYGOTT WLK
C8
1 LOMOND GR
2 DERWENT DR
3 BUTTERMERE CRES
4 LITTLEBECK RD
5 PAUL CRES
6 QUEEN ELIZABETH RD
7 ST PETER'S CRES
8 ST JOHN'S RD
9 THE CROFTS
10 STEPHEN CRES
11 ST MATTHEW'S RD
12 ST LUKE'S CRES
13 ST MARK'S RD
14 ST THOMAS' RD
F8
1 3RD AVE
2 5TH AVE
3 6TH AVE
4 7TH AVE
5 8TH AVE
6 9TH AVE
7 10TH AVE
A6
1 CARMEN CRES
2 CAMBRIAN WY
3 FORGE WY
4 EDINBURGH DR
5 GLEBE CL
6 HERON WY
7 WORSLEY CL
B5
1 RAVENDALE CL
2 EVENDINE CT
D4
1 NORTH END RD
2 NORTHFIELD CL
3 CHAPEL GARTH
4 DIXON CL
5 HILLSTEAD CL
6 HILLS DR
7 THE LANES
8 NORTH HOLME
9 FOURWAYS
10 STAVES CT
11 BUNKERS HILL CL
12 INGHAMS LA
13 NORTH END CRES
A1098
A16
Wilton Road Ind Est
Humberston Park Special Sch
Cloverfields Prim Sch
Humberston Comp Sch
CH
CHURCH AVE
Humberston CE Prim Sch
Liby
Humberston
DN35
Humberston Fitties
Thorpe Park Holiday Centre
Wad Farm
SOUTH SEA LANE
12TH AVE
11TH AVE
B1219
HUMBERSTON AVENUE
STATION RD
New Waltham Prim Sch
HEWITTS MANOR
ABBOTTS GRANGE
OLD PADDOCK CT
CANNON OAKES CT
Enfield Prim Sch
Cemy
TETNEY ROAD A1031
LONSDALE CL
South Sea Lane Farm
COTTAGE YD LA
STRATHMORE CT
New Waltham
Kirby Farm
Poplar Farm
Waltham House Farm
Pine Farms
Bishopthorpe Farm
Low Farm
NEWTON MARSH LANE
Eastfield Farm
HUMBERSTON ROAD
Sewage Works
LOUTH ROAD
Works
Highfield House
Holton le Clay Inf Sch
Holton le Clay
DN36
COW MARSH LANE
Grange Farm
HOLTON ROAD
Oil Terminal
Southfields Farm
Willow Farm
Yew Tree Farm
Holton le Clay Jun Sch
Tetney Hall Farm
A1031
LANCASTER GATE
North End
Brookfield Farm
CHEAPSIDE RD
DN37
Beech Farm
TETNEY LOCK RD
STATION ROAD
Lodge Farm
Holton Lodge
Holton Grange
Rose Wood
CH
Tetney
Tetney Prim Sch
Cemy
PH
MILL LANE
SCHOOL LA
TODDS CL
Willow Creek Farm
Waithe Beck
Waithe
CHURCH LANE
Tetney Drain
New Delights
Holme Farm
Tetney Blow Wells
OUT HOLME LANE
Eastfield Farm
Outholme Farm
Holme Farm
GRAINSBY LANE
Second Holme Farm
THORESBY ROAD
Bridge Farm
Waithe House Farm
Bowlings Park
Thoresby Bridge
FEN LANE
Blow Wells
Grainsby Bridge
STAINHOLME LA
TEMPLEMANS LA
Eastfield House
B1201
Westbrook Farm
PH
North Thoresby
THE FOUNDRY
HIGH ST
STATION RD
B1201
North Thoresby Prim Sch
PH
Top Farm
Fulstow Top
LN11
Low Farm
Brickyard Farm
A5
1 PELHAM RD
2 YARBOROUGH CL
3 HAYS CL
4 EASTFIELD RISE
5 BEAUMONDE
6 WOLD VW
7 HOLTON MT
8 HOLTON CT
9 MOUNT PLEASANT
10 ST PETER'S CL
11 PEPPERCORN WK
12 CAMPIONS CL
13 GARTHWAY
14 PINFOLD GDNS
15 SOUTHFIELD RD
16 SARGE CL
17 NURSERY GDNS
18 BEVERLEY CL
19 NICKERSON WY
B1
1 PLUMTREE LA
2 OLD PLUMTREE LA
3 BORMAN'S LA
4 SMITH FIELD
5 HIGHFIELD CL
6 CAMPIONS' LA
7 MUMBY CL
113
121

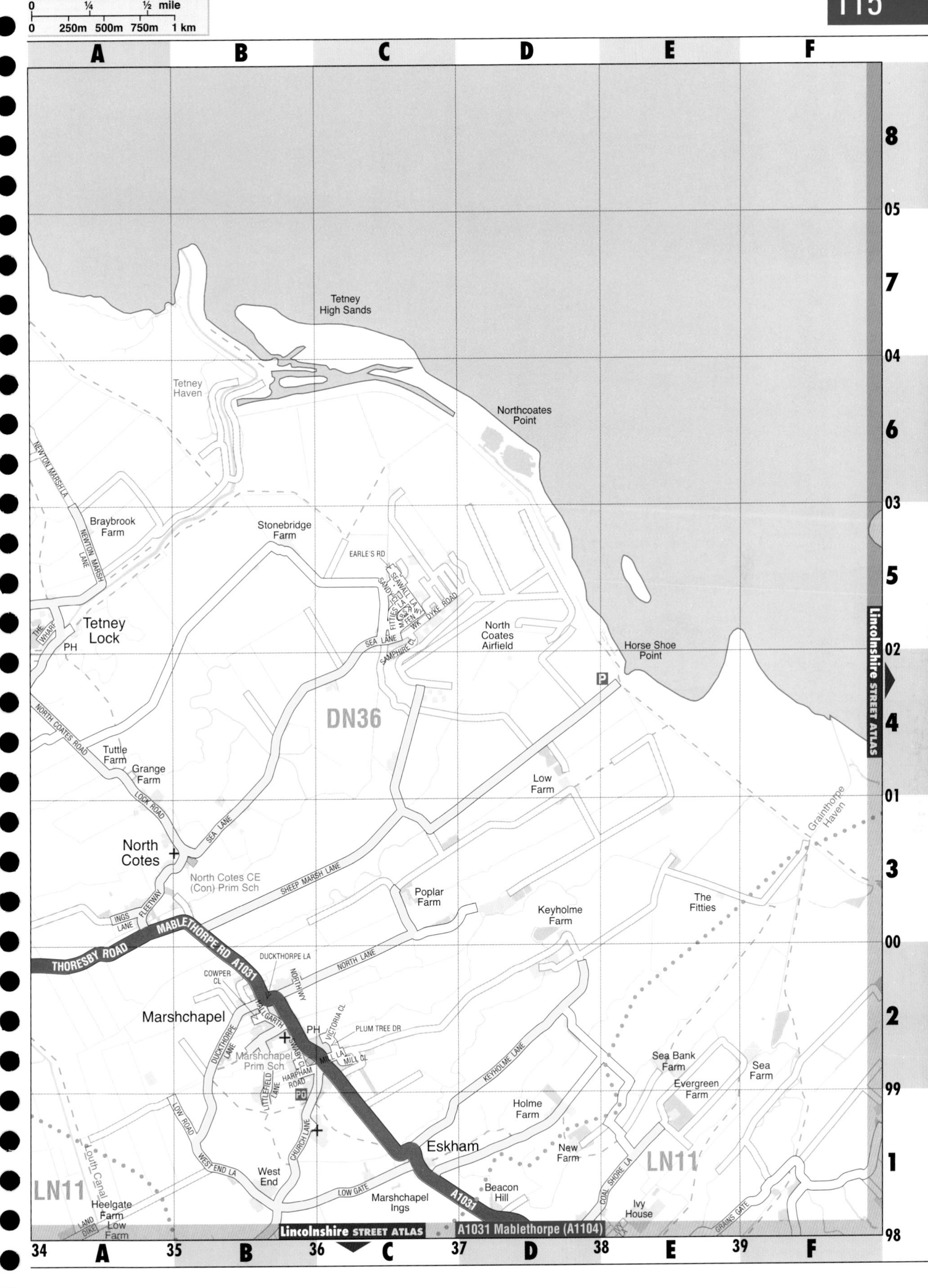

Scale: 1¾ inches to 1 mile

0   ¼   ½   mile
0   250m 500m 750m 1 km

Lincolnshire STREET ATLAS

Tetney
High Sands

Tetney
Haven

Northcoates
Point

Braybrook
Farm

Stonebridge
Farm

EARLE'S RD

North
Coates
Airfield

Horse Shoe
Point

Tetney Lock

PH

North Cotes Road

Tuttle
Farm

Grange
Farm

LOCK ROAD

SEA LANE

North
Cotes

North Cotes CE
(Con) Prim Sch

DN36

Low
Farm

Grainthorpe
Haven

SHEEP MARSH LANE

Poplar
Farm

Keyholme
Farm

The
Fitties

INGS
LANE

FLEETWAY

MABLETHORPE RD A1031

THORESBY ROAD

Marshchapel

COWPER
CL

DUCKTHORPE LA

NORTH LANE

DUCKTHORPE LANE

HALTGARTH LANE

ANTHONY

VICTORIA CL

PLUM TREE DR

KEYHOLME LANE

Holme
Farm

Sea Bank
Farm

Evergreen
Farm

Sea
Farm

PH

Marshchapel
Prim Sch

MILL LA

MILL CL

HARPHAM
ROAD

PO

LITTLEFIELD LANE

CHURCH LANE

Eskham

New
Farm

Holme
Farm

LN11

COAL SHORE LA

LN11

Louth Canal

Heelgate
Farm

Low
Farm

LOW ROAD

WEST END LA

West
End

LOW GATE

Marshchapel
Ings

A1031

Beacon
Hill

Ivy
House

GRAINS GATE

LAND DIKE

Lincolnshire STREET ATLAS

A1031 Mablethorpe (A1104)

34   A   35   B   36   C   37   D   38   E   39   F   98

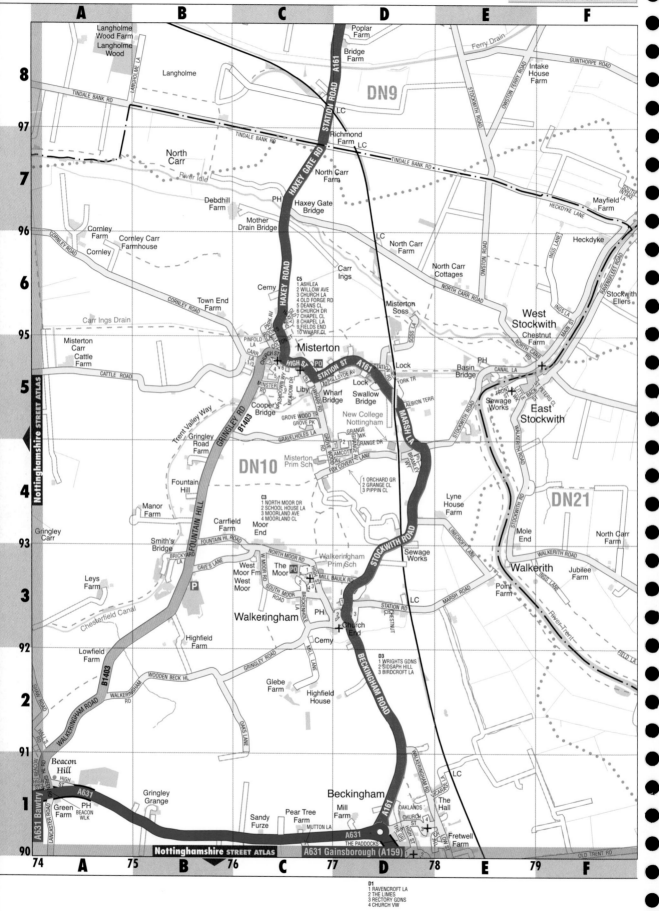

Scale: 1¾ inches to 1 mile
0   ¼   ½ mile
0 250m 500m 750m 1 km

DN9

Langholme Wood Farm
Langholme Wood
Langholme
TINDALE BANK RD
North Carr
River Idle
Debdhill Farm
Cornley Farm
Cornley Carr Farmhouse
Cornley
Town End Farm
Misterton Carr Cattle Farm
CATTLE ROAD
Carr Ings Drain

Poplar Farm
Bridge Farm
Ferry Drain
GUNTHORPE ROAD
Intake House Farm
OWSTON FERRY ROAD
Richmond Farm
LC
TINDALE BANK RD
North Carr Farm
Haxey Gate Bridge
Mother Drain Bridge
PH
Haxey Gate Bridge
HAXEY GATE RD
STATION ROAD
A161

HAXEY ROAD
Cemy
Carr Ings
North Carr Farm
North Carr Cottages
Heckdyke
Mayfield Farm
HECKDYKE LANE
SOUTH INTAKE
RAVENSFLEET ROAD
HECKDYKE LANE
INGS LANE

C5
1 ASHLEA
2 WILLOW AVE
3 CHURCH LA
4 OLD FORGE RD
5 DEANS CL
6 CHURCH DR
7 CHAPEL CL
8 CHAPEL LA
9 FIELDS END
10 WHARF CL

Misterton
Misterton Soss
HIGH ST PO STATION ST A161
Liby
Lock
Wharf Bridge
Swallow Bridge
Lock
ALBION TERR
York TR
STOCKWITH ROAD
Stockwith Ellers
West Stockwith
Chestnut Farm
PH
Basin Bridge
CANAL LA
Sewage Works
East Stockwith
MAIN ST
NORTH CARR RD
PETERS CL
FRONT
TITLE BACK
WALKERITH ROAD

Cooper's Bridge
Trent Valley Way
Gringley Road Farm
GRINGLEY RD
B1403
New College Nottingham
GROVE WOOD TR
GROVE PK
GRAVELHOLES LA
GRANGE WK
GRANGE DR
AMCOTT AV
FOX COVERT LANE
BRAMLEY PKWY
MARSH LA

DN10
Fountain Hill
Manor Farm
Carrfield Farm
Moor End
FOUNTAIN HILL
FOUNTAIN HL ROAD

Gringley Carr
Misterton Prim Sch
1 ORCHARD GR
2 GRANGE CL
3 PIPPIN CL
Lyne House Farm
DN21
North Carr Farm

Smith's Bridge
BRICKYARD LA
CAVE'S LANE
NORTH MOOR RD
W MOOR RD
SOUTH MOOR ROAD
West Moor Fm
West Moor
The Moor PO
Walkeringham Prim Sch
MILL BAULK RD
Sewage Works
Mole End
WALKERITH ROAD
Walkerith
Jubilee Farm
LINEGROFT LANE
Point Farm

Leys Farm
Chesterfield Canal
Highfield Farm
BRACKENHOE LA
PH
Walkeringham
STATION RD
CHESTNUT
LC
MARSH RD
River Trent
FIELD LA

Lowfield Farm
B1403
WALKERINGHAM RD
WOODEN BECK HL
GRINGLEY ROAD
Cemy
MILL LANE
Glebe Farm
Highfield House
Church End
BECKINGHAM ROAD

D3
1 WRIGHTS GDNS
2 SIDSAPH HILL
3 BIRDCROFT LA

Beacon Hill
HIGH ST
Green Farm
PH BEACON WLK
Gringley Grange
Sandy Furze
Pear Tree Farm
MUTTON LA
Mill Farm
Beckingham
A631
A161
OAKLANDS
CHURCH
The Hall
LC
WALKERINGHAM RD
Fretwell Farm
OLD TRENT RD

A631 Bawtry
LANCASTER ROAD
SHAW ROAD
OAKES LANE
HALL'S
A631
WALKERINGHAM RD
A631 Gainsborough (A159)
THE PADDOCKS
THE GB

D1
1 RAVENCROFT LA
2 THE LIMES
3 RECTORY GDNS
4 CHURCH VW

74   A   75   B   76   C   77   D   78   E   79   F

8 97 7 96 6 95 5 4 93 3 92 2 91 1 90

Nottinghamshire STREET ATLAS

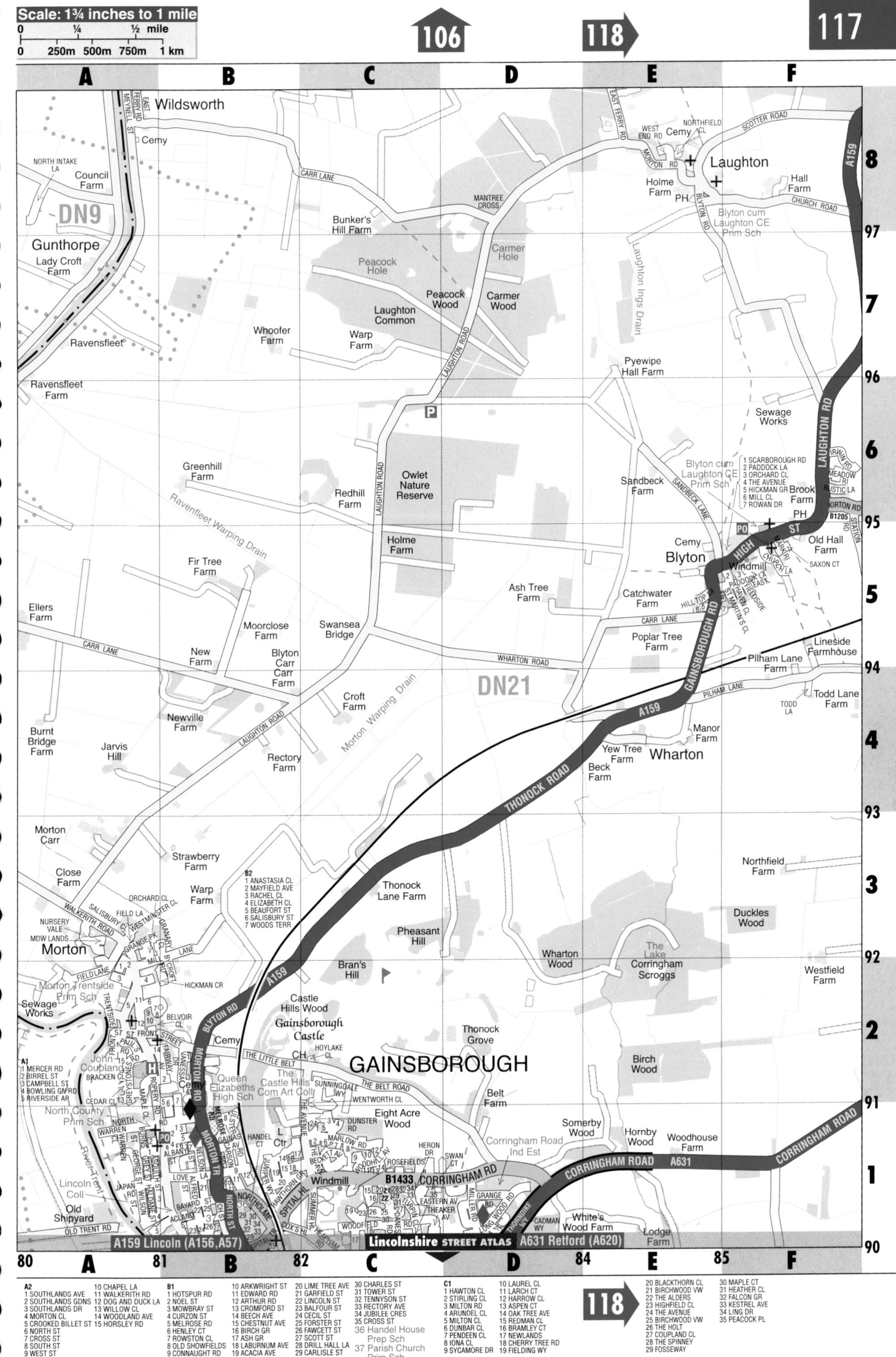

A2
1 SOUTHLANDS LA
2 SOUTHLANDS GDNS
3 SOUTHLANDS DR
4 MORTON CL
5 CROOKED BILLET ST
6 NORTH ST
7 CROSS ST
8 SOUTH ST
9 WEST ST
10 CHAPEL LA
11 WALKERITH RD
12 DOG AND DUCK LA
13 WILLOW CL
14 WOODLAND AVE
15 HORSLEY RD

B1
1 HOTSPUR RD
2 NOEL ST
3 MOWBRAY ST
4 CURZON ST
5 MELROSE RD
6 HENLEY CT
7 ROWSTON CL
8 OLD SHOWFIELDS
9 CONNAUGHT RD
10 ARKWRIGHT ST
11 EDWARD RD
12 ARTHUR RD
13 CROMFORD ST
14 BEECH AVE
15 CHESTNUT AVE
16 BIRCH GR
17 ASH GR
18 LABURNUM AVE
19 ACACIA AVE
20 LIME TREE AVE
21 GARFIELD ST
22 LINCOLN ST
23 BALFOUR ST
24 CECIL ST
25 FORSTER ST
26 FAWCETT ST
27 SCOTT ST
28 DRILL HALL LA
29 CARLISLE ST
30 CHARLES ST
31 TOWER ST
32 TENNYSON ST
33 RECTORY AVE
34 JUBILEE CRES
35 CROSS ST
36 Handel House Prep Sch
37 Parish Church Prim Sch

C1
1 HAWTON CL
2 STIRLING CL
3 MILTON RD
4 ARUNDEL CL
5 MILTON CL
6 DUNBAR CL
7 PENDEEN CL
8 IONA CL
9 SYCAMORE DR
10 LAUREL CL
11 LARCH CT
12 HARROW CL
13 ASPEN CT
14 OAK TREE AVE
15 REDMAN CL
16 BRAMLEY CT
17 NEWLANDS
18 CHERRY TREE RD
19 FIELDING WY
20 BLACKTHORN CL
21 BIRCHWOOD VW
22 THE ALDERS
23 HIGHFIELD CL
24 THE AVENUE
25 BIRCHWOOD VW
26 THE HOLT
27 COUPLAND CL
28 THE SPINNEY
29 FOSSEWAY
30 MAPLE CT
31 HEATHER CL
32 FALCON GR
33 KESTREL AVE
34 LING DR
35 PEACOCK PL

B2
1 ANASTASIA CL
2 MAYFIELD AVE
3 RACHEL CL
4 ELIZABETH CL
5 BEAUFORT ST
6 SALISBURY ST
7 WOODS TERR

A1
1 MERCER RD
2 BIRREL ST
3 CAMPBELL ST
4 BOWLING GA FRD
5 RIVERSIDE AR

117

107

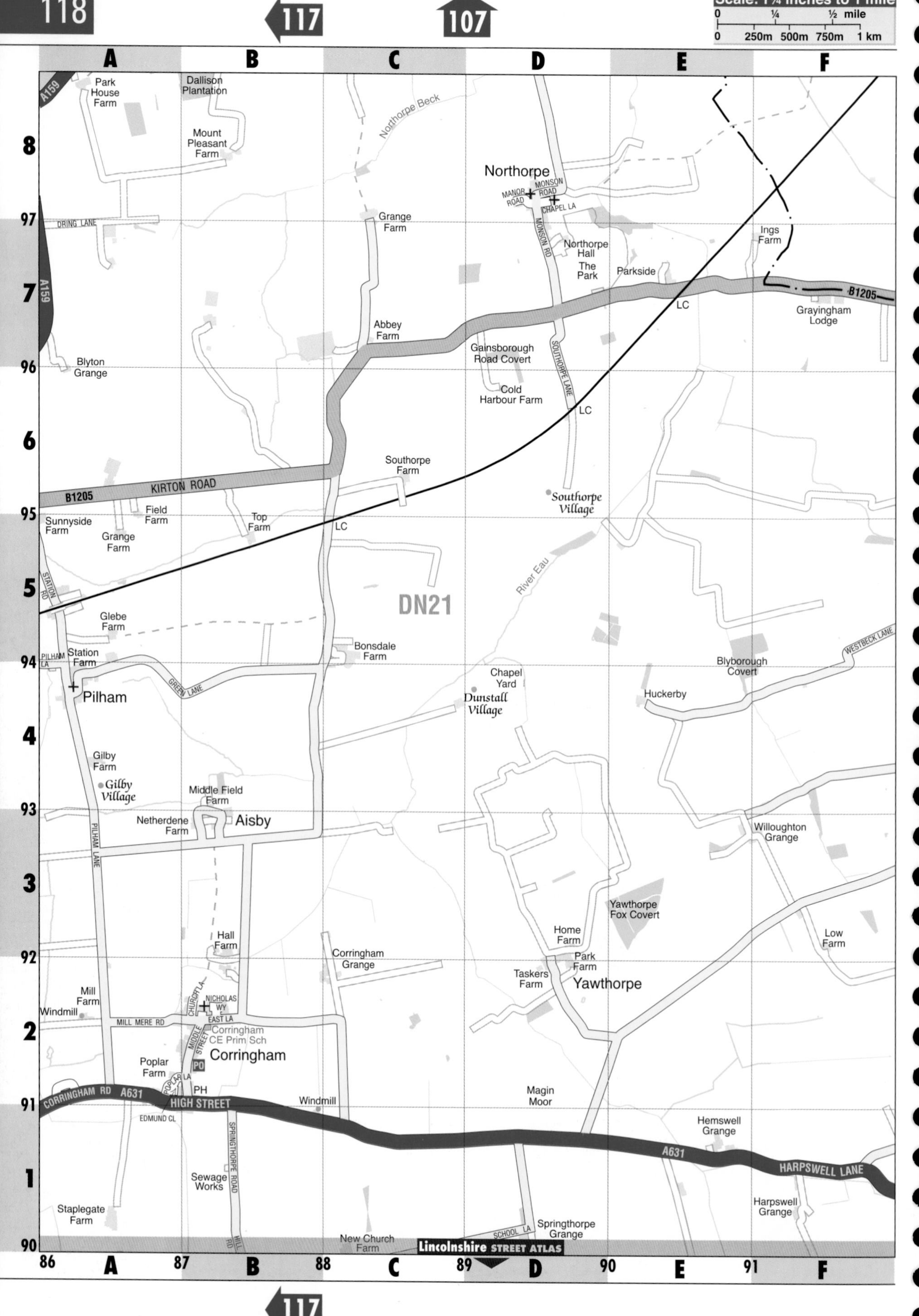

Scale: 1¾ inches to 1 mile
0 ¼ ½ mile
0 250m 500m 750m 1 km
A B C D E F
8 97 7 96 6 95 5 94 4 93 3 92 2 91 1 90
86 87 88 89 90 91
A159
Park House Farm
Dallison Plantation
Mount Pleasant Farm
Northorpe Beck
Northorpe
MANOR ROAD
MONSON ROAD
CHAPEL LA
MONSON RD
Grange Farm
DRING LANE
Northorpe Hall
The Park
Parkside
Ings Farm
B1205
LC
Grayingham Lodge
Abbey Farm
Gainsborough Road Covert
SOUTHORPE LANE
Blyton Grange
Cold Harbour Farm
Southorpe Farm
KIRTON ROAD
Southorpe Village
Sunnyside Farm
Field Farm
Top Farm
Grange Farm
STATION RD
River Eau
DN21
Glebe Farm
Bonsdale Farm
WESTBECK LANE
PILHAM LA
Station Farm
Blyborough Covert
Chapel Yard
GREEN LANE
Pilham
Dunstall Village
Huckerby
Gilby Farm
Gilby Village
Middle Field Farm
Netherdene Farm
Aisby
Willoughton Grange
PILHAM LANE
Yawthorpe Fox Covert
Low Farm
Hall Farm
Home Farm
Corringham Grange
Park Farm
Taskers Farm
Yawthorpe
Mill Farm
CHURCH LA
NICHOLAS WY
Windmill
EAST LA
MILL MERE RD
Corringham CE Prim Sch
MIDDLE STREET
Corringham
PO
Poplar Farm
POPLAR LA
PH
Magin Moor
CORRINGHAM RD
A631
HIGH STREET
Windmill
EDMUND CL
Hemswell Grange
SPRINGTHORPE ROAD
A631
HARPSWELL LANE
Sewage Works
Staplegate Farm
Harpswell Grange
Springthorpe Grange
SCHOOL LA
MILL RD
New Church Farm
Lincolnshire STREET ATLAS

117

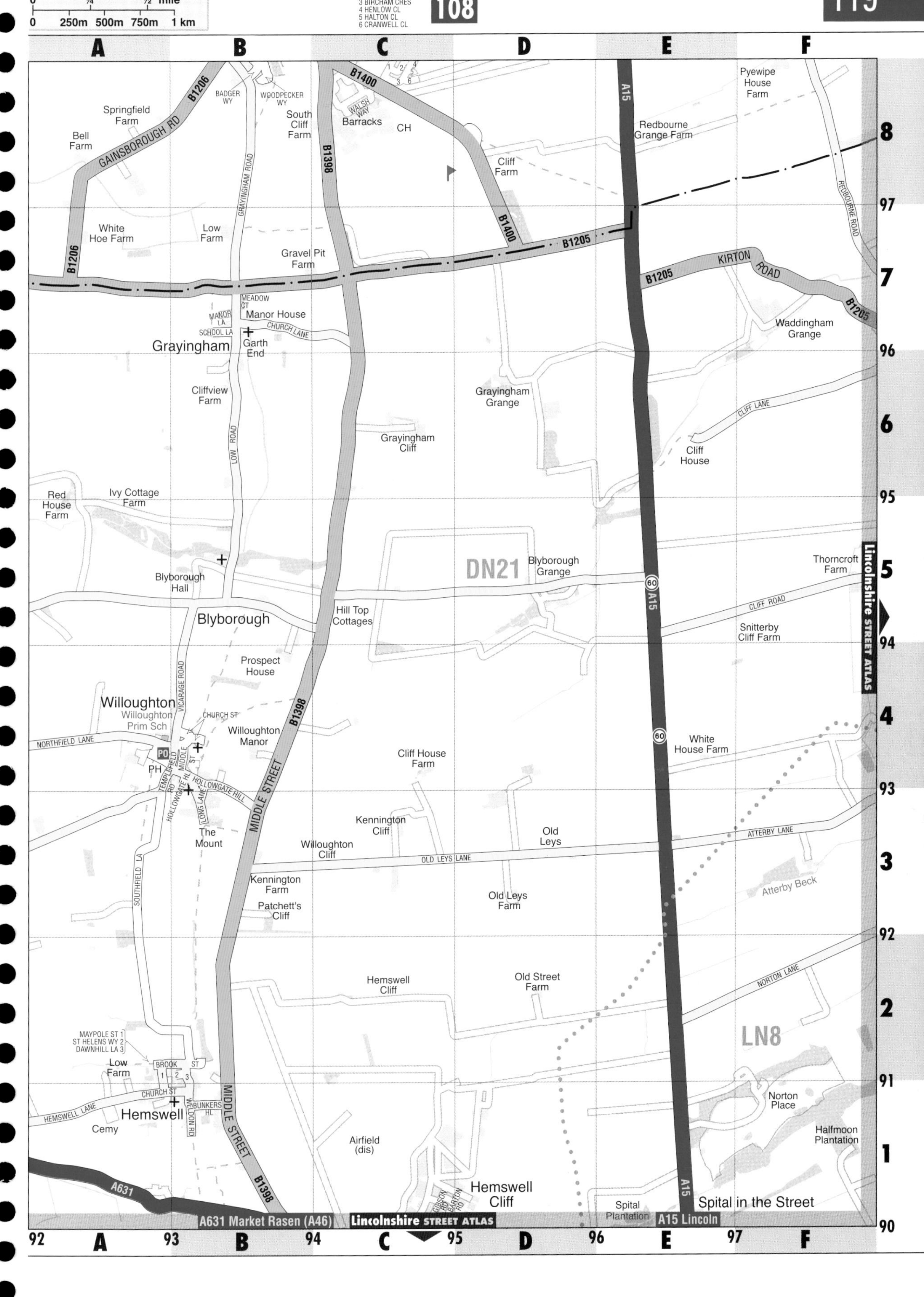
Scale: 1¾ inches to 1 mile
0 ¼ ½ mile
0 250m 500m 750m 1 km
C8
1 YORK RD
2 LINCOLN CRES
3 BIRCHAM CRES
4 HENLOW CL
5 HALTON CL
6 CRANWELL CL
108
A
B
C
D
E
F
8
97
7
96
6
95
5
94
4
93
3
92
2
91
1
90
92
93
94
95
96
97
B1206
GAINSBOROUGH RD
Springfield Farm
Bell Farm
BADGER WY
WOODPECKER WY
South Cliff Farm
B1400
WALSH WAY
Barracks
CH
B1398
A15
Pyewipe House Farm
Redbourne Grange Farm
Cliff Farm
GRAYINGHAM ROAD
REDBOURNE ROAD
White Hoe Farm
Low Farm
B1400
B1205
Gravel Pit Farm
B1205
KIRTON ROAD
B1205
MEADOW CT
MANOR LA
Manor House
SCHOOL LA
CHURCH LANE
Grayingham
Garth End
Waddingham Grange
Cliffview Farm
Grayingham Grange
CLIFF LANE
LOW ROAD
Grayingham Cliff
Cliff House
Red House Farm
Ivy Cottage Farm
DN21
Blyborough Grange
Thorncroft Farm
Blyborough Hall
60
A15
CLIFF ROAD
Blyborough
Hill Top Cottages
Snitterby Cliff Farm
Prospect House
VICARAGE ROAD
Willoughton
Willoughton Prim Sch
CHURCH ST
B1398
Willoughton Manor
60
White House Farm
NORTHFIELD LANE
PO
PH
TEMPLEFIELD RD
MIDDLE ST
Cliff House Farm
HOLLOWGATE HL
HOLLOWGATE HILL
LONG LANE
The Mount
MIDDLE STREET
Kennington Cliff
Old Leys
ATTERBY LANE
Willoughton Cliff
OLD LEYS LANE
Kennington Farm
Old Leys Farm
Atterby Beck
SOUTHFIELD LA
Patchett's Cliff
Hemswell Cliff
Old Street Farm
NORTON LANE
LN8
MAYPOLE ST 1
ST HELENS WY 2
DAWNHILL LA 3
Low Farm
BROOK ST
CHURCH ST
HEMSWELL LANE
Hemswell
BUNKERS HL
WELDON RD
MIDDLE STREET
Cemy
Norton Place
Halfmoon Plantation
Airfield (dis)
A631
B1398
GIBSON RD
BARTON RD
Hemswell Cliff
Spital Plantation
A15
Spital in the Street
A631 Market Rasen (A46)
Lincolnshire STREET ATLAS
A15 Lincoln
Lincolnshire STREET ATLAS

113

Scale: 1¾ inches to 1 mile
0   ¼   ½   mile
0   250m 500m 750m 1 km

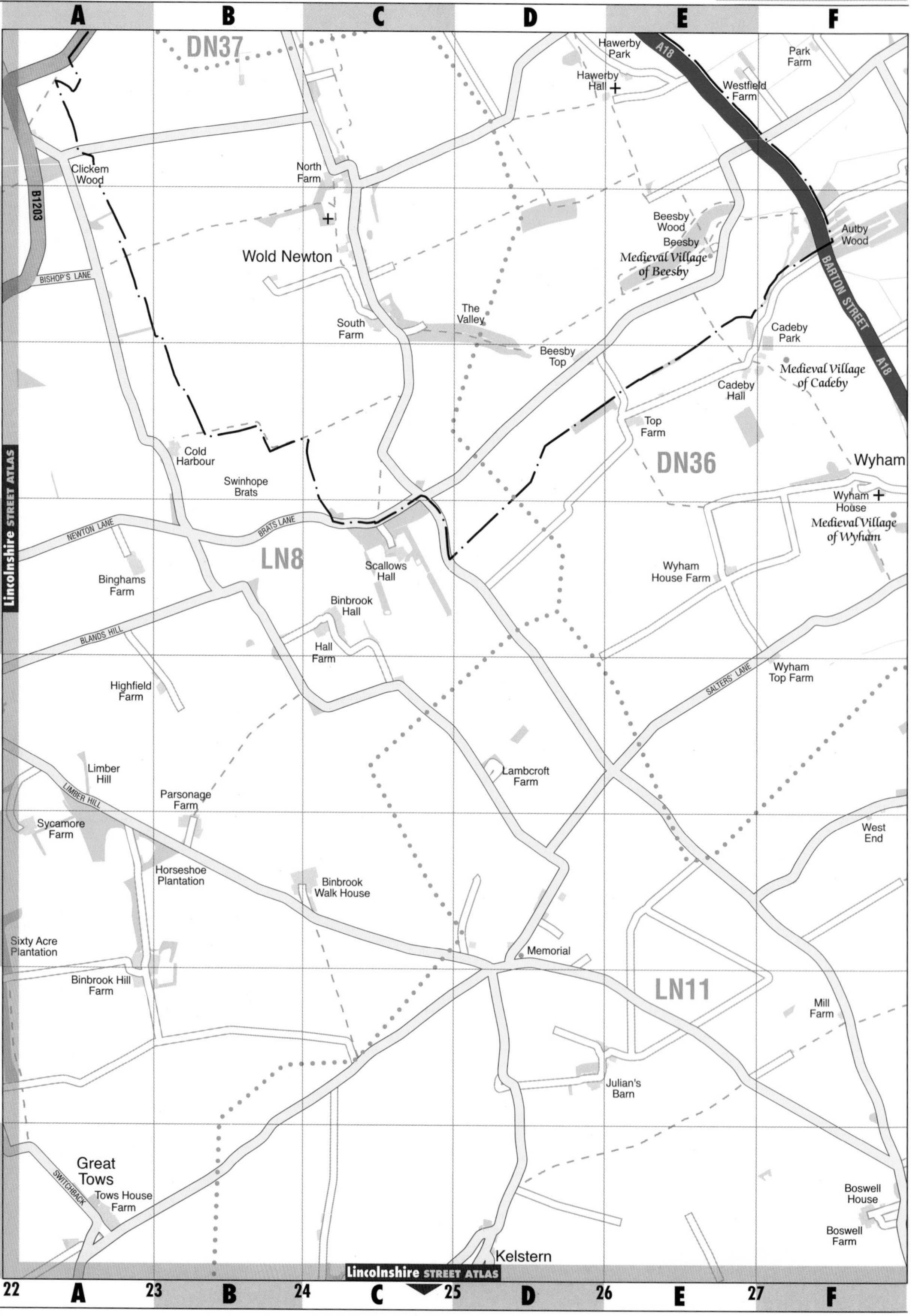

DN37

Hawerby
Park

Park
Farm

A18

Hawerby
Hall

Westfield
Farm

Clickem
Wood

North
Farm

Beesby
Wood

Autby
Wood

Beesby

Wold Newton

Medieval Village
of Beesby

BARTON STREET

South
Farm

The
Valley

Beesby
Top

Cadeby
Park

A18

Medieval Village
of Cadeby

Cold
Harbour

Cadeby
Hall

Wyham

BISHOP'S LANE

B1203

Swinhope
Brats

DN36

Top
Farm

Wyham
House

NEWTON LANE

BRATS LANE

LN8

Scallows
Hall

Wyham
House Farm

Medieval Village
of Wyham

Binghams
Farm

Binbrook
Hall

BLANDS HILL

Hall
Farm

SALTERS LANE

Wyham
Top Farm

Highfield
Farm

Limber
Hill

Parsonage
Farm

Lambcroft
Farm

West
End

LIMBER HILL

Sycamore
Farm

Horseshoe
Plantation

Binbrook
Walk House

Sixty Acre
Plantation

Memorial

LN11

Mill
Farm

Binbrook Hill
Farm

Julian's
Barn

SWITCHBACK

Great
Tows

Boswell
House

Tows House
Farm

Boswell
Farm

Kelstern

Lincolnshire STREET ATLAS

A   22   23   B   24   C   25   D   26   E   27   F

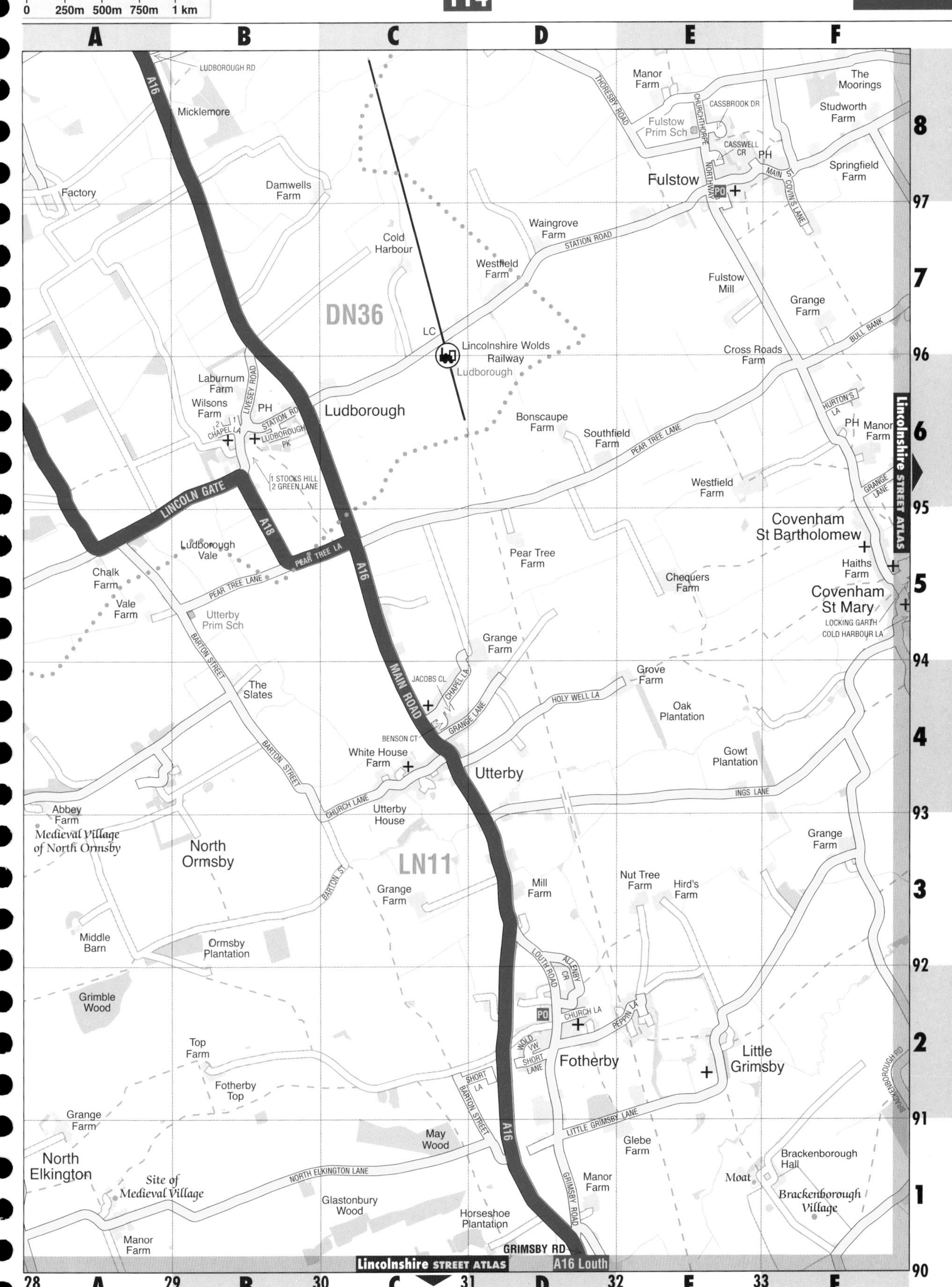

A B C D E F

8
97
7
96
6
95
5
94
4
93
3
92
2
91
1
90

LUDBOROUGH RD
Micklemore
Factory
Damwells Farm
Cold Harbour
DN36
LC
Lincolnshire Wolds Railway
Ludborough
Westfield Farm
Waingrove Farm
STATION ROAD
Manor Farm
CASSBROOK DR
Fulstow Prim Sch
CASSWELL CR
PH
Fulstow
PO
The Moorings
Studworth Farm
Springfield Farm
CHURCHTHORPE
NORTHWAY
MAIN ST
ST COVINS LANE
Fulstow Mill
Grange Farm
BULL BANK
Cross Roads Farm
HURTON'S LA
PH
Manor Farm
GRANGE LANE
Laburnum Farm
Wilsons Farm
LIVESEY ROAD
STATION RD
CHAPEL LA
PH
LUDBOROUGH PK
Ludborough
Bonscaupe Farm
Southfield Farm
PEAR TREE LANE
Westfield Farm
Covenham St Bartholomew
Haiths Farm
Covenham St Mary
LOCKING GARTH
COLD HARBOUR LA
1 STOCKS HILL
2 GREEN LANE
LINCOLN GATE
A18
A16
Ludborough Vale
PEAR TREE LA
PEAR TREE LANE
Chalk Farm
Vale Farm
Utterby Prim Sch
Pear Tree Farm
Grange Farm
Chequers Farm
Grove Farm
HOLY WELL LA
Oak Plantation
Gowt Plantation
BARTON STREET
The Slates
MAIN ROAD
JACOBS CL
CHAPEL LA
GRANGE LANE
BENSON CT
White House Farm
Utterby
INGS LANE
Grange Farm
BARTON STREET
CHURCH LANE
Utterby House
LN11
BARTON ST
Abbey Farm
Medieval Village of North Ormsby
North Ormsby
Grange Farm
Mill Farm
Nut Tree Farm
Hird's Farm
Grange Farm
Grimble Wood
Middle Barn
Ormsby Plantation
Top Farm
Fotherby Top
LOUTH ROAD
ALLENBY CR
PO
MALD VW
SHORT LANE
CHURCH LA
REPPON LA
Fotherby
Little Grimsby
BRACKENBOROUGH RD
Grange Farm
SHORT LA
BARTON STREET
A16
LITTLE GRIMSBY LANE
May Wood
Glebe Farm
Brackenborough Hall
Moat
North Elkington
Site of Medieval Village
NORTH ELKINGTON LANE
Glastonbury Wood
Horseshoe Plantation
GRIMSBY ROAD
Manor Farm
Brackenborough Village
Manor Farm
GRIMSBY RD

Lincolnshire STREET ATLAS

10

4

D6
1 TRENTHAM MEWS
2 PINFOLD WY NORTH
3 PINFOLD CT
4 PINFOLD CL
5 CHATSWORTH CL
6 SANDRINGHAM CL
7 THORESBY MEWS
8 BALMORAL CL

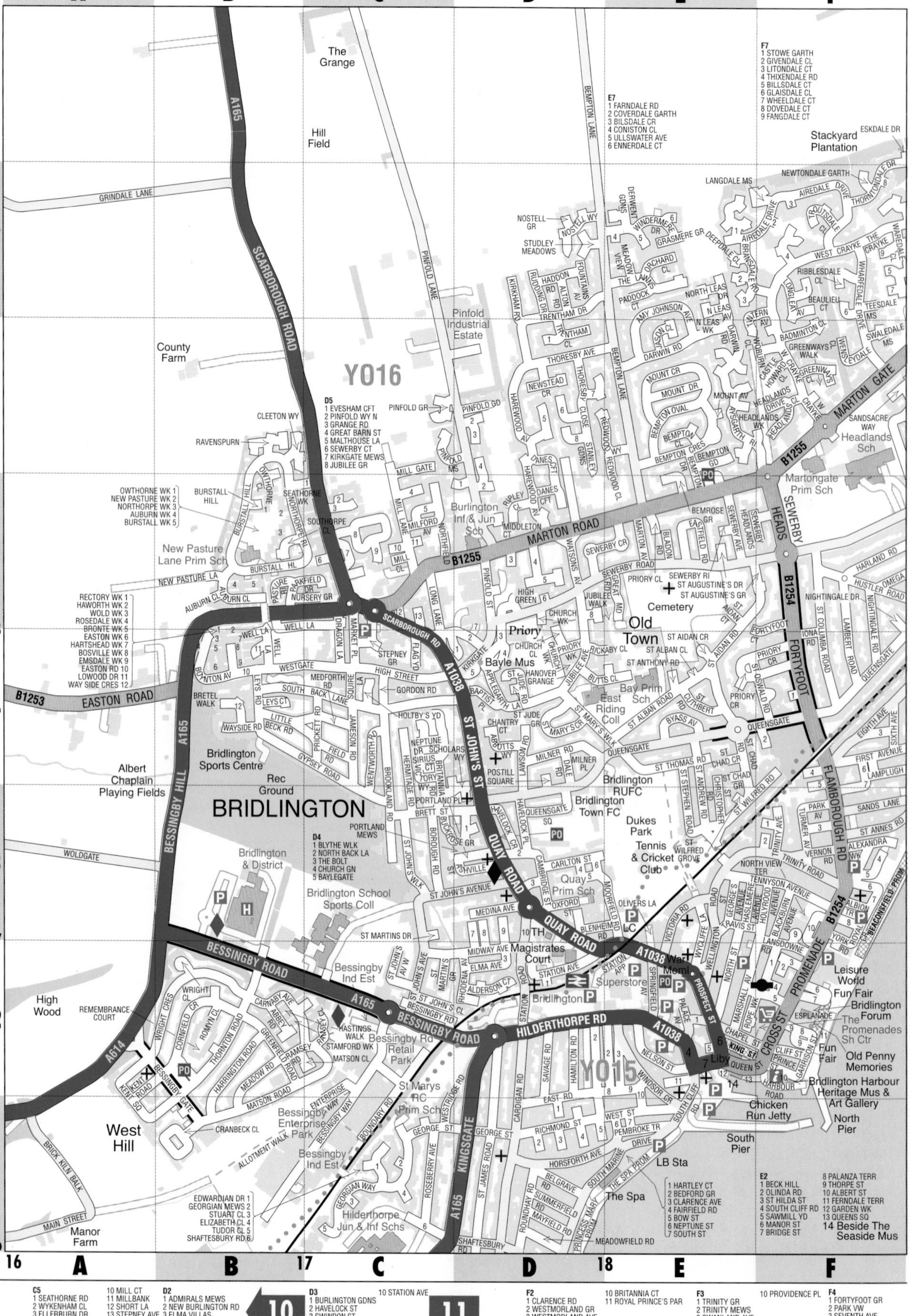

C5
1 SEATHORNE RD
2 WYKENHAM CL
3 ELLERBURN DR
4 MILLFIELD RD
5 MILFORD CRES
6 NEW PASTURE CL
7 SCARBOROUGH RD
8 SCARBOROUGH CRES
9 THE HOLLOWS
10 MILL CT
11 MILLBANK
12 SHORT LA
13 STEPNEY AVE

D2
1 ADMIRALS MEWS
2 NEW BURLINGTON RD
3 ELMA VILLAS

10

D3
1 BURLINGTON GDNS
2 HAVELOCK ST
3 SWINDON ST
4 GILBERT ST
5 THOMPSON ST
6 HILL ST
7 MELBOURNE AVE
8 WESTBOURNE AVE
9 ASHBOURNE AVE
10 STATION AVE

11

F2
1 CLARENCE RD
2 WESTMORLAND GR
3 WESTMORLAND AVE
4 PRINCESS ST
5 PRINCESS TERR
6 FORT TERR
7 REGENT TERR
8 MARLBOROUGH TERR
9 THE CRESCENT
10 BRITANNIA CT
11 ROYAL PRINCE'S PAR

F3
1 TRINITY GR
2 TRINITY MEWS
3 SWANLAND AVE
4 ALEXANDRA CT
5 ALEXANDRA DR
6 GLADSTONE TERR
7 BRIGHT CR
8 CARLISLE RD
9 LANSDOWNE CRES
10 PROVIDENCE PL

F4
1 FORTYFOOT GR
2 PARK VW
3 SEVENTH AVE
4 EDGECLIFFE VILLAS
5 CANTON VILLAS
6 LAMPLUGH SQ
7 LAMPLUGH LA

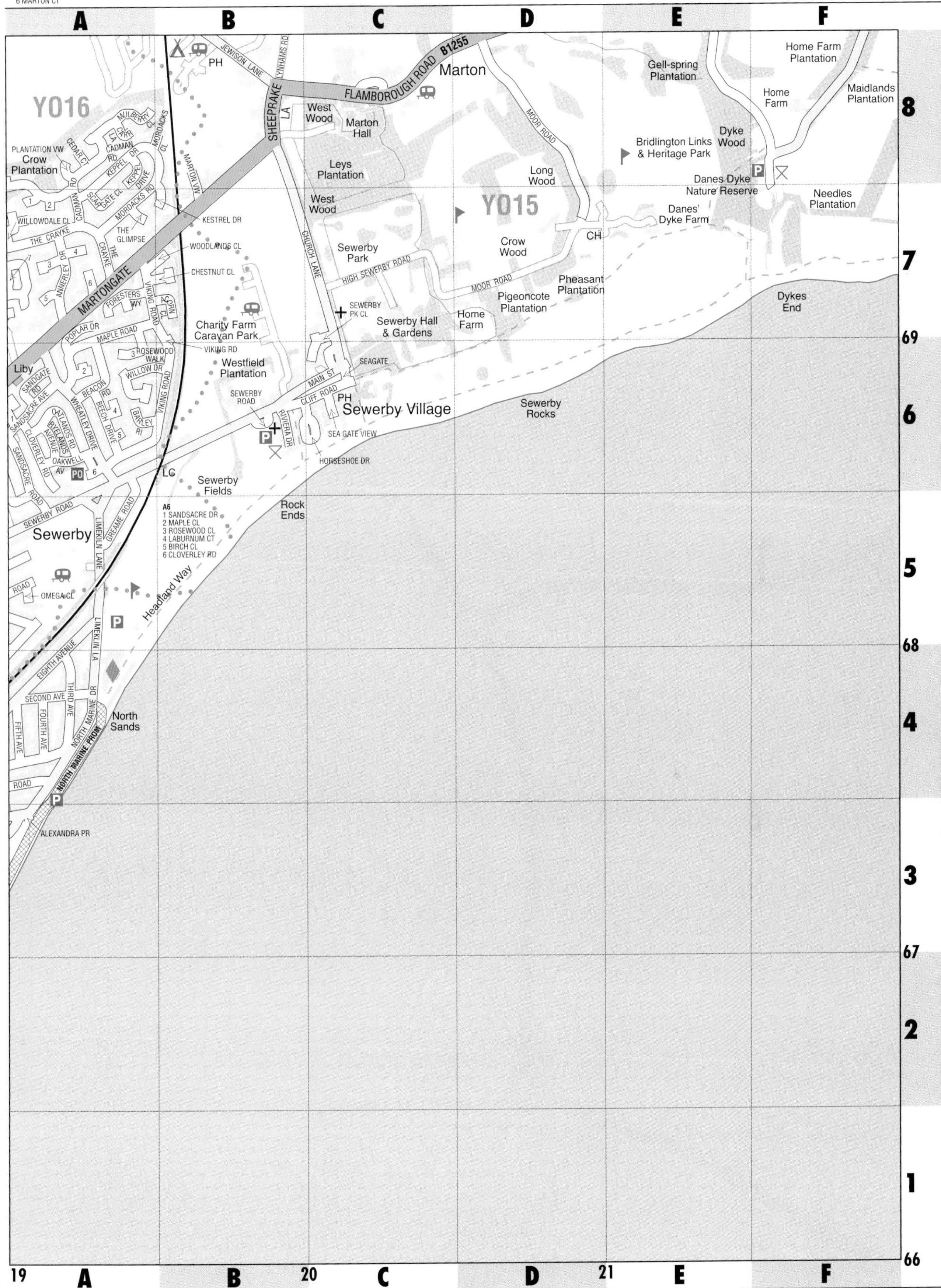

A7
1 NIDDERDALE CL   7 COTTERDALE CL
2 CALDERDALE CL
3 YORDAS CT
4 CARROWAY CL
5 LYTH CL
6 MARTON CT

YO16

Crow
Plantation

PLANTATION VW

Marton

FLAMBOROUGH ROAD   B1255

West
Wood

Marton
Hall

Leys
Plantation

Gell-spring
Plantation

Home Farm
Plantation

Home
Farm

Maidlands
Plantation

8

West
Wood

Long
Wood

YO15

Bridlington Links
& Heritage Park

Dyke
Wood

Danes Dyke

Nature Reserve

Needles
Plantation

Sewerby
Park

Crow
Wood

Danes'
Dyke Farm

CH

7

HIGH SEWERBY ROAD

MOOR ROAD

Pheasant
Plantation

Dykes
End

Charity Farm
Caravan Park

SEWERBY
PK CL

Sewerby Hall
& Gardens

Home
Farm

Pigeoncote
Plantation

69

Westfield
Plantation

SEAGATE

Sewerby
Rocks

6

SEWERBY
ROAD

PH

Sewerby Village

SEA GATE VIEW

Sewerby
Fields

HORSESHOE DR

Rock
Ends

A6
1 SANDSACRE DR
2 MAPLE CL
3 ROSEWOOD CL
4 LABURNUM CT
5 BIRCH CL
6 CLOVERLEY RD

5

Sewerby

OMEGA CL

Headland Way

68

EIGHTH AVENUE

North
Sands

4

SECOND AVE

FOURTH AVE

FIFTH AVE

ROAD

3

ALEXANDRA PR

67

2

1

66

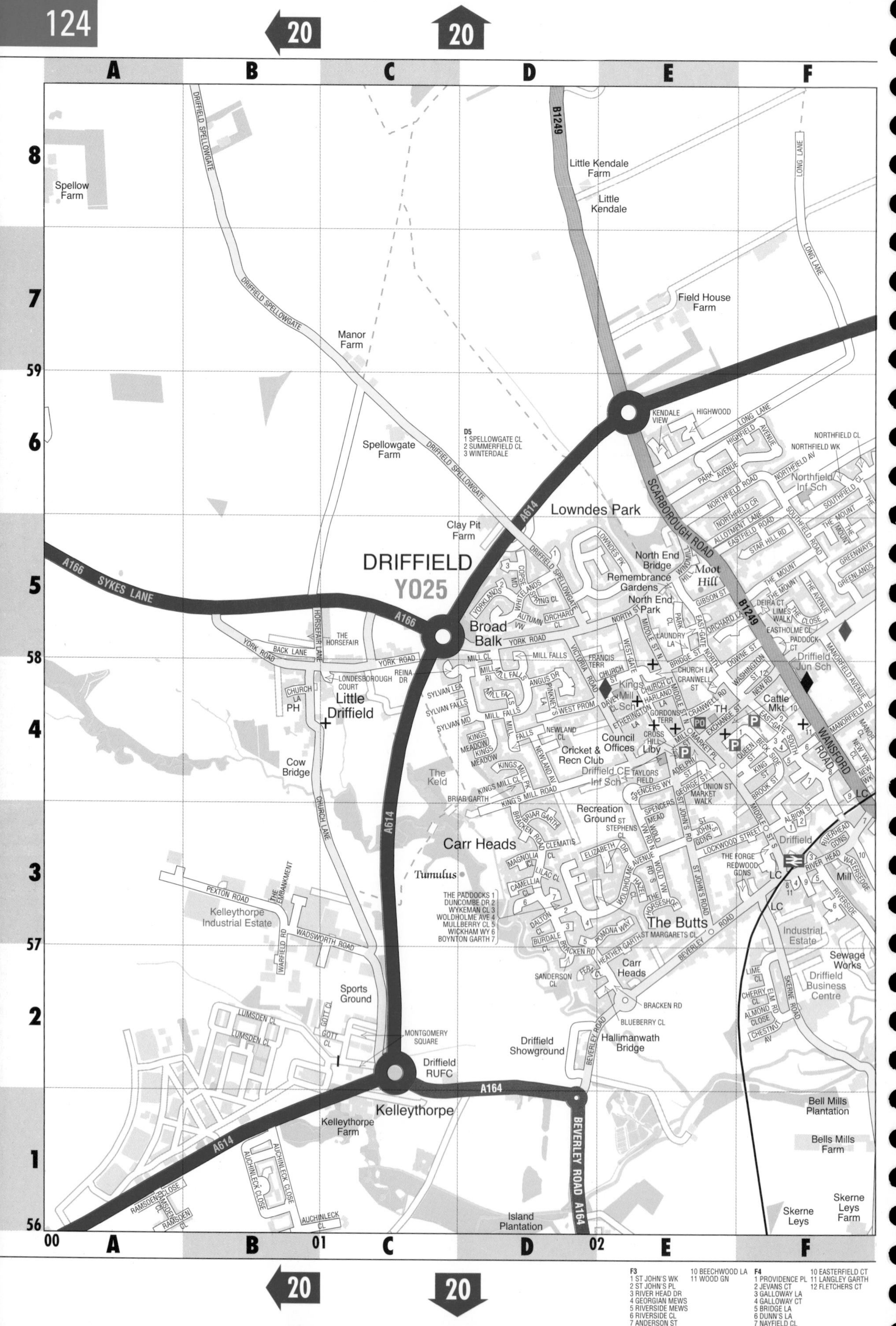

DRIFFIELD
YO25

Spellow Farm

Little Kendale Farm

Little Kendale

Field House Farm

Manor Farm

Spellowgate Farm

Clay Pit Farm

D5
1 SPELLOWGATE CL
2 SUMMERFIELD CL
3 WINTERDALE

Lowndes Park

KENDALE VIEW
HIGHWOOD

North End Bridge

Remembrance Gardens

Moot Hill

North End Park

Northfield Inf Sch

Broad Balk

Little Driffield

Driffield Jun Sch

Cattle Mkt

Cow Bridge

Council Offices

Cricket & Recn Club

Kings Mill El Sch

Driffield CE Inf Sch

The Keld

Carr Heads

Tumulus

THE PADDOCKS 1
DUNCOMBE DR 2
WYKEMAN CL 3
WOLDHOLME AVE 4
MULLBERRY CL 5
WICKHAM WY 6
BOYNTON GARTH 7

Recreation Ground

The Butts

Pexton Road

Kelleythorpe Industrial Estate

Carr Heads

Industrial Estate

Sewage Works

Driffield Business Centre

Sports Ground

Montgomery Square

Driffield RUFC

Driffield Showground

Hallimanwath Bridge

Lumsden Cl

Kelleythorpe Farm

Kelleythorpe

Bell Mills Plantation

Bells Mills Farm

Island Plantation

Skerne Leys

Skerne Leys Farm

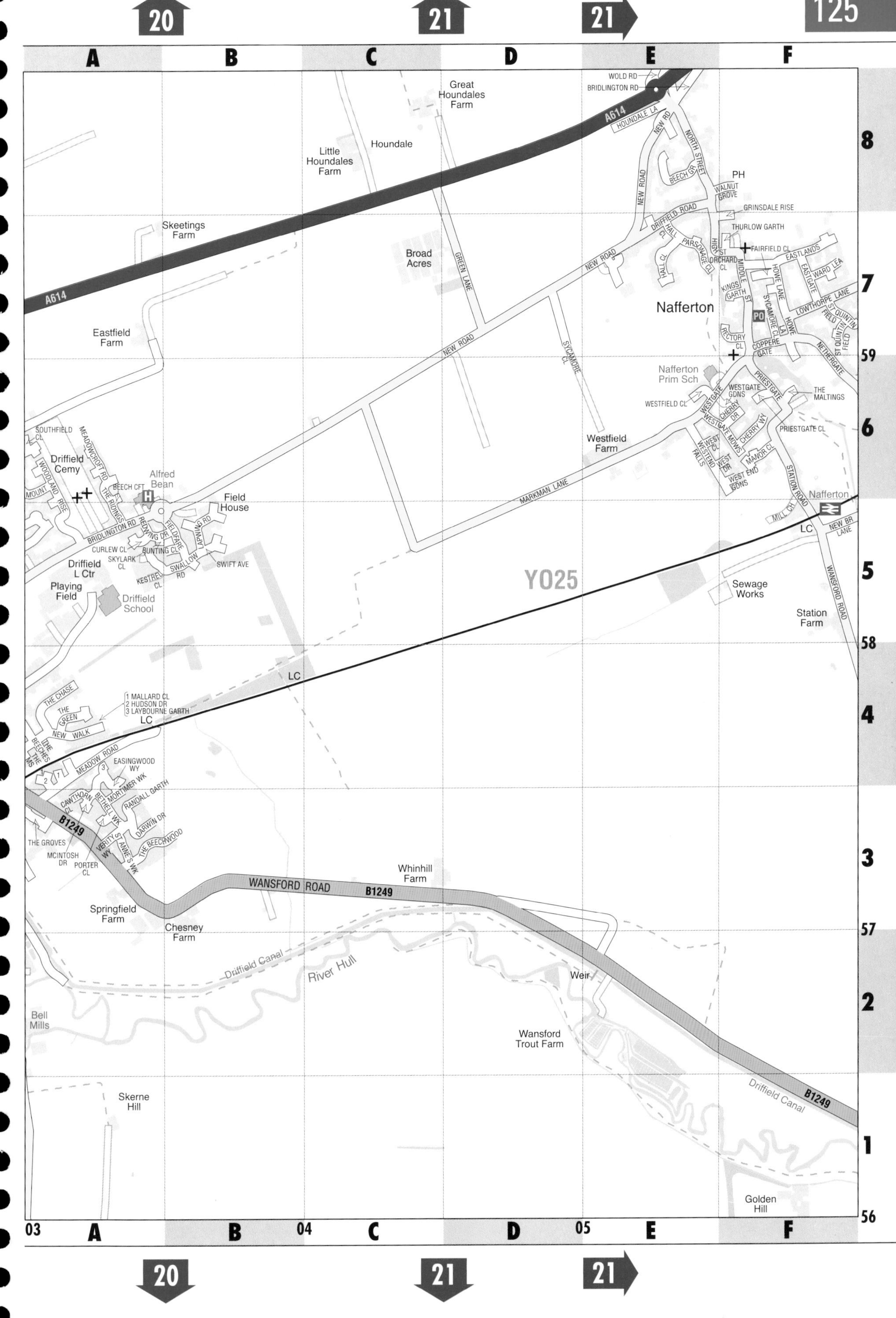
20
21
21
A
B
C
D
E
F
8
7
59
6
5
58
4
3
57
2
1
56
03
04
05
WOLD RD
BRIDLINGTON RD
Great Houndales Farm
A614
HOUNDALE LA
NEW RD
NORTH STREET
Little Houndales Farm
Houndale
BEECH GR
PH
NEW ROAD
WALNUT GROVE
GRINSDALE RISE
DRIFFIELD ROAD
THURLOW GARTH
Skeetings Farm
HALL CL
PARSONAGE CL
HIGH ST
FAIRFIELD CL
Broad Acres
GREEN LANE
NEW ROAD
ORCHARD CL
MIDDLE ST
EASTLANDS
HOWE LANE
EASTGATE
WARD LEA
KINGS GARTH
Nafferton
LOWTHORPE LANE
SYCAMORE CL
PO
ST QUINTIN FIELD
Eastfield Farm
RECTORY CL
COPPERGATE
HOWE LA
NETHERGATE
SYCAMORE CL
NEW ROAD
Nafferton Prim Sch
PRIESTGATE
WESTGATE GDNS
THE MALTINGS
WESTFIELD CL
WESTGATE
CHERRY DR
WESTGATE MEWS
CHERRY WY
PRIESTGATE CL
SOUTHFIELD CL
MEADOWCROFT RD
Westfield Farm
WEST CL
WESTEND FALLS
WEST DR
MANOR CL
WEST END GDNS
STATION ROAD
Driffield Cemy
WOODLAND RISE
Alfred Bean
BEECH CFT
MOUNT
THE RIDINGS
H
Field House
MARKMAN LANE
Nafferton
MILL CT
LAPWING RD
BRIDLINGTON RD
REDWING DR
FIELDFARE
NEW BR LANE
LC
CURLEW CL
BUNTING CL
SKYLARK CL
SWALLOW RD
SWIFT AVE
Driffield L Ctr
KESTREL CL
YO25
Playing Field
Driffield School
Sewage Works
WANSFORD ROAD
Station Farm
LC
THE CHASE
1 MALLARD CL
2 HUDSON DR
3 LAYBOURNE GARTH
THE GREEN
LC
NEW WALK
THE BEECHES
THE MS
MEADOW ROAD
EASINGWOOD WY
MORTIMER WK
CAWTHORN CL
BETHELL WK
RANDALL GARTH
DARWIN DR
B1249
THE GROVES
VERITY WY
ST ANNE'S WK
THE BEECHWOOD
MCINTOSH DR
PORTER CL
Whinhill Farm
WANSFORD ROAD
B1249
Springfield Farm
Chesney Farm
Driffield Canal
River Hull
Weir
Bell Mills
Wansford Trout Farm
Driffield Canal
B1249
Skerne Hill
Golden Hill
20
21
21

12 13

A B C D E F

8

Hall Moor

Wide Open Farm
Woodside Farm
CH

SKELTON LANE

Park Farm

YO32

Wigginton Moor

7

A19

Hurns Bridge
HURNS LA

MOOR LANE

Glebe Farm

57

Skelton Moor

Nova Scotia Plantation

6

New Farm

ST GILES ROAD
THE VILLAGE
Hall
Skelton
MOORLANDS LANE

St Catherines

Skelton Moor

MOOR LANE

Skelton Prim Sch

Skelton Plantation

CHURCH LANE
THE VILLAGE

B5
1 THE GREEN
2 THE MEADOWS
3 ORCHARD VIEW
4 THE WHEELHOUSE
5 THE DELL
6 ARTHUR PLACE

BRECKSFIELD

PH
PO

1 RATCLIFFE CT
2 GREGORY CL
3 ST CATHERINES CL

Rawcliffe Moor

5

ST GILES
THE VALE
GRANGE CL
FAIRFIELDS CL
PASTURE CL
SYCAMORE CL

STRIPE LANE

56

CH
BIRTREE AV
PARK CL

1 THE ROWMANS
2 THE BEECHES

Rawcliffe Moor Farm

Folly Bridge

Skelton Park Trading Estate

YO30

E3
1 CAITHNESS CL
2 CONWAY CL
3 HATFIELD CL
4 OSBOURNE DR
5 GREENWICH CL
6 SOMERSET CL
7 HIGHGROVE CL
8 LONGWOOD LINK
9 WINSCAR GR
10 BROADSTONE WY
11 MITCHELL WY

1 LANGSETT GR
2 RINGSTONE RD
3 BLAKELEY GR
4 ROSEBERRY GR

4

Hotel

Poplar Plantation

SHIPTON ROAD

A1237

Clifton Moor Sh Ctr

E2
1 CONINGHAM AVE
2 MANOR PK GR
3 ELMA GR
4 BARTON CL
5 RAWCLIFFE CL
6 CHESHIRE CL
7 DEANHEAD GR
8 SWINTON CL

3

Overton Ings

River Ouse

Skelton Bridge

Rawcliffe Farm

Rawcliffe Landing

BLENHEIM CT

MARLBOROUGH CL

Clifton Moor Retail Park

Rawcliffe Village
HURRICANE WAY

Rawcliffe Ind Est

STIRLING RD

Pioneer Bsns Pk

AMY JOHNSON WY

Moat
Manor Farm
CHURCH LANE
POPPLETON HALL GD

Tom Cobleighs Riverside Farm

HOLLYWOOD DR

LINDLEY WOOD
LONGWOOD RD
DEER HL GR
KINGSWOOD GR

AVIATOR CT

FOX GARTH
HILLCREST AV

A1237

A19

HAREWOOD CL 1
KENSINGTON RD 2

ST JAMES CL
ECCLES CL
MANOR LA

RAWCLIFFE CFT

MANOR PARK RD
VILLAGE STREET

BROADSTONE WY
RIBBLEHEAD

GOUTHWAITE CL

2

Nether Poppleton

NETHER WAY
TREBOR WY
NURSERY ROAD
MIDWAY AVE

MILLFIELD LANE
MILLFIELD CT

NURSERY RD

YO26

P&R
SHIPTON ROAD

FLORENCE GR
MANOR PARK RD
ST MARK'S GR
BILSDALE

STAINDALE CL
DALE DIKE GR

Rawcliffe Inf Sch

Rawcliffe
GOUTHWAITE CL

Lakeside County Prim Sch
OAKDALE
FOVELEY CL

ELDWICK CL

1

ALLERTON DRIVE
EASTHORPE DR
LANDYRIDGE
LONG RIDGE CL
LONG RIDGE LANE

ORCHARD RD

Hotel
WESTMINSTER PLACE
WHITE ROSE CL
WHITE ROSE WY
INGS LA

Poppleton Ings

Sewage Works

Rawcliffe Ings

FURNESS DR
BOWNESS DR
RUTTERMERE DR

EASTHOLME DR
WESTHOLME
KENTMERE DR
BORROWDALE

BEAVERDYKE

PO
RAWCLIFFE LA

A1237

A19

SHELLEY WY

NORTHOLME DRIVE
ALWYNE DRIVE
ALWYNE GR

CHELKER WY

54

56 A 57 B C 58 D E F

12 129

E1
1 CONISTON CL
2 WASDALE CL
3 GARBURN GR
4 SCAFELL CL
5 LOWESWATER RD
6 FYLINGDALES AVE

F1
1 EMBLETON DR
2 COLEDALE CL
3 LEIGHTON CFT
4 BARMBY CL
5 GRASMERE GR
6 BARDEN CT
7 SOUTHOLME DR
8 MILTON CARR
9 FEWSTON DR

10 REIGHTON DR
F2
1 MOREHALL CL
2 WHARNSCLIFFE DR
3 RYBURN CL

13

128

Map grid columns: A B C D E F
Map grid rows: 8 57 7 6 5 56 4 3 55 2 1 54

B1363
Plantation Farm
WIGGINTON ROAD
Villa Farm
Wigginton Lodge
Wigginton Moor
Brecks Farm
Wigginton Cottage Farm
Moor Plantation
Clifton Gate Farm
A1237
STIRLING RD
Clifton Moor Retail Park
B1363
Whitehall Grange
Clifton Moor
Clifton Moor Industrial Estate
Clifton Moor Ind Est
Kettlestring Farm
Coppins Farm
York Eco Bsns Ctr
Clifton Moor Ind Est
Sterling Park
Lysander Bsns Pk
Centurion Pk
Clifton Moor
Clifton Moor Bsns Village
Tower Ct Bsns Ctr
Bootham Stray
YO30
Green La Trad Est
DEVONSHIRE CT
WIGGINTON ROAD
B1363
LC
Burton GN
Works

Headlands Prim Sch
Haxby
YO32
Haxby Gates
Crompton Terrace
Crompton Farm
Haxby Road Farm
Mast
The Joseph Rowntree School
Hall Farm
Garth End
Manor House
Huntington Prim Sch
Greenacres
Lock House
Foss Bank Farm
Sewage Works
Ebor Way
Earswick Village
Centenary Way
A1237
River Foss
Foss Walk
Park Estate
The Avenue
York Road
Calf Close
Lady Kell

New Earswick
New Earswick Prim Sch
Sports Club
Huntington Sch
Huntington
YO31
Ebor Way
Works
Sports Ground
Playing Fields
Sports Ground
Yearsley Grove Prim Sch

130

128

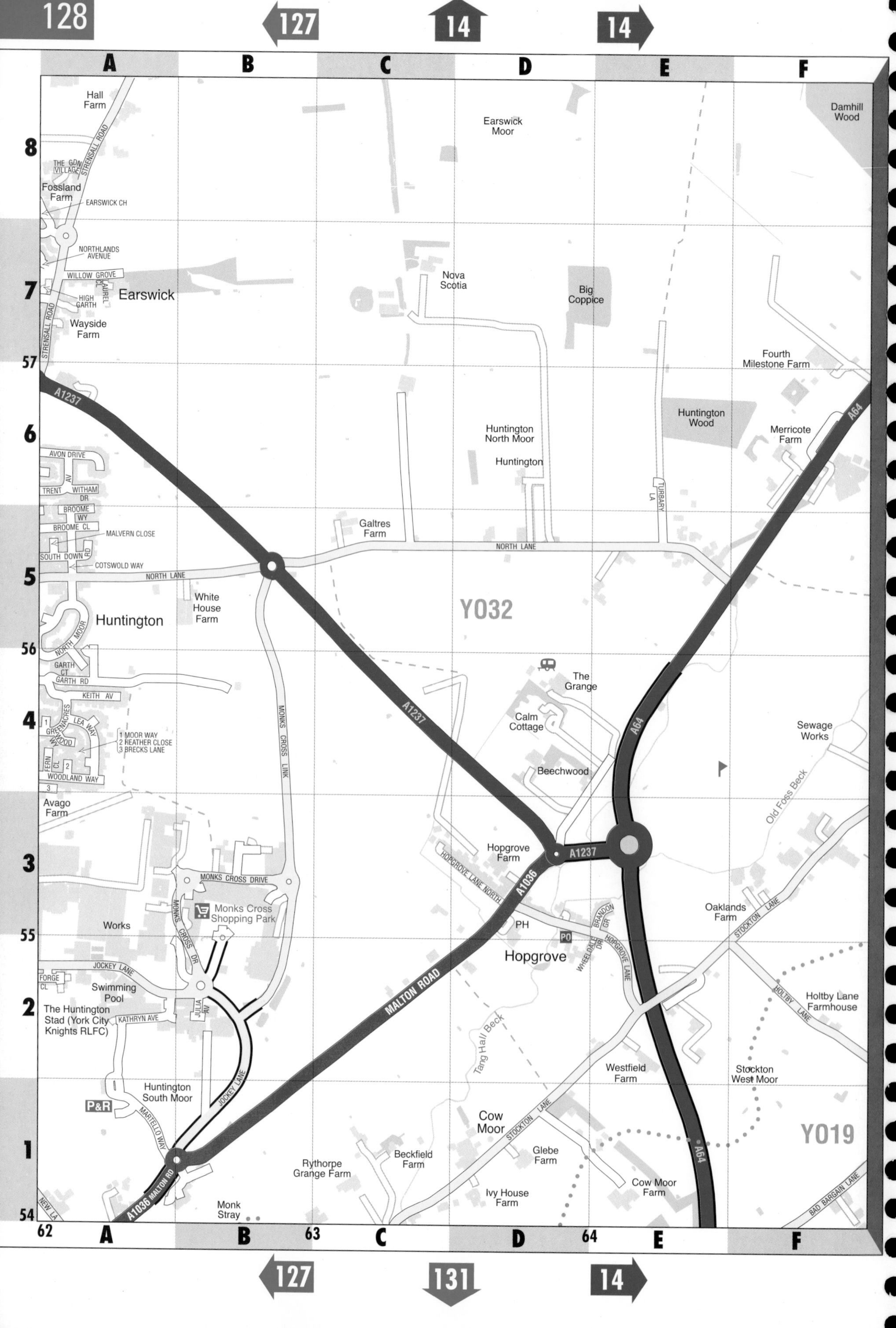
A
B
C
D
E
F
Hall Farm
Earswick Moor
Damhill Wood
8
THE GDN VILLAGE
STRENSALL ROAD
Fossland Farm
EARSWICK CH
NORTHLANDS AVENUE
WILLOW GROVE
LAUREL CL
7
HIGH GARTH
Earswick
Nova Scotia
Big Coppice
Wayside Farm
STRENSALL ROAD
57
Fourth Milestone Farm
A1237
Huntington Wood
6
Huntington North Moor
Merricote Farm
AVON DRIVE
AV
TRENT
WITHAM DR
Huntington
TURBARY LA
BROOME WY
BROOME CL
MALVERN CLOSE
Galtres Farm
NORTH LANE
SOUTH DOWN RD
COTSWOLD WAY
5
NORTH LANE
White House Farm
YO32
Huntington
NORTH MOOR
56
GARTH CT
GARTH RD
The Grange
KEITH AV
A1237
GREENACRES
LEA WAY
Calm Cottage
A64
Sewage Works
4
WOOD WY
1 MOOR WAY
2 HEATHER CLOSE
3 BRECKS LANE
MONKS CROSS LINK
FERN CL
Beechwood
WOODLAND WAY
Avago Farm
Old Foss Beck
Hopgrove Farm
3
MONKS CROSS DRIVE
A1237
HOPGROVE LANE NORTH
A1036
Monks Cross Shopping Park
MONKS CROSS DR
Oaklands Farm
STOCKTON LANE
Works
BRANDON GR
PH
55
PO
WHEELDALE DR
HOPGROVE LANE
Hopgrove
JOCKEY LANE
FORGE CL
Swimming Pool
MALTON ROAD
HOLTBY LANE
Holtby Lane Farmhouse
2
The Huntington Stad (York City Knights RLFC)
KATHRYN AVE
JULIA AV
Tang Hall Beck
Westfield Farm
Stockton West Moor
Huntington South Moor
JOCKEY LANE
P&R
MARTELLO WAY
Cow Moor
STOCKTON LANE
YO19
1
Rythorpe Grange Farm
Beckfield Farm
Glebe Farm
A64
A1036 MALTON RD
Cow Moor Farm
BAD BARGAIN LANE
NEW LA
Ivy House Farm
Monk Stray
54
62
A
B
63
C
D
64
E
F

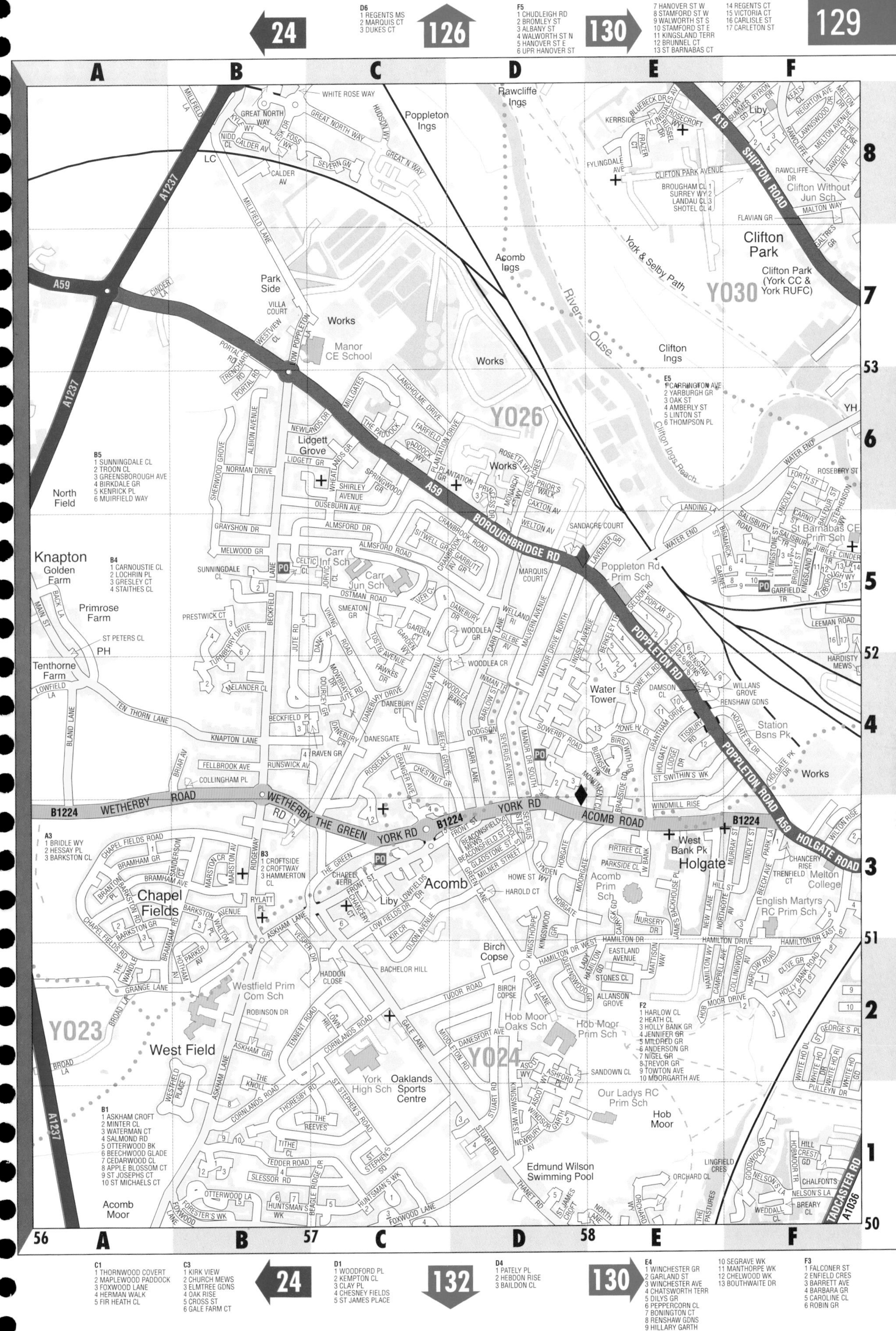

← 24
126
130

D6
1 REGENTS MS
2 MARQUIS CT
3 DUKES CT

F5
1 CHUDLEIGH RD
2 BROMLEY ST
3 ALBANY ST
4 WALWORTH ST N
5 HANOVER ST E
6 UPR HANOVER ST

7 HANOVER ST W
8 STAMFORD ST W
9 WALWORTH ST S
10 STAMFORD ST E
11 KINGSLAND TERR
12 BRUNNEL CT
13 ST BARNABAS CT

14 REGENTS CT
15 VICTORIA CT
16 CARLISLE ST
17 CARLETON ST

Map grid columns: A B C D E F
Map grid rows: 8 7 53 6 52 5 4 51 2 1 50

Rawcliffe Ings
Poppleton Ings
White Rose Way
Great North Way
Great N Way
Poppleton Ings
KERRSIDE
Clifton Without Jun Sch
BROUGHAM CL 1
SURREY WY 2
LANDAU CL 3
SHOTEL CL 4
FLAVIAN GR
Clifton Park
Clifton Park (York CC & York RUFC)
YO30
York & Selby Path
Acomb Ings
Clifton Ings
River Ouse
Clifton Ings Reach
Water End

E5
1 CARRINGTON AVE
2 YARBURGH GR
3 OAK ST
4 AMBERLY ST
5 LINTON ST
6 THOMPSON PL

YH

Manor CE School
Park Side
Villa Court
Works
Works
YO26

B5
1 SUNNINGDALE CL
2 TROON CL
3 GREENSBOROUGH AVE
4 BIRKDALE GR
5 KENRICK PL
6 MUIRFIELD WAY

North Field

B4
1 CARNOUSTIE CL
2 LOCHRIN PL
3 GRESLEY CT
4 STAITHES CL

Knapton
Golden Farm
Primrose Farm
St PETERS CL
PH
Tenthorne Farm
Ten Thorn Lane

Lidgett Grove
Carr Inf Sch
Carr Jun Sch
BOROUGHBRIDGE RD
Works
St Barnabas CE Prim Sch
ROSEBERY ST

Marquis Court
Poppleton Rd Prim Sch
POPPLETON RD
Water Tower
Station Bsns Pk
Works
HARDISTY MEWS

A3
1 BRIDLE WY
2 HESSAY PL
3 BARKSTON CL

WETHERBY ROAD
B1224
THE GREEN
YORK RD
B1224
YORK RD
ACOMB ROAD
HOLGATE ROAD
A59
POPPLETON ROAD

B3
1 CROFTSIDE
2 CROFTWAY
3 HAMMERTON

Chapel Fields
Acomb
Holgate
West Bank Pk
B1224
Chancery Rise
Trenfield Ct
Melton College
English Martyrs RC Prim Sch

YO23
West Field
Westfield Prim Com Sch
Birch Copse
Birch Copse
Hob Moor Oaks Sch
Hob Moor Prim Sch
Eastland Avenue
Allanson Grove

B1
1 ASKHAM CROFT
2 MINTER CL
3 WATERMAN CT
4 SALMOND RD
5 OTTERWOOD BK
6 BEECHWOOD GLADE
7 CEDARWOOD CL
8 APPLE BLOSSOM CT
9 ST JOSEPHS CT
10 ST MICHAELS CT

Acomb Moor
York High Sch
Oaklands Sports Centre
YO24
Edmund Wilson Swimming Pool
Our Ladys RC Prim Sch
Hob Moor
LINGFIELD CRES

F2
1 HARLOW CL
2 HEATH CL
3 HOLLY BANK GR
4 JENNIFER GR
5 MITFORD GR
6 ANDERSON GR
7 NIGEL GR
8 TREVOR GR
9 TOWTON AVE
10 MOORGARTH AVE

A1237
A1036
TADCASTER RD

← 24
132
130

C1
1 THORNWOOD COVERT
2 MAPLEWOOD PADDOCK
3 FOXWOOD LANE
4 HERMAN WALK
5 FIR HEATH CL

C3
1 KIRK VIEW
2 CHURCH MEWS
3 ELMTREE GDNS
4 OAK RISE
5 CROSS ST
6 GALE FARM CT

D1
1 WOODFORD PL
2 KEMPTON CL
3 CLAY PL
4 CHESNEY FIELDS
5 ST JAMES PLACE

D4
1 PATELY PL
2 HEBDON RISE
3 BAILDON CL

E4
1 WINCHESTER GR
2 GARLAND ST
3 WINCHESTER AVE
4 CHATSWORTH TERR
5 DILYS GR
6 PEPPERCORN CL
7 BONINGTON CT
8 RENSHAW GDNS
9 HILLARY GARTH

10 SEGRAVE WK
11 MANTHORPE WK
12 CHELWOOD WK
13 BOUTHWAITE DR

F3
1 FALCONER ST
2 ENFIELD CRES
3 BARRETT AVE
4 BARBARA GR
5 CAROLINE CL
6 ROBIN GR

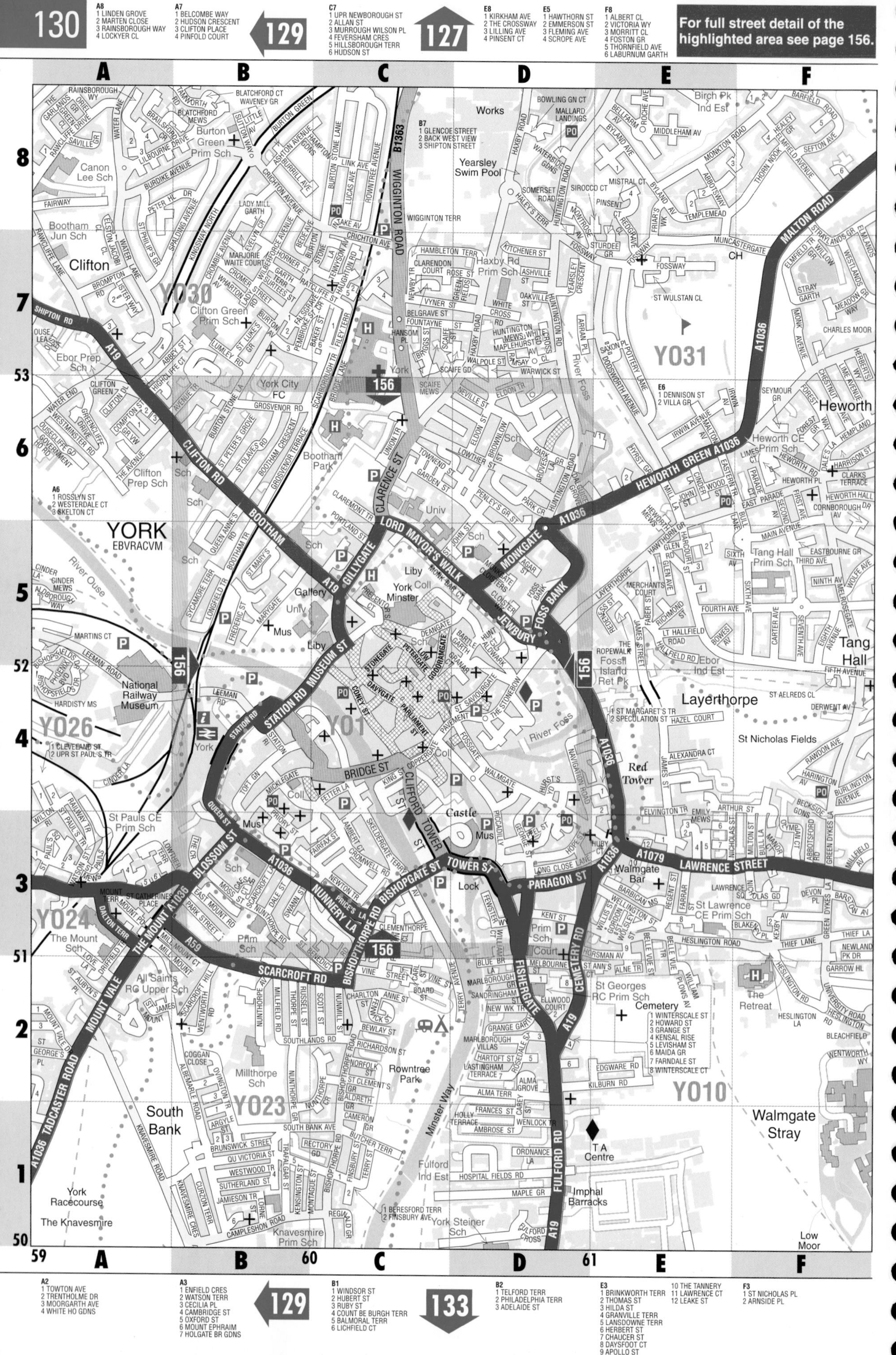

130

A8
1 LINDEN GROVE
2 MARTEN CLOSE
3 RAINSBOROUGH WAY
4 LOCKYER CL

A7
1 BELCOMBE WAY
2 HUDSON CRESCENT
3 CLIFTON PLACE
4 PINFOLD COURT

129

C7
1 UPR NEWBOROUGH ST
2 ALLAN ST
3 MURROUGH WILSON PL
4 FEVERSHAM CRES
5 HILLSBOROUGH TERR
6 HUDSON ST

127

E8
1 KIRKHAM AVE
2 THE CROSSWAY
3 LILLING AVE
4 PINSENT CT

E5
1 HAWTHORN ST
2 EMMERSON ST
3 FLEMING AVE
4 SCROPE AVE

F8
1 ALBERT CL
2 VICTORIA WY
3 MORRITT CL
4 FOSTON GR
5 THORNFIELD AVE
6 LABURNUM GARTH

For full street detail of the
highlighted area see page 156.

A2
1 TOWTON AVE
2 TRENTHOLME DR
3 MOORGARTH AVE
4 WHITE HO GDNS

A3
1 ENFIELD CRES
2 WATSON TERR
3 CECILIA PL
4 COUNT DE BURGH TERR
5 OXFORD ST
6 MOUNT EPHRAIM
7 HOLGATE BR GDNS

129

B1
1 WINDSOR ST
2 HUBERT ST
3 ADELAIDE ST

133

B2
1 TELFORD TERR
2 PHILADELPHIA TERR
3 BALMORAL TERR

E3
1 BRINKWORTH TERR
2 THOMAS ST
3 HILDA ST
4 GRANVILLE TERR
5 LANSDOWNE TERR
6 HERBERT ST
7 CHAUCER ST
8 DAYSFOOT CT
9 APOLLO ST

10 THE TANNERY
11 LAWRENCE CT
12 LEAKE ST

F3
1 ST NICHOLAS PL
2 ARNSIDE PL

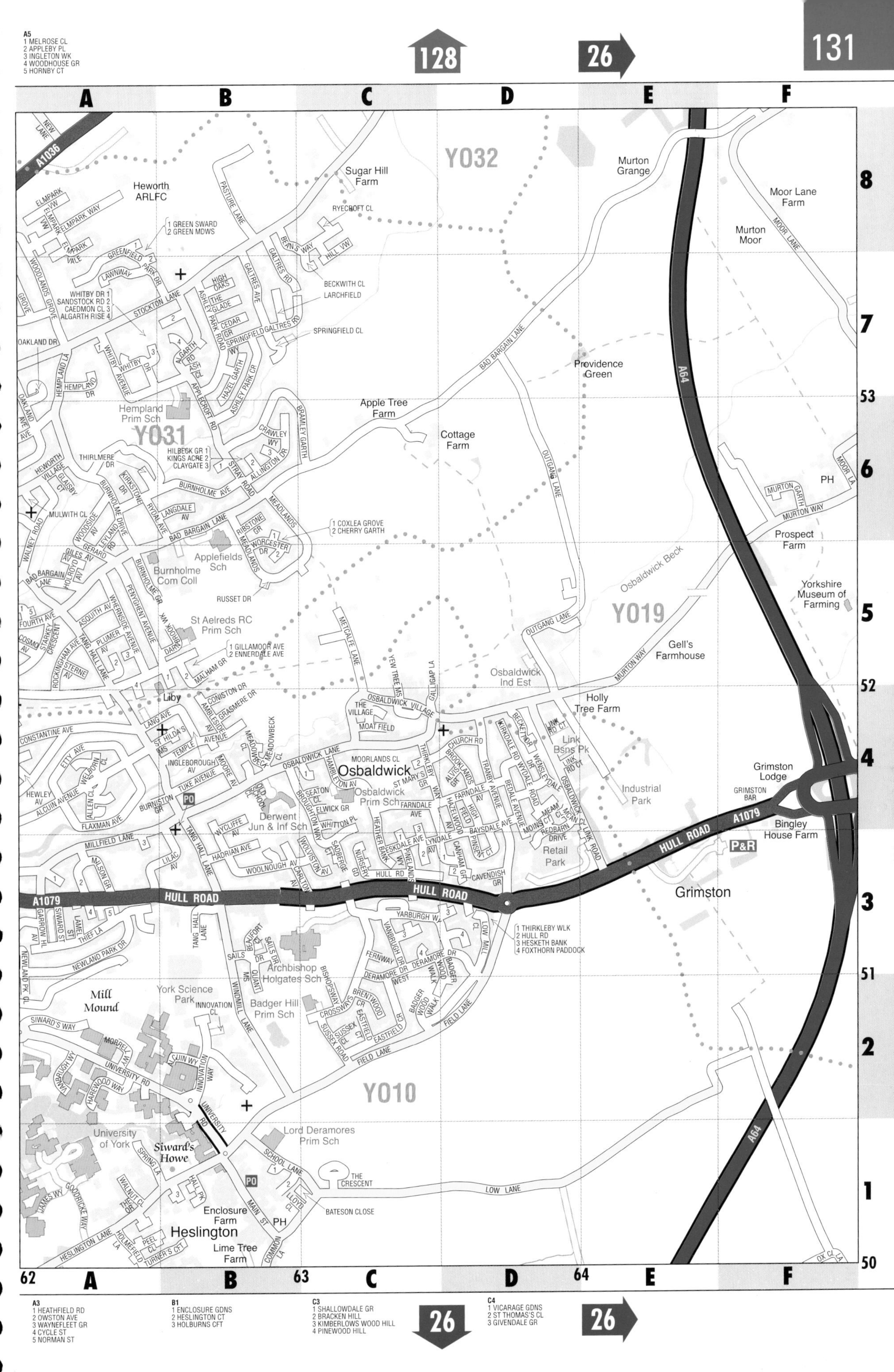
A5
1 MELROSE CL
2 APPLEBY PL
3 INGLETON WK
4 WOODHOUSE GR
5 HORNBY CT
128
26
A
B
C
D
E
F
8
7
53
6
5
52
4
3
51
2
1
50
62
63
64
A1036
NEW LANE
Heworth ARLFC
Sugar Hill Farm
YO32
Murton Grange
Moor Lane Farm
Murton Moor
MOOR LANE
PASTURE LANE
RYECROFT CL
1 GREEN SWARD
2 GREEN MDWS
ELMPARK VW
ELMPARK WAY
ELMPARK VALE
GREENFIELD PARK DR
LAWNWAY
HIGH OAKS
THE GLADE
CEDAR GR
GALTRES AVE
GALTRES RD
BEAN'S WAY
HILL VW
BECKWITH CL
LARCHFIELD
SPRINGFIELD CL
SPRINGFIELD WY
WHITBY DR 1
SANDSTOCK RD 2
CAEDMON CL 3
ALGARTH RISE 4
STOCKTON LANE
WOODLANDS GROVE
GROVE
OAKLAND DR
WHITBY AVENUE
WHITBY DR
ALGARTH RD
ASH CL
HAZEL GARTH
ASHLEY PARK CR
ASHLEY PARK ROAD
HEMPLAND LA
HEMPLAND DR
OAKLAND AVE
BAD BARGAIN LANE
Providence Green
A64
Apple Tree Farm
Cottage Farm
Hempland Prim Sch
YO31
APPLECROFT RD
CRAWLEY WY
BRAMLEY GARTH
ALLINGTON DR
STRAY RD
HILBECK GR 1
KINGS ACRE 2
CLAYGATE 3
THIRLMERE DR
HEWORTH VILLAGE
GLAISBY CT
BURNHOLME AVE
BURNHOLME DRIVE
KIRKSTONE DR
RYDAL AVE
LANGDALE AV
MEADLANDS
OUTGANG LANE
MURTON GARTH
MURTON WAY
PH
MOOR LA
MULWITH CL
WOODSIDE AV
LEYLAND RD
GERARD AV
GILES AV
HOLROYD AV
WALNEY ROAD
RIBSTONE GR
WORCESTER DR
1 COXLEA GROVE
2 CHERRY GARTH
Prospect Farm
Applefields Sch
Burnholme Com Coll
Osbaldwick Beck
Yorkshire Museum of Farming
BURNHOLME GR
PENYGHENT AVENUE
BROOK WK
RUSSET DR
YO19
FOURTH AVE
ASQUITH AV
WHERNSIDE AVENUE
St Aelreds RC Prim Sch
DARN
METCALFE LANE
OUTGANG LANE
Gell's Farmhouse
COSMO AV
STARKEY CRESCENT
ROCKINGHAM AVE
PLUMER AV
TANG HALL LANE
STERNE AV
1 GILLAMOOR AVE
2 ENNERDALE AVE
MALHAM GR
YEW TREE MS
GALLIGAP LA
MURTON WAY
Osbaldwick Ind Est
Liby
CONISTON DR
GRASMERE DR
AMBLESIDE AV
THE VILLAGE
OSBALDWICK VILLAGE
MOAT FIELD
Holly Tree Farm
CONSTANTINE AVE
LANG AVE
ST HILDA'S MS
TEMPLE AVENUE
MEADOWBECK CL
MEADOWBECK
CHURCH RD
BECKETT DR
LINK RD CT
Link Bsns Pk
ETTY AVE
WELBORN CL
INGLEBOROUGH AV
MOORE AV
OSBALDWICK LANE
MOORLANDS CL
Osbaldwick
HAMBLETON AV
ST MARY'S GR
THIRKLEBY WAY
ALVIS GR
BROOKLANDS
TRANBY AVENUE
KIRKDALE RD
WYDALE ROAD
WENSLEYDALE DR
OSBALDWICK LINK ROAD
Grimston Lodge
HEWLEY AV
ALCUIN AVENUE
ALLEN CL
TUKE AVENUE
OLD SCHOOL CL
SEATON CL
Osbaldwick Prim Sch
FARNDALE AVE
FARNDALE AV
BEDALE AVENUE
Industrial Park
GRIMSTON BAR
BURNISTON GR
PO
ELWICK GR
HAZELWOOD AV
HIGH FIELD
MEAM CL
MCAN CL
Bingley House Farm
FLAXMAN AVE
WYCLIFFE AV
Derwent Jun & Inf Sch
BROUGHTON WAY
WHITTON PL
HEATHER BANK
BAYSDALE AVE
MOINS CT
REDBARN DRIVE
A1079
HULL ROAD
MILLFIELD LANE
HADRIAN AVE
WOOLNOUGH AV
WOLVISTON AV
SADBERGE CT
NURSERY GD
ESKDALE AVE
PINELANDS WY
LYNDALE AV
CANHAM GR
PINSENT CT
Retail Park
P&R
MILSON GR
LILAC AV
CARLTON AV
HULL RD
CAVENDISH GR
Grimston
GARROW HL
SIWARD ST
LAMEL ST
THIEF LA
TANG HALL LANE
YARBURGH WY
LOW MILL CL
1 THIRKLEBY WLK
2 HULL RD
3 HESKETH BANK
4 FOXTHORN PADDOCK
NEWLAND PARK DR
NEWLAND PK CL
BEAUFORT CL
SAILS DR
SAILS
VANBRUGH DR
FERNWAY
DERAMORE DR
DERAMORE DR WEST
WOOD WALK
BADGER WOOD
Archbishop Holgates Sch
QUANT MS
BISHOPSWAY
BRENTWOOD CR
Mill Mound
York Science Park
INNOVATION CL
Badger Hill Prim Sch
WINDMILL LANE
CROSSWAYS
EASTFIELD CT
SUSSEX CL
SUSSEX ROAD
EASTFIELD CR
BADGER WOOD WALK
FIELD LANE
SIWARD'S WAY
MORRELL WY
ALCUIN WY
INNOVATION WAY
UNIVERSITY RD
VANBRUGH WY
HAREWOOD WAY
YO10
UNIVERSITY RD
University of York
Siward's Howe
SPRING LA
Lord Deramores Prim Sch
SCHOOL LANE
THE CRESCENT
LOW LANE
WALNUT CL
THE OR
HALL PK
LLOYD CL
JAMES WY
GOODRICKE WAY
Enclosure Farm
Heslington
MAIN ST
PH
BATESON CLOSE
HESLINGTON LANE
HOLMEFIELD LA
PEEL CL
TURNER'S CFT
Lime Tree Farm
COMMON LA
OX CL LA
A3
1 HEATHFIELD RD
2 OWSTON AVE
3 WAYNEFLEET GR
4 CYCLE ST
5 NORMAN ST
B1
1 ENCLOSURE GDNS
2 HESLINGTON CT
3 HOLBURNS CFT
C3
1 SHALLOWDALE GR
2 BRACKEN HILL
3 KIMBERLOWS WOOD HILL
4 PINEWOOD HILL
C4
1 VICARAGE GDNS
2 ST THOMAS'S CL
3 GIVENDALE GR
26
26

24   129

	A	B	C	D	E	F

Great Knoll

B8
1 REDCOAT WY
2 KITEMERE PL
3 HAWKSHEAD CL
4 OSPREY CL
5 PHEASANT DR
6 HOUNDSWAY
7 EATON CT
8 HATFIELD WLK

Acomb Moor

High Moor Close

B7
1 HALLADALE CL
2 TARBERT CRES
3 WANSBECK
4 CAIRNBORROW

Woodthorpe Prim Sch

Woodthorpe

1 CHALONER'S CR
2 WAIN'S GR
3 SILVERDALE CT

YO24

Hogg's Pond

Dringhouses

Sports & Social Club

Mast

Eastfield Farm

C7
1 QUAKER GN
2 LINDALE
3 CRUMMOCK
4 MITERDALE
5 STONETHWAITE
6 BANNISDALE
7 TROUTBECK

Marsh Farm

P&R

Superstore

The Grove

York Coll

Whin Garth

Sim Hills

Askham Bogs

Askham Bog Nature Reserve

Bond Hill Ash Farm

A64

Middlethorpe Grange Farm

Tadcaster Road

CH

Cotton End

Copmanthorpe Prim Sch

Copmanthorpe

YO23

Glebe Farm

Ploughman's Cl
Whistler Cl
Herdsman Dr
Thatchers Cft
Fletcher's Cft
Ostler's Cl
Sawyer's Cr
Wheel Wright Cl
Town Ings Drain

Liby

Copmanthorpe & District Recn Ctr
Sewage

1 BEADLE GARTH
2 BELLMANS CFT
3 VAVASOUR CT

Temple Hill Farm

HOMEFIELD CL 1
PADDOCK CL 2
BARNFIELD WY 3

Cemy

North Moor

LEADLEY CFT 1
MOORLAND GDNS 2

56	A	57	B	C	58	D	E	F

24   36

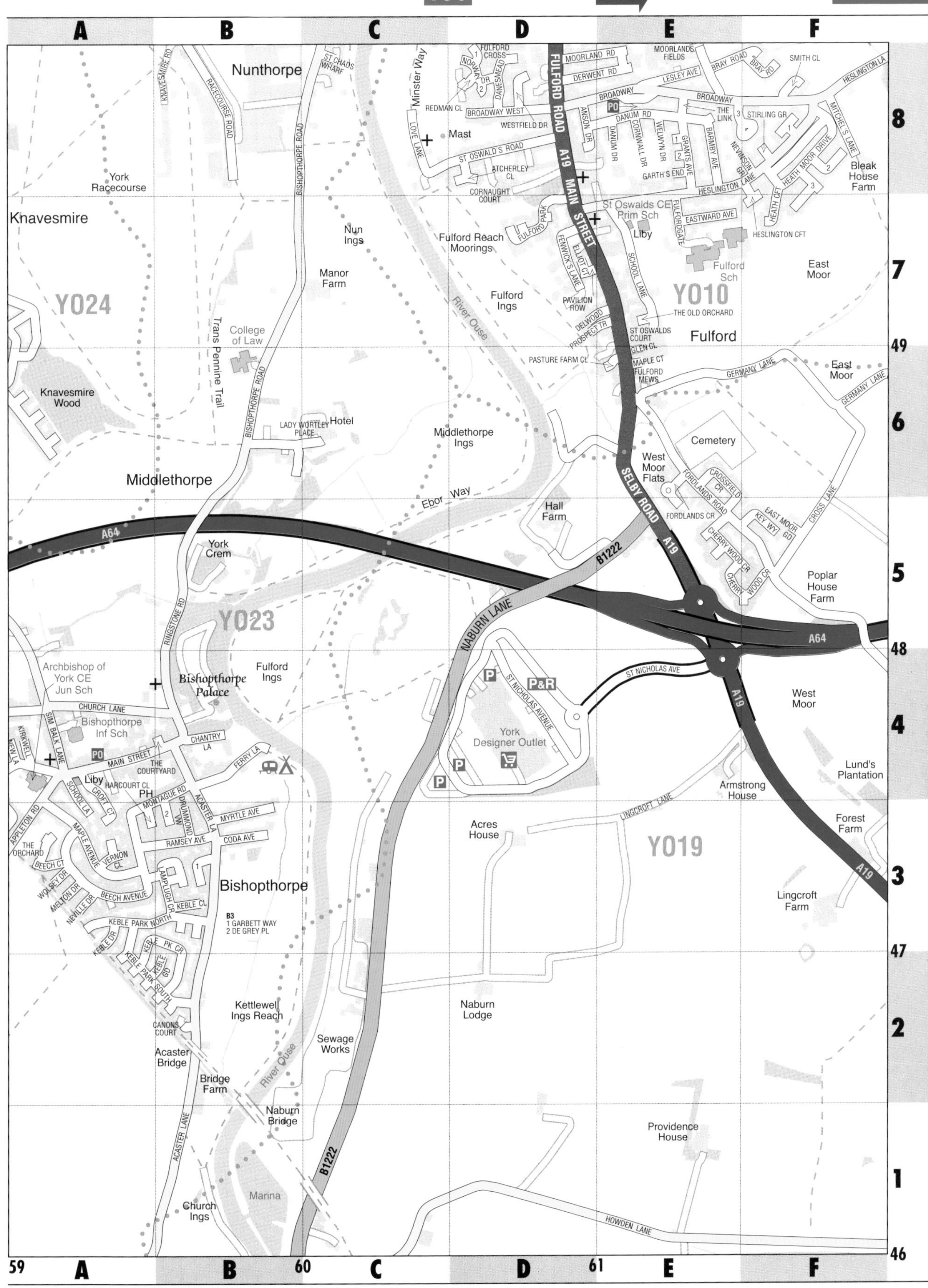

130

D8
1 STOCKHOLM CL
2 DANES CFT

26

E8
1 ENDFIELDS RD
2 CROSSLANDS RD
3 BROADWAY GR

F8
1 WILSTHORPE GR
2 TILMIRE CL
3 LOW MOOR AVE

133

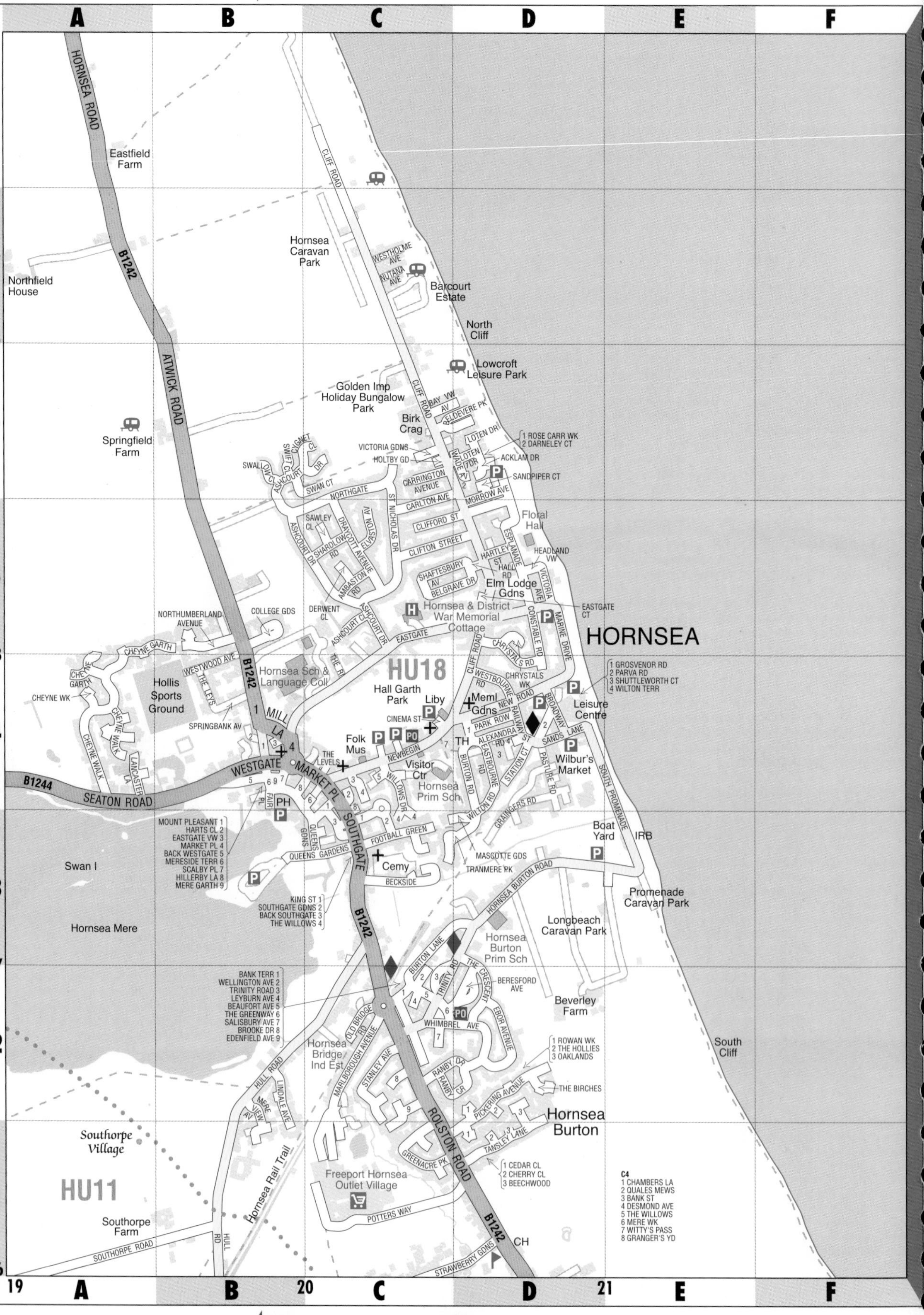

A B C D E F

8

7

49

6

5

48

4

3

47

2

1

46

HORNSEA

HU18

HU11

Hornsea Road

Eastfield Farm

Northfield House

B1242

Atwick Road

Springfield Farm

Hornsea Caravan Park

Cliff Road

Westholme Ave

Nutana Ave

Barcourt Estate

North Cliff

Lowcroft Leisure Park

Golden Imp Holiday Bungalow Park

Birk Crag

Bay Vw Av

Seldevere Pk

Loten Dr

1 Rose Carr Wk
2 Darneley Ct

Victoria Gdns

Holtby Gd

Acklam Dr

Sandpiper Ct

Swallow Cl

Swift Cl

Comet Cl

Ashcourt Dr

Swan Ct

Northgate

St Nicholas Dr

Dragocet Avenue

Carlton Ave

Carrington Avenue

Morrow Ave

Sawley Cl

Shardlow Rd

Clifford St

Clifton Street

Floral Hall

Headland Vw

Shaftesbury Av

Belgrave Dr

Hartley Hall Rd

Victoria Ave

Elm Lodge Gdns

Eastgate Ct

Northumberland Avenue

College Gds

Derwent Cl

Ashcourt Cl

Eastgate

Hornsea & District War Memorial Cottage

Chrystals Rd

Westborough

New Road

Marine Drive

Constable Rd

1 Grosvenor Rd
2 Parva Rd
3 Shuttleworth Ct
4 Wilton Terr

Cheyne Garth

Cheyne Wk

Cheyne Walk

Hollis Sports Ground

Westwood Ave

The Leys

B1242

Hornsea Sch & Language Coll

Hall Garth Park

Mill La

Springbank Av

Folk Mus

Cinema St

Meml Gdns

Park Row

TH

Alexandra Rd

Eastbourne Rd

Broadway

Sands Lane

Leisure Centre

Wilbur's Market

Westgate

Market Pl

The Levels

Newbegin

Burton Rd

Wilton Rd

Station Ct

Past The Rd

South Promenade

Visitor Ctr

Hornsea Prim Sch

B1244

Seaton Road

Mount Pleasant 1
Harts Cl 2
Eastgate Vw 3
Market Pl 4
Back Westgate 5
Mereside Terr 6
Scalby Pl 7
Hillerby La 8
Mere Garth 9

PH

Fair Pl

Queens Gardens

Southgate

Football Green

Cemy

Beckside

Graingers Rd

Masgotte Gds

Tranmere Pk

Boat Yard

IRB

Swan I

Hornsea Mere

King St 1
Southgate Gdns 2
Back Southgate 3
The Willows 4

Burton Lane

Hornsea Burton Road

Hornsea Burton Prim Sch

Beresford Ave

Longbeach Caravan Park

Promenade Caravan Park

Bank Terr 1
Wellington Ave 2
Trinity Road 3
Leyburn Ave 4
Beaufort Ave 5
The Greenway 6
Salisbury Ave 7
Brooke Dr 8
Edenfield Ave 9

Hornsea Bridge Ind Est

Old Bridge Road

Marlborough Avenue

Stanley Ave

Trinity Rd

The Crescent

Whimbrel Ave

Ranby Dr

Fibor Avenue

1 Rowan Wk
2 The Hollies
3 Oaklands

The Birches

Pickering Avenue

Tansley Lane

Hornsea Burton

Beverley Farm

South Cliff

Southorpe Village

Hull Road

Mere View Av

Lindale Ave

Hornsea Rail Trail

Greenacre Pk

1 Cedar Cl
2 Cherry Cl
3 Beechwood

Southorpe Farm

Southorpe Road

Hull Rd

Freeport Hornsea Outlet Village

Potters Way

Rolston Road

B1242

Strawberry Gdns

CH

C4
1 Chambers La
2 Quales Mews
3 Bank St
4 Desmond Ave
5 The Willows
6 Mere Wk
7 Witty's Pass
8 Granger's Yd

19 A B 20 C D 21 E F

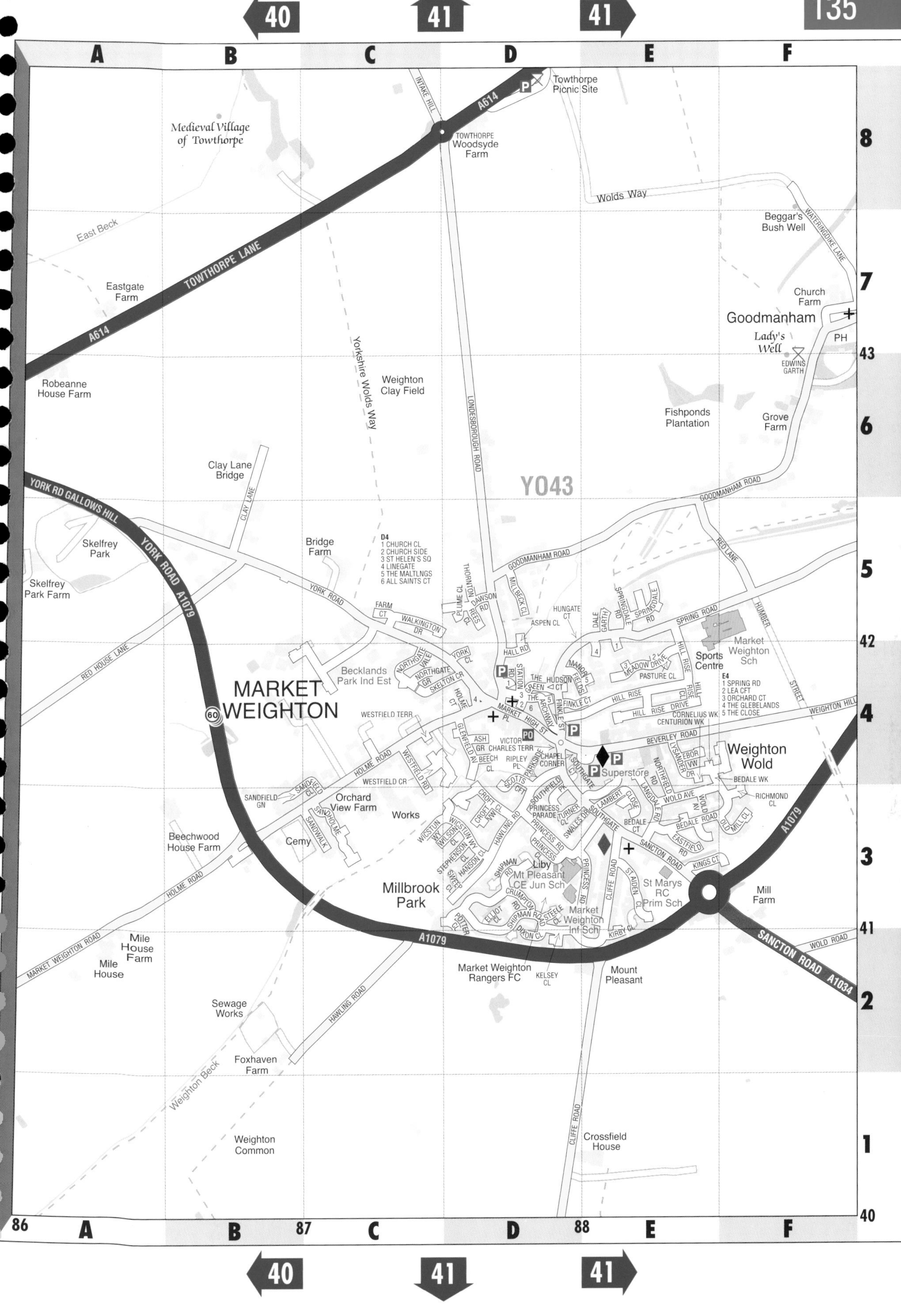
40
41
41
A
B
C
D
E
F
Towthorpe Picnic Site
Medieval Village of Towthorpe
INTAKE HILL
A614
TOWTHORPE Woodsyde Farm
Wolds Way
East Beck
TOWTHORPE LANE
Eastgate Farm
Beggar's Bush Well
WATERINGDIKE LANE
Church Farm
Goodmanham
Lady's Well
PH
EDWINS GARTH
Robeanne House Farm
Yorkshire Wolds Way
Weighton Clay Field
LONDESBOROUGH ROAD
Fishponds Plantation
Grove Farm
Clay Lane Bridge
CLAY LANE
YO43
GOODMANHAM ROAD
YORK RD GALLOWS HILL
Skelfrey Park
Skelfrey Park Farm
YORK ROAD
A1079
Bridge Farm
D4
1 CHURCH CL
2 CHURCH SIDE
3 ST HELEN'S SQ
4 LINEGATE
5 THE MALTLNGS
6 ALL SAINTS CT
RED LANE
HUMBER STREET
SPRING ROAD
Market Weighton Sch
Sports Centre
E4
1 SPRING RD
2 LEA CFT
3 ORCHARD CT
4 THE GLEBELANDS
5 THE CLOSE
RED HOUSE LANE
MARKET WEIGHTON
Becklands Park Ind Est
WESTFIELD TERR
MARKET PL
HIGH ST
BEVERLEY ROAD
WEIGHTON HILL
Weighton Wold
Superstore
HOLME ROAD
WESTFIELD CR
SANDFIELD GN
Orchard View Farm
Works
BEDALE WK
RICHMOND CL
Beechwood House Farm
Cemy
Millbrook Park
Liby
Mt Pleasant CE Jun Sch
St Marys RC Prim Sch
Market Weighton Inf Sch
SANCTON ROAD
Mill Farm
HOLME ROAD
MARKET WEIGHTON ROAD
Mile House Farm
Mile House
Market Weighton Rangers FC
KELSEY CL
Mount Pleasant
WOLD ROAD
A1034
Sewage Works
HAWLING ROAD
Foxhaven Farm
Weighton Beck
Weighton Common
CLIFFE ROAD
Crossfield House
8
7
43
6
5
42
4
3
41
2
1
40
86
87
88

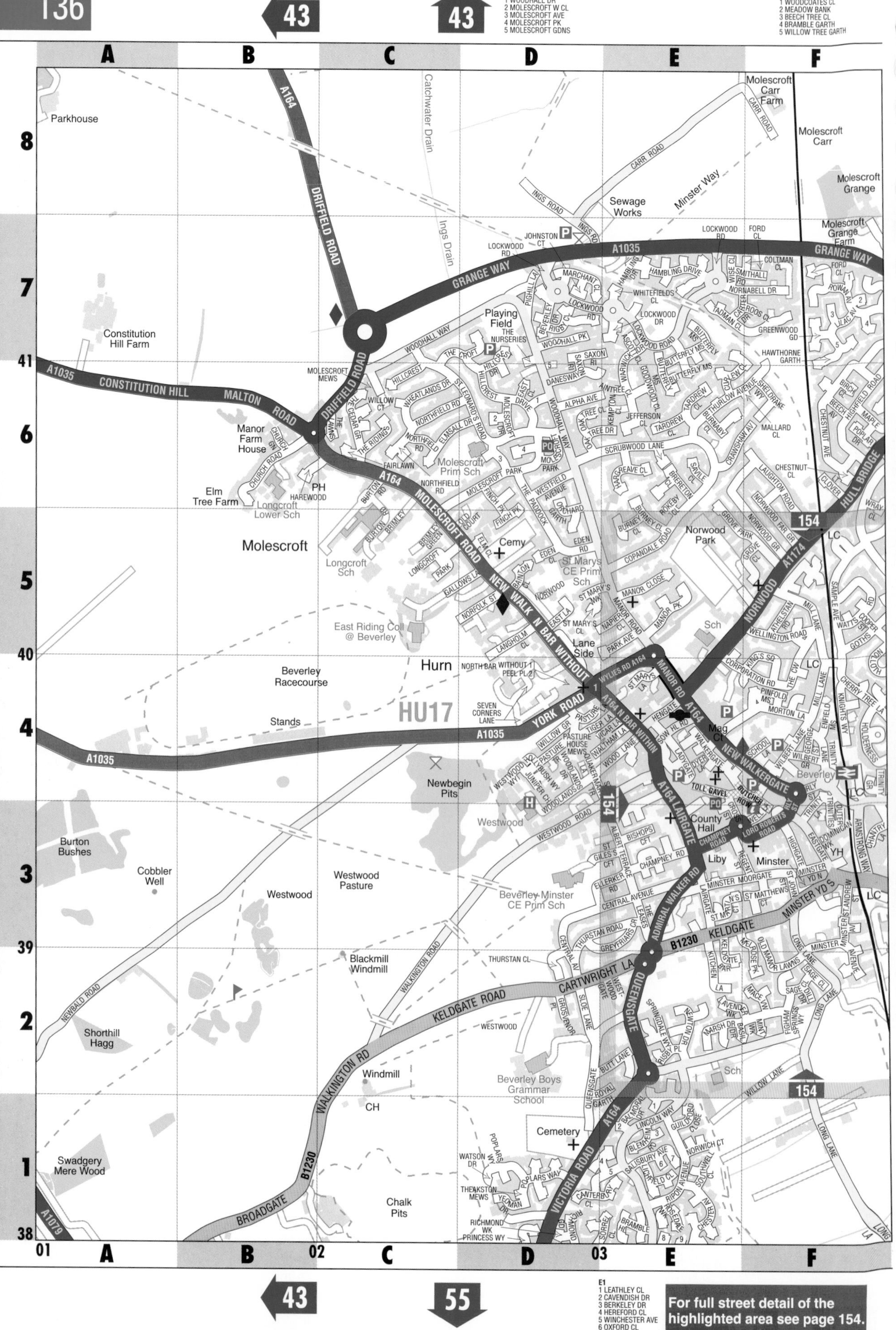

43
43

D6
1 WOODHALL DR
2 MOLESCROFT W CL
3 MOLESCROFT AVE
4 MOLESCROFT PK
5 MOLESCROFT GDNS

F7
1 WOODCOATES CL
2 MEADOW BANK
3 BEECH TREE CL
4 BRAMBLE GARTH
5 WILLOW TREE GARTH

Molescroft Carr Farm
Molescroft Carr
Molescroft Grange
Molescroft Grange Farm

Parkhouse

Constitution Hill Farm

Sewage Works

Minster Way
GRANGE WAY
A1035

Playing Field
THE NURSERIES

A1035 CONSTITUTION HILL
MALTON ROAD
DRIFFIELD ROAD

Manor Farm House

Elm Tree Farm
PH HAREWOOD
Longcroft Lower Sch

Molescroft Prim Sch
Molescroft Park

Molescroft
Longcroft Sch

Norwood Park

Cemy

East Riding Coll @ Beverley

Hurn

HU17

Beverley Racecourse

Stands

North Bar Without (PEEL PL 2)

SEVEN CORNERS LANE

York Road
A1035

Burton Bushes

Cobbler Well

Westwood Pasture

Westwood

Newbegin Pits

Westwood

Beverley Minster CE Prim Sch

County Hall
Liby
Minster

KELDGATE
B1230
CARTWRIGHT LA
QUEENSGATE

Blackmill Windmill

KELDGATE ROAD
WESTWOOD

WALKINGTON RD

Shorthill Hagg

Windmill
CH

Beverley Boys Grammar School

Cemetery

Swadgery Mere Wood

BROADGATE
B1230
A1079

Chalk Pits

43
55

E1
1 LEATHLEY CL
2 CAVENDISH DR
3 BERKELEY DR
4 HEREFORD CL
5 WINCHESTER AVE
6 OXFORD CL
7 ST ALBANS CL
8 CATHEDRAL CL
9 WELTON CL

For full street detail of the highlighted area see page 154.

A6
1 SOUTHFIELD DR
2 SIGSTON RD
3 EASTFIELD CL
4 SYMMONS CL

44
44

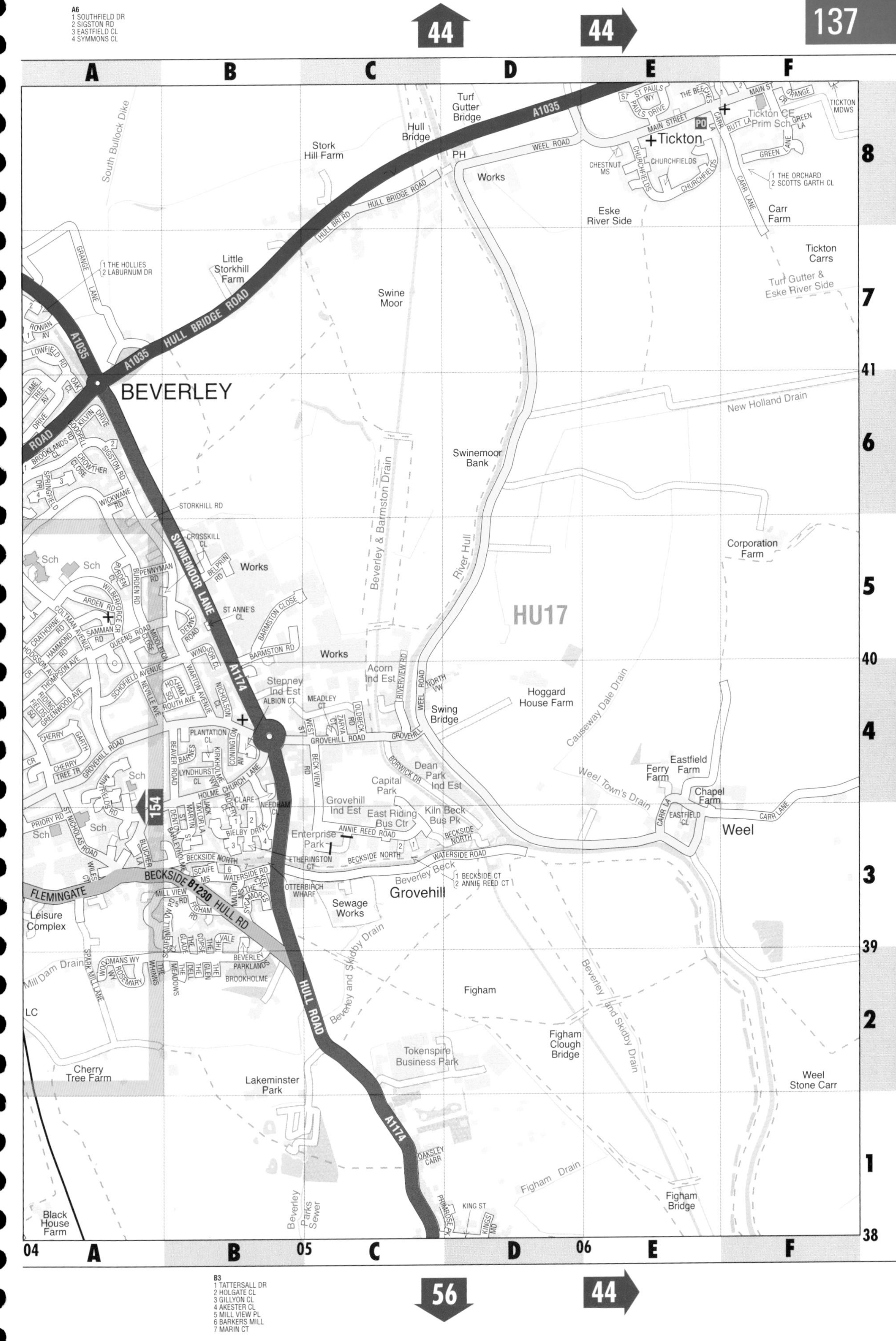

B3
1 TATTERSALL DR
2 HOLGATE CL
3 GILLYON CL
4 AKESTER CL
5 MILL VIEW PL
6 BARKERS MILL
7 MARIN CT

56
44

A   B   C   D   E   F

8

Pit (dis)
Sewage Works
CH
Field House Farm
Rogers Wood
PARK LANE
Church Hill
Skidby
Carolines Pl
Eastfield PH Farm
Skidby Hill Farm
Main Street
Townend Farm
David's Cl
Apple Cft
B1233
Cottingham High Sch
HARLAND WAY
FERENS GD
The Lawns
Little Weighton Rd
Orchard Rd
St Michael's
Skidby CE Prim Sch
South Rd
Forge Pl
Mill
Beverley Road
Mill Road
Keldgate Road
Mill Road
THE WOODLANDS
MILL LANE
WEST END RD

7

Cemy
Gallows Hill
Skidby Windmill & Museum of East Riding Rural Life
Keldgate Reservoirs
HU16
Keldgate
Keldgate Springs
Cemetery

E6
1 NEWBALD WY
2 WELTON AVE
3 SWANLAND WY
4 ELLOUGHTON GR
5 BRANTINGHAM CL
6 GOODMANHAM WY

33

Eppleworth Road
STEWART GARTH
RYDAL GR
PARKSIDE
DENE ROAD
WESTFIELD RD

6

Eppleworth Head
THE DALES
SANCTON CL
THE WOLDS
ST MARGARETS CL
LUND AV
HOLME CR
MAYLAND DR
BONDYKE CL
ST MARGARETS AVE
SPENCER
CHURCHILL AV
THE RINGS
WINSTON RD
WOODSTOCK
Westfield Prim Sch
WESTFIELD RD
SOUTHWOOD AVE

Near Stions Farm
Far Stions Farm
Westfield Rd
Castle Hill
BECK RD
CASTLE GN
ARRAS DR
DRIFFIELD CL
CAVE CR
SOUTHWOOD ROAD

5

Grange Farm
East Cottage Farm
Quarry (dis)
A164
P
H
P
GREENDALE CT
HOLLY DR
BIRDSALL CL
ETTON CL
Tower
P
Castle Road
CANADA DRIVE
OTTERBECK DR
ST LAWRENCE
BURTON RD
MURRAY CT
SOUTHWOOD CL
THE CLOSE

White House Farm
Westfield Road
CANADA DRIVE
MEADOW WY
TRAVIS RD

32

Hindhouse Farm
Eppleworth
Willerby Hill Farm
AWMAND GREEN
Plattwood Farm
BELTHAM GN

Stackyard Farm
GREEN LA
F5
1 TOWNSHEND DR
2 INVEREWE WY
3 CHELSEA CT
4 MONTREAL CRES
5 SOUTH FIELD CT
6 OTTAWA CL
7 WOLFE CL
8 MONTCALM WK
9 MAPLELEAF CT
10 MONKTON CL
11 RAMSDEN PL

4

Green Lane Farm
Willerby Hl Bsns Pk
Haltenprice Crem
Low Farm

3

Chalk Pit (dis)
Landfill
Haggs Lane
Haggs Farm
Haggs House Farm
HAGGS LA

Hotel
Main Street

31

Mast
ALBION LANE
Hotel
White House Cl
OAK HL
HU10
ABBEY LANE

2

Church End Farm
PH
Church Farm
Rawdales Farm
B1232
GRANGE PARK LANE
YORK WAY
VIKING
Main Street
VICTORIA AV
GREAT GUTTER LA
BEECHFIELD
THE REDWOODS
DERRYMORE RD
EDEN RISE
ELLERKER RISE
FISHER CL
Bellfield Farm
Abbey Grove
WELL LANE
BELLFIELD DR
SHGATE RD
GLOUCESTER RD
SOUTHGATE
THE HOLMES
WHEATCROFT AVE
SWADDALE AV
BRIMINGTON RD
BESSACARR AV

A164
Great Gutter Lane West
Beverley Road
ST STEPHEN'S CL
DR
Factory
Hotel
Liby
John Gray Ct
Wolfreton Lower Sch
Carr Lane Inf Sch
NORTHSTEAD CL
Carr Lane Prim Sch
LADYSMITH RD
REGENT CL
THE PARKWAY
THE CLOSE

1

Willerby Bottom
ASHWORTH DR
Parson Pit
WILLINGHAM WY
GARTH
ANNANDALE CL
LAXTON
CHILTON
GLENFIELD DR
GLENDALE CL
FAIRFIELD AVE
APPLETREE MS
OAKLANDS DR
TUDOR CT
KINGSLEY DR
PO
CARR LANE
THE OCTAGON
ASH GROVE
WILLOW CT
LILAC AV
LIME AVENUE
BIRCH DR
OVERTON CL
WOLFRETON LANE
CHURCHILLS

30

RIPLINGHAM ROAD
THE GLEN
Willerby
KINGSTON RD
B1232 RD
FERNDALE AV
HAWTHORNE AVENUE

01   A   B   02   C   D   03   E   F

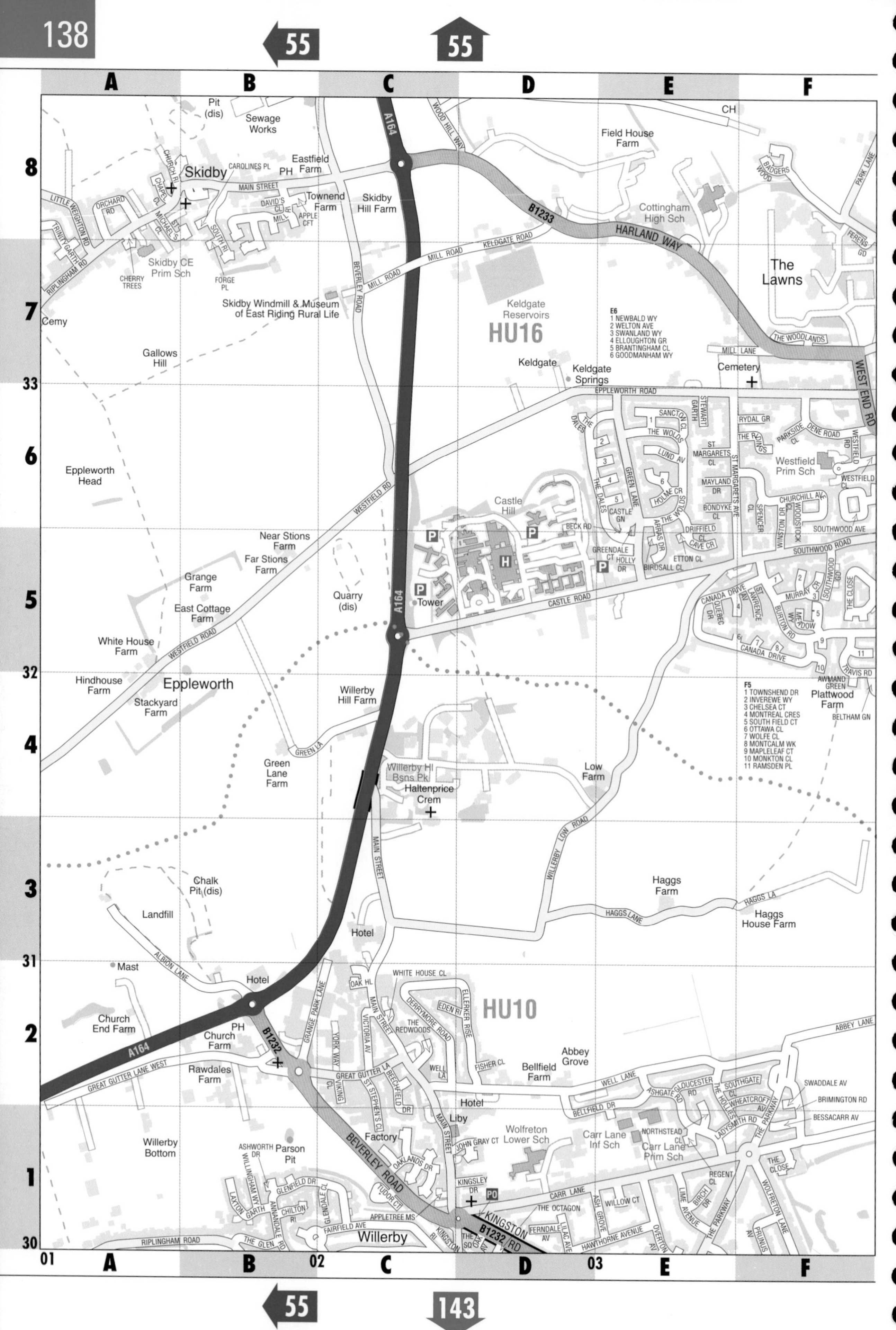

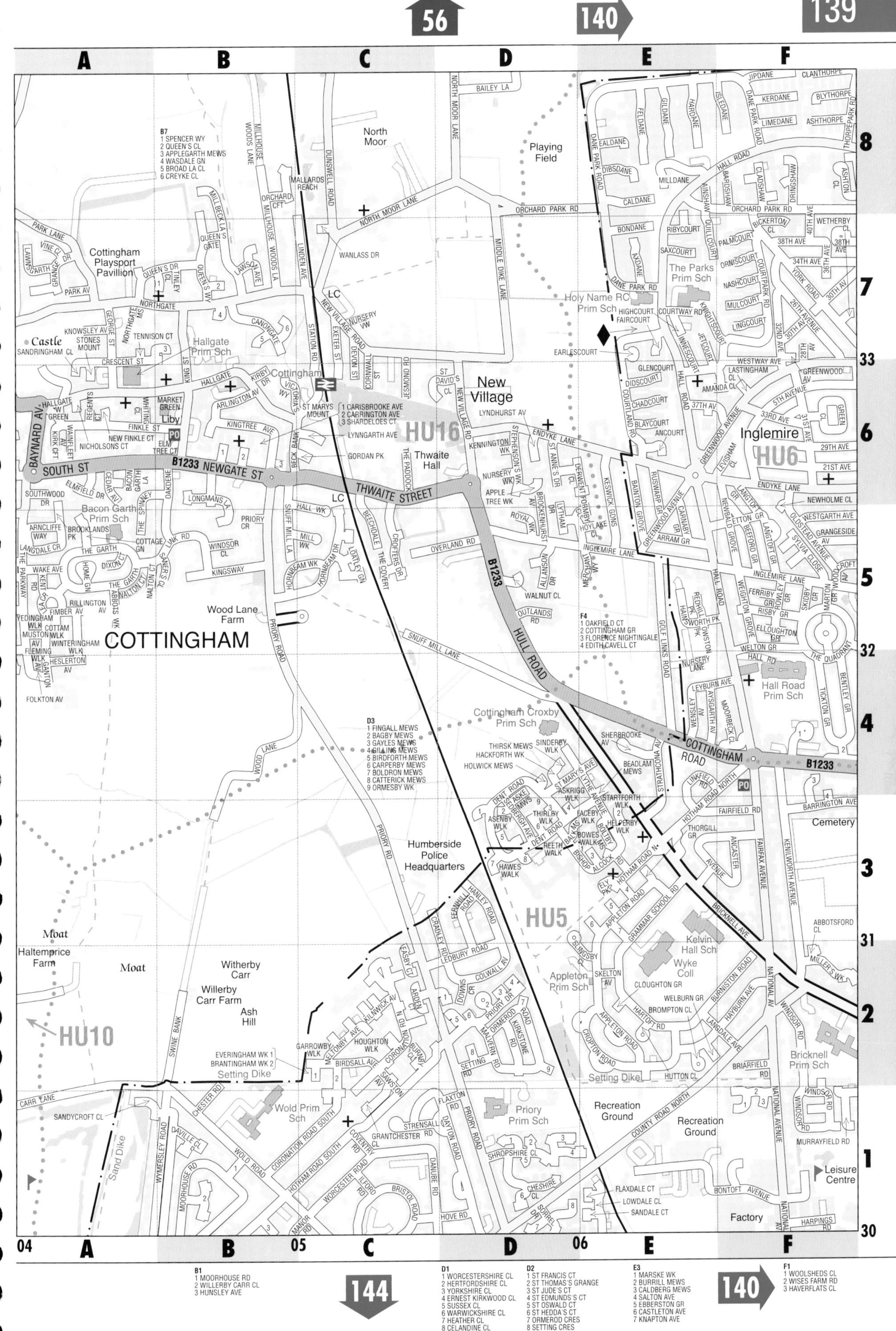
56
140
A
B
C
D
E
F
8
7
33
6
5
32
4
3
31
2
1
30
04
05
06
COTTINGHAM
New Village
Inglemire
North Moor
Playing Field
Cottingham Playsport Pavillion
Castle
Hallgate Prim Sch
Cottingham
Thwaite Hall
HU16
HU6
HU5
HU10
Bacon Garth Prim Sch
Wood Lane Farm
The Parks Prim Sch
Holy Name RC Prim Sch
Hall Road Prim Sch
Cottingham Croxby Prim Sch
Humberside Police Headquarters
Cemetery
Kelvin Hall Sch
Wyke Coll
Appleton Prim Sch
Moat
Haltemprice Farm
Witherby Carr
Willerby Carr Farm
Ash Hill
Setting Dike
Wold Prim Sch
Priory Prim Sch
Recreation Ground
Bricknell Prim Sch
Leisure Centre
Factory
Sand Dike
SOUTH ST
B1233 NEWGATE ST
THWAITE STREET
HULL ROAD
COTTINGHAM ROAD
B1233
B7
1 SPENCER WY
2 QUEEN'S CL
3 APPLEGARTH MEWS
4 WASDALE GN
5 BROAD LA CL
6 CREYKE CL
1 CARISBROOKE AVE
2 CARRINGTON AVE
3 SHARDELOES CT
F4
1 OAKFIELD CT
2 COTTINGHAM GR
3 FLORENCE NIGHTINGALE
4 EDITH CAVELL CT
D3
1 FINGALL MEWS
2 BAGBY MEWS
3 GAYLES MEWS
4 GILLING MEWS
5 BIRDFORTH MEWS
6 CARPERBY MEWS
7 BOLDRON MEWS
8 CATTERICK MEWS
9 ORMESBY WK
EVERINGHAM WK 1
BRANTINGHAM WK 2
B1
1 MOORHOUSE RD
2 WILLERBY CARR CL
3 HUNSLEY AVE
144
D1
1 WORCESTERSHIRE CL
2 HERTFORDSHIRE CL
3 YORKSHIRE CL
4 ERNEST KIRKWOOD CL
5 SUSSEX CL
6 WARWICKSHIRE CL
7 HEATHER CL
8 CELANDINE CL
D2
1 ST FRANCIS CT
2 ST THOMAS'S GRANGE
3 ST JUDE'S CT
4 ST EDMUNDS'S CT
5 ST OSWALD CT
6 ST HEDDA'S CT
7 ORMEROD CRES
8 SETTING CRES
9 MALVERN CRES
E3
1 MARSKE WK
2 BURRILL MEWS
3 CALDBERG MEWS
4 SALTON AVE
5 EBBERSTON GR
6 CASTLETON AVE
7 KNAPTON AVE
140
F1
1 WOOLSHEDS CL
2 WISES FARM RD
3 HAVERFLATS CL

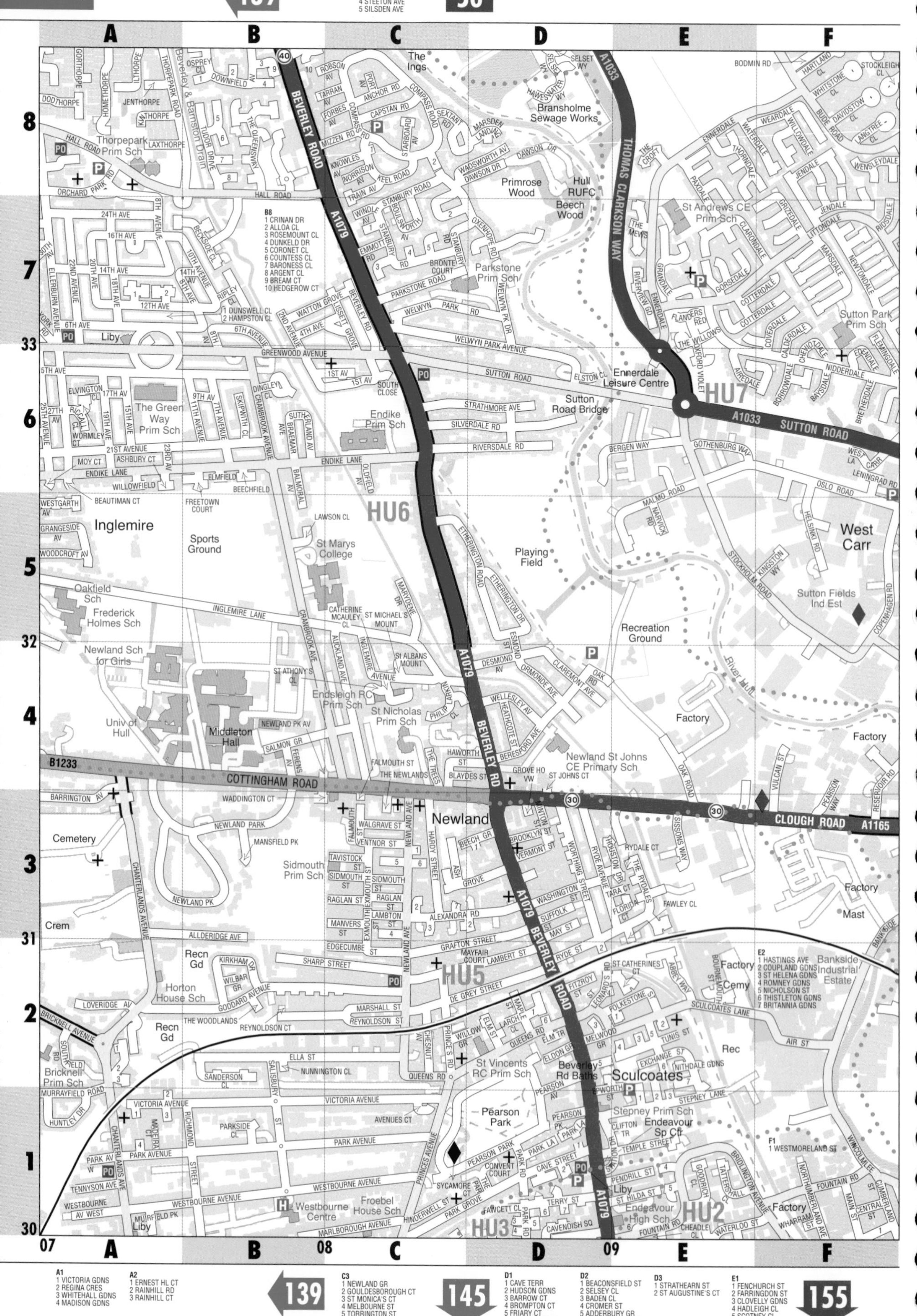

◀ 139

C8
1 FLAG WK
2 LARARD AVE

C7
1 BEECHCLIFFE AVE
2 CULLINGWORTH AVE
3 DENHOLME AVE
4 STEETON AVE
5 SILSDEN AVE

56 ▶

B8
1 CRINAN DR
2 ALLOA CL
3 ROSEMOUNT CL
4 DUNKELD DR
5 CORONET CL
6 COUNTESS CL
7 BARONESS CL
8 ARGENT CL
9 BREAM CT
10 HEDGEROW CT

1 DUNSWELL CL
2 HAMPSTON CL

A1
1 VICTORIA GDNS
2 REGINA CRES
3 WHITEHALL GDNS
4 MADISON GDNS

A2
1 ERNEST HL CT
2 RAINHILL RD
3 RAINHILL CT

◀ 139

C3
1 NEWLAND GR
2 GOULDESBOROUGH CT
3 ST MONICA'S CT
4 MELBOURNE ST
5 TORRINGTON ST
6 WALTER'S TERR
7 THEARNE CL

145

D1
1 CAVE TERR
2 HUDSON GDNS
3 BARROW CT
4 BROMPTON CT
5 FRIARY CT
6 HAMPSTEAD CT
7 KNIGHTSBRIDGE CT

D2
1 BEACONSFIELD ST
2 SELSEY CL
3 BADEN CL
4 CROMER ST
5 ADDERBURY GR
6 BEACONSFIELD ST

D3
1 STRATHEARN ST
2 ST AUGUSTINE'S CT

E1
1 FENCHURCH ST
2 FARRINGDON CL
3 CLOVELLY GDNS
4 HADLEIGH CL
5 SCOTNEY CL
6 STAFFORD ST

155 ▼

57

142

B7
1 PEVENSEY CL
2 PEACEHAVEN CL

D8
1 GOLDCREST CL
2 CORMORANT CL
3 LOWLAND CL
4 HOUSEMARTIN DR

F5
1 HAMMERSMITH RD
2 SHOREDITCH CL
3 TOTTENHAM CL
4 WILLESDEN CL

D7
1 WYKEHAM CL
2 WHEELDALE CL
3 STONEGATE CL
4 OAKTREE DR
5 FINCH GT
6 SWALLOW GRANGE
7 DUNNOCK CL
8 WINSCAR GFT
9 STRILES GR
10 WORSBOROUGH CL
11 LEALHOLM CT
12 KILTON CT

E7
1 BROADSTAIRS CL
2 CANTERBURY DR
3 WHITSTABLE CL
4 LADYBOWER CL
5 BROOMHEAD CL
6 SHETLAND CL
7 ORKNEY CL
8 SOUTHCROFT DR
9 NORDALE CL
10 HIRNCROFT CL

11 KELGATE CL
12 THE HAWTHORNS
13 NORTHCROFT DR
14 DARNHOLM CT
15 SABRINA CT
16 GILLAMOOR CL
17 HOVINGHAM CL
18 PETULA CT

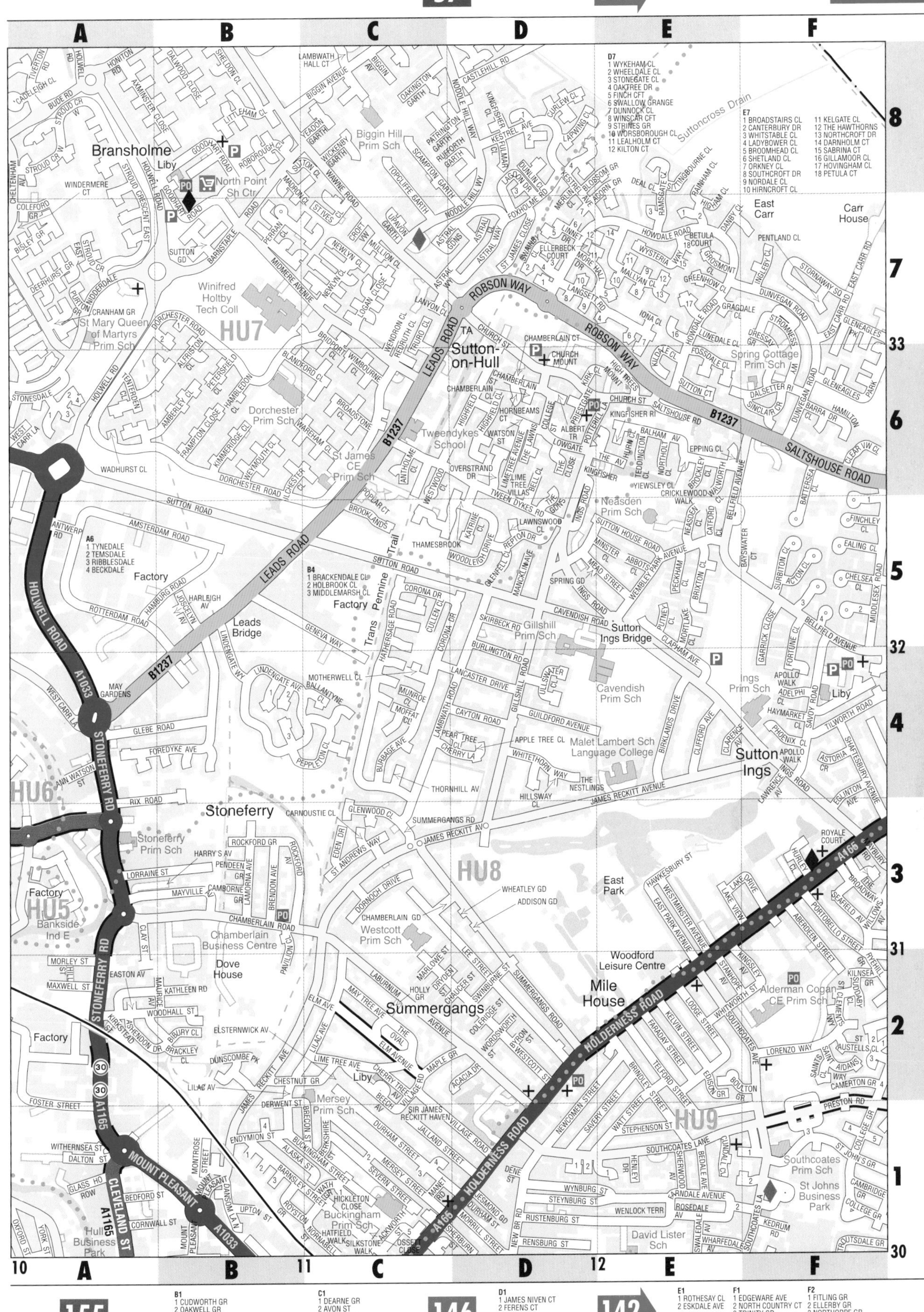

B1
1 CUDWORTH GR
2 OAKWELL GR
3 WOMBWELL GR
4 ALSTON AVE

C1
1 DEARNE GR
2 AVON ST
3 DUNELM CL
4 BRANDON CT
5 BUCKINGHAM ST

D1
1 JAMES NIVEN CT
2 FERENS CT

E1
1 ROTHESAY CL
2 ESKDALE AVE

F1
1 EDGEWARE AVE
2 NORTH COUNTRY CT
3 TRINITY GR
4 WADHAM GR
5 MERTON GR

F2
1 FITLING GR
2 ELLERBY GR
3 NORTHORPE GR
4 ELLERBY GR

A5
1 PETERSHAM CL
2 TWICKENHAM CL
3 CHISWICK CL
4 WIMBLEDON CL
5 BELLFIELD AVE
6 HAUXWELL GR

7 PINDERFIELD CL
8 GUY'S CRES
9 ALDER HEY DR

B5
1 ALWOODLEY CL
2 ATLANTA CT
3 GANTON CL
4 BELTON CL
5 HARLESTON CL

141

C5
1 DUNMOW CL
2 SHORWELL CL
3 ROOKLEY CL
4 COLDSTREAM CL
5 DRAYTON CL
6 FOYNES GN

57

C6
1 BICKLEIGH GR
2 HARLOW CL
3 ST MARGARETS CT
4 PARKHURST CL

58

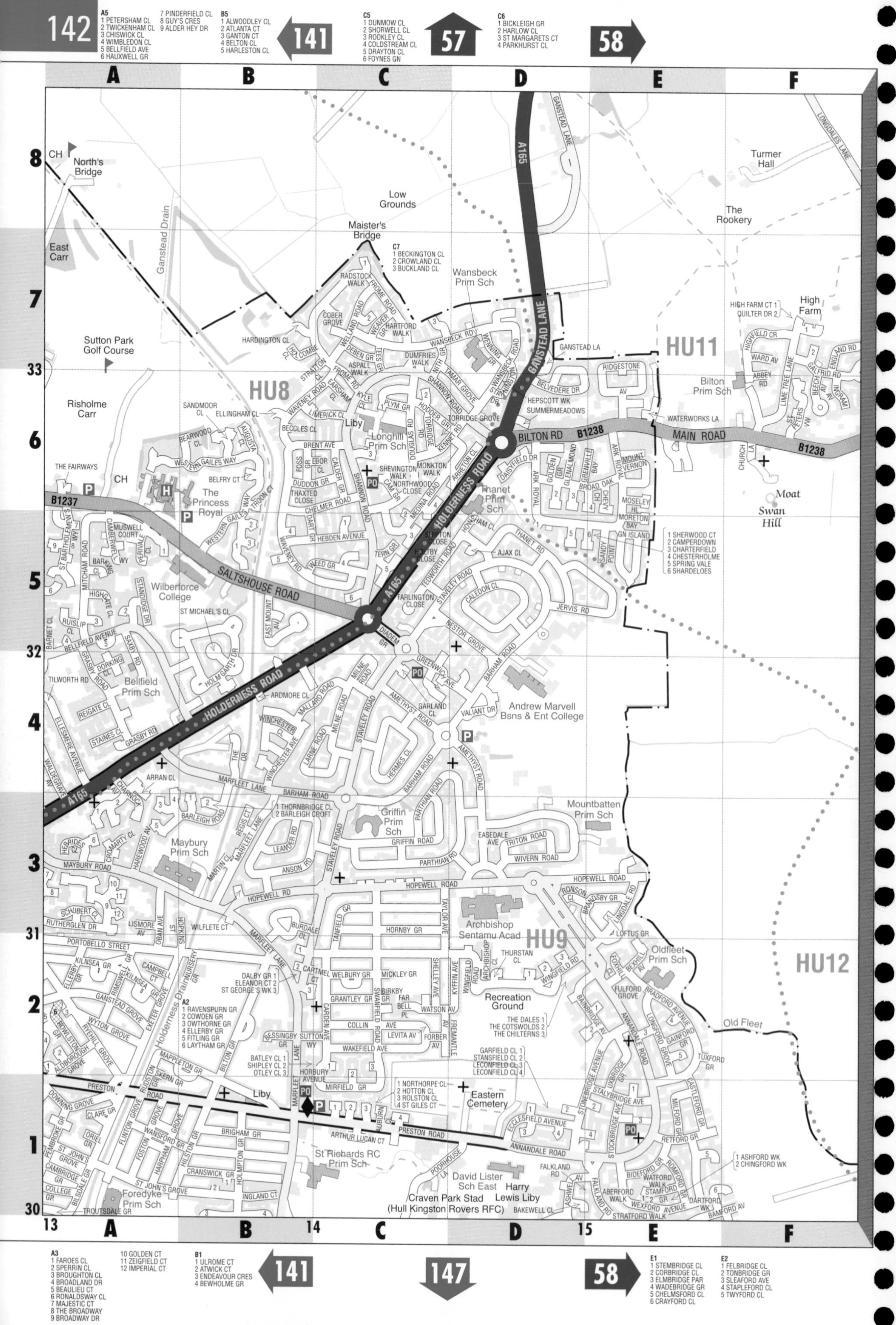

A3
1 FAROES CL
2 SPERRIN CL
3 BROUGHTON CL
4 BROADLAND DR
5 BEAULIEU CT
6 RONALDSWAY CL
7 MAJESTIC CT
8 THE BROADWAY
9 BROADWAY DR

10 GOLDEN CT
11 ZEIGFIELD CT
12 IMPERIAL CL

B1
1 ULROME CT
2 ATWICK CT
3 ENDEAVOUR CRES
4 BEWHOLME GR

141

147

58

E1
1 STEMBRIDGE CL
2 CORBRIDGE CL
3 ELMBRIDGE PAR
4 WADEBRIDGE GR
5 CHELMSFORD CL
6 CRAYFORD CL

E2
1 FELBRIDGE CL
2 TONBRIDGE GR
3 SLEAFORD AVE
4 STAPLEFORD CL
5 TWYFORD CL

69 138 144

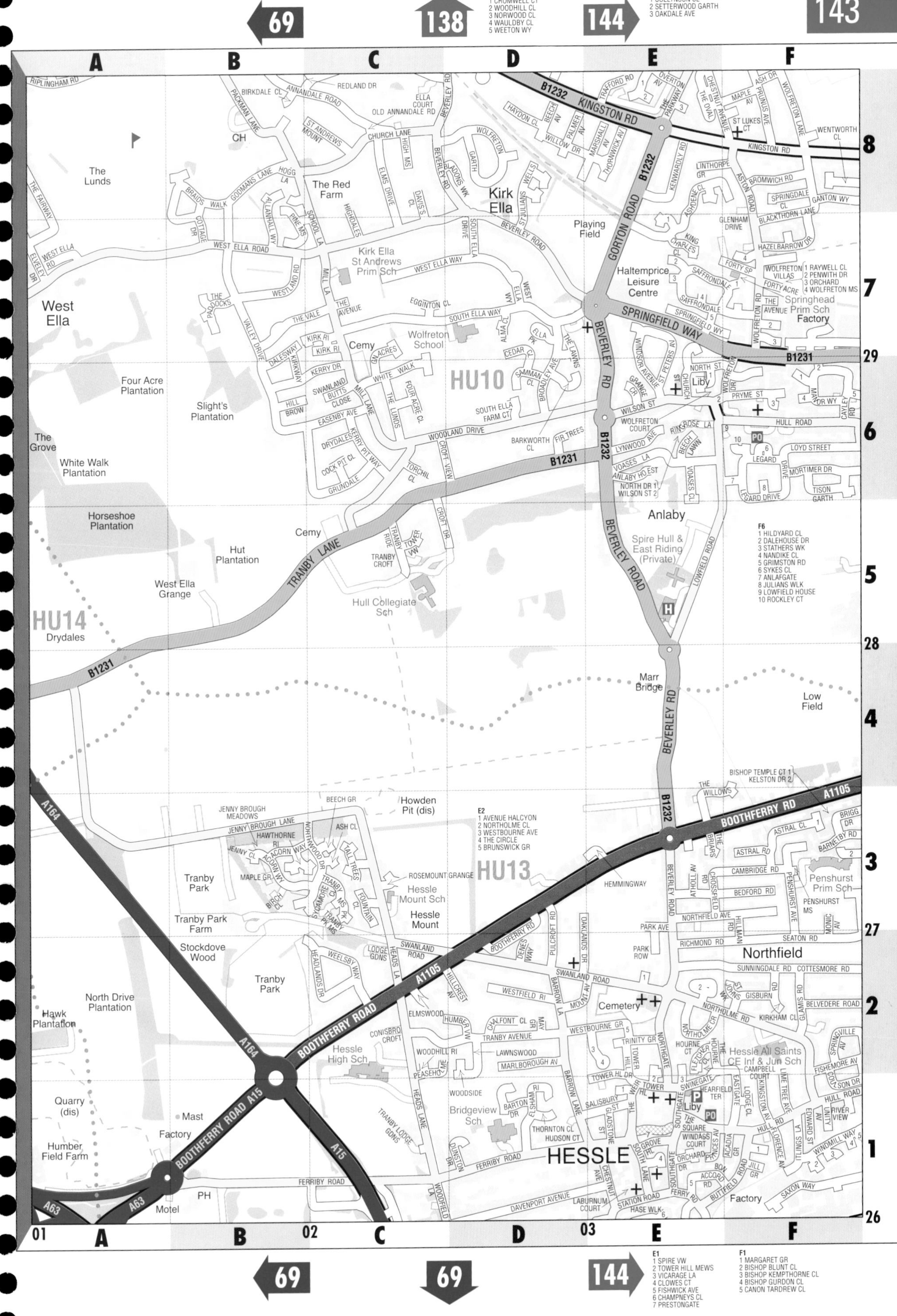

69 69 144

E1
1 SPIRE VW
2 TOWER HILL MEWS
3 VICARAGE LA
4 CLOWES CT
5 FISHWICK AVE
6 CHAMPNEYS CL
7 PRESTONGATE

F1
1 MARGARET GR
2 BISHOP BLUNT CL
3 BISHOP KEMPTHORNE CL
4 BISHOP GURDON CL
5 CANON TARDREW CL

A3
1 BARNETBY RD
2 KELSTON DR
3 YARMOUTH AVE
4 WINTHORPE RD
5 BROCKLESBY CL
6 CORRAN GARTH
7 CHURCH FIELD

B7
1 LANGFORD WK
2 HOLLYTREE AVE
3 LABURNUM DR
4 ROSEWOOD CL

143

139

D8
1 LOCKTON GR
2 HACKNESS GR
3 BARGATE GR
4 SNAINTON GR
5 SORREL DR

E6
1 AIRMYN AVE
2 ST MARTINS AVE
3 BUTTERMERE CL

F6
1 HAWTHORN CT

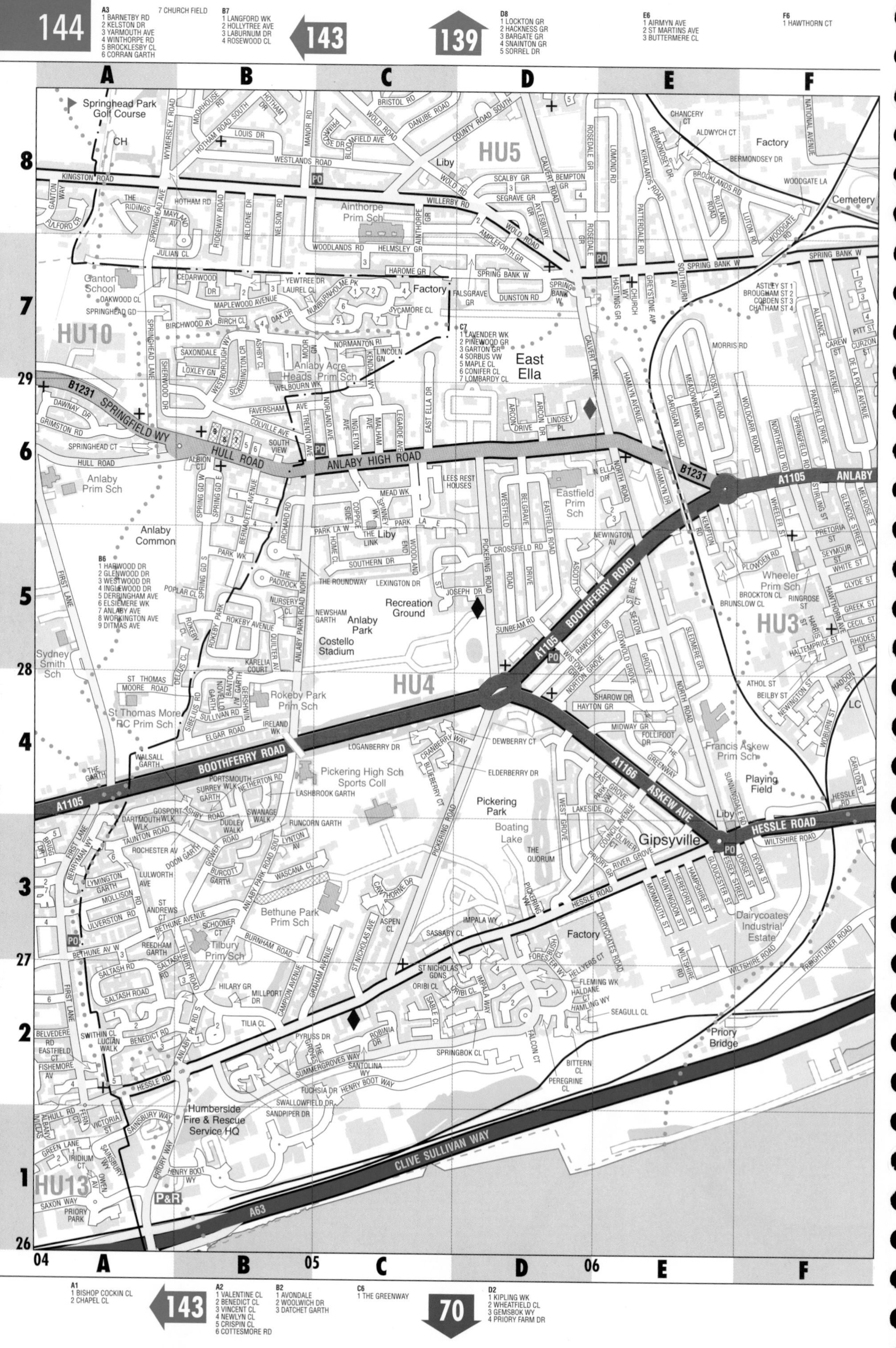

A1
1 BISHOP COCKIN CL
2 CHAPEL CL

143

A2
1 VALENTINE CL
2 BENEDICT CL
3 VINCENT CL
4 NEWLYN CL
5 CRISPIN CL
6 COTTESMORE RD

B2
1 AVONDALE
2 WOOLWICH DR
3 DATCHET GARTH

C6
1 THE GREENWAY

70

D2
1 KIPLING WK
2 WHEATFIELD CL
3 GEMSBOK WY
4 PRIORY FARM DR

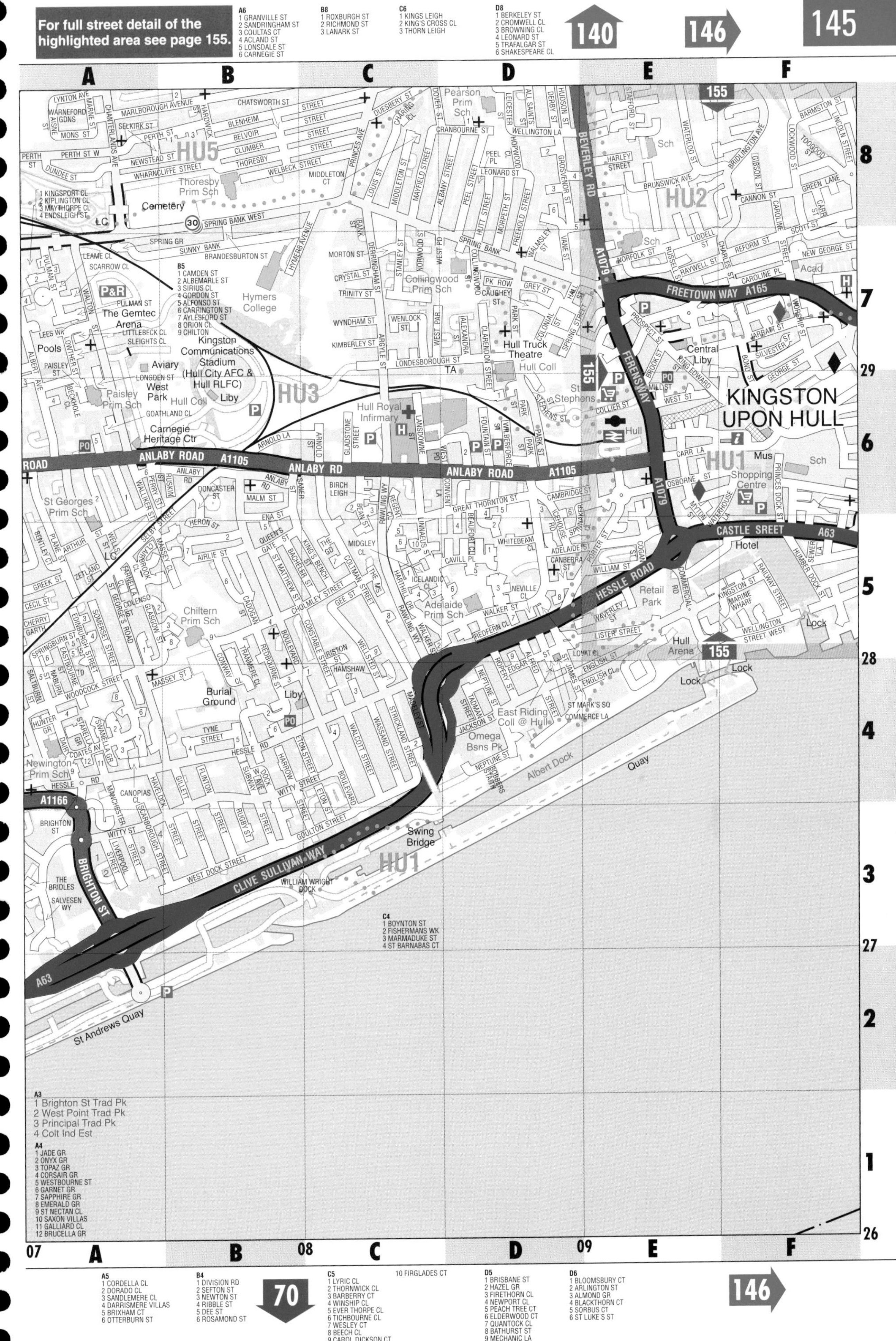

For full street detail of the highlighted area see page 155.
A6
1 GRANVILLE ST
2 SANDRINGHAM ST
3 COULTAS CT
4 ACLAND ST
5 LONSDALE ST
6 CARNEGIE ST
B8
1 ROXBURGH ST
2 RICHMOND ST
3 LANARK ST
C6
1 KINGS LEIGH
2 KING'S CROSS CL
3 THORN LEIGH
D8
1 BERKELEY ST
2 CROMWELL CL
3 BROWNING CL
4 LEONARD ST
5 TRAFALGAR ST
6 SHAKESPEARE CL
140
146
145
A
B
C
D
E
F
HU5
HU2
HU3
HU1
Thoresby Prim Sch
Cemetery
SPRING BANK WEST
Pearson Prim Sch
BEVERLEY RD
155
1 KINGSPORT CL
2 KIPLINGTON CL
3 MAYTHORPE CL
4 ENDSLEIGH ST
B5
1 CAMDEN ST
2 ALBEMARLE ST
3 SIRIUS CL
4 GORDON ST
5 ALFONSO ST
6 CARRINGTON ST
7 AYLESFORD ST
8 ORION CL
9 CHILTON
The Gemtec Arena
Kingston Communications Stadium (Hull City AFC & Hull RLFC)
Hymers College
Collingwood Prim Sch
Hull Truck Theatre
Hull Coll
FREETOWN WAY A165
FERENSWAY
Central Liby
KINGSTON UPON HULL
Hull Royal Infirmary
Paisley Prim Sch
West Park
Carnegie Heritage Ctr
ANLABY ROAD A1105
ANLABY RD
St Georges Prim Sch
Shopping Centre
CASTLE STREET A63
HESSLE ROAD
Retail Park
Chiltern Prim Sch
Adelaide Prim Sch
Burial Ground
East Riding Coll @ Hull
Omega Bsns Pk
Albert Dock
Quay
Hull Arena
Newington Prim Sch
A1166
BRIGHTON ST
Swing Bridge
CLIVE SULLIVAN WAY
WILLIAM WRIGHT DOCK
C4
1 BOYNTON ST
2 FISHERMANS WK
3 MARMADUKE ST
4 ST BARNABAS CT
A63
St Andrews Quay
A3
1 Brighton St Trad Pk
2 West Point Trad Pk
3 Principal Trad Pk
4 Colt Ind Est
A4
1 JADE GR
2 ONYX GR
3 TOPAZ GR
4 CORSAIR GR
5 WESTBOURNE ST
6 GARNET GR
7 SAPPHIRE GR
8 EMERALD GR
9 ST NECTAN CL
10 SAXON VILLAS
11 GALLIARD CL
12 BRUCELLA GR
8
7
29
6
5
28
4
3
27
2
1
26
07
08
09
A5
1 CORDELLA CL
2 DORADO CL
3 SANDLEMERE CL
4 DARRISMERE VILLAS
5 BRIXHAM CT
6 OTTERBURN ST
B4
1 DIVISION RD
2 SEFTON ST
3 NEWTON ST
4 RIBBLE ST
5 DEE ST
6 ROSAMOND ST
70
C5
1 LYRIC CL
2 THORNWICK CL
3 BARBERRY CT
4 WINSHIP CL
5 EVER THORPE CL
6 TICHBOURNE CL
7 WESLEY CT
8 BEECH CL
9 CAROL DICKSON CT
10 FIRGLADES CT
D5
1 BRISBANE ST
2 HAZEL GR
3 FIRETHORN CL
4 NEWPORT CL
5 PEACH TREE CT
6 ELDERWOOD CT
7 QUANTOCK CL
8 BATHURST ST
9 MECHANIC LA
D6
1 BLOOMSBURY CT
2 ARLINGTON ST
3 ALMOND GR
4 BLACKTHORN CT
5 SORBUS CT
6 ST LUKE'S ST
146

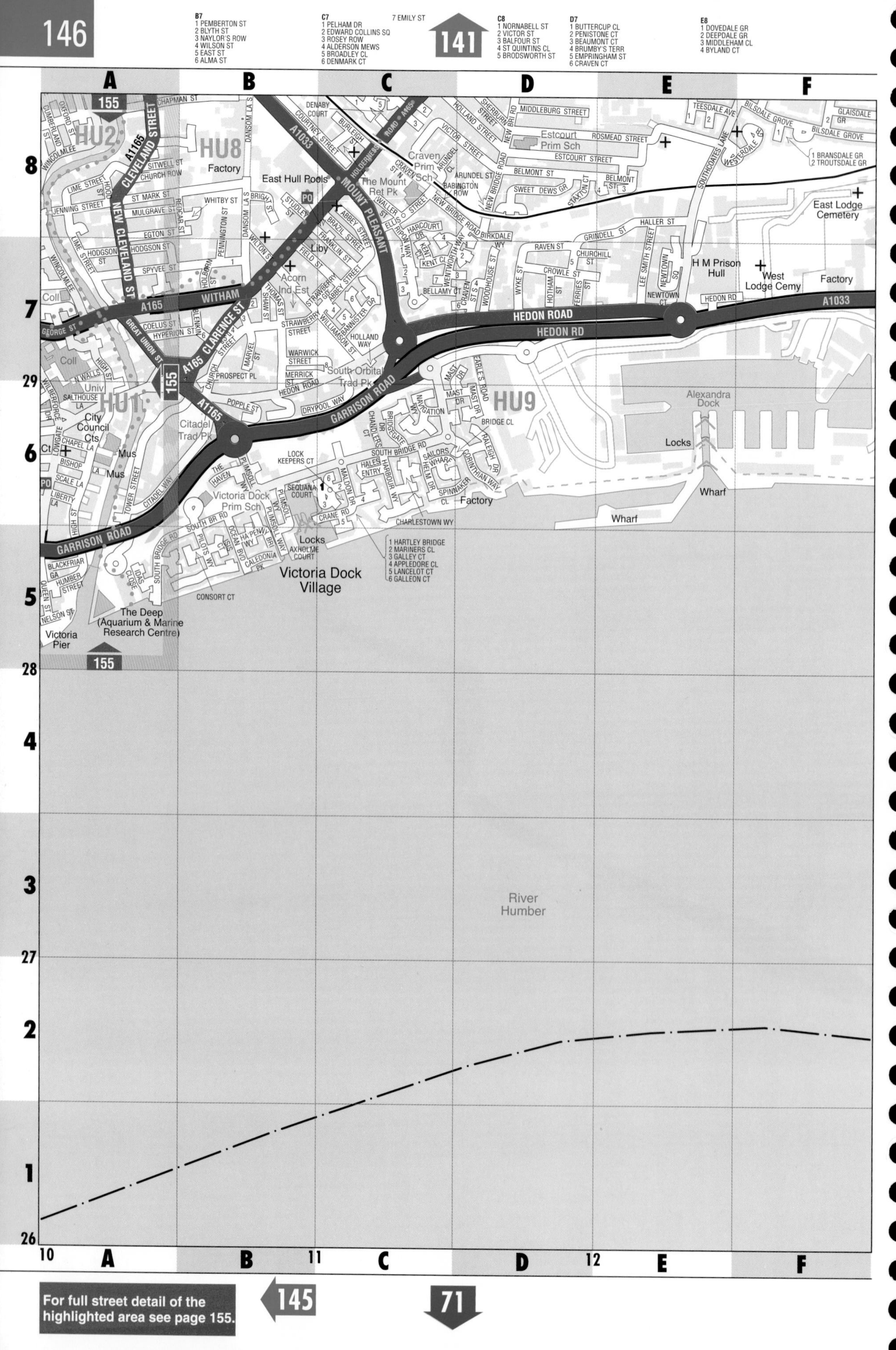

141

145

71

B7
1 PEMBERTON ST
2 BLYTH ST
3 NAYLOR'S ROW
4 WILSON ST
5 EAST ST
6 ALMA ST

C7
1 PELHAM DR
2 EDWARD COLLINS SQ
3 ROSEY ROW
4 ALDERSON MEWS
5 BROADLEY CL
6 DENMARK CT

7 EMILY ST

C8
1 NORNABELL ST
2 VICTOR ST
3 BALFOUR ST
4 ST QUINTINS CL
5 BRODSWORTH ST

D7
1 BUTTERCUP CL
2 PENISTONE CT
3 BEAUMONT CT
4 BRUMBY'S TERR
5 EMPRINGHAM ST
6 CRAVEN CT

E8
1 DOVEDALE GR
2 DEEPDALE GR
3 MIDDLEHAM CL
4 BYLAND CT

1 HARTLEY BRIDGE
2 MARINERS CL
3 GALLEY CT
4 APPLEDORE CL
5 LANCELOT CT
6 GALLEON CT

1 BRANSDALE GR
2 TROUTSDALE GR

For full street detail of the
highlighted area see page 155.

142

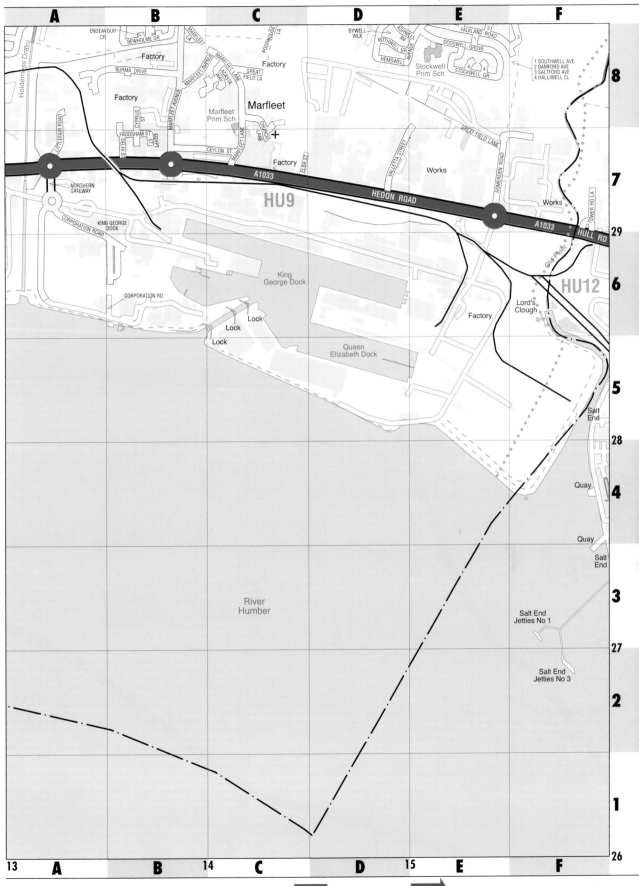

A B C D E F

ENDEAVOUR CR
BEWHOLME GR
MARFLEET LA
POORHOUSE LA
BYWELL WLK
ASHWELL AV
BOTHWELL GR
HEMSWELL AVENUE
HEMSWELL
FALKLAND ROAD
DODSWELL GROVE
STOCKWELL GR
Stockwell Prim Sch
1 SOUTHWELL AVE
2 BAMFORD AVE
3 SALTFORD AVE
4 HALLIWELL CL
Holderness Drain
Factory
BURMA DRIVE
MARFLEET AVENUE
MARFLEET LANE
ACASTA WAY
GREAT FIELD LA
Factory
Factory
Marfleet
Marfleet Prim Sch
CYPRUS ST
LITTLEFAIR ROAD
FRODSHAM ST
DELHI ST
EGYPT ST
MARFLEET AVENUE
CHURCH LANE
MARFLEET LANE
CEYLON ST
ELBA ST
Factory
GREAT FIELD LANE
VALLETTA STREET
Works
SOMERDEN ROAD
Works
TOWER HO LA
A1033
HEDON ROAD
A1033
HULL RD
NORTHERN GATEWAY
HU9
CORPORATION ROAD
KING GEORGE DOCK
Old Fleet
HU12
King George Dock
CORPORATION RD
Lord's Clough
Factory
Lock
Lock
Lock
Queen Elizabeth Dock
Salt End
Quay
Quay
Salt End
River Humber
Salt End Jetties No 1
Salt End Jetties No 3

8 7 29 6 5 28 4 3 27 2 1 26

13 A B 14 C D 15 E F

71

72

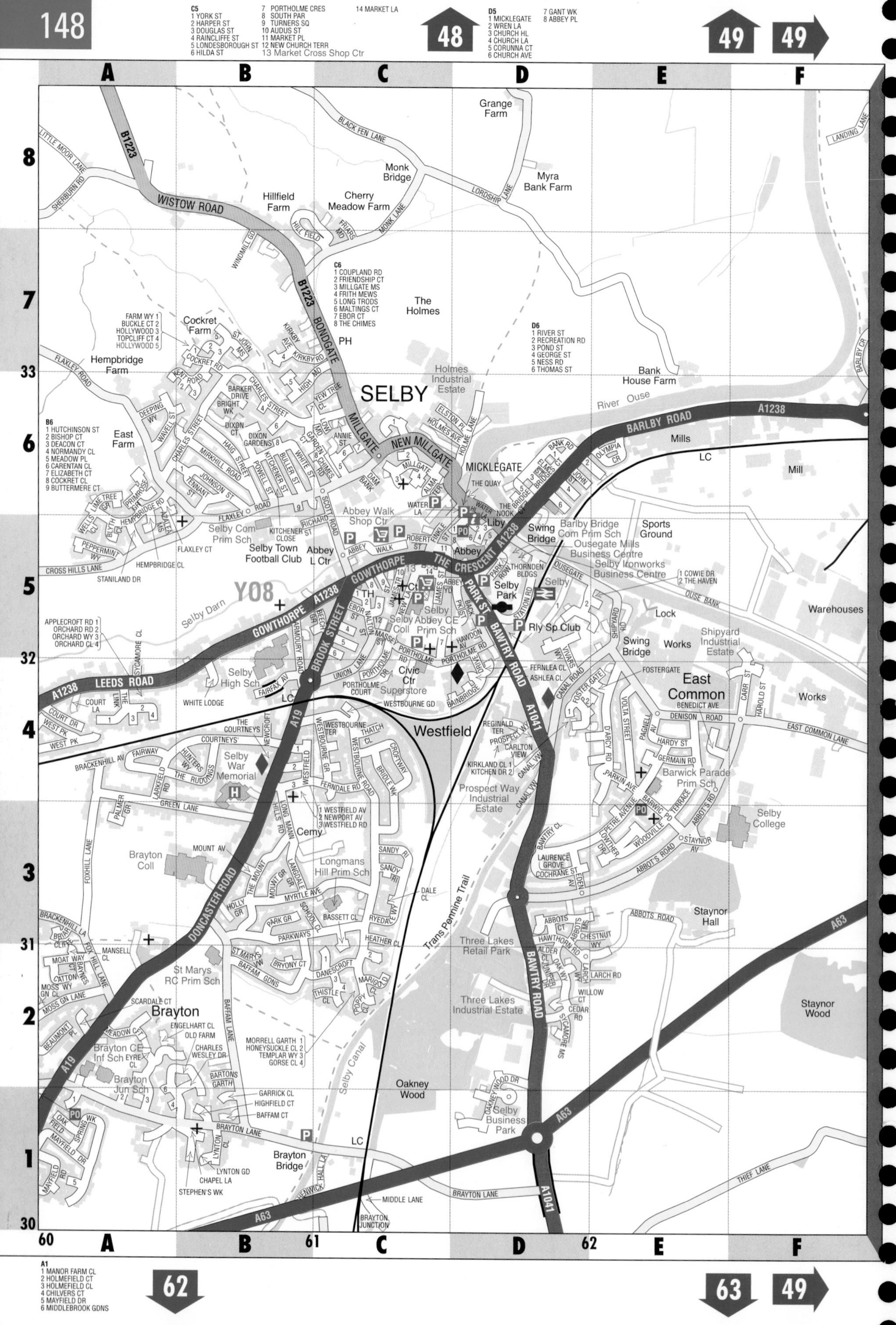

148
C5
1 YORK ST
2 HARPER ST
3 DOUGLAS ST
4 RAINCLIFFE ST
5 LONDESBOROUGH ST
6 HILDA ST
7 PORTHOLME CRES
8 SOUTH PAR
9 TURNERS SQ
10 AUDUS ST
11 MARKET PL
12 NEW CHURCH TERR
13 Market Cross Shop Ctr
14 MARKET LA
48
D5
1 MICKLEGATE
2 WREN LA
3 CHURCH HL
4 CHURCH LA
5 CORUNNA CT
6 CHURCH AVE
7 GANT WK
8 ABBEY PL
49
49
A
B
C
D
E
F
8
7
33
6
5
32
4
3
31
2
1
30
60
61
62
Grange Farm
Monk Bridge
Myra Bank Farm
Hillfield Farm
Cherry Meadow Farm
WISTOW ROAD
B1223
BLACK FEN LANE
LORDSHIP LANE
LITTLE MOOR LANE
SHERBURN RD
C6
1 COUPLAND RD
2 FRIENDSHIP CT
3 MILLGATE MS
4 FRITH MEWS
5 LONG TRODS
6 MALTINGS CT
7 EBOR CT
8 THE CHIMES
The Holmes
D6
1 RIVER ST
2 RECREATION RD
3 POND ST
4 GEORGE ST
5 NESS RD
6 THOMAS ST
Bank House Farm
FARM WY 1
BUCKLE CT 2
HOLLYWOOD 3
TOPCLIFF CT 4
HOLLYWOOD 5
Cockret Farm
Hempbridge Farm
FLAXLEY ROAD
BONDGATE
PH
SELBY
Holmes Industrial Estate
River Ouse
BARLBY ROAD
A1238
Mills
LC
Mill
B6
1 HUTCHINSON ST
2 BISHOP CT
3 DEACON CT
4 NORMANDY CL
5 MEADOW PL
6 CARENTAN CL
7 ELIZABETH CT
8 COCKRET CL
9 BUTTERMERE CT
East Farm
MILLGATE
NEW MILLGATE
MICKLEGATE
THE QUAY
Abbey Walk Shop Ctr
Selby Com Prim Sch
Selby Town Football Club
Abbey L Ctr
Liby
Abbey
Swing Bridge
Barlby Bridge Com Prim Sch
Sports Ground
Ousegate Mills Business Centre
Selby Ironworks Business Centre
1 COWIE DR
2 THE HAVEN
OUSE BANK
Warehouses
CROSS HILLS LANE
STANILAND DR
HEMPBRIDGE CL
FLAXLEY CT
GOWTHORPE
THE CRESCENT
Selby Park
Selby
YO8
Selby Dam
Lock
APPLECROFT RD 1
ORCHARD RD 2
ORCHARD WY 3
ORCHARD CL 4
Selby Abbey CE Coll Prim Sch
Rly Sp Club
Swing Bridge
Works
Shipyard Industrial Estate
LEEDS ROAD
BROOK STREET
BAWTRY ROAD
Selby High Sch
Civic Ctr
Superstore
FOSTERGATE
East Common
Works
WHITE LODGE
LC
Westfield
DENISON ROAD
EAST COMMON LANE
A19
A1041
Selby War Memorial
Cemy
Prospect Way Industrial Estate
Barwick Parade Prim Sch
Selby College
1 WESTFIELD AV
2 NEWPORT AV
3 WESTFIELD RD
Brayton Coll
Longmans Hill Prim Sch
DOUCASTER ROAD
Trans Pennine Trail
Staynor Hall
Three Lakes Retail Park
ABBOTS ROAD
A63
St Marys RC Prim Sch
Brayton
Three Lakes Industrial Estate
Staynor Wood
MORRELL GARTH 1
HONEYSUCKLE CL 2
TEMPLAR WY 3
GORSE CL 4
Brayton CE Inf Sch
Brayton Jun Sch
Selby Canal
Oakney Wood
Selby Business Park
BRAYTON LANE
Brayton Bridge
LC
MIDDLE LANE
BRAYTON JUNCTION
THIEF LANE
A1
1 MANOR FARM CL
2 HOLMEFIELD CT
3 HOLMEFIELD CL
4 CHILVERS CT
5 MAYFIELD DR
6 MIDDLEBROOK GDNS
62
63
49

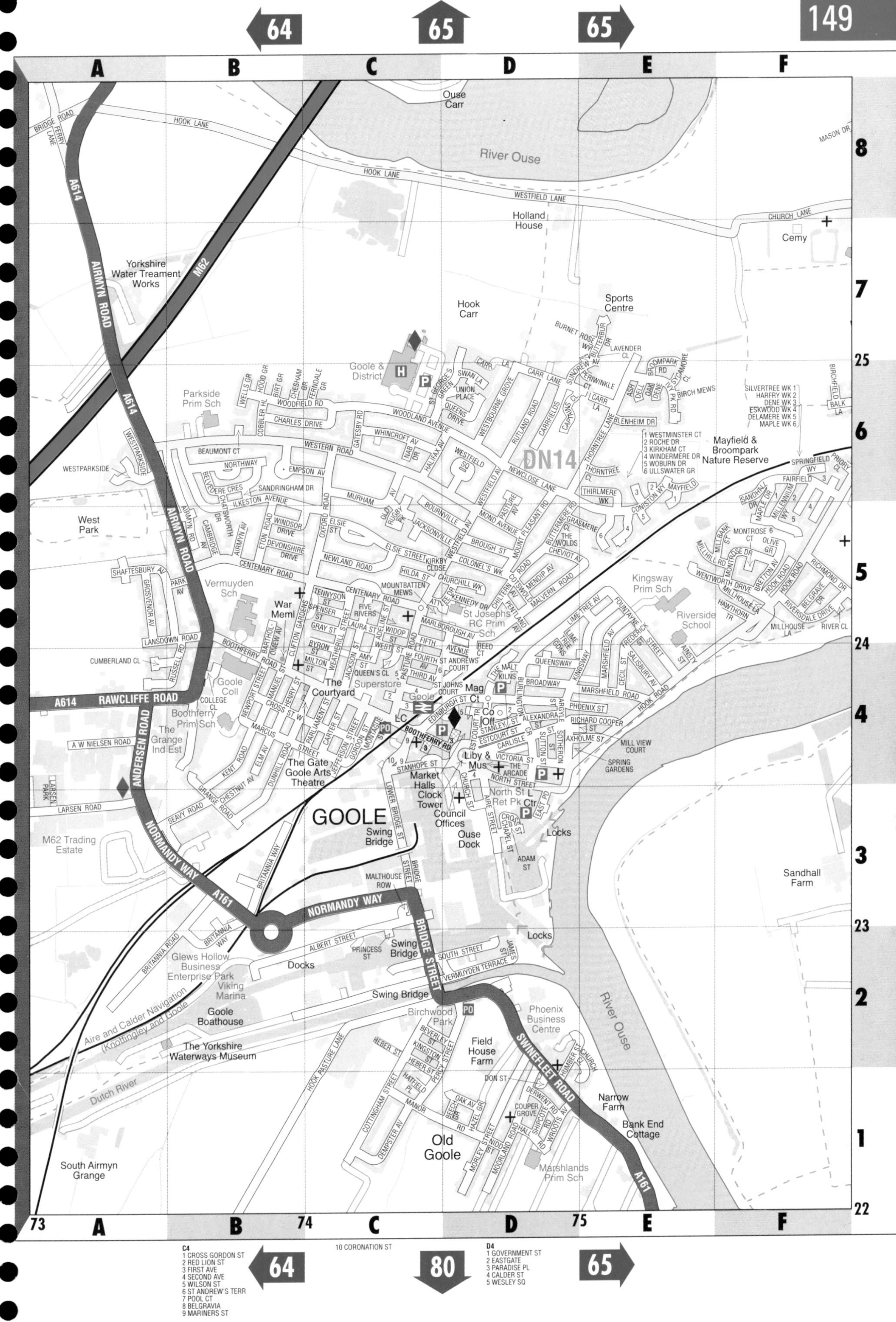

GOOLE

DN14

River Ouse

Ouse Carr

River Ouse

West Park

Vermuyden Sch

Goole Coll

South Airmyn Grange

Old Goole

Sandhall Farm

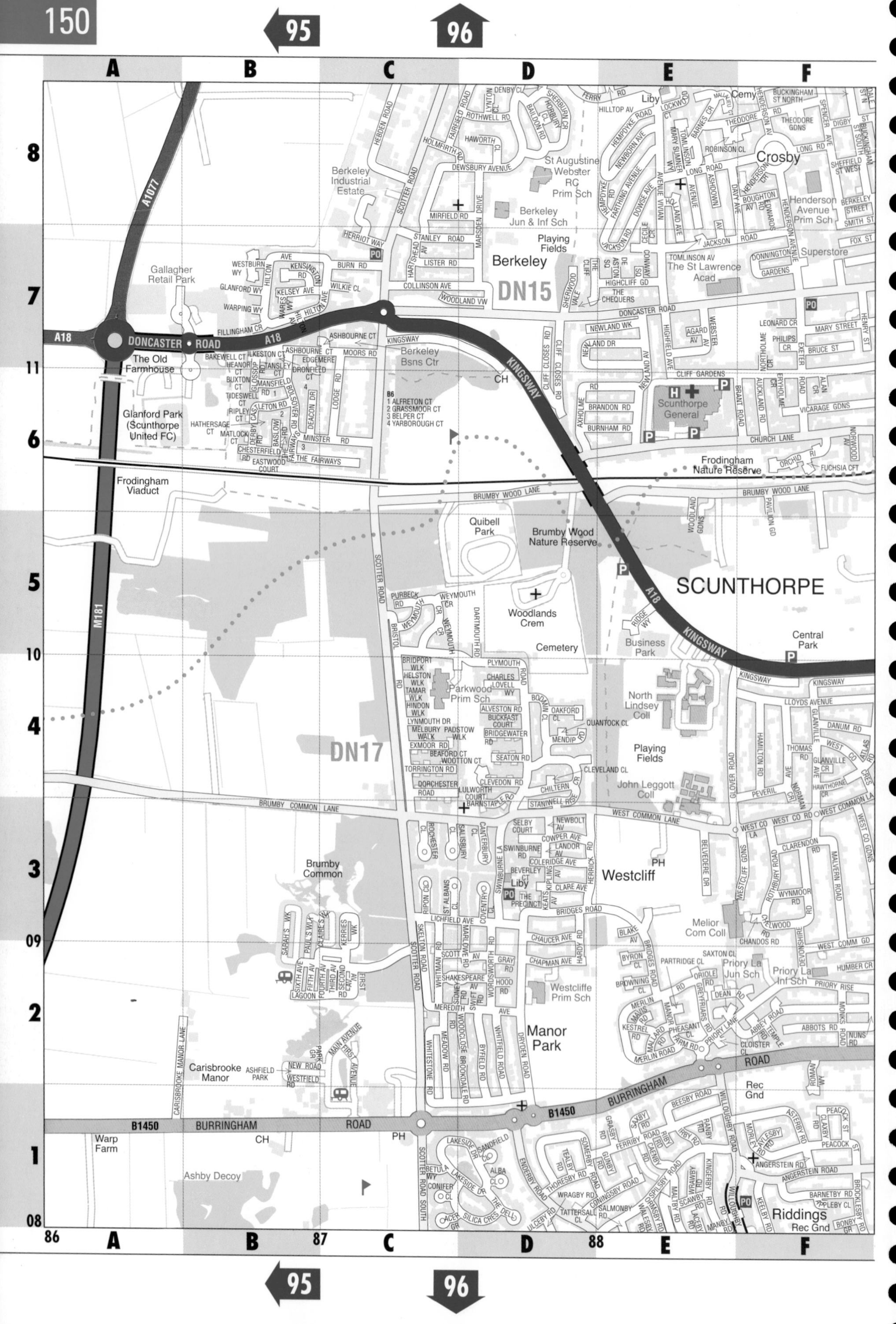

95
96
A
B
C
D
E
F
8
7
11
6
5
10
4
3
09
2
1
08
86
87
88
A1077
A18
DONCASTER ROAD
M181
Gallagher Retail Park
The Old Farmhouse
Glanford Park (Scunthorpe United FC)
Frodingham Viaduct
Berkeley Industrial Estate
Berkeley Bsns Ctr
B6
1 ALFRETON CT
2 GRASSMOOR CT
3 BELPER CT
4 YARBOROUGH CT
St Augustine Webster RC Prim Sch
Berkeley Jun & Inf Sch
Playing Fields
Berkeley
DN15
Liby
Cemy
Crosby
Henderson Avenue Prim Sch
Superstore
The St Lawrence Acad
Scunthorpe General
KINGSWAY
Frodingham Nature Reserve
BRUMBY WOOD LANE
Quibell Park
Brumby Wood Nature Reserve
SCUNTHORPE
Woodlands Crem
Cemetery
Business Park
Central Park
North Lindsey Coll
Playing Fields
John Leggott Coll
DN17
Parkwood Prim Sch
BRUMBY COMMON LANE
WEST COMMON LANE
Brumby Common
Westcliff
Melior Com Coll
Priory La Jun Sch
Priory La Inf Sch
Westcliffe Prim Sch
Manor Park
Carisbrooke Manor
Rec Gnd
B1450
BURRINGHAM ROAD
Warp Farm
Ashby Decoy
Riddings Rec Gnd
SCOTTER ROAD
SCOTTER ROAD SOUTH
CARISBROOKE MANOR LANE

B7
1 BELGRAVE SQ
2 SOUTHGATE
3 ETHEL CT
4 LESLIE CT
5 KINSLEY WK
6 JUBILEE WY
7 WILSONS CL
8 WALKERS CL
9 GREENS CL
10 MANLEY ST
11 CARLTON ST
12 The Parishes Shop Ctr
13 The Base Youth Arts Ctr

B8
1 NORTH ST
2 CROSS ST

C7
1 DAWES LA

96
97

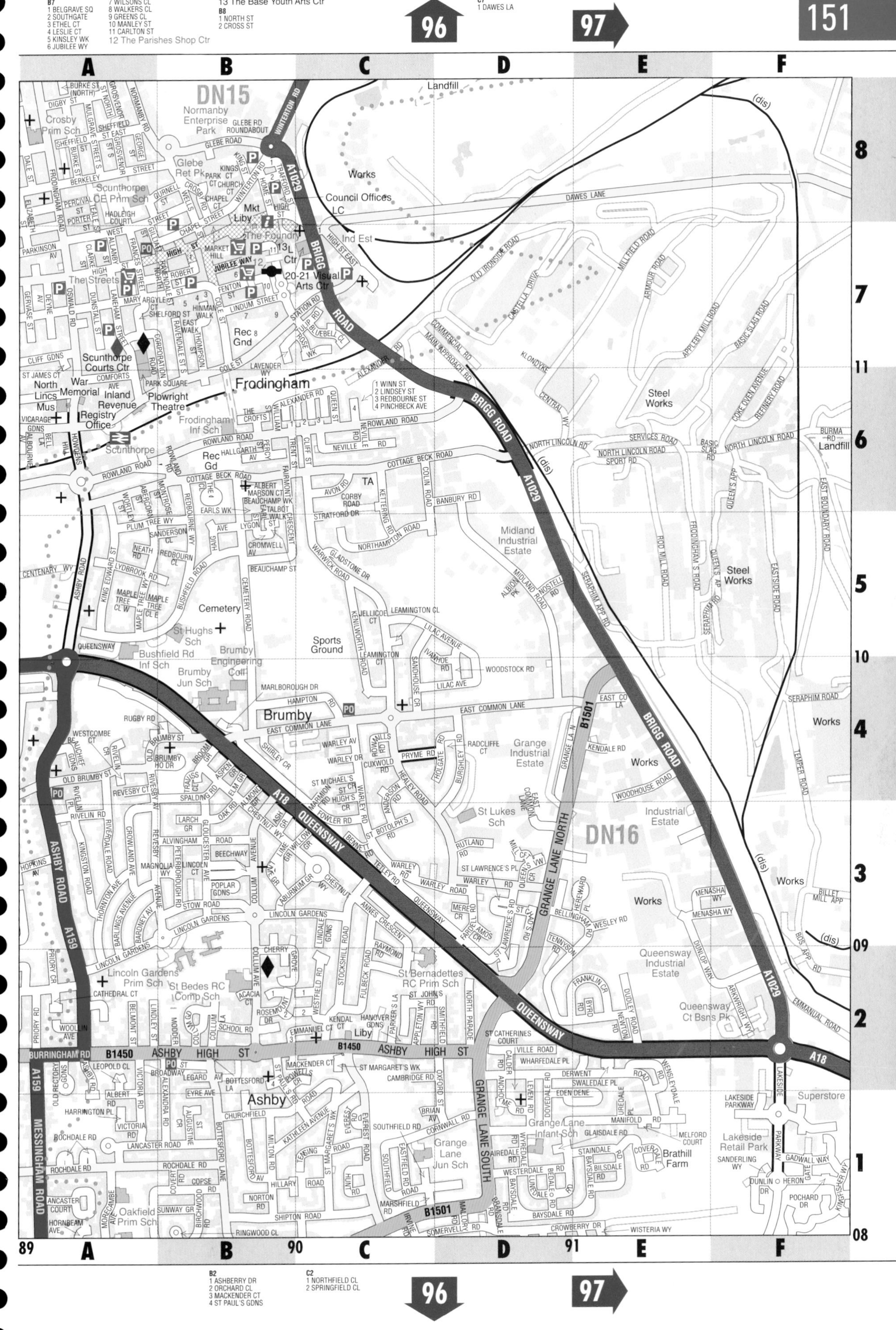

B2
1 ASHBERRY DR
2 ORCHARD CL
3 MACKENDER CT
4 ST PAUL'S GDNS

C2
1 NORTHFIELD CL
2 SPRINGFIELD CL

96
97

A B C D E F

8

River Humber

Pyewipe

Dock Tower
Locks   Locks   Locks

Works   Works

7

BROWN ST 1
HENDERSON ST 2
SMITH ST 3
SIDEBOTTOM ST 4
SMITTON ST 5

Water Reclamation Works

LC

Sports Ground

Royal Dock

11

Europa Business Park

LC

Moody Lane

Sewage Works

DN31

Stuart Wortley St

Jetty

A180

6

Ventura Business Park

Appian Wy

Estate Rd No 1

Lock Hill

Marina

Murray

Cherry Tree's Business Park

West Coates Road

Westside Rd

Alexandra Dock North

Westside Road

Rowlandson St

South Humberside Industrial Estate

Alexandra Dock

Works

CLEETHORPE RD

A180

5

Littlecoates Prim Sch

Birchin Wy Ind Est

A180   WESTGATE

Grimsby Docks

Strand Com Sch

West Marsh

Adam Watkin St   Smith St

High

Alexandra Dock Ret Pk Ret Pk Development

Industrial Estate

East Marsh

10

West Marsh

LAWRENCE ST 1
SAUNDERS ST 2
HUMBER TERR 3
FRESHNEY DR 4

Duke of York Gdns

Corporation Road

Victoria Retail Park

Superstore

Grimsby Leisure Centre

St Leonard's Av   St Francis Av

Rec Gnd   Liby

Boulevard Gardens

Swing Bridge

P.S Lincoln Castle

Superstore

4

Grimsby Auditorium

Macaulay Sch

Macaulay Wk

Fishing Heritage Ctr

Mag Ct

St Marys

Superstore

RC Prim Sch

ELLIS WAY

FREDERICK WARD WAY

Riverhead

Eastgate

Telford Place

YARBOROUGH ROAD   A1136

CROMWELL RD   A1136

Freshney Pl

Mkt Hall

Crown & Cty Ct

Hall East

Liby   Lincoln

TH

Bowling Gn La

Sheepfold

Peaks Parkway Ret Pk

Holme Hill

Edward Heneage Prim Sch

3

Yarborough

A1136

DUDLEY ST

Prince's

Grimsby Town

Rec Gnd

GRIMSBY

09

Gosport Gr

Cross Coates Rd

Vicarage Lawn

St James'

Wellgate Mews

Cyril Cooper Court

Wintringham

Welholme Prim Sch

2

Sports Field

Littlefield

PELHAM RD 1
THE SPINNEY 2
CHELMSFORD PL 3
MALMESBURY DR 4
TEWKESBURY DR 5
THE LAWNS 6
ST JAMES CT 7
BEECHFIELD CT 8
SELMESTON CT 9

College St

The Grimsby Institute

Abbey Park Mews

DN32

WELHOLME RD

Maningtree Close

Intax Farm Mews

Welholme Galleries

1 PETERHOUSE RD
2 PEMBROKE WK

Works

DN34

Regent Gardens

Nairn Wy

B1212   WELHOLME ROAD

People's Park

Wellow

Peaksfield Avenue

1

Cambridge Park Sch

WESTWARD HO

Hereford Technology School

Grimsby Institute of FE & HE

St Martins Prep Sch

B1212   BARGATE

Grange

Franklin College

A46   WEELSBY ROAD

WEELSBY RD

08

25   A   26   B   C   27   D   E   F

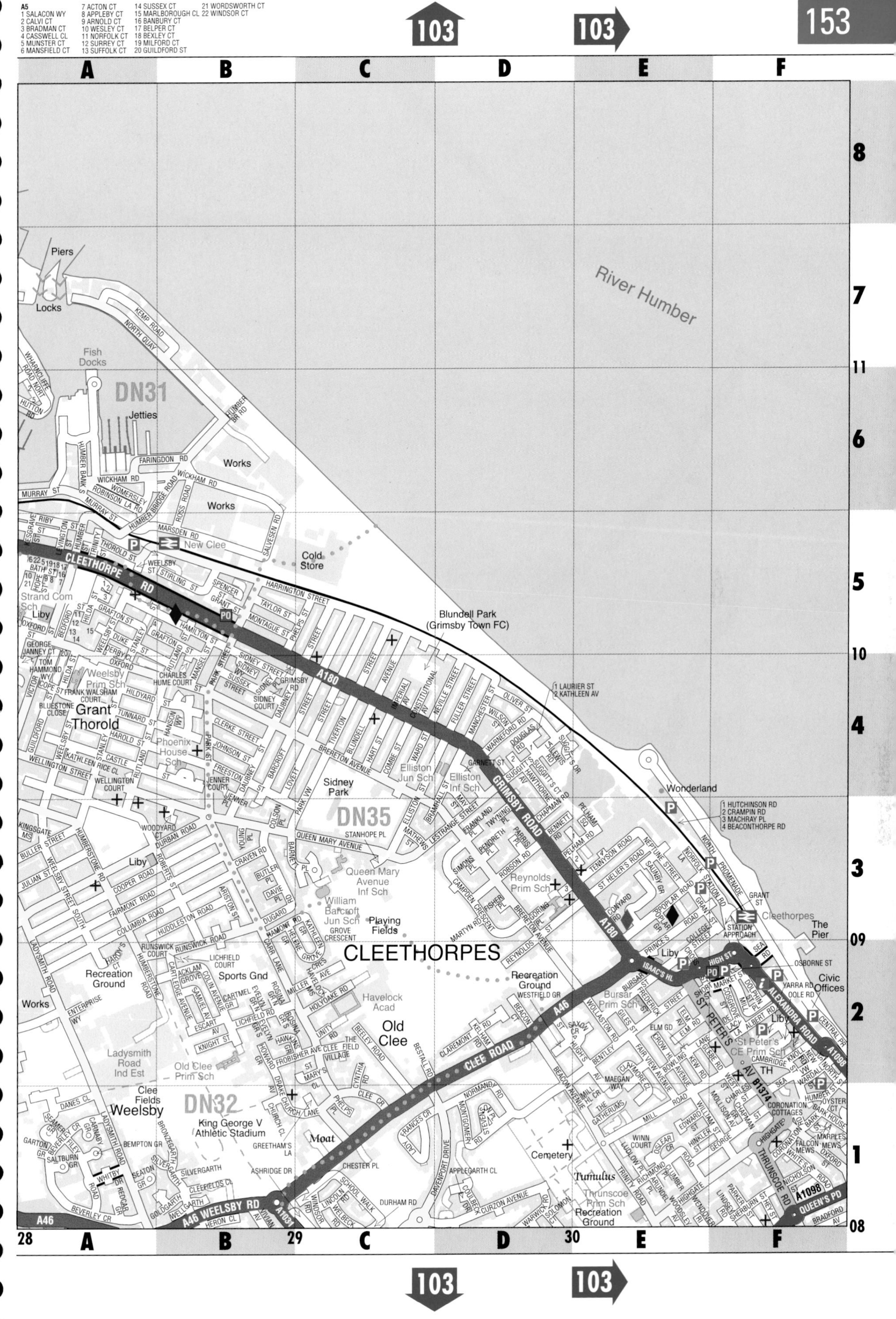
A5
1 SALACON WY
2 CALVI CT
3 BRADMAN CT
4 CASSWELL CL
5 MUNSTER CT
6 MANSFIELD CT
7 ACTON CT
8 APPLEBY CT
9 ARNOLD CT
10 WESLEY CT
11 NORFOLK CT
12 SURREY CT
13 SUFFOLK CT
14 SUSSEX CT
15 MARLBOROUGH CL
16 BANBURY CT
17 BELPER CT
18 BEXLEY CT
19 MILFORD CT
20 GUILDFORD ST
21 WORDSWORTH CT
22 WINDSOR CT
103
103
A
B
C
D
E
F
8
7
11
6
5
10
4
3
09
2
1
08
28
29
30
River Humber
Piers
Locks
Fish Docks
DN31
Jetties
Works
Works
New Clee
Cold Store
Blundell Park (Grimsby Town FC)
CLEETHORPE RD
A180
GRIMSBY ROAD
Strand Com Sch
Weelsby Prim Sch
Grant Thorold
Phoenix House Sch
Sidney Park
DN35
Elliston Jun Sch
Elliston Inf Sch
Queen Mary Avenue Inf Sch
William Barcroft Jun Sch
Playing Fields
Reynolds Prim Sch
CLEETHORPES
Wonderland
1 LAURIER ST
2 KATHLEEN AV
1 HUTCHINSON RD
2 CRAMPIN RD
3 MACHRAY PL
4 BEACONTHORPE RD
NORTH PROMENADE
Cleethorpes
The Pier
Civic Offices
ALEXANDRA ROAD
Recreation Ground
Sports Gnd
Havelock Acad
Old Clee
Bursar Prim Sch
St Peter's CE Prim Sch
CLEE ROAD
A46
Ladysmith Road Ind Est
Old Clee Prim Sch
Clee Fields
Weelsby
DN32
King George V Athletic Stadium
Moat
Cemetery
Tumulus
Thrunscoe Prim Sch
Recreation Ground
A46 WEELSBY RD
A1098
QUEEN'S PD
B1374
Works
Liby

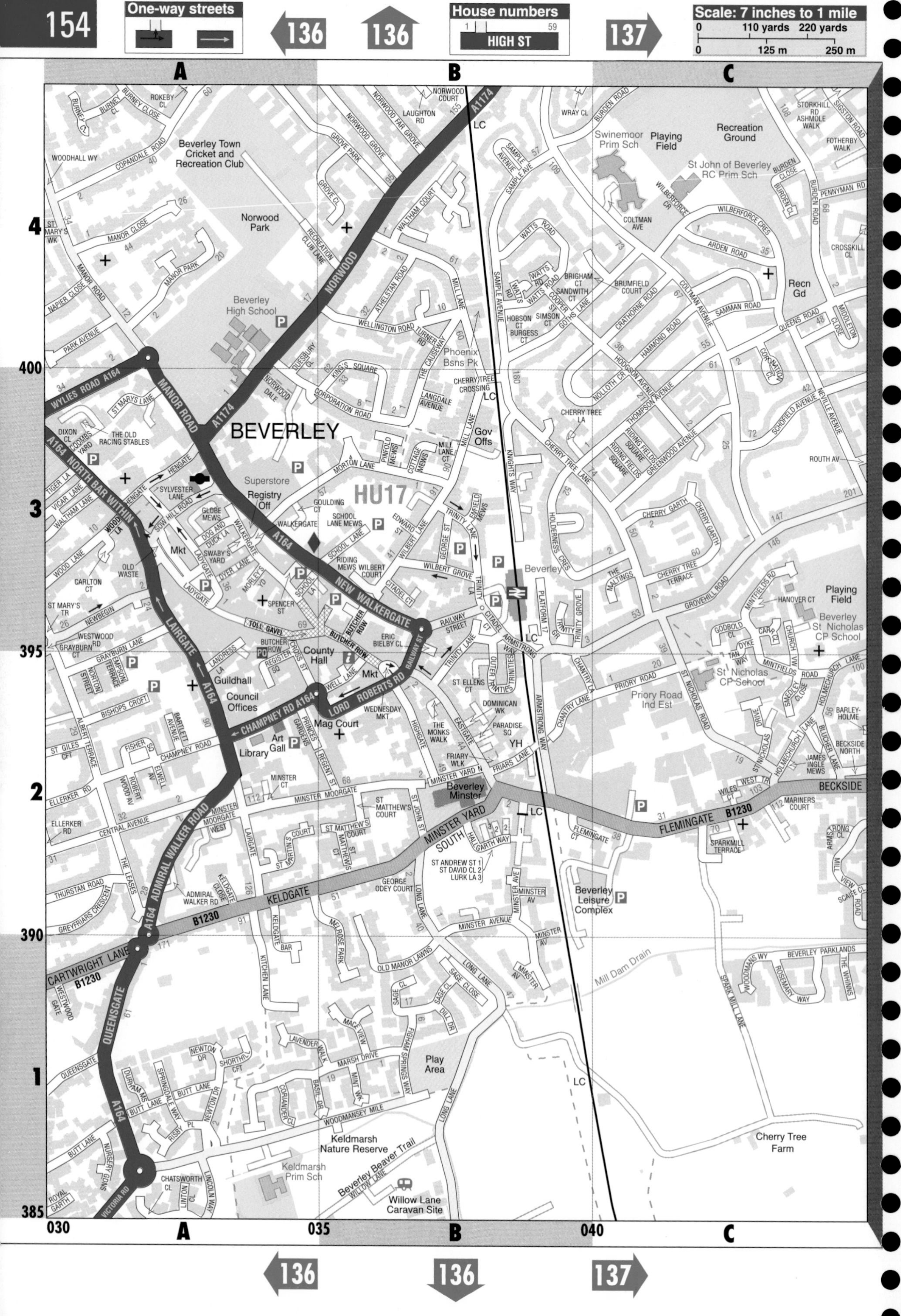
One-way streets
136
136
House numbers
1
59
HIGH ST
137
Scale: 7 inches to 1 mile
0
110 yards
220 yards
0
125 m
250 m
A
B
C
4
3
2
1
400
395
390
385
030
035
040
BEVERLEY
HU17
Beverley Town Cricket and Recreation Club
Norwood Park
Beverley High School
Swinemoor Prim Sch
Playing Field
Recreation Ground
St John of Beverley RC Prim Sch
Recn Gd
Phoenix Bsns Pk
Gov Offs
Superstore
Registry Off
Mkt
Guildhall
Council Offices
County Hall
Library
Art Gall
Mag Court
Beverley
Beverley Minster
YH
Priory Road Ind Est
St Nicholas CP School
Beverley St Nicholas CP School
Beverley Leisure Complex
Play Area
Keldmarsh Nature Reserve
Keldmarsh Prim Sch
Beverley Beaver Trail
Willow Lane Caravan Site
Cherry Tree Farm
Mill Dam Drain
LC
NORWOOD
A1174
MANOR ROAD
WYLIES ROAD A164
A164 NORTH BAR WITHIN
NEW WALKERGATE
A164
LAIRGATE
CHAMPNEY RD A164
LORD ROBERTS RD
RAILWAY ST
ADMIRAL WALKER ROAD
KELDGATE
B1230
CARTWRIGHT LANE
QUEENSGATE
MINSTER YARD SOUTH
FLEMINGATE
BECKSIDE
ARMSTRONG WAY
TOLL GAVEL
BUTCHER ROW
WEDNESDAY MKT
HIGHGATE
EASTGATE
WILBERFORCE CRES
ARDEN ROAD
SAMMAN ROAD
QUEENS ROAD
COLTMAN AVENUE
CHERRY TREE LANE
GROVEHILL ROAD
PRIORY ROAD
ST NICHOLAS ROAD
CHANTRY LANE
HOLMECHURCH LANE
MINSTER AVENUE
LONG LANE
MARSH DRIVE
WOODMANSEY MILE
BUTT LANE
VICTORIA RD
SPARK MILL LANE
BEVERLEY PARKLANDS

136
136
137

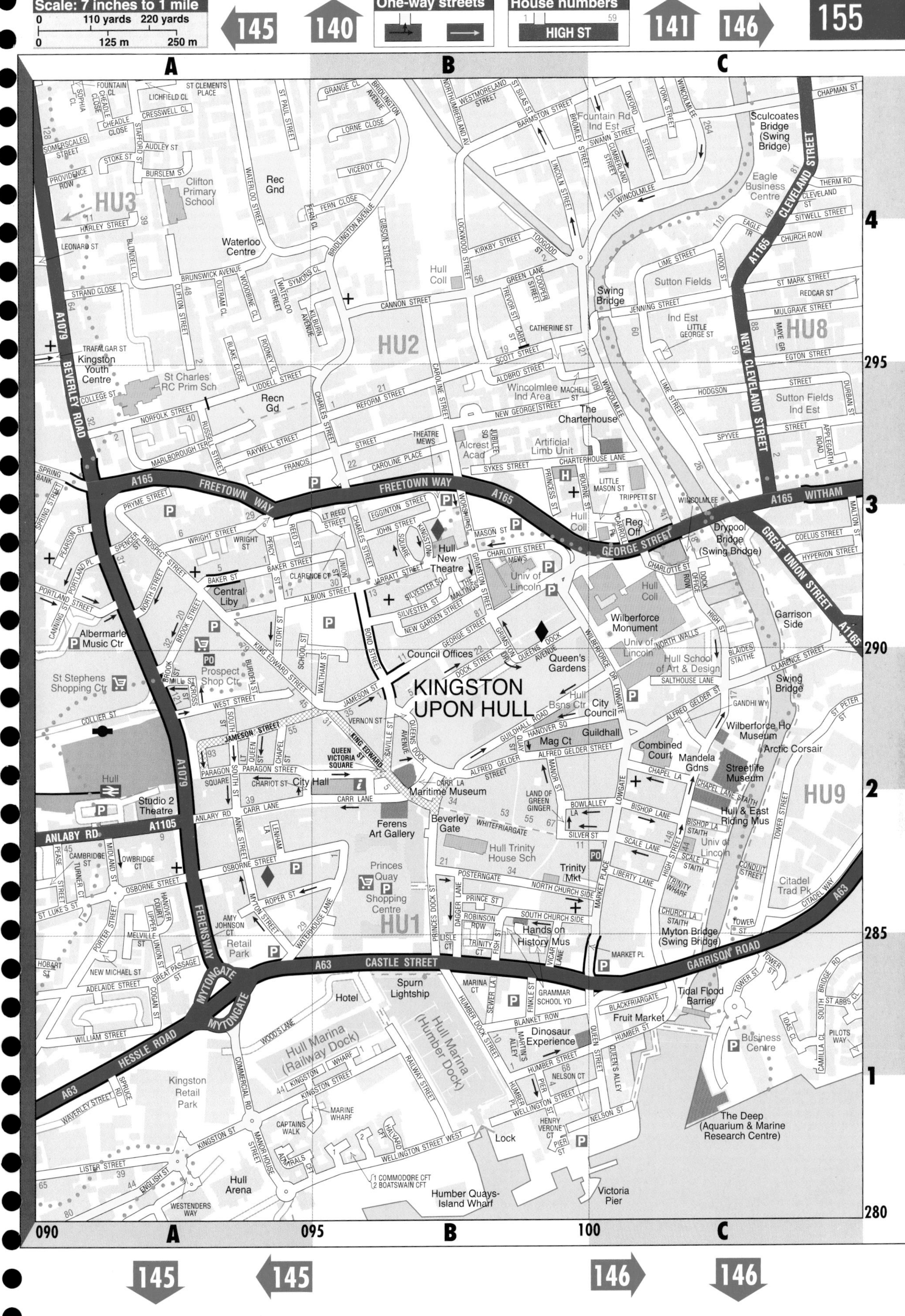
Scale: 7 inches to 1 mile
110 yards 220 yards
125 m 250 m
One-way streets
House numbers
HIGH ST
145
140
141
146
KINGSTON UPON HULL
HU1
HU2
HU3
HU8
HU9
FREETOWN WAY
BEVERLEY ROAD
FERENSWAY
CASTLE STREET
GARRISON ROAD
GEORGE STREET
NEW CLEVELAND STREET
GREAT UNION STREET
HESSLE ROAD
ANLABY RD
Hull Marina (Railway Dock)
Hull Marina (Humber Dock)
The Deep (Aquarium & Marine Research Centre)
Maritime Museum
Ferens Art Gallery
Princes Quay Shopping Centre
Guildhall
City Hall
Hull New Theatre
Wilberforce Monument
Queen's Gardens
Victoria Pier
Humber Quays-Island Wharf
Hull Arena
Kingston Retail Park
145
145
146
146

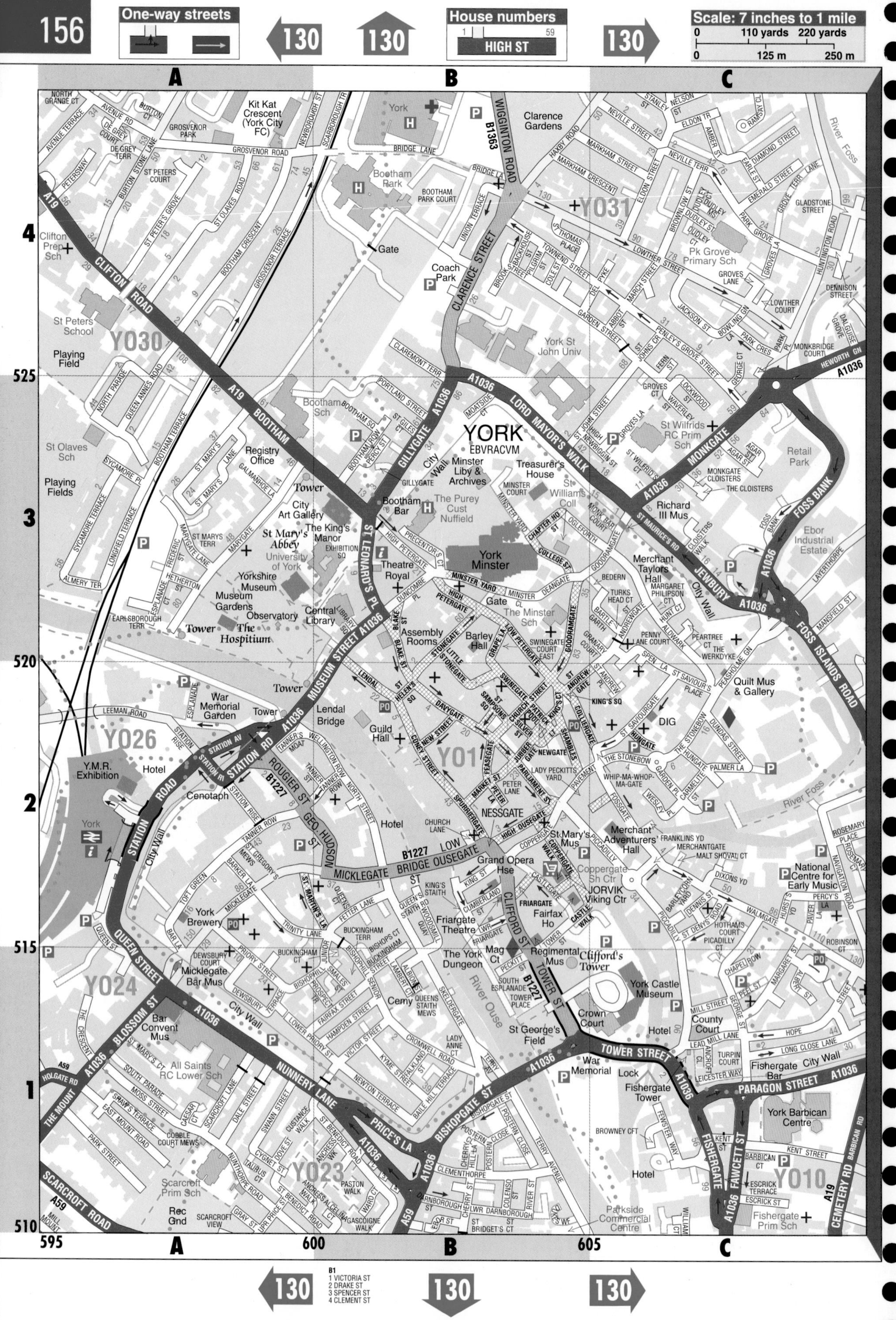

One-way streets

House numbers
1 | 59
HIGH ST

Scale: 7 inches to 1 mile
0   110 yards   220 yards
0   125 m   250 m

130 | 130 | 130

Index

Place name May be abbreviated on the map

Location number Present when a number indicates the place's position in a crowded area of mapping

Locality, town or village Shown when more than one place has the same name

Postcode district District for the indexed place

Page and grid square Page number and grid reference for the standard mapping

Church Rd 6 Beckenham BR2..........53 C6

Cities, towns and villages are listed in CAPITAL LETTERS

Public and commercial buildings are highlighted in magenta   **Places of interest** are highlighted in blue with a star★

Abbreviations used in the index

Acad	Academy	Comm	Common	Gd	Ground	L	Leisure	Prom	Promenade
App	Approach	Cott	Cottage	Gdn	Garden	La	Lane	Rd	Road
Arc	Arcade	Cres	Crescent	Gn	Green	Liby	Library	Recn	Recreation
Ave	Avenue	Cswy	Causeway	Gr	Grove	Mdw	Meadow	Ret	Retail
Bglw	Bungalow	Ct	Court	H	Hall	Meml	Memorial	Sh	Shopping
Bldg	Building	Ctr	Centre	Ho	House	Mkt	Market	Sq	Square
Bsns, Bus	Business	Ctry	Country	Hospl	Hospital	Mus	Museum	St	Street
Bvd	Boulevard	Cty	County	HQ	Headquarters	Orch	Orchard	Sta	Station
Cath	Cathedral	Dr	Drive	Hts	Heights	Pal	Palace	Terr	Terrace
Cir	Circus	Dro	Drove	Ind	Industrial	Par	Parade	TH	Town Hall
Cl	Close	Ed	Education	Inst	Institute	Pas	Passage	Univ	University
Cnr	Corner	Emb	Embankment	Int	International	Pk	Park	Wk, Wlk	Walk
Coll	College	Est	Estate	Intc	Interchange	Pl	Place	Wr	Water
Com	Community	Ex	Exhibition	Junc	Junction	Prec	Precinct	Yd	Yard

Index of towns, villages, streets, hospitals, industrial estates, railway stations, schools, shopping centres, universities and places of interest

Akeferry Rd *continued*
Westwoodside DN9 . . . . . . 105 B2
Akester Cl 4 HU17 . . . . . . 137 B3
Alan Cres DN15 . . . . 150 F6
Alaska St HU8 . . . . 141 B1
Alba Cl DN17 . . . . 150 D1
Albany St
Gainsborough DN21 . . . . . 117 B1
Kingston upon Hull HU3 . . 145 D8
3 York YO26 . . . . 129 F5
Albany Villas HU13 . . . . . . 144 A1
Albatross Dr DN37 . . . . . . 102 A4
Albemarle Cl 5 HU15 . . . . 68 B5
Albemarle Rd
Bilton HU11 . . . . 58 A3
2 Keyingham HU12 . . . . . . 73 C4
York YO23 . . . . 130 B2
Albemarle St 2 HU3 . . . . 145 B5
Albermarle Music Ctr*
HU2 . . . . 155 A2
Alberta Cres 7 DN17 . . . . . 96 C2
Albert Ave HU3 . . . . 145 A7
Albert Avenue Pools
HU3 . . . . 145 A7
Albert Cl
4 Grimsby DN32 . . . . 152 F5
1 York YO32 . . . . 130 F8
Albertine Ct 5 DN37 . . . . 113 D7
Albert Marson Ct DN16 . . 151 B6
Albert Pl 3 DN32 . . . . 152 F5
Albert Rd
Cleethorpes DN35 . . . . 153 F2
Scunthorpe DN16 . . . . 151 A1
Albert St
10 Bridlington YO15 . . . . . 122 E2
Brigg DN20 . . . . 98 C2
Goole DN14 . . . . 149 C2
5 New Holland DN19 . . . . . 70 E2
3 Thorne/Moorends DN8 . . 93 B8
York YO10 . . . . 156 C1
Albert Street E DN32 . . . . 152 F5
Albert Street W DN32 . . . 152 F5
Albert Terr
Beverley HU17 . . . . 154 A2
Kingston upon Hull HU7 . . 141 D6
Welwick HU12 . . . . 90 A7
Albery Way DN36 . . . . 114 A8
Albina Garth 1 HU12 . . . . 72 D7
Albion Ave YO26 . . . . 129 B6
Albion Ct
Beverley HU17 . . . . 137 B4
Kingston upon Hull HU4 . . 144 B6
Albion Hill DN9 . . . . 105 E6
Albion La HU10 . . . . 138 A3
Albion Pk DN16 . . . . 151 D5
Albion St
Great Driffield YO25 . . . . . 124 F3
Grimsby DN32 . . . . 152 F4
Kingston upon Hull HU1 . . 155 A3
York YO1 . . . . 156 B1
Albion Terr
Bridlington YO15 . . . . 122 F3
Misterton DN10 . . . . 116 D5
Albourne Ave DN15 . . . . . 151 A6
Albright Cl 31 YO42 . . . . . . 29 A3
Alcelina Ct YO23 . . . . 156 B1
Alcrest Acad HU2 . . . . 155 B3
Alcuin Ave YO10 . . . . 131 A4
Alcuin Way YO10 . . . . 131 B2
Aldam Dr DN9 . . . . 94 F1
Aldborough Gr HU9 . . . . . . 142 A2
Aldborough Way YO26 . . . 129 F5
Aldbro' St HU2 . . . . 155 B3
ALDBROUGH 47 C1
Aldbrough La HU11 . . . . . . 59 A6
Aldbrough Prim Sch
HU11 . . . . 47 C1
Aldbrough Rd
East Garton HU11 . . . . 59 D7
Withernwick HU11 . . . . 46 E3
Alden Cl DN40 . . . . 87 C1
Aldenham Pk HU7 . . . . 56 E5
Alder Cl
16 Brough HU15 . . . . 68 D5
Selby YO8 . . . . 148 D2
Alder Gr 6 DN8 . . . . 79 B2
Alder Hey Dr 9 HU9 . . . . . 142 A5
Alderley Ct YO32 . . . . 127 E3
Alderley Edge 6 DN37 . . 113 D6
Alderman Cogan CE Prim
Sch 16 HU9 . . . . 141 F2
Aldermans Way 10 YO25 . . 34 B2
Alderney Way 2 DN40 . . . 101 C8
Alderson Ct YO16 . . . . 122 D2
Alderson Mews 5 HU9 . . 146 C7
Alders The 22 DN21 . . . . . 117 C1
Aldersyde YO24 . . . . 132 E7
Aldersyde Ct YO24 . . . . . . 132 E7
Aldersyde Mews YO24 . . . 132 E7
Alder View 22 DN33 . . . . . 102 C2
Alder Way YO32 . . . . 127 D2
Aldreth Gr YO23 . . . . 130 C2
Aldrich Rd DN35 . . . . 103 C2
Aldwark YO1 . . . . 156 C3
Aldwych Croft 6 DN36 . . 114 A7
Aldwych Ct HU5 . . . . 144 E8
Alexander Ave YO31 . . . . . 127 E2
Alexander Rd DN16 . . . . . 151 B6
Alexandra Ct
4 Bridlington YO15 . . . . . 122 F3
York YO10 . . . . 130 E4
Alexandra Dock N DN31 . 152 C6
Alexandra Dock Ret Pk
DN31 . . . . 152 D5
Alexandra Dr
1 Beverley HU17 . . . . 55 E8
5 Bridlington YO15 . . . . . 122 F3
Alexandra Prom YO15 . . . 123 A3
Alexandra Rd
Cleethorpes DN35 . . . . 153 F2
Grimsby DN31 . . . . 152 D4
Hornsea HU18 . . . . 134 D4
Kingston upon Hull HU5 . . 140 C3
Scunthorpe DN16 . . . . 151 B2
Strensall YO32 . . . . 14 A6
Thorne/Moorends DN8 . . . . 79 B2
Alexandra Road N DN40 . . 87 D3
Alexandra Road S DN40 . . 87 D2
Alexandra St
Goole DN14 . . . . 149 D4
Kingston upon Hull HU3 . . 145 D7
Thorne DN8 . . . . 79 A1
Alexandra Wlk YO15 . . . . 122 F3
Alfonso St 5 HU3 . . . . 145 B5
Alfred Bean Hospl YO25 125 A6
Alfred Gelder St HU1 . . . . 155 B2
Alfred St
Gainsborough DN21 . . . . . 117 B1
Grimsby DN31 . . . . 152 D4
Kingston upon Hull HU3 . . 145 D5
Alfreton Ct 1 DN15 . . . . . 150 B6
Alfriston Cl HU7 . . . . 141 B6
Algarth Rd
Pocklington YO42 . . . . 29 A4
York YO31 . . . . 131 B7
Algarth Rise
Pocklington YO42 . . . . 28 F4
York YO31 . . . . 131 B7
Algernon St DN32 . . . . 152 F1
Alison Garth 29 HU12 . . . . . 72 D7
ALKBOROUGH 82 C8
Alkborough Flats* DN15 . 67 B1
Alkborough La DN15 . . . . . 82 D7
Alkborough Prim Sch
DN15 . . . . 82 C8
Alkborough Turf Maze
(Julian Bower)* DN15 . . 82 B8
Allanby St DN15 . . . . 151 A7
Allanhall Way HU10 . . . . . 143 B8
Allanson Dr HU16 . . . . 139 D5
Allanson Gr YO24 . . . . 129 E2
Allan St 2 YO30 . . . . 130 C7
Allderidge Ave HU5 . . . . . 140 B3
Allenby Ave DN34 . . . . 152 A2
Allenby Cres LN11 . . . . . . 121 D3
Allen Cl YO10 . . . . 131 A4
Allendale YO24 . . . . 132 D8
Allerford Dr 8 HU7 . . . . . . 57 A5
ALLERTHORPE 28 E2
Allerthorpe Comm Nature
Reserve* YO42 . . . . 28 B2
Allerthorpe Lakeland Pk*
YO42 . . . . 28 E1
Allerton Dr
1 Immingham DN40 . . . . . 87 C1
22 Poppleton YO26 . . . . 12 F1
Allerton Prim Sch 37
DN40 . . . . 87 B1
Allestree Dr 2 DN33 . . . . 113 E8
All Hallows Rd 3 HU17 . . . 55 B7
Alliance Ave HU3 . . . . 144 F7
Alliance La HU3 . . . . 144 F7
Allington Dr
Great Coates DN31 . . . . . . 102 C5
York YO31 . . . . 131 B6
Allinson Yd HU17 . . . . 45 A7
Allison Cl DN17 . . . . 107 D7
Allison La
14 Flamborough YO15 . . . . . 5 A2
Ulrome YO25 . . . . 22 F4
Alloa Cl 2 HU6 . . . . 140 B8
Allotment La YO25 . . . . . . 124 E5
Allotment Wlk YO16 . . . . . 122 B1
All Saints Cl
4 Kingston upon Hull
HU13 . . . . 69 F4
11 Waltham DN37 . . . . . . 113 E6
All Saints Ct 6 YO43 . . . . 135 D4
All Saints Mews HU12 . . . . 58 C1
All Saints RC Lower Sch
YO23 . . . . 156 A1
All Saints RC Upper School
YO29 . . . . 130 B2
All Saints' St HU3 . . . . . . 145 D8
Alma Cl HU10 . . . . 143 D7
Alma Gr YO10 . . . . 130 D2
Alma St
6 Kingston upon Hull
HU9 . . . . 146 B7
4 Withernsea HU19 . . . . . . 74 F7
Alma Terr
Selby YO8 . . . . 148 C6
York YO10 . . . . 130 D2
Almery Terr YO30 . . . . 156 A3
Almond Cl
Great Driffield YO25 . . . . . 124 F2
Hambleton YO8 . . . . 48 B1
Almond Gr
Brigg DN20 . . . . 98 B2
3 Kingston upon Hull
HU3 . . . . 145 D6
Scunthorpe DN16 . . . . 151 B4
York YO32 . . . . 127 D4
Almond Tree Ave DN14 . . . 63 C3
Almsford Dr YO26 . . . . 129 C5
Almsford Rd YO26 . . . . . . 129 C5
Alness Dr YO24 . . . . 132 B7
Alne Terr YO10 . . . . 130 E2
Alpha Ave HU17 . . . . 136 D6
Alpha Ct DN8 . . . . 92 F8
Alsenham Pk 9 HU7 . . . . . . 56 E5
Alston Ave 4 HU8 . . . . . . 141 B1
ALTHORPE 95 D4
Althorpe & Keadby Prim Sch
DN17 . . . . 95 D5
Althorpe Park 17 HU7 . . . . 56 E5
Althorpe Sta DN17 . . . . 95 D5
Altoft Cl
2 Brandesburton YO25 . . . 34 B2
12 Laceby DN37 . . . . 101 F1
Alton Park Mews YO25 . . . 22 C1
Alton Rd YO16 . . . . 122 D7
Altyre Way DN36 . . . . 103 B1
Alured Garth 9 HU12 . . . . 72 D7
Alveston Rd DN17 . . . . . . 150 D4
Alvingham Ave 25 DN35 . 103 C2
Alvingham Rd DN16 . . . . . 151 B3
Alvin Wlk 9 YO41 . . . . 27 B2
Alvis Gr YO10 . . . . 131 D4
Alwoodley Cl 1 HU8 . . . . 142 B5
Alwyne Dr YO30 . . . . 126 E1
Alwyne Gr YO30 . . . . 126 E1
Alwyn Rd 19 DN8 . . . . 93 B8
Amanda Cl HU6 . . . . 139 E6
Amanda Dr DN7 . . . . 92 D4
Ambaston Rd HU18 . . . . . 134 C5
Amber Ct YO31 . . . . 156 C4
Amberley Cl HU7 . . . . 141 B6
Amberly St 4 YO26 . . . . . 129 E5
Amber St YO31 . . . . 156 C4
Ambler's La YO30 . . . . 12 F7
Ambleside Ave YO10 . . . . 131 B4
Ambrey Cl 16 YO14 . . . . 2 F8
Ambrose Ave 1 DN7 . . . . . . 92 E4
Ambrose St YO10 . . . . 130 D1
Amcott Ave DN10 . . . . 116 D4
AMCOTTS 81 F1
Amcotts Rd 14 DN33 . . . . 102 D1
Amelia Ct 15 DN36 . . . . . . 114 D8
Amen La YO43 . . . . 53 D5
Amesbury Ave DN33 . . . . . 113 D8
Amethyst Ct 11 DN36 . . . . 114 A8
Amethyst La DN14 . . . . 65 F8
Amethyst Rd HU9 . . . . 142 C4
Amos Cl 9 DN33 . . . . 113 D8
Amos Cres DN16 . . . . 151 D3
Ampleforth Gr HU5 . . . . . 144 D8
Amsterdam Rd HU7 . . . . . 141 A5
Amwell Gn 8 DN7 . . . . 92 D3
Amy Johnson Ave YO16 . 122 E6
Amy Johnson Ct HU1 . . . . 155 A1
Amy Johnson Way YO30 . 127 A3
Amy St DN14 . . . . 149 C4
Anastasia Cl 1 DN21 . . . . 117 B2
Ancaster Ave
Grimsby DN33 . . . . 113 D8
Kingston upon Hull HU5 . . 139 F3
Ancaster Ct DN16 . . . . . . 151 A1
Ancholme Ave 10 DN40 . . . 87 B1
Ancholme Gdns 11 DN20 . 98 C2
Ancholme L Ctr DN20 . . . . 98 B1
Ancholme Rd DN16 . . . . . 151 D2
Ancholme Way DN20 . . . . . 98 B2
Anchorage St 7 DN20 . . . . 98 B2
Anchor Cl 31 DN8 . . . . 93 A8
Anchor Rd
Kingston upon Hull HU6 . . 140 C8
Scunthorpe DN16 . . . . 97 A3
Anchors Way 16 DN20 . . . . 98 B2
Ancient La DN7 . . . . 92 F3
Ancourt HU6 . . . . 139 E6
Ancress Wlk YO23 . . . . . . 156 A1
Ancroft Cl YO1 . . . . 156 C1
Anderby Dr DN37 . . . . 102 B4
Anderson Gr 6 YO24 . . . . 129 F2
Anderson Rd
Goole DN14 . . . . 149 A4
Scunthorpe DN16 . . . . 151 C3
Andersons Cl 17 HU12 . . . . 72 D7
Anderson St
7 Great Driffield YO25 . . . 124 F3
Grimsby DN31 . . . . 152 D3
Andrew Dr 4 YO32 . . . . . . 127 F1
Andrew La 3 HU12 . . . . . . 72 C7
Andrew Marvell Bsns & Ent
Coll HU9 . . . . 142 D4
Andrew Paddock DN20 . . 108 F5
Andrew Rd 11 DN36 . . . . . 114 D8
Andrew's Ct 15 YO42 . . . . . 28 F4
Andrews Rd DN18 . . . . 84 A7
Andrews Way 8 DN40 . . . . 87 B1
Angerstein Rd DN17 . . . . 150 F1
Anglesey Dr DN40 . . . . . . 101 C8
ANGRAM 24 C3
Angram Cl YO30 . . . . 126 F1
Angram La YO8 . . . . 49 A6
Angram Rd YO26 . . . . 24 A5
Angus Dr YO25 . . . . 124 D4
ANLABY 143 E5
Anlaby Acre Head Prim Sch
HU4 . . . . 144 B7
Anlaby Ave 7 HU4 . . . . . . 144 B6
Anlaby High Rd HU4 . . . . 144 C6
Anlaby House Est HU10 . . 143 E6
Anlaby Park Road N
HU4 . . . . 144 B5
Anlaby Park Road S HU4 144 B2
Anlaby Prim Sch HU10 . . . 144 A6
Anlaby Rd HU3 . . . . 155 A2
Anlafgate 7 HU10 . . . . 143 F6
Anlary Rd HU1 . . . . 155 A2
Annan Cl YO24 . . . . 132 C6
Annandale Rd
Kingston upon Hull HU9 . . 142 E2
Willerby HU10 . . . . 138 B1
Annerley Dr YO16 . . . . 123 A7
Annes Cres DN16 . . . . 151 C3
Annesley St DN31 . . . . . . 152 D5
Anne St
Kingston upon Hull HU1 . . 155 A2
Anne St *continued*
York YO23 . . . . 130 C2
Ann Gr DN35 . . . . 103 B2
Annie Med La HU15 . . . . . . 53 F1
Annie Reed Rd HU17 . . . . 137 C3
Annie Road Ct HU17 . . . . 137 C3
Annie St YO8 . . . . 148 C6
Anningson La 6 DN36 . . 114 A8
Annumhills Rd YO8 . . . . . . 50 D7
Ann Watson St HU7 . . . . . 141 A4
Anserdam La HU15 . . . . . . 52 C2
Anson Dr YO10 . . . . 133 D8
Anson Rd HU9 . . . . 142 B3
Antelope Rd DN18 . . . . 70 A1
Anthea Dr YO31 . . . . 127 E1
Antholme Cl HU7 . . . . 141 C6
Anthony's Bank Rd DN35 103 E1
Anthony Way 1 DN41 . . . . 101 D6
Antrim Way 4 DN33 . . . . . 102 E1
Antwerp Rd HU7 . . . . 141 A5
Anvil Wlk DN15 . . . . 82 F3
Apollo St 9 YO10 . . . . 130 E3
Apollo Wlk HU8 . . . . 141 F4
Apperston Ct 21 YO42 . . . . 29 A4
Appian Way DN31 . . . . 152 A6
Appin Cl 7 HU7 . . . . 57 A6
Apple Blossom Ct 8
YO24 . . . . 129 B1
APPLEBY 83 C1
Appleby Cl DN17 . . . . 150 F1
Appleby Ct 8 DN32 . . . . . 153 A5
Appleby Gdns DN20 . . . . . . 97 D4
Appleby Glade YO32 . . . . 127 D7
Appleby La
Broughton DN20 . . . . 97 D4
Burstwick HU12 . . . . 73 A7
Appleby Mill Rd DN16 . . . 151 E7
Appleby Pl 2 YO31 . . . . . . 131 A5
Apple Croft HU16 . . . . 138 B8
Applecroft Rd
Selby YO8 . . . . 148 A4
York YO31 . . . . 131 B7
Appledore Cl HU9 . . . . . . 146 C6
Applefields DN20 . . . . 98 D3
Applefields Sch YO31 . . . 131 B5
Applegarth 8 HU15 . . . . . . 66 D7
Apple Garth
21 Hedon HU12 . . . . 72 D7
15 Poppleton YO26 . . . . 12 F1
Applegarth Cl DN35 . . . . . 153 D1
Applegarth La
Bainton YO25 . . . . 31 E7
Bridlington YO16 . . . . 122 D4
Applegarth Mews 3
HU16 . . . . 139 B7
Applegarth Rd HU8 . . . . . 155 C3
Appleton Ct YO23 . . . . 132 F3
Appleton Gdns 8 HU15 . . . 53 F1
Appleton Prim Sch HU5 . 139 E2
Appleton Rd
Bishopthorpe YO23 . . . . . . 133 A3
Kingston upon Hull HU5 . . 139 E3
Appleton Way DN16 . . . . . 151 C2
Apple Tree Cl
Kingston upon Hull HU8 . . 141 D4
1 Long Riston/Arnold
HU11 . . . . 45 C5
Apple Tree Ct 1 DN41 . . . 101 F5
Apple Tree Garth 5
HU17 . . . . 45 A8
Appletree Mews HU10 . . . 138 C1
Apple Tree Wlk HU16 . . . . 139 D6
Appleyard Dr DN18 . . . . . . 84 E8
Arables La HU12 . . . . 74 C4
Arcade The DN14 . . . . 149 D4
Archbishop Cl HU9 . . . . . 142 D2
Archbishop Holgates Sch
YO10 . . . . 131 B3
Archbishop of York CE Jun
Sch YO23 . . . . 133 A4
Archbishop Sentamu Acad
HU9 . . . . 142 D3
Archer Rd DN37 . . . . 113 D6
Archers Cl DN20 . . . . 98 D4
Archibald Cl 16 YO42 . . . . . 28 F4
Archway The YO43 . . . . . . 135 D4
Arcon Dr HU4 . . . . 144 D6
Arctic Corsair* HU1 . . . . . 155 C2
Arden Ct HU5 . . . . 139 C2
Arden Rd HU17 . . . . 154 C4
Ardent Rd DN18 . . . . 70 A1
Arden Village 21 DN35 . . 103 C1
Ardmore Cl HU9 . . . . 142 B4
Arenhall Cl 2 YO32 . . . . . 127 C8
Argam Dikes*
Grindale YO25 . . . . 3 B2
Rudston YO25 . . . . 10 A7
Argam La YO25 . . . . 2 F1
Argent Cl 8 HU6 . . . . 140 B8
Arglam La YO43 . . . . 51 F6
Argyle Ct DN15 . . . . 151 A7
Argyle St
Goole DN14 . . . . 149 D4
Kingston upon Hull HU3 . . 145 C7
York YO23 . . . . 130 B1
Ariston St DN32 . . . . 153 B3
Arkley Cl 18 HU15 . . . . 68 C5
Ark Royal HU11 . . . . 142 E6
Arkwright St 10 DN21 . . . . 117 B1
Arkwright Way DN16 . . . . 151 F2
Arlington Ave HU16 . . . . . 139 B6
Arlington Rd YO30 . . . . . . 127 A1
Arlington St 2 HU3 . . . . . 145 D6
Armeria Dr 23 DN17 . . . . . . 96 D1
Armour Rd DN16 . . . . 151 E7
Armoury Rd YO8 . . . . 148 B5
Armstrong Cl HU17 . . . . . 154 C2
Armstrong Place E DN31 152 C5
Armstrong Place W
DN31 . . . . 152 C5
Armstrong St DN31 . . . . . 152 C5
Armstrong Way
Beverley HU17 . . . . 154 B2
Rawcliffe YO32 . . . . 126 E3
Armthorpe La DN3 . . . . 92 A3
Arncliffe Cl 1 HU7 . . . . 56 F6
Arncliffe Way HU16 . . . . . 139 A5
ARNOLD 45 C4
Arnold Cl DN37 . . . . 101 F2
Arnold Ct 9 DN32 . . . . 153 A5
Arnold La HU3 . . . . 145 B6
Arnold Lane E HU11 . . . . . 45 C5
Arnold Lane W HU11 . . . . . 45 C4
Arnold St HU3 . . . . 145 B6
Arnside Pl 2 YO10 . . . . . . 130 F3
ARRAM 44 A7
Arram Gr HU6 . . . . 139 E5
Arram Rd HU17 . . . . 43 D6
Arram Sta HU17 . . . . 43 F7
Arran Cl
Immingham DN40 . . . . 101 C8
Kingston upon Hull HU9 . . 142 A4
19 New Waltham DN36 . . . 114 A8
Arrandale DN21 . . . . 107 C4
Arran Pl YO31 . . . . 130 D7
Arras Dr HU16 . . . . 138 E6
Arreton Cl HU8 . . . . 142 D6
Art College Mews DN32 . 152 F4
Arthur Lucan Ct HU9 . . . . 142 C1
Arthur Pl 6 YO30 . . . . 126 B5
Arthur Rd 12 DN21 . . . . . . 117 B1
Arthur St
Grimsby DN31 . . . . 152 C4
Kingston upon Hull HU3 . . 145 A5
Withernsea HU19 . . . . 74 F7
York YO10 . . . . 130 E4
Arundel Cl
4 Gainsborough DN21 . . . 117 C1
Kingston upon Hull HU9 . . 146 C8
Arundel Gr YO24 . . . . 132 C7
Arundel Pl DN35 . . . . 153 E1
Arundel Rd 5 DN6 . . . . 76 E2
Arundel Wlk DN34 . . . . . . 152 A3
Ascot Rd
23 Waltham DN37 . . . . 113 D6
Wigginton YO32 . . . . 13 D5
Ascott Cl
Beverley HU17 . . . . 136 E7
Kingston upon Hull HU4 . . 144 D5
Ascot Way YO24 . . . . 129 D1
Asenby Wlk HU5 . . . . 139 D3
Asgard Way 5 DN33 . . . . . 102 D1
Ash Ave HU15 . . . . 68 C6
Ashberry Dr
Messingham DN17 . . . . 107 D7
1 Scunthorpe DN16 . . . . . 151 B2
Ashbourne 7 DN37 . . . . . . 113 D6
Ashbourne Ct DN15 . . . . . 150 B7
Ashbourne Way YO24 . . . 132 C8
Ashburnham Cl 4 DN6 . . . 76 F2
Ashburnham Rd 14 DN8 . . 93 A8
Ashburnham Wlk 5 DN6 . 76 F2
Ashbury Ct HU6 . . . . 140 A6
ASHBY 151 B1
Ashby Cl
Grimsby DN37 . . . . 102 B4
Holton le Clay DN36 . . . . . 114 B5
Kingston upon Hull HU4 . . 144 B7
ASHBY CUM FENBY 113 D3
Ashby High St DN16 . . . . . 151 A2
ASHBY HILL 113 C3
Ashby Hill DN37 . . . . 113 C3
Ashby La DN37 . . . . 113 C4
Ashby Rd
Cleethorpes DN35 . . . . 103 B2
Kingston upon Hull HU4 . . 144 B4
Scunthorpe DN16 . . . . 151 A5
Ash Cl
Hessle HU13 . . . . 143 C3
Newton on Derwent YO41 . . 27 E4
Sproatley HU11 . . . . 58 D5
York YO31 . . . . 131 B7
Ashcombe Rd HU7 . . . . 56 E5
Ashcourt Cl HU18 . . . . 134 C5
Ashcourt Dr HU18 . . . . 134 B5
Ash Ct 13 DN35 . . . . 103 B1
Ashdale Pk 14 HU14 . . . . . . 69 A5
Ashdale Rd 19 YO19 . . . . . . 26 F7
Ash Dell DN14 . . . . 149 E6
Ash Dene 7 HU17 . . . . 55 D8
Ashdene Cl HU10 . . . . 143 E7
Ashdown Ave DN15 . . . . . 150 E8
Ashdown Cl DN20 . . . . 98 D2
Ashdown Way
Gringley on the Hill
DN10 . . . . 116 A1
Misterton DN10 . . . . 116 C5
Ash Dr
Kingston upon Hull HU10 . 143 F8
Scalby HU15 . . . . 66 D7
Thorngumbald HU12 . . . . . . 72 E5
Ashendon Dr HU8 . . . . 141 A2
Ashfield YO43 . . . . 40 A1
Ashfield Ave 1 DN8 . . . . . . 93 A7
Ashfield Ct
Crowle DN17 . . . . 94 D7
York YO24 . . . . 132 E7
Ashfield Gr 6 DN7 . . . . 92 C6
Ashfield Pk DN17 . . . . 150 B2
Ashfield Rd
Hatfield DN7 . . . . 92 C4
Thorne DN8 . . . . 92 F7
Ashford Pl YO24 . . . . 129 D2
Ashford Wlk HU9 . . . . 142 E1
Ashgate Rd HU10 . . . . 138 E2

Barrow Rd
Barrow upon Humber DN19... 70 E1
Barton-upon-Humber DN18. 85 A8
New Holland DN19... 70 E2
The Hallands DN18... 85 F7
BARROW UPON HUMBER... 85 D7
Barry Ave DN34... 102 C2
Barstow Ave YO10... 130 F3
Bartholomew Ave DN14. 149 B5
Bartindale Rd YO14... 3 A5
Bartle Garth YO1... 156 C3
Bartlett Ave HU17... 154 A2
Bartlett Cl 9 HU12... 58 D1
Barton Dr HU13... 143 D1
Barton La DN19... 85 C8
Barton-on-Humber Sta DN18... 69 F1
Barton Rd
Caenby Corner Estate DN21... 119 C1
Wrawby DN20... 98 D3
Barton St Peters CE Prim Sch DN18... 69 F1
Bartons Garth YO8... 148 B2
Barton St
Barrow upon Humber DN19... 85 D8
Irby DN37... 112 F7
Keelby DN41... 101 A4
Wyham cum Cadeby DN36. 120 F7
BARTON-UPON-HUMBER... 84 D7
BARTON WATERSIDE... 69 F2
Bartrams HU15... 68 D6
Barwick Parade Prim Sch YO8... 148 E4
Barwic Par YO8... 148 E4
Base Youth Arts Ctr The DN15... 151 B7
Basic Slag Rd DN16... 151 E6
Basil Dr HU17... 154 A1
Baslow Rd DN15... 150 B6
Bassett Cl
1 Broughton DN20... 97 E3
Selby YO8... 148 C3
Bassett Rd 2 DN35... 103 D2
Bate La DN14... 78 A4
Bateson Cl YO10... 131 C1
Bath St DN32... 153 A5
Bathurst St 8 HU3... 145 D5
Batley Cl HU9... 142 C2
Battersea Cl HU8... 141 F5
Battery Rd HU12... 72 A4
Battery St DN40... 87 C1
Battleflats Way YO41... 15 D2
Battle Gn DN9... 105 D7
Batty La 7 DN14... 65 A7
Bawtry Cl YO8... 148 D3
Bawtry Rd
Hatfield DN7... 92 F3
Selby YO8... 148 D3
Baxter Gate HU12... 72 D7
Bayard St DN21... 117 B1
Baylegate 6 YO16... 122 D4
Bayle Mus* YO16... 122 D4
Baynard Ave HU16... 139 A6
Baynes Ct YO8... 148 A2
Bayons Ave 13 DN33... 113 D8
Bay Prim Sch YO16... 122 E4
Baysdale HU7... 140 F6
Baysdale Ave YO10... 131 D3
Baysdale Rd DN16... 151 D1
Baysgarth House Mus* DN18... 84 F8
Baysgarth L Ctr DN18... 84 F8
Baysgarth Sch DN18... 84 F8
Baysgarth View DN18... 84 F7
Bayswater Ct HU8... 141 E5
Bayswater Pl 2 DN33... 113 D8
Baytree Ave DN34... 152 A2
Bay View Ave HU18... 134 C6
Beach Holt La DN37... 101 D2
Beacon Ave
14 Barton-upon-Humber DN18... 84 E8
Cleethorpes DN35... 153 D2
Beacon Cl 5 HU13... 69 F4
Beacon Ct DN32... 153 D2
Beacon Hill* DN10... 116 A1
Beacon Hill Rd DN10... 116 A1
Beacon La YO25... 21 B8
Beacon Rd
Bridlington YO16... 123 A6
Millington YO42... 17 B1
Beaconsfield HU19... 74 F6
Beaconsfield Mews YO24... 129 D3
Beaconsfield Prom YO15 122 F3
Beaconsfield St
1 Kingston upon Hull HU5... 140 D2
6 Sculcoates HU5... 140 D2
York YO24... 129 D3
Beaconthorpe Rd DN35.. 153 E3
Beacon View YO43... 40 B1
Beadlam Mews HU5... 139 E4
Beadle Garth YO23... 132 B2
Beaford Ct DN17... 150 C4
Beagle Cl 12 DN20... 97 E4
Beagle Croft YO41... 15 C1
Beagle Ridge Dr YO24... 129 C1
Beagle Spinney YO41... 15 C1
BEAL... 61 D4
Bealey's La YO25... 32 B1
Beal La
Beal DN14... 61 D4
Cridling Stubbs WF11... 61 C1
Beamsley Way 18 HU7... 56 F5
Bean Gdns 3 DN14... 78 C8
Beanland La YO32... 14 D2
Bean St HU3... 145 C6
Bean's Way YO31... 131 B8
Bearwood Cl HU9... 142 B6
Beatty Ave 13 DN33... 113 E8
Beauchamp St DN16... 151 B5
Beauchamp Wlk DN16... 151 B6
Beauchief Gdns DN16... 151 A4
Beaufort Ave HU18... 134 C2
Beaufort Cl
Kingston upon Hull HU3.. 145 D6
York YO10... 131 B3
Beaufort Cres 5 DN35... 103 B1
Beaufort St 5 DN21... 117 B2
Beaulahland 2 DN18... 84 A7
Beaulah Villas 1 DN18... 84 A7
Beaulieu Cl 1 YO32... 127 F5
Beaulieu Ct
Bridlington YO16... 122 F7
5 Kingston upon Hull HU9... 142 A3
Beaumonde 5 DN36... 114 A5
Beaumont Ct
Goole DN14... 149 B6
3 Kingston upon Hull HU9... 146 D7
Beaumont Pl YO8... 148 A2
Beautiman Ct HU6... 140 A5
Beaverdyke YO30... 126 F1
Beaver Rd HU17... 137 B4
Beccles Cl HU8... 142 B6
Beck Bank HU16... 139 C6
Beck Cl
6 Elvington YO41... 27 B2
14 Howden DN14... 65 B7
Keelby DN41... 101 A4
Beckdale 4 HU7... 141 A6
Beckett Ave DN21... 117 C1
Beckett Dr YO10... 131 D4
Beck Farm Mews DN37.. 113 B6
Beckfield La YO26... 129 B5
Beckfield Pl YO26... 129 B4
Beck Garth 12 HU12... 72 D7
Beck Hill
6 Barton-upon-Humber DN18... 84 F8
1 Bridlington YO15... 122 E2
Beckhole Cl HU3... 145 A6
Beckhythe Cl DN33... 102 F1
BECKINGHAM... 116 D1
Beckingham Rd DN10... 116 D2
Beckington Cl 1 HU8... 142 C7
Beck La
Appleby DN15... 83 D1
5 Barrow upon Humber DN19... 85 D8
Broughton DN20... 97 E3
Easington HU12... 90 F6
Redbourne DN21... 108 F2
Scunthorpe DN16... 96 D2
Wheldrake YO19... 38 A8
Becklands Park Ind Est YO43... 135 C4
Beck Rd
Cottingham HU16... 138 E6
North Cave HU15... 53 D2
Willerby HU10... 138 D1
Beck Row YO41... 16 D5
Becks Cl 5 YO32... 127 C8
Beckside
Beverley HU17... 154 C2
4 Brough HU15... 68 D6
7 Elvington YO41... 27 B2
Hornsea HU18... 134 C3
Rothwell LN7... 111 F2
Stillingfleet YO19... 36 D3
Wilberfoss YO41... 27 F6
Beck Side
Barmby Moor YO42... 28 D3
Great Driffield YO25... 124 F4
Hibaldstow DN20... 108 F5
Beckside Cl
4 Humberston DN35... 103 C1
Kingston upon Hull HU6.. 140 B7
Beckside Ct HU17... 137 C3
Beckside Gdns YO10... 130 F4
Beckside Manor HU12... 60 B1
Beckside N HU17... 154 C2
Becks La DN21... 107 A3
Beck St HU12... 90 F6
Beck View 14 YO42... 29 A3
Beck View Rd HU17... 137 C4
Beckwith Cl YO31... 131 C7
Beckwith Hall Dr 7 YO19 49 A8
Beck Wlk 7 DN35... 103 C1
Bedale Ave
Kingston upon Hull HU9.. 141 E1
York YO10... 131 D4
Bedale Ct YO43... 135 E3
Bedale Mews 31 HU15... 68 C5
Bedale Pl 28 DN35... 103 C2
Bedale Rd
Market Weighton YO43... 135 E3
Scunthorpe DN16... 151 D1
Bedale Wlk YO43... 135 F4
Bede Ave YO30... 130 B7
Bedern YO1... 156 C3
Bedford Gr YO15... 122 D1
Bedford Rd
Humberston DN35... 103 D1
Kingston upon Hull HU13. 143 F3
Bedfords Fold 6 LS25... 61 A7
Bedford St
Grimsby DN32... 153 A5
Kingston upon Hull HU8.. 141 A1
Bedford Way 2 DN15... 96 D7
Beech Ave
3 Airmyn DN14... 64 E4
Beverley HU17... 136 F6
Bishopthorpe YO23... 133 A3
3 Flamborough YO15... 5 A2
Flixborough DN15... 96 A7
14 Gainsborough DN21... 117 B1
14 Grimsby DN33... 102 E2
Gunness DN15... 95 E6
Kingston upon Hull HU8.. 141 C2
4 Naburn YO23... 36 C7
7 Preston HU12... 72 C7
York YO24... 129 F3
Beech Cl
4 Broughton DN20... 97 D3
Burstwick HU12... 73 A6
2 Elvington YO41... 27 B2
Garton-on-the-Wolds YO25. 19 F6
Kilham YO25... 9 B3
8 Kingston upon Hull HU3... 145 C5
Market Weighton YO43... 135 D4
Sproatley HU11... 58 C5
Beechcliffe Ave 1 HU6. 140 C7
Beech Cres 7 DN7... 92 C6
Beech Croft
Barlby with Osgodby YO8.. 49 B6
Driffield YO25... 125 A5
Beech Ct
Bishopthorpe YO23... 133 A3
6 Pocklington YO42... 29 A4
Beechdale HU16... 139 C5
Beech Dr
Bridlington YO16... 123 A6
2 North Ferriby HU14... 69 A4
11 Patrington HU12... 74 D1
Beeches Ave 23 DN16... 96 D2
Beeches The
Great Driffield YO25... 125 A4
Pocklington YO42... 29 A4
Skelton YO30... 126 C4
Tickton HU17... 137 E8
26 Upper Poppleton YO26.. 12 F1
Beechfield
Kingston upon Hull HU6.. 140 B6
Newton-on-Ouse YO30... 12 B6
Beechfield Cl 15 YO8... 48 B1
Beechfield Ct DN34... 152 C2
Beechfield Dr HU10... 138 C2
Beechfield Rd DN7... 92 C4
Beech Garth DN19... 85 C7
Beech Glade YO31... 127 F2
Beech Gr
1 Airmyn DN14... 64 E4
Burton upon Stather DN15. 82 B5
Camblesforth YO8... 63 C5
2 Flamborough YO15... 5 A2
Goole DN14... 149 D1
Holton le Clay DN36... 114 B5
Nafferton YO25... 125 E8
Newland HU5... 140 C3
Northfield HU13... 143 C3
Selby YO8... 148 C5
1 Swanland HU14... 69 C7
York YO26... 129 C4
Beech Hill Rd HU14... 69 C7
Beechlands 9 YO25... 124 F3
Beechlands The 9 YO25 124 F3
Beech Lawn HU10... 143 E6
Beech Pk YO19... 49 A8
Beech Pl 5 YO32... 14 A6
Beech Rd
Brough HU15... 68 C6
Campsall DN6... 76 E1
Beech Rise HU12... 72 A4
Beech Tree Ave 21 DN8.. 93 B7
Beech Tree Cl 3 HU17.. 136 F7
Beech Tree La YO8... 63 C5
Beechtree Way 2 HU17.. 44 F6
Beech View
Hutton Cranswick YO25... 32 E6
Walkington HU17... 55 C8
Beechway DN16... 151 B3
Beech Way
10 Cleethorpes DN36... 103 B1
25 Upper Poppleton YO26.. 12 F1
Beechwood HU18... 134 D1
Beechwood Ave
25 Grimsby DN33... 102 C2
3 Immingham DN40... 87 C1
Beechwood Cl 9 DN3... 92 A1
Beechwood Cres 3 DN20 97 E4
Beechwood Ct 17 DN7... 92 D3
Beechwood Dr
Scawby DN20... 108 E8
3 Scotter DN21... 107 C3
Beechwood Glade 6 YO24... 129 B1
Beechwood La 10 YO25.. 124 F2
Beechwood The YO25... 125 A3
Beechwood Views HU12... 60 B1
BEEFORD... 22 C1
Beeford CE Prim Sch YO25... 22 C1
Beeford Gr HU6... 139 F5
Beeford Rd YO25... 22 F1
Beeforth Cl YO32... 127 D5
Beeley Rd DN32... 153 C2
BEELSBY... 112 F5
Beelsby Rd LN7... 112 C5
Beel's Rd DN41... 101 E8
Beesby Dr 22 DN35... 103 C2
Beesby Medieval Village* DN36... 120 E7
Beesby Rd DN17... 150 E1
Beeson Gr DN31... 152 C5
Beeson St DN31... 152 C5
Beggar Hill DN21... 107 D5
Beilby St HU3... 144 F4
Belcombe Way 1 YO30. 130 A7
Beldevere Pk HU18... 134 C6
Belfry Ct HU8... 142 B6
Belgrave Cl
6 Belton DN9... 94 E1
Belton DN9... 105 E8
Belgrave Dr
Goole DN14... 149 F5
Hornsea HU18... 134 C5
Kingston upon Hull HU4.. 144 D5
7 North Cave HU15... 53 D3
Belgrave Rd
Bridlington YO15... 122 D1
1 Grimsby DN33... 102 D1
Belgrave Sq 1 DN15... 151 B7
Belgrave St YO31... 130 C7
Belgravia 8 DN14... 149 C4
Bellamy Ct HU9... 146 C7
Bellasize La DN14... 66 C6
Bellasize Pk HU15... 66 D8
Bellbutts View 1 DN21.. 107 B3
Bell Cl
Haxby YO32... 127 C8
Kingston upon Hull HU7.. 141 D5
Bellcroft La HU12... 72 E4
Bellcroft Rd HU12... 72 F5
Bellcross La 7 DN14... 65 B7
Belleisle Rd 12 DN34... 102 B3
Bellerby Way YO42... 28 F3
Belle Vue St YO10... 130 E3
Belle Vue Terr
19 Thorne/Moorends DN8... 93 A8
York YO10... 130 E3
Bellfarm Ave YO31... 130 E8
Bellfield Ave 5 HU8... 142 A5
Bellfield Dr HU10... 138 D1
Bellfield Prim Sch HU8.. 142 A4
Bell Gn DN14... 78 B2
Bellground La YO30... 12 D4
Bell Hall* YO19... 36 E6
Bellhouse Way YO24... 132 B8
Bellingham Rd DN16... 151 D3
Bell La
Cawood YO8... 48 A7
Foggathorpe YO8... 51 B7
Rawcliffe DN14... 64 A2
Scunthorpe DN15... 151 A6
Bellmans Croft YO23... 132 B2
Bell Mills YO25... 125 A2
Bells Dr 9 DN20... 108 F5
Bells Rd 2 HU12... 72 B7
Bellwin Dr DN15... 82 A1
Bellwood Cres 7 DN8... 93 A8
Bellwood Dr YO24... 132 B8
Belmont DN36... 114 A5
Belmont Cl
13 Cleethorpes DN35... 103 B2
3 York YO30... 127 A1
Belmont St
Kingston upon Hull HU9.. 146 D8
Scunthorpe DN16... 151 A2
Belper Ct
17 Cleethorpes DN31... 153 A5
3 Scunthorpe DN15... 150 B6
Belprin Rd HU17... 137 B5
Belshaw La DN9... 94 D1
Beltham Gn HU16... 138 F4
Belthorn Rd 1 DN17... 81 F1
Belthorpe La YO42... 16 E1
BELTOFT... 95 A1
BELTON... 94 E1
Belton All Saints CE Prim Sch DN9... 94 E2
Belton Cl 4 HU8... 142 B5
Belton Fields DN9... 94 D1
Belton Gr 7 DN33... 102 D2
Belton Rd
Belton DN9... 95 A1
Epworth DN9... 105 E7
Sandtoft DN8... 94 B3
Belt Rd The DN21... 117 C2
Belvedere Cl YO15... 11 B4
Belvedere Cres DN14... 149 B6
Belvedere Dr
Kingston upon Hull HU11... 142 D6
Scunthorpe DN17... 150 E3
7 Thorne/Moorends DN8.. 79 B2
Belvedere Gr YO15... 11 B4
Belvedere Par YO15... 11 B4
Belvedere Rd
Bridlington YO15... 11 B4
Kingston upon Hull HU13. 143 F2
Belvoir Ave 8 YO41... 27 B2
Belvoir Cl DN21... 117 A2
Belvoir Rd DN35... 103 B1
Belvoir St HU5... 145 C8
Belwood Dr DN9... 94 E2
BEMPTON... 4 D4
Bempton Cl YO16... 122 E6
Bempton Cliffs Nature Reserve* YO15... 4 D5
Bempton Cres YO16... 122 E6
Bempton Dr YO16... 122 E6
Bempton Gdns YO16... 122 E6
Bempton Gr
Grimsby DN32... 153 A1
Kingston upon Hull HU5.. 144 D8
Bempton La
Bempton YO16... 4 B1
Bridlington YO16... 122 D8
Bempton Oval YO16... 122 E6
Bempton Prim Sch YO15.. 4 C4
Bempton Sta YO16... 4 C2
Bemrose Gr YO16... 122 E5
Bemrose Way DN31... 152 C4
Bence The YO42... 17 C3
Benedict Ave YO8... 148 E4
Benedict Cl 2 HU4... 144 A2
Benedict Rd HU4... 144 A2
BENINGBROUGH... 12 D4
Beningbrough Hall & Gdns* YO30... 12 B5
Beningbrough La YO30... 12 D5
Benjy La YO19... 37 E7
BENNETLAND... 66 C7
Bennetland La HU15... 66 C7
Bennett Dr DN15... 83 A4
Bennett Rd
Cleethorpes DN35... 153 D3
Scunthorpe DN16... 151 C3
Benningholme La HU11.. 45 D2
Bennington Cl 48 HU12... 72 D7
Bennymoor La YO8... 49 C4
Benson Ct LN11... 121 C4
Bentinck La HU11... 45 F8
BENTLEY... 55 D7
Bentley Ct HU3... 145 A5
Bentley Gr HU6... 139 F4
Bentley La DN38... 110 E7
Bentley St DN35... 153 E2
Berea The DN34... 152 C1
Beresford Ave
Hornsea HU18... 134 D2
Kingston upon Hull HU6.. 140 D4
Beresford Terr YO23... 130 C1
Beretun Gn 11 DN18... 84 E8
Bergen Way HU7... 140 D6
BERKELEY... 150 D7
Berkeley Bsns Ctr DN15. 150 C7
Berkeley Dr
3 Beverley HU17... 136 E1
32 Hedon HU12... 72 D7
Berkeley Ind Est DN15... 150 C8
Berkeley Jun & Inf Sch DN15... 150 D8
Berkeley Rd DN35... 103 D1
Berkeley St
1 Kingston upon Hull HU3... 145 D8
Scunthorpe DN15... 150 F8
Berkeley Terr YO26... 129 E5
Berkshire Cl 4 HU17... 55 F8
Berkshire St HU8... 141 C1
Bermondsey Dr HU5... 144 E8
Bermuda Ave HU11... 45 D2
Bernadette Ave HU4... 144 B5
Berners Rd 15 DN35... 103 D1
Berridge La DN14... 78 A6
Berriman's La YO25... 9 B3
Berryman Way HU13... 144 A3
Berwick Ct 5 DN40... 87 C1
Beside the Seaside Mus* 14 YO16... 122 E2
Bessacarr Ave HU10... 138 F1
Bessemer Way DN15... 96 D7
BESSINGBY... 10 F4
Bessingby Gate YO16... 122 A2
Bessingby Gr HU9... 142 B2
Bessingby Hill YO16... 122 B3
Bessingby Rd YO16... 122 C2
Bessingby Road Ret Pk YO16... 122 C2
Bessingby Way YO16... 122 C1
Bestall Rd DN32... 153 C2
BESWICK... 32 D3
Beswick Hall* YO25... 32 D3
Beswick Heads YO25... 32 C3
Beswick Rd YO25... 32 E2
Beswick & Walton CE Prim Sch YO25... 32 D3
Bethell Ct 6 HU12... 72 D7
Bethell Wlk YO25... 125 A3
Bethlehem St DN32... 152 D3
Bethune Ave HU4... 144 A3
Bethune Avenue W HU13... 144 A3
Bethune Park Prim Sch HU4... 144 C3
Betony Cl 4 DN15... 96 B7
Betteras Hill Rd LS25... 61 A8
Betula Ct HU8... 141 E7
Betula Way DN17... 150 C1
Between Dikes Rd YO8... 63 F8
Between Rivers La DN14.. 78 E7
BEVERLEY... 154 A3
Beverley Balk YO41... 15 B2
Beverley Boys Gram Sch HU17... 136 D2
Beverley Cl 18 DN36... 114 A5
Beverley Cres DN32... 153 A1
Beverley Ct
11 Healing DN41... 101 F5
Scunthorpe DN17... 150 D3
Beverley Dr HU17... 136 D7
Beverley High Sch HU17 154 A4
Beverley La YO43... 41 E2
Beverley L Complex HU17... 154 C2
Beverley Minst* HU17.. 154 B2
Beverley Minst CE Prim Sch HU17... 136 D3
Beverley Parklands HU17... 154 C1
Beverley Parks Nature Reserve* HU17... 55 F7
Beverley Racecourse HU17... 136 B4
Beverley Rd
Beeford YO25... 22 D1

Bray Gate YO42 ... 16 E2
Bray Rd YO10 ... 133 F8
BRAYTON ... 148 A2
Brayton CE Inf Sch YO8 . 148 A2
Brayton Coll YO8 ... 148 A3
Brayton Junc YO8 ... 148 C1
Brayton Jun Sch YO8 ... 148 A2
Brayton La YO8 ... 148 B1
Brazil St HU9 ... 146 C8
Breamar Ct 2 DN14 ... 62 A2
Bream Ct 9 HU6 ... 140 B8
Breamer La HU11 ... 35 A2
Breary Cl YO24 ... 129 F1
Breck La HU15 ... 53 B3
Brecksfield YO30 ... 126 C5
Brecks La
Kirk Sandall DN3 ... 92 A2
Strensall YO32 ... 14 B7
York YO32 ... 127 F4
Breckstreet La YO42 ... 39 C3
Brecon Dr 22 HU7 ... 56 F6
Brecon St HU8 ... 141 B1
Breeze La YO25 ... 22 D1
Breezemount Ct 4 DN7 .. 92 C6
BREIGHTON ... 50 D5
Breighton Aerodrome★ YO8 ... 50 D5
Breighton Rd
Bubwith YO8 ... 50 D6
Wressle YO8 ... 50 C3
Bremerhaven Way 24 DN33 ... 102 C2
Brendon Ave HU8 ... 141 B3
Brent Ave HU8 ... 142 B6
Brentwood Cl HU15 ... 68 B6
Brentwood Cres YO10 ... 131 C2
Brereton Ave DN35 ... 153 C4
Brereton Cl HU17 ... 136 E6
Bretel Wlk YO16 ... 122 B4
Bretherdale HU7 ... 140 F6
Brethergate DN9 ... 105 B2
Bretton Ave DN14 ... 149 F5
Bretton Cl 5 DN7 ... 92 D3
Brett St YO16 ... 122 C3
Brevere Rd HU12 ... 72 D7
Brewery Gdns DN17 ... 94 D8
Brewery Rd DN17 ... 94 D8
Brewster Ave 17 DN40 ... 87 C1
Breydon Ct 4 DN15 ... 82 B4
Brian Ave
Cleethorpes DN35 ... 103 B2
Scunthorpe DN16 ... 151 C1
Waltham DN37 ... 113 D6
Briar Ave YO26 ... 129 B4
Briar Cl
4 Newport HU15 ... 52 F1
South Killingholme DN40 ... 86 F3
Briar Cliffe YO8 ... 148 A3
Briar Ct 10 DN19 ... 86 A8
Briar Dr YO31 ... 127 F2
Briarfield Rd HU5 ... 139 F2
Briar Garth
Driffield YO25 ... 124 D4
Great Driffield YO25 ... 124 D3
Briar La
4 Grimsby DN33 ... 113 D8
Healing DN41 ... 101 F5
15 Scartho DN33 ... 113 D8
Briarsfield YO42 ... 28 D4
Briars La DN7 ... 92 C7
Briars The HU13 ... 143 E3
Briar Way DN15 ... 96 B7
Briarwood Cl
10 Bransholme HU7 ... 57 B5
Gateforth YO8 ... 61 F7
Brick Dike La HU20 ... 54 C5
Brickenhole La DN10 ... 116 C3
Brickhill La YO8 ... 63 F4
Brick Kiln Balk YO16 ... 122 A1
Brick Kiln La YO8 ... 62 D6
Brick La DN40 ... 86 E5
Brick Lands La DN14 ... 62 F4
Bricknell Ave HU5 ... 139 E3
Bricknell Prim Sch HU5 . 139 F2
Brick Rd HU12 ... 88 F6
Brickyard DN37 ... 100 D3
Brickyard La
Melton HU14 ... 68 F4
Walkeringham DN10 ... 116 B3
Wrawby DN20 ... 98 C3
Bridge Cl
Haxby YO32 ... 127 C7
Kingston upon Hull HU9 .. 146 D6
Bridge Cres YO8 ... 64 C8
Bridge Ct YO8 ... 148 D6
Bridge Farm DN14 ... 77 F6
Bridgegate DN14 ... 65 A7
Bridgegate Dr HU9 ... 146 C6
Bridge Gdns DN31 ... 152 A5
Bridge Hill DN7 ... 92 C6
Bridge Hill Cl DN14 ... 79 B8
Bridge La
Cadney DN20 ... 109 C6
5 Great Driffield YO25 ... 124 F4
Horkstow DN18 ... 83 F5
Pollington DN14 ... 77 F6
Rawcliffe DN14 ... 79 B8
York YO30 ... 156 B4
Bridge Rd
Airmyn DN14 ... 149 A8
Bishopthorpe YO23 ... 132 F3
Broughton DN20 ... 97 F5
South Cave HU15 ... 53 F1
Bridges Ct YO8 ... 148 D6
Bridges La YO42 ... 38 E4
Bridges Rd DN17 ... 150 E3
Bridge St
7 Bridlington YO15 ... 122 E2
10 Brigg DN20 ... 98 B2
Goole DN14 ... 149 C3
Great Driffield YO25 ... 124 E4
Pocklington YO42 ... 29 A4
Thorne/Moorends DN8 ... 93 A8
York YO1 ... 156 B2
Bridges The DN18 ... 84 F8
Bridge Street North DN31 ... 152 F5
Bridgeview Sch HU13 ... 143 D1
Bridgewater Rd DN17 ... 150 D4
Bridles The
9 Goxhill DN19 ... 86 A8
Kingston upon Hull HU3 .. 144 F2
Bridle Way 1 YO26 ... 129 A3
Bridle Wlk YO8 ... 148 C4
BRIDLINGTON ... 122 B3
Bridlington Ave HU2 ... 155 B4
Bridlington Balk YO25 ... 34 A8
Bridlington Bay Rd YO15 . 10 E4
Bridlington & District Hospl YO16 ... 122 B3
Bridlington Forum YO15. 122 F2
Bridlington Harbour Heritage Mus & Art Gallery★ YO15 ... 122 F2
Bridlington Leisure World YO15 ... 122 F2
Bridlington Rd
Barmston YO25 ... 22 F6
Brandesburton YO25 ... 34 C3
Flamborough YO15 ... 4 F1
Hunmanby YO14 ... 3 A7
Sledmere YO25 ... 7 C4
1 Stamford Bridge YO41 .. 15 D2
Ulrome YO25 ... 23 A2
Wold Newton YO25 ... 2 A4
Bridlington Sch Sports Coll YO16 ... 122 C3
Bridlington Sports Ctr YO16 ... 122 B4
Bridlington St YO14 ... 2 F8
Bridlington Sta YO15 ... 122 D2
Bridport Cl HU7 ... 141 C7
Bridport Wlk DN17 ... 150 C4
Briergate YO32 ... 127 C7
Brierholme Carr Rd DN7 . 92 F5
Brierholme Cl DN7 ... 92 F5
Brierholme Ings Rd DN7 .. 92 F5
Brier La YO8 ... 64 A4
Brierley Cl
10 Howden DN14 ... 65 A7
Snaith DN14 ... 78 C8
BRIGG ... 98 D2
Briggate Dr DN17 ... 107 D7
Brigg Dr HU13 ... 143 F3
Brigg Farm Ct YO8 ... 63 D5
Brigg La YO8 ... 63 D5
Brigg Prep Sch DN20 ... 98 C1
Brigg Prim Sch DN20 ... 98 B2
Brigg Rd
Barton-upon-Humber DN18 ... 84 E5
Broughton DN20 ... 97 F3
Cadney DN20 ... 109 C7
Grasby LN7 ... 111 A6
Hibaldstow DN21 ... 108 F6
Messingham DN17 ... 107 D7
North Kelsey LN7 ... 110 A5
Scunthorpe DN15 ... 151 C7
South Kelsey LN7 ... 110 A1
Wrawby DN20 ... 98 D3
Briggs St YO31 ... 130 C7
Brigg Sta DN20 ... 98 C1
BRIGHAM ... 33 E8
Brigham Ct HU17 ... 154 B4
Brigham Gr HU9 ... 142 B1
Brigham La
Brigham YO25 ... 33 E8
Foston YO25 ... 21 E1
Brighowgate DN34 ... 152 D2
Bright Cres 7 YO15 ... 122 F3
Brighton St HU3 ... 145 A3
Brighton Street Trading Pk 1 HU3 ... 145 A3
Bright St
Kingston upon Hull HU8 .. 146 B8
York YO26 ... 129 F5
Bright Wlk YO8 ... 148 B6
BRIGSLEY ... 113 D4
Brigsley Rd DN37 ... 113 D6
Brimington Rd HU10 ... 138 F2
Brimley HU17 ... 136 C5
Brimley Gn HU17 ... 136 C5
BRIND ... 51 A2
Brind La DN14 ... 50 F2
Brindlegate 4 YO42 ... 29 A4
Brindleys La DN14 ... 50 F3
Brindley St HU9 ... 141 E2
Brinkworth Rush YO41 ... 27 A2
Brinkworth Terr 1 YO10 130 E3
Brisbane St HU3 ... 145 D5
Bristol Rd
Kingston upon Hull HU5 .. 144 C8
Scunthorpe DN17 ... 150 C5
Britannia Cres 7 DN34 .. 102 B3
Britannia Ct 10 YO16 ... 122 F2
Britannia Gdns 7 HU5 ... 140 E2
Britannia Rd
Bridlington YO16 ... 122 C4
Goole DN14 ... 149 A2
Britannia Way DN14 ... 149 B3
Britton Cl DN17 ... 81 D3
Brixham Ct
5 Kingston upon Hull HU3 ... 145 A5
Waltham DN33 ... 113 E7
Brixton Cl HU8 ... 141 E5
Broach La
Heck DN14 ... 62 D1
Kellington DN14 ... 61 F3
Broach Rd
Heck DN14 ... 77 D8
Hensall DN14 ... 62 C1
Broadacre Pk 1 HU15 ... 68 D5
Broadacre Prim Sch HU7. 56 F6
Broadacres
Carlton DN14 ... 63 D3
Keyingham HU12 ... 73 D4
Broad Acres YO32 ... 127 C7
Broadacres Ave DN14 ... 63 D3
Broadacres Garth DN14 .. 63 D3
BROAD BALK ... 124 D6
Broad Balk YO17 ... 6 A5
Broadbent Gate Rd DN8 .. 79 B1
Broadgate HU17 ... 136 B1
Broad Highway YO19 ... 37 F8
Broad La
Appleton Roebuck YO23 ... 36 A6
6 Beal DN14 ... 61 D4
Catton YO41 ... 27 C7
Cawood YO8 ... 48 A6
Howden DN14 ... 65 B6
Rufforth YO23 ... 129 A2
Sykehouse DN14 ... 78 B4
Upper Poppleton YO26 ... 12 D2
Wistow YO8 ... 48 A5
Broad La Cl 5 HU16 ... 139 B7
Broadland Dr 4 HU9 ... 142 A3
Broadlands YO19 ... 38 A8
Broadlands Cl 33 DN7 ... 92 D4
Broadley Ave HU10 ... 143 D6
Broadley Cl 6 HU9 ... 146 C7
Broadley Croft 3 HU15 ... 68 D5
Broadley Way HU15 ... 68 D5
Broadmanor
North Duffield YO8 ... 50 A7
Pocklington YO42 ... 29 A3
Broad Manor YO42 ... 29 A3
Broad Oak HU11 ... 142 D6
Broad Oak La 18 YO32 ... 13 E5
Broadstairs Cl 1 HU8 ... 141 E7
Broadstone Cl HU7 ... 141 C6
Broadstone Way
10 Rawcliffe YO30 ... 126 E3
York YO30 ... 126 E3
Broadwater Dr 34 DN7 ... 92 D4
Broadwaters 1 HU7 ... 56 E5
Broadway
Goole DN14 ... 149 D4
5 Grimsby DN34 ... 102 B2
Hatfield DN7 ... 92 C3
Hornsea HU18 ... 134 D4
7 Keelby DN41 ... 101 A5
Scunthorpe DN16 ... 151 A2
York YO10 ... 133 E8
Broadway Dr 9 HU9 ... 142 A3
Broadway Gr 3 YO10 ... 133 E8
Broadway Nook DN7 ... 92 C3
Broadway The 8 HU9 ... 142 A3
Broadway W YO10 ... 133 D8
Brockadale Nature Reserve★ WF8 ... 76 B4
Brock Cl
15 Epworth DN9 ... 105 D6
1 Grimsby DN33 ... 102 E1
Brockenhurst Ave HU16 . 139 D6
Brockenhurst Rd 7 DN7 . 92 E4
Brockett Ind Est YO23 ... 36 B6
BROCKFIELD ... 14 E2
Brockfield Park Dr YO31 127 F2
Brockfield Rd YO31 ... 127 E2
Brockle Bank Ct 9 HU12 . 58 C1
BROCKLESBY ... 100 E6
Brocklesby Ave DN40 ... 87 B1
Brocklesby Cl 5 HU13 ... 144 A3
Brocklesby Junc DN39 ... 100 B8
Brocklesby Park Prim Sch DN37 ... 100 E4
Brocklesby Pl 11 DN34 ... 102 C2
Brocklesby Rd
10 Grimsby DN34 ... 102 C2
Scunthorpe DN17 ... 150 F1
Ulceby DN41 ... 100 B8
Brockley Cl HU8 ... 141 E6
Brockton Cl HU3 ... 144 F5
Broc-o-Bank 1 DN6 ... 76 E2
Brodsworth St 5 HU9 ... 146 C8
Bromley St
Kingston upon Hull HU2 .. 155 B4
2 York YO26 ... 129 F5
Brompton Cl HU5 ... 139 E2
Brompton Ct 4 HU3 ... 140 D1
Brompton Rd YO30 ... 130 A7
Bromwich Rd HU10 ... 143 F8
Bronte Ct HU6 ... 140 C7
Bronte Wlk YO16 ... 122 B4
Bronzegarth DN32 ... 153 B1
Brookdale Rd DN17 ... 150 D2
Brooke Dr HU18 ... 134 C2
Brooke Prim Sch DN8 ... 93 B7
Brookes Cl DN21 ... 108 B1
Brooke St DN8 ... 93 A8
Brookfield Cl
Carnaby YO16 ... 10 E4
1 Kingston upon Hull HU7. 56 F5
8 Thorne/Moorends DN8 .. 93 A8
Brookfield Rd DN33 ... 102 D1
Brookholme HU17 ... 137 B3
Brook La DN20 ... 98 A1
Brookland Rd YO16 ... 122 C4
Brooklands
2 Broughton DN20 ... 97 E3
Kingston upon Hull HU7 .. 141 C5
York YO10 ... 131 D4
Brooklands Ave
Broughton DN20 ... 97 D4
Cleethorpes DN35 ... 103 D3
Brooklands Cl HU17 ... 137 A6
Brooklands Pk HU16 ... 139 A5
Brooklands Rd HU5 ... 144 E8
Brooklyn Dr DN36 ... 114 D8
Brooklyn St HU5 ... 140 D3
Brooks Cl 17 DN37 ... 101 F1
Brookside 2 HU15 ... 68 D6
Brookside Cl YO42 ... 28 D3
Brook St
Great Driffield YO25 ... 124 F4
Hemswell DN21 ... 119 A2
Kingston upon Hull HU2 .. 155 A3
Selby YO8 ... 148 C4
York YO31 ... 156 B4
Broome Cl YO32 ... 127 F5
Broome Way YO32 ... 128 A5
Broomfield Way YO25 ... 23 A6
BROOMFLEET ... 67 B6
Broomfleet Carr La HU15. 67 B7
Broomfleet Sta HU15 ... 67 B6
Broom Gr DN16 ... 151 B4
Broomhead Cl 5 HU8 ... 141 E7
Broomhill Cl 23 WF11 ... 61 A2
Broomhill Cres 25 WF11 ... 61 A2
Broomhill Dr 26 WF11 ... 61 A2
Broomhill Gr 19 WF11 ... 61 A2
Broomhill Pl 22 WF11 ... 61 A2
Broomhill Sq 24 WF11 ... 61 A2
Broomhill Wlk 21 WF11 .. 61 A2
Broompark Rd DN14 ... 149 E6
Broomston La DN9 ... 104 F1
Brosley Ave DN3 ... 92 A4
BROUGH ... 68 C5
Brougham Cl YO30 ... 129 F8
Brougham St HU3 ... 144 F7
Brough Prim Sch HU15 ... 68 C6
Brough Rd HU15 ... 54 A1
Brough Sh Pl 32 HU15 ... 68 C5
Brough St DN14 ... 149 D5
Brough Sta HU15 ... 68 B5
BROUGHTON ... 97 E4
Broughton Cl 1 HU9 ... 142 A3
Broughton Inf Sch DN20 .. 97 E3
Broughton Jun Sch DN20. 97 E3
Broughton Way YO10 ... 131 B4
Brow La
Kilpin DN14 ... 65 E7
Snaith DN14 ... 78 B8
Brown Cow Rd YO8 ... 63 C8
Browney Croft YO10 ... 156 C1
Browning Cl
3 Kingston upon Hull HU3 ... 145 D8
Scunthorpe DN17 ... 150 E2
Browning Rd 20 YO42 ... 29 A3
Brownlow St YO31 ... 156 C4
Brown Moor 27 YO41 ... 15 D2
Brownmoor La YO32 ... 13 B8
Browns La 15 DN8 ... 93 A8
Browns Orch DN32 ... 152 D2
Brown St DN31 ... 152 F7
Bruce Cl 6 DN20 ... 97 D3
Brucella Gr 12 HU3 ... 145 A4
Bruce St DN15 ... 150 F7
BRUMBY ... 151 B4
Brumby Comm La DN17 . 150 C3
Brumby Engineering College DN16 ... 151 B5
Brumby House Dr DN16 . 151 A4
Brumby Jun Sch DN16 ... 151 B4
Brumby's Terr 4 HU9 ... 146 D7
Brumby Wood La DN17 .. 150 D6
Brumby Wood Nature Reserve★ DN17 ... 150 D5
Brumfield Ct HU17 ... 154 C4
Brunel Cl
Grimsby DN32 ... 152 F1
4 Scunthorpe DN16 ... 96 D2
Brunel Ct 12 YO26 ... 129 F5
Brunslow Cl HU3 ... 144 E5
Brunswick Ave HU2 ... 155 A4
Brunswick Cl 2 YO32 ... 14 C8
Brunswick Gr 5 HU13 ... 143 E2
Brunswick St YO23 ... 130 B1
Brunton Way DN36 ... 114 A7
Bryan Mere 3 HU17 ... 43 A2
Bryants The HU17 ... 45 A7
Bryony Ct YO8 ... 148 B2
Bryson Cl DN8 ... 79 B1
BUBWITH ... 50 D7
Bubwith Prim Sch YO8 ... 50 D7
Buccaneer Ct YO41 ... 27 A3
Buccaneer Way 16 HU15 .. 68 C5
Buck Beck Way 12 DN36 . 103 B1
Buckfast Ct DN17 ... 150 D4
Buckingham Ave DN15 ... 96 C7
Buckingham Ct YO1 ... 156 A1
Buckingham Gr 17 DN33 102 D1
Buckingham Prim Sch HU8 ... 141 C1
Buckingham St
5 Kingston upon Hull HU8 ... 141 C1
York YO1 ... 156 B1
Buckingham Street N DN15 ... 150 F8
Buckingham Street S DN15 ... 150 F8
Buckingham Terr YO1 ... 156 B2
Buck Inn Yd 35 YO42 ... 29 A3
Buckland Cl 3 HU8 ... 142 C7
Buckle Cl YO8 ... 50 A8
Buckle Ct YO8 ... 148 B7
Buckrose Gr YO16 ... 122 C3
BUCKTON ... 4 C4
Buckton Gate YO15 ... 4 C3
Buddleia Cl DN41 ... 101 F5
Bude Cl 2 DN36 ... 114 A8
Bude Park Prim Sch HU7. 56 F5
Bude Rd HU7 ... 140 F8
Budworth Pk 4 HU7 ... 56 E5
BUGTHORPE ... 16 D4
Bugthorpe CE Prim Sch YO41 ... 16 D4
Bugthorpe La YO41 ... 16 D5
Bugthorpe Lane Town E YO41 ... 16 E5
Bull Alley La DN14 ... 63 B3
Bull Balk YO41 ... 27 E4
Bull Bank LN11 ... 121 F7
Buller St
Grimsby DN32 ... 153 A3
Selby YO8 ... 148 B6
Bullfinch La 5 DN35 ... 103 C1
Bullivant Rd DN7 ... 92 E4
Bull La
Everingham YO42 ... 40 C4
Huby YO32 ... 13 B7
York YO10 ... 130 F3
Bull Moor La YO60 ... 15 A8
Bull Moor Rd DN7 ... 93 A4
Bull Pasture 14 HU15 ... 53 F1
Bull Ring La 11 DN31 ... 152 D3
Bulmer La YO43 ... 51 E8
Bulwick Ave DN33 ... 113 E8
Bunkers Hill DN21 ... 119 B1
Bunkers Hill Cl 11 DN36 . 114 D4
Bunting Cl YO25 ... 125 A5
Burbage Ave HU8 ... 141 C4
Burcom Ave 7 DN36 ... 114 D8
Burcott Garth HU4 ... 144 B3
Burdale Cl
Great Driffield YO25 ... 124 D3
Kingston upon Hull HU9 .. 142 B3
Burden Cl HU17 ... 154 C4
Burden Rd HU17 ... 154 C4
Burden St HU1 ... 155 A2
Burdike Ave YO30 ... 130 A8
Burdock Rd DN16 ... 96 E2
Burgar Rd DN8 ... 93 A7
Burgate
4 Barton-upon-Humber DN18 ... 84 F8
North Newbald YO43 ... 53 F7
Burgess Ct HU17 ... 154 B4
Burgess Rd DN20 ... 98 C2
Burgess Sq 46 HU12 ... 72 D7
Burgess Wlk YO24 ... 132 C8
Burghley Cl LN7 ... 111 A3
Burghley Rd DN16 ... 151 D4
Burgon Cres DN15 ... 83 B5
Burke St DN15 ... 151 A8
Burke Street N DN15 ... 151 A8
Burlands La YO26 ... 24 F7
Burleigh St HU8 ... 146 C8
Burley Ave 18 DN35 ... 103 C2
Burley Cl DN37 ... 101 F2
Burlington Ave YO10 ... 130 F4
Burlington Cres DN14 ... 149 D4
Burlington Gdns YO16 ... 122 D3
Burlington Inf Sch YO16 122 D5
Burlington Jun Sch YO16 ... 122 C5
Burlington Rd HU8 ... 141 D5
Burlyn Rd 3 YO14 ... 3 A8
Burma Dr HU9 ... 147 B8
Burma Rd DN16 ... 151 F6
BURN ... 62 D7
Burnaby Cl HU17 ... 136 E6
Burnbutts La YO25 ... 32 C7
BURNBY ... 29 D1
Burnby Cl HU5 ... 139 C2
Burnby Hall Gdns★ YO42 . 29 A3
Burnby La YO42 ... 29 A3
Burn Est YO32 ... 127 E4
Burnet Dr 12 DN16 ... 96 E2
Burnet Rose Way DN14 .. 149 E7
Burnett's Yd LN7 ... 111 C4
Burney Cl HU17 ... 154 A4
Burn Hall Cl YO8 ... 62 D7
BURNHAM ... 85 C3
Burnham Ave 4 HU12 ... 73 A6
Burnham La DN39 ... 85 E4
Burnham Rd
Barton-upon-Humber DN18 ... 85 A6
Epworth DN9 ... 105 E6
Kingston upon Hull HU4 .. 144 B3
Owston Ferry DN9 ... 106 A3
Scunthorpe DN15 ... 150 D6
Burnham Reach 26 DN35 ... 103 C1
Burnham Sq DN9 ... 106 A3
Burnholme Ave YO31 ... 131 B6
Burnholme Com Coll YO31 ... 131 A5
Burnholme Dr YO31 ... 131 A6
Burnholme Gr YO31 ... 131 A5
Burniston Gr YO10 ... 131 A4
Burniston Rd HU5 ... 139 E2
Burn La YO8 ... 62 D6
Burn Rd DN15 ... 150 C7
Burnsall Dr YO26 ... 129 E4
Burnsalls Rd HU12 ... 72 C7
Burns Cl 2 YO42 ... 28 F4
Burns Ct YO24 ... 132 B7
Burns Gr 31 DN33 ... 102 D2
Burnside DN20 ... 97 D3
Burns St DN21 ... 117 A1

Cavendish Gr YO10 131 D3
Cavendish Pk 8 HU15 68 C5
Cavendish Prim Sch HU8 141 E4
Cavendish Rd
Kingston upon Hull HU8 141 D5
9 Scunthorpe DN16 96 D2
Cavendish Sq HU3 140 D1
Cavendish Way DN32 152 F3
Cave Rd HU15 68 B6
Cave's La DN10 116 B3
Cave St HU5 140 D1
Cave Terr 1 HU5 140 D1
Cavill Dr 12 DN14 65 B7
Cavill Pl HU3 145 D5
CAWKELD 32 B5
CAWOOD 48 B8
Cawood CE Aided Prim Sch YO8 48 B8
Cawood Cl HU11 45 D2
Cawood Cres HU11 45 D2
Cawood Dr HU11 45 D2
Cawood Rd
Stillingfleet YO19 36 D3
Wistow YO8 48 C7
Cawthorn Cl YO25 125 A3
Cawthorne Dr HU4 144 C3
Caxton Ave YO26 129 D6
Cayley Cl YO30 126 F1
Cayley Rd HU10 143 F6
Cayton Rd HU8 141 D4
Cecil Cl 10 DN21 107 C3
Cecile Cres DN15 150 E7
Cecilia Pl 3 YO24 130 A3
Cecil Rd 7 YO14 3 A8
Cecil St
24 Gainsborough DN21 117 B1
Goole DN14 149 E4
Kingston upon Hull HU3 144 F5
Cedar Ave
Flixborough DN15 96 A7
Kingston upon Hull HU16 139 A6
Stainforth DN7 92 D6
Cedar Cl
11 Cleethorpes DN35 103 B1
Gainsborough DN21 117 A2
Hambleton YO8 48 B1
Hornsea HU18 134 D1
Kingston upon Hull HU10 143 D7
Scawby DN20 108 F8
7 Scotter DN21 107 C3
Wawne HU7 56 F8
Cedar Cres YO8 48 D2
Cedar Ct
Bridlington YO16 123 A8
8 Hedon HU12 72 C7
Scunthorpe DN15 151 B8
Cedar Dr 2 DN40 87 C2
Cedar Glade YO19 26 E7
Cedar Gr
2 Aldbrough HU11 47 C1
Stainforth DN7 92 D6
York YO31 131 B7
Cedar Gr The HU17 136 C6
Cedar Rd
Selby YO8 148 D2
2 Thorne/Moorends DN8 79 B1
Cedarwood 5 HU15 66 D7
Cedarwood Cl 7 YO24 129 B1
Cedarwood Dr HU5 144 B7
Cedric Rd DN3 92 A1
Celandine Cl
8 Kingston upon Hull HU5 139 D1
8 South Killingholme DN40 86 E3
Celery Bank DN14 66 A4
Celtic Cl YO26 129 B5
Cemetery Cres 7 DN37 101 F1
Cemetery La
North Kelsey LN7 110 A5
Pocklington YO42 29 A3
Cemetery Rd
Hatfield DN7 92 F4
Laceby DN37 101 F1
Scunthorpe DN16 151 B5
Winterton DN15 83 B5
York YO10 156 C1
Centenary Rd DN14 149 B5
Centenary Way DN17 151 A5
Central Ave
Beverley HU17 154 A2
Ulrome YO25 23 B3
Central Parade DN34 152 A3
Central Promenade DN35 153 F2
Central St HU2 140 F1
Central Way DN16 151 D6
Centurion Pk YO30 127 B2
Centurion Way
Brough HU15 68 C5
Caistor LN7 111 A4
Clifton YO30 127 B3
Centurion Wlk YO43 135 E4
Century Rd HU12 72 A8
Ceylon St HU9 147 C7
Chadcourt HU6 139 E6
Chadwell Springs DN37 113 C6
Chaffinch Cl DN15 96 B7
Chaffinch Dr 14 DN35 103 C1
Chaldon Cl 4 YO32 14 A6
Chalfont Cl HU13 143 D2
Chalfonts YO24 129 F1
Chaloner's Cres YO24 132 D7
Chaloner's Rd YO24 132 D8
Chamberlain Bsns Pk HU8 141 B3
Chamberlain Cl HU7 141 D6
Chamberlain Ct HU7 141 D7
Chamberlain Gdns HU8 141 C3
Chamberlain Rd HU8 141 B3
Chamberlain St HU7 141 D6
Chambers La 1 HU18 134 C4
Chamomile Cl 17 DN16 96 E2
Champney Rd HU17 154 A2
Chancel Rd DN16 96 D2
Chancel Wlk 8 DN20 97 E3
Chancery Ct
Kingston upon Hull HU5 144 E8
York YO24 129 C3
Chancery La 2 DN17 94 D7
Chancery Rise YO24 129 F3
Chancewaters 5 HU7 56 E5
Chandlers Cl 2 DN36 114 A7
Chandlers Ct HU9 146 C6
Chandos Rd DN17 150 F3
Channel Rd HU12 89 B6
Chanterlands Ave HU5 140 A1
Chantreys Dr 13 HU15 68 C6
Chantry Ave 14 YO26 12 F1
Chantry Cl
Grimsby DN31 152 C3
York YO24 132 C8
Chantry Ct YO16 122 D4
Chantry Gap 11 YO26 12 F1
Chantry Gr 13 YO26 12 F1
Chantry La
Beverley HU17 154 B2
Bishopthorpe YO23 133 B4
Etton HU17 43 A6
Grimsby DN31 152 C3
Rimswell HU12 74 C5
Chantry Mdws 1 YO25 9 C3
Chantry Way 13 HU14 69 B7
Chantry Way E 9 HU14 69 B7
Chapel Balk Rd YO8 49 F1
Chapel Cl
Barrow upon Humber DN19 85 D7
27 Flamborough YO15 5 A2
8 Howden DN14 65 A6
2 Kingston upon Hull HU4 144 A1
7 Misterton DN10 116 C5
North Duffield YO8 50 A7
12 Preston HU12 58 C1
Rawcliffe DN14 64 A1
Skidby HU16 138 A8
Skirlaugh HU11 45 E2
4 Westwoodside DN9 105 B2
Chapel Cnr YO43 135 D4
Chapel Ct
Alkborough DN15 82 C8
7 Hibaldstow DN20 108 F5
Scotter DN21 107 C4
Scunthorpe DN15 151 B8
Chapelfield Rd DN19 86 B7
CHAPEL FIELDS 129 B3
Chapel Fields
Coniston HU11 57 F6
Holme-on-Spalding-Moor YO43 40 A1
Chapel Fields Rd YO26 129 A3
Chapel Garth
Broomfleet HU15 67 B5
11 Gilberdyke HU15 66 D8
Holme-on-Spalding-Moor YO42 40 A1
Ottringham HU12 73 E3
Skipsea YO25 23 A1
3 Tetney DN36 114 D4
CHAPEL HADDLESEY 62 C5
Chapel Haddlesey CE Prim Sch YO8 62 B5
Chapel Hill 1 HU15 68 E6
Chapel Hill Rd YO42 29 A4
Chapel La
Ashby cum Fenby DN37 113 D3
Askham Bryan YO23 24 F3
Barmston YO25 23 A6
Barnoldby le Beck DN37 113 B6
14 Barton-upon-Humber DN18 69 E1
Brayton YO8 148 B1
Broughton DN20 97 E3
Elsham DN20 98 F7
10 Gainsborough DN21 117 A2
Habrough DN40 100 E8
Horkstow DN18 84 A5
Keadby with Althorpe DN17 95 C6
13 Keyingham HU12 73 C4
Kilham YO25 9 B3
Kingston upon Hull HU1 155 C2
Langtoft YO25 8 D5
Laxton DN14 65 F4
Little Smeaton WF8 76 B3
Ludborough DN36 121 B6
Middleton YO25 31 C4
8 Misterton DN10 116 C5
Northorpe DN21 118 D8
Ottringham HU12 73 E3
Rawcliffe DN14 64 A2
Reighton YO14 3 E5
3 Riccall YO19 37 A1
Scawby DN20 108 E8
Skeffling HU12 90 C6
Swallow LN7 112 B5
Sykehouse DN14 78 A4
18 Thorne/Moorends DN8 93 A8
Utterby LN11 121 C4
Wansford YO25 21 C3
1 Wawne HU7 56 E7
West/East Butterwick DN17 95 D1
West Ella HU10 69 C8
Chapel La *continued*
Whitton DN15 67 E3
Winterton DN15 83 A5
Wrawby DN20 98 D4
Chapel Lane Staith HU1 155 C2
Chapel Mdws 8 HU15 66 D8
Chapel Mews 3 HU15 68 C6
Chapel Rd
Broughton DN20 97 E3
Habrough DN40 100 E8
Tetney DN36 114 D4
Chapel Row YO10 156 C1
Chapelry Garth 28 HU12 72 D7
Chapel St
2 Amcotts DN17 81 F1
Barmby Moor YO42 28 D3
Bridlington YO15 122 E2
13 Caistor LN7 111 B4
5 Crowle DN17 94 D8
6 Epworth DN9 105 E6
6 Flamborough YO15 5 A2
Goole DN14 149 D3
Goxhill DN19 86 A8
Hillam LS25 61 B7
Kingston upon Hull HU1 155 A2
Lockington YO25 32 B2
North Kelsey LN7 110 A4
Scunthorpe DN15 151 B7
Chapel Terr YO24 129 C3
Chapel Way 21 DN20 98 C2
Chapel Wlk 4 YO19 37 A1
Chapman Ave DN17 150 D2
Chapman Cl 1 YO32 14 C8
Chapman Ct DN31 152 D4
Chapman Gr DN35 153 F1
Chapman Rd DN35 153 D3
Chapmans Ct YO24 132 D6
Chapman's La YO30 12 E7
Chapman St HU8 155 C4
Chapter House St YO1 156 B3
Chapter Wk DN20 97 E3
Charing Cl HU3 145 C8
Chariot St HU1 155 A2
Chariot Way 6 YO25 19 B6
Charles Ave
Grimsby DN33 102 E1
Laceby DN37 101 E1
17 New Waltham DN36 114 A7
15 Scotter DN21 107 C3
Charles Ct 7 DN8 79 B1
Charles Dr DN14 149 B6
Charles Hume Ct DN32 153 B4
Charles Lovell Way DN17 150 D4
Charles Moor YO31 130 F7
Charles St
Cleethorpes DN35 153 F1
30 Gainsborough DN21 117 B1
22 Hedon HU12 72 D7
Kingston upon Hull HU2 155 B3
Selby YO8 148 B6
Charlestown Way HU9 146 C6
Charles Wesley Dr YO8 148 B2
Charlotte St Mews HU1 155 B3
Charlotte St HU1 155 C3
Charlton St
Grimsby DN31 152 C4
York YO23 130 C2
Charnock Ave HU9 142 A4
Charnwood Cl 29 HU7 56 F6
Charter Ave DN14 64 A1
Charterfield HU11 142 D6
Charterhouse Dr 3 DN16 96 E2
Charterhouse La HU2 155 B3
Charterhouse The★ HU2 155 C3
Charter's La 4 YO25 34 B2
Charters The YO8 49 B5
Chase Hill Rd DN40 86 E5
Chase Sch 45 DN7 92 D4
Chase Side Ct YO24 132 E8
Chase The
Driffield YO25 125 A4
2 Snaith DN14 78 C8
Chatham St HU3 144 F7
Chatsworth Cl
Beverley HU17 154 A1
5 Bridlington YO16 122 D6
Chatsworth Dr
Goole DN14 149 B6
16 Haxby YO32 13 F5
Chatsworth Pl 1 DN35 103 B2
Chatsworth St HU5 145 B8
Chatsworth Terr 4 YO26 129 E4
Chatsworth Way 12 DN9 105 D2
Chatterton Cres DN15 96 D7
Chaucer Ave DN17 150 D3
Chaucer La YO32 14 B8
Chaucer St
Kingston upon Hull HU8 141 C2
7 York YO10 130 E3
Chaumont Way 1 YO32 14 D2
Chaytor Cl 16 HU12 72 D6
Cheadle Cl
Kingston upon Hull HU2 155 A4
Sculcoates HU2 140 E1
Cheapside
Kingston upon Hull HU8 155 C4
Waltham DN37 113 E5
Cheapside Rd DN37 113 F4
Cheapsides La HU15 66 D8
Checker La YO19 49 A7
Cheesemans Cl 9 DN37 113 E6
Cheesemans La 8 DN37 113 E6
Chelkar Way YO30 126 F1
Chellsway HU19 74 F6
Chelmer Rd HU8 142 B5
Chelmsford Ave DN34 152 A1
Chelmsford Cl 5 HU9 142 E1
Chelmsford Pl DN34 152 B2
Chelsea Cl HU8 141 F5
Chelsea Ct 3 HU16 138 F5
Chelsea Wlk 1 DN35 103 D1
Cheltenham Ave HU7 141 A8
Cheltenham Cl 8 DN16 96 E2
Cheltenham Way 30 DN35 103 C1
Chelwood Dr 30 DN33 102 D2
Chelwood Rd DN17 150 F3
Chelwood Wlk 12 YO26 129 E4
Chepstow Gr DN34 152 A1
Chequers The DN15 150 E7
Cheriton Cl 14 HU7 56 F5
CHERRY BURTON 43 B5
Cherry Burton CE Prim Sch HU17 43 B5
Cherry Cl
Great Driffield YO25 124 F2
Hornsea HU18 134 D1
34 Humberston DN35 103 C1
17 Humberston DN36 114 D8
Cherry Cobb Sands Rd HU12 87 F8
Cherry Cres YO43 40 A1
Cherry Ct 16 HU15 66 D8
Cherry Dale 11 DN35 103 B2
Cherry Dr
Holme-on-Spalding-Moor YO43 40 A1
Nafferton YO25 125 F6
Cherry Garth
Beverley HU17 154 C3
Kingston upon Hull HU3 145 A5
Lund YO25 31 F2
York YO31 131 B5
Cherry Gr
5 Belton DN9 94 E1
Belton DN9 105 E8
16 Poppleton YO26 12 F1
Scunthorpe DN16 151 B2
Cherry Hill La YO23 156 B1
Cherry Hill Pk HU12 74 B8
Cherry Holt 7 LN7 111 B4
Cherry La
Barrow upon Humber DN19 85 D8
Kingston upon Hull HU8 141 C4
Wootton DN39 85 E2
York YO24 132 F8
Cherry Mount 1 DN16 96 E2
Cherry Orch
16 Epworth DN9 105 E6
2 Haxby YO32 127 D8
Cherry Orchard Mews 12 YO42 29 A4
Cherry Paddock
4 Haxby YO32 127 D8
Kexby YO41 15 C2
Cherry Rd 4 YO14 3 A8
Cherry St YO23 156 B1
Cherry Tree Ave
1 Brigg DN20 98 B2
Kingston upon Hull HU8 141 C2
Newton-on-Ouse YO30 12 B6
9 Withernsea HU19 75 A6
York YO32 127 D4
Cherry Tree Cl
Bilton HU11 58 A3
13 Brayton YO8 48 D1
Little Burton YO25 34 B2
Cherry Tree Cres DN34 102 C4
Cherry Tree Crossing HU17 154 B3
Cherry Tree Ct 12 YO8 49 B4
Cherrytree Dr YO8 48 D6
Cherry Tree Dr
Hatfield DN7 92 D5
5 Naburn YO23 36 C7
3 Thorne/Moorends DN8 79 A1
Cherry Tree Gdns 17 DN17 94 D7
Cherry Tree Gr DN7 92 C5
Cherry Tree La
Beverley HU17 154 B3
31 Hedon HU12 72 D7
Cherry Tree Rd 18 DN21 117 C1
Cherry Tree Rise DN21 107 D4
Cherry Trees HU16 138 A7
Cherry Tree's Bsns Pk DN31 152 A6
Cherry Tree Terr HU17 154 C3
Cherry Tree Wlk 7 YO8 49 B4
Cherry Way
Messingham DN17 107 D7
Nafferton YO25 125 F6
Cherry Wood Cres YO19 133 E5
Chesham Gr DN14 149 B6
Cheshire Ave YO32 14 A6
Cheshire Cl
Kingston upon Hull HU5 139 D1
6 Rawcliffe YO32 126 E2
Chesney Dr DN16 96 D2
Chesney Fields 4 YO24 129 D1
Chesnut Ave HU5 140 C2
Chesnut Way 6 DN19 86 A8
Chessingham Gdns YO24 132 E6
Chessingham Pk YO19 26 F6
Chesswick Ave DN17 95 D5
Chesswick Cres DN17 95 D5
Chester Ave HU17 136 E1
Chester Court Rd YO8 63 A6
Chesterfield Rd DN15 150 B6
Chester Grange DN33 102 F1
Chesterholme HU11 142 E6
Chester Pl DN35 153 C1
Chester Rd HU5 139 B1
Chester Wlk DN34 152 A1
Chestnut Ave
2 Airmyn DN14 64 E4
Beverley HU17 136 F6
15 Gainsborough DN21 117 B1
Goole DN14 149 B3
Great Driffield YO25 124 F2
Grimsby DN31 152 B3
Hedon HU12 72 C8
10 Hemingbrough YO8 49 F1
Hessle HU13 143 E1
Immingham DN40 87 D2
Kirk Ella HU10 143 E8
Stainforth DN7 92 D6
3 Thorne/Moorends DN8 93 B7
2 Thorngumbald HU12 72 E5
Withernsea HU19 75 A5
York YO31 130 F6
Chestnut Cl
Beverley HU17 136 F6
Bridlington YO15 123 B7
6 Burstwick HU12 73 A6
4 Scotter DN21 107 C3
Snaith DN14 78 B8
Walkeringham DN10 116 D3
17 Waltham DN37 113 D6
Chestnut Cres YO43 40 A1
Chestnut Croft 17 YO8 49 F1
Chestnut Ct
9 Hemingbrough YO8 49 F1
York YO32 127 F5
Chestnut Dr
15 Gilberdyke HU15 66 D8
8 Hemingbrough YO8 49 F1
Holme-on-Spalding-Moor YO43 40 A1
Messingham DN17 107 D7
Chestnut Garth
Burton Pidsea HU12 59 C2
4 Hemingbrough YO8 49 F1
Roos HU12 60 A1
Chestnut Gn 10 LS25 61 A8
Chestnut Gr
Acomb YO26 129 C4
8 Barnetby le Beck DN38 99 B4
5 Broughton DN20 97 E4
Huntington YO32 127 E4
Kingston upon Hull HU8 141 B2
Sproatley HU11 58 D5
Withernsea HU19 75 A5
Chestnut Mews
Cawood YO8 48 A8
Tickton HU17 137 E8
Chestnut Pk YO41 28 C8
Chestnut Rd
Cawood YO8 48 A8
Waltham DN37 113 D6
Chestnut Rise
Barrow upon Humber DN19 85 C8
6 Hemingbrough YO8 49 F1
Chestnuts The
6 Haxby YO32 127 C8
Hensall DN14 62 D2
Searby DN38 110 D8
Chestnut View YO42 29 B3
Chestnut Way
Scunthorpe DN16 151 B3
Selby YO8 148 E3
Chestnut Wlk DN41 102 A5
Chevering Pk 8 HU7 56 E5
Cheverton Ave 19 HU19 75 A6
Cheviot Ave DN14 149 D5
Cheviot Cl
3 Thorne/Moorends DN8 93 A7
1 York YO32 127 F3
Cheviotdale HU7 140 F6
Chevy Chase HU11 142 E6
Cheyne Garth HU18 134 A4
Cheyne Wlk HU18 134 A4
Chichester Dr 19 LN7 111 B4
Chichester Rd DN35 103 C2
Chiltern Cres DN17 150 D4
Chiltern Dr 19 DN37 113 D6
Chiltern Prim Sch HU3 145 B5
Chiltern Rd DN14 149 D5
Chilterns The HU9 142 D2
Chiltern Way
26 Grimsby DN33 113 E8
York YO32 127 F5
Chilton Cl 19 DN40 87 B1
Chilton Rise HU10 138 B1
Chilton St 9 HU3 145 B5
Chilvers Ct 4 YO8 148 A1
Chimes Rd YO8 148 C6
Chimes The 9 YO8 148 C6
Chimney Field Rd HU12 74 B6
Chingford Ave 1 DN34 102 D2
Chingford Wlk HU9 142 E1
Chippendale Cl 2 DN36 114 D8
Chiswick Cl 3 HU8 142 A5
Cholmley St HU3 145 B5
Christine Pl 4 DN33 113 F8
Chrystals Rd HU18 134 D5
Chrystals Wlk HU18 134 D5
Chudleigh Rd 1 YO26 129 F5
Church Acres DN14 65 D1
Church Ave
Humberston DN36 114 C8
6 North Ferriby HU14 69 A4
6 Selby YO8 148 D5
Church Balk
Dunnington YO19 26 E7
Thorne/Moorends DN8 93 B8
Church Cl
Askham Bryan YO23 24 F3

Church Cl *continued*
Bonby DN20 84 C2
Bridlington YO16 122 D4
4 Bubwith YO8 50 D7
25 Flamborough YO15 5 A2
Goole DN14 149 E2
Grimsby DN32 153 B1
Kingston upon Hull HU7 141 D6
Laxton DN14 65 F4
1 Market Weighton YO43 135 D4
10 Riccall YO19 48 F8
8 Thorne/Moorends DN8 93 B8
5 Wetwang YO25 19 B5
Wheldrake YO19 38 A7
Church Cres
Owston Ferry DN9 106 A3
4 Wawne HU7 56 E7
Church Ct
Great Driffield YO25 124 E4
Scunthorpe DN15 151 B8
Church Dike La YO8 63 F5
Church Dr
Leven HU17 45 A8
6 Misterton DN10 116 C5
CHURCH END 33 F8
Church End YO8 48 B8
Church Farm Cl YO23 62 C4
Church Farm Ct YO25 2 E3
Churchfield DN14 63 C2
Church Field 7 HU13 144 A3
Churchfield Dr 28 YO32 13 E5
Churchfield La WF8 76 C4
Churchfield Rd DN16 151 B1
Church Field Rd DN6 76 E1
Churchfields HU17 137 E8
Church Fields DN15 83 A5
Church Gate 21 HU12 72 C7
Church Gn
Beverley HU17 136 B6
5 Bridlington YO16 122 D4
3 Elvington YO41 27 C2
Church Hill
Grasby DN38 110 E7
10 Hunmanby YO14 2 F8
Reighton YO14 3 C6
Riby DN37 101 B2
3 Selby YO8 148 D5
South Cave HU15 53 F2
Stillingfleet YO19 36 D3
Whitton DN15 67 E3
8 Wistow YO8 48 D6
Church Hill Rd YO25 31 C4
Churchill Ave
Brigg DN20 98 C2
Burstwick HU12 73 A7
Hatfield DN7 92 F4
Hutton Cranswick YO25 32 E7
10 Keelby DN41 101 A5
Kingston upon Hull HU16 138 F6
Churchill Rise HU12 73 A7
Churchill St HU9 146 D7
Churchill Way DN32 152 F3
Churchill Wlk DN14 149 C5
Church La
Appleby DN15 83 C1
Atwick YO25 35 C5
Aylesby DN37 101 E2
Barnetby le Beck DN37 113 B6
1 Beeford YO25 22 D1
Beswick YO25 32 B4
Bilton HU11 142 F6
Bishop Burton HU17 43 B2
Bishopthorpe YO23 133 A4
Blyton DN21 117 F5
Bonby DN20 84 C2
Bradley DN37 102 C1
Brandesburton YO25 34 B2
Bridlington YO15 123 B7
Brigsley DN37 113 D4
3 Brough HU15 68 C7
Broughton DN20 97 E3
6 Buckton/Bempton YO15 4 D3
Burstwick HU12 73 A7
Cadney DN20 109 D6
Carlton DN14 63 C3
Carnaby YO16 10 D5
Catton YO41 27 D8
Catwick HU17 45 C8
Corringham DN21 118 B2
Driffield YO25 124 B4
Dunnington YO19 26 E7
4 Elvington YO41 27 C2
Fishlake DN7 92 D8
24 Flamborough YO15 5 A2
Fotherby LN11 121 D2
Fridaythorpe YO25 18 B7
Garton YO25 124 B4
Gateforth YO8 61 F8
Grayingham DN21 119 B7
Great Driffield YO25 124 E4
Great Limber DN37 100 D3
Grimsby DN32 152 D3
12 Grimsby DN33 102 E1
17 Haxby YO32 13 E5
Haxey DN9 105 C2
Hedon HU12 72 C7
Hensall DN14 62 C1
Hollym HU19 75 A4
Holton le Clay DN36 114 A5
Hook DN14 149 F7
Hotham YO43 53 D5
Humberston DN36 114 D8
Hutton Cranswick YO25 32 E8
Immingham DN40 86 E4
Irby DN37 112 D7
Keadby with Althorpe DN17 95 D4
Kellington DN14 61 E3
Keyingham HU12 73 C4

Church La *continued*
2 Kilham YO25 9 C3
Kirk Ella HU10 143 C8
Laceby DN37 101 F1
Langtoft YO25 8 C1
Lockington YO25 32 B1
Luddington & Haldenby DN17 81 D4
Marfleet HU9 147 C8
Marsh Chapel DN36 115 B1
Millington YO42 29 D6
3 Misterton DN10 116 C5
4 Monk Fryston LS25 61 A8
Moor Monkton YO26 12 B2
Nether Poppleton YO26 126 B3
New Earswick YO32 127 F5
4 North Cave HU15 53 D3
North Frodingham YO25 33 F8
North Kelsey LN7 110 A4
North Killingholme DN40 86 E4
North Thoresby DN36 114 B1
Nunburnholme YO42 29 E2
Patrington HU12 74 D1
Poppleton YO26 126 A3
Rudston YO25 9 F6
Saxby All Saints DN20 84 B3
Scawby DN20 98 A1
Scotter DN21 107 C3
Scunthorpe DN15 150 F6
Seaton Ross YO42 39 E4
4 Selby YO8 148 D5
Sigglesthorne HU11 45 F8
Skelton YO30 126 B5
Skirlaugh HU11 45 E2
2 Snaith DN14 63 C1
Sproatley HU11 58 D5
Stallingborough DN41 101 D6
10 Stamford Bridge YO41 15 D2
Strensall YO32 14 A7
Swinefleet DN14 65 D1
Tetney DN36 114 D3
Thorngumbald HU12 72 E5
Thwing YO25 2 A1
Twin Rivers DN14 81 A8
Ulceby DN39 86 A1
Utterby LN11 121 C3
Waithe DN36 114 A3
4 Waltham DN37 113 E6
Watton YO25 32 D4
6 Wawne HU7 56 F7
Wetwang YO25 19 B6
Wheldrake YO19 38 A7
Withernwick HU11 46 D3
York YO1 156 B2
Church Lane Staith HU1 155 C2
Church Mews
Barlby YO8 49 A5
Swanland HU14 69 C7
2 York YO26 129 C3
Church Mount
Kingston upon Hull HU7 141 D6
9 North Newbald YO43 53 F7
Church Rd
Beverley HU17 136 B6
33 Dunswell HU7 56 F6
Laughton DN21 117 F8
North Ferriby HU14 69 A4
Rimswell HU19 74 D7
Skeffling HU12 90 D6
Stainforth DN7 92 C6
Stamford Bridge YO41 15 D2
Thornton YO42 39 B7
Wawne HU7 56 E7
York YO10 131 D4
Church Rise
Holtby YO19 14 F1
Skidby HU16 138 A8
Church Row HU8 155 C4
Churchside 4 DN19 85 D8
Church Side
Alkborough DN15 82 C8
Appleby DN15 83 D2
Goxhill DN19 86 A7
Grasby DN38 110 E7
2 Market Weighton YO43 135 D4
West Halton DN15 82 E7
16 Winterton DN15 83 A5
Church St
7 Aldbrough HU11 47 C1
Amcotts DN17 81 F1
Anlaby HU10 143 E6
Bainton YO25 31 E7
Beckingham DN10 116 D1
6 Brough HU15 68 D6
Bubwith YO8 50 D7
Burton Pidsea HU12 59 D1
14 Caistor LN7 111 B4
Copmanthorpe YO23 132 B2
Dunnington YO19 26 E7
Elsham DN20 98 F7
4 Epworth DN9 105 E6
Fishlake DN7 92 D8
19 Flamborough YO15 5 A2
Gainsborough DN21 117 B1
Goole DN14 149 D4
5 Goxhill DN19 86 A8
Great Driffield YO25 124 D4
Grimsby DN32 152 F5
Haxey DN9 105 C2
Hemswell DN21 119 A1
Hibaldstow DN20 108 F5
Huggate YO42 18 C2
Hutton Cranswick YO25 32 E8
4 Kilham YO25 9 C3
Kingston upon Hull HU7 141 E6
Kirton in Lindsey DN21 108 B1
Messingham DN17 107 D7
Misterton DN10 116 C5

Church St *continued*
Nettleton LN7 111 B3
North Cave HU15 53 D3
North Kelsey LN7 110 A4
Owston Ferry DN9 106 A3
3 Riccall YO19 48 F8
Scawby DN20 108 E8
South Cave HU15 53 F1
Thorne/Moorends DN8 93 A8
Willoughton DN21 119 B4
York YO1 156 B2
Churchthorpe LN11 121 E8
CHURCH TOWN 94 E1
Churchtown DN9 94 E1
Church View
12 Airmyn DN14 64 E4
Alkborough DN15 82 C8
8 Barton-upon-Humber DN18 84 F8
4 Beckingham DN10 116 D1
Beverley HU17 154 C3
4 Brough HU15 68 C7
Eastrington DN14 65 F8
Grimsby DN34 102 C4
22 Hemingbrough YO8 49 F1
Norton DN6 76 E1
Ottringham HU12 73 E3
7 Patrington HU12 74 D1
Swallow LN7 112 B5
1 Waltham DN37 113 E6
Church View Cl DN9 94 E1
Church Way
East Ella HU5 144 E7
Nettleton LN7 111 B3
Church Wlk
Bridlington YO16 122 D5
Holton le Clay DN36 114 A5
Owston Ferry DN9 106 A3
5 Wistow YO8 48 D6
Cinder La
Upper Poppleton YO26 129 A7
York YO26 129 F5
Cinder Mews YO26 130 A5
Cinema St HU18 134 C4
Circle The 4 HU13 143 E2
Cissplatt La DN41 101 A5
Citadel Ct HU17 154 B3
Citadel Trading Pk HU9 155 C2
Citadel Way HU9 155 C2
City Art Gallery* YO30 156 B3
Cladshaw HU6 139 F8
Claire's Wlk DN17 150 C3
Clanthorpe HU6 139 F8
Clapham Ave HU8 141 E5
Clapson's La 19 HU14 69 E1
Clare Ave DN17 150 D3
Clare Ct
Beverley HU17 137 B4
Grimsby DN34 152 A1
Clare Gr HU9 142 A1
Claremont Ave HU6 140 D4
Claremont Rd DN32 153 D2
Claremont Terr YO31 156 B4
Clarence Ave
Bridlington YO15 122 D1
Kingston upon Hull HU8 141 E4
Clarence Cl 25 DN40 87 B1
Clarence Ct HU2 155 A3
Clarence Rd 1 YO16 122 F2
Clarence St
Kingston upon Hull HU9 155 C2
York YO31 156 B4
Clarendon Ct YO31 130 C7
Clarendon Rd
6 Grimsby DN34 102 C2
Scunthorpe DN17 150 F3
Clarendon St HU3 145 D7
Clark Ave DN31 152 A3
Clarke Cres 9 YO15 4 D3
Clarkes Rd DN40 86 E4
Clarke St DN15 151 A7
Clarks La 10 HU12 74 D1
Clark's La YO43 53 D6
Clarksons Dr DN41 101 E6
Clarks Terr YO31 130 F6
Clarondale HU7 140 E7
Clavering St DN31 152 B5
Claxby Rd DN17 150 F1
CLAXTON 15 B7
Clay Bank Rd DN8 93 C6
Clayden St DN31 152 B5
Clayfield Cl 18 YO42 29 A4
Clayfield La
Pocklington YO42 29 A4
Shipton Thorpe YO43 40 F6
Clayfield Rd
Pocklington YO42 29 A3
Scunthorpe DN15 96 C7
Claygate YO31 131 B6
Clay Hill YO41 16 C3
Clay La
Bubwith YO8 50 C5
Camblesforth YO8 63 C6
Cliffe YO8 49 D4
Holton le Clay DN36 114 A6
Kirton in Lindsey DN21 108 B1
Market Weighton YO43 135 B5
Millington YO42 29 C6
Scotter DN21 107 C4
Claymore Cl DN35 153 E2
Claypit La DN14 63 C3
Clay Pl 3 YO24 129 D1
Clay St HU8 141 A3
Claytons Fold 18 HU15 66 D8
Clear View Cl HU8 141 F6
Clearwaters 6 HU7 56 E5
Cleatham Rd DN21 108 A3
Cleaves Ave HU15 54 A2

Clee Cres DN32 153 C1
Cleefields Cl DN32 153 B1
Clee Ness Dr 16 DN36 103 D1
Clee Rd DN35 153 D2
Cleethorpe Rd DN32 153 A5
CLEETHORPES 153 C2
Cleethorpe Sands Nature Reserve* DN35 103 E1
Cleethorpes Coast Light Rly* DN35 103 E2
Cleethorpes Ctry Pk* DN35 103 C1
Cleethorpes Discovery Ctr* DN35 103 D2
Cleethorpes L Ctr DN35 103 D2
Cleethorpes Sta DN35 153 F3
Cleeton La YO25 23 A2
Cleeton Way YO16 122 B6
Cleeve Dr 12 HU7 57 A5
Cleeve Prim Sch HU7 57 A5
Cleeve Rd HU12 72 D6
Clee Village DN32 153 C2
Clematis Ave DN41 101 F5
Clematis Cl YO25 124 D3
Clematis Way DN16 96 E2
Clementhorpe YO23 156 B1
Clementhorpe La HU15 66 D8
Clementhorpe Rd HU15 66 D8
Clement St 4 YO23 156 B1
Clerke St DN35 153 B4
Clevedon Rd DN17 150 D4
Cleveland Cl
Hook DN14 65 B5
4 Immingham DN40 87 B1
Scunthorpe DN17 150 D4
Cleveland Gdns
Grimsby DN31 152 B5
Stockton on the Forest YO32 14 D3
Cleveland St
Grimsby DN31 152 B5
Kingston upon Hull HU8 155 C4
York YO24 130 A4
Cleveland Terr YO32 127 F4
Cleveland Way
41 Hatfield DN7 92 D4
York YO32 127 F3
Cliff Ave DN15 82 F5
Cliff Closes Rd DN15 150 D6
Cliff Dr DN15 82 B5
CLIFFE 49 E2
Cliffe La YO43 52 D8
Cliffe Prim Sch YO8 49 E2
Cliffe Rd
Market Weighton YO43 135 D1
Newbald YO43 53 C7
Cliff Gdns DN15 150 E6
Cliff Gr DN18 84 E8
Cliff Hill Rd DN6 76 D2
Cliff House Dr 3 HU13 69 E4
Cliff La
Bempton YO15 4 D4
Mappleton HU18 47 A6
Waddingham DN21 119 F6
Clifford Ave HU8 141 E4
Clifford's Cl DN20 98 A1
Clifford St
Hornsea HU18 134 C5
York YO1 156 B2
Clifford's Twr* YO1 156 B1
Cliff Rd
Atwick YO25 35 D5
Bridlington YO15 123 B6
Hessle HU13 69 E4
Hornsea HU18 134 C6
Snitterby DN21 119 F5
South Ferriby DN18 84 A8
Winteringham DN15 83 A8
Cliff St
Bridlington YO15 122 F2
Scunthorpe DN16 151 C6
Cliff The DN15 150 D7
Cliff Top La 2 HU13 69 E4
CLIFTON 130 A7
Clifton Ct 27 DN8 93 A8
Clifton Dale YO30 130 A6
Clifton Gdns DN14 149 B4
Clifton Gn YO30 130 A6
Clifton Green Prim Sch YO30 130 B7
Clifton Moor Bsns Village YO30 127 A2
Clifton Moorgate YO30 127 B3
Clifton Moor Gate YO30 127 A2
Clifton Moor Ind Estate YO30 127 A3
Clifton Moor Retail Pk YO30 127 A4
Clifton Moor Sh Ctr YO30 126 F3
Clifton Park Ave YO30 129 E8
Clifton Park (York CC & York RUFC) YO30 129 F7
Clifton Pl 3 YO30 130 A7
Clifton Prep Sch YO30 156 A4
Clifton Prim Sch HU2 155 A4
Clifton Rd
Grimsby DN34 152 A2
York YO30 156 A4
Clifton St
Hornsea HU18 134 C5
Kingston upon Hull HU2 155 A4
Clifton Terr HU5 140 E1
Clifton Without Jun Sch YO30 129 F8
Clive Gr YO24 129 F2
Clive Sullivan Way HU4 144 C1
CLIXBY 111 A7

Clixby Cl DN35 103 D2
Clixby La DN38 110 E7
Clockmill La YO42 29 A4
Cloeberry Way 14 HU12 72 C7
Cloister Cl DN17 150 F2
Cloisters The
6 Grimsby DN37 102 B4
15 Hemingbrough YO8 49 F1
Humberston DN36 114 D8
Wilberfoss YO41 27 F6
York YO31 156 C3
Cloisters Wlk YO31 156 C3
Cloister Wk DN20 97 E3
Close The
9 Acaster Malbis YO32 36 C7
Cawood YO8 48 A7
Goxhill DN19 71 A1
Great Driffield YO25 124 F5
Grimsby DN34 152 C3
Kingston upon Hull HU10 138 F1
4 Leven HU17 45 A8
5 Market Weighton YO43 135 E4
Norton DN6 76 E2
12 Patrington HU12 74 D1
Riccall YO19 49 A8
Scunthorpe DN16 151 B6
Sutton-on-Hull HU7 141 D6
8 Withernsea HU19 75 A6
York YO30 129 F8
Clouds La
Belton DN9 95 B1
West Butterwick DN17 106 C8
Clough Garth HU12 72 D8
Clough La DN40 86 F6
Clough Rd HU5 140 F3
Cloughton Gr HU5 139 E2
Clovelly Gdns 3 HU5 140 E1
Clover Bank View 11 HU6 56 E5
Clover Ct 26 DN20 98 B2
Cloverfields Prim Sch DN36 114 C8
Cloverley Cl YO41 15 C2
Cloverley Rd 6 YO16 123 A6
Clowes Ct 4 HU13 143 E1
Clumber Pl DN35 153 E1
Clumber St HU5 145 C8
Clyde St
Grimsby DN32 152 F4
Kingston upon Hull HU3 144 F5
Clyfton Cres DN40 87 B1
Coach House Garth YO42 28 D3
Coach House Gdns DN20 108 E8
Coachings The 4 HU13 69 E4
Coachyard Mews DN21 108 B1
Coal Pit La WF8 76 A2
Coal Shore La LN11 115 E1
Coastguard Hill YO14 3 E5
Coates Ave DN15 83 A5
Coates Marsh La DN14 63 B2
Cobble Court Mews YO24 156 A1
Cobble La DN14 51 F1
Cobbler Hill DN14 149 B6
Cobcroft La WF11 76 B8
Cobdale La YO42 29 F7
Cobden St HU3 144 F7
Cobden Street North End DN32 152 F4
Cober Gr HU8 142 C7
Cobham Way YO32 126 E3
Cochrane St YO8 148 D3
Cockerell La YO25 22 B4
Cocketts La DN20 108 F5
COCK HILL 12 B2
Cock Pit Cl HU10 143 C6
Cockret Cl 3 YO8 148 B6
Cockret Ct YO8 148 B7
Cockret Rd YO8 148 B7
Cockthorne La DN15 83 C7
Coda Ave YO23 133 B3
Coelus St HU9 155 C3
Coeside YO24 132 B7
Cogan St HU1 155 A1
Coggan Cl YO23 130 B2
Coggan Way YO23 132 F4
Cohort Cl 10 HU15 68 C5
Coke Oven Ave DN16 151 F6
Cold Harbour La LN11 121 F4
Cold Harbour Rd HU17 43 A1
Cold Harbour View 5 HU17 43 A2
Coldstream Cl 4 HU8 142 C5
COLEBY 82 E6
Coleby Rd DN15 82 E7
Coledale Cl 2 YO30 126 F1
Coleford Gr HU7 141 A7
Colemans Rd 4 HU12 72 C7
Colenso St
Kingston upon Hull HU3 145 A5
York YO23 156 B1
Coleridge Ave DN17 150 D3
Coleridge St HU8 141 D2
Cole St
Scunthorpe DN15 151 B6
York YO31 156 B4
Colin Ave DN32 153 B2
Colin Rd DN16 151 C6
Colins Wlk DN21 107 C4
College Ave 31 DN33 113 E8
College Cl
Alkborough DN15 82 C8
Goole DN14 149 B4
College Farm Cl DN14 77 A8
College Gdns
32 Grimsby DN33 113 E8

Dog & Duck La *continued*
12 Gainsborough DN21 ... 117 A2
Dog & Duck Sq 13 YO15 ... 5 A2
Dog Kennel La HU17 ... 43 C3
Doherty Wlk YO24 ... 132 C8
Dolby Vale 23 DN34 ... 102 C2
Dolegate YO41 ... 15 F4
Dole Rd DN17 ... 80 B1
Doll La 2 DN20 ... 98 F7
Dollyth Howe* YO17 ... 6 F6
Dolman Cres 11 DN17 ... 96 C2
Dolphin St DN35 ... 153 F2
Dominican Wlk HU17 ... 154 B2
Dominion Cl 9 DN36 ... 114 A7
Don Ave YO24 ... 132 E8
Doncaster Coll DN8 ... 93 B8
Doncaster Rd
Brayton YO8 ... 148 B3
Gunness DN15 ... 95 E6
Hatfield DN7 ... 92 D3
Haxey DN9 ... 104 F2
North Elmsall WF8 ... 76 A1
Scunthorpe DN15 ... 150 A7
Stainforth DN7 ... 92 B6
Doncaster St HU3 ... 145 B6
Don Cl DN14 ... 78 B8
Donna Fields YO25 ... 9 F6
Donnington Gdns DN15 ... 150 F7
Donnington St DN32 ... 152 F3
Don St DN14 ... 149 D1
Donville Rd DN17 ... 81 A3
Dooks Cl DN21 ... 107 C1
Doon Garth HU4 ... 144 A3
Dorado Cl 2 HU3 ... 145 A5
Dorchester Prim Sch HU7 ... 141 B6
Dorchester Rd
Kingston upon Hull HU7 ... 141 B7
Scunthorpe DN17 ... 150 C4
Doriam Ave YO31 ... 127 F2
Doriam Dr YO31 ... 127 F2
Dorking Cl HU8 ... 142 A4
Dornoch Dr HU8 ... 141 C3
Dorothy Ave
Thorne/Moorends DN8 ... 92 F8
6 Waltham DN37 ... 113 E7
Dorrington Cl 23 YO42 ... 29 A3
Dorr La DN14 ... 78 A8
Dorset Ave HU11 ... 45 E2
Dorset Close E 2 DN15 ... 82 B4
Dorset Close W 1 DN15 ... 82 B4
Dorset St HU4 ... 144 F3
Dorsey Way 5 HU15 ... 68 C7
Dot Hill Cl 3 YO43 ... 53 F7
Double Bridges Rd DN8 ... 93 B6
Doughty Cl 2 DN37 ... 113 E7
Doughty Rd DN32 ... 152 E3
Douglas Ave DN31 ... 152 A4
Douglas Rd
Cleethorpes DN35 ... 153 D4
Kingston upon Hull HU8 ... 142 C6
Douglas St 3 YO8 ... 148 C5
Dove Cl HU12 ... 74 A8
Dovecote Garth 5 YO41 ... 27 B2
Dove Cote Gdns DN14 ... 62 D2
Dovecote Mdws DN20 ... 98 D3
Dovedale Cl DN15 ... 83 A6
Dovedale Ct YO16 ... 122 F7
Dovedale Dr 18 DN33 ... 113 E8
Dovedale Gr 1 HU9 ... 146 E8
Dovedale Rd DN16 ... 151 D1
Dove La HU12 ... 74 B8
Dover St
Grimsby DN31 ... 152 C4
Kingston upon Hull HU3 ... 145 C8
Dove St YO23 ... 156 A1
Dower Chase YO19 ... 37 A6
Dower Pk YO19 ... 37 B6
Dower Rise 11 HU14 ... 69 B7
Downe Cl DN14 ... 78 D7
Downe St YO25 ... 124 E4
Downfield Ave HU6 ... 140 B8
Downhill Dr 7 HU7 ... 57 B5
Downing Cl 6 DN34 ... 102 C3
Downing Cres 11 DN16 ... 96 D2
Downing Gr HU9 ... 142 A1
Download Cres WF11 ... 61 A1
Downs Cres HU5 ... 139 D2
Dowse Ave DN15 ... 150 E8
Dowsons La DN14 ... 78 E8
DRAGONBY ... 82 E1
Dragonby Rd 3 DN17 ... 96 C2
Dragon La YO16 ... 122 C5
Drain Bank HU15 ... 67 B8
Drain La
Gilberdyke HU15 ... 52 D2
Holme-on-Spalding-Moor YO43 ... 51 F8
Drake Ave DN32 ... 153 B2
Drakes Cl YO32 ... 127 F5
Drake St 2 YO23 ... 156 B1
Dr Anderson Ave 9 DN7 ... 92 C6
Drapers Croft YO23 ... 132 B4
Draper's La 17 HU12 ... 72 C7
DRAX ... 63 F5
Drax Castle Earthworks* YO8 ... 63 F4
Drax Prim Sch YO8 ... 63 F5
Draycot LN7 ... 111 A2
Draycott Ave HU18 ... 134 C5
Dray Dr HU17 ... 43 E5
Drayton Cl 5 HU8 ... 142 C5
Dressay Gr HU8 ... 141 F7
Drew Ave DN32 ... 102 F2
Drewry La 7 DN9 ... 105 A2
Drewton Ct 8 DN14 ... 65 A7
Drewton La HU15 ... 54 A4
DRIFFIELD ... 124 C5
Driffield Bsns Ctr YO25 ... 124 F2
Driffield CE Inf Sch YO25 ... 124 E4
Driffield Cl HU16 ... 138 E6
Driffield Jun Sch YO25 ... 124 F5
Driffield L Ctr YO25 ... 125 A5
Driffield Rd
Beverley HU17 ... 136 C6
Huggate YO42 ... 18 C1
Kilham YO25 ... 9 C2
Langtoft YO25 ... 8 C4
Molescroft HU17 ... 136 B8
Nafferton YO25 ... 125 E7
Skerne & Wansford YO25 ... 21 A2
Driffield Sch YO25 ... 125 A5
Driffield Showground* YO25 ... 124 D2
Driffield Spellowgate YO25 ... 124 B7
Driffield Sports Ctr YO25 ... 125 A5
Driffield Sta YO25 ... 124 F3
Driffield Terr YO24 ... 130 A2
Driffil Way DN15 ... 83 A4
Drill Hall La 28 DN21 ... 117 B1
Dringfield Cl 2 YO24 ... 132 D8
DRINGHOUSES ... 132 E8
Dringhouses Prim Sch YO24 ... 132 F8
Dringhouses Sports Club YO24 ... 132 F8
Dring La DN21 ... 118 A7
Dringshaw HU6 ... 139 F8
Dringthorpe Rd YO24 ... 132 F7
Drive The
Cherry Burton HU17 ... 43 A4
Kirk Sandall DN3 ... 92 A1
Waltham DN37 ... 113 E6
Drome Rd YO23 ... 132 C2
Dronfield Ct DN15 ... 150 B7
Drove La HU7 ... 44 E1
Drovers Rise 1 HU15 ... 68 C6
Drummer's Well* YO25 ... 21 F8
Drummond Ct 5 HU7 ... 57 B5
Drummond View YO23 ... 133 B4
Drury Cl 1 DN37 ... 113 D6
Drury La 3 DN36 ... 114 A7
Drydales HU10 ... 143 C6
Dryden Rd DN17 ... 150 D2
Dryden St HU8 ... 141 C2
Dryham La HU15 ... 53 C3
Dryhurst Cl 9 DN6 ... 76 F2
Drypool Way HU9 ... 146 B6
Duchess St DN32 ... 152 D2
Duck La
Ganton YO12 ... 1 A8
Kirton in Lindsey DN21 ... 108 B1
Duckthorpe La DN36 ... 115 B2
Duddon Gr HU8 ... 142 B6
Dudley Ct YO31 ... 156 C4
Dudley Mews YO31 ... 156 C4
Dudley Pl DN35 ... 103 B2
Dudley Rd
28 Brigg DN20 ... 98 C2
Scunthorpe DN16 ... 151 E2
Dudley St
Grimsby DN34 ... 152 C3
York YO31 ... 156 C4
Dudley Wlk HU4 ... 144 B3
Duesbery St HU5 ... 145 C8
Duesbury Cl HU17 ... 154 A3
Dugard Rd DN32 ... 153 B3
DUGGLEBY ... 6 B6
Duggleby Howe* YO17 ... 6 C5
Dukes Ct 3 YO26 ... 129 D6
Duke's La YO25 ... 2 A1
Duke St
Grimsby DN32 ... 153 A5
13 Stainforth DN7 ... 92 C6
Dukes Wharf YO23 ... 156 B1
Dulverton Cl 4 HU7 ... 56 F5
Dumfries Wlk HU8 ... 142 C7
Dunbar Ave 5 DN36 ... 114 A7
Dunbar Cl 6 DN21 ... 117 C1
Duncan Dr DN18 ... 69 E1
Dunce Mire Rd LS25 ... 61 A8
Duncombe Ct HU12 ... 72 E7
Duncombe Dr
Great Driffield YO25 ... 124 D3
Strensall YO32 ... 14 B8
Duncombe Gdns DN32 ... 152 F5
Duncombe La YO32 ... 14 B8
Duncombe Pl YO1 ... 156 B3
Duncombe St DN32 ... 152 F4
Dundas St YO1 ... 156 C2
Dundee St HU5 ... 145 A8
Dunelm Cl 3 HU8 ... 141 C1
Dunelm Cres 18 DN8 ... 79 B2
Dunflat Gate HU17 ... 55 D6
Dunflat La HU16 ... 55 B5
Dunflat Rd HU17 ... 55 D6
Dunhill Rd DN14 ... 149 B4
Dunkeld Dr 4 HU6 ... 140 B8
Dunken Hill Highgate HU17 ... 42 F4
Dunlin Cl HU7 ... 141 D8
Dunlin Dr DN16 ... 151 F1
Dunlop Way DN16 ... 151 E3
Dunmires La DN14 ... 80 E8
Dunmow Cl 1 HU8 ... 142 C5
Dunmow St DN31 ... 152 B5
DUNNINGTON
Driffield ... 26 F7
Hornsea ... 34 F7
Dunnington La
Beeford YO25 ... 34 D7
Skipsea YO25 ... 22 F1
Dunnington Prim Sch YO19 ... 26 E7
Dunnock Cl
7 Kingston upon Hull HU8 ... 141 D7
26 Yaddlethorpe DN17 ... 96 D1
Dunnscroft YO15 ... 5 A2
Dunn's La 6 YO25 ... 124 F4
Dunns Paddock 3 DN20 ... 98 F7
Dunscombe Pk HU8 ... 141 B2
DUNSCROFT ... 92 C3
Dunstall St DN15 ... 151 A7
Dunstan Dr
30 Canal Side DN8 ... 93 A8
26 Thorne/Moorends DN8 ... 93 A8
Dunstan Hill DN21 ... 108 B1
Dunstan Villas 17 DN21 ... 108 B1
Dunstan Wlk 34 DN8 ... 93 A8
Dunster Rd DN21 ... 117 C1
Dunston Dr HU13 ... 143 D1
Dunston Rd HU5 ... 144 D7
DUNSVILLE ... 92 B3
Dunsville Prim Sch DN7 ... 92 D3
DUNSWELL ... 56 D5
Dunswell Cl HU6 ... 140 A7
Dunswell La HU6 ... 56 C6
Dunswell Prim Sch HU6 ... 56 D6
Dunswell Rd
Cottingham HU16 ... 56 B6
Kingston upon Hull HU16 ... 139 C8
Dunvegan Rd HU8 ... 141 F6
Durban Rd DN32 ... 153 B3
Durban St HU8 ... 155 C3
Durham Ave
Grimsby DN34 ... 152 A3
10 Thorne/Moorends DN8 ... 93 A8
Durham Cl 18 YO8 ... 49 F1
Durham Mews HU17 ... 154 A1
Durham Rd
Cleethorpes DN35 ... 153 C1
Hatfield DN7 ... 92 D4
Durham St HU8 ... 141 C1
Durlston Dr YO32 ... 14 A7
Dursley Ave 1 DN36 ... 113 F7
Dyer La HU17 ... 154 A3
Dyke Cl 2 HU13 ... 69 F4
Dykelands Cl YO19 ... 37 F7
Dyke Rd DN36 ... 115 C5
Dykes La YO23 ... 132 A1
Dymoke Dr DN37 ... 102 B3
Dyon La YO8 ... 50 B3
Dyon Rd YO8 ... 50 D7
Dyon Way YO8 ... 50 D7

E

Eadon Pl DN14 ... 78 B8
Eagle Bsns Ctr HU2 ... 155 C4
Eagle Terr HU8 ... 155 C4
EALAND ... 94 E6
Ealand Rd DN17 ... 95 C6
Ealdane HU6 ... 139 E8
Ealing Cl HU8 ... 141 F5
Earfit La YO23 ... 36 A8
Earl Ave 24 DN36 ... 114 A8
Earlescourt HU6 ... 139 E7
Earle's Rd
Kingston upon Hull HU9 ... 146 D7
North Cotes DN36 ... 115 C5
Earle St YO31 ... 156 C4
Earlsborough Terr YO30 ... 156 A3
Earlsgate Gdns DN15 ... 82 F5
Earlsgate Rd DN15 ... 83 A5
Earl St
Grimsby DN31 ... 152 C3
Scunthorpe DN16 ... 151 B6
Earls Wlk DN16 ... 151 B6
Earsham Cl HU8 ... 142 C6
EARSWICK ... 128 A7
Earswick Chase YO32 ... 127 F7
Earswick Village YO32 ... 127 F7
Easby Ct HU5 ... 139 C2
Easedale Ave HU9 ... 142 D3
Easenby Ave HU10 ... 143 C6
Easenby Cl 3 HU14 ... 69 C7
EASINGTON ... 91 A6
Easington CE VC Prim Sch HU12 ... 90 F5
Easington Rd
Easington HU12 ... 91 B2
Skeffling HU12 ... 90 E6
Easingwood Way YO25 ... 125 A4
Eason Rd
8 Grimsby DN33 ... 102 D1
York YO24 ... 132 E8
Eason View YO24 ... 132 E8
East Acridge 7 DN18 ... 84 F8
East Back Side YO25 ... 10 C3
East Bank DN7 ... 92 C7
East Boundary Rd DN16 ... 151 F6
Eastbourne Gr YO31 ... 130 F5
Eastbourne Rd HU18 ... 134 D4
Eastbourne St HU3 ... 145 A5
Eastbourne Way 12 DN33 ... 113 E8
EASTBURN ... 20 B2
EAST BUTTERWICK ... 106 E8
EAST CARLTON ... 47 A2
East Carr Rd
Keyingham HU12 ... 73 D5
Kingston upon Hull HU8 ... 141 F7
East Cl HU17 ... 136 D6
East Comm La
Brumby DN16 ... 151 D3
East Comm La *continued*
Scunthorpe DN16 ... 151 B4
Selby YO8 ... 148 F4
EAST COMMON ... 148 E4
EAST COTTINGWITH ... 38 C5
EAST COWICK ... 78 D8
East Cross St 15 DN21 ... 108 B1
East Dale Dr DN21 ... 108 B2
East Dale Rd HU14 ... 68 E5
East Dock Rd DN40 ... 87 E2
EAST ELLA ... 144 D7
East Ella Dr HU4 ... 144 C6
East End
Humberside Airport DN39 ... 100 A6
Walkington HU17 ... 55 C8
East End Cl DN33 ... 102 E1
East End Rd HU12 ... 58 D1
Easterfield Ct 10 YO25 ... 124 F4
Eastern Ave DN21 ... 117 C1
Eastern Inway DN34 ... 152 A1
Eastern Terr YO31 ... 130 E6
Easterwood Cl 12 HU7 ... 57 B5
East Ferry Rd
Laughton DN21 ... 106 D1
Wildsworth DN21 ... 117 A8
Eastfield
5 Humberston DN36 ... 114 D8
Hunmanby YO14 ... 2 F8
Eastfield Ave
Grimsby DN33 ... 113 E8
Haxby YO32 ... 127 C7
Eastfield Cl
3 Beverley HU17 ... 137 A6
North Frodingham YO25 ... 34 A8
Eastfield Cres YO10 ... 131 C2
Eastfield Ct
Northfield HU15 ... 144 A2
York YO10 ... 131 C2
Eastfield Est HU12 ... 60 B1
Eastfield La
Dunnington YO19 ... 26 F8
Kellington DN14 ... 61 F4
Rise HU17 ... 45 F6
Eastfield Prim Sch
Immingham DN40 ... 87 C1
Kingston upon Hull HU4 ... 144 D6
Eastfield Rd
Barton-upon-Humber DN18 ... 84 F7
Brandesburton YO25 ... 34 C2
Bridlington YO16 ... 122 E5
Brigg DN20 ... 98 C2
Easington HU12 ... 91 A5
Epworth DN9 ... 105 E6
Fangfoss YO41 ... 28 D7
Great Driffield YO25 ... 124 E5
1 Keelby DN41 ... 101 A5
Keyingham HU12 ... 73 D4
Kingston upon Hull HU4 ... 144 D6
Market Weighton YO43 ... 135 E3
Messingham DN17 ... 107 D7
North Killingholme DN40 ... 86 F4
Scunthorpe DN16 ... 151 C1
East Field Rd DN7 ... 92 C8
Eastfield Rise 4 DN36 ... 114 A5
Eastgate
Beverley HU17 ... 154 B2
2 Goole DN14 ... 149 D4
Grimsby DN32 ... 152 E4
Hornsea HU18 ... 134 C5
Kingston upon Hull HU13 ... 143 E2
Lund YO25 ... 31 F2
Nafferton YO25 ... 125 F7
North Newbald YO43 ... 53 F7
Patrington HU12 ... 74 D1
Scotton DN21 ... 107 C2
East Gate
Rudston YO25 ... 9 F6
Thorne/Moorends DN8 ... 79 B2
Eastgate Ct HU18 ... 134 C5
East-Gate N YO25 ... 124 E5
East-Gate S YO25 ... 124 F4
Eastgate View HU18 ... 134 B4
East Gn DN17 ... 107 D7
East Gr
Barton-upon-Humber DN18 ... 69 F1
Kingston upon Hull HU4 ... 144 D4
Easthall Rd LN7 ... 110 B4
EAST HALTON ... 86 E7
East Halton Prim Sch DN40 ... 86 D6
East Halton Rd DN40 ... 86 E3
East Hann La DN19 ... 70 E1
Eastholme Cl YO25 ... 124 F5
Eastholme Dr YO30 ... 126 E1
Eastholme Gdns 9 DN15 ... 82 B4
Eastholme La HU12 ... 73 C7
Easthorpe Dr YO26 ... 126 A1
East Hull Pools HU9 ... 146 C8
East La
Beverley HU17 ... 136 D5
Corringham DN21 ... 118 B2
Sigglesthorne HU11 ... 45 F8
Stainforth DN7 ... 92 C6
East Lambwath Rd HU11 ... 46 D3
Eastland Ave YO24 ... 129 E2
Eastlands YO25 ... 125 F7
Eastlands Rd YO25 ... 19 E2
EAST LOUND ... 105 E3
East Lound Rd
Haxey DN9 ... 105 D2
Owston Ferry DN9 ... 106 A3
EAST LUTTON ... 7 C8
EAST MARSH ... 152 F5
East Marsh Rd DN19 ... 71 C3
East Mid Mere Rd DN40 ... 86 F4
East Moor Gdns YO19 ... 133 F5
East Mount 8 HU14 ... 69 A4
East Mount Ave HU8 ... 142 B5
East Mount Rd YO24 ... 156 A1
Eastmount Recn Ctr HU8 ... 142 B6
EAST NEWTON ... 59 F8
East Newton Rd HU11 ... 47 D1
EASTOFT ... 81 A3
Eastoft CE Prim Sch DN17 ... 81 A3
Eastoft Rd
Crowle DN17 ... 94 D8
Luddington & Haldenby DN17 ... 81 C3
Easton Ave HU8 ... 141 A2
Easton Rd YO16 ... 122 A4
Easton Wlk YO16 ... 122 B4
East Parade
Brigg DN20 ... 98 C2
Goole DN14 ... 149 D3
York YO31 ... 130 F6
East Park Ave HU8 ... 141 E3
East Pk HU17 ... 45 B8
EAST RAVENDALE ... 113 C2
East Ravendale CE Prim Sch DN37 ... 113 B2
East Rd
Bridlington YO15 ... 122 D1
Keadby with Althorpe DN17 ... 95 C6
East Riding Bsns Pk HU17 ... 137 C3
East Riding Coll @ Beverley HU17 ... 136 C5
East Riding Coll @ Bridlington YO16 ... 122 D4
East Riding Coll @ Carnaby YO25 ... 10 D2
East Riding Coll @ Hull HU3 ... 145 D4
EASTRINGTON ... 51 F1
Eastrington Ponds Nature Reserve* DN14 ... 65 E8
Eastrington Prim Sch DN14 ... 51 F1
Eastrington Sta DN14 ... 66 A8
East Riverside DN40 ... 87 E3
East St Mary's Gate 3 DN31 ... 152 D3
East Scar YO15 ... 5 A3
Eastside Rd
Grimsby DN31 ... 152 F5
Scunthorpe DN16 ... 151 F5
East St
Dalton Holme HU17 ... 31 E1
Grimsby DN31 ... 152 E3
Hibaldstow DN20 ... 108 F5
Kilham YO25 ... 9 C3
5 Kingston upon Hull HU9 ... 146 B7
Leven HU17 ... 45 A8
Roxby cum Risby DN15 ... 83 A4
EAST STOCKWITH ... 116 F5
East View
7 Campsall DN6 ... 76 E1
10 Knottingley WF11 ... 61 A2
Eastville Rd 10 DN33 ... 102 D2
Eastward Ave YO10 ... 133 E7
East Way YO31 ... 127 E2
East Wlk DN15 ... 151 B7
Eastwold 2 YO43 ... 53 F7
Eastwood Ave DN32 ... 102 E2
Eastwood Ct DN15 ... 150 B6
Eastwood Dr 8 DN20 ... 97 E4
Eaton Ct
Grimsby DN34 ... 152 C2
7 York YO24 ... 132 B8
Eaton Rd 18 DN40 ... 87 C1
Ebberston Gr 5 HU5 ... 139 E3
Ebor Ave HU18 ... 134 D2
Ebor Cl HU8 ... 142 B6
Ebor Ct 7 YO8 ... 148 C6
Ebor Ind Est YO31 ... 156 C3
Ebor Manor 1 HU12 ... 73 C4
Ebor Prep Sch YO30 ... 130 A7
Ebor St
Selby YO8 ... 148 C5
York YO23 ... 156 B1
Ebor View YO43 ... 135 E4
Ebor Way YO26 ... 126 A2
Ebsay Dr YO30 ... 127 A1
Eccles Cl YO30 ... 126 D2
Eccles Ct DN20 ... 98 D4
Ecclesfield Ave HU9 ... 142 D1
Eccleston Rd DN3 ... 92 A3
Eddlemere La YO25 ... 32 E7
Eden Ave YO8 ... 148 D3
Eden Cl
Beverley HU17 ... 136 D5
York YO24 ... 132 C7
Edencroft Dr 14 DN3 ... 92 A2
Edendale HU7 ... 140 F6
Eden Dene DN16 ... 151 D1
Eden Dr HU8 ... 141 C3
Edenfield Ave HU18 ... 134 C2
Eden Field Rd 12 DN3 ... 92 A2
Eden Gdns YO15 ... 4 D2
Eden Gr Rd 1 DN3 ... 92 A1
Eden Rd HU17 ... 136 D5
Eden Rise HU10 ... 138 C2
Edenthorpe Hall Prim Sch DN3 ... 92 A1
Edgar Cl DN21 ... 107 C4
Edgar St HU3 ... 145 D5
Edgbaston Ave 27 DN17 ... 96 C2
Edge Ave DN33 ... 102 E1
Edgecliffe Villas 4 YO15 ... 122 F4

172 Gox–Hag

Goxhill Rd DN19 .... 85 E8
Goxhill Sta DN19......... 85 F8
Grafton St
Grimsby DN32.......... 153 A5
Kingston upon Hull HU5 .. 140 C2
Gragdale Cl HU8 .... 141 E7
Graham Ave HU4........ 144 C2
Graingers Rd HU18...... 134 D3
GRAINSBY.............. 113 F2
Grainsby Ave
Cleethorpes DN35....... 103 B2
Holton le Clay DN36 ..... 114 B5
Grainsby Healing★
DN36.................. 113 F3
Grainsby La
Grainsby DN36.......... 113 E1
Tetney DN36 .... 114 D3
Grains Gate LN11 .... 115 E1
GRAISELOUND 105 C1
Graizelound Fields Rd
DN9 .... 105 D1
Grammar School La DN20 98 C3
Grammar School Rd
Brigg DN20 .... 98 C2
Kingston upon Hull HU5 .. 139 E2
Grammar School Road S 7
DN20 .... 98 C2
Grammar School Wlk
DN16 .... 96 E2
Grammar School Yd
HU1 .... 155 B1
Grampian Cl 4 YO32.... 127 F5
Grampian Way
23 Grimsby DN33 .... 113 E8
Kingston upon Hull HU7 ... 57 A6
Thorne/Moorends DN8 .... 93 A7
Grampion Sh Ctr HU7 .... 57 A6
Granary Cl DN21 .... 117 A3
Granary Croft 7 DN9 ... 105 D2
Granary Ct
Elloughton HU15 .... 68 C7
York YO1 .... 156 B3
Granary Fold DN21...... 107 C4
Granary The DN21 ...... 107 C4
Grandale HU7 .... 140 E7
Grand Opera House York★
YO1.................... 156 B2
GRANGE................ 152 A1
Grange Ave
12 Barton-upon-Humber
DN18................. 84 E8
Hatfield DN7 .... 92 D4
14 Laceby DN37 .... 101 F1
Misterton DN10......... 116 D5
Grange Cl
2 Buckton/Bempton YO15.. 4 C3
Full Sutton YO41 .... 16 A2
5 Hatfield DN7.......... 92 D4
Kingston upon Hull HU2 .. 155 B4
Misterton DN10......... 116 D4
Skelton YO30........... 126 B5
Grange Cres
Kingston upon Hull HU10 . 143 E6
Tickton HU17........... 137 F8
Grange Ct 7 DN9....... 105 B2
Grange Dr
Kingston upon Hull HU16 . 139 A7
Misterton DN10......... 116 D4
Grange Farm Cl YO8 ..... 49 B5
Grange Farm La 20
DN36 .... 114 A7
Grange Field DN20....... 98 D8
Grange Garth
10 Wistow YO8 .... 48 D6
York YO10 .... 130 D2
Grange Gr 3 DN8........ 79 B2
Grange Ind Est DN15.... 151 D4
Grange Ind Est The
DN14.................. 149 B4
Grange Jun & Inf Sch
DN34.................. 102 C3
Grange La
Covenham St Bartholomew
LN11................ 121 F6
Molescroft HU17........ 137 A7
North Kelsey LN7........ 110 A3
Rufforth YO26 .... 129 A2
Utterby LN11........... 121 C4
Grangeland Wlk YO42.... 28 E3
Grange Lane Inf Sch
DN16.................. 151 D1
Grange Lane Jun Sch
DN16.................. 151 D1
Grange Lane N DN16.... 151 D3
Grange Lane S
25 Bottesford DN16 ...... 96 E2
Scunthorpe DN16 .... 151 D1
Grange Park La HU10 ... 138 B2
Grange Pk
1 Brough HU15 .... 68 C5
Gainsborough DN21 ..... 117 A3
2 Kirk Sandall DN3 ...... 92 A2
Swanland HU14.......... 69 B6
Granger Ave YO26 ...... 129 C4
Grange Rd
3 Bridlington YO16 ..... 122 D5
8 Campsall DN6.......... 76 E1
Gainsborough DN21 ..... 117 D1
Garthorpe & Fockerby DN14 81 E8
Goole DN14............. 149 B4
7 Leconfield HU17....... 43 D6
North Frodingham YO25 ... 34 B6
Snaith DN14............. 78 C8
Thorne/Moorends DN8 .... 79 B2
Thorngumbald HU12 ...... 72 F5
Granger's Yd 8 HU18... 134 C4
Grangeside Ave HU6 .... 139 F5
Grange St YO10......... 130 D2
Grange Way HU17....... 136 E7
Grange Wlk
Grimsby DN34.......... 152 A2
Misterton DN10......... 116 D5
GRANSMOOR 22 C6
Gransmoor La YO25....... 22 A5
Gransmoor Rd YO25...... 22 D5
Grantchester Cl HU5 .... 139 C1
Grantham Ave
Grimsby DN33 .... 102 E1
11 Kingston upon Hull HU7. 56 F6
Grantham Dr YO26 ...... 129 E4
Grantley Gr HU9 .... 142 C2
Grants Ave YO10........ 133 E8
Grant St
Cleethorpes DN31 .... 153 E3
Grimsby DN31 .... 153 B5
GRANT THOROLD........ 153 A4
Granville Rd 1 DN15..... 96 D7
Granville St
Grimsby DN32 .... 152 F2
1 Kingston upon Hull
HU3................. 145 A6
Granville Terr 4 YO10 .. 130 E3
Grape La YO1........... 156 B3
GRASBY................ 110 E7
Grasby All Saints CE Prim
Sch DN38............. 110 E8
Grasby Cres DN37....... 102 B4
Grasby Rd
Great Limber DN37 ...... 100 C3
Kingston upon Hull HU8 .. 142 A4
North Kelsey LN7........ 110 D5
Scunthorpe DN17 .... 150 E1
Grasby Wold La DN38 ... 110 F8
Grasmere Cl
Gainsborough DN21 ..... 117 C1
Goole DN14............ 149 D5
Grasmere Dr YO10 ...... 131 B4
Grasmere Gr
Bridlington YO16 .... 122 E7
11 Humberston DN36 .... 103 C1
5 York YO30........... 126 F1
Grassam Cl 3 HU12...... 58 D1
Grassdale Pk 3 HU15 .... 68 B5
Grassholme YO24 .... 132 C7
Grassington Cl 11 HU7 ... 57 A6
Grassmoor Ct 2 DN15 .. 150 B6
Gravelhill La DN14 .... 76 F7
Gravelholes La DN10 .... 116 C4
Gravel Pit Hill DN20..... 109 D6
Gravelpit La
Kirkburn YO25 .... 19 F1
Sancton YO43............ 41 E2
Gravel Pit La
Kirmington DN39........ 100 A6
Yaddlethorpe DN17 .... 96 C1
Gravel Pit Rd
Barton-upon-Humber
DN18................. 84 D8
Scotter DN21........... 107 C4
Graves La YO42 .... 39 B6
Grayburn Ct HU17....... 154 A3
Grayburn La HU17 ...... 154 A2
Gray Friars DN37 .... 102 B4
GRAYINGHAM........... 119 B7
Grayingham Rd 19 DN21. 108 B1
Grayling Cl 15 DN37..... 102 B4
Gray Rd DN17 .... 150 D2
Grays Croft HU12 .... 59 C2
Grayshon Dr YO26 ...... 129 B5
Gray St
Goole DN14............ 149 C5
York YO23 .... 156 A1
Greame Rd YO16........ 123 A5
Great Barn St 4 YO16... 122 D5
Great Cl YO8............. 48 B8
GREAT COATES 102 B5
Great Coates Prim Sch
DN37.................. 102 B5
Great Coates Rd
Grimsby DN37 .... 102 B4
Healing DN41........... 101 F5
Great Coates Sta DN37 .. 102 B5
GREAT COWDEN 47 A5
Great Field La HU9...... 147 C7
GREAT GIVENDALE 29 B8
Great Grimsby Bsns Pk
DN37.................. 102 C6
Great Gutter La HU10 .... 55 C1
Great Gutter Lane E
HU10 .... 138 C2
Great Gutter Lane W
HU10 .... 138 A2
GREAT HATFIELD......... 46 D6
Great Hatfield Rd HU11... 46 D4
GREAT HECK............. 77 D7
GREAT KELK 22 A5
GREAT KENDALE 20 D7
GREAT LIMBER......... 100 D3
Great Meadow Rd YO16 . 122 E5
Great North Way YO26 .. 129 B8
Great Passage St HU1... 155 A1
Great Stather Cl DN15.... 82 A5
Great Thornton St HU3.. 145 D6
GREAT TOWS 120 A1
Great Union St HU9 ..... 155 C3
Grebe Rd HU15 .... 52 F1
Greek St HU3........... 144 F5
Greenacre 23 HU12 ...... 73 C4
Greenacre Cl
Dunsville DN7 .... 92 D2
Pocklington YO42......... 29 B3
Greenacre Pk
Gilberdyke HU15 .... 66 D8
Greenacre Pk *continued*
Hornsea HU18.......... 134 C1
Greenacres
4 Swanland HU14 .... 69 C7
York YO32 .... 127 F4
Green Acres HU10 ...... 143 C6
Greenacres Cl 3 YO8 .... 48 D1
Greenacres Cres 7 YO8.. 48 D1
Greenacres Dr 4 YO8.... 48 D1
Greenacres Gr 3 YO8.... 48 D1
Greenacres Pk HU12 ..... 60 B1
Green Balk YO42 .... 17 D1
Green Bank DN8 .... 93 D6
Green Cl
Kingston upon Hull HU6 .. 139 F6
York YO30 .... 130 A8
Greencliffe Dr YO30..... 130 A6
Greencroft Ct 14 YO19.... 26 F7
Greencroft La 17 YO19 ... 26 F7
Greendale DN17 .... 107 D7
Greendale Ct HU16...... 138 E5
Green Dike YO32........ 127 C8
Green Dikes La YO25....... 8 F1
Green Dykes La YO10 ... 130 F3
Greenfield Cl 6 DN3..... 92 A3
Greenfield Dr
6 Brayton YO8.......... 48 D1
Hibaldstow DN20........ 109 A5
Greenfield Garth 5 HU6 . 56 D5
Greenfield La YO25 ...... 31 C4
Greenfield Park Dr YO31 131 A7
Greenfield Rd
Bridlington YO16 .... 122 B2
Middleton-on-the-Wolds
YO25................. 31 C4
Greenfields
Pollington DN14.......... 77 F6
York YO31 .... 130 D7
Greenfinch Dr 8 DN35.. 103 C1
Greengales Ct YO19...... 38 A8
Greengales La YO19...... 38 A8
Greengarth DN17 .... 96 C1
Greengate DN9 .... 105 E6
Greengate La
Cliffe YO8............... 49 F6
2 Goxhill DN19 .... 86 A8
Greengate Rd WF8........ 76 C1
Greenhill 8 DN20........ 97 D3
Green Hill 10 DN35...... 103 B2
Greenhill Rd DN9 .... 105 C2
Green Hills YO60......... 15 B7
Greenhoe Rd DN17....... 96 B2
Greenholme Bank DN9.. 105 A6
Greenhow Cl HU8....... 141 E7
Green Island HU11 ...... 142 E5
Green La
Acomb YO24........... 129 D2
Appleton Roebuck YO23.... 36 B6
Barmby on the Marsh DN14 64 A6
Barrow upon Humber DN19 85 D8
Belton DN9 .... 94 D2
Brigsley DN37 .... 113 D4
Broughton DN20 .... 97 E3
Buckton/Bempton YO15 .... 4 D3
Cottingham HU16........ 138 E6
Cottingwith YO42......... 38 C5
Fimber YO25 .... 18 F6
Hatfield DN7 .... 92 E1
Heck DN14............. 77 D8
Kingston upon Hull HU2 .. 155 B4
Langtoft YO25 .... 8 D5
Ludborough DN36 .... 121 B6
Moor Monkton YO26 ...... 24 A8
Nafferton YO25 .... 125 D7
North Duffield YO8....... 49 F8
North Kelsey LN7........ 110 A4
Pilham DN21 .... 118 A4
Rawcliffe YO30 .... 127 A1
Selby YO8.............. 148 A3
Skidby HU10 .... 138 B4
South Cave HU15......... 53 D1
Sutton Ings HU13 .... 144 A1
Swine HU11............. 57 E7
Tibthorpe YO25 .... 19 D2
Tickton HU17........... 137 F8
Weaverthorpe YO25 .... 8 A8
Wetwang YO25 .... 18 D5
Wigginton YO32.......... 13 D5
Wressle DN14............ 64 D8
Greenland La DN14 ...... 78 F7
Greenlands YO25 .... 124 F5
Greenlands Ave 13 DN36 114 A7
Greenlands La YO8....... 48 C3
Green Lane Trading Est
YO30.................. 127 A1
Green Marsh Rd HU12.... 72 E4
Green Mdws YO31 ...... 131 A7
Greenoak La DN14 .... 66 B7
Green Rd
Gringley on the Hill
DN10................ 116 A1
15 Hedon HU12.......... 72 C7
Greensborough Ave 3
YO26 .... 129 B5
Greens Cl 9 DN15 ...... 151 B7
Greenshaw Dr YO32..... 127 C8
Greenshaw La HU12...... 74 D1
Greenside
18 Dunnington YO19 ...... 26 F7
8 Flamborough YO15...... 5 A2
Greenside Cl 24 YO19 .... 26 F7
Greenside Wlk 23 YO19... 26 F7
Greens La
Burstwick HU12.......... 73 B8
Burton Pidsea HU12 ...... 59 C1
Wawne HU7.............. 56 E7
Green's Rd DN7.......... 92 C3
Greenstiles La HU14...... 69 C7
Green Sward YO31 ...... 131 A8
Green The
Barmby Moor YO42 .... 28 D3
5 Brough HU15 .... 68 D6
20 Dunnington YO19 ...... 26 F7
Great Driffield YO25 ..... 125 A4
Lund YO25 .... 31 F3
7 Market Weighton YO43 135 D4
Rawcliffe DN14 .... 64 A1
20 Scotter DN21 .... 107 C3
1 Skelton YO30 .... 126 B5
Sproatley HU11 .... 58 D5
Stillingfleet YO19......... 36 D3
1 Swanland HU14 .... 69 B7
20 Thorne/Moorends DN8.. 93 A8
Wistow YO8 .... 48 D6
York YO26 .... 129 C3
Green Top Prim Sch 14
DN8................... 93 A7
Greenway
8 Barton-upon-Humber
DN18................. 69 F1
10 Waltham DN37....... 113 E6
Green Way YO32 .... 127 F4
Green Way Prim Sch The
HU6................... 140 A6
Greenways
Great Driffield YO25 ..... 124 F5
2 North Ferriby HU14 .... 69 A5
Greenways Cl YO16 ..... 122 F6
Green Ways Ct 2 YO8.... 48 D6
Greenways Dr 1 YO8 .... 48 D6
Greenways Wlk YO16.... 122 F6
Greenway The
2 Haxby YO32 .... 127 C7
Hornsea HU18.......... 134 C2
1 Kingston upon Hull
HU4................. 144 C6
Greenwich Ave HU9..... 142 C4
Greenwich Cl
3 Frodingham DN15 ..... 96 D7
5 York YO30........... 126 E3
Greenwood Ave
Beverley HU17.......... 154 C3
Inglemire HU6.......... 139 F6
Kingston upon Hull HU6 .. 139 E5
Greenwood Gdns HU17.. 136 F7
Greenwood Gr YO24 .... 132 C8
Greetham's La DN32 .... 153 B1
Greet's Hill YO17......... 16 E7
GREETWELL 108 C7
Gregory Cl YO30 .... 126 C5
Grenley St 8 WF11 ...... 61 A2
Grenville Bay HU11 ..... 142 D6
Gresley Ct 3 YO26 ..... 129 B4
Gresley Way DN40 .... 87 D2
Greville Rd HU12......... 72 D7
Greyfriars Cres HU17.... 154 A1
Greyfriars Rd DN20 ...... 97 E3
Greygarth Cl 14 HU7 ..... 56 F6
GREY GREEN............. 94 E2
Greylees Ave 6 HU6 ..... 56 D5
Grey St
Gainsborough DN21 ..... 117 A1
Kingston upon Hull HU2 .. 145 D7
Greystoke Rd YO30...... 126 E1
Greystone Ave HU5 ..... 144 E7
Greystone Ct YO32 ..... 127 C7
Greystones Rd DN21 .... 117 A2
GRIBTHORPE 51 B6
Griffin Prim Sch HU9.... 142 C3
Griffin Rd HU9.......... 142 C3
Griffiths Way 18 HU12.... 73 C4
Grime St DN31.......... 152 E4
GRIMSBY............... 152 E2
Grimsby Auditorium★
DN31.................. 152 A4
Grimsby Docks Sta DN32 152 F5
Grimsby Institute of FE & HE
DN34.................. 152 C1
Grimsby Institute (The
Towers International Ctr)
The DN34 .... 152 C2
Grimsby L Ctr DN31..... 152 A4
Grimsby Rd
Caistor LN7 .... 111 C4
Cleethorpes DN35....... 153 D4
Fotherby LN11........... 121 D1
Humberston DN36....... 103 B1
Laceby DN37 .... 101 F1
Swallow LN7 .... 112 B6
Waltham DN37.......... 113 E7
Grimsby Swimming Pool
DN33.................. 102 E2
Grimsby Town Sta DN31 . 152 D3
Grimscott Cl 2 HU7 ..... 56 F5
GRIMSTON 131 E3
Grimston Bar YO19...... 131 F4
Grimston Dr HU1 .... 155 B3
Grimston Rd
12 Hunmanby YO14........ 3 A8
5 Kingston upon Hull
HU10................ 143 F6
Grimston St HU1........ 155 B3
Grimthorpe Hill YO42 .... 29 B7
Grimwith Garth YO30.... 126 F2
GRINDALE 3 D2
Grindale La YO16 .... 122 A7
Grindale Rd
Bempton YO16............ 4 A3
Grindale YO16 .... 3 E2
Grindell St HU9......... 146 D8
Gringley Rd DN10....... 116 B4
Grinsdale Rise YO25..... 125 F7
Grizedale HU7 .... 140 F7
Grosmont Cl HU8 .... 141 E7
Grosvenor Ave DN14 .... 149 A5
Grosvenor Cres 2 DN32 152 D3
Grosvenor Ct DN7......... 92 D8
Grosvenor House YO30.. 156 A4
Grosvenor Pk YO30 ..... 156 A4
Grosvenor Pl HU17...... 136 D2
Grosvenor Rd
Hornsea HU18.......... 134 D4
York YO30 .... 156 A4
Grosvenor St
Grimsby DN32.......... 152 D2
Kingston upon Hull HU3 .. 145 D8
Grosvenor Street N
DN15 .... 151 A8
Grosvenor Street S
DN15 .... 151 A8
Grosvenor Terr YO30.... 156 A4
Grove Cl HU17 .... 154 B4
Grove Cres DN35........ 153 C2
Grove Ct YO25 .... 124 F3
Grove Gdns 12 YO26...... 12 F1
GROVEHILL............. 137 C3
Grovehill HU17 .... 137 C4
Grove Hill HU13......... 143 E1
Grovehill Ind Est HU17 .. 137 C4
Grovehill Rd HU17 ...... 154 C3
Grove House View HU5.. 140 D3
Grove La DN37.......... 113 E6
Grovenor Ct 11 DN35.... 103 D1
Grove Pk
7 Barlby YO8 .... 49 B5
Beverley HU17.......... 154 A4
Misterton DN10......... 116 C5
Grove Rd DN7 .... 92 D8
Groves Ct YO31 .... 156 C3
Groves La YO31 .... 156 C3
Grove St DN21.......... 108 A1
Groves The
Great Driffield YO25 ..... 125 A3
Kingston upon Hull HU4 .. 144 B2
Northfield HU4.......... 144 B2
Grove Terr La YO31 ..... 156 C4
Grove The
Barrow upon Humber
DN19................ 85 D8
Beckingham DN10....... 116 D1
Kellington DN14.......... 62 A3
York YO24 .... 132 E6
Grove View YO30 .... 130 A6
Grove Wharf★ DN15 ..... 95 E7
Grove Wood Rd DN10 ... 116 C5
Grove Wood Terr DN10.. 116 C5
Grundale HU10 .... 143 C6
Grundell's Yd 4 YO16... 122 D4
Grundill La
Hatfield HU11 .... 46 A8
Seaton HU11............. 35 A1
Guardians Rd 2 HU12.... 74 D1
Guernsey Gr 1 DN40.... 101 C8
Guest Field HU11 .... 47 B1
Guildford Ave HU8 ..... 141 D4
Guildford Cl HU17....... 136 E1
Guildford St 20 DN32.... 153 A5
Guildhall Rd HU1 .... 155 B2
Guilicarr La LN7 .... 109 E4
Guisefield Rd 5 DN9.... 105 D6
Gullane Dr 7 HU6 .... 56 D5
Gull Nook YO15........... 5 A2
GUNBY................... 50 D6
Gunby Pl 9 DN35 ...... 103 C2
Gunby Rd
Bubwith YO8 .... 50 D5
Scunthorpe DN17 .... 150 E1
Gunbywood Rd YO8...... 50 D6
GUNNESS 95 E6
Gunness & Burringham CE
Prim Sch DN17 .... 95 E5
Gunness La DN15 .... 95 F8
GUNTHORPE............ 117 A7
Gunthorpe Rd DN9...... 116 F8
Gurnell St DN15......... 151 A8
Gurth Ave DN3........... 92 A1
Gus Walker Dr YO42 ..... 29 B4
Guy Garth 1 HU12....... 72 D7
Guy's Cres 8 HU9 ...... 142 A5
Gypsey Rd YO16 .... 122 B4

H

HABROUGH............. 100 E8
Habrough Ct 9 DN40 .... 86 E3
Habrough La DN39...... 100 C6
Habrough Rd
Immingham DN40 .... 87 A1
South Killingholme DN40... 86 E2
Habrough Sta DN40..... 100 E8
Hackforth Wlk HU5 ..... 139 D4
Hackness Gr 2 HU5 .... 144 D8
Haddlesey Rd WF11 ...... 61 D5
Haddon Cl YO24 .... 129 C2
Haddon Rd YO16........ 122 D7
Haddon St HU3 .... 144 F4
Hadds La DN8 .... 78 F3
Hadds Nook Rd DN8 ..... 78 F2
Hadleigh Cl 4 HU2 ..... 140 E1
Hadleigh Ct DN15....... 151 A8
Hadleigh Gn 4 DN17..... 95 D4
Hadleigh Rd DN40 .... 87 C1
Hadrian Ave YO10....... 131 B3
Hagg La
Belton DN9 .... 94 E3
Cottingwith YO42......... 38 E8
Dunnington YO19 .... 26 F6
Hemingbrough YO8 .... 49 F3
Haggs La
Fenwick DN6 .... 77 D2
Kingston upon Hull HU10 . 138 E3
Haggwood Wlk YO19..... 26 F1
Hag La YO42............. 38 C4

Hague Park La 12 YO25 . . 124 F4
Haig Ave DN16 . . . 151 B5
Haigh Ct DN32 . . . 102 F2
Haigh La DN14 . . . 77 A6
Haigh St DN35 . . . 103 D3
Haig Rd DN8 . . . 79 B2
Haig St YO8 . . . 148 B6
Haile Rd DN36 . . . 103 D1
Hailgate DN14 . . . 65 A7
Hailgate Cl 8 DN14 . . . 65 B7
Hainsworth Pk HU6 . . . 139 E5
Hainton Ave DN32 . . . 152 F2
HAISTHORPE . . . 10 C3
Haith's La DN36 . . . 114 B1
Haldane Ct HU4 . . . 144 D2
Haldane St DN21 . . . 117 A1
Halecroft 24 HU7 . . . 56 E5
Hale Hill La DN7 . . . 92 E3
Hales Cl 3 DN16 . . . 96 D1
Hales Cres 12 HU12 . . . 72 C7
Hales Entry HU9 . . . 146 C6
Hales La YO8 . . . 63 E5
Haley's Terr YO31 . . . 130 D8
Halfacres La YO42 . . . 40 A6
Half Acre Wood 1 DN17 . . 95 D4
Halifax App DN20 . . . 99 A8
Halifax Ave DN14 . . . 149 C6
Halifax Cl
Full Sutton YO41 . . . 16 A2
8 Pocklington YO42 . . . 28 F4
Halifax Ct 7 YO30 . . . 127 A1
Halifax Way
Elvington YO41 . . . 27 A3
Pocklington YO42 . . . 28 E3
Halkon Cl DN17 . . . 81 D3
Halladale Cl 1 YO24 . . . 132 B7
HALLANDS THE . . . 85 F7
Hallard Way 7 YO32 . . . 14 B7
Hallbrook Ct 4 DN16 . . . 96 D1
Hall Cl
5 Airmyn DN14 . . . 64 E4
Cawood YO8 . . . 36 D1
Nafferton YO25 . . . 125 E7
7 Snaith DN14 . . . 78 C8
Hallcroft 1 DN39 . . . 86 A1
Hallcroft La YO23 . . . 132 A3
Hallcroft Rd 1 DN9 . . . 105 D2
Hall Ct DN17 . . . 81 A3
Haller St HU9 . . . 146 E8
Hall Farm Cl 4 YO19 . . . 48 F8
Hall Farm Ct YO42 . . . 16 F2
Hallfield Rd YO31 . . . 130 E5
HALL GARTH . . . 26 F6
Hallgarth DN36 . . . 115 B2
Hall Garth YO8 . . . 49 C4
Hallgarth Ave DN16 . . . 151 B6
Hallgarth Way HU17 . . . 154 B2
Hallgate
Kingston upon Hull HU16 . 139 A6
10 Pocklington YO42 . . . 29 A4
Hallgate Prim Sch HU16 . 139 B7
Hall Gdns
Rawcliffe DN14 . . . 64 B2
Winterton DN15 . . . 83 B5
Halliwell Cl HU9 . . . 147 E8
Hall La
Elsham DN20 . . . 98 F7
Stainforth DN7 . . . 92 A6
Hall Leys Park 22 HU7 . . . 56 E5
Hall Mdw DN20 . . . 84 C2
Hall Park Rd
Hunmanby YO14 . . . 2 F8
Immingham DN40 . . . 87 C2
Hall Pk
Swanland HU14 . . . 69 C6
Wistow YO8 . . . 49 A5
York YO10 . . . 131 B1
Hall Rd
Goole DN14 . . . 149 D1
Hornsea HU18 . . . 134 D5
Kingston upon Hull HU6 . . 139 E5
Market Weighton YO43 . . . 135 D4
Sproatley HU11 . . . 58 D5
Hall Rise
12 Haxby YO32 . . . 13 F5
Messingham DN17 . . . 107 D7
Hall Road Prim Sch HU6 139 F4
Halls La
13 Keelby DN41 . . . 101 A4
North Kelsey LN7 . . . 110 A4
Hall Spinney The 5 DN14 65 B7
Hall Spout YO42 . . . 28 D3
Hall's Rd DN10 . . . 116 A2
Hall St HU2 . . . 145 D7
Hall View DN17 . . . 107 D7
Hall Way DN39 . . . 99 F5
Hall Wlk
1 Brough HU15 . . . 68 D6
Kingston upon Hull HU16 . 139 B6
Walkington HU17 . . . 55 B8
Hallytreeholme Rd YO25 . 33 E3
HALSHAM . . . 73 F6
Haltemprice L Ctr HU10 . 143 E7
Haltemprice St HU3 . . . 144 F5
Halton Cl 5 DN21 . . . 119 C8
Halton Pl DN35 . . . 103 B2
Halton Way DN34 . . . 102 D2
Halyard Croft HU1 . . . 155 B1
Hambledon Cl HU7 . . . 141 B6
Hambleton Ave YO10 . . . 131 C4
Hambleton Terr YO31 . . . 130 C7
Hambleton View 10 YO32 . 13 D5
Hambleton Way YO32 . . . 127 F3
Hambling Dr HU17 . . . 136 E7
Hamburg Rd HU7 . . . 141 A5
Hamden Rd YO42 . . . 28 E3
Hamerton Cl 11 YO14 . . . 3 A8
Hamerton Rd 10 YO14 . . . 3 A8
Hamilton Cl 7 DN34 . . . 102 B2
Hamilton Dr
Kingston upon Hull HU8 . . 141 F6
York YO24 . . . 129 E2
Hamilton Drive E YO24 . . 129 F2
Hamilton Drive W YO24 . 129 D2
Hamilton Hill Rd YO25 . . . 23 A6
Hamilton Rd
Bridlington YO15 . . . 122 D2
Scunthorpe DN17 . . . 150 F4
Hamilton St DN32 . . . 153 B5
Hamilton Way YO24 . . . 129 E2
Hamish Wlk 27 DN40 . . . 87 B1
Hamlet The 8 DN14 . . . 61 F2
Hamling Way HU4 . . . 144 D2
Hamlyn Ave HU4 . . . 144 E7
Hamlyn Dr HU4 . . . 144 E6
Hammersike Rd YO8 . . . 48 A4
Hammersmith Rd 1
HU8 . . . 141 F5
Hammerton Cl 3 YO26 . . 129 B3
Hammerton Rd 25 DN17 . . 96 C2
Hammond Rd HU17 . . . 154 C4
Hamont Rd DN32 . . . 153 B3
Hampden Cres 1 DN7 . . 104 A8
Hampden St YO1 . . . 156 B1
Hampshire St HU4 . . . 144 E3
Hampson Gdns
19 Kirk Sandall DN3 . . . 92 A2
York YO30 . . . 130 B8
Hampstead Ct 6 HU3 . . . 140 D1
Hampstead Pk 6 DN33 . . 102 D1
Hampston Cl HU6 . . . 140 A7
Hampton Cl 18 DN35 . . . 103 C1
Hampton Gdns YO30 . . . 130 C8
Hampton Rd
Hatfield DN7 . . . 92 C4
Scunthorpe DN16 . . . 151 B4
Hamshaw Ct HU3 . . . 145 C4
Handel Ct DN21 . . . 117 B1
Handel House Prep Sch
DN21 . . . 117 B1
Handley Cl YO30 . . . 127 A2
Hands on History Mus★
HU1 . . . 155 B2
Hanger La DN14 . . . 63 B3
Hankins La YO42 . . . 38 D1
Hanley Rd HU5 . . . 139 D3
Hanover Ct
Beverley HU17 . . . 154 C3
Kingston upon Hull HU1 . . 155 A2
Hanover Dr 25 HU15 . . . 68 C5
Hanover Gdns DN16 . . . 151 C2
Hanover Grange YO16 . . . 122 D4
Hanover St W 7 YO26 . . . 129 F5
Hanover Sq HU1 . . . 155 B2
Hanover Street E 5
YO26 . . . 129 F5
Hansard Cres
6 Caistor LN7 . . . 111 B4
5 Gilberdyke HU15 . . . 66 D8
Hansard Dr 6 HU15 . . . 66 D8
Hansom Pl YO31 . . . 130 C7
Hanson Cl YO43 . . . 135 D3
Hanson Way DN32 . . . 153 B4
Ha'penny Bridge Way
HU9 . . . 146 B5
Harborough Cl 20 YO14 . . . 2 F8
Harbour Rd YO15 . . . 122 F2
Harbour Way HU9 . . . 146 C6
Harcourt Cl
Bishopthorpe YO23 . . . 133 A4
Wheldrake YO19 . . . 37 F7
Harcourt Dr HU9 . . . 146 C8
Harcourt St YO31 . . . 130 E5
Hardane HU6 . . . 139 E8
Harden Cl YO30 . . . 126 F2
Hardenshaw La YO8 . . . 63 B4
Hardington Cl HU8 . . . 142 B7
Hardisty Mews YO26 . . . 130 A4
Hardmoor La YO43 . . . 53 C5
Hardrada Way 3 YO41 . . . 15 D1
Hardwick St HU5 . . . 145 B8
Hardy Rd DN17 . . . 150 D2
Hardy's Ct DN32 . . . 153 A2
Hardys Rd HU12 . . . 72 C7
Hardy's Rd DN35 . . . 103 C2
Hardy St
Kingston upon Hull HU5 . . 140 C3
Selby YO8 . . . 148 E4
Hare St DN32 . . . 152 F2
Harewood HU17 . . . 136 B6
Harewood Ave
Bridlington YO16 . . . 122 D6
Kingston upon Hull HU9 . . 142 A3
4 Kirk Sandall DN3 . . . 92 A2
Harewood Cl
Rawcliffe YO30 . . . 126 D2
5 Wigginton YO32 . . . 13 D5
Harewood Crest 21 HU15 . 68 D5
Harewood Gr 17 DN35 . . . 103 C1
Harewood Way YO10 . . . 131 A2
Harfry Wlk DN14 . . . 149 F6
Hargrave St DN31 . . . 152 B5
Hargreave Cl HU17 . . . 136 E6
Hargreaves Way DN15 . . . 96 D7
Hariff La HU12 . . . 73 B4
Harington Ave YO10 . . . 130 F4
Harker St 12 WF11 . . . 61 A2
Harland La YO25 . . . 124 E4
Harland Rd
Bridlington YO16 . . . 122 F5
6 Brough HU15 . . . 68 C6
Harland Way HU16 . . . 138 E8
Harlech Cl 1 HU7 . . . 57 A6
Harlech Way DN32 . . . 152 F4
Harleigh Ave
Kingston upon Hull HU7 . . 141 A5
Harleigh Ave *continued*
Stoneferry HU7 . . . 141 B5
Harlequin Dr 15 HU7 . . . 56 F5
Harleston Cl 5 HU8 . . . 142 B5
Harlestone Ct 8 DN34 . . 102 B3
Harley St HU2 . . . 155 A4
Harlow Cl
2 Kingston upon Hull
HU8 . . . 142 C6
1 York YO24 . . . 129 F2
Harlow Rd YO24 . . . 129 F2
Harlow St DN31 . . . 152 B5
HARLTHORPE . . . 51 A8
Harlthorpe Gn YO8 . . . 51 A8
Harneis Cres DN37 . . . 101 F1
Harold Ct YO24 . . . 129 D3
Harold St
Grimsby DN32 . . . 153 A4
Selby YO8 . . . 148 F4
Harolds Way 1 YO41 . . . 15 D1
Harome Gr HU5 . . . 144 C7
Harpenden Cl 12 DN7 . . . 92 D3
Harpendon Dr 6 DN7 . . . 92 D3
Harper Cl YO42 . . . 29 A3
Harper St
8 Great Driffield YO25 . . . 124 F4
2 Selby YO8 . . . 148 C5
HARPHAM . . . 21 F8
Harpham Gr HU9 . . . 142 A1
Harpham La YO25 . . . 9 D2
Harpham Rd DN36 . . . 115 B2
Harpings Rd HU5 . . . 139 F1
Harpswell Hill DN21 . . . 119 B1
Harpswell La DN21 . . . 118 F1
Harrier Ct YO41 . . . 27 A3
Harrier Rd 2 DN18 . . . 69 F1
Harrington Ct 33 HU12 . . . 72 D7
Harrington Pl DN16 . . . 151 A1
Harrington Rd YO16 . . . 122 B2
Harrington St DN35 . . . 153 B5
Harrison Cl
Sproatley HU11 . . . 58 D5
Winteringham DN15 . . . 83 B8
Harrison St
Grimsby DN31 . . . 152 C3
York YO31 . . . 130 F6
Harris St HU3 . . . 144 F5
Harrow Cl 12 DN21 . . . 117 C1
Harrowdyke 10 DN18 . . . 84 E8
Harrow Gdns 12 DN17 . . . 96 C2
Harrow Glade 5 YO30 . . 127 A1
Harrow St HU3 . . . 145 B4
Harrybeck La YO43 . . . 53 D4
Harry Moor La YO8 . . . 48 B2
Harry's Ave HU8 . . . 141 B3
Harrys Dream 3 DN20 . . . 97 E3
Harsell La HU11 . . . 34 F2
HARSWELL . . . 40 C3
Harswell La
Everingham YO43 . . . 40 D5
Holme-on-Spalding-Moor
YO42 . . . 40 C2
Hart Dr 26 YO42 . . . 29 A3
Hartendale Cl 22 YO15 . . . 5 A2
Hartford Wlk HU8 . . . 142 C7
Harthill YO25 . . . 31 B7
Harthill Ave HU17 . . . 43 D6
Hart Hill Cres YO41 . . . 16 A2
Harthill Dr HU3 . . . 145 C5
Hart La DN15 . . . 83 B5
Hartland Cl HU7 . . . 140 F8
Hartley Bridge HU9 . . . 146 C6
Hartley Ct YO15 . . . 122 D1
Hartley St HU18 . . . 134 D5
Hartoft Rd HU5 . . . 139 E2
Hartoft St YO10 . . . 130 D2
HARTON . . . 15 C8
Harts Cl HU18 . . . 134 B4
Hartshead Ave DN15 . . . 150 C7
Hartshead Wlk YO16 . . . 122 B4
Hartsholme Pk 27 HU7 . . . 56 F5
Hart St DN35 . . . 153 C4
Harvest Ave 19 DN18 . . . 84 E8
Harvest Cl
13 Kirk Sandall DN3 . . . 92 A2
11 Strensall YO32 . . . 14 B7
Harvest Cres 4 DN37 . . . 113 D6
Harvester Cl DN9 . . . 105 F6
Harvest Rise 1 DN19 . . . 85 C8
Harwood Dr 1 HU4 . . . 144 B6
Harwood Rd YO26 . . . 24 F7
Hase Wlk HU13 . . . 143 E1
Haslemere Ave YO15 . . . 122 E3
Hassacarr La YO19 . . . 26 F6
Hastings Ave 1 HU5 . . . 140 E2
Hastings Cl 4 YO30 . . . 127 A1
Hastings Gr HU5 . . . 144 E7
Hastings Wlk YO16 . . . 122 C2
HATCLIFFE . . . 112 F3
Hatcliffe Cl 20 DN33 . . . 102 D2
HATFIELD . . . 92 D5
Hatfield Cl 3 YO30 . . . 126 E3
Hatfield La
Barnby Dun DN3 . . . 92 A4
Edenthorpe DN3 . . . 92 A1
Hatfield Manor CE Jun Sch
DN7 . . . 92 E4
Hatfield Pl DN14 . . . 149 C1
Hatfield Rd DN7 . . . 93 A6
Hatfield & Stainforth Sta
DN7 . . . 92 C5
Hatfield Travis VA CE Inf Sch
DN7 . . . 92 E4
Hatfield Visual Arts Coll
DN7 . . . 92 D4
Hatfield Water Pk★ DN7 . 92 E5
Hatfield Wlk
Kingston upon Hull HU8 . . 141 C1
Hatfield Wlk *continued*
York YO24 . . . 132 B8
HATFIELD WOODHOUSE . . . 93 A3
Hatfield Woodhouse Prim
Sch DN7 . . . 93 A3
Hathersage Ct DN15 . . . 150 B6
Hathersage Rd HU7 . . . 141 C4
Hatkill La YO41 . . . 16 B1
Hatters Cl YO23 . . . 132 B3
Hatton Gr 32 DN33 . . . 102 D2
Haugh La YO8 . . . 61 F8
Haugh Pk 14 HU7 . . . 56 E5
Haughton Rd YO30 . . . 130 C7
Hauling La YO23 . . . 36 C8
Hauxwell Gr 6 HU8 . . . 142 A5
Havelock Acad DN32 . . . 153 C2
Havelock Cres YO16 . . . 122 D3
Havelock Mews DN32 . . . 153 C2
Havelock Pl YO16 . . . 122 D3
Havelock St
Bridlington YO16 . . . 122 D3
Kingston upon Hull HU3 . . 145 A4
Haven Ave
2 Brough HU15 . . . 68 B5
Grimsby DN31 . . . 152 C4
Haven Basin Rd HU12 . . . 72 C6
Haven Cl DN21 . . . 117 F5
Haven Garth
1 Brough HU15 . . . 68 B5
2 Hedon HU12 . . . 72 D7
Haven Gdns DN31 . . . 152 A5
Haven Rd
Barton-upon-Humber
DN18 . . . 69 E1
North Killingholme DN40 . . . 87 A6
Patrington HU12 . . . 89 C8
Haven Staithes 24 HU12 . . 72 C7
Haven Terr DN31 . . . 152 C4
Haven The
Kingston upon Hull HU9 . . 146 B6
Selby YO8 . . . 148 D5
2 Walkington HU17 . . . 55 D8
Haverah Ct YO30 . . . 126 F1
Havercroft Rd 15 YO14 . . . 3 A8
Haverflats Cl 3 HU5 . . . 139 F1
Haverstoe Pl 7 DN35 . . . 103 B2
Hawdon Ave YO8 . . . 148 D5
Hawerby Rd DN37 . . . 101 F1
Haweswater Way HU6 . . . 140 D8
Hawes Wlk HU5 . . . 139 D3
Hawke Garth 5 YO14 . . . 3 A8
Hawkesbury St HU8 . . . 141 E3
Hawkins Gr DN32 . . . 153 B2
Hawkins Way 3 DN40 . . . 86 E3
Hawkshead Cl 3 YO24 . . . 132 B8
Hawling Rd YO43 . . . 135 C2
Haworth Cl DN15 . . . 150 D8
Haworth St HU6 . . . 140 C4
Haworth Wlk YO16 . . . 122 B4
Hawse Rd YO8 . . . 63 E8
Hawthorn Ave
2 Brigg DN20 . . . 98 C2
1 Immingham DN40 . . . 87 D2
Kingston upon Hull HU3 . . 144 F5
Hawthorn Cl
Burstwick HU12 . . . 73 B6
Healing DN41 . . . 101 F6
5 Newport HU15 . . . 52 F1
Wootton DN39 . . . 85 E2
Hawthorn Ct 1 HU3 . . . 144 F6
Hawthorn Dr
Wilberfoss YO41 . . . 27 E5
Wistow YO8 . . . 49 A5
Hawthorne Ave
Cleethorpes DN35 . . . 153 D4
29 Grimsby DN33 . . . 113 E8
Hatfield DN7 . . . 92 C2
12 Haxby YO32 . . . 13 E5
Kingston upon Hull HU10 . 138 D1
5 New Waltham DN36 . . . 113 F7
Scunthorpe DN17 . . . 150 F4
4 Thorne/Moorends DN8 . . 79 A1
Hawthorne Cl
10 Thorpe Willoughby
YO8 . . . 48 B2
12 Winterton DN15 . . . 83 A5
Hawthorne Cres DN17 . . . 150 F4
Hawthorne Dr YO43 . . . 40 A1
Hawthorne Garth HU17 . . 136 F7
Hawthorne Gdns DN19 . . . 86 A8
Hawthorne Gr
5 Thorne/Moorends
DN8 . . . 79 A1
York YO31 . . . 130 E5
Hawthorne Mews YO32 . . . 14 B7
Hawthorne Rd DN8 . . . 79 A1
Hawthorne Rise HU13 . . . 143 B3
Hawthorn Garth DN14 . . . 61 F4
Hawthorn Gate 17 DN18 . . 84 F8
Hawthorn Gr
Gainsborough DN21 . . . 117 B1
York YO31 . . . 130 E5
Hawthorn Pl YO32 . . . 127 E4
Hawthorn Rd YO8 . . . 148 D3
Hawthorn Rise 6 DN19 . . . 85 C8
Hawthorns 2 YO19 . . . 48 F8
Hawthorn Spinney YO31 . 127 E3
Hawthorn St 1 YO31 . . . 130 E5
Hawthorns The
12 Kingston upon Hull
HU8 . . . 141 E7
5 Long Riston/Arnold
HU11 . . . 45 C5
Hawthorn Terr
Goole DN14 . . . 149 F5
York YO32 . . . 127 D4
Hawthorn Terrace N
YO32 . . . 127 D4
Hawthorn Terrace S
YO32 . . . 127 D3
Hawthorn Terr Cent 2
YO32 . . . 127 D3
Hawthorn Way
6 Althorpe DN17 . . . 95 D4
9 Gilberdyke HU15 . . . 66 D7
Hawton Cl 1 DN21 . . . 117 C1
HAXBY . . . 127 D7
Haxby Moor Rd
Haxby YO32 . . . 13 F7
Towthorpe YO32 . . . 14 A7
Haxby Rd
Clifton YO31 . . . 127 D1
New Earswick YO32 . . . 127 D6
York YO31 . . . 156 B4
Haxby Rd Prim Sch
YO31 . . . 130 D7
HAXEY . . . 105 C3
HAXEY CARR . . . 105 B4
Haxey CE Prim Sch DN9 105 D3
Haxey Gate Rd DN10 . . . 116 C7
Haxey Grange 8 DN9 . . . 105 D2
Haxey La DN9 . . . 105 D2
Haxey Rd DN10 . . . 116 C6
Hayburn Ave HU5 . . . 139 F2
Haycroft Ave
Grimsby DN31 . . . 152 C3
West Marsh DN31 . . . 152 C3
Haycroft St DN31 . . . 152 C3
Haydock Garth 6 HU7 . . . 57 A5
Haydon Cl HU10 . . . 143 D8
Hayes La DN7 . . . 78 D1
Hayfield Cl
Barnby Dun DN3 . . . 92 A4
9 Haxey DN9 . . . 105 D2
Hayforth Cl YO30 . . . 127 A2
Hayling Mere 29 DN35 . . . 103 C1
Haymarket Cl HU8 . . . 141 F4
Haymer Dr 43 HU12 . . . 72 D7
Haynes Cl 2 DN8 . . . 93 B7
Haynes Gdns 15 DN8 . . . 93 B8
Haynes Gn 9 DN8 . . . 93 B8
Haynes Gr 1 DN8 . . . 93 B7
Haynes Rd DN8 . . . 93 B8
Hays Cl 3 DN36 . . . 114 A5
HAYTON . . . 40 C8
Hayton Cl DN15 . . . 83 A5
Hayton Gr HU4 . . . 144 D4
Hayton's La DN15 . . . 83 D2
Hayward Cl 3 HU17 . . . 55 D8
Hazel Ave
Crowle DN17 . . . 94 D8
Withernsea HU19 . . . 75 A5
Hazelbarrow Dr HU10 . . . 143 F7
Hazel Cl
Great Driffield YO25 . . . 124 E3
Messingham DN17 . . . 107 C7
York YO32 . . . 127 D2
Hazel Cres 12 HU15 . . . 66 D7
Hazel Croft 5 DN40 . . . 87 B1
Hazel Ct
23 Brough HU15 . . . 68 C5
York YO10 . . . 130 E4
Hazel Garth YO31 . . . 131 B7
Hazel Gr
Goole DN14 . . . 149 D1
2 Kingston upon Hull
HU3 . . . 145 D5
20 Yaddlethorpe DN17 . . . 96 D1
Hazelmere Ct YO32 . . . 127 E3
Hazelnut Gr YO30 . . . 127 B2
Hazel Old La DN14 . . . 62 C2
Hazel Rd DN7 . . . 92 C5
Hazelwood Ave YO10 . . . 131 D4
Hazing La DN14 . . . 77 B6
Headingley Ave 20 DN17 . 96 C2
Headingley Rd 7 DN6 . . . 76 E2
Headland Cl 30 YO32 . . . 13 E5
Headlands Cl YO16 . . . 122 F6
Headlands Dr
Aldbrough HU11 . . . 47 C1
Bridlington YO16 . . . 122 F6
Kingston upon Hull HU13 . 143 C2
Headlands Prim Sch
YO32 . . . 127 D8
Headlands Rd HU11 . . . 47 C1
Headlands Sch YO16 . . . 122 F5
Headlands Wlk YO16 . . . 122 E6
Headland View HU18 . . . 134 D5
Headley Cl 2 YO30 . . . 127 B1
Heads La HU13 . . . 143 C1
Healey Gr YO31 . . . 130 F8
Healey Rd DN16 . . . 151 C4
HEALING . . . 102 A5
Healing Prim Sch DN41 . 101 F5
Healing Rd DN41 . . . 101 D6
Healing Sch DN41 . . . 101 F5
Healing Sta DN41 . . . 101 F6
Health Pl 29 DN20 . . . 98 C2
Heanor Ct DN15 . . . 150 B7
Heapham Rd DN21 . . . 117 C1
Hearfield Terr HU13 . . . 143 E1
Heater Cnr HU17 . . . 31 F1
Heath Cl 2 YO24 . . . 129 F2
Heathcote St HU6 . . . 140 D4
Heath Croft YO10 . . . 133 F7
Heather Bank
13 Stamford Bridge YO41 . . 15 D2
York YO10 . . . 131 C4
Heather Cl
31 Gainsborough DN21 . . . 117 C1
7 Kingston upon Hull
HU5 . . . 139 D1
Selby YO8 . . . 148 C3

Heather Cl *continued*
York YO32 128 A4
Heather Croft 4 YO31 127 E2
Heatherdale Cl 9 DN33 113 E8
Heather Garth YO25 124 E2
Heather Gr 1 DN16 96 F2
Heatherwood Cl 11 HU7 57 B5
Heathfield Cl 8 DN3 92 A3
Heathfield Ct DN34 152 B1
Heathfield Rd 1 YO10 131 A3
Heath Moor Dr YO10 133 F8
Heath Ride YO32 14 B8
Hebden Ave HU8 142 C5
Hebden Rd DN15 150 C8
Hebdon Rise 2 YO26 129 D4
Heber St DN14 149 C2
Hebrides Cl HU9 142 A3
Heckdyke La DN10 116 F7
Heck La
Heck DN14 77 C7
Hensall DN14 62 D1
Heck & Pollington Lake DN14 77 E7
Hedgerow Cl 4 DN19 85 C8
Hedgerow Ct 10 HU6 140 B8
Hedgerow La 24 DN20 98 C2
Hedgerows The YO8 49 E3
Hedley Cl 7 HU15 53 F1
HEDON 72 C8
Hedon Mus* HU12 72 C7
Hedon Prim Sch HU12 72 C7
Hedon Rd
Kingston upon Hull HU9 146 B6
Marfleet HU9 147 D7
Heigholme La HU17 44 F8
Heigholm La YO25 34 A1
Height Lands La YO23 24 D6
Heimdal Rd DN33 102 E1
Helen Cres 9 DN40 87 B1
Helene Gr DN32 153 B3
Hellyer Cl HU14 69 A5
Hellyers Ct HU4 144 D2
Helm Dr HU9 146 C6
Helms Ave 6 HU12 58 C1
Helmsdale YO24 132 C6
Helmsley Gr
16 Haxby YO32 13 D5
Kingston upon Hull HU5 144 C7
Helperby Wlk HU5 139 E3
Helsinki Rd HU7 140 F5
Helston Wlk DN17 150 C4
Helvellyn Cl 10 HU7 57 A6
Hemble Way HU7 56 F5
HEMINGBROUGH 49 F1
Hemingbrough Prim Sch YO8 49 F1
Hemlock Ave YO31 127 E1
Hemmingway Wlk HU13 143 E3
Hempbridge Cl YO8 148 A5
Hempbridge Rd YO8 148 A5
Hempdyke Rd DN15 150 E8
Hempland Ave YO31 130 F6
Hempland Dr YO31 131 A7
Hempland La YO31 131 A7
Hempland Prim Sch YO31 131 B6
HEMSWELL 119 A1
Hemswell Ave HU9 147 D8
HEMSWELL CLIFF 119 D1
Hemswell Dr 6 DN37 102 C4
Hemswell La DN21 119 A1
Henderson Ave DN15 150 F8
Henderson Ave Prim Sch DN15 150 F8
Henderson Cres DN15 150 F8
Henderson St DN31 153 A6
Henderson Way DN15 83 A5
Hendon Garth YO30 127 A1
Heneage Rd DN32 152 F2
Hengate HU17 154 A3
Henley Ct 6 DN21 117 B1
Henley Dr HU9 141 E1
Henlow Cl 4 DN21 119 C8
Henry Boot Way HU4 144 C2
Henry Ct 8 DN8 79 B1
Henry St
Goole DN14 149 B4
Grimsby DN31 152 C4
Scunthorpe DN15 150 F7
Henry Verone Ct HU2 155 B1
HENSALL 62 D2
Hensall Prim Sch DN14 62 C1
Hensall Sta DN14 62 C1
Henwick Hall La YO8 148 C1
Hepscott Wlk HU8 142 D6
Hepworth's La DN14 63 C2
Herbert St 6 YO10 130 E3
Herberts Way YO31 130 F7
Herdsman Dr YO23 132 C3
Herdsman Rd 3 YO24 132 D8
Herdwick Cl 1 YO30 127 B1
Hereford Ave DN34 152 C1
Hereford Cl 4 HU17 136 E1
Hereford Rd YO42 28 E3
Hereford St HU4 144 E3
Hereford Tech Sch DN34 152 B1
Hereward Pl DN16 151 E3
Herman Wlk YO24 132 C8
Hermes Cl HU9 142 C4
Hermitage Rd YO16 122 C4
Hermitage The 5 DN8 79 B2
Heron Ave YO24 132 C8
Heron Cl
Grimsby DN32 103 A2
10 Scunthorpe DN15 96 B7
Heron Dr DN21 117 C1
Heron Gate DN16 151 F1
Heron Holt 1 DN20 97 D4
Heron Mews YO15 11 B4
Heron Rise YO32 127 F5
Heron St HU3 145 B5
Heron Way
26 Barton Upon Humber DN18 84 E8
6 Holton le Clay DN36 114 A6
Herrick Rd DN17 150 D3
Herriot Way DN15 150 C7
Hersey Rd 24 LN7 111 B4
Hertfordshire Cl 2 HU5 139 D1
Hesketh Bank YO10 131 D3
Hesketh Dr DN3 92 A2
Heslerton Ave HU16 139 A4
Heslin Cl 8 YO32 127 C8
HESLINGTON 131 B1
Heslington Croft YO10 133 F7
Heslington Ct 2 YO10 131 B1
Heslington La
Heslington YO10 131 A1
York YO10 130 F3
Heslington Rd YO10 130 E3
HESSAY 24 C8
Hessay Ind Est YO26 24 C8
Hessay Pl 2 YO26 129 A3
HESSLE 143 E1
Hessle All Saints CE Inf Sch HU13 143 F2
Hessle All Saints CE Jun Sch HU13 143 F2
Hessle High Sch HU13 143 C2
Hessle Mount Sch HU13 143 C3
Hessle Rd HU1 155 A1
Hessleskew La YO43 42 A4
Hessle Station HU13 69 E4
Hessle View 22 DN18 84 E8
Hetherton St YO30 156 A3
Hewde La DN15 83 A8
Hewitt's Ave DN36 114 A8
Hewitts Ave Bsns Pk DN36 103 B1
Hewitt's Cir DN36 103 B1
Hewitts Cir Ret Pk DN35 103 B1
Hewitts Manor
3 Cleethorpes DN35 103 B1
New Waltham DN36 114 B8
Hewley Ave YO10 131 A4
HEWORTH 130 F6
Heworth YO31 131 A6
Heworth CE Prim Sch YO31 130 F6
Heworth Gn YO31 156 C4
Heworth Hall Dr YO31 130 F6
Heworth Mews YO31 130 E6
Heworth Pl YO31 130 F6
Heworth Rd YO31 130 F6
Heworth Village YO31 131 A6
Hewson Rd DN36 114 D8
Hewson's La DN18 69 E1
Hewson St DN17 107 D7
Heyford Rd YO42 28 E3
Hey St DN35 153 F1
Heythrop Rd DN35 103 C2
HIBALDSTOW 108 F5
Hibaldstow Cl 21 DN34 102 C2
Hibaldstow Prim Sch DN20 109 A5
Hickleton Cl HU8 141 C1
Hickman Cres DN21 117 B2
Hickman Gr DN21 117 E5
Higham Cl HU8 141 E7
Higham Way HU15 68 D5
Highbields YO42 28 F7
High Bridge Rd DN8 93 C7
High Brighton St 18 HU19 75 A6
High Burgage 2 DN15 68 B1
HIGH CATTON 27 D8
High Catton Rd YO41 27 D8
Highcliffe Ct YO30 130 A6
Highcliff Gdns DN15 150 E7
Highcourt HU6 139 E7
Highcroft HU17 43 A5
High Croft 7 YO14 2 F8
Highdales HU10 143 C8
High Eggborough La DN14 62 A1
High Farm Ct HU11 142 F7
HIGHFIELD 50 E7
Highfield
Kingston upon Hull HU7 141 D6
Pollington DN14 77 F7
Withernsea HU19 75 A6
High Field YO10 131 D4
Highfield Ave
Great Driffield YO25 124 E6
Grimsby DN32 152 E1
22 Immingham DN40 87 B1
Scunthorpe DN15 150 E7
Highfield Cl
Barnby Dun DN3 92 A4
Fangfoss YO41 28 C8
Gainsborough DN21 117 C1
Hatfield DN7 92 D5
Kingston upon Hull HU7 141 D6
North Frodingham YO25 34 A8
5 North Thoresby DN36 114 B1
Wold Newton YO25 2 A4
Highfield Cres
Barlby with Osgodby YO8 49 B5
15 Barton-upon-Humber DN18 84 F8
Kingston upon Hull HU11 142 F7
9 Thorne/Moorends DN8 79 A1
2 Westwoodside DN9 105 B2
Highfield Ct YO8 148 B1
Highfield Dr 1 DN21 108 B1
Highfield Gr
4 Brigg DN20 98 C3
Highfield YO8 50 E7
Highfield La
Fangfoss YO41 16 B1
Womersley DN6 76 D5
Highfield Rd
Beverley HU17 136 F6
Highfield YO8 50 D7
North Thoresby DN36 114 B1
High Field Rd DN20 98 D3
Highfield Rise 1 HU12 58 D1
Highfields
10 Barrow upon Humber DN19 85 C8
Crowle DN17 94 D8
South Cave HU15 54 A2
Highfield View 3 YO8 49 B4
Highfield Way HU14 69 A4
High Garth
Earswick YO32 128 A7
Scunthorpe DN17 96 C1
Highgate
Balne DN14 77 D6
Cherry Burton HU17 42 E4
Cleethorpes DN35 153 E1
Highgate Cl HU8 142 A5
High Gn YO16 122 D5
Highgrove DN17 107 D7
Highgrove Cl 7 YO30 126 E3
Highgrove Way HU7 56 F6
High Hazel Rd DN8 79 B2
HIGH HUNSLEY 54 D6
High La
Carnaby YO25 10 C3
Sutton upon Derwent YO41 27 D3
Highlands Ave 5 YO32 14 B7
Highlands Prim Sch HU7 57 A6
Highland Tarn 31 DN40 87 B1
High Levels Bank
Belton DN8 94 A4
Hatfield DN8 93 A6
High Leys Rd DN17 96 C2
High Mdw
Gowdall DN14 63 A1
Selby YO8 148 B6
High Mdws HU10 143 C8
Highmoor Cl YO24 132 D8
High Moor La YO30 12 C8
Highmoor Rd YO24 132 D8
HIGH MOWTHORPE 6 D7
High Newbiggin St YO31 156 B3
High Oaks YO31 131 B7
High Ousegate YO1 156 B2
High Petergate YO1 156 B3
High Peter La YO25 20 D7
High Point Ret Pk DN31 152 E5
High Rd
Elloughton-cum-Brough HU15 68 D6
North Cave HU15 53 E3
HIGH RISBY 82 F1
High Risby Medieval Village* DN15 83 A1
High Row YO41 16 D4
High Sewerby Rd YO15 123 C7
High Side YO25 34 A8
High St
Airmyn DN14 64 E3
Aldbrough HU11 47 C1
Barmby on the Marsh DN14 64 A7
Barrow upon Humber DN19 85 D8
Barton-upon-Humber DN18 69 E1
Beckingham DN10 116 D1
Belton DN9 94 E1
Blyton DN21 117 F5
Boynton YO16 10 D7
Bridlington YO16 122 C4
Broughton DN20 97 D3
Buckton/Bempton YO15 4 C3
Burringham DN17 95 D4
Burton upon Stather DN15 82 B4
Caistor LN7 111 B4
Carlton DN14 63 C2
Cawood YO8 48 B8
Cleethorpes DN35 153 E2
Corringham DN21 118 A1
Cottam YO25 7 E5
4 Crowle DN17 94 D7
Easington HU12 90 F6
East Butterwick DN17 106 D8
East Ferry DN21 106 B2
Eastoft DN17 81 A3
Eastrington DN14 65 F8
Epworth DN9 105 E6
7 Flamborough YO15 5 A2
Flixborough DN15 82 B1
Garthorpe & Fockerby DN17 81 E5
Goole DN14 65 C4
Great Limber DN37 100 D3
Gringley on the Hill DN10 116 A1
Hatfield DN7 92 C2
Haxey DN9 105 D2
Holme-on-Spalding-Moor YO43 40 A1
Humberside Airport DN39 100 A6
Kilham YO25 9 A8
Kingston upon Hull HU1 155 C1
Kirby Grindalythe YO17 6 D8
Kirton in Lindsey DN21 108 B1
Laceby DN37 101 F1
Langtoft YO25 8 C8
Luddington & Haldenby DN17 81 C4
Market Weighton YO43 135 D4
Messingham DN17 107 D7
Misterton DN10 116 C5
High St *continued*
Nafferton YO25 125 E7
Nettleton LN7 111 C2
North Ferriby HU14 69 A5
North Kelsey LN7 110 A4
North Thoresby DN36 114 A1
14 Norton DN6 76 E1
Owston Ferry DN9 106 B3
Rawcliffe DN14 64 A1
Redbourne DN21 108 F2
Roxby cum Risby DN15 82 E1
Sancton YO43 41 D2
Scotter DN21 107 C3
Scotton DN21 107 C1
Scunthorpe DN15 151 A7
Snaith DN14 63 B1
South Ferriby DN18 84 A7
Swinefleet DN14 65 D1
Ulceby DN39 86 A1
Walkeringham DN10 116 C3
Waltham DN37 113 E6
West/East Butterwick DN17 95 D1
Wharram YO17 6 A6
Winterton DN15 83 A5
Withernwick HU11 46 D3
Wootton DN39 85 E2
Wroot DN9 104 D6
High Stile HU17 45 B8
High Street E DN15 151 C7
High Street W DN21 107 C4
Highthorn Rd YO31 127 E2
High Thorpe Cres DN35 103 B2
High Trees Mount HU8 141 E6
Highwood YO25 124 E6
Higrove Way 32 HU7 56 F6
Hilary Gr HU4 144 B2
Hilary Rd 11 DN33 113 E8
Hilbeck Gr YO31 131 B6
Hilbra Ave YO32 127 D6
Hilda St
Goole DN14 149 C5
Grimsby DN32 153 A4
6 Selby YO8 148 C5
3 York YO10 130 E3
HILDERTHORPE 11 B4
Hilderthorpe Inf Sch YO15 122 C1
Hilderthorpe Jun Sch YO15 122 C1
Hilderthorpe Rd YO15 122 D2
Hildyard Cl
19 Hedon HU12 72 D7
1 Kingston upon Hull HU10 143 F6
Hildyard St DN32 153 A4
Hiles Ave DN15 83 A5
HILLAM 61 A7
Hillam Comm La LS25 61 B7
Hillam Hall La 4 LS25 61 A7
Hillam Hall View 3 LS25 61 A7
Hillam House Cl 5 LS25 61 A7
Hillam La LS25 61 A7
Hillam Rd YO8 61 F8
Hillary Garth 9 YO26 129 E4
Hillary Rd DN16 151 B1
Hillary Way DN37 102 C4
Hill Brow HU10 143 B6
Hillcrest
Beverley HU17 136 C6
8 Monk Fryston LS25 61 A8
Hill Crest YO19 14 F1
Hillcrest Ave
Kingston upon Hull HU13 143 C2
Poppleton YO26 126 A2
Hillcrest Dr
Beverley HU17 136 D6
Burton upon Stather DN15 82 A4
Hill Crest Gdns YO24 129 F1
Hillerby La HU18 134 B4
Hill Field YO8 148 B8
Hillfield Dr HU11 45 D2
Hillfoot Dr 22 DN17 96 C2
Hillgarth Ct 4 YO41 27 B2
Hillman Rd HU13 143 F3
Hill Rd DN21 118 B1
Hill Rise
Brough HU15 68 C6
Market Weighton YO43 135 E4
Hill Rise Cl YO43 135 E4
Hill Rise Dr YO43 135 E4
Hillsborough Terr 5 YO30 130 C7
Hills Dr 6 DN36 114 D4
Hillside Cl
Bootham Stray YO30 127 B2
9 Monk Fryston LS25 61 A8
Hillside Cres DN38 99 B5
Hillside Dr DN18 84 E8
Hillside Gdns YO25 8 D5
Hillside Rd DN20 97 E4
Hillside Way YO17 7 B8
Hillsmere Gr 5 DN15 83 A5
Hill St
Bridlington YO16 122 D3
Kingston upon Hull HU8 141 A2
York YO24 129 E3
Hillstead Cl 5 DN36 114 D4
Hillsway Cl HU8 141 D4
Hillsyde Ave DN10 116 C5
Hill The DN20 98 D8
Hilltop Ave DN15 150 E8
Hilltop Gdns DN17 107 C7
Hill Top La DN21 117 E5
Hill Top Pl DN34 102 B2
Hill Top Rd 4 YO8 48 D6
Hill Top View HU11 57 F6
Hill View YO31 131 C7
HILSTON 60 B4
Hilston Gr HU9 142 B1
Hilton Ave DN15 150 B7
Hilton Cl DN9 94 E2
Hilton Ct DN35 103 D1
Hinch Garth HU12 60 B1
Hinderwell St HU5 140 C1
Hindon Wlk DN17 150 C4
Hinkler St DN35 153 E1
Hinkley Dr 2 DN40 87 B2
Hinman Wlk DN15 151 B7
Hinsley La DN14 63 C2
Hinton Ave 1 YO24 132 C8
Hirncroft Cl 10 HU8 141 E7
HIRST COURTNEY 62 F3
Hirst Courtney & Temple Hirst Prim Sch YO8 62 E3
Hirst Rd DN14 63 A3
HIVE 52 C2
Hive La HU15 52 B1
Hobart St HU3 155 A1
Hobb La 14 DN21 107 C3
Hobby Cl DN31 102 B5
Hobgate YO24 129 D3
Hobman La YO25 32 E7
Hob Moor Dr YO24 129 E2
Hob Moor Oaks Sch YO26 129 D2
Hob Moor Prim Sch YO24 129 E2
Hobmoor Terr YO24 129 F1
Hobson Cl YO23 132 B1
Hobson Ct HU17 154 B4
Hobson Rd 5 HU15 68 C5
Hobson Way DN41 101 F8
Hodder Gr HU8 142 C6
Hoddesdon Cres 13 DN7 92 D3
Hoddy Cows La YO15 4 C3
Hodge Ct 3 HU9 146 C7
Hodge La WF8 76 B3
Hodgson Ave HU17 154 B4
Hodgson La
Roos HU12 60 A1
Upper Poppleton YO26 24 F8
Hodgson's Fields Nature Reserve* HU12 90 D7
Hodgson St HU8 155 C3
Hodsow Fields YO42 28 E4
Hodsow La YO42 28 F3
Hoggard La DN14 81 E8
Hogg La HU10 143 B8
Hogsea La HU11 60 B4
Holbeck Pl 17 DN40 87 B1
Holborn St HU9 146 B7
Holbrook Cl 2 HU7 141 B4
Holburns Croft 3 YO10 131 B1
Holcombe Cl HU8 142 B7
Holcroft Garth 10 HU12 72 D7
Holden Gdns YO8 48 D2
Holderness Cres HU17 154 B3
Holderness Rd HU9 146 C8
HOLGATE 129 F3
Holgate Bridge Gdn 7 YO24 130 A3
Holgate Cl 2 HU17 137 B3
Holgate Lodge Dr YO26 129 E4
Holgate Pl 12 HU14 69 B7
Holgate Rd
Scunthorpe DN16 151 D4
York YO24 156 A1
Holland Ave
Crowle DN17 94 D8
Scunthorpe DN15 150 E8
Holland Dr DN38 110 E7
Holland St HU9 146 C8
Holland Way HU9 146 C7
Holles St DN32 152 E3
Hollicarrs Cl YO19 37 A2
Hollies The
Barlby with Osgodby YO8 49 C4
Beverley HU17 137 A7
Hornsea HU18 134 D2
Kingston upon Hull HU10 138 E2
Snaith & Cowick DN14 78 C8
Stockton on the Forest YO19 14 D3
Hollin Bridge La DN7 93 A3
Hollingsworth Ave 12 DN40 87 B1
Hollingsworth Cl 14 DN35 103 B1
Hollingsworth La 22 DN9 105 E6
Hollis Cres YO32 14 B6
Hollowgate Hill DN21 119 A3
Hollows The 9 YO16 122 C5
Holly Bank Gr 3 YO24 129 F2
Holly Bank Rd YO24 129 F2
Hollybush Cl DN14 77 A7
Hollybush Way HU17 136 D4
Holly Cl
Acaster Malbis YO23 36 C8
Full Sutton YO41 16 A2
13 Scunthorpe DN16 96 E2
Stallingborough DN41 101 D6
Hollycroft YO25 23 A6
Holly Dr HU16 138 E5
Hollygarth La DN14 61 D4
Holly Gr
11 Gilberdyke HU15 66 D7
Selby YO8 148 B3
Summergangs HU8 141 C2
8 Thorpe Willoughby YO8 48 B2
Holly Hill HU15 68 E6
HOLLYM 75 A4
Hollym Rd
Patrington HU19 74 F3
Withernsea HU19 75 A5

Kingsgate *continued*
Carnaby YO15 10 F2
Cleethorpes DN32 153 A3
Kingsgate Mews DN32 153 A3
Kingsland Terr 11 YO26 129 F5
Kings Lea YO8 50 A8
Kings Leigh 1 HU3 145 C6
Kingsley Ave HU9 141 E2
Kingsley Cl 6 HU15 68 B5
Kingsley Dr HU10 138 D1
Kingsley Gr 4 DN33 102 E2
Kings Mdw YO25 124 D4
Kingsmead 20 DN8 79 B2
Kings Mead
Great Driffield YO25 124 D4
Woodmansey HU17 137 D1
Kings Mews DN35 103 E1
Kings Mill Cl YO25 124 D4
Kings Mill Pk YO25 124 D4
King's Mill Rd YO25 124 D3
Kings Mill Sch YO25 124 E4
Kings Moor Rd YO32 14 D2
King's Pl 23 HU12 72 C7
Kingsport Cl HU3 145 A7
Kings Rd DN40 87 D1
King's Rd
Barnetby le Wold DN38 99 B5
Cleethorpes DN35 103 D2
King's Sq
Beverley HU17 154 B3
York YO1 156 C2
King's Staith YO1 156 B2
King St
1 Barton-upon-Humber DN18 84 F8
Bridlington YO15 122 E2
6 Cawood YO8 48 B8
Cottingham HU16 139 B6
East Halton DN40 86 D7
Goxhill DN19 86 A8
Great Driffield YO25 124 F4
1 Hornsea HU18 134 C3
19 Keelby DN41 101 A4
Sancton YO43 41 E2
Scunthorpe DN15 151 B8
Thorne/Moorends DN8 93 A8
Winterton DN15 83 A5
17 Withernsea HU19 75 A6
Woodmansey HU17 137 D1
York YO1 156 B2
Kingsthorpe YO24 129 D2
Kingsthorpe Pk 11 YO8 48 D6
Kingston Ave
Grimsby DN34 152 A2
Kingston upon Hull HU13 143 F1
Kingston Cl
Hilderthorpe YO15 11 B4
8 Humberston DN35 103 D1
Kingston Communications Stadium (Hull City AFC & Hull RLFC) HU3 145 B7
Kingston Cres YO15 11 B4
Kingston Rd
Bridlington YO15 11 B4
Kingston upon Hull HU10 138 D1
Scunthorpe DN16 151 A3
Kingston Ret Pk HU1 155 A1
Kingston Rise
Kingston upon Hull HU10 138 C1
Willerby HU10 138 C1
Kingston Sq HU2 155 B3
Kingston St
Goole DN14 149 C2
Kingston upon Hull HU1 155 B1
KINGSTON UPON HULL 155 B2
Kingston View 27 DN18 84 F8
Kingston Way HU7 140 F5
Kingston Wharf HU1 155 A1
Kingsway
2 Brigg DN20 98 B2
Cleethorpes DN35 103 D3
Goole DN14 149 D4
Kingston upon Hull HU16 139 B5
Scunthorpe DN15 150 C7
14 Stainforth DN7 92 C6
6 Stamford Bridge YO41 15 D2
Kingsway N YO30 130 B7
Kingsway Prim Sch DN14 149 E5
Kingsway Sta DN35 103 D2
Kingsway W YO24 129 D1
Kingswood College of Arts HU7 57 A5
Kingswood Gr YO24 129 D3
Kingswood Ret Pk HU7 56 E5
Kingtree Ave HU16 139 B6
Kinloch Way 28 DN40 87 B1
Kinloss Garth 2 HU7 57 B5
Kinsbourne Gn 37 DN7 92 D4
Kinsley Wlk 5 DN15 151 B7
Kinthorpe HU6 140 A8
Kiplin Dr 14 DN6 76 E2
Kipling Ave DN17 150 D3
Kipling Cl YO25 31 C4
Kiplingcotes Chalk Pit Nature Reserve* YO43 41 F6
Kiplingcotes La YO43 42 A5
Kipling Cotes Medieval Village* YO25 30 D2
Kiplingcotes Racecourse* YO25 30 E1
Kiplington Cl HU3 145 A7
Kipling Wlk 1 HU4 144 D2
Kirby Cl YO43 135 E2
Kirby Dr
Cottingham HU16 139 B6
Kingston upon Hull HU16 139 B6
KIRBY GRINDALYTHE 6 E6
Kirby La YO25 7 A4
KIRBY UNDERDALE 17 A5
Kir Cres YO24 129 C3
Kirk Balk YO17 16 E8
Kirk Balk La YO60 15 B7
KIRK BRAMWITH 92 A6
KIRKBURN 20 A2
Kirkby Ave YO8 148 B7
Kirkby Cl DN14 149 C5
Kirkby Rd
Scunthorpe DN17 96 C2
Selby YO8 148 B7
Kirkby St HU2 155 B4
Kirk Cl HU7 141 D6
Kirkcroft YO32 127 C8
Kirk Croft HU16 139 A6
Kirkdale Rd YO10 131 D4
Kirkden Paddocks DN9 94 C2
KIRK ELLA 143 D8
Kirkfield Rd HU19 75 A6
Kirkgate
Bridlington YO16 122 D4
8 Pocklington YO42 29 A4
Kirk Gate DN37 113 E6
Kirkgate Mews YO16 122 D5
Kirkham Ave 1 YO31 130 E8
Kirkham Cl HU13 143 F2
Kirkham Ct DN14 149 E6
Kirkham Dr HU5 140 B2
Kirkham Rd YO16 122 D7
Kirkholme Way HU17 137 B4
Kirkhouse Green Rd DN7 92 A8
Kirk La
Sykehouse DN14 78 B4
Walkington HU17 55 B7
Kirkland Cl YO8 148 D4
Kirklands YO32 14 B6
Kirklands La YO41 16 C2
Kirklands Rd HU5 144 E8
Kirkland St YO42 29 A4
Kirk Rd 2 HU12 58 C1
Kirk Rise HU10 143 C7
Kirkside 2 DN37 113 E6
KIRK SMEATON 76 B3
Kirk Smeaton CE Prim Sch WF8 76 B3
Kirkstead Cres DN33 102 D2
Kirkstead St HU8 141 A2
Kirkstone Dr YO31 131 A6
Kirkstone Rd HU5 139 D2
Kirk View 1 YO26 129 C3
Kirkway HU10 143 B7
Kirkwell YO23 133 A4
Kirman Cres 18 DN17 96 C2
KIRMINGTON 100 A6
Kirmington CE Prim Sch DN39 100 A6
Kirmington Gdns DN34 152 A2
Kirncroft Cl 16 HU12 73 C4
KIRTON IN LINDSEY 108 B1
Kirton in Lindsey Prim Sch DN21 108 A1
Kirton La DN7 92 E6
Kirton Lane Prim Sch DN7 92 D7
Kirton Lindsey Sta DN21 108 B2
Kirton Rd
Blyton DN21 117 F6
Holme DN16 97 B2
Kirton in Lindsey DN21 108 A3
Messingham DN17 107 E6
Scawby DN20 108 C8
Scotton DN21 107 D2
Kishorn Ct 30 DN40 87 B1
Kissing Gate HU12 59 D2
Kitchen Dr YO8 148 D4
Kitchener Cl YO8 148 B5
Kitchener St
Selby YO8 148 B6
York YO31 130 D7
Kitchen La HU17 154 A1
Kitemere Pl 2 YO24 132 B8
Kit Kat Crescent (York City FC) YO31 130 B7
Kitty Garth YO19 38 A7
Kitty Hill (Tumulus)* YO41 16 E3
Klondyke DN16 151 D7
KNAPTON 129 A5
Knapton Ave 7 HU5 139 E3
Knapton Cl 1 YO32 14 B6
Knapton Ct LN7 111 C4
Knapton La YO26 129 B4
KNAVESMIRE 133 A7
Knavesmire Cres YO23 130 B1
Knavesmire Prim Sch YO23 130 B1
Knavesmire Rd
Nunthorpe YO23 133 B8
York YO23 130 A1
KNEDLINGTON 64 E6
Knedlington Rd DN14 65 A6
Knedlington Wlk 7 DN14 65 A6
Knightly Way HU7 56 E5
Knightsbridge 7 DN36 114 A8
Knightsbridge Ct 7 HU3 140 D1
Knightsbridge Rd DN17 107 D7
Knights Cl
Belton DN9 94 E2
8 Laceby DN37 101 F1
Knightscourt HU6 139 F7
Knights Ct HU17 154 B2
Knight's Ct 16 DN16 96 D2
Knight St DN32 153 B2
Knights Way HU17 154 B3
Knole Pk HU7 56 F5
Knoll St DN35 153 F2
Knoll The YO24 129 B2
KNOTTINGLEY 61 B2
Knottingley High Sch WF11 61 A2
Knowle Rd 25 HU7 56 F5
Knowles Ave HU6 140 C8
Knowle Way 54 HU12 72 D7
Knowsley Ave HU16 139 A7
Kyffin Ave HU9 142 D2
Kyle Cl HU8 142 C6
Kyle Way YO26 129 B8
Kyme St YO1 156 B1

L

Labrador Dr 11 DN20 97 E4
Laburnham Ave 21 DN37 113 D6
Laburnham Cl 22 DN37 113 D6
Laburnum Ave
18 Gainsborough DN21 117 B1
Gunness DN15 95 E6
Hutton Cranswick YO25 32 E7
Kingston upon Hull HU8 141 C2
11 Thorne/Moorends DN8 79 B2
Laburnum Cl
Rufforth YO23 24 C6
7 Snaith DN14 63 C1
3 Thorpe Willoughby YO8 48 B1
Laburnum Ct
Barlow YO8 63 D7
4 Bridlington YO16 123 A6
Kingston upon Hull HU13 143 D1
Laburnum Dr
Beverley HU17 137 A7
7 Church Town DN9 94 E1
Grimsby DN34 102 C4
3 Kingston upon Hull HU4 144 B7
Laburnum Farm Cl YO26 24 C8
Laburnum Garth 6 YO31 130 F8
Laburnum Gr
Burton upon Stather DN15 82 B5
10 Crowle DN17 94 D7
Scunthorpe DN16 151 B3
Stillingfleet YO19 36 D4
Laburnum Wlk 17 HU15 66 D8
LACEBY 101 E2
LACEBY ACRES 102 B2
Laceby Acres Prim Sch DN34 102 B3
Laceby Rd
Grimsby DN34 102 C2
Laceby Acres DN34 102 B2
Scunthorpe DN17 150 E1
Lady Anne Ct YO1 156 B1
Ladybower Cl 4 HU8 141 E7
Lady Frances Cres DN35 153 C1
Ladygate HU17 154 A3
Lady Hamilton Gdns YO24 129 E2
Lady Kell Gdns YO32 127 E8
Lady Mill Garth YO30 130 B8
Lady Peckitts Yd YO1 156 B2
Lady Rd YO30 130 B7
Ladyside Cl 17 HU7 57 A6
Ladysmith Ind Est DN32 153 A2
Ladysmith Mews 13 YO32 14 A7
Ladysmith Rd
Grimsby DN32 152 F3
Kingston upon Hull HU10 138 E1
Lady's Well* YO43 135 F7
Ladywell Gate 3 HU15 68 E6
Lady Wortley Pl YO23 133 B6
Laforey Rd DN37 102 C6
Lagoon Dr HU7 141 D8
Lagoon Rd DN17 150 B2
Lairgate HU17 154 A2
Lairs La YO42 30 A5
Lake Dr HU8 141 E3
Lakeside
Acaster Malbis YO23 36 C7
Great Coates DN31 102 B6
Little Leven HU17 44 F6
Lakeside County Prim Sch YO30 126 F2
Lakeside Dr DN17 150 C1
Lakeside Gr
Kingston upon Hull HU4 144 D4
1 Strensall YO32 14 B8
Lakeside Parkway DN16 151 F1
Lakeside Ret Pk DN16 151 F1
Lakeside Sta DN35 103 E2
Lakeview 6 HU17 44 F6
Lake View HU8 141 E3
Laking La YO25 2 A3
Lalrgate Pl 20 DN36 103 C1
Lambert Ave 16 HU15 68 C6
Lambert Cl YO43 135 E3
Lambert Ct YO1 156 B1
Lambert Park Rd 23 HU12 72 C7
Lambert Rd
Bridlington YO16 122 F5
Grimsby DN32 152 E2
Lambert St HU5 140 D2
Lamb Inn Rd 9 WF11 61 A2
Lamb La
Newport HU15 67 B8
Roos HU12 60 A1
Lambourn Ct 25 DN35 103 C1
Lambourne Rise 7 DN16 96 D1
Lambton St HU5 140 C3
Lambwath Hall Ct HU7 141 C8
Lambwath La HU11 46 A3
Lambwath Rd HU8 141 C4
Lambwell Hill HU15 54 E2
Lamel St YO10 131 A3
Lamorna Ave HU8 141 B3
Lamplugh Cres YO23 133 B3
Lamplugh La 7 YO15 122 F4
Lamplugh Rd YO15 122 F4
Lamplugh Sq 6 YO15 122 F4
Lampton Gr DN32 152 D2
Lanark St 3 HU5 145 B8
Lancar Cl 18 YO32 13 D5
Lancaster App DN40 86 D4
Lancaster Ave DN31 152 B3
Lancaster Ct 13 DN33 102 D1
Lancaster Dr
Kingston upon Hull HU8 141 D4
2 Moorland Prison DN7 104 A8
7 South Killingholme DN40 86 E3
Lancaster Gate DN36 114 A4
Lancaster La HU18 134 A4
Lancaster Rd
Carnaby YO15 10 D2
Gringley on the Hill DN10 116 A1
Pocklington YO42 28 E3
Scunthorpe DN16 151 A1
Lancaster Way
26 Brough HU15 68 C5
York YO30 127 A1
Lancelot Ct HU9 146 C6
Lancing Way 24 DN33 113 E8
Landalewood Rd YO30 126 F2
Landau Cl YO30 129 F8
Land Dike LN11 115 A1
Landeck Ave DN34 152 B2
Land Ends Rd DN8 78 F1
Landing La
Asselby DN14 64 D6
Barlby with Osgodby YO8 148 F8
Broomfleet HU15 67 A7
Gilberdyke HU15 52 D1
Haxby YO32 127 E7
Hemingbrough YO8 63 F8
Newport HU15 52 E1
Riccall YO19 48 F8
York YO26 129 E6
Landing Rd YO8 62 A7
Landings The 21 YO32 13 F5
Land of Green Ginger HU1 155 B2
Landor Ave DN17 150 D3
Landress La HU17 154 A2
Laneham St DN15 151 A7
Lanes End 24 DN21 108 B1
Lanes The 7 DN36 114 D4
Lane The YO41 15 B2
Lang Ave YO10 131 A4
Langdale Ave
Beverley HU17 154 B3
Grimsby DN33 113 D8
Kingston upon Hull HU5 139 E2
York YO31 131 B6
Langdale Cres HU16 139 A5
Langdale Dr 4 HU12 73 C4
Langdale Gr YO8 148 B3
Langdale Mews YO16 122 E7
Langdale Rd YO43 135 E4
Langford Wlk 1 HU4 144 B7
Langham Rd 13 HU12 72 E5
Langholm Cl HU17 136 D5
Langholme Dr YO26 129 C6
Langholme La DN9 116 B8
Langley Ct 1 YO32 127 F6
Langley Dr DN16 96 D1
Langley Garth
11 Driffield YO25 124 F4
Great Driffield YO25 124 F4
Langley Pk 25 HU7 56 F5
Langley Pl 5 DN35 103 D2
Langleys Rd 6 DN6 76 E1
Langold Dr 15 DN6 76 E2
Lang Rd
Bishopthorpe YO23 132 F4
York YO32 127 F6
Langrick Ave 9 DN14 65 B7
Langrickgate La YO42 38 C5
Langsett Gr YO30 126 F3
Langsett Rd HU8 141 D7
Langthorpe Rd HU11 45 F2
Langthwaite Cl 18 HU15 68 D5
LANGTOFT 8 D5
Langtoft Gr HU6 139 F5
Langtoft Prim Sch YO25 8 C5
Langton Cl 16 DN33 102 D2
Langton Ct 1 YO32 14 A6
Langton Dr DN33 102 D2
Langton Rd DN36 114 B5
Langtree Cl HU7 140 F8
Langwith Stray YO10 26 C2
Lansdowne Ave DN33 102 E2
Lansdowne Cres 9 YO15 122 F3
Lansdowne Rd YO15 122 F2
Lansdowne St HU3 145 C6
Lansdowne Terr 5 YO10 130 E3
Lansdown Link 17 DN35 103 C2
Lansdown Rd
Goole DN14 149 A5
13 Immingham DN40 87 B1
Lansdown Way 7 YO32 13 F5
Lanshaw Croft YO30 126 F1
Lanyon Cl HU7 141 C7
Laporte Rd DN40 87 E2
Lapwing Cl HU7 141 D8
Lapwing Rd YO25 125 B5
Lapwing Way 17 DN18 69 E1
Larard Ave 2 HU6 140 C8
Larch Cl
2 Immingham DN40 87 D2
Kingston upon Hull HU5 140 D2
Larch Ct 11 DN21 117 C1
Larch Dr HU12 72 E5
Larchfield YO31 131 C7
Larch Gr
Scawby DN20 108 F8
Scunthorpe DN16 151 B3
Larchmont Cl 7 HU15 68 C6
Larch Rd 6 DN35 103 B1
Larch Road YO8 148 E2
Larch Way
35 Haxby YO32 13 E5
Selby YO8 148 D2
Larden Ave 1 DN33 113 E8
Larkfield Cl 1 YO23 132 A3
Larkfield Rd YO8 148 A4
Lark Rise 2 DN21 107 B3
Larkspur Ave DN41 101 F5
Larmour Rd DN37 102 B4
Larne Rd HU9 142 B4
Larsen Pk DN14 149 A3
Larsen Rd DN14 149 A3
Lascelles Ave HU19 74 F6
Lasenby Cl YO32 127 D5
Lashbrook Garth HU4 144 B4
Lastingham 12 HU15 68 C6
Lastingham Cl HU6 139 F6
Lastingham Terr YO10 130 D2
LAUGHTON 117 F8
Laughton Rd
Beverley HU17 154 B4
Blyton DN21 117 B4
Laundry La YO25 124 E5
Laura St DN14 149 C5
Laurel Ave DN8 79 B2
Laurel Cl
Earswick YO32 128 A7
10 Gainsborough DN21 117 C1
Gateforth YO8 48 B1
3 Grimsby DN33 102 E1
Kingston upon Hull HU5 144 B7
Laurel Gr LN7 110 A1
Laurels Cl 1 DN40 100 E8
Laurels The
Barlby YO8 49 B5
Barmby Moor YO42 28 D3
Laurel Way 19 DN16 96 E2
Laurence Gr YO8 148 D3
Lauridson Cl 2 DN37 101 E1
Laurier St DN35 153 D4
Laurold Ave DN7 93 A3
Lauty La HU11 45 C5
Lavender Cl
23 Dunswell HU7 56 F5
Goole DN14 149 E7
Lavender Gr
10 New Waltham DN36 113 F8
York YO26 129 E5
Lavender Way DN15 151 B6
Lavender Wlk
Beverley HU17 154 A1
1 Kingston upon Hull HU5 144 C7
Lavenham Rd DN33 113 D8
Laveracks Ind Est YO41 27 B3
Lawn La DN6 77 E3
Lawnsgarth HU16 139 A7
LAWNS THE 138 F7
Lawns The
Beverley HU17 136 C6
Bridlington YO16 122 E7
Grimsby DN34 152 C2
Kirk Ella HU10 143 D7
Sutton-on-Hull HU7 141 D6
Lawnswood HU13 143 D2
Lawnswood Cl HU7 141 D5
Lawnswood Dr YO30 129 F8
Lawnway YO31 131 A7
Lawrence Ave
Bewholme HU11 34 E3
Kingston upon Hull HU8 141 F3
Lawrence Ct 11 YO10 130 E3
Lawrence Sq YO10 130 F3
Lawrence St
Grimsby DN31 152 C4
York YO10 130 E3
Lawson Ave
Grimsby DN31 152 B3
Kingston upon Hull HU16 139 B7
Lawson Cl
Kingston upon Hull HU6 140 B5
1 Walkington HU17 55 B7
Lawson Rd
Bridlington YO16 122 D4
York YO24 132 F7
Lawsons Cl YO14 2 F7
Laxthorpe HU6 140 A8
LAXTON 65 F4
Laxton Garth HU10 138 B1
Laxton Gr 5 DN16 96 D1
Laybourne Garth YO25 125 A4
LAYERTHORPE 130 E4
Layerthorpe YO31 156 C3
LAYTHAM 39 B2
Laytham Gr 6 HU9 142 A2
Leaburn Rd DN17 107 D7
Lea Cres HU16 139 A5
Lea Croft 2 YO43 135 E4
Leadhills Way 6 HU7 57 B5
Leadley Croft YO23 132 A1
Lead Mill La YO1 156 C1
Lea Dr DN32 102 F2
Leads Rd HU7 141 C6
Lea Field Rd YO25 31 E6
Lea Garth DN17 107 D7
Leake St 12 YO10 130 E3
Lealand Cl 1 DN37 101 E1
Lealholm Ct 11 HU8 141 D7

Melton Rd
North Ferriby HU14 69 A5
Wrawby DN20 98 F4
MELTON ROSS 99 C5
Melville Cl 10 HU12 73 C4
Melville St HU1 155 A1
Melwood Cl DN9 105 F6
Melwood Gr
Kingston upon Hull HU5 140 D2
York YO26 129 B5
Melwood Hill DN9 105 F6
Melwood View DN9 105 F6
Memorial Ave 14 HU19 75 A6
Menasha Way DN16 151 E3
Mendip Ave
Goole DN14 149 D5
Grimsby DN33 113 E8
Mendip Cl 2 YO32 127 F5
Mendip Rd DN17 150 D4
Menson Dr DN7 92 D4
MENTHORPE 50 C5
Mercer Rd 1 DN21 117 A1
Merchant Adventurers' Hall* YO1 156 C2
Merchantgate YO1 156 C2
Merchants Ct YO31 130 E5
Merchant Way
Copmanthorpe YO23 132 B3
New Village HU16 139 E5
Mercia Way DN15 96 C8
Mere Cres DN16 151 D3
Meredith Ave DN17 150 C2
Meredyke Rd DN17 81 D3
Mere Garth HU18 134 B4
Mere Grange YO25 18 B6
Mere La
Dalton Holme HU17 42 F8
Edenthorpe DN3 92 A1
Winterton DN15 83 A7
Mereside 9 YO15 5 A2
Mereside Terr HU18 134 B4
Mereside View YO15 5 A2
Mere View Ave HU18 134 B2
Mere Way HU14 69 B7
Mere Wlk 6 HU18 134 C4
Meridian Point Ret Pk DN35 103 D2
Merlin Cl HU7 141 D7
Merlin Covert 4 YO31 127 F3
Merlin Dr DN20 99 A8
Merlin Rd DN17 150 E2
Merrick St HU9 146 B7
Merryman Garth HU12 72 C7
Merryweather Ct 14 DN16 96 D1
Mersey Prim Sch HU8 141 C1
Mersey St HU8 141 C1
Merton Gr 5 HU9 141 F1
Merton Rd DN16 96 D2
MESSINGHAM 107 C7
Messingham La DN20 108 C7
Messingham Prim Sch DN17 107 D7
Messingham Rd
East Butterwick DN17 106 D8
Scotter DN21 107 C4
16 Scunthorpe DN17 96 C2
Metcalfe La YO19 131 C5
Metham La DN14 65 F4
Mews The
Bransholme HU7 29 B3
Kingston upon Hull HU3 145 C5
Meynell St DN21 117 A8
Micklegate
1 Selby YO8 148 D5
York YO1 156 A2
Micklegate Bar Mus* YO24 156 A1
Micklethwaite Gr 2 DN8 79 B2
Micklethwaite Rd 1 DN8 79 B2
Mickley Gr HU9 142 C2
Middle Banks 24 YO32 13 E5
Middle Barn Hill DN20 84 D1
Middlebrook Gdns YO8 148 A2
Middlebrook La 23 DN8 93 A8
Middleburg St HU9 146 D8
Middlecroft YO41 27 F5
Middlecroft Dr YO32 14 A7
Middlecroft Gr 2 YO32 14 B7
Middle Ct DN31 152 E4
Middle Dike La HU16 139 D7
Middledyke La HU16 139 D6
Middlefield La WF8 76 A2
Middle Garth Dr HU15 54 A2
Middlegate Cl 9 DN19 85 C8
Middlegate La
Saxby All Saints DN20 84 B4
South Ferriby DN18 84 B7
Middlegate Mews DN38 99 D5
Middleham Ave YO31 130 E8
Middleham Cl 3 HU9 146 E8
Middlehowe Gn 2 HU17 55 B8
Middlehowe Rd HU17 55 A8
Middle La
Amcotts DN17 95 E8
Brayton YO8 148 C1
14 Knottingley WF11 61 A2
Preston HU12 58 B1
5 Seaton HU11 35 A1
Middlemarsh Cl 3 HU7 141 B4
Middleplatt Rd DN40 87 D2
Middlesex Rd HU8 141 F5
Middle St
Corringham DN21 118 B2
Foggathorpe YO42 39 A2
Kilham YO25 9 B3
Nafferton YO25 125 F7
North Kelsey LN7 110 A4
Rudston YO25 9 F6
Middle St *continued*
Scotton DN21 107 C1
Wilberfoss YO41 27 F5
Willoughton DN21 119 B3
Middle Street N YO25 124 E4
Middle Street S YO25 124 F3
MIDDLETHORPE 133 B6
Middlethorpe Dr YO24 132 E7
Middlethorpe Gr YO24 132 F7
Middlethorpe Prim Sch DN35 103 B2
Middle Thorpe Rd DN35 103 B2
Middleton CE Prim Sch YO25 31 C4
Middleton Cl
Beverley HU17 154 C4
Messingham DN17 107 D7
Middleton Ct
Bridlington YO16 122 D5
Kingston upon Hull HU5 145 B8
Middleton Hall* HU6 140 B4
MIDDLETON-ON-THE-WOLDS 31 B4
Middleton Rd
Bainton YO25 31 D5
Scunthorpe DN16 96 D2
York YO24 129 C2
Middleton St HU3 145 C8
Middlewood Cl YO23 24 C6
Midfield Pl DN36 114 D8
Midfield Rd DN36 114 D8
Midfield Way 1 DN41 101 A4
Midgley Cl
Kingston upon Hull HU3 145 C5
21 Stamford Bridge YO41 15 D2
Midland Ind Est DN15 151 D5
Midland Rd DN16 151 D5
Midland St HU1 155 A2
Midmere Ave HU7 141 B7
Midway Ave
Bridlington YO16 122 D2
Poppleton YO26 126 A1
Midway Gr HU4 144 E4
Milcroft Cres 13 DN7 92 D4
Mildred Gr 5 YO24 129 F2
Mile End Ave DN7 92 D3
Mile End Pk YO42 29 A4
MILE HOUSE 141 E2
Miles La HU17 43 C6
Milestone Ave YO23 24 C6
Mile The YO42 29 A4
Milford Ave YO16 122 C5
Milford Cres 5 YO16 122 C5
Milford Ct 19 DN31 153 A5
Milford Gr HU9 142 E1
Milford Mews 7 YO32 127 D7
Milford Way 8 YO32 127 D7
Millard Ave DN7 92 D4
Millard Nook 18 DN7 92 D4
Mill Ave DN31 152 C4
Mill Balk DN14 77 C8
Mill Balk Pl DN14 78 B8
Millbank 11 YO16 122 C5
Millbank St DN14 149 F5
Mill Baulk Rd DN10 116 C3
Millbeck Bank HU15 67 E8
Millbeck Cl YO43 135 D5
Mill Beck La HU16 139 B8
MILLBROOK PARK 135 C3
Millbrook Way 23 DN18 84 F8
Mill Cl
Blyton DN21 117 F5
Bridlington YO16 122 C5
15 Broughton DN20 98 B2
Great Driffield YO25 124 D4
Marshchapel DN36 115 C2
Monk Fryston LS25 61 A8
7 Waltham DN37 113 E6
Mill Cres 11 DN21 107 C3
Millcroft 15 YO8 48 D1
Mill Croft
Scawby DN20 108 F8
11 Scunthorpe DN16 96 E2
Millcroft Cl 32 DN8 93 A8
Mill Ct 10 YO16 122 C5
Milldane HU16 139 E8
Mill Dr HU17 45 A8
Millennium Way DN14 149 F5
Miller Ave DN32 153 C2
Miller Cl
Barmby Moor YO42 28 F4
10 Thorne/Moorends DN8 93 B7
Miller La
Thorne/Moorends DN8 93 B7
Yapham YO42 29 A6
Miller Rd DN21 117 D1
Millers Brook DN9 94 E1
Millers Cl 3 DN21 108 B2
Millers Croft 6 YO23 132 B3
Millers Quay 14 DN20 98 B2
Millers Way DN20 97 E3
Miller's Wlk HU5 139 F2
Mill Falls YO25 124 D4
Millfield Ave
16 Grimsby DN33 102 E2
York YO10 130 F3
Millfield Cl YO41 27 E5
Millfield Ct YO19 37 F7
Mill Field Ct 5 DN3 92 A3
Millfield Dr YO8 63 D4
Millfield Garth YO25 31 C4
Millfield Gdns YO26 126 A2
Millfield Ind Est YO19 37 F7
Millfield La
Nether Poppleton YO26 129 B8
Poppleton YO26 126 A2
York YO10 131 A3
Millfield Rd
4 Bridlington YO16 122 C5
17 Hemingbrough YO8 49 F1
Hemingbrough YO8 63 F8
Thorne/Moorends DN8 93 A8
York YO23 130 B2
Mill Field Rd
Chapel Haddlesey YO8 62 B5
Fishlake DN7 92 C8
Scunthorpe DN16 151 E7
Millfields
Barton-upon-Humber DN18 84 E8
23 Caistor LN7 111 B4
Millfields Way 7 DN19 85 C8
Millfield The DN20 109 A6
Mill Garth
12 Cleethorpes DN35 103 B2
14 Hemingbrough YO8 49 F1
Millgate YO8 148 C6
Mill Gate YO16 122 C5
Millgate Mews 3 YO8 148 C6
Millgates YO26 129 C6
Mill Hill
Ellerker HU15 68 A8
Escrick YO19 37 B5
Mill Hill Cres DN35 153 E1
Mill Hill Dr
6 Scunthorpe DN16 96 E2
York YO32 127 F4
Millhill Rd DN14 149 E5
Mill Hill Rd DN7 92 E3
Millhouse La DN14 149 F5
Mill House La DN15 83 B5
Millhouse St Rise 3 DN40 87 B1
Mill House Way HU11 45 D2
Millhouse Woods La HU16 139 B8
Millias Cl 13 HU14 68 D5
MILLINGTON 29 C6
Millington Woods Nature Reserve* YO42 29 D8
Mill La
Acaster Malbis YO23 36 C8
Askham Richard YO23 24 D2
Barlow YO8 63 B7
Barrow upon Humber DN19 85 C8
Beverley HU17 154 B4
Bielby YO42 39 E6
Bishop Burton HU17 43 B2
Brandesburton YO25 34 B2
Brayton YO8 62 C8
Bridlington YO16 122 C5
Brigg DN20 98 B1
Brough HU15 68 C6
Broughton DN20 97 E3
Caistor LN7 111 C4
Carlton DN14 63 D3
Drax YO8 63 F5
East Halton DN40 86 D6
Eastrington HU15 52 A1
Elstronwick HU12 58 F3
Foston YO25 21 F1
Gainsborough DN21 117 A2
Gilberdyke HU15 52 D1
Goxhill DN19 71 A1
Harpham YO25 21 E7
Haxby YO32 13 D5
Haxey DN9 105 B2
Hayton YO42 29 D1
2 Hemingbrough YO8 49 F1
Hessay YO23 24 B7
Holton le Clay DN36 114 B4
Hornsea HU18 134 B4
Huggate YO42 18 B1
Immingham DN40 87 A1
Inglemire HU16 138 E7
14 Keelby DN41 101 A4
Kilpin DN14 65 D5
Kirk Ella HU10 143 C6
Kirton in Lindsey DN21 108 C1
Langtoft YO25 8 C7
Laxton DN14 65 F3
Marshchapel DN36 115 C2
Newbald YO43 53 E6
Newland YO8 64 A3
Newport HU15 52 E1
3 North Cave HU15 53 D3
North Dalton YO25 31 C7
North Kelsey LN7 110 A4
Rawcliffe DN14 63 F1
1 Riccall YO19 37 A1
Rise HU17 45 E6
Scawby DN20 108 F8
Seaton HU11 35 A2
Seaton Ross YO42 39 D4
Skipsea YO25 23 B2
Sledmere YO25 6 F3
Snaith & Cowick DN14 78 C8
South Ferriby DN18 84 A7
Walkeringham DN10 116 C3
Warter YO42 30 A4
Watton YO25 32 D4
Welwick HU12 90 A7
Wilberfoss YO41 27 E6
Wrawby DN20 98 E3
York YO31 130 E6
Mill Lane Ct HU17 154 B3
Mill Lane W HU15 68 B6
Mill Mere Rd DN21 118 A2
Mill Mount YO24 130 A3
Mill Mount Ct YO24 130 A3
Millom Way DN32 152 F4
Mill Pl DN35 153 F2
Millport Dr HU4 144 B2
Mill Race DN36 114 E4
Mill Rd
Aldbrough HU11 47 C2
Burton Constable HU11 58 D7
Burton Fleming YO25 2 D4
Cleethorpes DN35 153 E1
Crowle DN17 94 D8
Hibaldstow DN20 108 E4
Keadby DN17 95 D5
Keyingham HU12 73 C4
Luddington & Haldenby DN17 81 C4
Skidby HU16 138 C7
Sproatley HU11 58 D5
Swanland HU14 69 A6
Mill Rise
Great Driffield YO25 124 D4
Skidby HU16 138 B8
Swanland HU14 69 A6
Mills Dr DN7 104 A8
Millside YO25 9 C3
Mill Side Cl 6 YO25 9 C3
Mills Service Rd DN16 97 A4
Mill St
Great Driffield YO25 124 E4
Hutton Cranswick YO25 32 E8
Kingston upon Hull HU1 155 A2
York YO1 156 C1
Millstone Cl 4 DN21 108 B2
Millthorpe Sch YO23 130 B2
Mill View
Hut Green DN14 62 A2
Waltham DN37 113 D6
Mill View Cl DN9 105 D7
Mill View Cres YO25 22 C1
Mill View Ct DN14 149 E4
Millview Gdns DN20 98 E3
Mill View Pl 5 HU17 137 B3
Mill View Rd HU17 154 C2
Mill Wlk HU16 139 C5
Milne Rd HU9 142 C4
Milner Pl YO16 122 D4
Milner Rd YO16 122 D4
Milner St YO24 129 D3
Milson Cl
4 Barton-upon-Humber DN18 84 E8
Broughton DN20 97 D4
Milson Gr YO10 131 A3
Milson Rd 8 DN41 101 A4
Milton Carr 8 YO30 126 F1
Milton Cl
5 Gainsborough DN21 117 C1
12 Howden DN14 65 A7
Milton Rd
3 Gainsborough DN21 117 C1
Grimsby DN33 102 D2
Scunthorpe DN16 151 B1
Milton St
Goole DN14 149 C4
York YO10 130 F3
Mimosa Ct DN15 96 F2
Minchin Cl 3 YO30 127 B1
Minehead Rd HU7 57 A5
Mineral Quay Rd DN40 87 C3
Minnow Cl 14 DN37 102 B4
Minshull Rd 12 DN35 103 C2
Minster Ave
Beverley HU17 154 B2
York YO31 127 F2
Minster Cl
3 Haxby YO32 127 C8
Kingston upon Hull HU8 141 D5
40 Wigginton YO32 13 E5
York YO1 156 B3
Minster Ct
Beverley HU17 154 A2
11 Howden DN14 65 A7
York YO1 156 B3
Minster Moorgate HU17 154 A2
Minster Moorgate W HU17 154 A2
Minster Rd
Misterton DN10 116 C5
Scunthorpe DN15 150 B6
Minster Sch The YO1 156 B3
Minster View YO32 127 C8
Minster Yard N HU17 154 B2
Minster Yard S HU17 154 B2
Minster Yd YO1 156 B3
Minter Cl 2 YO24 129 B1
Mintfields Rd HU17 154 C3
Minton St HU5 140 D3
Mint Wlk HU17 154 B1
Mires La HU15 53 D2
Mires The YO43 53 F7
Mirfield Gr HU9 142 C1
Mirfield Rd
Grimsby DN32 102 F2
Scunthorpe DN15 150 C8
Mirkhill Rd YO8 148 B6
Misson Bank DN9 104 C3
MISTERTON 116 C5
Misterton Prim Sch DN10 116 C4
Mistral Ct YO31 130 E8
Mitcham Rd HU8 142 A5
Mitchell Cl DN7 92 D5
Mitchell La YO41 27 D8
Mitchell Way 11 YO30 126 E3
Mitchel's La YO10 133 F8
Miterdale 4 YO24 132 C7
Mitford Cl 3 YO14 2 F8
Mitford Rd 2 YO14 2 F8
Mitten Ave 10 DN14 78 C8
Mizzen Rd HU6 140 B8
MLS Bsns Centres YO30 127 A2
Moat Field YO10 131 C4
Moat House Rd DN21 108 A1
Moat La 4 DN40 86 E3
Moat Rd DN15 82 C1
Moatside Ct YO31 156 B3
Moat The 45 HU12 72 D7
Moat Way YO8 148 A2
Modder St DN16 151 B2
Model Farm La DN39 86 B1
Moffat Cl HU8 141 C4
Moins Ct YO10 131 D4
Moira Cl DN7 92 D7
Moiser Cl YO32 127 D4
MOLESCROFT 136 B5
Molescroft Ave 3 HU17 136 D6
Molescroft Dr HU17 136 D6
Molescroft Gdns 5 HU17 136 D6
Molescroft Mews HU17 136 C6
Molescroft Pk 4 HU17 136 D6
Molescroft Prim Sch HU17 136 D6
Molescroft Rd HU17 136 C6
Molescroft West Cl 2 HU17 136 D6
Mollison Ave DN35 153 F1
Mollison Rd HU4 144 A3
Monarch Way YO26 129 D6
Monckton Rise YO43 53 F6
Mond Ave DN14 149 D5
Money Hill (Tumulus)* YO43 42 A8
Monic Ave HU13 143 F2
Monk Ave YO31 130 F7
Monk Bar Ct YO1 156 B3
Monkbridge Ct YO31 156 C4
MONK FRYSTON 61 B8
Monk Fryston CE Prim Sch LS25 61 A8
Monkgate YO31 156 C3
Monkgate Cloisters YO31 156 C3
Monk La YO8 148 C7
Monks Cl DN7 92 D5
Monks Cross Dr YO32 128 A3
Monks Cross Link YO32 128 B4
Monks Cross Sh Pk YO32 128 B3
Monks Rd DN17 150 F2
Monks Way (West) HU14 68 F5
Monks Wlk The HU17 154 B2
Monkton 11 HU15 68 D6
Monkton Cl 10 HU16 138 F5
Monkton Rd 5 YO31 127 F1
Monkton Wlk HU8 142 C6
Monmouth St HU4 144 E3
Monson Rd DN21 118 D8
Mons St HU5 145 A8
Montague Rd YO23 133 A3
Montague St
Cleethorpes DN35 153 B5
Goole DN14 149 C4
York YO23 130 C1
Montague Wlk 6 YO26 12 F1
Montbretia Dr 25 DN16 96 D1
Montcalm Wlk 8 HU16 138 F5
Montgomery Rd DN35 153 D1
Montgomery Sq YO25 124 C2
Montreal Cres 4 HU16 138 F5
Montrose Ave YO31 130 D8
Montrose Ct DN14 149 F5
Montrose Dr DN14 149 F5
Montrose St
Kingston upon Hull HU8 141 B1
Scunthorpe DN16 151 B6
Monument Cl YO24 129 E3
Moody La DN31 152 A7
Mook St YO60 16 B8
Moorbeck Cl HU6 139 F4
Moor Carr La
Barlby with Osgodby YO8 49 B5
Barlby YO8 49 B5
Moor Cl YO19 37 F8
Moor Cottage Rd YO25 34 D5
Moorcroft Rd YO24 132 D7
Moor Dike Rd DN7 104 A8
Moore Ave YO10 131 B4
Moor Edges Rd DN8 93 B8
MOOR END 52 B8
Moor End YO43 52 B8
MOORENDS 79 C2
Moorends Rd DN8 79 A4
Moorfield Dr YO41 27 E6
Moorfield Rd YO16 122 D3
Moorfields 3 YO8 48 D6
Moorfields La DN14 65 D3
Moorfield Way YO41 27 E6
Moorfoot Cl 8 HU7 57 A6
Moorgarth Ave 10 YO24 129 F2
Moorgate YO24 129 D3
Moor Gn HU4 144 B7
Moor Gr YO24 132 E8
Moorhouse Rd 1 HU5 139 B1
Moorings Ct DN14 65 C4
Moorings The DN20 98 A2
Moor La
6 Barlby YO8 49 B5
Bilbrough LS24 24 B1
Bishopthorpe YO23 132 E2
Burton Agnes YO25 10 C2
Caistor LN7 111 A4
Carnaby YO16 10 E4
Cliffe YO8 49 F4
Copmanthorpe YO23 132 A1
Earswick YO32 128 C8
Full Sutton YO41 15 F1
Harpham YO25 22 A8

Oak Tree Cl
Beverley HU17 136 D6
Strensall YO32 14 B7
Oak Tree Ct
Bubwith YO8 50 D7
4 Wigginton YO32 127 D7
Oaktree Dr 4 HU8 141 D7
Oak Tree Dr HU17 136 D6
Oak Tree Est 10 HU12 58 C1
Oak Tree Gr YO32 127 D3
Oak Tree La YO32 127 C7
Oak Tree Way
Little Burton YO25 34 B2
10 Strensall YO32 14 B7
Oak Tree Wlk DN17 94 D7
Oakville St YO31 130 D7
Oak Way
Cleethorpes DN35 103 B1
Selby YO8 148 D2
Oakwell Ave YO16 123 A6
Oakwell Gr 2 HU8 141 B1
Oakwood Cl HU5 144 A7
Oakwood Dr DN37 102 B3
Oakwood Pk DN14 77 F6
Oakwood Rise 1 DN16 96 D2
Oasis Acad Immingham DN40 87 C1
Oasis Acad Wintringham DN32 102 F2
Oatfield Cl 16 DN33 113 D8
Oatlands Rd YO16 123 A6
Oban Ave HU9 142 A2
Oban Ct 32 DN40 87 B1
Occupation La
North Kelsey LN7 110 A4
Swanland HU14 69 B8
Ulceby DN39 86 B1
Ocean Bvd HU9 146 B6
Ocean Dr 7 HU15 52 F1
Ochrepit Hill YO42 17 A2
Octagon The HU10 138 D1
OCTON 8 F8
Octon Rd YO25 9 A8
Oderin Dr DN36 114 B8
Odin Ct DN31 102 D2
Ogilvy Dr DN17 96 C2
Ogleforth YO1 156 B3
Ogle Rd 11 YO15 5 B2
O'hanlon Ave DN20 98 C2
Old Annandale Rd HU10 143 C8
Old Barn La DN15 83 A3
Oldbeck Rd HU17 137 C4
Old Boys Sch La 4 YO8 48 B8
Old Bridge Rd HU18 134 C2
Old Brumby St DN16 151 A4
Old Carpenter's Yd DN7 92 B6
Old Chapel Cl 2 HU11 45 C5
Old Chapel La DN37 101 F1
OLD CLEE 153 C2
Old Clee Jun & Inf Sch DN32 153 B2
Old Coppice 14 YO32 13 F5
Old Courts Rd 6 DN20 98 C2
Old Crosby DN15 96 D7
Old Ct HU17 136 D5
Old Dairy DN19 85 D8
Old Dairy Cl DN8 93 A8
Old Dike Lands YO32 127 C8
OLD ELLERBY 58 A8
Old Epworth Road E DN7 92 F4
Old Epworth Road W 9 DN7 92 E4
Old Farm Cl HU12 73 E3
Old Farm Ct 5 DN37 113 D6
Old Farm Way YO8 148 B2
Oldfield Ave HU6 140 C6
Oldfield Cl
Barnby Dun DN3 92 A4
Stainforth DN7 92 B6
Oldfield Cres DN7 92 C6
Oldfield La DN7 92 B6
Old Field La DN7 92 A5
Oldfield Rd 11 DN8 93 B7
Old Fleet 2 DN37 102 B3
Oldfleet Prim Sch HU9 142 E2
Old Forge Rd 4 DN10 116 C5
Old Forge Way
North Frodingham YO25 34 C8
Skirlaugh HU11 45 D2
OLD GOOLE 149 C1
Old Green La YO41 28 A5
Old Hall La YO41 27 C5
Old Haxey Rd DN10 116 C6
Old Highway The 9 YO32 14 B6
Old House Gdns YO8 62 A5
Old Howe La YO25 22 A3
Old Ironside Rd DN15 151 D7
Old La
Blacktoft DN14 66 C4
Hirst Courtney YO8 62 F3
Long Marston YO26 24 A6
Reedness DN14 80 E7
Sigglesthorne HU11 45 F8
Oldlane Gate DN14 80 D4
Old Lea YO43 40 B1
Old Leys La DN21 119 C3
Old Main Rd
Barnetby le Beck DN37 113 B6
Irby DN37 112 D7
Oldman Ct
Woodthorpe YO24 132 C8
York YO24 132 C8
Old Manor Dr DN20 108 E8
Old Manor Lawns HU17 154 B2
Old Mill Cl YO43 135 F3
Old Mill La
7 Broughton DN20 97 E3
Whitton DN15 67 E3
Wrawby DN20 98 D4
Old Mkt Pl 6 DN31 152 D3
Old Moorings The DN17 81 A3
Old Moor La YO24 132 E7
Old Nursery Yd 24 DN8 93 B7
Old Orchard YO32 127 D8
Old Orchard The
Fulford YO10 133 E7
Shipton YO30 12 F5
Old Paddock Ct DN36 114 B7
Old Penny Memories★ YO15 122 F2
Old Plumtree La 2 DN36 114 B1
Old Pond Pl 16 HU14 69 A4
Old Post Office La
Barnetby le Wold DN38 99 B4
5 South Ferriby DN18 84 A7
Old Quarry The DN38 110 E7
Old Rd
Healing DN37 102 B5
Holme-on-Spalding-Moor YO43 40 B1
Leconfield HU17 43 C6
Ottringham HU12 73 E3
Old Rectory Gdns DN17 151 A1
Old Row The DN15 82 A5
Old Rugby Pk DN14 149 C5
Old School Cl
Osbaldwick YO10 131 B4
Sykehouse DN14 78 B4
Old School Dr DN20 108 F5
Old School La
Allerthorpe DN17 95 D5
Barlby with Osgodby YO8 49 B5
Keadby DN17 95 D5
North Kelsey LN7 110 A4
20 Scunthorpe DN16 96 D2
Old School Yd 8 DN21 108 B1
Old Showfields 8 DN21 117 B1
Old Smithy & Heritage Ctr The★ DN9 106 B3
Old Stack Yd The DN20 98 D3
Oldstead Ave HU6 139 F5
Old Sunderlandwick La YO25 20 D1
Old Tatham YO43 40 B1
Old Thorne Rd DN7 92 E4
OLD TOWN 122 E5
Old Trent Rd DN10 116 F1
Old Trough La HU15 52 C2
Old Vicarage Dr DN15 83 D1
Old Vicarage La 5 LS25 61 A8
Old Vicarage Pk DN20 108 E8
Old Village Rd HU20 55 A4
Old Village St DN15 95 E6
Old Village The YO32 127 F5
Old Warp La DN18 84 A7
Old Waste HU17 154 A3
Old Woodyard The 23 HU19 75 A6
Olinda Rd 2 YO15 122 E2
Olive Dr DN16 96 F2
Olive Gr DN14 149 F5
Oliver Ct DN31 152 D4
Oliver's Cl 18 YO14 2 F8
Olivers La YO16 122 E3
Oliver St DN35 153 D4
Olivier Ct HU4 144 E3
Olympia Cres YO8 148 E6
Olympian Ct YO10 130 F4
Ombler Cl 11 HU12 73 C4
Omega Bsns Pk HU3 145 D4
Omega Bvd DN8 92 F8
Omega Cl YO16 123 A5
Omega Rd YO16 122 F5
On Hill HU14 69 B6
Ontario Rd DN17 96 B2
Onyx Gr 2 HU3 145 A4
Oole Rd DN35 153 F2
Opsa Bsns Ctr YO1 156 B2
Opus Ave YO26 126 C1
Orb La DN15 96 D8
Orby Gr 6 DN33 102 D2
Orchard Ave 8 DN21 107 C3
Orchard Cl
2 Barrow upon Humber DN19 85 C7
13 Barton-upon-Humber DN18 84 F8
Blyton DN21 117 F5
Bridlington YO16 122 E7
3 Burringham DN17 95 D4
Burton upon Stather DN15 82 B5
Driffield YO25 125 E7
Eggborough DN14 61 F2
Great Driffield YO25 124 D5
Hatfield DN7 92 C3
Kingston upon Hull HU10 143 F7
2 Kirton in Lindsey DN21 108 B1
Messingham DN17 107 D7
6 Monk Fryston LS25 61 A8
Morton DN21 117 A3
9 Norton DN6 76 E2
10 Pocklington YO42 28 F4
Roos HU12 74 A8
2 Scunthorpe DN16 151 B2
Selby YO8 148 A4
13 Snaith DN14 63 C1
Wilberfoss YO41 27 E6
York YO24 129 E1
Orchard Cotts 4 YO19 26 F7
Orchard Croft
3 Epworth DN9 105 D7
10 Grimsby DN33 113 E8
Orchard Croft *continued*
Kingston upon Hull HU16 139 B8
Orchard Ct
3 Market Weighton YO43 135 E4
10 Waltham DN37 113 D6
Orchard Dr
Burton upon Stather DN15 82 B5
Goole DN14 65 C4
Gunness DN15 95 E6
Hatfield DN7 92 C3
Kingston upon Hull HU13 143 E1
Middleton-on-the-Wolds YO25 31 C4
1 Winteringham DN15 68 B1
Orchard End 20 YO8 49 F1
Orchard Garth
Beverley HU17 136 D6
Copmanthorpe YO23 132 B2
Orchard Gdns
4 Pocklington YO42 28 F4
York YO31 127 E2
Orchard Gr
Hatfield DN7 92 D5
Misterton DN10 116 D4
Orchard Grange 8 DN9 94 E1
Orchard La
Great Driffield YO25 124 E5
Hutton Cranswick YO25 32 E8
Thorne/Moorends DN8 79 B2
Orchard Paddock 3 YO32 127 D8
Orchard Park Rd HU6 139 F8
Orchard Pk YO42 39 B6
Orchard Rd
Kingston upon Hull HU4 144 B5
Selby YO8 148 A4
Skidby HU16 138 A8
Upper Poppleton YO26 126 A1
Orchard St DN8 93 A8
Orchards The YO25 32 E8
Orchard The
Beverley HU17 137 F8
Bishopthorpe YO25 133 A3
Cherry Burton HU17 43 A5
Fangfoss YO41 28 C8
Heslington YO10 131 A1
Kingston upon Hull HU9 142 B4
Leven HU17 45 A7
14 New Waltham DN36 114 A7
Orchard View 3 YO30 126 B5
Orchard Way
1 Gilberdyke HU15 66 D7
Hensall DN14 62 C2
Howden DN14 65 A6
7 Long Riston HU11 45 C5
9 Pocklington YO42 28 F4
Selby YO8 148 A4
Skirlaugh HU11 45 D2
1 Strensall YO32 14 B7
Thorpe Willoughby YO8 48 B2
York YO24 129 E1
Orchid Rise DN15 150 F6
Ordnance La YO10 130 D1
Ore Blending Rd DN16 97 A4
Oribi Cl HU4 144 C2
Oriel Cl 6 HU17 55 D8
Oriel Gr
Kingston upon Hull HU9 142 A1
York YO30 130 A8
Oriole Rd DN17 150 E2
Orion Cl 8 HU3 145 B5
Orion Way DN34 102 B2
Orkney Cl 7 HU8 141 E7
Orkney Pl 11 DN40 87 C1
Ormerod Cres 7 HU5 139 D2
Ormerod Rd HU5 139 D2
Ormesby Wlk 9 HU5 139 D3
Ormonde Ave HU6 140 D4
Ormsby Cl 9 DN35 103 B2
Ormsby Rd DN17 150 E1
Orniscourt HU6 139 F7
Orrin Cl YO24 132 C7
Orwell St DN31 152 F5
OSBALDWICK 131 C4
Osbaldwick Ind Est YO19 131 D5
Osbaldwick La YO10 131 B4
Osbaldwick Link Rd YO10 131 D4
Osbaldwick Prim Sch YO10 131 C4
Osbaldwick Village YO10 131 C4
Osborne Dr DN36 114 A5
Osborne Rd DN41 101 E8
Osborne St
Cleethorpes DN35 153 F2
Grimsby DN31 152 D3
Kingston upon Hull HU1 155 A2
Osbourne Dr
Keyingham HU12 73 D4
4 York YO30 126 E3
OSGODBY 49 C4
OSGODBY COMMON 49 C6
Oshawa Dell YO42 29 A2
Oslear Cres DN35 153 E1
Oslo Rd HU7 140 F6
Osmington Gdns 10 YO32 14 A7
Osprey Cl
Kingston upon Hull HU6 140 B8
4 York YO24 132 B8
Osprey Dr DN31 102 B5
Ossett Cl HU8 141 C1
Ostler's Cl YO23 132 C3
Ostler's La DN18 84 A5
Ostman Rd YO26 129 C5
Oswald Rd DN15 151 A7
Otley Cl HU9 142 C2
Ottawa Cl 6 HU16 138 F5
Ottawa Rd 6 DN17 96 C2
Otterbirch Wharf HU17 137 B3
Otterburn St 6 HU3 145 A5
Otterwood Bank 5 YO24 129 B1
Otterwood La YO24 129 B1
Otterwood Paddock YO41 15 C2
OTTRINGHAM 73 F3
Ottringham Rd HU12 73 D4
Oubrough La HU11 57 F8
Oundle Cl 5 DN16 96 E2
Our Ladys RC Prim Sch YO24 129 E1
Ouse Acres YO26 129 D6
Ouse Bank YO8 148 E5
Ouseburn Ave YO26 129 C6
Ousecliffe Gdns YO30 130 A6
OUSEFLEET 66 D2
Ousegate YO8 148 D5
Ousegate Mills Business Centre YO8 148 D5
Ouse Lea YO30 130 A7
Ouse Way DN14 78 B8
Outer Trinities HU17 154 B2
Outgaits Cl 4 YO14 2 F8
Outgaits La YO14 3 A8
Outgang La YO19 131 D6
Outgang The
Brantingham HU15 68 B7
South Cliffe YO43 53 B6
Outgate DN17 94 E6
Out Gates
Foston YO25 22 B3
Harpham YO25 21 E6
Out Holme La DN36 114 E3
Outlands Rd HU16 139 D5
OUT NEWTON 90 E8
Out Newton Rd
Holmpton HU19 75 C1
Skeffling HU12 90 D6
Outram Cl HU2 155 A4
Outstray Rd HU12 89 C7
Oval The
Brough HU15 68 C6
Grimsby DN33 102 E1
Hatfield DN7 92 C5
Kellingley DN14 61 C3
Kirk Ella HU10 143 E8
Pocklington YO42 29 A4
23 Scunthorpe DN17 96 C2
Summergangs HU8 141 C2
Overdale Cl YO24 132 D8
Overland Rd HU16 139 C5
Overstrand Dr HU7 141 D6
OVERTON 12 F2
Overton Ave HU10 143 E8
Overton Ct 6 DN18 69 F1
Overton Rd YO30 12 F3
Ovington Terr YO23 130 B2
Owbridge Ct HU2 155 A2
Owen Ave HU13 144 A1
Owlet Nature Reserve★ DN21 117 C6
Owlwood Ct 7 YO19 26 E7
Owlwood La 6 YO19 26 E7
OWMBY 110 D7
Owmby Cl DN40 87 A1
Owmby Hill DN38 110 D8
Owmby La LN7 110 C5
Owmby Mount DN38 110 D8
Owmby Rd DN38 110 D8
Owmby Wold La DN38 110 E8
Owsthorpe La DN14 52 A1
Owston Ave 2 YO10 131 A3
Owston Castle★ DN9 106 A3
OWSTON FERRY 106 A2
Owston Ferry Castle Nature Reserve★ DN9 106 A3
Owston Ferry Rd DN9 116 E8
Owston Rd
1 Hunmanby YO14 2 F8
West Stockwith DN10 116 E6
Owst Rd HU12 73 C4
OWSTWICK 59 E3
OWTHORNE 74 F7
Owthorne Cl YO16 122 B6
Owthorne Gr 3 HU9 142 A2
Owthorne Grange HU19 74 F6
Owthorne Wlk
Bridlington YO16 122 B5
Withernsea HU19 74 F7
Ox Calder Cl 16 YO19 26 F7
Ox Carr La YO32 14 B6
Ox Cl YO41 15 D2
Ox Close La YO10 26 C4
Oxcombe Cl DN37 113 D8
Oxenhope Rd HU6 140 D7
Oxen La YO8 49 E3
Oxford Cl 6 HU17 136 E1
Oxford Rd DN14 149 C5
Oxford St
Bridlington YO16 122 D3
Cleethorpes DN35 153 F1
Grimsby DN32 153 A4
Kingston upon Hull HU2 155 C4
Scunthorpe DN16 151 D2
5 York YO24 130 A3
Oxford Violet HU7 140 E6
Oxmardyke La HU15 66 E6
Oxmarsh La DN19 70 E2
Ox Pasture La DN17 81 C2
Oyster Ct DN35 153 F1
Oyster Way YO14 3 C8

P

Packman La HU10 143 B8
Paddock Cl
Askham Richard YO23 24 D3
Copmanthorpe YO23 132 A2
Huntington YO32 127 F4
Paddock Ct
Bridlington YO16 122 E7
Great Driffield YO25 124 F5
33 Immingham DN40 87 B1
Paddock La
Blyton DN21 117 F5
West Butterwick DN17 95 C1
Paddock Lane E DN21 117 F5
Paddock Rise 8 DN19 85 C8
Paddocks The
Barnoldby le Beck DN37 113 B6
Beckingham DN10 116 D1
6 Crowle DN17 94 D7
Great Driffield YO25 124 D3
Hutton Cranswick YO25 32 E7
Kingston upon Hull HU10 143 B7
Middleton YO25 31 C4
Wheldrake YO19 38 A7
Paddock The
14 Airmyn DN14 64 E4
Beverley HU17 136 D6
1 Buckton/Bempton YO15 4 D3
3 Burton upon Stather DN15 82 B4
Cottingham HU16 139 C6
East Ella HU4 144 B5
Fangfoss YO41 28 C8
13 Gilberdyke HU15 66 D8
1 North Ferriby HU14 69 A5
8 Selby YO8 148 C6
2 Swanland HU14 69 C7
Wilberfoss YO41 27 E5
York YO26 129 C6
Paddock View HU11 58 B3
Paddock Way YO26 129 C6
Pademoor Terr DN17 81 A2
Padstow Cl 7 HU7 56 F5
Padstow Wlk DN17 150 C4
Pagehall Cl DN33 102 E1
Paghill Est HU12 72 A5
Pagnell Ave YO8 148 E4
Paignton Ct DN33 113 E7
PAINSTHORPE 17 B5
Painsthorpe La YO41 17 B5
Paisley Prim Sch HU3 145 A6
Paisley St HU3 145 A7
Palace Ave YO15 122 E2
Palanza Terr 8 YO15 122 E2
Pale La YO8 61 F7
Palmcourt HU6 139 F7
Palmer Ave HU10 143 D8
Palmer Gr YO8 148 A3
Palmer La
Barrow upon Humber DN19 85 D8
York YO1 156 C2
Palmes Cl YO19 36 E8
Palm Farm★ DN39 85 F5
Pam Cl 19 DN40 87 C1
Pamela Rd DN40 87 C1
Panama Dr HU11 45 D2
Panman La YO19 26 F8
Paper Mill Rd DN14 79 B8
Parade Ct YO31 130 F6
Parade The
Hunmanby YO14 3 B8
Kingston upon Hull HU5 140 D1
Paradise Cotts YO17 17 F8
Paradise Pl
9 Brigg DN20 98 B2
3 Goole DN14 149 D4
Paradise Sq HU17 154 B2
Paragon Sq HU1 155 A2
Paragon St
Kingston upon Hull HU1 155 A2
York YO10 156 C1
Parcevall Dr 32 HU7 56 F5
Parish Church Prim Sch DN21 117 B1
Parishes Sh Ctr The 12 DN15 151 B7
Park Ave
Barlow YO8 63 C7
Barton-upon-Humber DN18 84 E8
Beverley HU17 154 A4
1 Brandesburton YO25 34 B2
Bridlington YO15 122 F3
Cottingham HU16 139 A7
Crowle DN17 94 D7
Goole DN14 149 B5
Great Driffield YO25 124 E6
Grimsby DN32 152 D1
Misterton DN10 116 C6
New Earswick YO32 127 D5
Northfield HU13 143 E3
Scunthorpe DN17 96 C2
Snaith DN14 78 D8
Withernsea HU19 75 A6
Park Avenue W HU5 140 A1
Park Cl
6 Airmyn DN14 64 E4
Great Driffield YO25 124 E5
Immingham DN40 87 C1
Melbourne YO42 39 A7
Skelton YO30 126 B4
Westwoodside DN9 105 A2
Park Cres
11 Thorne/Moorends DN8 93 A7
York YO31 156 C4

RAWCLIFFE *continued*
York . . . 126 E2
Rawcliffe Ave YO30 . . . 129 F8
RAWCLIFFE BRIDGE . . . 79 C8
Rawcliffe Bridge Prim Sch DN14 . . . 79 B8
Rawcliffe Cl 5 YO30 . . . 126 E2
Rawcliffe Croft YO30 . . . 126 D2
Rawcliffe Dr YO30 . . . 129 F8
Rawcliffe Gr HU4 . . . 144 D5
Rawcliffe Ind Est YO30 . . . 126 E3
Rawcliffe Inf Sch YO30 . . . 126 E1
Rawcliffe La YO30 . . . 126 F1
Rawcliffe Landing YO30 . . . 126 C3
Rawcliffe Prim Sch DN14 . . . 64 A1
Rawcliffe Rd DN14 . . . 149 A4
Rawcliffe Sta DN14 . . . 79 A8
Rawcliffe Village YO30 . . . 126 E3
Rawcliffe Way YO30 . . . 126 E2
Rawdale Cl HU15 . . . 54 A2
Rawdon Ave YO10 . . . 130 F4
Rawling Way HU3 . . . 145 C5
Rawlinson Ave 22 LN7 . . . 111 B4
Raymond Rd DN16 . . . 151 C3
Raynard Cl YO25 . . . 32 E7
Raywell Cl HU10 . . . 143 F7
Raywell St HU2 . . . 155 A3
Read Cl YO8 . . . 63 F5
Reading Gate
Reedness DN17 . . . 80 C3
Swinefleet DN14 . . . 80 D7
Reading Room Yd 4 HU14 . . . 69 A4
Read Sch YO8 . . . 63 F5
Reangamoor La YO42 . . . 39 D2
Reaper's Rise 15 DN9 . . . 105 E6
Reaper's Way 6 DN9 . . . 105 D2
Recreation Club La HU17 . . . 154 A4
Recreation Rd 2 YO8 . . . 148 D6
Recto Ave DN32 . . . 152 F1
Rectory Ave 33 DN21 . . . 117 B1
Rectory Cl YO25 . . . 125 F7
Rectory Gdns
3 Beckingham DN10 . . . 116 D1
York YO23 . . . 130 B1
Rectory La
Beeford YO25 . . . 22 C1
Preston HU12 . . . 58 C1
Roos HU12 . . . 60 C3
Rectory Rd HU12 . . . 74 A8
Rectory St DN9 . . . 105 E6
Rectory View
9 Beeford YO25 . . . 22 D1
Lockington YO25 . . . 32 C2
Rectory Way YO43 . . . 40 B1
Rectory Wlk YO16 . . . 122 B4
Redbarn Dr YO10 . . . 131 D4
Redbourn Cl DN16 . . . 151 B5
REDBOURNE . . . 108 F3
Redbourne East Rd DN16 . . . 97 A6
Redbourne Mere DN21 . . . 108 E2
Redbourne Rd
Grimsby DN33 . . . 102 D2
Hibaldstow DN20 . . . 108 F4
Waddingham DN21 . . . 119 F8
Redbourne St
Kingston upon Hull HU3 . . . 145 B5
3 Scunthorpe DN16 . . . 151 C6
Redbourn Way DN16 . . . 151 B6
Redcap La YO42 . . . 38 C5
Redcar Gr DN32 . . . 153 A1
Redcar St HU8 . . . 155 C4
Redcliff Dr 19 HU14 . . . 69 A4
Redcliff Rd
Kingston upon Hull HU13 . . . 69 E4
Melton HU14 . . . 68 F5
Redcoat Way 1 YO24 . . . 132 B8
Redcombe La DN20 . . . 98 B2
Redeness St YO31 . . . 130 E5
Redfern Cl HU3 . . . 145 D5
Redgates HU17 . . . 55 B7
Redgrave Cl 4 YO31 . . . 130 E8
Redhall Cl 7 DN3 . . . 92 A2
Redhill Field La YO23 . . . 24 D1
Redhill Pk HU6 . . . 139 E5
Redhouse La YO8 . . . 63 F6
Red House La YO43 . . . 135 A4
Red La
Market Weighton YO43 . . . 135 E5
South Ferriby DN18 . . . 83 F7
Redland Cres 2 DN8 . . . 93 B8
Redland Dr HU10 . . . 143 C8
Red Lion St 2 DN14 . . . 149 C4
Redman Cl
15 Gainsborough DN21 . . . 117 C1
York YO10 . . . 133 C8
Redmayne Sq YO32 . . . 14 B8
Redmire Cl HU7 . . . 57 A6
Redmires Cl YO30 . . . 127 A2
Redruth Cl HU7 . . . 141 C6
Redthorn Dr YO31 . . . 127 F1
Red Twr★ YO1 . . . 130 E4
Redwing Dr YO25 . . . 125 A5
Redwood Cl YO16 . . . 122 E6
Redwood Ct DN16 . . . 96 E2
Redwood Dr
7 Cleethorpes DN35 . . . 103 B1
6 Haxby YO32 . . . 13 E5
Redwood Gdns YO25 . . . 124 F3
Redwoods The HU10 . . . 138 C2
Redwood Way YO16 . . . 122 D6
Reed Ct DN14 . . . 149 D4
Reedham Garth HU4 . . . 144 A3
Reedholme La DN8 . . . 78 F4
REEDNESS . . . 65 F2
Reedness Prim Sch DN14 . . . 66 A1
Reed St HU2 . . . 155 A3
Reedsway 12 YO25 . . . 34 B2
Rees Cl YO43 . . . 135 D5
Reeth Wlk HU5 . . . 139 D3
Reeves The YO24 . . . 129 C1
Refinery Rd DN16 . . . 151 F6
Reform St HU2 . . . 155 B3
Regency Ct 3 DN18 . . . 69 E1
Regency Mews 2 YO24 . . . 132 F8
Regent Arc DN32 . . . 152 D3
Regent Cl
Kingston upon Hull HU3 . . . 145 C6
Willerby HU10 . . . 138 E1
Regent Dr 15 DN17 . . . 94 D7
Regent Gdns DN34 . . . 152 C1
Regents Ct
Cottingham HU16 . . . 139 A6
14 York YO26 . . . 129 F5
Regents Mews 1 YO26 . . . 129 D6
Regent St
Beverley HU17 . . . 154 B2
Pocklington YO42 . . . 29 A3
York YO10 . . . 130 E3
Regent Street Pavement 8 YO42 . . . 29 A3
Regent Terr 7 YO15 . . . 122 F2
Regimental Mus★ YO1 . . . 156 B1
Regina Cres 2 HU5 . . . 140 A1
Reginald Gr YO23 . . . 130 C1
Reginald Rd DN15 . . . 96 C7
Reginald Terr YO8 . . . 148 D4
Regis Ct HU9 . . . 142 B3
Register Sq HU17 . . . 154 A2
Reid Pk YO32 . . . 13 E5
Reigate Cl HU8 . . . 142 A4
REIGHTON . . . 3 D6
Reighton Ave YO30 . . . 129 F8
Reighton Dr 10 YO30 . . . 126 F1
Reilly Way YO42 . . . 28 E4
Reina Dr YO25 . . . 124 C4
Rein The DN9 . . . 105 A2
Reldene Dr HU5 . . . 144 B7
Remembrance Ct YO16 . . . 122 A2
Remillo Ave DN32 . . . 152 F1
Remington Ave HU11 . . . 34 E3
Remple Ave DN7 . . . 93 A3
Remple Comm Rd DN7 . . . 92 F2
Remple La DN7 . . . 93 A3
Rendel St DN31 . . . 152 D5
Rensburg St HU9 . . . 141 D1
Renshaw Gdns 8 YO26 . . . 129 E4
Renton Ct HU13 . . . 143 F6
Reporto Ave DN32 . . . 152 F1
Repton Dr
Kingston upon Hull HU7 . . . 141 D5
21 Scunthorpe DN16 . . . 96 D2
Reservoir Rd HU6 . . . 140 F3
Responso Ave DN32 . . . 152 F1
Reston Ct 8 DN35 . . . 103 D2
Reston Gr 25 DN33 . . . 102 D2
Retford Gr HU9 . . . 142 E1
Retreat Hospl The
York YO10 . . . 130 F2
York YO10 . . . 130 F2
Revenser Ct 53 HU12 . . . 72 D7
Revesby Ave
13 Grimsby DN34 . . . 102 C2
Scunthorpe DN16 . . . 151 A3
Revesby Ct DN16 . . . 151 A4
Revigo Ave DN32 . . . 152 F1
Revill Cl 17 DN21 . . . 107 C3
Reygate Gr YO23 . . . 132 B2
Reynolds Cl HU14 . . . 68 E5
Reynoldson Ct HU5 . . . 140 B2
Reynoldson St HU5 . . . 140 C2
Reynolds Prim Sch DN35 . . . 153 D3
Reynolds St DN35 . . . 153 D2
Rhodena Ave YO16 . . . 122 D2
Rhodes St HU3 . . . 144 F5
Rhyl Cl 4 HU7 . . . 56 F7
Rialto Ave DN32 . . . 152 F1
Ribblesdale 3 HU7 . . . 141 A6
Ribblesdale Cl YO16 . . . 122 F7
Ribble St 4 HU3 . . . 145 B4
Ribston Cl 9 DN16 . . . 96 D1
Ribstone Gr YO31 . . . 131 B6
RIBY . . . 101 C2
Ribycourt HU6 . . . 139 E7
Riby Ct DN36 . . . 114 B5
Riby Rd
Cabourne LN7 . . . 111 D6
Keelby DN41 . . . 101 A4
Scunthorpe DN17 . . . 150 E1
Stallingborough DN41 . . . 101 C4
Swallow LN7 . . . 112 A7
Riby Sq DN32 . . . 152 F5
Riby St DN31 . . . 153 A5
RICCALL . . . 49 A8
Riccall Cl HU6 . . . 140 A6
Riccall La YO19 . . . 36 D1
Riccall Prim Sch YO19 . . . 36 F1
Richard Cooper St DN14 . . . 149 E4
Richard III Mus★ YO31 . . . 156 C3
Richardson Cl DN36 . . . 114 D8
Richardson Rd 35 HU12 . . . 72 C7
Richardson St YO23 . . . 130 C2
Richard St
Grimsby DN31 . . . 152 C4
Selby YO8 . . . 148 B5
Richdale Ave DN21 . . . 108 B1
Richmond Cl YO43 . . . 135 F3
Richmond Dr
Goole DN14 . . . 149 F5
10 Scunthorpe DN16 . . . 96 E2
Richmond Gdns HU17 . . . 136 D1
Richmond La HU7 . . . 56 E6
Richmond Rd
Cleethorpes DN35 . . . 153 E1
Richmond Rd *continued*
Grimsby DN34 . . . 152 A2
Kingston upon Hull HU13 . . . 143 E2
24 Thorne/Moorends DN8 . . . 79 B2
Richmond St
Bridlington YO15 . . . 122 D1
2 Kingston upon Hull HU5 . . . 145 B8
York YO31 . . . 130 E5
Richmond Way
2 Beverley HU17 . . . 55 E8
Dunswell HU6 . . . 56 E6
Richmond Wlk HU17 . . . 136 D1
Rickaby Cl YO16 . . . 122 D4
Ridding Cres DN14 . . . 64 A1
Ridding La DN14 . . . 64 A1
RIDDINGS . . . 150 F1
Riddings Inf Sch DN17 . . . 96 C2
Riddings Jun Sch DN17 . . . 96 C2
Riddings Pool DN17 . . . 96 B2
Ridgestone Ave HU11 . . . 142 E7
Ridge View DN20 . . . 98 C2
Ridgeway YO26 . . . 129 B3
Ridge Way DN17 . . . 150 E5
Ridgeway Rd HU5 . . . 144 B7
Ridgeway The DN34 . . . 102 B2
Ridgewood Ave 6 DN3 . . . 92 A1
Ridgewood Dr DN15 . . . 82 A4
Riding Fields Sq HU17 . . . 154 C3
Riding Mews HU17 . . . 154 B3
Ridings The
Beverley HU17 . . . 136 C6
Cottingham HU16 . . . 138 E6
East Ella HU5 . . . 144 A8
Great Driffield YO25 . . . 125 A6
15 North Ferriby HU14 . . . 69 A4
Ridsdale HU7 . . . 140 F7
Rifle Butts Quarry Nature Reserve★ YO43 . . . 41 D5
Rigby Cl HU17 . . . 136 D7
Rileston Pl 12 DN16 . . . 96 D1
Rillington Ave HU16 . . . 139 A5
RIMSWELL . . . 74 D7
Rimswell Gr HU9 . . . 142 A2
Ring Beck La HU15 . . . 68 A8
Ringley Mdws 5 YO15 . . . 4 C3
Ringrose La HU10 . . . 143 E6
Ringrose St HU3 . . . 144 F5
Ringstead Garth 4 HU7 . . . 57 A5
Ringstone Rd
Bishopthorpe YO23 . . . 133 B5
York YO30 . . . 126 F3
Ringwood Cl DN16 . . . 151 B1
Ripley Cl
Bridlington YO16 . . . 122 D5
Kingston upon Hull HU6 . . . 140 B7
Ripley Ct DN15 . . . 150 B6
Ripley Gr 3 YO32 . . . 13 E5
Ripley Pl YO43 . . . 135 D4
RIPLINGHAM . . . 54 E2
Riplingham Rd
Kingston upon Hull HU10 . . . 143 A8
Skidby HU10 . . . 138 A1
Ripon Ave HU17 . . . 136 E1
Ripon Cl DN17 . . . 150 C3
Ripon St DN31 . . . 152 C3
Ripon Way HU9 . . . 146 C8
RISBY . . . 55 C5
Risby Garth HU16 . . . 55 C4
Risby Gr HU6 . . . 139 F5
Risby Hill HU20 . . . 55 A4
Risby La HU17 . . . 55 B7
Risby Pl HU17 . . . 154 A1
Risby Rd DN15 . . . 82 F1
RISE . . . 45 F5
Rise Cl HU11 . . . 45 C5
Risedale 21 LN7 . . . 111 B4
Rise La
Catwick HU17 . . . 45 D8
Rise HU11 . . . 45 D5
Rise Rd HU11 . . . 45 F7
Rise The
Hornsea HU18 . . . 134 C4
7 North Ferriby HU14 . . . 69 A5
Scunthorpe DN17 . . . 96 C2
South Ferriby DN18 . . . 84 A8
Riseway HU11 . . . 45 C5
Risewood YO41 . . . 15 B2
Rishworth Cl 5 HU7 . . . 57 A6
Rishworth Gr YO30 . . . 126 F2
Riston CE Prim Sch HU11 . . . 45 C5
Riston Rd HU17 . . . 45 C7
Riston St HU3 . . . 145 C5
Rivan Ave 5 DN33 . . . 113 E8
Rivan Gr 6 DN33 . . . 113 E8
Rivelin Cres DN16 . . . 151 A4
Rivelin Park 23 HU7 . . . 56 E5
Rivelin Pl DN16 . . . 151 A4
Rivelin Rd DN16 . . . 151 A3
Rivelin Way YO30 . . . 126 F2
Riverbank Cl DN17 . . . 95 D5
Riverbank Rise
24 Barton-upon-Humber DN18 . . . 84 E8
20 Barton upon Humberside DN18 . . . 69 E1
River Cl
2 Barlby YO8 . . . 49 B5
Goole DN14 . . . 149 F5
Riverdale 4 DN14 . . . 61 D4
Riverdale Rd
Kilpin DN14 . . . 65 C1
Scunthorpe DN16 . . . 151 A3
River Gr HU4 . . . 144 E3
Riverhead★ DN31 . . . 152 E3
River Head YO25 . . . 124 F3
River Head Dr 3 YO25 . . . 124 F3
Riverhead Gdns YO25 . . . 124 F3
River La
Fishlake DN7 . . . 92 D8
Market Weighton YO43 . . . 40 F2
West Haddlesey YO8 . . . 62 A5
River Mdw DN20 . . . 98 B1
Riversdale 7 YO32 . . . 13 F5
Riversdale Dr DN14 . . . 149 F5
Riversdale Rd HU6 . . . 140 D6
Riverside
11 Broughton DN20 . . . 98 B2
Great Driffield YO25 . . . 124 F3
Rawcliffe DN14 . . . 64 A2
Scotter DN21 . . . 107 C4
Riverside App 5 DN21 . . . 117 A1
Riverside Cl
1 Elvington YO41 . . . 27 C2
6 Great Driffield YO25 . . . 124 F3
West Haddlesey YO8 . . . 62 A5
Riverside Cres YO32 . . . 127 F6
Riverside Ct
5 Hessle HU13 . . . 69 E4
Rawcliffe DN14 . . . 64 A2
Riverside Dr DN35 . . . 103 D1
Riverside Gdns
2 Elvington YO41 . . . 27 C2
2 Poppleton YO26 . . . 12 F1
Riverside Mews 5 YO25 . . . 124 F3
Riverside Sch DN14 . . . 149 E5
Riverside Wlk
1 Poppleton YO26 . . . 12 F1
5 Strensall YO32 . . . 14 A7
River St
1 Selby YO8 . . . 148 D6
York YO23 . . . 156 B1
Riversvale Dr 21 YO26 . . . 12 F1
River View
1 Barlby YO8 . . . 49 B5
26 Barton-upon-Humber DN18 . . . 84 F8
Goole DN14 . . . 65 C3
Kingston upon Hull HU13 . . . 143 F1
Riverview Ave HU14 . . . 69 A4
Riverview Gdns HU7 . . . 140 E7
Riverview Rd HU17 . . . 137 C4
River Wlk DN14 . . . 65 C4
Rivesby Ave DN16 . . . 151 A3
Riviera Dr YO15 . . . 123 B6
Rix Rd HU7 . . . 141 A3
Roall La DN14 . . . 61 F4
Robert Cl
Immingham DN40 . . . 87 B1
3 Withernsea HU19 . . . 75 A6
Robertson Cl YO42 . . . 29 A3
Roberts St DN32 . . . 153 A3
Robert St
Scunthorpe DN15 . . . 151 B7
Selby YO8 . . . 148 C5
Robert Wilkinson Prim Sch YO32 . . . 14 A7
Robert Wood Ave HU17 . . . 154 A2
Robin Cl 28 HU15 . . . 68 D5
Robin Gr 6 YO24 . . . 129 F3
Robin Hood Cres 5 DN3 . . . 92 A1
Robin Hood Rd 3 DN3 . . . 92 A1
Robinia Dr HU4 . . . 144 C2
Robinson Cl DN15 . . . 150 E8
Robinson Ct YO1 . . . 156 C2
Robinson Dr YO24 . . . 129 B2
Robinson La DN31 . . . 153 A6
Robinson Rd DN40 . . . 87 E2
Robinson Row HU1 . . . 155 B2
Robinson's Gr DN20 . . . 109 A5
Robinson's La DN36 . . . 114 B1
Robinson Street E DN32 . . . 152 E3
Robin Wlk DN31 . . . 102 B5
Roborough Cl HU7 . . . 141 B8
Robson Ave HU6 . . . 140 B8
Robson Rd DN35 . . . 153 D3
Robson Way
Kingston upon Hull HU8 . . . 141 D7
6 Preston HU12 . . . 72 C7
Rochdale Rd DN16 . . . 151 A1
Roche Ave YO31 . . . 130 E8
Roche Dr DN14 . . . 149 E6
Rochester Ave HU4 . . . 144 A3
Rochester Cl DN17 . . . 150 C3
Rochester Ct 2 DN35 . . . 103 D1
Rockford Ave HU8 . . . 141 B3
Rockford Gr HU8 . . . 141 B3
Rockingham Ave HU8 . . . 131 A5
Rockingham Ct 10 DN34 . . . 102 B2
Rockley Ct HU10 . . . 143 F6
Rod Mill Rd DN16 . . . 151 E5
Rodney Cl HU2 . . . 155 A4
Roecliffe Ct YO26 . . . 24 C8
Roe La LS25 . . . 61 C7
Rogers Ct
Woodthorpe YO24 . . . 132 C8
York YO24 . . . 132 C8
Rokeby Ave HU4 . . . 144 B5
Rokeby Cl
Beverley HU17 . . . 154 A4
Kingston upon Hull HU4 . . . 144 B5
Rokeby Park Prim Sch HU4 . . . 144 B4
Rokeby Pk HU4 . . . 144 B5
Roladan Cl 27 DN36 . . . 114 A8
Roland Ct YO32 . . . 127 E3
Roland Simpson Cl 1 DN14 . . . 78 C8
ROLSTON . . . 46 E8
Rolston Ave 3 YO31 . . . 127 E2
Rolston Cl HU9 . . . 142 C1
Rolston Rd HU18 . . . 134 C2
Roman Avenue N 17 YO41 . . . 15 D2
Roman Avenue S YO41 . . . 15 D1
Roman Cl YO42 . . . 40 C8
Roman Rd DN20 . . . 108 D8
Roman Rigg YO43 . . . 53 D8
Romans Cl YO19 . . . 48 F8
Roman Way
Riddings DN17 . . . 150 F2
Scunthorpe DN17 . . . 150 F2
Rombalds Croft 26 HU15 . . . 68 C6
Romford Gr HU9 . . . 142 E1
Romney Gdns 4 HU5 . . . 140 E2
Romsey Ct 11 DN34 . . . 102 B3
Romwood Cl 17 HU15 . . . 68 D6
Romyn Cl YO16 . . . 122 B2
Ronaldsway Cl 6 HU9 . . . 142 A3
Ronson Cl HU9 . . . 142 D3
Rookery Ave 10 DN33 . . . 102 E2
Rookery Croft 9 DN9 . . . 105 E6
Rookery Rd 18 DN41 . . . 101 F5
Rookery The
Scawby DN20 . . . 108 F8
22 Scotter DN21 . . . 107 C3
Rooklands 2 DN21 . . . 107 C3
Rookley Cl 3 HU8 . . . 142 C5
Rook's La DN10 . . . 116 C5
ROOS . . . 60 A1
Roos CE Prim Sch HU12 . . . 60 B1
Roos Cl HU17 . . . 136 F7
Rootas La HU17 . . . 43 A6
Ropers Ct YO23 . . . 132 C3
Roper St HU1 . . . 155 A2
Ropery Cl
Beverley HU17 . . . 137 B4
Keyingham HU12 . . . 73 D3
3 Kilham YO25 . . . 9 C3
Thorngumbald HU12 . . . 72 E5
Ropery La 1 DN18 . . . 69 E1
Ropery Rd DN21 . . . 117 A2
Ropery St
Grimsby DN32 . . . 152 F3
Kingston upon Hull HU3 . . . 145 D5
Ropery Walk 36 YO42 . . . 29 A3
Ropery Wlk YO42 . . . 29 A3
Ropewalk The★ DN18 . . . 69 F1
Ropewalk The
9 Caistor LN7 . . . 111 B4
York YO31 . . . 130 E5
Rope Wlk
Bridlington YO15 . . . 122 E2
Thorne/Moorends DN8 . . . 93 A8
Rosaire Pl DN33 . . . 113 E8
Rosalind Ave DN34 . . . 152 B3
Rosamond St 6 HU3 . . . 145 B4
Rosbrook Way 11 DN19 . . . 86 A8
Roseacres DN14 . . . 65 C4
Roseberry Ave
Bridlington YO15 . . . 122 C1
15 Hatfield DN7 . . . 92 D4
Roseberry Gr YO30 . . . 126 F3
Rosebery St YO26 . . . 129 F6
Rose Carr Wlk HU18 . . . 134 D6
Rosecomb Way 6 YO32 . . . 127 D7
Rosecroft Way YO30 . . . 129 E8
Rosedale
Leven HU17 . . . 45 B8
Scunthorpe DN17 . . . 96 C1
Skipsea YO25 . . . 23 B2
Waltham DN37 . . . 113 D7
Rosedale Ave
Kingston upon Hull HU9 . . . 141 E1
York YO26 . . . 129 C4
Rosedale Gr HU5 . . . 144 D7
Rosedale St YO10 . . . 130 D2
Rosedale Wlk
Beverley HU17 . . . 136 E1
Bridlington YO16 . . . 122 B4
Rosefields DN21 . . . 117 C1
Rose Gdns 4 DN40 . . . 87 C2
Rose La HU17 . . . 43 C5
Rose Lea Cl 2 LS25 . . . 61 A7
Rosemary Ave DN34 . . . 102 C3
Rosemary Ct YO1 . . . 156 C2
Rosemary Pl YO1 . . . 156 C2
Rosemary Way
Beverley HU17 . . . 154 C1
Humberston DN36 . . . 103 C1
Rosemoor Cl 19 YO14 . . . 2 F8
Rosemount Cl 3 HU6 . . . 140 B8
Rosemount Dr DN16 . . . 151 B2
Rosemount Grange HU13 . . . 143 C3
Rose St YO31 . . . 130 C7
Rose Tree Gr YO32 . . . 127 D4
Rosetta Way YO26 . . . 129 D6
Roseveare Ave DN34 . . . 152 A3
Rose Wlk DN15 . . . 151 C7
Rosewood Cl
3 Bridlington YO16 . . . 123 A6
4 Kingston upon Hull HU4 . . . 144 B7
Rosewoods DN14 . . . 65 C8
Rosewood Way 25 DN16 . . . 96 D2
Rosewood Wlk YO16 . . . 123 A6
Rosey Row 4 HU9 . . . 146 C7
Rosina Grove N DN32 . . . 153 B2
Rosina Grove S DN32 . . . 153 B2
Roslyn Cres HU12 . . . 72 C7
Roslyn Rd HU3 . . . 144 E7
Rosmead St HU9 . . . 146 D8
Rosper Rd DN40 . . . 87 A4
Rossall Cl 4 DN16 . . . 96 E2
Ross La
Bainton YO25 . . . 31 D7
Winterton DN15 . . . 83 B5
Rosslyn St 1 YO30 . . . 130 A6
Ross Rd DN31 . . . 153 B5
Rostun Rd HU12 . . . 60 B2
Rothbury Rd DN17 . . . 150 F3

188 Rot–St M

Rothesay Cl 1 HU9 . . . . . 141 E1
Roth Hill La YO19 . . . . 37 E3
ROTHWELL 111 F2
Rothwell Ave 15 DN33 . . . 102 D2
Rothwell Rd
Cabourne LN7 . . . . 111 C3
Scunthorpe DN15 . . . . 150 D8
Rotsea La YO25 . . . . 33 B7
Rotterdam Rd HU7 . . . . . . 141 A5
Rotton Sykes La DN15 . . . . 67 F2
Rougier St YO1 . . . . 156 A2
Roundhay Rd YO15 . . . . . . 122 D1
Round Hill Link YO30 . . . . 126 F2
Roundway
Grimsby DN34 . . . . 152 C1
7 Immingham DN40 . . . . . 87 C1
Roundway The HU4 . . . . . 144 C5
ROUTH 44 F5
Routh Ave HU17 . . . . 154 C3
Roval Dr DN40 . . . . 87 B1
Rowan Ave
Beverley HU17 . . . . 136 F7
York YO32 . . . . 127 D4
Rowan Cl
3 Barrow upon Humber DN19 . . . . 85 C8
Gateforth YO8 . . . . 48 B1
4 Hut Green DN14 . . . . . . 62 A2
2 Keelby DN41 . . . . 101 A4
10 Thorne/Moorends DN8 . . 79 B2
Rowan Cres 2 DN16 . . . . . 96 E2
Rowan Ct
7 Goxhill DN19 . . . . 86 A8
Little End YO43 . . . . 40 A1
Rowan Dr
Blyton DN21 . . . . 117 F5
Healing DN41 . . . . 101 F5
6 Humberston DN36 . . . . 114 D8
Rowan Garth HU16 . . . . 55 C4
Rowan Pl YO32 . . . . 127 D4
Rowans The
23 Gainsborough DN21 . . . 117 C1
Holme-on-Spalding-Moor YO42 . . . . 40 A1
1 Little Leven HU17 . . . . . . 44 F6
1 Westwoodside DN9 . . . 105 A2
Rowan Wlk HU18 . . . . 134 D2
Rowedale Cl 15 YO14 . . . . 2 F8
Row La HU12 . . . . 90 A7
Rowlandhall La DN14 . . . . 50 E1
Rowland Rd DN16 . . . . 151 A6
Rowlandson St DN31 . . . . 152 F6
Rowley Ct 2 YO32 . . . . . . 127 F7
Rowley Gr HU6 . . . . 139 F5
Rowley Mews
Pocklington YO42 . . . . 29 A3
37 Pocklington YO42 . . . . . 29 A3
Rowley Rd HU20 . . . . 54 F3
Rowlston Gr HU9 . . . . 142 A2
Rowmans The YO30 . . . . . 126 C4
Rowmills Rd DN16 . . . . . . 151 C4
Rowntree Ave YO30 . . . . . 130 C8
Rowpit La HU17 . . . . 45 C8
Rowston Cl 7 DN21 . . . . . 117 B1
Rowston St DN35 . . . . 103 D3
Rowton Dr HU11 . . . . 45 D2
Roxburgh St 1 HU5 . . . . . 145 B8
ROXBY 83 A3
Roxby Cswy DN15 . . . . 83 C4
Roxby Rd DN15 . . . . 82 F4
Roxton Ave DN41 . . . . 101 A5
Roxton Hall Dr 13 HU14 . . 69 A5
Roxton Medieval Village* DN40 . . . . 101 A7
Royal Chase YO24 . . . . 132 F8
Royal Cres YO15 . . . . 122 F2
Royal Ct 25 DN35 . . . . 103 D1
Royal Dr DN14 . . . . 79 A8
Royale Ct HU9 . . . . 141 F3
Royal Garth HU17 . . . . 154 A1
Royal Prince's Par 11 YO15 . . . . 122 F2
Royal St DN31 . . . . 152 E6
Royal Wlk HU16 . . . . 139 D5
Royd's Rd YO8 . . . . 61 F6
Royston Gr HU8 . . . . 141 B1
Ruard Rd DN19 . . . . 86 B8
Ruards La DN19 . . . . 71 A1
Ruby St 3 YO23 . . . . 130 B1
Rudcarr La YO19 . . . . 14 E1
Rudding Dr YO16 . . . . 122 D7
Ruddings YO19 . . . . 38 A8
Ruddings Cl 9 YO32 . . . . . 127 C8
Ruddings La YO42 . . . . 38 E2
Ruddings The
Selby YO8 . . . . 148 A4
Wheldrake YO19 . . . . 38 A8
Rudgate La DN14 . . . . 78 E4
Rudham Ave DN32 . . . . 102 F2
RUDSTON 9 F6
Rudston Beacon* YO25 . . . . 9 F4
Rudston Gr HU9 . . . . 142 A1
Rudston Monolith* YO25 . . 9 F6
Rudston Rd YO25 . . . . 9 F2
Rue de Nozay 2 DN20 . . . 97 E4
Ruffhams Cl YO19 . . . . 37 F8
Rufford Rd 3 DN35 . . . . . 103 C2
RUFFORTH 24 C6
Rufforth Dr HU17 . . . . 43 D5
Rufforth Garth HU7 . . . . . 141 C8
Rufforth Prim Sch YO23 . . 24 C6
Rugby Cl 21 HU19 . . . . 75 A6
Rugby Rd DN16 . . . . 151 A4
Ruislip Cl HU8 . . . . 142 A5
Runcorn Garth HU4 . . . . . 144 B3
Rundle Ct 29 YO42 . . . . 29 A3
Runner End YO43 . . . . 40 A1
Runnymede Ave 1 HU7 . . 56 E6
Runnymede Way HU7 . . . . 56 E5
Runswick Ave YO26 . . . . . 129 B4
Runswick Ct DN32 . . . . . . 153 A2
Runswick Rd DN32 . . . . . . 153 B2
Rupert Rd 9 DN33 . . . . . . 102 E2
Rushcarr La DN17 . . . . 95 C1
Rushes The 14 DN18 . . . . . 69 E1
Rusholme La YO8 . . . . 64 A5
Rushtons Way DN20 . . . . . 108 F5
Rushwood Cl 6 YO32 . . . . 13 F5
Ruskington Cl DN31 . . . . . 102 C5
Ruskin St HU3 . . . . 145 B6
Ruskin Way 20 HU14 . . . . . 68 D5
Russel Cl 6 DN15 . . . . 96 D7
Russell Ct 13 DN35 . . . . . . 103 D1
Russell Dr
20 Keyingham HU12 . . . . . . 73 C4
York YO30 . . . . 129 E8
Russell Rd DN14 . . . . 149 B4
Russell St
Kingston upon Hull HU2 . . 155 A3
York YO23 . . . . 130 B2
Russell Wlk DN17 . . . . 107 D7
Russet Cl
12 Scunthorpe DN15 . . . . . . 96 B7
Wrawby DN20 . . . . 98 D3
Russet Dr YO31 . . . . 131 B5
Rustenburg St HU9 . . . . . 141 D1
Rustic La DN21 . . . . 117 F6
Ruston Ct 18 HU12 . . . . 74 D1
RUSTON PARVA 21 C8
Ruston Terr 17 HU12 . . . . . 74 D1
Ruswarp Gr HU6 . . . . 139 E6
Rutherglen Dr HU9 . . . . . . 142 A3
Rutland Cl YO23 . . . . 132 A3
Rutland Dr 18 DN36 . . . . . 114 A7
Rutland Rd
Goole DN14 . . . . 149 D6
Kingston upon Hull HU5 . . 144 E8
Scunthorpe DN16 . . . . 151 D3
Rutland St DN32 . . . . 153 A4
Ryburn Cl YO30 . . . . 126 F2
Rydal Ave
11 Grimsby DN33 . . . . 113 D8
York YO31 . . . . 131 A6
Rydale Ct HU5 . . . . 140 E3
Rydales The HU5 . . . . 140 E3
Rydal Gr HU16 . . . . 138 E6
Ryde Ave HU5 . . . . 140 D3
Ryde St HU5 . . . . 140 D2
Rye Cl YO32 . . . . 127 C8
Rye Cres 31 HU15 . . . . 68 D5
Ryecroft 7 YO32 . . . . 14 A6
Ryecroft Ave
10 Norton DN6 . . . . 76 E2
York YO24 . . . . 132 C7
Ryecroft Cl YO31 . . . . 131 C8
Ryecroft Dr HU19 . . . . 75 A6
Ryecroft Gdns DN14 . . . . . . 62 A2
Ryecroft Rd DN6 . . . . 76 E1
Ryedale 12 HU15 . . . . 68 D6
Ryedale Ave DN15 . . . . 83 A6
Ryedale Way YO8 . . . . 148 C3
RYEHILL 73 A4
Ryehill Cl YO32 . . . . 127 D5
Ryehill Gr HU9 . . . . 141 F2
Ryehill La HU12 . . . . 73 A4
Ryelands Ave YO16 . . . . . . 123 A6
Ryemoor Rd YO32 . . . . 127 C8
Rylatt Pl YO26 . . . . 129 B3
Rymer Pl DN35 . . . . 103 D2
Rysome La HU19 . . . . 75 C1
Rysome Rd HU12 . . . . 90 B7
Rythergate 8 YO8 . . . . 48 B8

S

Sabina Ct HU8 . . . . 141 E7
Sable Cl HU4 . . . . 144 C2
Sabrina Ct 15 HU8 . . . . . . 141 E7
Sackville Cl
5 Beverley HU17 . . . . 55 E8
14 Immingham DN40 . . . . . 87 C1
Sackville Rd 15 DN40 . . . . . 87 C1
Sackville St DN34 . . . . 152 C3
Sacred Gate HU12 . . . . 72 D6
Sadberge Ct YO10 . . . . 131 C3
Saddleback La YO25 . . . . . . 31 B7
Saddle Cl DN19 . . . . 86 A8
Saddlers Cl
1 Copmanthorpe YO23 . . 132 B3
Huntington YO32 . . . . 127 F2
Saddlers Way YO26 . . . . 24 A6
Saddler's Way DN9 . . . . . . 105 D3
Saddlers Wlk YO19 . . . . 37 A5
Saddleworth Cl 19 HU7 . . . 57 A6
Saffre Cl 17 DN15 . . . . 83 A5
Saffrondale HU10 . . . . 143 E7
Saffron Dr 6 DN14 . . . . 63 C1
Saffron Garth 15 HU12 . . . . 74 D1
Saffron Way 16 DN17 . . . . . 94 D7
Sage Cl HU17 . . . . 154 B1
Sagefield Cl 6 DN33 . . . . . 113 D8
Sailors Wharf HU9 . . . . . . 146 C6
Sails Dr YO10 . . . . 131 B3
Sainsbury Way HU13 . . . . . 144 A1
St Abbs Cl HU9 . . . . 155 C1
St Aelreds Cl YO31 . . . . . . 130 F4
St Aelreds RC Prim Sch YO31 . . . . 131 B5
St Aidan Cres YO16 . . . . . . 122 E4
St Aidan Ct YO16 . . . . 122 E5
St Aidan Rd YO16 . . . . 122 E4
St Aiden Cl YO43 . . . . 135 E3
St Aiden's Way HU9 . . . . . 141 F2
St Alban Cl YO16 . . . . 122 E4
St Alban Rd YO16 . . . . 122 E4
St Albans Ave DN31 . . . . . 152 A4
St Albans Cl
7 Beverley HU17 . . . . 136 E1
Hibaldstow DN20 . . . . 108 F5
Scunthorpe DN17 . . . . 150 C3
St Alban's Cl HU11 . . . . 46 D3
St Albans Mount HU6 . . . 140 C4
St Ambrose Ct 23 HU7 . . . . 57 A5
St Andrewgate YO1 . . . . . 156 B2
St Andrew Pl YO1 . . . . 156 C2
St Andrew Rd YO16 . . . . . . 122 E4
St Andrews Ave DN17 . . . . 96 C1
St Andrews CE Prim Sch HU7 . . . . 140 E8
St Andrews Cl YO25 . . . . . . 31 E7
St Andrew's Cl
Middleton-on-the-Wolds YO25 . . . . 31 C4
Paull HU12 . . . . 72 A5
Redbourne DN21 . . . . 108 E3
St Andrews Ct
Goole DN14 . . . . 149 C4
Northfield HU4 . . . . 144 A3
St Andrew's Dr DN15 . . . . . 82 A4
St Andrews Gr 10 DN7 . . . . 92 D4
St Andrews La 5 DN40 . . . 87 B2
St Andrew's Mount HU10 . . . . 143 C8
St Andrews Prim Sch HU10 . . . . 143 C7
St Andrew's St DN21 . . . . 108 A1
St Andrew St HU17 . . . . . . 154 B2
St Andrew's Terr 6 DN14 . . . . 149 C4
St Andrews Way HU8 . . . . 141 C3
St Andrew's Way
2 Barnby Dun DN3 . . . . 92 A3
Epworth DN9 . . . . 105 E7
St Andrews Wlk YO25 . . . . 22 A2
St Ann Ct YO10 . . . . 130 E2
St Anne's Cl HU17 . . . . 137 B5
St Anne's Dr HU16 . . . . . . 139 D6
St Annes Rd YO15 . . . . 122 F3
St Anne's Rd 8 DN41 . . . . 101 A5
St Annes Sch HU15 . . . . 68 E5
St Anne's Wlk
9 Brough HU15 . . . . 68 D6
Driffield YO25 . . . . 125 A3
St Ann's Ave DN34 . . . . . . 152 B2
St Ann's Ct YO10 . . . . 130 D2
St Anthony Rd YO16 . . . . . 122 E4
St Anthony's Dr 24 HU12 . . 72 D7
St Anthony's Pk 25 HU12 . . 72 D7
St Athony's Cl HU6 . . . . . . 140 B4
St Aubyn's Pl YO24 . . . . . . 130 A2
St Augustine Ave DN32 . . 152 E1
St Augustine Cres DN16 . 151 B1
St Augustine Dr HU11 . . . . 45 E2
St Augustines Ct 40 HU12 . 72 C7
St Augustine's Ct 2 HU5 . . . . 140 D3
St Augustine's Dr YO16 . . 122 E5
St Augustine's Gate 30 HU12 . . . . 72 C7
St Augustine's Gr YO16 . . 122 E5
St Augustine Webster RC Prim Sch DN15 . . . . 150 D8
St Austells Cl HU9 . . . . . . 141 F2
St Barbara's Cres 8 DN15 82 B4
St Barnabas CE Prim Sch
Barnetby le Wold DN38 . . . . 99 B4
Clifton Park YO26 . . . . 129 F5
St Barnabas Ct
4 Kingston upon Hull HU3 . . . . 145 C4
13 York YO26 . . . . 129 F5
St Barnabas Dr HU14 . . . . . 69 C7
St Barnabas Rd
Barnetby DN38 . . . . 99 C4
Barnetby le Wold DN38 . . . . 99 B4
St Bartholemew's Way HU8 . . . . 142 A5
St Bartholomew's Cl 17 DN41 . . . . 101 A4
St Bede Ct
East Ella HU4 . . . . 144 E5
Kingston upon Hull HU4 . . 144 E5
St Bedes RC Comp Sch DN16 . . . . 151 B2
St Benedict Cl 21 HU7 . . . . 57 B5
St Benedict Rd YO23 . . . . 156 A1
St Bernadettes RC Prim Sch DN16 . . . . 151 C2
St Bernard's Cl 9 DN20 . . 97 E4
St Boltophs Cl 4 WF11 . . . 61 A2
St Botolph's Rd DN16 . . . 151 C3
St Bridget's Ct YO23 . . . . 156 B1
St Catherines Cl YO30 . . . 126 C5
St Catherines Cres 8 DN16 . . . . 96 D2
St Catherines Ct
6 Grimsby DN34 . . . . 102 C3
Kingston upon Hull HU5 . . 140 E2
Scunthorpe DN16 . . . . 151 D2
St Catherines Dr HU17 . . . 43 C6
St Catherine's Dr DN7 . . . . 92 C2
St Catherines Pl YO24 . . . 130 A3
St Chad DN19 . . . . 85 D8
St Chad Cres YO16 . . . . . . 122 E4
St Chad Gr YO16 . . . . 122 E4
St Chad Rd YO16 . . . . 122 E4
St Chad's Rd DN16 . . . . . . 151 D3
St Chads Wharf YO23 . . . . 133 C8
St Charles' RC Prim Sch HU2 . . . . 155 A3
St Christopher Rd YO16 . 122 E4
St Christopher's Rd DN36 . . . . 114 C8
St Clares Wlk 12 DN20 . . . . 98 C2
St Clement's Field DN20 . . 98 D8
St Clement's Gr YO23 . . . 130 C2
St Clements Pl HU2 . . . . . 155 A4
St Clements Way
17 Holton le Clay DN36 . . . 114 A5
Kingston upon Hull HU9 . . 141 F2
St Columba Rd YO16 . . . . 122 F5
St Crispins Cl DN40 . . . . . . 86 E4
St Cuthbert Rd YO16 . . . . 122 E4
St David Cl HU17 . . . . 154 B2
St David La YO15 . . . . 5 B3
St David's Cl HU16 . . . . . . 139 D6
St Davids Cres DN17 . . . . . 96 C2
St David's View 9 DN14 . . 64 E4
St Deny's Cl 1 DN40 . . . . . 86 E3
St Denys' Rd YO1 . . . . 156 C2
St Edmunds YO41 . . . . 15 D2
St Edmunds's Ct 4 HU5 139 D2
St Edward's Cl YO24 . . . . 132 F8
St Edwin Reach DN7 . . . . . 92 C5
St Edwins Cl 27 DN7 . . . . . 92 D4
St Ellens Ct HU17 . . . . 154 B2
St Francis Ave DN31 . . . . . 152 A4
St Francis Ct 1 HU5 . . . . . 139 D2
St Francis Gr DN37 . . . . . . 101 E1
St George's Ave
Bridlington YO15 . . . . 122 E3
Hatfield DN7 . . . . 92 C3
St Georges Cl 19 DN8 . . . . 93 B7
St George's Ct DN21 . . . . . 108 F3
St George's Gn DN14 . . . . 149 D6
St George's Pl YO24 . . . . . 129 F2
St Georges Prim Sch HU3 . . . . 145 A6
St Georges RC Prim Sch YO10 . . . . 130 D2
St Georges Rd 16 DN8 . . . . 93 B7
St George's Rd HU3 . . . . . 145 A5
St George's Wlk HU9 . . . . 142 B2
St Giles' Ave DN33 . . . . . . 102 E1
St Giles Croft HU17 . . . . . 154 A2
St Giles Ct
Kingston upon Hull HU9 . . 142 C1
York YO31 . . . . 156 B3
St Giles Rd YO30 . . . . 126 B5
St Giles Way YO23 . . . . . . 132 A2
St Gregory's Mews YO1 . 156 A2
St Hedda's Ct 6 HU5 . . . . 139 D2
St Helena Gdns 3 HU5 . . 140 E2
St Helens Ave 13 DN33 . . 102 E2
St Helen's Ave YO42 . . . . . . 29 B4
St Helen's Cl YO42 . . . . 29 B4
St Helen's Cres DN37 . . . . 113 D5
St Helen's Dr 10 HU15 . . . . 68 D6
St Helen's La YO14 . . . . 3 C6
St Helen's Rd
Brigg DN20 . . . . 98 C2
Pocklington YO42 . . . . 29 B4
5 York YO24 . . . . 132 E8
St Helen's Rise YO19 . . . . . 38 A7
St Helen's Sq
Barmby Moor YO42 . . . . 28 D4
3 Market Weighton YO43 135 D4
York YO1 . . . . 156 B2
St Helens Way DN21 . . . . 119 B2
St Helen's Well* YO43 . . . 41 D5
St Helier's Rd DN35 . . . . . 153 E3
St Hilda's Ave DN34 . . . . . 152 B2
St Hildas Mews YO10 . . . . 131 B4
St Hilda St
3 Bridlington YO15 . . . . . 122 E2
Kingston upon Hull HU3 . . 140 E1
St Hugh's Ave DN35 . . . . . 153 D2
St Hugh's Cres DN16 . . . . . 151 C4
St Hughs Hospl DN32 . . . . 102 F2
St Hughs Sch DN16 . . . . . . 151 B5
St Hybald's Gr DN20 . . . . . 108 F7
St Ives Cl HU7 . . . . 141 C7
St Ives Cres DN34 . . . . 102 C3
St James Ave
Grimsby DN34 . . . . 152 A2
Hatfield DN7 . . . . 92 C3
St James CE Prim Sch HU7 . . . . 141 C6
St James Cl
12 Crowle DN17 . . . . 94 D7
Kingston upon Hull HU7 . . 141 D7
York YO30 . . . . 126 E3
St James Croft YO24 . . . . 129 D1
St James Ct
Rawcliffe DN14 . . . . 64 A1
Scunthorpe DN15 . . . . 151 A6
St James' Ct DN34 . . . . . . 152 C2
St James Mount YO23 . . . 130 A2
St James Pl
31 Bottesford DN16 . . . . . . 96 E2
5 York YO24 . . . . 129 D1
St James Rd
Bridlington YO15 . . . . 122 D1
22 Brigg DN20 . . . . 98 C2
Welton HU14 . . . . 68 F5
St James' Sch DN34 . . . . . 152 C2
St James's Rd DN20 . . . . . 108 E8
St James St HU3 . . . . 145 D5
St James Terr YO8 . . . . . . 148 C5
St Joan's Dr DN20 . . . . . . 108 E8
St John Mews YO8 . . . . . . 148 B7
St John's Ave YO16 . . . . . . 122 C3
St John's Avenue W YO16 . . . . 122 C2
St Johns Bsns Pk HU9 . . . 141 F1
St Johns Cl
1 Beverley HU17 . . . . 55 F8
12 Goxhill DN19 . . . . 86 A8
St John's Cl
Bridlington YO16 . . . . 122 C2
11 Pocklington YO42 . . . . . . 28 F4
St John's Cres YO31 . . . . . 156 C4
St Johns Ct
Goole DN14 . . . . 149 C4
Grimsby DN34 . . . . 152 A1
Kingston upon Hull HU6 . . 140 D4
St John's Gdns YO25 . . . . 124 E3
St John's Gr HU9 . . . . 141 F1
St John's Pl 2 YO25 . . . . 124 F3
St John's Rd
Great Driffield YO25 . . . . . 124 E3
8 Humberston DN36 . . . . 114 C8
Scunthorpe DN16 . . . . 151 C2
9 Stamford Bridge YO41 . . 15 D2
St John's St
Bridlington YO16 . . . . 122 D4
15 Howden DN14 . . . . 65 A7
St John St
Beverley HU17 . . . . 154 B2
York YO31 . . . . 156 B3
St John's Well* YO25 . . . . 21 F8
St John's Wlk
Bridlington YO16 . . . . 122 C3
1 Great Driffield YO25 . . . 124 F3
Kingston upon Hull HU13 . 143 F2
St Joseph Dr HU4 . . . . 144 C5
St Josephs Ct 9 YO24 . . . 129 B1
St Josephs RC Prim Sch
Cleethorpes DN35 . . . . 103 B2
Goole DN14 . . . . 149 D5
St Jude Gr YO16 . . . . 122 D4
St Jude Rd YO16 . . . . 122 D4
St Jude's Ct 3 HU5 . . . . . . 139 D2
St Julian's Wells HU10 . . 143 D7
St Katherine's Rd 2 HU15 53 F1
St Lawrence Acad The DN15 . . . . 150 E7
St Lawrence Ave
Kingston upon Hull HU16 . 138 F5
Snaith DN14 . . . . 78 B8
St Lawrence Rd DN7 . . . . . . 92 C4
St Lawrences CE Prim Sch YO10 . . . . 130 E3
St Lawrence's Pl DN16 . . 151 D3
St Lawrence Sq HU11 . . . . . 45 F8
St Lawrence's Rd DN16 . . 151 D2
St Leonards Ave YO8 . . . . . 49 B4
St Leonard's Ave DN31 . . 152 A4
St Leonard's Cl 2 YO25 . . 22 D1
St Leonard's Pl YO30 . . . . 156 B3
St Leonard's Rd
Beverley HU17 . . . . 136 C6
Kingston upon Hull HU5 . . 140 D2
St Luke's Cl DN7 . . . . 92 C2
St Luke's Cres 12 DN36 . . 114 C8
St Lukes Ct HU10 . . . . 143 F8
St Luke's Ct DN32 . . . . 152 F4
St Luke's Gr YO30 . . . . 130 B7
St Lukes Sch DN16 . . . . . . 151 D3
St Luke's St
6 Kingston Upon Hull HU3 . . . . 145 D6
Kingston upon Hull HU3 . . 155 A2
St Margarets Ave HU16 . . 138 E6
St Margarets Cl
Driffield YO25 . . . . 124 E3
Kingston upon Hull HU16 . 138 E6
St Margaret's Cl 9 DN37 101 F1
St Margaret's Cres 4 DN40 . . . . 100 E8
St Margarets Ct 3 HU8 . . 142 C6
St Margaret's Terr YO1 . . 130 E4
St Margarets View 4 HU11 . . . . 45 C5
St Margaret's Wlk DN16 . 151 C1
St Mark's Gr YO30 . . . . . . 126 E2
St Mark's Rd 13 DN36 . . . 114 C8
St Mark's Sq HU3 . . . . 145 D4
St Mark St HU8 . . . . 155 C4
St Martins Ave 2 HU4 . . . 144 E6
St Martins CE Prim Sch
Fangfoss YO41 . . . . 28 C8
Owston Ferry DN9 . . . . 106 A3
St Martin's Cl
Blyton DN21 . . . . 117 F5
2 Burton Agnes YO25 . . . . 10 A2
Fangfoss YO41 . . . . 28 C8
St Martin's Cres
6 Grimsby DN33 . . . . 102 E2
Scawby DN20 . . . . 108 E8
St Martin's Ct HU17 . . . . . 154 A2
St Martins Dr YO16 . . . . . 122 C3
St Martin's Dr 1 YO25 . . . 10 A2
St Martin's Gr YO16 . . . . . 122 C2
St Martin's La YO1 . . . . . . 156 A2
St Martins Pk 1 DN9 . . . . 106 A3
St Martin's Pl 16 DN41 . . 101 A4
St Martins Prep Sch DN32 . . . . 152 D1
St Martin's Rd
Scawby DN20 . . . . 108 E8
Thorngumbald HU12 . . . . . . 72 E5
St Mary Queen of Martyrs Prim Sch HU7 . . . . 141 A7
St Mary's YO30 . . . . 156 A3
St Mary's Abbey* YO1 . . . 156 A3
St Mary & St Josephs RC Prim Sch 20 YO42 . . . . 29 A4
St Mary's Ave
1 Barnetby le Wold DN38 . . . . 99 B4
12 Hemingbrough YO8 . . . . 49 F1
Kingston upon Hull HU5 . . 139 D4
St Marys CE Prim Sch
Askham Richard YO23 . . . . . 24 D3
Beverley HU17 . . . . 136 D5

Somerby Dr 3 DN9 106 A3
Somerby Gn DN38 99 C1
Somerby Rd DN17 150 D1
Somerby Wold La DN38 99 C1
Somerden Rd HU9 147 E7
Somersby St DN31 152 D4
Somerscales St HU3 155 A4
Somerset Cl 6 YO30 126 E3
Somerset Dr 6 DN15 82 B4
Somerset Rd YO31 130 D8
Somerset St HU3 145 A5
Somerton Dr DN7 92 F4
Somerton Rd DN40 87 C1
Somervell Rd DN16 151 C1
Sonia Crest DN40 87 B1
Sophia Ave 7 DN33 102 E1
Sophia Cl HU2 155 A4
Sorbus Ct 5 HU3 145 D6
Sorbus View 4 HU5 144 C7
Sorrel Cl HU17 136 E1
Sorrel Dr 5 HU5 144 D8
Sorrell La DN14 78 D1
Sorrel Way DN15 96 B7
Soss La DN10 116 D5
Sotheron St DN14 149 D4
Sour La DN8 92 E8
Soutergate 12 DN18 69 F1
South Ave YO25 31 F2
South Axholme Com Sch DN9 105 D6
South Back La YO16 122 B4
SOUTH BANK 130 A1
South Bank DN17 95 D6
South Bank Ave YO23 130 B1
SOUTH BRAMWITH 92 B6
South Bridge Rd HU9 155 C1
SOUTHBURN 20 B1
Southburn Ave HU5 144 E7
Southburn Rd
Bainton YO25 32 A8
Kirkburn YO25 20 A1
South Carr Dales Rd HU19 75 A4
South Carr La DN20 109 B4
South Carr Rd DN20 109 A4
South Carrs HU17 45 A8
SOUTH CAVE 54 A2
South Cave CE Prim Sch HU15 53 F1
South Cave Sports Ctr HU15 53 F1
South Church Side
2 Easington HU12 90 F6
Kingston upon Hull HU1 155 B2
South Cl
7 Kilham YO25 9 C3
Kingston upon Hull HU6 140 C6
SOUTH CLIFFE 53 B7
Southcliffe Rd 12 DN21 107 C3
Southcliff Rd HU19 75 A6
South Cliff Rd
4 Bridlington YO15 122 E2
Kirton in Lindsey DN21 108 B1
Southcoates Ave HU9 141 E2
Southcoates La HU9 146 E8
Southcoates Prim Sch HU9 141 F1
Southcote Cl 4 HU15 54 A2
Southcroft Dr 8 HU8 141 E7
South Dale LN7 111 B4
South-Dale Cl 1 DN21 108 B2
SOUTH DALTON 42 E8
South Down Rd 3 YO32 127 F5
South Dr YO25 31 C4
SOUTH DUFFIELD 50 A4
South Duffield Rd YO8 49 C4
South Ella Dr HU10 143 D7
South Ella Farm Ct HU10 143 D6
South Ella Way HU10 143 D7
SOUTH END
Hornsea 46 D3
Patrington 90 F5
South End
Seaton Ross YO42 39 E3
South Ferriby DN18 84 A7
Thorne/Moorends DN8 93 A7
Wike Well End DN8 93 B7
South End La DN14 77 B4
South End Rd
Ottringham HU12 73 E3
Roos HU12 60 B1
Southern Dr HU4 144 C5
Southern Way DN40 87 C3
Southern Wlk DN33 113 E8
South Esplande YO1 156 B1
South Farm Rd HU12 88 D5
SOUTH FERRIBY 84 B7
South Ferriby Prim Sch DN18 84 A7
SOUTH FIELD 69 E4
Southfield
1 Belton DN9 94 E1
Kingston upon Hull HU13 69 E4
Southfield Cl
Great Driffield YO25 124 F6
Rufforth YO23 24 D6
14 Thorne/Moorends DN8 93 B7
Ulceby DN39 86 B1
Wetwang YO25 19 B5
Southfield Cres 2 YO24 132 E8
South Field Ct 5 HU16 138 F5
Southfield Dr
1 Beverley HU17 137 A6
4 Epworth DN9 105 D6
North Ferriby HU14 69 A4
Southfield La
Barmston YO25 23 A6
Southfield La *continued*
Elstronwick HU12 59 C3
Everingham YO42 40 B4
Kellington DN14 61 E2
Roos HU12 60 C1
Seaton Ross YO42 39 D1
Skipsea YO25 23 B2
Willoughton DN21 119 A3
Southfield Pk YO43 135 D3
Southfield Rd
1 Broughton DN20 97 D3
8 Crowle DN17 94 D7
Elstronwick HU12 59 A2
Great Driffield YO25 124 F6
Grimsby DN33 113 E8
15 Holton le Clay DN36 114 A5
Kingston upon Hull HU5 140 A2
North Kelsey LN7 109 E2
Pocklington YO42 28 F4
Scunthorpe DN16 151 C1
Thorne/Moorends DN8 93 B7
Wetwang YO25 19 A5
Winterton DN15 82 F5
Southfields HU15 52 E1
Southfields Rd YO32 14 B7
Southfield Well Balk YO25 19 B5
South Furlong Croft 17 DN9 105 E6
Southgate
Hornsea HU18 134 C3
Kingston upon Hull HU13 143 E1
Market Weighton YO43 135 E3
2 Scunthorpe DN15 151 B7
South Gate YO25 32 E6
Southgate Cl HU10 138 E2
Southgate Ct YO43 135 D4
Southgate Gdns 2 HU18 134 C3
South Glebe YO25 32 B1
South Gr 8 YO25 9 C3
South Holderness Sports Ctr HU12 72 D8
South Holderness Tech Coll HU12 72 D8
South Humberside Ind Est DN31 152 A5
South Hunsley Sch HU14 68 E5
South Ings La HU15 53 C2
South Intake La DN9 116 F7
SOUTH KELSEY 110 A1
SOUTH KILLINGHOLME 86 E3
South La
Bishop Wilton YO42 16 F1
Burton Fleming YO25 2 E2
Cawood YO8 48 B7
Kingston upon Hull HU13 143 E1
South Landing Nature Reserve* YO15 5 A1
Southlands
4 Haxby YO32 13 E5
16 Hemingbrough YO8 49 F1
Southlands Ave 1 DN21 117 A2
Southlands Cl YO19 37 B6
Southlands Dr 3 DN21 117 A2
Southlands Gdns 2 DN21 117 A2
Southlands Rd YO23 130 B2
South Lawn Way HU14 68 F5
South Leys Rd HU19 75 A4
South Marine Dr YO15 122 D1
South Marsh Rd DN41 101 F7
Southmoor La WF11 61 B1
Southmoor Rd
Crowle DN17 94 C8
Thorganby YO19 37 F5
South Moor Rd DN10 116 C3
SOUTH NEWBALD 53 F7
South Newbald Rd YO43 53 F7
Southolme Dr 7 YO30 126 F1
South Orbital Trading Pk HU9 146 C7
Southorpe Cl YO16 122 B5
Southorpe La DN21 118 D7
Southorpe Nature Reserve* HU11 46 D8
Southorpe Rd HU11 134 A1
South Osbourne Way DN40 87 C2
South Parade
Grimsby DN31 152 D4
Leven HU17 45 A7
8 Selby YO8 148 C5
Thorne DN8 93 A7
York YO23 156 A1
South Park Rd DN17 96 B2
South Parkway 4 DN14 78 C8
South Pk HU12 60 B1
South Prom HU18 134 D4
South Rd
Keadby with Althorpe DN17 95 C6
Thorne/Moorends DN8 79 B2
South Rise HU16 138 B8
South Rise Cres 20 DN17 96 C2
South Ruddings La YO19 37 F7
South St Mary's Gate 4 DN31 152 D3
South Sea Ave 26 YO15 5 A2
South Sea La DN36 114 D7
South Sea Mews YO15 5 A2
South Sea Rd YO15 5 A2
Southside HU12 74 D1
South Side
Kilham YO25 9 B3
Winteringham DN15 68 A1
South Side La YO25 9 F6
Southside Rd HU12 73 F5
South St
Barmby on the Marsh DN14 64 A7
Barnetby le Wold DN38 99 B4
Bridlington YO15 122 E1
Burton Fleming YO25 2 E2
Cottingham HU16 139 A6
8 Gainsborough DN21 117 A2
Goole DN14 149 C2
Keelby DN41 101 A5
Kingston upon Hull HU1 155 A2
Leven HU17 45 A7
Middleton-on-the-Wolds YO25 31 C4
North Kelsey LN7 110 A4
Owston Ferry DN9 106 B2
Roxby cum Risby DN15 82 F3
West Butterwick DN17 106 D8
Winterton DN15 83 A5
South Townside Rd YO25 34 A8
South View
Broughton DN20 97 D4
Grimsby DN34 152 A2
Healaugh LS24 24 A2
Holton le Clay DN36 114 B5
6 Humberston DN36 103 D1
Kingston upon Hull HU4 144 B6
South View Ave
Brigg DN20 98 C2
Burringham DN17 95 D4
Southwell Ave HU9 147 E8
Southwell Cl HU17 136 E1
South Wold HU20 55 A4
Southwold Cres 25 DN33 113 E8
Southwood Ave HU16 138 F6
Southwood Dr HU16 139 A6
South Wood Dr 12 DN8 93 A7
Southwood Gdns HU16 138 F5
Southwood Pk YO25 20 D2
Southwood Rd
Kingston upon Hull HU16 138 F5
Sutton upon Derwent YO41 38 C8
Soutter Gate HU12 72 C7
Sovereign Cl 14 DN34 102 B2
Sovereign Way 7 HU7 56 E5
Sowerby Rd YO26 129 D4
Sowers La DN15 83 A5
Sow Hill Rd HU17 154 A3
Spa Hill DN21 108 B1
Spalding Ave YO30 130 B7
Spalding Rd DN16 151 B4
SPALDINGTON 51 C4
Spa Prom The YO15 122 E1
Spark Mill La HU17 154 C1
Sparkmill Terr HU17 154 C2
Spark St DN34 152 A3
Sparrowcroft La DN14 66 E3
Spa The* YO15 122 E1
Spawd Bone La 27 WF11 61 A2
Spa Well La DN14 78 C8
Speculation St YO1 130 E4
Speedwell Cres DN15 96 B7
Speedwell La 1 HU17 55 D8
SPEETON 3 F5
Speeton Gate YO15 4 B4
Spellowgate YO25 20 C7
Spellowgate Cl YO25 124 D5
Spencer Ave DN15 150 F8
Spencer Cl
22 Hedon HU12 72 C7
Kingston upon Hull HU16 138 F6
Spencers Mead YO25 124 E3
Spencer St
Beverley HU17 154 A3
Grimsby DN31 153 B5
Kingston upon Hull HU2 155 A3
3 York YO23 156 B1
Spencers Way YO25 124 E4
Spencer Way 1 HU16 139 B7
Speng La YO23 24 B4
Spen La
Holme-on-Spalding-Moor YO43 39 F2
York YO1 156 C3
Spenser St DN14 149 C5
Sperrin Cl 2 HU9 142 A3
Spey Bank YO24 132 C6
Spicer's Rd HU12 72 C6
Spilsby Rd DN17 150 E1
Spindle Cl YO24 132 C8
Spindlewood 1 HU15 68 C7
Spinnaker Cl HU3 145 D5
Spinney Cl 2 DN40 87 C1
Spinney Croft Cl 12 HU14 69 A5
Spinney The
1 Barnby Dun DN3 92 A3
8 Barrow upon Humber DN19 85 D8
Brigg DN20 98 C1
28 Gainsborough DN21 117 C1
Grimsby DN34 152 C3
Kingston upon Hull HU16 139 A5
6 Newport HU15 52 F1
7 Swanland HU14 69 B7
York YO24 132 F7
Spinney Wlk HU4 144 C6
Spire Hull & East Riding Hospl HU10 143 E5
Spire View
21 Hemingbrough YO8 49 F1
1 Kingston upon Hull HU13 143 E1
Spital Hill DN21 117 B1
SPITAL IN THE STREET 119 E1
Spital Terr DN21 117 B1
Spittlerush La DN6 76 D2
Sport Rd DN16 151 E6
Spout Hill HU15 68 C8
Spratton Ct 2 DN37 102 B2
Springbank DN20 98 C2
Spring Bank
Grimsby DN34 152 A3
Kingston upon Hull HU3 155 A3
4 North Newbald YO43 53 F7
Springbank Ave
Dunnington YO19 26 E7
Hornsea HU18 134 B4
Spring Bank W HU5 144 D7
Springbok Cl HU4 144 D2
Springburn St HU3 145 A5
Spring Cl YO25 124 D5
Spring Cottage Prim Sch HU8 141 F6
Springdale Cl HU10 143 F8
Springdale Rd YO43 135 E5
Springdale Way HU17 154 A1
Springfield
Holme-on-Spalding-Moor YO43 40 A1
6 Howden DN14 65 B7
Springfield Ave
Bridlington YO15 122 E2
18 Brough HU15 68 C6
5 Hatfield DN7 92 E4
Springfield Cl
Barlby with Osgodby YO8 49 B5
Heworth YO31 131 C7
2 Scunthorpe DN16 151 C2
Spring Field Cl HU11 45 F8
Springfield Cres 3 WF8 76 C3
Springfield Dr
9 Barlby YO8 49 B5
Beverley HU17 137 A6
Springfield Gdns YO43 40 A1
Springfield Prim Sch DN33 113 D8
Springfield Rd
26 Brigg DN20 98 C2
Grimsby DN33 113 D8
Kingston upon Hull HU3 144 F6
Pocklington YO42 29 B3
4 Poppleton YO26 12 F1
Springfield Rise DN20 98 D2
Springfields 18 WF11 61 A2
Springfields Ave 17 WF11 61 A2
Springfield Way
Hook DN14 149 F6
Kingston upon Hull HU10 143 E7
York YO31 131 B7
Spring Gardens E HU4 144 B6
Spring Gardens S HU4 144 B5
Spring Gardens W HU4 144 B6
Spring Gdns
Goole DN14 149 E4
Kingston upon Hull HU8 141 D5
Spring Gr HU3 145 A7
Springhead Ave HU5 144 A7
Springhead Cl 6 DN14 65 A7
Springhead Ct HU10 144 A6
Springhead Gdns HU5 144 A7
Springhead La HU5 144 A7
Springhead Prim Sch HU10 143 F7
Spring La
2 Buckton/Bempton YO15 4 D3
11 Laceby DN37 101 F1
Long Marston YO26 24 A5
York YO10 131 A1
Spring Rd 1 YO43 135 E4
Springs Rd DN10 104 C1
Spring St
Immingham DN40 87 C1
Kingston upon Hull HU2 155 A3
Springs Way DN20 98 B2
Springthorpe Rd DN21 118 B1
Spring Vale HU11 142 D5
Springville Ave HU13 143 F2
Springway Cres DN34 152 A3
Spring Wlk YO8 148 A1
Springwood YO32 127 D7
Springwood Cres 7 DN33 113 D8
Springwood Gr
Knapton YO26 129 C6
16 Welton HU15 68 D6
SPROATLEY 58 C5
Sproatley Endowed Prim Sch HU11 58 D5
Sproatley Rd HU12 58 D3
Spruce Cl YO32 127 D2
Spruce La DN39 86 A1
Spruce Rd
Kingston upon Hull HU1 155 A1
Leven HU17 45 B8
Spurn Ave 16 DN33 113 E8
Spurn Lightship* YO23 155 B1
Spurn National Nature Reserve* HU12 91 D6
Spurn Rd HU12 91 B2
Spurr Ct YO24 132 C8
Spurriergate YO1 156 B2
Spurr Rd DN39 99 F5
Spyvee St HU8 155 C3
Square The
4 Easington HU12 90 F6
Goxhill DN19 86 A8
Kingston upon Hull HU10 138 D1
Kingston upon Hull HU13 143 E1
Skerne & Wansford YO25 21 C3
Yapham YO42 28 E7
Squire La YO16 122 C4
Stable La 4 DN18 69 E1
Stabler Cl 15 YO32 13 D5
Stable Rd YO8 63 D7
Stablers Wlk YO32 127 F7
STADDLETHORPE 66 D7
Staddlethorpe Broad La HU15 66 D7
Stafford St
6 Kingston upon Hull HU2 140 E1
Kingston upon Hull HU2 155 A4
Staindale Cl YO30 126 E2
Staindale Rd DN16 151 E1
Staines Cl HU8 142 A4
STAINFORTH 92 C7
Stainforth Moor Rd DN7 93 C3
Stainforth Rd DN7 92 A5
Stainton Dr
Grimsby DN33 102 D2
15 Immingham DN40 87 B1
9 Scunthorpe DN17 96 C2
Staithes Cl 4 YO26 129 B4
Staithes Rd HU12 72 B8
Staithe St 3 YO8 50 D7
STALLINGBOROUGH 101 E6
Stallingborough CE Prim Sch DN41 101 E6
Stallingborough Rd
Healing DN41 101 E5
Immingham DN40 87 B1
Keelby DN41 101 A5
Stallingborough Sta DN41 101 E6
Stalybridge Ave HU9 142 E1
STAMFORD BRIDGE 15 E2
Stamford Bridge Prim Sch YO41 15 D2
Stamford Bridge Rd YO19 26 E7
Stamford Bridge W YO41 15 C2
Stamford Gr HU9 142 E1
Stamford Street E 10 YO26 129 F5
Stamford Street W 8 YO26 129 F5
Stamford Wlk YO16 122 C2
Stanage Wlk DN32 152 F4
Stanbury Rd HU6 140 C7
Standage Rd 12 HU12 72 E5
Standidge Dr HU8 142 A5
Standish La 1 DN40 87 B2
Stanfield Rd 2 DN9 105 D6
Stanford Cl DN37 101 F1
Stanford Jun & Inf Sch DN37 101 F1
Stanholme La DN36 114 A1
Stanhope Ave HU9 141 E2
Stanhope Pl DN35 153 C3
Stanhope St DN14 149 C4
Staniland Dr YO8 148 A5
Staniland Way 1 DN36 114 D8
Staniwell Rise DN17 150 D3
Staniwells Dr 9 DN20 97 D3
Stanley Ave
Haxby YO32 127 D7
Hornsea HU18 134 C2
Stanley Gdns
Bridlington YO16 122 D6
15 Stainforth DN7 92 C6
Stanley Rd
Scunthorpe DN15 150 C7
16 Stainforth DN7 92 C6
Stanley St
Goole DN14 149 D4
Grimsby DN32 153 A4
Kingston upon Hull HU3 145 C7
York YO31 156 C4
Stannington Dr HU8 142 D6
Stansfield Cl HU9 142 D1
Stansted St DN31 152 B5
Stan Valley 2 WF8 76 C3
Stapleford Cl 4 HU9 142 E2
Staple Rd DN40 86 F3
Starboard Ave HU6 140 C8
Starcarr La YO25 34 A1
Star Carr La DN20 98 C4
Starella Gr HU3 145 A4
Starham Rd LN7 109 C4
Star Hill Rd YO25 124 F5
Starkbridge La DN14 78 A3
Starkey Cres YO31 131 A5
Startforth Wlk HU5 139 E3
Stather Rd
Burton upon Stather DN15 82 A5
Flixborough DN15 82 A1
Stathers Wlk 3 HU10 143 F6
Station App
Bridlington YO15 122 E2
Cleethorpes DN35 153 F3
Station Ave
10 Bridlington YO16 122 D3
New Earswick YO32 127 D3
New Waltham DN36 114 A7
York YO1 156 A2
Station Bsns Pk YO26 129 F4
Station Ct
33 Canal Side DN8 93 A8
46 Hatfield DN7 92 D4
Hornsea HU18 134 D4
Station Dr HU3 140 D1
Station Hill YO25 19 B6
Station La
Barmby on the Marsh DN14 64 B7
Cliffe YO8 49 E3
Hedon HU12 72 C8
Holme-on-Spalding-Moor YO43 39 F1
Searby cum Owmby DN38 110 D7
Shipton YO30 12 E5
Station Mews HU18 134 D4

192 Sta–Tam

Station Rd
Bainton YO25 31 E6
Blyton DN21 117 F6
Bridlington YO15 122 D2
Brough HU15 68 B5
Burringham DN17 95 D4
7 Burstwick HU12 73 A6
Burton Agnes YO25 10 A1
Carlton DN14 63 C3
Cleethorpes DN35 153 E3
Copmanthorpe YO23 132 B2
Cottingham HU13 143 E1
East Halton DN40 86 D7
Eastrington DN14 65 F8
Epworth DN9 105 D7
Fulstow LN11 121 D7
Garthorpe & Fockerby DN17 81 E6
Garton YO25 20 A5
Gilberdyke HU15 66 D8
Grasby DN38 110 E6
Grimsby DN37 102 B5
Gunness DN15 95 E5
Habrough DN40 100 E8
Harpham YO25 21 E8
Hatfield DN7 92 D4
Haxby YO32 13 F5
Haxey DN9 116 C7
Healing DN41 101 F5
Hensall DN14 62 C1
Holton le Clay DN36 114 A4
Howden DN14 65 B8
Hutton Cranswick YO25 32 E7
Keadby with Althorpe DN17 95 D6
Keyingham HU12 73 C4
Killingholme High DN40 87 B5
Kingston upon Hull HU16 139 C7
Kirton in Lindsey DN21 108 B2
Lockington YO25 32 D1
Ludborough DN36 121 B6
Market Weighton YO43 135 D4
Middleton YO25 31 C5
Misterton DN10 116 D5
Nafferton YO25 125 F6
New Waltham DN36 114 A7
North Cave HU15 53 D3
North End DN19 71 A1
North Ferriby HU14 69 A4
North Kelsey LN7 110 A4
North Thoresby DN36 114 B1
Norton DN6 76 F2
Ottringham HU12 73 F4
Owston Ferry DN9 106 A2
Patrington HU12 74 C2
Pocklington YO42 29 A3
24 Poppleton YO26 12 F1
Preston HU12 72 C8
Rawcliffe DN14 64 A1
Riccall YO19 49 A8
Scawby DN20 108 F7
Scunthorpe DN15 151 B6
Selby YO8 148 D5
South Cave HU15 54 A2
South Kelsey LN7 110 D2
South Killingholme DN40 87 A5
Stallingborough DN41 101 D6
Thorngumbald HU12 73 A5
Thornton Curtis DN39 85 F5
Ulceby DN39 86 B1
Walkeringham DN10 116 D3
Waltham DN37 113 E7
Wharram YO17 6 A4
Whitton DN15 67 D3
Wistow YO8 48 C6
5 Withernsea HU19 75 A6
Womersley DN6 76 D5
York YO24 156 A2
Station Rise YO1 156 A2
Station Sq 4 YO32 14 B7
Station St DN10 116 C5
Station View
Cliffe YO8 49 D3
Little Weighton HU20 55 A4
Staunton Pk HU7 56 E5
Staveley Rd HU9 142 C3
Staves Ct 10 DN36 114 D4
Staxton Ct HU9 146 D8
Staxton Hill YO12 1 C8
Staynor Ave YO8 148 E3
Steadings The DN15 82 B1
Steele Cl YO43 135 D3
Steep Hill HU15 54 B2
Steeping Dr 11 DN40 87 B1
Steeple Cl 4 YO32 13 D5
Steeton Ave 4 HU6 140 C7
Stembridge Cl 1 HU9 142 E1
Stephen Cl 2 DN39 86 A1
Stephen Cres
14 Barton-upon-Humber DN18 84 F8
Grimsby DN34 102 C2
10 Humberston DN36 114 C8
Stephenson Cl
37 Hedon HU12 72 D7
Market Weighton YO43 135 C3
York YO31 127 E1
Stephenson St HU9 141 E1
Stephenson's Wlk HU16 139 D6
Stephenson Way YO26 129 F5
Stephen's Wlk YO8 148 B1
Stephenwath La YO41 16 C5
Stepney Ave 13 YO16 122 C5
Stepney Gr YO16 122 C4
Stepney Ind Est HU17 137 B4
Stepney La HU5 140 E1
Stepney Prim Sch HU5 140 E1
Sterling Cres DN37 113 D6
Sterling Pk YO30 127 A3
Sterne Ave
7 Broughton DN20 97 D3
York YO31 131 A5
Stevenson Pl DN35 153 D1
Stevenson's Way 18 DN18 84 E8
Steward Cl YO8 48 D1
Stewart Garth HU16 138 E6
Stewart La YO19 36 C4
Steynburg St HU9 141 D1
STILLINGFLEET 36 C3
Stirling Cl 2 DN21 117 C1
Stirling Gr YO10 133 F8
Stirling Rd
Barmby Moor YO42 28 E3
York YO30 126 F3
Stirling St
Grimsby DN31 153 B5
Kingston upon Hull HU3 144 F6
Stirrup Cl YO24 132 B8
Stockbridge Ave HU9 142 E1
Stockbridge La YO25 32 F6
Stockbridge Pk 2 HU15 68 C7
Stockbridge Rd HU15 68 B7
Stockham Ct 21 DN33 102 D1
Stockhill Cl 1 YO19 26 E7
Stockholm Cl 1 YO10 133 D8
Stockholm Pk 23 HU12 72 D7
Stockholm Rd
Kingston upon Hull HU7 140 E5
16 Thorngumbald HU12 72 E5
Stocking La
Hillam LS25 61 B7
Knottingley WF11 61 B2
Stockleigh Cl HU7 140 F8
Stocks Dr DN14 79 B8
Stocks Hill
Belton DN9 94 E1
Huggate YO42 18 C1
Ludborough DN36 121 B6
Stockshill Rd DN16 151 C2
Stockton Hall Hospl YO32 14 D3
Stockton La
Heworth YO32 128 D1
York YO31 131 A7
STOCKTON ON THE FOREST 14 D3
Stockton on the Forest Prim Sch YO32 14 D3
Stockwell Gr HU9 147 E8
Stockwell La 13 YO25 34 B2
Stockwell Prim Sch HU9 147 E8
Stockwith La DN14 63 A4
Stockwith Rd
Haxey DN9 105 E1
Owston Ferry DN9 116 E8
Walkeringham DN10 116 D3
Walkerith DN21 116 E4
Stoke St HU2 155 A4
Stonebow The YO1 156 C2
Stonebridge Ave HU9 142 D1
Stone Bridge Dr YO41 27 F5
Stonecarr Ct 2 HU7 56 F7
Stone Creek HU12 88 C5
Stone Dale YO42 17 D3
STONEFERRY 141 B3
Stoneferry Prim Sch HU8 141 A3
Stoneferry Rd HU8 141 A2
Stonegate
Hunmanby YO14 2 F8
Thorne/Moorends DN8 93 A8
York YO1 156 B3
Stonegate Cl 3 HU8 141 D7
Stone Hill DN7 93 A4
Stone Hill Rd DN7 93 A4
Stoneknowle Hill YO43 54 A8
Stone La DN17 95 D4
Stonelands Ct 2 YO30 127 A1
Stonepit Balk YO17 6 C5
Stonepit Hill YO17 6 C4
Stonepit La YO15 4 E3
Stonepit Rd HU15 54 A1
Stone Riggs YO32 14 D2
Stones Cl YO24 129 E2
Stonesdale HU7 141 A6
Stones Mount HU16 139 A7
Stonethwaite 5 YO24 132 C7
Stonewall Cottage La 25 YO41 15 D2
Stoney La HU15 53 A3
Stoney Way DN36 114 D4
Stony Cl DN7 92 C7
Stony La HU15 53 A2
Stool Close Rd DN9 94 E1
Stoop Cl YO32 127 C8
Storkhill Rd HU17 154 C4
Storking La YO41 27 F6
Stornaway Sq HU8 141 F7
Stortford St DN31 152 B5
Story St HU1 155 A3
Stothards La 1 DN19 86 A8
Stottlebink 17 YO15 5 A2
Stovin Cres DN15 83 A5
Stow Cl 11 DN37 102 B4
Stow Ct YO32 127 E3
Stowe Garth 1 YO16 122 F7
Stowgarth 29 DN18 84 F8
Stow Rd
Atwick YO25 35 D5
Scunthorpe DN16 151 B3
Straight La YO19 26 F8
Straits Rd HU11 46 D2
Strand Cl HU3 155 A4
Strand Com Sch DN32 153 A5
Strand St DN32 152 F5
Stratford Ave 4 DN33 102 D2
Stratford Dr DN16 151 C5
Stratford Way YO32 127 E3
Stratford Wlk HU9 142 E1
Strathcona Ave HU5 139 E4
Strathearn St 1 HU5 140 D3
Strathmore Ave
Burstwick HU12 73 A7
Kingston upon Hull HU6 140 C6
Strathmore Ct DN36 114 A7
Stratton Cl HU8 142 B7
Stratton Pk 3 HU14 69 B6
Strawberry Gdns
Hornsea HU18 134 C1
Kingston upon Hull HU9 145 B7
Strawberry Hill 2 DN37 113 C6
Strawberry St HU9 146 B7
Stray Garth YO31 130 F7
Straylands Gr YO31 130 F8
Stray Rd
Sunk Island HU12 89 B6
York YO31 131 B6
Stray The HU15 54 A2
Street La
Bubwith DN14 50 F5
North Kelsey LN7 110 B4
Streetlife Mus* HU1 155 C2
Streets The' DN15 151 A7
Street The YO42 28 A2
STRENSALL 14 A7
STRENSALL CAMP 14 B6
Strensall Comm Nature Reserve* YO60 14 D8
Strensall Pk YO32 14 A5
Strensall Rd
Earswick YO32 128 A7
Kingston upon Hull HU5 139 C1
York YO32 127 F6
Strickland Rd
Eastoft DN17 81 A2
13 Hunmanby YO14 3 A8
Strickland St HU3 145 C4
Strines Gr 9 HU8 141 D7
Stripe La YO30 126 B5
Stromness Way HU8 141 F7
Stroud Crescent E HU7 141 A7
Stroud Crescent W HU7 141 A8
Strouther Cl YO42 29 A3
Stroykins Cl DN34 102 C3
Strubby Cl 6 DN35 103 D2
Stuart Cl
Bridlington YO15 122 C1
Scunthorpe DN17 96 C1
4 Strensall YO32 14 C8
Stuart Gr
Eggborough DN14 62 A2
9 Thorpe Willoughby YO8 48 B1
Stuart Rd YO24 129 D1
Stuart Wortley St DN31 152 F6
Stubbs Cl 30 HU15 68 D5
Stubbs La
Cridling Stubbs WF11 76 A8
Norton DN6 76 E2
Stubbs Rd WF8 76 D3
Stubden Gr YO30 126 F2
Studcross DN9 105 D6
Studio 2 Theatre* HU1 155 A2
Studley Mdws YO16 122 D7
Studley St HU8 146 B8
Sturdee Gr YO31 130 D7
Sturmer Ct 15 DN16 96 D1
STURTON 108 F7
Sturton Gr 23 DN33 102 D2
Sturton La DN20 108 E7
Stygate La DN6 76 E1
Stylefield Rd 15 YO15 5 A2
Styles Croft HU14 69 C7
Subway St HU3 145 B3
Subway The DN16 97 A4
Suddaby Cl HU9 141 F2
Suddle Way 4 DN41 101 A4
Sudforth La DN14 61 C3
Suffolk Ct 13 DN32 153 A5
Suffolk St HU5 140 D3
Sugar Mill Ponds Nature Reserve* DN14 79 B8
Suggitt's Ct DN35 153 D4
Suggitt's La DN35 153 D4
Suggitt's Orch DN35 153 D4
Sullivan Rd HU4 144 B4
Summerdale DN18 84 E8
Summerfield Ave 3 DN37 113 E7
Summerfield Cl
Great Driffield YO25 124 D5
4 Waltham DN37 113 E7
Summerfield Rd
Bridlington YO15 122 D1
York YO24 132 C7
SUMMERGANGS 141 C2
Summergangs Dr 17 HU12 72 E5
Summergangs Rd HU8 141 C3
Summer Gdns YO30 129 F8
Summergroves Way HU4 144 B2
Summer Hill DN21 117 C1
Summermeadows HU11 142 D6
Sunbeam Rd HU4 144 D5
Sundrew Ave DN14 149 D6
Sunk Island Rd HU12 88 E8
Sunningdale 12 DN37 113 D6
Sunningdale Ave 1 DN20 98 C3
Sunningdale Cl
Knapton YO26 129 B5
1 York YO26 129 B5
Sunningdale Dr 7 DN40 87 C2
Sunningdale Rd
Gipseyville HU4 144 E4
Sunningdale Rd *continued*
Northfield HU13 143 F2
Scunthorpe DN17 96 B2
Sunningdale Way DN21 117 C2
Sunnybank 1 DN18 84 E8
Sunny Bank
Kingston upon Hull HU3 145 B7
3 Knottingley WF11 61 A2
Sunny Cnr 13 DN33 102 E1
Sunnydale 3 YO32 127 D7
Sunny Hill 9 DN21 108 B1
Sunnyside Cl HU12 73 C4
Sunrise Dr YO14 3 C8
Sunway Gr DN16 151 A1
Surbiton Cl HU8 141 F5
Surrey Ct 12 DN32 153 A5
Surrey Garth HU4 144 B4
Surrey Way YO30 129 F8
Surtees St
Grimsby DN31 152 F6
York YO30 130 B7
Sussex Cl
5 Kingston upon Hull HU5 139 D1
York YO10 131 C2
Sussex Ct 14 DN32 153 A5
Sussex Rd YO10 131 C2
Sussex St DN35 153 B4
Sussex Way 14 YO32 14 A7
Susworth Rd DN17 106 D4
Sutcliffe Ave 18 DN33 102 D2
Sutherland Ave HU6 140 B6
Sutherland St YO23 130 B1
Sutor Cl YO23 132 B3
Sutton Bridge* YO41 27 C2
Sutton Cl HU7 141 B8
Sutton Ct HU8 141 E6
Sutton Fields Ind Est
Kingston upon Hull HU2 155 C4
West Carr HU7 140 F5
Sutton Gdns HU7 141 B7
Sutton House Rd HU8 141 D5
SUTTON INGS 141 F4
Sutton La
Barmby Moor YO42 28 B3
Byram cum Sutton WF11 61 A4
SUTTON-ON-HULL 141 D6
Sutton Park Prim Sch HU7 140 F7
Sutton Pl DN20 108 F7
Sutton Rd
Howden DN14 65 A6
Kingston upon Hull HU6 140 D6
12 Kirk Sandall DN3 92 A3
Wawne HU7 56 F7
Wigginton YO32 13 D7
Sutton St DN14 149 D4
SUTTON UPON DERWENT 27 C1
Sutton upon Derwent CE Prim Sch YO41 27 C2
Sutton Way
Kingston upon Hull HU9 142 B2
York YO30 130 B8
Swaby Cl DN36 115 B2
Swaby Dr DN35 103 B2
Swaby's Yd HU17 154 A3
Swaddale Ave HU10 138 F2
Swainby Cl HU8 141 D7
Swale Ave YO24 132 E8
Swaledale Ave HU9 141 E1
Swaledale Mews YO16 122 F6
Swaledale Pl DN16 151 D2
Swale Rd 29 HU15 68 D5
Swales Dr YO43 135 D3
Swales Rd DN36 114 D8
SWALLOW 112 B5
Swallow Cl HU18 134 B6
Swallow Ct 4 DN9 105 D7
Swallow Dr 3 DN41 101 F5
Swallowfield Dr HU4 144 B2
Swallow Grange 6 HU8 141 D7
Swallow La DN39 85 E2
Swallow Rd YO25 125 B5
Swanage Wlk HU4 144 B4
Swan Cl YO19 37 A7
Swan Ct
Gainsborough DN21 117 D1
Hornsea HU18 134 C6
Swanella Gr HU3 145 A4
Swan Farm Ct YO19 37 A7
Swanfield Rd HU9 142 C2
Swan La DN14 149 D6
SWANLAND 69 B6
Swanland Ave 3 YO15 122 F3
Swanland Butts Cl HU10 143 C6
Swanland Cl 17 DN8 93 B7
Swanland Ct 23 DN8 93 B7
Swanland Dale HU14 69 B8
Swanland Garth 4 HU14 69 A5
Swanland Hill 16 HU14 69 A5
Swanland Prim Sch HU14 69 B6
Swanland Rd HU13 143 C2
Swanland Way 3 HU16 138 E6
Swannacks View DN20 108 F7
Swann St
Kingston upon Hull HU2 155 C4
York YO23 156 A1
Swan Syke Dr 8 DN6 76 F2
Sweep Cl YO43 135 D3
Sweet Briar Cl 7 DN37 113 D7
Sweet Dews Gr HU9 146 D8
Sweyne Garth DN14 65 D1
Swift Ave YO25 125 B5
Swift Cl HU18 134 B6
Swift Dr DN20 98 B2
Swift Rd DN17 150 D2
Swiftsure Cres 16 DN34 102 B2
Swinburne La DN17 150 D3
Swinburne Rd DN17 150 D3
Swinburne St HU8 141 D2
Swinderby Garth 19 HU7 57 A5
Swinderby Gdns DN34 152 A1
Swindon St YO16 122 D3
SWINE 57 D6
Swine Bank HU5 139 B2
SWINEFLEET 65 D1
Swinefleet Prim Sch DN14 65 C1
Swinefleet Rd
Goole DN14 149 D2
Goole Fields DN14 80 C8
Swinegate
Kingston upon Hull HU13 143 E1
York YO1 156 B2
Swinegate Court E YO1 156 B3
Swine La HU11 57 E5
Swinemoor La HU17 137 B5
Swinemoor Prim Sch HU17 154 C4
Swine Rd HU11 45 C1
Swineridge Hill YO42 29 B6
Swineridge La YO42 29 C6
Swinescaif Hill Swine HU15 54 A3
Swinescaif Rd
South Cave HU15 54 A3
South Cave HU15 54 B3
Swinster La DN40 86 E6
Swinsty Ct YO30 126 F1
Swinton Cl 8 YO30 126 E2
Switchback LN8 120 A1
Swithin Cl HU13 144 A2
Sycamore Ave
15 Grimsby DN33 102 E2
1 Hut Green DN14 62 A2
York YO32 127 D4
Sycamore Cl
3 Barnetby le Wold DN38 99 B4
2 Broughton DN20 97 D3
East Ella HU5 144 C7
14 Gilberdyke HU15 66 D8
Goole DN14 149 E6
1 Haxby YO32 127 D7
Hessle HU13 143 C3
Nafferton YO25 125 F7
8 Preston HU12 58 C1
Selby YO8 148 A4
Skelton YO30 126 C5
12 Snaith & Cowick DN14 78 C8
Sycamore Cres
Bottesford DN16 96 F2
Hutton Cranswick YO25 32 E7
Sycamore Ct
Kingston upon Hull HU5 140 C1
Sproatley HU11 58 D5
Sycamore Dr
9 Gainsborough DN21 117 C1
3 Thorngumbald HU12 72 E5
Sycamore Mews YO8 148 D2
Sycamore Pl
New Earswick YO32 127 D4
York YO30 156 A3
Sycamore Rd YO8 49 B5
Sycamores The HU17 137 B3
Sycamore Terr YO30 156 A3
Sycamore View 17 YO26 12 F1
Sydney Smith Sch HU10 144 A5
SYKEHOUSE 78 B3
Sykehouse Rd DN14 78 C4
Sykes Balk YO25 21 E8
Sykes Cl
6 Kingston upon Hull HU10 143 F6
Swanland HU14 69 B7
Sykes La
Garton YO25 124 A5
Goxhill DN19 71 A2
Sykes St HU2 155 B3
Sylvan Falls YO25 124 C4
Sylvan Lea YO25 124 C4
Sylvan Mead YO25 124 C4
Sylvester La HU17 154 A3
Sylvester Sq HU1 155 B3
Sylvester St 13 DN21 108 B1
Sylvia Cl HU6 139 F5
Symmons Cl 4 HU17 137 A6
Symons Cl HU2 155 A4
Symons Way 13 YO42 29 A3

T

Tabard Hamlet 5 DN14 61 F2
Tabard Rd 6 DN14 61 F2
Tabards The 7 DN14 61 F2
Tadcaster Rd
Copmanthorpe YO23 132 C4
York YO24 129 F1
Tadcaster Rd Dringhouses YO23 132 E5
Tadman Cl HU17 136 E7
Tadman St HU3 145 D4
Tailler Rd 44 HU12 72 D7
Talbot Circ DN3 92 A4
Talbot Rd DN40 87 C1
Talbot Wlk DN16 151 B6
Talisman Dr 6 DN16 96 D1
Tallert Way 28 DN33 102 C2
Tall Trees HU13 143 C3
Tamar Dr 14 DN36 114 A8
Tamar Gr HU8 142 C7
Tamarisk Way 18 DN16 96 E2
Tamar Wlk DN17 150 C4
Tamworth Rd 9 YO30 127 A1